Fodor's

BARCELONA

12

WELCOME TO BARCELONA

The capital of Catalonia is a banquet for the senses, with its beguiling mix of ancient and modern architecture, tempting cafés and markets, and sun-drenched Mediterranean beaches. A stroll along La Rambla and through waterfront Barceloneta, as well as a tour of Gaudí's majestic Sagrada Família and his other unique creations, are part of a visit to Spain's second-largest city. Modern art museums and chic shops call for attention, too. Barcelona's vibe stays lively well into the night, when you can linger over regional wine and cuisine at buzzing tapas bars.

TOP REASONS TO GO

★ **Gaudí:** The iconic Sagrada Família, undulating Casa Batlló, and playful Park Güell.

★ **Food:** From the Boqueria market's bounty to tapas bars to avant-garde restaurants.

★ **Museums:** Museu Picasso and the Museu Nacional d'Art de Catalunya lead the list.

★ **Architecture:** Roman and medieval in the Barri Gòtic, Moderniste in the Eixample.

★ **Shopping:** Stylish fashion boutiques and innovative design emporia tempt buyers.

★ **Beautiful Beaches:** Sandy havens and surfing hubs delight urban sun worshippers.

Fodor's BARCELONA

Publisher: Amanda D'Acierno, *Senior Vice President*

Editorial: Arabella Bowen, *Editor in Chief*; Linda Cabasin, *Editorial Director*

Design: Fabrizio La Rocca, *Vice President, Creative Director*; Tina Malaney, *Associate Art Director*; Chie Ushio, *Senior Designer*; Ann McBride, *Production Designer*

Photography: Melanie Marin, *Associate Director of Photography*; Jessica Parkhill and Jennifer Romains, *Researchers*

Maps: Rebecca Baer, *Senior Map Editor*; David Lindroth, Mark Stroud (Moon Street Cartography), *Cartographers*

Production: Linda Schmidt, *Managing Editor*; Evangelos Vasilakis, *Associate Managing Editor*; Angela L. McLean, *Senior Production Manager*

Sales: Jacqueline Lebow, *Sales Director*

Marketing & Publicity: Heather Dalton, *Marketing Director*; Katherine Punia, *Senior Publicist*

Business & Operations: Susan Livingston, *Vice President, Strategic Business Planning*; Sue Daulton, *Vice President, Operations*

Fodors.com: Megan Bell, *Executive Director, Revenue & Business Development*; Yasmin Marinaro, *Senior Director, Marketing & Partnerships*

Writers: Jared Lubarsky, Steve Tallantyre, Suzanne Wales

Editors: Kristan Schiller, Andrew Collins

Editorial Contributor: Steven Montero

Production Editor: Jennifer DePrima

5th Edition

ISBN 978-0-8041-4228-1

ISSN 1554-5865

SPECIAL SALES

This book is available at special discounts for bulk purchases for sales promotions or premiums. For more information, e-mail specialmarkets@randomhouse.com

PRINTED IN THE UNITED STATES OF AMERICA

10 9 8 7 6 5 4 3 2 1

CONTENTS

Fodor's Features

CONTENTS

MAPS

ABOUT THIS GUIDE

Fodor's Recommendations

Everything in this guide is worth doing—we don't cover what isn't—but exceptional sights, hotels, and restaurants are recognized with additional accolades. **Fodor's Choice★** indicates our top recommendations; and **Best Bets** call attention to notable hotels and restaurants in various categories. Care to nominate a new place? Visit Fodors.com/contact-us.

Trip Costs

We list prices wherever possible to help you budget well. Hotel and restaurant price categories from **$** to **$$$$** are noted alongside each recommendation. For hotels, we include the lowest cost of a standard double room in high season. For restaurants, we cite the average price of a main course at dinner or, if dinner isn't served, at lunch. For attractions, we always list adult admission fees; discounts are usually available for children, students, and senior citizens.

Hotels

Our local writers vet every hotel to recommend the best overnights in each price category, from budget to expensive. Unless otherwise specified, you can expect private bath, phone, and TV in your room. For expanded hotel reviews, facilities, and deals visit Fodors.com.

Top Picks

★ Fodor's Choice

Listings

- ✉ Address
- Branch address
- ☎ Telephone
- Fax
- Website
- E-mail
- Admission fee
- Open/closed times
- Ⓜ Subway
- Directions or Map coordinates

Hotels & Restaurants

- Hotel
- Number of rooms
- Meal plans
- ✕ Restaurant
- Reservations
- Dress code
- No credit cards
- $ Price

Other

- ⇨ See also
- ☞ Take note
- Golf facilities

Restaurants

Unless we state otherwise, restaurants are open for lunch and dinner daily. We mention dress code only when there's a specific requirement and reservations only when they're essential or not accepted. To make restaurant reservations, visit Fodors.com.

Credit Cards

The hotels and restaurants in this guide typically accept credit cards. If not, we'll say so.

1

EXPERIENCE BARCELONA

BARCELONA TODAY

Capital of the autonomous Community of Catalonia, bilingual Barcelona (Catalan and Spanish) is the unrivaled visitor destination in Spain, and with good reason: dazzling art and architecture, creative cuisine, great weather, and warm hospitality. It's a city proud of its cultural past and confident about its future.

A Tale of Two Cities

Restive for centuries in the shadow of Madrid, where Spain ruled from the center—more often than not, with an iron hand—Barcelona has a drive to innovate and excel that stems largely from a determination to eclipse its longtime rival. A powerful sense of national identity (Catalans consider themselves a "nation" and decidedly not a province of Spain) motivates designers, architects, merchants, and industrialists to ever-higher levels of originality and achievement. Especially since the smashing success of the 1992 Olympic Games, national pride and confidence have grown stronger and stronger, and today fully half the Catalan population favors the holding of a referendum on complete independence.

Cuisine: Haute and Hot

Since Ferran Adrià's northern Catalonian phenomenon elBulli closed, *chef d'auteur* successes in Barcelona have proliferated. Some two-dozen superb restaurants (and more on the way) have won international recognition, so keeping abreast of the city's culinary rock stars can be a dizzying pursuit. Here's a quick primer: Adrià disciples Sergi Arola at the Hotel Arts and Carles Abellán at Comerç 24 still compete with Adrià precursor Jean Louis Neichel. Rising stars such as Jordi Artal of Cinc Sentits, Jordi Vilà of Alkimia, the Torres twins at Dos Cielos, and Jordi Herrera of Manairó join established masters Carles Gaig and Mey Hofmann in a dazzling galaxy of gastronomical creativity. Meanwhile, the Roca brothers from Girona (whose Celler de Can Roca was designated in 2013 the best restaurant in the world), Raül Balam from Sant Pol de Mar, and Martin Berasategui from San Sebastián have opened award-winning hotel restaurants in, respectively, the Omm (Moo), the Mandarin Oriental (Moments), and the Condes de Barcelona (Lasarte). Add to this list up-and-comers like Xavier Franco of the restaurant Saüc (in the

WHAT WE'RE TALKING ABOUT

Bullfights in Barcelona were prohibited as of January 1, 2012, but it remains to be seen whether the conservative (Partido Popular) political victory will reintroduce what many regard as a fundamental part of Spanish culture.

The Sagrada Família, Gaudí's yet-unfinished masterpiece, is coming right along. The nave and transept of the interior are open and dazzling visitors; the basilica was consecrated by Pope Benedict XVI in 2010; the entire project, with its 520-foot central spire, is expected to be finished by the centenary of Gaudí's death, in 2026. Drawing some three million visitors a year, it is Barcelona's most iconic structure.

Can FC Barcelona continue to dominate world *fútbol*? The chance to win a third Champions title in four years

Ohla Hotel), Dani Lechuga of Caldeni, and Oriol Ivern of Hisop, and you begin to appreciate what a gastronomic haven Barcelona has become.

Design, Architecture, Fashion, Style

Barcelona's cutting-edge achievements in interior design and couture continue to threaten the traditional dominance of Paris and Milan, while "starchitect" landmarks like Jean Nouvel's Torre Agbar, Norman Foster's communications tower on the Collserola skyline, and Ricardo Bofill's W Barcelona hotel (nicknamed Vela: the Sail) on the waterfront transform the city into a showcase of postmodern visual surprises.

Fútbol Nirvana

Barcelona's always amazing FC Barcelona soccer juggernaut seemed as if it had peaked in 2006 when Brazilian import Ronaldinho led the team to its second European title—but the best was yet to come. Former star-midfielder-turned-coach Pep Guardiola and an almost entirely homegrown team of stars dazzled the world in 2009, winning the *triplete*, or Triple Crown: the Spanish Liga, the King's Cup, and the Champions League European title. With star player Leo Messi still only in his twenties, and the farm system producing a steady supply of new players committed to Barcelona's razzle-dazzle style of attacking, creative play, the team has grown from strength to strength. Even without Guardiola, who stepped down in May 2012, FC Barcelona's creative choreography and dedication to exciting, offensive soccer seems here to stay.

New Toys

With a new airport terminal, a behemoth new convention center complex, a new AVE high-speed train connection that makes once-distant Madrid into little more than a Barcelona suburb, Barcelona is again on the move. City planners predict that the new AVE terminal at Plaça de les Glòries will someday shift the city center eastward, and that the new Barcelona hub will surround the Torre Agbar and the Fòrum at the Mediterranean end of Diagonal.

---

fell short in spring of 2012 with Barcelona's semifinal defeat by Chelsea; also in 2012, Barcelona came in behind Real Madrid in the Liga for the first time in four years, and beloved coach Pep Guardiola left the team for German Bundesliga club Bayern Munich. Two coaches later, Barcelona is back as the Liga powerhouse, and its faithful fans are on the edge of their maroon-and-blue seats in anticipation of what comes next.

It's a post-elBulli world in gastronomy in Barcelona; the award-winning Costa Brava restaurant by superstar chef and founder Ferran Adrià closed in 2011. With chefs such as the late Santi Santimaria, the momentarily retired Fermín Puig, and the redirected Ferran Adrià no longer at the top of the culinary heap, it's a novel time as new stars emerge to fill the void.

BARCELONA PLANNER

When to Go

For optimal weather and marginally fewer tourists, the best times to visit Barcelona, Catalonia, and Bilbao are April through June and mid-September through mid-December. Catalans and Basques vacation in August, causing epic traffic jams at both ends of the month. Major cities are relaxed and, except for tourists, empty in August, though Gràcia's Festa Major in Barcelona and Semana Grande in Bilbao keep these two cities alive during the summer season. Some shops and restaurants shut down for part of the month, but museums remain open, and a range of star-studded music and theater festivals ensure that there's no slack in the city's cultural calendar.

Summers in Barcelona are occasionally very hot, but temperatures rarely surpass 100°F (38°C), and air-conditioning is becoming more widespread. In any case, dining alfresco on a warm summer night is one of northern Spain's finest pleasures. All in all, spring and fall offer the best temperatures at both ends of the Pyrenees. Barcelona winters are chilly enough for overcoats, but never freezing: ideal for walking, fireside dining, and hearty winter cuisine.

Getting Around

The best way to get around Barcelona is on foot; the occasional resort to subway, taxi, or tram will help you make the most of your visit. The comfortable FGC (Ferrocarril de la Generalitat de Catalunya) trains that run up the center of the city from Plaça de Catalunya to Sarrià put you within 20- to 30-minute walks of nearly everything. (The metro and the FGC close just short of midnight Monday through Thursday and Sunday, and at 2 am on Friday; on Saturday, the metro runs all night. The main attractions you need a taxi or the metro to reach are Montjuïc (Miró Foundation, MNAC, Mies van der Rohe Pavilion, CaixaFòrum, and Poble Espanyol), most easily accessed from Plaça Espanya; Park Güell above Plaça Lesseps; and the Auditori at Plaça de les Glòries. You can reach Gaudí's Sagrada Família by two metro lines (2 and 5), but you may prefer the walk from the FGC's Provença stop, as it's an enjoyable half-hour jaunt that passes by three major Moderniste buildings: Palau Baró de Quadras, Casa Terrades (les Punxes), and Casa Macaia.

Sarrià and Pedralbes are easily explored on foot. The Torre Bellesguard and the Col.legi de les Teresianes are uphill treks; you might want to take a cab. It's a pleasant stroll from Sarrià down through the Jardins de la Vil.la Cecilia and Vil.la Amèlia to the Cátedra Gaudí (the pavilions of the Finca Güell, with Gaudí's amazing wrought-iron dragon gate); from there, you can get to the Futbol Club Barcelona through the Jardins del Palau Reial de Pedralbes and the university campus, or catch a two-minute taxi.

All of Ciutat Vella (Barri Gòtic, Rambla, El Raval, Born-Ribera, and Barceloneta) is best explored on foot. If you stay in Barceloneta for dinner (usually not more than €12), have the restaurant call you a taxi to get back to your hotel.

The city bus system is also a viable option—you get a better look at the city as you go—but the metro is faster and more comfortable. The tramway offers a quiet ride from Plaça Francesc Macià out Diagonal to the Futbol Club Barcelona, or from behind the Ciutadella Park out to Glòries and the Fòrum at the east end of Diagonal.

Leave Barcelona with Everything You Brought—or Bought

Although violent muggings are practically unheard-of in Barcelona, petty thievery is common. Handbags, backpacks, camera cases, and wallets are favorite targets, so tuck those away. Coat pockets with zippers work well for indispensable gear, while cash and a few credit cards wedged into a front trouser pocket are almost unassailable. Handbags hooked over chairs, on the floor or sidewalk under your feet, or dangling from hooks under bars are easy prey. Even a loosely carried bag is tempting for bag-snatchers. If you carry a purse, use one with a short strap that tucks tightly under your arm without room for nimble hands to unzip. A plastic shopping bag for your essentials will attract even less attention.

Catalan for Beginners

Anyone who questions how different Catalan and Spanish are need only have a look at the nonsensical Catalan tongue twister *"Setze jutges d'un jutjat menjen fetge d'un penjat"* (Sixteen judges from a courthouse eat the liver of a hanged man); in Spanish, it's *"Dieciseis jueces de un juzgado comen el higado de un ahorcado."* Catalan is derived from Latin and Provençal French, whereas Spanish has a heavy payload of Arabic vocabulary and phonetics. For language exchange (*intercambios*), check the bulletin board at the Central University Philosophy and Letters Faculty on Gran Via or any English bookstore for free half-hour language exchanges of English for Catalan (or Spanish). It's a great way to get free private lessons, meet locals, and, with the right chemistry, even begin a cross-cultural fling. Who said French is the only language of love?

Top Festivals and Events

Carnaval (*Carnestoltes*) arrives in Barcelona in February or early March, just before Lent, a colorful fling that rivals its more flamboyant counterpart in Sitges, down the coast.

Semana Santa (Holy Week), the week before Easter, is Spain's most important celebration everywhere but Barcelona, as the locals depart in droves for vacations elsewhere.

La Diada de Sant Jordi is Barcelona's Valentine's Day, celebrated April 23 with gifts of flowers and books in observance of International Book Day and to honor the 1616 deaths of Miguel de Cervantes and William Shakespeare.

La Fira de Sant Ponç brings farmers to town for an open-air market in the Raval on May 11.

La Verbena de Sant Joan celebrates the summer solstice and Midsummer's Eve with fireworks and all-night beach parties on the night of June 23.

La Festa Major de Gràcia honors Santa Maria with street dances and concerts in Barcelona's village-turned-neighborhood, Gràcia, in mid-August.

Festes de La Mercé honors Barcelona's patron saint, Nostra Senyora de la Mercé, for a week beginning September 24.

WHAT'S WHERE

1 La Rambla. This is the city's most emblematic promenade, once a seasonal watercourse that flowed along the outside of the 13th-century city walls. A stroll on La Rambla—where tourists mix with pickpockets, buskers, scammers, street performers, and locals—passes the Boqueria market, the Liceu opera house, and, at the port end, Drassanes, the medieval shipyards. Just off La Rambla is Plaça Reial, a stately neoclassical square; off the other side is Gaudí's masterly Palau Güell.

2 Barri Gòtic. The medieval Gothic Quarter surrounds the Catedral de la Seu on the high ground that the Romans settled in the 1st century BC. The medieval Jewish quarter, the antiquers' row, Plaça Sant Jaume, and the Sant Just neighborhood are quintessential Barcelona.

3 El Raval. Once a slum, this area west of La Rambla has brightened considerably, thanks partly to the Barcelona Museum of Contemporary Art, designed by Richard Meier. Behind the Boqueria market is the stunning Antic Hospital de la Santa Creu, with its high-vaulted Gothic Biblioteca de Catalunya reading room; just steps away is Sant Pau del Camp, Barcelona's earliest church.

4 Sant Pere, La Ribera, and El Born. Northeast of La Rambla, Sant Pere is the city's old textile neighborhood. The narrow cobblestone streets of La Ribera and El Born are filled with interesting shops and restaurants; this area is perhaps best known for the grand urban palaces of Barcelona's medieval nobles and merchant princes—five of which linked together now house the Picasso Museum. Passeig del Born, once the medieval jousting ground, draws crowds to its shops by day and to its saloons by night.

5 Barceloneta. This waterfront neighborhood, just east of Born-Ribera, was open water until the mid-18th century, when it was filled in to provide housing for barcelonins displaced by the construction of Ciutadella—at the time the largest fortress in Europe and a symbol of the hated Bourbon regime. Some of the city's best seafood restaurants make Barceloneta a favorite for Sunday-afternoon paella gatherings.

6 The Eixample. The Eixample (Expansion) is the post-1860 grid square of city blocks uphill from Ciutat Vella containing most of Barcelona's Moderniste (Art Nouveau) architecture, including Gaudí's unfinished work, the Sagrada Família church. Passeig de Gràcia is the city's premier shopping street. It also offers more Gaudí at Casa Batlló, Casa Milà (La Pedrera), and Casa Calvet.

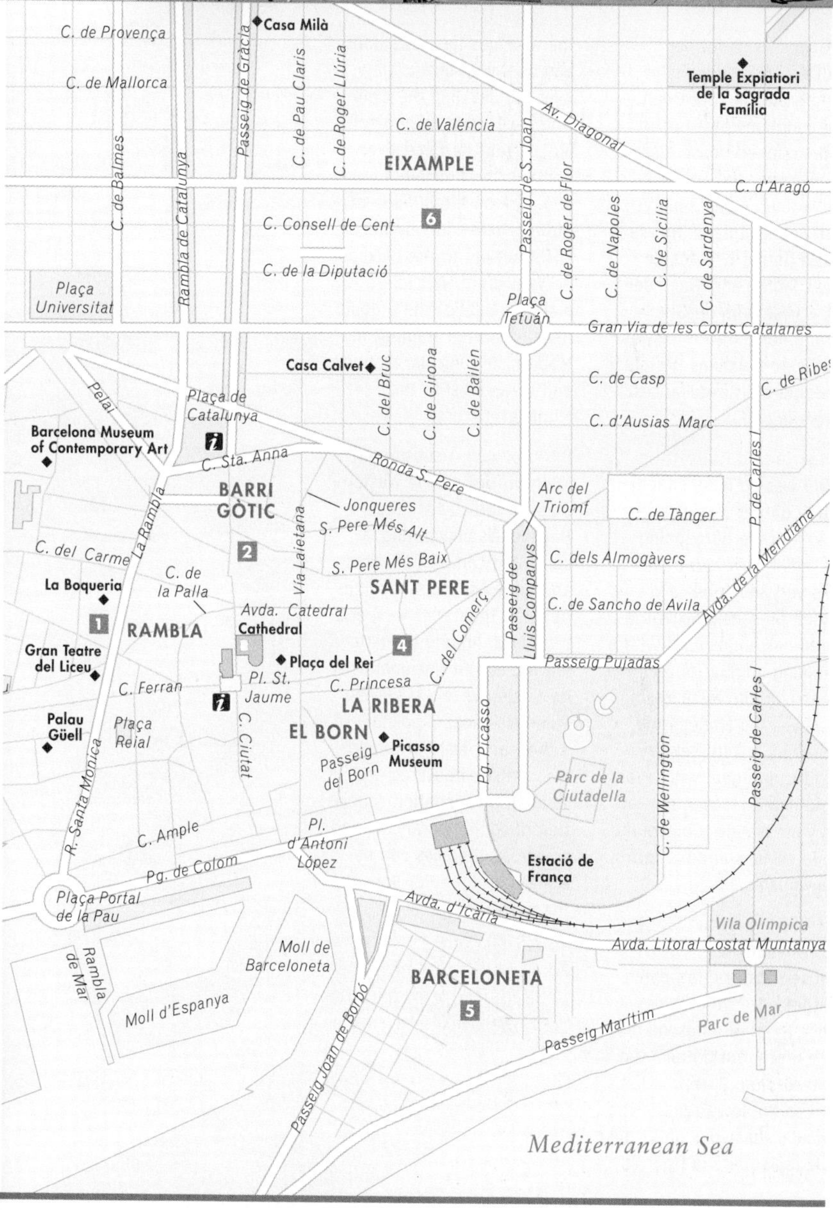

C. de Provença
Casa Milà
C. de Mallorca
Passeig de Gràcia
C. de Pau Claris
C. de Roger Llúria
Temple Expiatiori de la Sagrada Família
Av. Diagonal
C. de Valéncia
EIXAMPLE
C. de Balmes
Rambla de Catalunya
Passeig de S. Joan
C. de Roger de Flor
C. de Napoles
C. de Sicilia
C. de Sardenya
C. d'Aragó
C. Consell de Cent
6
C. de la Diputació
Plaça Universitat
Plaça Tetuán
Gran Via de les Corts Catalanes
Casa Calvet
C. del Bruc
C. de Girona
C. de Bailén
C. de Casp
C. de Ribes
Pelai
Plaça de Catalunya
C. d'Ausias Marc
Barcelona Museum of Contemporary Art
C. Sta. Anna
Ronda S. Pere
P. de Carles I
BARRI GÒTIC
Jonqueres
Arc del Triomf
C. de Tànger
S. Pere Més Alt
La Rambla
C. del Carme
2
Via Laietana
S. Pere Més Baix
C. dels Almogàvers
Avda. de la Meridiana
La Boqueria
C. de la Palla
SANT PERE
Passeig de Lluís Companys
C. de Sancho de Avila
1
RAMBLA
Avda. Catedral
Cathedral
C. del Comerç
Gran Teatre del Liceu
4
Plaça del Rei
Passeig Pujadas
C. Ferran
Pl. St. Jaume
C. Princesa
Palau Güell
Plaça Reial
C. Ciutat
LA RIBERA
EL BORN
Picasso Museum
Passeig del Born
Pg. Picasso
Parc de la Ciutadella
C. de Wellington
Passeig de Carles I
R. Santa Monica
C. Ample
Pl. d'Antoni López
Estació de França
Pg. de Colom
Plaça Portal de la Pau
Avda. d'Icària
Vila Olímpica
Avda. Litoral Costat Muntanya
Rambla de Mar
Moll de Barceloneta
BARCELONETA
5
Moll d'Espanya
Passeig Joan de Borbó
Passeig Marítim
Parc de Mar
Mediterranean Sea

WHAT'S WHERE

7 Gràcia. This former outlying village begins at Gaudí's playful Park Güell and continues past his first commissioned house, Casa Vicens, through two markets and various pretty squares such as Plaça de la Vila de Gràcia (formerly Plaça de Rius i Taulet) and Plaça del Sol. Carrer Gran de Gràcia, though narrow and noisy, is lined with buildings designed by Gaudí assistant Francesc Berenguer.

8 Sarrià and Pedralbes. Sarrià was an independent village until it was incorporated into the burgeoning metropolis in 1927. It still feels very much like a village, though present-day gentrification has endowed it with a gratifying number of gourmet shops and fine restaurants. Nearby is the Monestir de Pedralbes, a 14th-century architectural gem with a rare triple-tiered cloister; not far away are Gaudí's Col.legi de les Teresianes and his Torre Bellesguard.

9 Tibidabo, Vallvidrera, and the Collserola Hills. Tibidabo, Barcelona's perch, is a place to avoid unless you're a fan of amusement-park kitsch. But do take the *Tramvia Blau* (Blue Tram) at least to the lower end of the funicular that goes up to the park: the square in front of the terminus has restaurants and bars with terrific views over the city, and the Gran Hotel la Florida up above it all is a tour de force. Even better is the Collserola forest and park on the far side of the hill, accessible by the FGC train out to the Baixador de Vallvidrera. Vallvidrera is a sleepy village with a good restaurant (Can Trampa), a Moderniste funicular station, and views west to the Montserrat massif.

10 Montjuïc. A substantial lump of rock on the western edge of the city, Montjuïc is Barcelona's playground: a sprawling complex of parks and gardens, sports facilities, open-air theater spaces, and museums. Among the latter are the Museu Nacional d'Art de Catalunya (MNAC) in the Palau Nacional, repository of a thousand years of Catalonia's artistic treasures; the Joan Miró Foundation collection of contemporary art and sculpture; the Mies van der Rohe Barcelona Pavilion; and the CaixaForum.

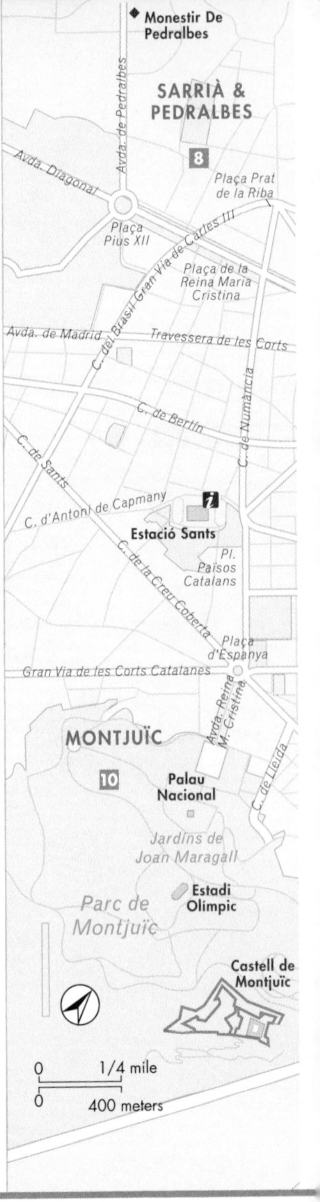

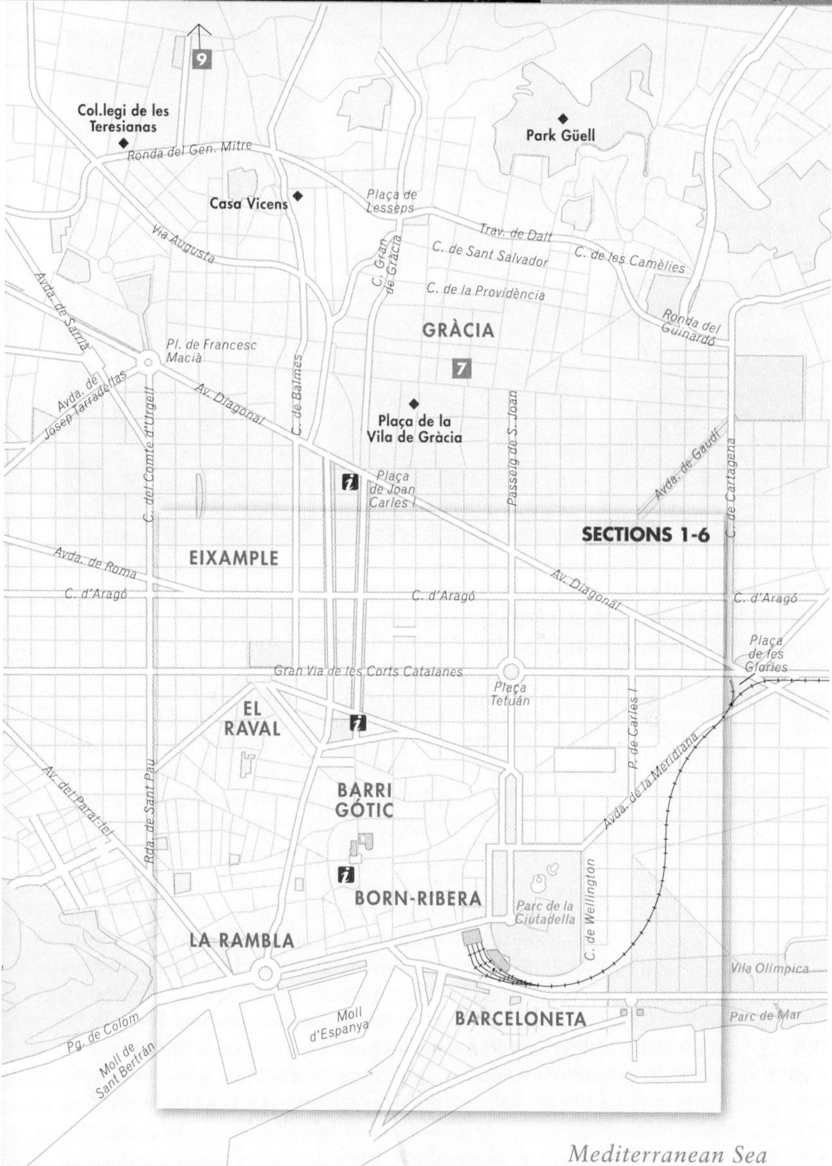
9
Col.legi de les Teresianas
Park Güell
Ronda del Gen. Mitre
Casa Vicens
Plaça de Lesseps
Via Augusta
Trav. de Dalt
C. de Sant Salvador
C. de les Camèlies
C. Gran de Gràcia
C. de la Providència
Avda. de Sarrià
Ronda del Guinardó
GRÀCIA
Pl. de Francesc Macià
7
Avda. de Josep Tarradellas
Av. Diagonal
C. de Balmes
Plaça de la Vila de Gràcia
Passeig de S. Joan
C. del Comte d'Urgell
Avda. de Gaudí
Plaça de Joan Carles I
C. de Cartagena
SECTIONS 1-6
EIXAMPLE
Avda. de Roma
C. d'Aragó
C. d'Aragó
Av. Diagonal
C. d'Aragó
Plaça de les Glòries
Gran Via de les Corts Catalanes
Plaça Tetuán
EL RAVAL
P. de Carles I
Av. del Paral·lel
BARRI GÒTIC
Avda. de la Meridiana
Rda. de Sant Pau
C. de Wellington
BORN-RIBERA
Parc de la Ciutadella
LA RAMBLA
Vila Olímpica
Moll d'Espanya
BARCELONETA
Parc de Mar
Pg. de Colom
Moll de Sant Bertrán
Mediterranean Sea

BARCELONA TOP ATTRACTIONS

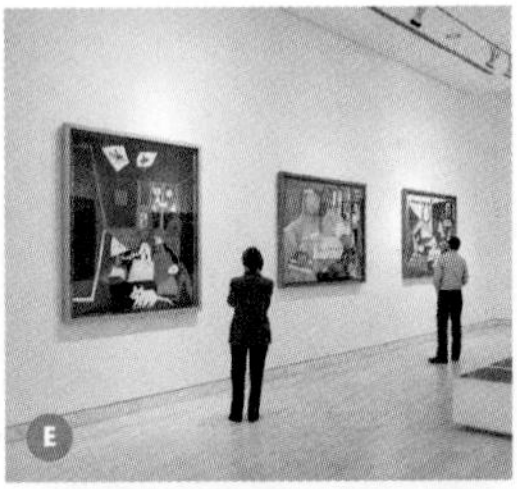

The Boqueria Market

(A) The oldest market of its kind in Europe, the Boqueria market is a labyrinth of stalls in a Moderniste wrought-iron shell just off La Rambla, selling edibles of every imaginable sort: the must-see source of fish, fowl, meat, fruits, and vegetables for Barcelona's home kitchens and restaurants.

Casa Batlló and the Manzana de la Discòrdia

(B) The Manzana de la Discòrdia (Apple of Discord) on Passeig de Gràcia is so called for its row of astonishing but utterly uncomplementary buildings by the three most famous Moderniste architects—Domènech i Montaner, Puig i Cadafalch, and Gaudí. Of the three, Gaudí's Casa Batlló, with its undulating roof, multicolor facade, and skull-and-bones balconies, is the most remarkable.

Gaudí's Sagrada Família

(C) The city's best-known landmark, Gaudí's soaring still-unfinished Temple Expiatori de la Sagrada Família (Expiatory Temple of the Holy Family) draws lines of visitors around the block. With the completion of the interior in the fall of 2010, the lofty nave and transept have become the city's premier sight.

Museu Nacional d'Art de Catalunya (MNAC)

(D) Atop the stairway leading up from Plaça d'Espanya, MNAC is Barcelona's answer to Madrid's Prado. It houses an unmatched collection of Catalonia's Romanesque art, from altarpieces to frescoes, most of it rescued from Pyrenean churches and monasteries and lovingly restored. Separate galleries display the work of 19th-century masters such as Marià Fortuny, Ramón Casas, and Santiago Rusiñol.

Museu Picasso

(E) Pablo Picasso's connection to Barcelona, where he spent key formative years and first showed his work in 1900, eventually bore fruit when his manager Jaume Sabartés donated his collection to the city in 1962. Nearly as stunning as the 3,500 Picasso works on display are the five medieval palaces that house them.

Palau de la Música Catalana

(F) Often described as the flagship of Barcelona's Modernisme, this dizzying tour de force by architect Lluís Domènech i Montaner is a showcase of Art Nouveau crafts and decorative techniques—every detail and motif symbolic of the Catalan cultural identity. Much criticized during the aesthetically somber 1939–75 Franco regime, the city's longtime prime concert venue is an exciting place to hear music.

Park Güell

(G) Gaudí's playful park in Gràcia was originally developed as a residential community. Gaudí's patron and principal investor in the project, Count Eusebi Güell, must have been disappointed when the idea failed to catch on; only two of the houses planned for this whimsical garden were built. What did get built were Moderniste gems: the gingerbread gatehouses, the dazzling central staircase, and the undulating ceramic tile bench around the central square.

Santa Maria del Mar Basilica

(H) For Mediterranean Gothic at its best, Santa Maria del Mar is the Sagrada Família's opposite. Burned back to its stone shell in a fire at the start of the Spanish Civil War in 1936, it was restored by post-Bauhaus architects who saw the purity of Berenguer de Montagut's 1329 design and maintained his spare, elegant lines.

LIKE A LOCAL

If you want to get a sense of local culture and indulge in some of the pleasures treasured by barcelonins, start with these few highlights in the rituals of daily life—activities and events you can share with the leisure-loving inhabitants of this most dynamic of cities.

Grazing: Tapas and Wine Bars

Few pastimes in Barcelona are more satisfying than wandering, tippling, and tapas hunting. By day or after dark, exploring Barri Gòtic, Gràcia, Barceloneta, or the Born-Ribera district offers an endless selection of taverns, cafés, bars, and restaurants, where you ballast your drinks with little portions of fish, sausage, cheese, peppers, wild mushrooms, or *tortilla* (potato omelet), lovingly prepared on the premises. If you find yourself on Passeig de Gràcia or La Rambla in a bar that serves microwaved tapas, know this: you're missing out. The areas around Passeig del Born, Santa Maria del Mar, Plaça de les Olles, and the Picasso Museum are the prime *tapeo* (tapa-tasting) and *txikiteo* (tippling) grounds.

Openings, Presentations, Lectures, and Musical Events

Check listings in the *Guía del Ocio* or in the daily newspapers *El País* or *La Vanguardia, or the online edition of Barcelona Time Out* to find announcements for art-gallery openings, book presentations, and free public concerts. Often serving *cava* (Catalan sparkling wine) and canapés, these little gatherings welcome visitors (if it's announced in the papers, you're invited). Famous authors from Richard Ford or Paul Auster to Martin Amis or local stars such as Javier Marías or Carlos Ruiz Zafón may be presenting new books at the British Institute or at bookstores such as La Central. Laie Libreria holds jazz performances in its café, while the travel bookstore Altair has frequent book signings and talks by prominent travel authors. Events in the town hall's Saló de Cent are usually open to the public.

Soccer: FC Barcelona

If FC Barcelona's playing, and you're in town, get thee to a sports bars—and the bigger the flat-screen TV, the better. The pubs down around La Rambla with fútbol on the tube are usually packed with foreign tourists; the taverns and cafés in Barceloneta, El Raval, Gràcia, and Sarrià are generally local *penyas* (fan clubs), where passions run high. Memorize the club song, in Catalan, so you can join in when Barça scores. For the real thing, there is the Camp Nou stadium—though tickets can be pricy.

Sunday Sardanas, Puppets, and Castellers

The Sunday-morning papers carry announcements for local neighborhood celebrations, flea markets and produce fairs, puppet shows, storytelling sessions for children, *sardana* folk-dancing, bell-ringing concerts, and, best of all, *castellers*. The castellers, complex human pyramids sometimes reaching as high as 10 stories, are a quintessentially Catalan phenomenon that originated in the Penedés region west of Barcelona; they're performed at neighborhood fiestas or on major holidays. Most Sunday-morning events are over by 2 pm, when lunchtime officially reigns supreme, so get an early start. The Barcelona town hall in Plaça Sant Jaume is a frequent venue for castellers and sardanas, as is the Plaça de la Catedral.

GREAT ITINERARIES

Ciutat Vella, Quintessential Barcelona

Stroll La Rambla and see the colorful Boqueria market before cutting over to the Catedral de la Seu in Barri Gòtic, unrivaled for the density and number of its surviving medieval buildings and monuments. Detour through stately Plaça Sant Jaume where the Palau de la Generalitat, Catalonia's seat of government, faces the Ayuntamiento (City Hall). The Gothic Plaça del Rei and the Neoclassical Plaça Reial—not to be confused—are short walks from Plaça Sant Jaume. The Museu Picasso is five minutes from the loveliest example of Catalan Gothic architecture, the basilica of Santa Maria del Mar. An evening concert at the Palau de la Música Catalana after a few tapas and before a late dinner is an unsurpassable way to end the day.

Budget another whole day, perhaps, for the Raval, behind the Boqueria, for the Museu d'Art Contemporani de Barcelona, the medieval Antic Hospital de la Santa Creu, the Sant Pau del Camp church, and the medieval shipyards at Drassanes Reiales. Palau Güell, just off the lower Rambla, is an important Gaudí work. A short hike away, the waterfront Barceloneta neighborhood is a prime place for a paella on the beach.

The Post-1860 Checkerboard Eixample

A morning touring the Eixample starts early and begins at Gaudí's magnum opus, the Temple Expiatori de la Sagrada Família (while there include a side-trip up Avinguda Gaudí to the Hospital de Sant Pau). Afterward head to the central Passeig de Gràcia, but en route swing past Moderniste architect Puig i Cadafalch's Casa Terrades and his Palau Baró de Quadras. Spend the afternoon in the Eixample with the undulating facades and stunning interiors of Casa Milà and Casa Batlló. Other Eixample masterpieces include Gaudí's Casa Calvet, not far from Plaça de Catalunya, the Fundació Tàpies, and more far-flung Moderniste gems such as the Casa Golferichs, and the Casa de la Papallona (the "Butterfly House") out toward Plaça de Espanya. Parallel to the Passeig de Gràcia is the Rambla Catalunya, a tree-shaded promenade lined with shops and cafés.

Upper Barcelona: Gràcia and Sarrià

For a more rustic and restful excursion, try the formerly outlying towns of Gràcia and Sarrià. Gràcia is home to Gaudí's first private residential commission, Casa Vicens, and his playful Park Güell above Plaça Lesseps; the tree-lined lower reaches of this bustling neighborhood are filled with houses by Gaudí's right-hand man, Francesc Berenguer. Sarrià is a village long since absorbed by the ever-expanding city, an intimate warren of narrow streets, neighborhood shops, and restaurants. A bit removed from the village itself are the Monestir de Pedralbes, with its superb Gothic cloister, Gaudí's Torre Bellesguard, and his Col.legi de les Teresianes (a convent school, not open to the public).

Art in Montjuïc

Montjuïc is the site of the Museu Nacional d'Art de Catalunya; the nearby Fundació Miró features Catalan artist Joan Miró's colorful paintings and textiles, and a stellar Calder mobile. Down the stairs toward Plaça d'Espanya are the Mies van der Rohe Barcelona Pavilion and the restored Casaramona textile mill, now the CaixaForum cultural center and gallery.

A WALK AROUND LA RAMBLA

It's a Mediterranean thing. Many towns have that one street in town (or barrio even) that runs from the town hall to the church or main street to the port (pick any two landmarks) where everyone comes. These streets are dedicated to the long tradition of the promenade—where you move slower (you don't walk, you stroll) and take in your surroundings, where you go to see and be seen, and where you share a table with friends at an outdoor café. In Barcelona, that's La Rambla.

La Rambla: Rite of Passage

Start from the top, at **Plaça de Catalunya.** La Rambla changes names and personalities as you descend toward the sea, bringing you first to **Rambla de Canaletes** (drink from the fountain here, and the inscription on the base promises that you will return to Barcelona, no matter how far away you go), then to **Rambla dels Ocells**—the old bird market now given over to ice cream vendors and souvenir stands—past Carrer de Portaferrissa to the flower stalls along **Rambla de les Flors.** (The **Boqueria market** is off to the right here.) From the **Liceu opera house, Rambla de Santa Mónica** takes you past the Plaça Reial on the left to the end of your promenade at Drassanes.

The Boqueria: Horn of Plenty

There's a stall in the Mercat de Sant Josep, popularly known as **La Boqueria,** for any and every imaginable ingredient in a Barcelona kitchen. Highlights are **Pinotxo,** the legendary dozen-stool gourmet counter, **Quim de la Boqueria,** with its famous *ous esclafats amb llanqueta* (eggs with tiny fish), and **Petràs,** the world-renowned wild mushroom stand at the back.

The Medieval Hospital: Gothic Splendor

Behind the Boqueria and through Plaça de la Gardunya is the medieval **Antic Hospital de la Santa Creu,** founded in the 13th century by King Martí l'Humà (Martin the Humane, now housing the Biblioteca (Library) de Catalunya. The library, well worth a visit, is up the stairway under the breathtaking Gothic stone arches of the courtyard, to the right.

Moderniste Raval: Gaudí and Domènech i Montaner

From the Hospital, walk back along Carrer Hospital to Plaça de Sant Agustí, and cut through Carrer de l'Arc de Sant Agustí to the **Hotel Espanya,** a Moderniste masterpiece by architect Lluís Domènech i Montaner. The mermaid murals in the dining room and the marble fireplace in the bar are highlights. From here, Carrer Sant Pau brings you to the **Liceu**—Barcelona's magnificent opera house.

An alternative detour off Rambla des Ocells also brings you to this point. (Why not do both?) Turn left on Carrer de Portaferrissa, and take the second right, down Carrer Petritxol (art galleries and to-die-for chocolate shops) into the square in front of **Santa Maria del Pi,** and admire this 14th-century masterpiece. Then return to La Rambla via Carrer Cardenal Casañas, which brings you out just in front of the Lieau. Farther down, the first street to the right is Carrer Nou de la Rambla; Gaudí's **Palau Güell** is 50 yards down the street. Directly across the Rambla here is the entrance to the neoclassical **Plaça Reial.**

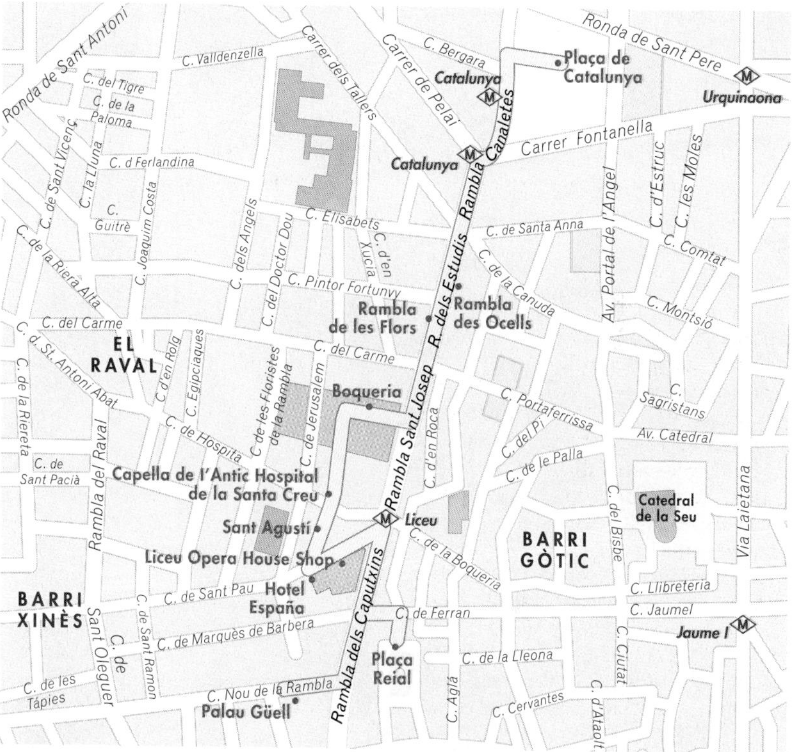

Highlights:	Canaletes fountain, Rambla de les Flors, La Boqueria, Antic Hospital de la Santa Creu, Hotel Espanya, the Liceu opera house, Palau Güell, Plaça Reial
Where to Start:	Top of La Ramblas at Plaça de Catalunya
Length:	Three hours with time for browsing through the Boqueria; two miles in all
Where to Stop:	Plaça Reial
Best Time to Go:	Before 2 pm, when everything is open and the market is at its busiest
Worst Time to Go:	Between 2 pm and 4 pm, when the market starts to slow down and Palau Güell closes
Where to Refuel:	Café Viena for the famous flautas de jamón ibérico (Iberico ham sandwiches); Bar Pinotxo, Quim de la Boqueria or Kiosko Universal in La Boqueria

GAUDÍ

ARCHITECTURE THROUGH THE LOOKING GLASS

(left) The undulating rooftop of Casa Batlló. (top) Right angles are notably absent in the Casa Milà façade.

Before his 75th birthday in 1926, Antonio Gaudí was hit by a trolley car while on his way to Mass. The great architect—initially unidentified—was taken to the medieval Hospital de la Santa Creu in Barcelona's Raval and left in a pauper's ward, where he died two days later without regaining consciousness. It was a dramatic and tragic end for a man whose entire life seemed to court the extraordinary and the exceptional.

Gaudí's singularity made him hard to define. Indeed, eulogists at the time, and decades later, wondered how history would treat him. Was he a religious mystic, a rebel, a bohemian artist, a Moderniste genius? Was he, perhaps, all of these? He certainly had a rebellious streak, as his architecture stridently broke with tradition. Yet the same sensibility that created the avant-garde benchmarks Park Güell and La Pedrera also created one of Spain's greatest shrines to Catholicism, the *Temple Expiatori de la Sagrada Família* (Expiatory Temple of the Holy Family), which architects agree is one of the world's most enigmatic structures; work on the cathedral continues to this day. And while Gaudí's works suggest a futurist aesthetic, he also reveled in the use of ornamentation, which 20th century architecture largely eschewed.

What is no longer in doubt is Gaudí's place among the great architects in history. Eyed with suspicion by traditionalists in the 1920s and 30s, vilified during the Franco regime, and ultimately redeemed as a Barcelona icon after Spain's democratic transition in the late 70s, Gaudí has finally gained universal admiration.

THE MAKING OF A GENIUS

Gaudí was born in 1852 the son of a boilermaker and coppersmith in Reus, an hour south of Barcelona. As a child, he helped his father forge boilers and cauldrons in the family foundry, which is where Gaudí's fascination with three-dimensional and organic forms began. Afflicted from an early age with reoccuring rheumatic fever, the young architect devoted his energies to studying and drawing flora and fauna in the natural world. In school Gaudí was erratic: brilliant in the subjects that interested him, absent and disinterested in the others. As a seventeen-year-old architecture student in Barcelona, his academic results were mediocre. Still, his mentors agreed that he was brilliant.

Unfortunately being brilliant didn't mean instant success. By the late 1870s, when Gaudí was well into his twenties, he'd only completed a handful of projects, including the Plaça Reial lampposts, a flower stall, and the factory and part of a planned workers' community in Mataró. Gaudí's career got the boost it needed when, in 1878, he met Eusebi Güell, heir to a textiles fortune and a man who, like Gaudí, had a refined sensibility. (The two bonded over a mutual admiration for the visionary Catalan poet Jacint Verdaguer.) In 1883 Gaudí became Güell's architect and for the next three decades, until Güell's death in 1918, the two collaborated on Gaudí's most important architectural achievements, from high-profile endeavors like Palau Güell, Park Güell, and Pabellones Güell to smaller projects for the Güell family.

(top) Interior of Casa Batlló. (bottom) Chimneys on rooftop of Casa Milà recall helmeted warriors or veiled women.

GAUDÍ TIMELINE

1883–1884

Gaudí builds a summer palace, *El Capricho* in Comillas, Santander for the brother-in-law of his benefactor, Eusebi Güell. Another gig comes his way during this same period when Barcelona ceramics tile mogul Manuel Vicens hires him to build his town house, *Casa Vicens*, in the Gràcia neighborhood.

El Capricho

1884–1900

Gaudí whips up the Pabellones Güell, Palau Güell, the Palacio Episcopal of Astorga, Barcelona's Teresianas school, the Casa de los Botines in León, Casa Calvet, and Bellesguard. These have his classic look of this time, featuring interpretation of Mudéjar (Moorish motifs), Gothic, and Baroque styles.

Palacio Episcopal

BREAKING OUT OF THE T-SQUARE PRISON

If Eusebi Güell had not believed in Gaudí's unusual approach to Modernisme, his creations might not have seen the light of day. Güell recognized that Gaudí was imbued with a vision that separated him from the crowd. That vision was his fascination with the organic. Gaudí had observed early in his career that buildings were being composed of shapes that could only be drawn by the compass and the T-square: circles, triangles, squares, and rectangles—shapes that in three dimensions became prisms, pyramids, cylinders and spheres. He saw that in nature these shapes are unknown. Admiring the structural efficiency of trees, mammals, and the human form, Gaudí noted ". . . neither are trees prismatic, nor bones cylindrical, nor leaves triangular." The study of natural forms revealed that bones, branches, muscles, and tendons are all supported by internal fibers. Thus, though a surface curves, it is supported from within by a fibrous network that Gaudí translated into what he called "ruled geometry," a system of inner reinforcement he used to make hyperboloids, conoids, helicoids, or parabolic hyperboloids.

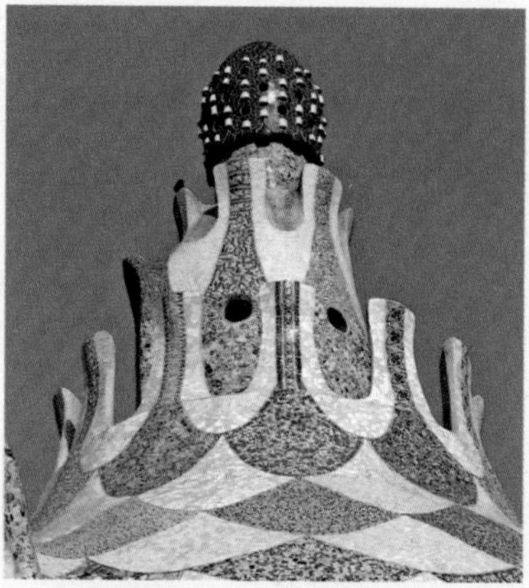

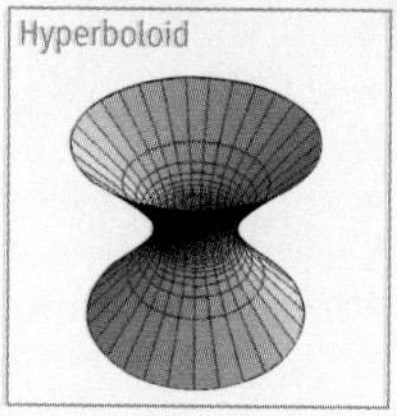

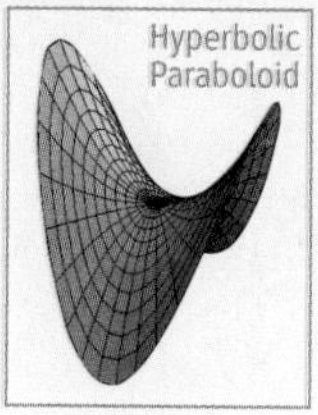

The top of the gatehouse in Park Güell at the main entrance; note the mushroom-like form.

These tongue-tying words are simple forms and familiar shapes: the femur is hyperboloid; the way shoots grow off a branch is helicoidal; the web between your fingers is a hyperbolic paraboloid. To varying degrees, these ideas find expression in all of Gaudí's work, but nowhere are they more clearly stated than in the two masterpieces La Pedrera and Park Güell.

1900–1917

Gaudí's Golden Years—his most creative, personal, and innovative period. Topping each success with another, he tackles Park Güell, the reform of Casa Batlló, the Güell Colony church, Casa Milà (La Pedrera), and the Sagrada Família school.

Casa Batlló's complex chimneys

1918–1926

A crushing blow: Gaudí suffers the death of his assistant, Francesc Berenguer. Grieving and rudderless, he devotes himself fully to his great unfinished opus, la Sagrada Família—to the point of obsession. On June 10th, 1926, he's hit by a trolley car. He dies two days later.

La Sagrada Família

Pabellones Güell. A mosaic dragon greets visitors on Park Güell's central staircase.

La Sagrada Família. Tubular bell towers over the Nativity façade were designed by Gaudí for an innovative carillon musical system.

Palau Güell. The rooftop chimneys display organic form. Using colorful broken tiles, each of a unique structure almost like a topiary garden.

Casa Calvet. The vestibule, elevator, and stairwell are beginning to warp and heave into organic suggestions.

Casa Milà (La Pedrera). The undulating stone façade seems to reflect the Mediterranean's rolling surface.

HOW TO SEE GAUDÍ IN BARCELONA

Few architects have left their stamp on a major city as thoroughly as Gaudí did in Barcelona. Paris may have the Eiffel Tower, but Barcelona has Gaudí's still unfinished masterpiece, the **Temple Expiatori de la Sagrada Família,** the city's most emblematic structure. Dozens of other buildings, parks, gateways and even paving stones around town bear Gaudí's personal Art Nouveau signature, but the continuing progress on his last and most ambitious project makes his creative energy an ongoing part of everyday Barcelona life in a unique and almost spectral fashion.

(top) The serpentine ceramic bench at Park Güell, designed by Gaudí collaborator Josep Maria Jujol, curves sinuously around the edge of the open square. (bottom) Sculptures by Josep María Subirachs grace the temple of the Sagrada Família.

In Barcelona, nearly all of Gaudí's work can be visited on foot or, at most, with a couple of metro or taxi rides. A walk from **Palau Güell** near the Mediterranean end of the Rambla, up past **Casa Calvet** just above Plaça Catalunya, and on to **Casa Batlló** and **Casa Milà** is an hour's stroll, which, of course, could take a full day with thorough visits to the sites. **Casa Vicens** is a half hour's walk up into Gràcia from **Casa Milà. Park Güell** is another thirty- to forty-minute walk up from that. **La Sagrada Família,** on the other hand, is a good hour's hike from the next nearest Gaudí point and is best reached by taxi or metro. The **Teresianas** school, the **Bellesguard Tower,** and **Pabellones Güell** are within an hour's walk of each other, but to get out to Sarrià you will need to take the comfortable Generalitat (FGC) train.

FLAVORS OF BARCELONA

These days chockablock with celebrity chefs and starred restaurants, Catalonia has become a foodie's dream destination. But long before that, there was traditional country cooking: a lush palette of tastes and textures, including sausages and charcuterie, wild mushrooms, spring onions with romescu sauce, and hams from acorn-fed pigs from southwestern Spain, all happily irrigated with sparkling wines from the Penedès. These items represent the "must eats" that every visitor should try—the quintessential flavors of this city.

Calçots

One of Catalonia's most beloved and authentic feasts is the winter *calçotada*: a celebration of the sweet, long-stemmed, twice-planted spring onions called *calçots*. These delicacies were originally credited to a 19th-century farmer named Xat Benaiges who discovered a technique for extending the scallions' edible portions by packing soil around the base, giving them stockings or shoes (*calçat*), so to speak. Valls and the surrounding region now produce upward of 5 million calçots annually. Calçot feasts take place in restaurants and homes between January and March, though the season is getting longer on both ends. On the last weekend of January, the town of Valls itself holds a public calçotada, hosting as many as 30,000 people who come to gorge on onions, sausage, lamb chops, and young red wine.

Casa Félix (✉ *Ctra. N240, Km 17, north of Tarragona* ☎ *977/609–0900* 🌐 *www.felixhotel.net*) is the classic Valls calçotada restaurant, with entire dining rooms enclosed by enormous wine barrels.

L'Antic Forn (✉ *Pintor Fortuny 28* ☎ *93/412–0286* 🌐 *www.lanticforn.com*) serves calçots in the middle of Barcelona a few steps from Plaça de Catalunya.

Restaurant Masia Bou (✉ *Ctra. de Lleida, Km 21.5* ☎ *977/600427* 🌐 *www.masiabou.com*) offers typical calçotades in a sprawling Valls *masia* (farmhouse) an hour and a half from Barcelona by car.

Cava

Catalan sparkling wine, called *cava,* is produced mainly in the Penedès region, 40 kilometers (25 miles) southwest of Barcelona. Cava was created in 1872 by local winemaker Josep Raventós after the Penedès vineyards had been devastated by the phylloxera plague and the predominantly red varietals were being replaced by vines producing white grapes. Impressed with the success of the Champagne region, Raventós decided to make his own dry sparkling wine, which has since become the region's runaway success story. Cava comes in different degrees of dryness: *brut nature, brut* (extra dry), *seco* (dry), *semiseco* (medium), and *dulce* (sweet). The soil and microclimate of the Penedès region, along with the local grape varietals, give cava a slightly earthier, darker taste than its French counterpart, with larger and zestier bubbles.

La Barcelonina de Vins i Esperits (✉ *València 304* ☎ *93/215–7083*) is a bar/restaurant in Barcelona's Eixample quarter with a huge list of wines and cavas.

La Vinya del Senyor (✉ *Pl. de Santa Maria 5* ☎ *93/310–3379*) offers top cavas and wines by the glass from a continually changing list.

Ibérico Ham

Jamón ibérico de bellota, or ham from free-range acorn-fed Ibérico pig, descendant from the *Sus mediterraneus* that once roamed the Iberian Peninsula, has become Spain's modern-day caviar. The meat is dark, red, and tastes of the roots, herbs, spices, tubers, and wild mushrooms of

southwestern Spain. The defining characteristic of this free-range pig is its ability to store monounsaturated fats from acorns in streaks or marbled layers that run through its muscle tissue. This is one of the few animal fats scientifically proven to fight the cholesterol that clogs arteries. The tastes and aromas, after two years of aging, are so complex—so nutty, buttery, earthy, and floral—that Japanese enthusiasts have declared Ibérico ham *umami,* a word used to describe a fifth dimension in taste, in a realm somewhere beyond delicious. In addition, jamón ibérico de bellota liquefies at room temperature, so it literally melts in your mouth.

Caveats: *Jamón serrano* refers to mountain-cured ham (from *sierra*) and should never be confused with jamón ibérico de bellota. What is commercialized in the U.S. as Serrano ham comes from white pigs raised on cereals and slaughtered outside of Spain. *Pata negra* means "black hoof." Not all ibérico pigs have black hooves, and some pigs with black hooves are not purebred ibéricos. *Jabugo* refers only to ham from the town of Jabugo in Huelva in the Sierra de Aracena. The term has been widely and erroneously applied to jamón ibérico de bellota in general.

For heavenly ham, try one of these spots: **Café Viena** (✉ *Rambla 115* ☎ *93/317–1492*) is famous for its *flauta de jamón ibérico* (flute or slender roll filled with tomato drizzlings and Ibérico ham), described by the *New York Times* as "the best sandwich in the world." **Mesón Cinco Jotas** (✉ *Rambla de Catalunya 91–93* ☎ *93/487–8942*) serves a complete selection of ham and charcuterie from the famous Sánchez Carvajal artisans in the town of Jabugo, Huelva.

Sausage

Catalonia's variations on this ancient staple cover a wide range of delicacies. Typically ground pork is mixed with black pepper and other spices, stuffed into casings, and dried to create a protein-rich, easily conservable meat product. If Castile is the land of roasts and Valencia is the Iberian rice bowl and vegetable garden, Catalonia may produce the greatest variety of sausages. Below are some of the most common:

Botifarra: pork sausage seasoned with salt and pepper. Grilled and served with stewed white beans and *allioli* (garlic mayonnaise). Variations include botifarra with truffles, apples, wild mushrooms, and even chocolate.

Botifarra Blanca: typical of El Vallès Oriental just north of Barcelona, made of tripe and pork jowls, seasoned and boiled. Served as a cold cut.

Botifarra Catalana Trufada: a tender, pink-hued sausage, seasoned and studded with truffles.

Botifarra de Huevo: Egg sausage with ingredients similar to botifarra but with egg yolks added.

Botifarra dolça: cured with sugar instead of salt and seasoned with spices such as cinnamon and nutmeg; served as a semi-dessert, this sausage is typical of the Empordà region.

Botifarra negra: Catalan blood sausage made with white bread soaked in pig blood with fat, salt, and black pepper.

Fuet: means "whip" for its slender shape; made of 60/40 lean meat to fat, also known as *secallona, espetec,* and *somalla.*

Llonganissa: classic pork sausage, made with 85/15 lean meat to fat, and ample salt and pepper.

Ready to have a sausage extravaganza? Shop at these places:

La Botifarreria de Santa Maria (✉ *Carrer de Santa Maria 4* ☎ *93/319–9123*) next to the Santa Maria del Mar basilica stocks a compendium of Catalonia's sausages and charcuterie, along with top hams from all over Spain.

La Masia de la Boqueria (✉ *Mercat de la Boqueria* ☎ *93/317–9420*) is one of the finest charcuterie and ham specialists in the Boqueria market.

Xarcuteria Margarit (✉ *Cornet i Mas 63, Sarrià* ☎ *93/203–3323*) up in the village of Sarrià has an excellent charcuterie (*xarcuteria* or *cansaladeria* in Catalan) on Cornet i Mas just below Plaça Sant Vicenç and another in the Sarrià market on Reina Elisenda.

Wild Mushrooms

Wild mushrooms are a fundamental taste experience in Catalan cuisine: the better the restaurant, the more chanterelles, morels, black trumpets, or 'shrooms of a dozen standard varieties are likely to appear on the menu. Wild mushrooms (in Spanish *setas,* in Catalan *bolets*) are valued for their aromatic contribution to gastronomy; they impart a musty, slightly gamey taste of the forest floor, a dark flavor of decay, to the raw materials such as meat or eggs with which they are typically cooked. Many barcelonins are proficient wild-mushroom stalkers and know how to find, identify, and prepare up to half a dozen kinds of bolets, from *rovellones* (*Lactarius deliciosus*) sautéed with parsley, olive oil, and a little garlic, to *camagrocs* (*Cantharellus lutescens*) scrambled with eggs. Wild mushrooms flourish in the fall, but different varieties appear in the spring and summer, and dried and reconstituted mushrooms are available year-round. Panlike Llorenç Petràs retired in 2010, but his Fruits del Bosc (Forest Fruits) stall at the back of the Boqueria market is still the place to go for a not-so-short course in mycology. Petràs and his sons supply the most prestigious chefs in Barcelona and around Spain with whatever they need; if morels are scarce this year in Catalonia but abundant in, say, Wisconsin, the Petràs family will dial them in. Llorenç's book *Cocinar con Setas* (Cooking with Wild Mushrooms) is a runaway best seller presently in its 10th edition.

Petràs—Fruits del Bosc. This shop (✉ *Mercat de la Boqueria, stands 867–870 and 962–964* ☎ *93/302–5273* 🌐 *www.boletspetras.com*) in the back of the Boqueria shows and sells the finest wild-mushroom collection in Barcelona.

2

EXPLORING BARCELONA

By Jared Lubarsky

The infinite variety of street life, the nooks and crannies of the medieval Barri Gòtic, the ceramic tile and stained glass of Art Nouveau facades, the art and music, the throb of street life, the food (ah, the food!)—one way or another, Barcelona will find a way to get your full attention.

The Catalonian capital greets the new millennium with a cultural and industrial rebirth comparable only to the late-19th-century Renaixença (Renaissance) that filled the city with its flamboyant Moderniste (Art Nouveau) buildings. An exuberant sense of style—from hip new fashions to cutting-edge interior design, to the extravagant visions of star-status Postmodern architects—gives Barcelona a vibe like no other in the world. Barcelona is Spain's most-visited city, and it's no wonder: it's a 2,000-year-old master of the art of perpetual novelty.

What sinks in first about Barcelona is its profoundly human scale—its dogged attention, in all matters of urban development, to the quality of life. Corner buildings in the Eixample are chamfered, leaving triangles of public space at the intersections for people to do what people have done on street corners since cities were invented: stop and schmooze, put out tables and chairs, survey the passing scene. Arteries like La Rambla, Diagonal, and Rambla de Catalunya send the vehicle traffic flowing down both sides of broad leafy pedestrian promenades. Benches and pocket parks are everywhere, graced as often as not with a striking piece of sculpture. You have to look hard for a building over nine stories high: barcelonins are reluctant to live too far up away from the street, where all the action is.

And the action never stops. Families with baby strollers are a common sight on La Rambla until well after midnight. Restaurants don't even begin to fill up for dinner until 9 or 10. At 2 am, the city's bar and club scene is barely in first gear. Creative, acquisitive, and playful in about equal doses, barcelonins seem to have learned to do without much sleep; they stay up late but then just get up in the morning and go about their business—buying and selling, planning, building, working in fields where Catalonia has established itself at the frontier, in everything from medical research to "smart city" green technologies, to hospitality.

Barcelona's present boom began on October 17, 1987, when Juan Antonio Samaranch, president of the International Olympic Committee, announced that his native city had been chosen to host the 1992 Olympics. This single masterstroke allowed Spain's so-called second city to throw off the shadow of Madrid and its 40-year "internal exile" under Franco, and resume its rightful place as one of Europe's most dynamic destinations. The Catalan administration lavished millions in subsidies from the Spanish government for the Olympics, then used the Games as a platform to broadcast the news about Catalonia's cultural and national identity from one end of the planet to the other. Madrid? Where's that? Calling Barcelona a second city of anyplace is playing with fire; its recent past as a provincial outpost is well behind it, and the city looks to the future with more creativity and raw energy than ever. More Mediterranean than Spanish, historically closer and more akin to Marseille or Milan than to Madrid, Barcelona has always been ambitious, decidedly modern (even in the 2nd century), and quick to accept the most recent innovations. (The city's electric light system, public gas system, and telephone exchange were among the first in the world.) Its democratic form of government is rooted in the so-called Usatges Laws instituted by Ramon Berenguer I in the 11th century, which amounted to a constitution. This code of privileges represented one of the earliest known examples of democratic rule; Barcelona's Consell de Cent (Council of 100), constituted in 1274, was Europe's first parliament and one of the cradles of Western democracy. The center of an important seafaring commercial empire, with colonies spread around the Mediterranean as far away as Athens, when Madrid was still a Moorish outpost on the arid Castilian steppe; it was Barcelona that absorbed new ideas and styles first. It borrowed navigation techniques from the Moors. It embraces the ideals of the French Revolution. It nurtured artists like Picasso and Miró, who blossomed in the city's air of freedom and individualism. Barcelona, in short, has always been ahead of the curve.

It must have something to do with the air. The temperature here is almost always just right; the sky is impossibly blue; the light dazzles and transforms. Every now and then a breeze from the sea reminds you that Barcelona is, after all, a beach city and one of the great ports of Europe, still flourishing—and bewitching visitors as it has for centuries.

LA RAMBLA

Sightseeing
★★★★★
Nightlife
★★★★☆
Dining
★★★☆☆
Lodging
★★★★☆
Shopping
★★★☆☆

The promenade in the heart of pre-modern Barcelona was originally a watercourse, dry for most of the year, that separated the walled Ciutat Vella from the outlying Raval. In the 14th century, the city walls were extended and the arroyo was filled in, so it gradually became a thoroughfare where peddlers, farmers, and tradesmen hawked their wares. (The watercourse is still there, under the pavement. From time to time a torrential rain will fill it, and the water rises up through the drains.) The poet-playwright Federico García Lorca called this the only street in the world he wished would never end—and in a sense, it doesn't.

Down the watercourse now flows a river of humanity, gathered here and there around the mimes, acrobats, jugglers, musicians, puppeteers, portrait artists, break dancers, rappers, and rockers competing for the crowd's attention. Couples sit at café tables no bigger than tea trays while nimble-footed waiters dodge traffic, bringing food and drink from kitchens. With the din of taxis and motorbikes in the traffic lanes on either side of the promenade, the revelers and rubberneckers, and the Babel of languages, the scene is as animated at 3 am as it is at 3 pm.

From the rendezvous point at the head of La Rambla at Café Zurich to the Boqueria produce market, the Liceu opera house, or La Rambla's lower reaches, there is something for everyone along this spinal column of Barcelona street life.

TOP ATTRACTIONS

Fodor's Choice ★ **Gran Teatre del Liceu.** Barcelona's opera house has long been considered one of the most beautiful in Europe, a rival to Milan's La Scala. First built in 1848, this cherished cultural landmark was torched in

1861, later bombed by anarchists in 1893, and once again gutted by an accidental fire in early 1994. During that most recent fire, Barcelona's soprano Montserrat Caballé stood on La Rambla in tears as her beloved venue was consumed. Five years later, a restored Liceu, equipped for modern productions, opened anew. Even if you don't see an opera, don't miss a tour of the building; some of the Liceu's most spectacular halls and rooms, including the glittering foyer known as the Saló dels Miralls (Room of Mirrors), were untouched by the fire of 1994, as were those of Spain's oldest social club, El Círculo del Liceu. The Espai Liceu downstairs in the annex has a cafeteria; a gift shop with a wide selection of opera-related books and recordings; and a 50-seat video theater, where you can see a documentary history of the Liceu and a media library of recordings and films of past productions. ✉ *La Rambla 51–59, Rambla* ☎ *93/485–9914, 93/485–9900 for backstage tour reservations* 🌐 *www.liceubarcelona.cat* 🎫 *Guided tours weekdays €11.50, weekends €10.50; 20-min express tour €5.50* ⏲ *Tours daily at 10 am in Spanish and English; guided express tours daily at 11:30, noon, 12:30, and 1. Backstage tours in Spanish at 9 am, including wardrobe and dressing rooms (€12.50), must be arranged by reservation* Ⓜ *Liceu.*

Fodor's Choice ★ **La Boqueria.** Barcelona's most spectacular food market, also known as the Mercat de Sant Josep, is an explosion of life and color graced with wonderful little tapas bar–restaurants (with counter seating only). Stall after stall of fruit, herbs, wild mushrooms, vegetables, nuts, candied preserves, cheese, ham, fish, poultry, and provender of every imaginable genus and strain greet you as you turn in from La Rambla and wade through the throng of shoppers and casual visitors. Under a Moderniste hangar of wrought-iron girders and stained glass, the market occupies a neoclassical square built in 1840 by architect Francesc Daniel Molina. The ionic columns visible around the edges of the market were part of the mid-19th-century neoclassical square constructed here after the original Sant Josep convent was torn down, uncovered in 2001 after more than a century of neglect. Highlights include the sunny greengrocer's market outside (to the right if you've come in from La Rambla), along with **Pinotxo** (Pinocchio), just inside to the right, where owner Juanito Bayén and his family serve some of the best food in Barcelona. (The secret? "Fresh, fast, hot, salty, and garlicky.") Pinotxo—marked with a ceramic portrait of the wooden-nosed prevaricator himself—is typically overbooked. But take heart; the **Kiosko Universal,** over toward the port side of the market, or **Quim de la Boqueria** both offer delicious alternatives. Don't miss the herb- and wild-mushroom stand at the back of La Boqueria, with its display of *fruits del bosc* (fruits of the forest): wild mushrooms, herbs, nuts, and berries. ✉ *La Rambla 91, Rambla* 🌐 *www.boqueria.info* ⏲ *Mon.–Sat. 8–8* Ⓜ *Liceu.*

FAMILY Fodor's Choice ★ **Museu Marítim.** The superb Maritime Museum, which is currently under renovation, is housed in the 13th-century **Drassanes Reials** (Royal Shipyards), at the foot of La Rambla adjacent to the harbor front. This vast covered complex launched the ships of Catalonia's powerful Mediterranean fleet directly from its yards into the port (the water once reached the level of the eastern facade of the building). Today

GETTING ORIENTED

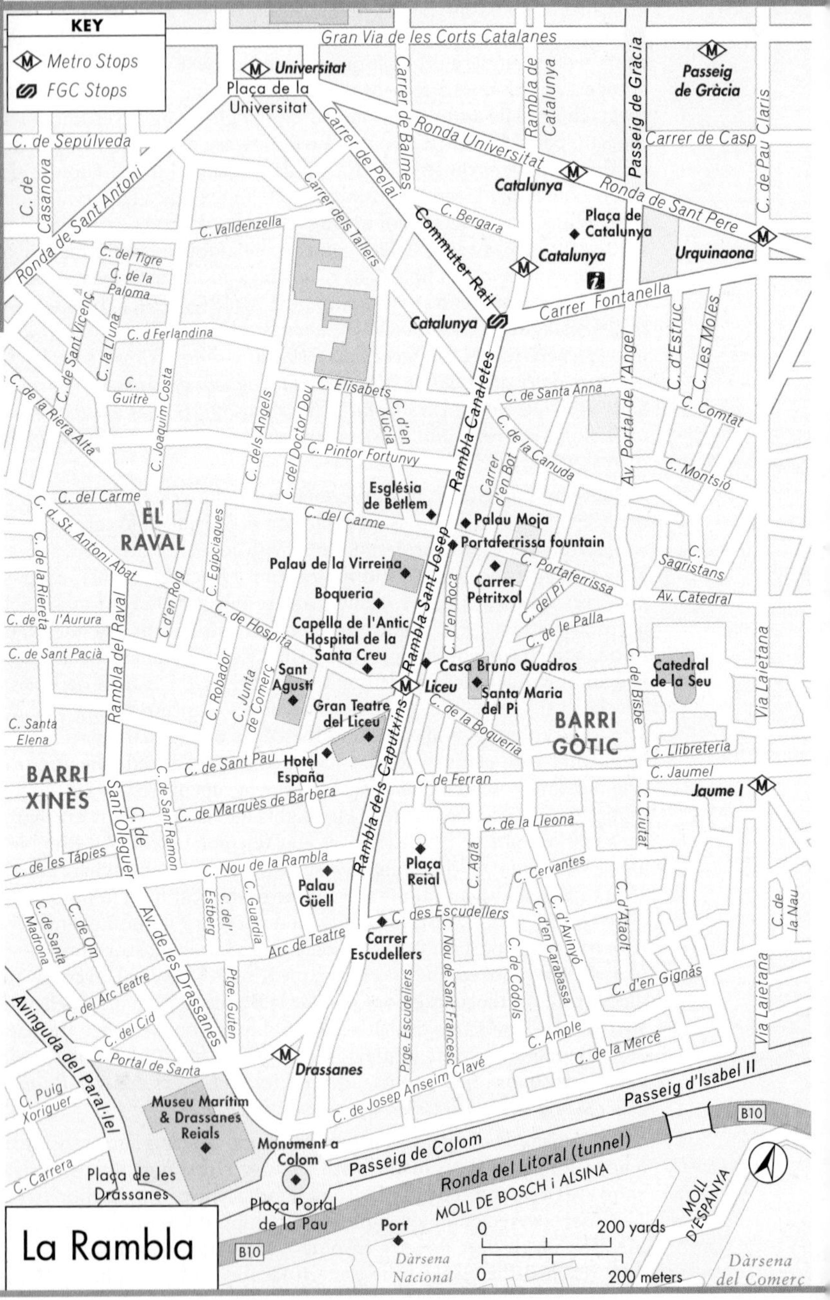

TIMING

Allow three to four hours, including stops, for exploring La Rambla. The best times to find things open are 9 to 2 and 4 to 8, although this popular promenade has a life of its own 24 hours a day. Some museums remain open through the lunch hour but others close—go online or ask at your nearest Tourist Information office to check. Most church hours are 9 to 1:30 and 4:30 to 8.

GETTING HERE

The Plaça de Catalunya metro stop will put you at the head of La Rambla in front of the Café Zurich, Barcelona's most famous rendezvous point. From here it's just a few steps down to the fountain on the right side of La Rambla de Canaletes.

QUICK BITES

Café de l'Opera. Across La Rambla from the Liceu opera house, Café de l'Opera is a favorite Barcelona hangout. The waiters are seasoned pros, the tapas come in ample portions, and the Thonet chairs and etched mirrors give the café historic charm. Always bustling, especially when a performance lets out at the Liceu, this is a place to keep a close eye on your belongings. ✉ *La Rambla 74, Rambla* ☏ *93/317–7585* Ⓜ *Liceu.*

WORD OF MOUTH

"La Boqueria is a fantastic market! It is true that a few of the stands near La Rambla entrance can be oriented toward tourists, but go behind those to the main body of the mercado and anyone interested in food will be in heaven! Yes, the prices might be a tad higher than they are in other local markets, but few foreign tourists will care about paying a few cents more per kilo of calçots." —ekscrunchy

TOP ATTRACTIONS

Boqueria

Gran Teatre del Liceu

Palau Güell

TOP EXPERIENCES

Browsing (and grazing) in the Boqueria market

Exploring Palau Güell

Strolling La Rambla

Taking a tour of the opera house

WHERE TO EAT (⇨ CH. 3)

Café Viena

Can Culleretes

El Irati

MariscCO

HAPPENING NIGHTLIFE (⇨ CH. 5)

Bar Pastis

Boadas

Glaciar

Jamboree-Jazz and Dance-Club

AREA SHOPS (⇨ CH. 7)

Art Escudellers

Custo Barcelona

Ganiveteria Roca

these are the world's largest and best-preserved medieval shipyards; centuries ago, at a time when Greece was a province of the House of Aragón (1377–88), they were of crucial importance to the sea power of Catalonia (then the heavyweight in an alliance with Aragón). On the Avinguda del Paral.lel side of Drassanes is a completely intact section of the 14th- to 15th-century walls—Barcelona's third and final ramparts—that encircled El Raval along the Paral.lel and the Rondas de Sant Pau, Sant Antoni, and Universitat. (*Ronda,* the term used for the "rounds" or patrols soldiers made atop the defensive walls, became the name for the avenues that replaced them.) The earliest part of Drassanes is the section farthest from the sea along Carrer de Portal de Santa Madrona. Subsequent naves were added in the 17th and 18th centuries.

Though the shipyards seem more like a cathedral than a naval construction site, the Maritime Museum is filled with vessels, including a spectacular collection of ship models. The life-size reconstruction of the galley of Juan de Austria, commander of the Spanish fleet in the Battle of Lepanto, is perhaps the most impressive display in the museum. Figureheads, nautical gear, early navigational charts, and medieval nautical lore enhance the experience, and headphones and infrared pointers provide a first-rate self-guided tour. Concerts, often featuring early-music master and viola de gamba virtuoso Jordi Savall, are occasionally held in this acoustic gem. The cafeteria is Barcelona's hands-down winner for dining in the midst of medieval elegance. Don't miss the small bronze reproduction of a sailing ship, commemorating the 1571 Battle of Lepanto, out on La Rambla corner nearest the port. ✉ *Av. de les Drassanes s/n, Rambla* ☎ *93/342–9920* 🌐 *www.mmb.cat* 🎟 *€3.50 (free on Sun.)* ⏲ *Daily 10–8* Ⓜ *Drassanes.*

Fodor's Choice ★ **Palau Güell.** Gaudí built this mansion in 1886–89 for textile baron Count Eusebi de Güell Bacigalupi, his most important patron. (The prominent four bars of the *senyera,* the banner of Catalonia, on the facade between the parabolic arches of the entrance attest to the nationalist fervor the two men shared.) Gaudí's principal obsession in this project was to find a way to illuminate this seven-story house, hemmed in as it is by other buildings in the cramped quarters of El Raval. The dark facade is a dramatic foil for the brilliance of the inside, where spear-shape Art Nouveau columns frame the windows, rising to support a series of detailed and elaborately carved wood ceilings.

The basement stables are famous for the "fungiform" (mushroom-like) columns carrying the weight of the whole building. Note Gaudí's signature parabolic arches between the columns and the way the arches meet overhead, forming a canopy of palm fronds. (The beauty of the construction was probably little consolation to the political prisoners held here during the 1936–39 Civil War.) The patio where the horses were groomed receives light through a skylight, one of many devices Gaudí used to brighten the space. Don't miss the figures of the faithful hounds, with the rings in their mouths for hitching horses, or the wooden bricks laid down in lieu of cobblestones in the entryway upstairs and on the ramp down to the basement grooming area, to deaden the sound of horses' hooves. The chutes on the Carrer Nou

A shipshape collection of nautical wonders is on display at the Museu Marítim.

de la Rambla side of the basement were for loading feed straight in from street level overhead; the catwalk and spiral staircase were for the servants to use, en route to their duties.

Upstairs are three successive receiving rooms; the wooden ceilings are progressively more spectacular, in the complexity of their richly molded floral motifs. The third receiving room, the one farthest in, with the most elaborate ornamentation, has a jalousie in the balcony: a double grate through which Güell was able to observe—and eavesdrop (like the name implies)—on his arriving guests. The main hall, with the three-story-tall tower reaching up above the roof, was for parties, dances, and receptions. Musicians played from the balcony; the overhead balcony window was for the principal singer. Double doors enclose a chapel of hammered copper with retractable *prie-dieux*; a small bench for two is built into the right side of the altar. Around the corner is a small organ, the flutes in rectangular tubes climbing the central shaft of the building.

The dining room is dominated by a beautiful mahogany banquet table seating ten, an Art Nouveau fireplace in the shape of a deeply curving horseshoe arch, and walls with floral and animal motifs. Note the Star of David in the woodwork over the window and the Asian religious themes in the vases on the mantelpiece. From the outside rear terrace, the polished Garraf marble of the main part of the house is exposed; the brick servants' quarters are on the left. The passageway built toward La Rambla was all that came of a plan to buy an intervening property and connect three houses into one grand structure, a scheme that never materialized.

STALINIST CHEKAS IN BARCELONA

The Stalinist purge carried out against Trotskyist elements in the Republican left, early in the Civil War, came very close to claiming the life of British novelist George Orwell, author of *Animal Farm* and *Nineteen Eighty-Four,* who had joined a Trotsky-affiliated militia unit when he volunteered to fight against the forces of fascism in Spain in 1936. Orwell joined the Workers' Party of Marxist Unification (POUM) but soon found himself embroiled in the internecine warfare of the various factions on the Left: the POUM against the Confederación Nacional del Trabajo (CNT), the CNT against the Unified Socialist Party of Catalonia (which was getting arms and directives from Moscow)—a stew of Stalinists, Trotskyites, and anarchists.

Orwell was wounded in May 1937, and sent to Barcelona to recuperate, by which time the political situation had more or less collapsed. His POUM affiliation put him in danger from the pro-Soviet Communists, and he left the country in June. Out of his experiences came the book *Homage to Catalonia* (1938).

A footnote to this is that the basement of Palau Güell was used as a *cheka* (the Russian word for prison or detention center) by the Stalinist faction, and it was into this dungeon that Andreu Nin, secretary-general of Barcelona's Trotskyist faction, disappeared in 1937, never to be seen again.

Gaudí is most himself on the roof, where his playful, polychrome ceramic chimneys seem like preludes to later works like the Park Güell and La Pedrera. Look for the flying-bat weather vane over the main chimney, a reference to the Catalan king Jaume I, who brought the house of Aragón to its 13th-century imperial apogee in the Mediterranean. Jaume I's affinity for bats is said to have stemmed from his Majorca campaign, when, according to one version, he was awakened by a fluttering *rat penat* (literally, "condemned mouse") in time to stave off a Moorish night attack. Another version attributes the presence of the bat in Jaume I's coat of arms to his gratitude to the Sufi sect that helped him to successfully invade Majorca, using the bat as a signal indicating when and where to attack. See if you can find the hologram of COBI, Javier Mariscal's 1992 Olympic mascot, on a restored ceramic chimney (hint: the all-white one at the Rambla end of the roof terrace). ✉ *Nou de la Rambla 3–5, Rambla* ☎ *93/472–5775* 🌐 *palauguell.cat/come-palace* 🎫 *€12* 🕒 *Apr.–Oct., Tues.–Sun. 10–8; Nov.–Mar., Tues.–Sun. 10–5:30* Ⓜ *Drassanes, Liceu.*

Plaça Reial. Nobel Prize–winning novelist Gabriel García Márquez, architect and urban planner Oriol Bohigas, and Pasqual Maragall, former president of the Catalonian Generalitat, are among the many famous people said to have acquired apartments overlooking this elegant square, a chiaroscuro masterpiece in which neoclassical symmetry clashes with big-city street funk. Plaça Reial is bordered by stately ocher facades with balconies overlooking the wrought-iron **Fountain of the Three Graces,** and an array of lampposts designed by Gaudí in 1879. Cafés and restaurants—several of them excellent—line the square. Plaça

Reial is most colorful on Sunday morning, when collectors gather to trade stamps and coins; after dark it's a center of downtown nightlife for the jazz-minded, the young, and the adventurous (it's best to be streetwise touring this area in the late hours). Bar Glaciar, on the uphill corner toward La Rambla, is a booming beer station for young international travelers. Tarantos has top flamenco performances, and Jamboree offers world-class jazz. ✉ *Pl. Reial, Rambla* Ⓜ *Liceu.*

Portaferrissa fountain. Both the fountain and the ceramic representation of Barcelona's second set of walls and the early Rambla are worth studying carefully. If you can imagine pulling out the left side of the ceramic scene and looking broadside at the amber yellow 13th-century walls that ran down this side of La Rambla, you will see a clear picture of what this spot looked like in medieval times. The sandy Rambla ran along outside the walls, while the portal looked down through the ramparts into the city. As the inscription on the fountain explains, the Porta Ferrica, or Iron Door, was named for the iron measuring stick attached to the wood and used in the 13th and 14th centuries to establish a unified standard for measuring goods. ✉ *La Rambla and Carrer Portaferrissa, Rambla* Ⓜ *Pl. de Catalunya, Liceu.*

WORTH NOTING

Carrer dels Escudellers. Named for the *terrissaires* (earthenware potters) who worked here making *escudellas* (bowls or stew pots), this colorful loop is an interesting subtrip off La Rambla. Go left at Plaça del Teatre and you'll pass the landmark **Grill Room** at No. 8, an Art Nouveau saloon with graceful wooden decor and an ornate oak bar; next is **La Fonda Escudellers,** another lovely, glass- and stone-encased dining emporium. (At neither—alas!—is the food especially good.) At Nos. 23–25 is Barcelona's most comprehensive ceramics display, **Art Escudellers.** Across the street, with chickens roasting over the corner, is **Los Caracoles,** once among the most traditional of Barcelona's restaurants and now mainly the choice of tourists with deep pockets. Still, the bar and the walk-through kitchen on the way in are picturesque, as are the dining rooms and the warren of little stairways between them. Another 100 yards down Carrer Escudellers is **Plaça George Orwell,** named for the author of *Homage to Catalonia,* a space created to bring light and air into this formerly iffy neighborhood. **■TIP→ The little flea market that hums along on Saturday is a great place to browse.**

Take a right on Carrer de la Carabassa and walk down this cobbled alley. It is arched over with graceful bridges that once connected the houses with their adjacent gardens. At the end of the street, looming atop her own basilica, is **Nostra Senyora de la Mercè** (Our Lady of Mercy). This giant representation of Barcelona's patron saint is a 20th-century (1940) addition to the 18th-century Església de la Mercè; the view of La Mercè gleaming in the sunlight, babe in arms, is one of the Barcelona waterfront's most impressive sights. As you arrive at Carrer Ample, note the **15th-century door** with a winged Sant Miquel Archangel delivering a squash backhand to a scaly Lucifer; it's from the Sant Miquel church, formerly part of City Hall, torn down in the early 19th century. From the Mercè, a walk out Carrer Ample (to the right) leads back to La Rambla. Don't miss the grocery store on the corner of Carrer

CLOSE UP

Barcelona's Lovers' Day

Barcelona's best day? Easy. April 23—St. George's Day, La Diada de Sant Jordi, Barcelona's "Valentine's Day." A day so sweet and playful, so goofy and romantic, that 6 million Catalans go giddy from dawn to dusk.

Legend has it that the patron saint of Catalonia, the knight-errant St. George (Sant Jordi in Catalan) slew a dragon that was about to devour a beautiful princess in the little village of Montblanc, south of Barcelona. From the dragon's blood sprouted a rosebush, from which the hero plucked the prettiest blossom for the princess. Hence the traditional Rose Festival celebrated in Barcelona since the Middle Ages, to honor chivalry and romantic love: a day for men to present their true loves with roses as well. In 1923 the festival merged with International Book Day to mark the anniversary of the all-but-simultaneous deaths of Miguel de Cervantes and William Shakespeare, on April 23, 1616; it then became the custom for the ladies to present their flower-bearing swains with a book in return.

More than 4 million roses and half a million books are sold in Catalonia on Sant Jordi's Day. In Barcelona, bookstalls run the length of nearly every major thoroughfare, and although it's an official workday, nearly everybody manages to duck out for at least a while and go browsing. There is a 24-hour reading of *Don Quixote*. Authors come to bookstalls to sign their works. Given Barcelona's importance as a publishing capital, the literary side of the holiday gets special attention.

A Roman soldier martyred for his Christian beliefs in the 4th century, St. George is venerated as the patron saint of 15 European countries—England, Greece, and Romania among them. Images of St. George are everywhere in Barcelona—most notably, perhaps, on the facade of the Catalonian seat of government, the Generalitat. Art Nouveau sculptor Eusebi Arnau depicted Sant Jordi skewering the unlucky dragon on the facade of the Casa Amatller, and on the corner of Els Quatre Gats café. Gaudí referenced the story with an entire building, the Casa Batlló, with the saint's cross implanted on the scaly roof and the skulls and bones of the dragon's victims framing the windows.

Sant Jordi's Day roses are tied with a spike of wheat (for his association with springtime and fertility) and a little red and yellow *senyera*, the Catalonian flag.

In Sarrià there are displays of 45 varieties of rose, representing 45 different kinds of love, from impossible to unrequited, from Platonic to filial and maternal. In the Plaça Sant Jaume the Generalitat, its patio filled with roses, opens its doors to the public. Choral groups sing love songs in the Barri Gòtic; jazz combos play in Plaça del Pi. La Rambla is packed solid from the Diagonal to the Mediterranean, with barcelonins basking in the warmth of spring and romance. Rare is the woman anywhere in town without a rose in hand, bound with a red-and-yellow ribbon that says "t'estimo": I love you.

Summer days bring strollers to Barcelona's main thoroughfare, La Rambla.

de la Carabassa—**La Lionesa,** at Carrer Ample 21, one of Barcelona's best-preserved 19th-century shops. At No. 7 is the **Solé** shoe store, with handmade shoes from all over the world. You might recognize Plaça Medinaceli, next on the left, from Pedro Almodovar's film *Todo Sobre Mi Madre* (*All About My Mother*); from the scene featuring the heroine's dog and her aging father. ✉ *Carrer dels Escudellers* Ⓜ *Drassanes.*

Carrer Petritxol. Just steps from La Rambla and one of Barcelona's most popular streets, lined with art galleries, *xocolaterías* (chocolate shops), and stationers, this narrow passageway dates back to the 15th century, when it was used as a shortcut through the backyard of a local property owner. Working up Petritxol from Plaça del Pi, stop to admire the late-17th-century *sgraffito* design (mural ornamentation made by scratching away a plaster surface), some of the city's best, on the facade over the **Ganiveteria Roca** knife store, *the* place for cutlery in Barcelona. Next on the right at Petritxol 2 is the 200-year-old **Dulcinea,** with a portrait of the great Catalan playwright Àngel Guimerà (1847–1924) over the fireplace; drop in for the house specialty, the *suizo* ("Swiss" hot chocolate and whipped cream). Also at Petritxol 2 is the **Llibreria Quera,** one of the city's best hiking and mountaineering bookstores.

Note the plaque to Àngel Guimerà over No. 4 and the **Art Box** gallery at Nos. 1–3 across the street. At No. 5 is **Sala Parès,** founded in 1840, the dean of Barcelona's art galleries, where major figures like Isidre Nonell, Santiago Russinyol, and Picasso have shown their work. Farther up are the gallery **Trama** at No. 8 and the **Galeria Petritxol** at No. 10. **Xocoa** at No. 9 is another popular chocolate shop. Look carefully at the "curtains" carved into the wooden door at No. 11 and the floral ornamentation around the edges of the ceiling inside; the store is **Granja la Pallaresa,** yet another enclave of chocolate and *ensaimada* (a light-looking but deadly sweet Majorcan pastry, with confectioner's sugar dusted on top). Finally on the left at No. 17 is the **Rigol** fine arts supply store. ✉ *Carrer PetrixolRambla* Ⓜ *Liceu, Pl. de Catalunya.*

Casa Bruno Quadros. Like something out of an amusement park, this former umbrella shop was whimsically designed (assembled is more like it) by Josep Vilaseca in 1885. A Chinese dragon with a parasol, Egyptian balconies and galleries, and a Peking lantern all bring exotic touches that were very much in vogue at the time of the Universal Exposition of 1888. Now housing a branch office of the bank Caixa de Sabadell, this prankster of a building is much in keeping with Art Nouveau's eclectic playfulness and fascination with things Oriental, though it has never been taken very seriously as an expression of Modernisme and, consequently, is generally omitted from most studies of Art Nouveau architecture. ✉ *La Rambla 82, Rambla* Ⓜ *Liceu.*

GEOMETRICAL BARCELONA

Barcelona's three geometrically named avenues, the Diagonal, the Meridiana, and the Paral.lel, were devised by Ildefons Cerdà (the urban planner who designed the post-1860 Eixample) as high-speed urban thoroughfares that would funnel traffic through and beyond the checkerboard of his urban grid. The Paral.lel is so named because it parallels the equator. The Meridiana is perpendicular to the Paral.lel and parallels the Greenwich Meridian. The Diagonal runs at an oblique angle across the Eixample.

Església de Betlem. The Church of Bethlehem is one of Barcelona's few Baroque buildings, and hulks stodgily on La Rambla just above Rambla de les Flors. Burned out completely at the start of the Civil War in 1936, the church is unremarkable inside; the outside, spruced up, is made of what looks like quilted stone. If you find this less than a must-see, worry not: you have all of Barcelona for company, with the possible exception of Betlem's parishioners. This was where Viceroy Amat claimed the hand of the young Virreina-to-be when in 1780 she was left in the lurch by the viceroy's nephew. In a sense, Betlem has compensated the city with the half-century of good works the young widow was able to accomplish with her husband's fortune. The Nativity scenes on display down the stairs at the side entrance on La Rambla at Christmastime are an old tradition here, allegedly begun by St. Francis of Assisi, who assembled the world's first such crèche in Barcelona in the early 13th century. ✉ *Carrer del Carme 2, Rambla* ☎ *93/318–3823* Ⓜ *Pl. de Catalunya.*

Monument a Colom (*Columbus Monument*). This Barcelona landmark to Christopher Columbus sits grandly at the foot of La Rambla along the wide harbor-front promenade of Passeig de Colom, not far from the very shipyards (**Drassanes Reials**) that constructed two of the ships of his tiny but immortal fleet. Standing atop the 150-foot-high iron column—the base of which is aswirl with gesticulating angels—Columbus seems to be looking out at "that far-distant shore" he discovered; in fact he's pointing, with his 18-inch-long finger, in the general direction of Sicily. The monument was erected for the 1888 Universal Exposition to commemorate the commissioning of Columbus's voyage, in Barcelona, by the monarchs Ferdinand and Isabella, in 1491. Since the royal court was at that time (and, until 1561, remained) itinerant, Barcelona's role in the discovery of the New World is, at best, circumstantial. In fact, Barcelona was consequently excluded from trade with the Americas by Isabella, so Catalonia and Columbus have never really seen eye to eye. For a bird's-eye view over La Rambla and the port, take the elevator to the small viewing platform (*mirador*) at the top of the column. The entrance is on the harbor side. ✉ *Portal de la Pau s/n, Rambla* ☎ *93/285–3832* 🎫 *€4* ⏲ *Mar.–Oct., daily 8:30–8:30; Nov.–Feb., daily 8:30–7:30* Ⓜ *Drassanes.*

Palau de la Virreina. The neoclassical Virreina Palace, built by a viceroy to Peru in 1778, is now a major center for themed exhibitions of paintings, photography, and historical artifacts. The **Tiquet Rambles** office on the ground floor, run by the municipal *Institut de Cultura* (daily 10–8:30) is the place to go for information and last-minute tickets to concerts, theater and dance performances, gallery shows, and museums. The portal to the palace, and the pediments carved with elaborate floral designs, are especially beautiful. ✉ *Rambla de les Flors 99, Rambla* ☎ *93/301–7775, 93/316–1000 for Tiquet Rambles* 🌐 *lavirreina.bcn.cat* 🎫 *Free; €3 charge for some exhibits* ⏲ *Tues.–Sun. 12–8* Ⓜ *Liceu.*

Palau Moja. The first palace to occupy this corner on La Rambla was built in 1702 and inhabited by the Marquès de Moja. The present austere palace was completed in 1790 and, with the Betlem church across the street, forms a small baroque-era pocket along La Rambla. The Palau is normally open to the public only on rare occasions, such as special exhibitions—when visitors also have the chance to see the handsome mural and painted ceiling by Francesc Pla, known as El Vigatà (meaning from Vic, a town 66 km north of Barcelona). In the late 19th century the Palau Moja was bought by Antonio López y López, Marquès de Comillas, and it was here that Jacint Verdaguer, Catalonia's national poet and chaplain of the marquess's shipping company, the Compañia Transatlántica, wrote his famous patriotic epic poem "L'Atlàntida." ✉ *Portaferrissa 1, Rambla* ☎ *93/316–2740* Ⓜ *Pl. de Catalunya.*

Port. Beyond the Columbus monument—behind the ornate Duana (now the Barcelona Port Authority headquarters)—is **Rambla de Mar,** a boardwalk with a drawbridge designed to allow boats into and out of the inner harbor. Rambla de Mar extends out to the **Moll d'Espanya,** with its Maremagnum shopping center, IMAX theater, and the excellent **Aquarium.** Next to the Duana you can board a Golondrina boat for a tour of the port and the waterfront or, from the Moll de Barcelona on the right, take a cable car to Montjuïc or Barceloneta. Trasmediterránea and the fleeter Buquebus passenger ferries leave for Italy and the Balearic Islands from the Moll de Barcelona; at the end of the quay is Barcelona's World Trade Center and the Eurostars Grand Marina Hotel. ✉ *Port* Ⓜ *Drassanes.*

THE BARRI GÒTIC

Sightseeing ★★★★★
Nightlife ★★☆☆☆
Dining ★★★★☆
Lodging ★★★☆☆
Shopping ★★★★☆

No city in Europe has an ancient quarter to rival Barcelona's Barri Gòtic in its historic atmosphere and the sheer density of its monumental buildings. It's a stroller's delight, where you can expect to hear the strains of a flute or a classical guitar from around the next corner. Thronged with sightseers by day, the quarter can be eerily quiet at night, a stone oasis of silence at the eye of the storm.

A labyrinth of medieval buildings, squares, and narrow cobblestone streets, the Barri Gòtic comprises the area around the Catedral de la Seu, built over Roman ruins you can still visit and filled with the Gothic structures that marked the zenith of Barcelona's power in the 15th century. On certain corners you feel as if you're making a genuine excursion back in time, and, for a brief flash, suddenly the 21st century, not the 15th, seems like a figment of your imagination.

The Barri Gòtic rests squarely atop the first Roman settlement. Sometimes referred to as the *rovell d'ou* (the yolk of the egg), this high ground the Romans called Mons Taber coincides almost exactly with the early 1st- to 4th-century fortified town of Barcino. Sights to see here include the Plaça del Rei, the remains of Roman Barcino underground beneath the Museum of the History of the City, the Plaça Sant Jaume and the area around the onetime Roman Forum, the medieval Jewish Quarter, and the ancient Plaça Sant Just.

TOP ATTRACTIONS

Baixada de Santa Eulàlia. Down Carrer Sant Sever from the side door of the cathedral cloister, past Carrer Sant Domènec del Call and the Església de Sant Sever, is a tiny shrine, in an alcove overhead, dedicated to the 4th-century martyr Santa Eulàlia, patron saint of the city. Down this hill, or *baixada* (descent), Eulàlia was rolled in a barrel filled with—as the Jacint Verdaguer verse in ceramic tile on the wall reads—*glavis i ganivets de dos talls* (swords and double-edged knives), the final of the

13 tortures to which she was subjected before her crucifixion at Plaça del Pedró. ✉ *Carrer Sant Sever s/n, Barri Gòtic* Ⓜ *Liceu, Jaume I.*

Casa de l'Ardiaca (*Archdeacon's House*). The interior of this 15th-century building, home of the Municipal Archives (upstairs), has superb views of the remains of the 4th-century Roman watchtowers and walls. Look at the Montjuïc sandstone carefully, and you will see blocks taken from other buildings, carved and beveled into decorative shapes, proof of the haste of the Romans to fortify the site as the Visigoths approached from the north, when the Pax Romana collapsed. The marble letter box by the front entrance was designed in 1895 by Lluís Domènech i Montaner for the Lawyer's Professional Association; as the story goes, it was meant to symbolize, in the images of the doves, the lofty flight to the heights of justice and, in the images of the turtles, the plodding pace of administrative procedures. In the center of the lovely courtyard here, across from the Santa Llúcia chapel, is a fountain; on the day of Corpus Christi in June the fountain impressively supports *l'ou com balla,* or "the dancing egg," a Barcelona tradition in which eggs are set to bobbing atop jets of water in various places around the city. ✉ *Carrer de Santa Llúcia 1, Barri Gòtic* ☎ *93/256–2255* 🌐 *www.bcn.es/arxiu/arxiuhistoric* ⏲ *Archives Sept.–June, weekdays 9–8:45, Sat. 9–1; July and Aug., weekdays 9–7:30* Ⓜ *Liceu, Jaume I.*

Ajuntament de Barcelona. The 15th-century city hall on Plaça Sant Jaume faces the Palau de la Generalitat, with its mid-18th-century neoclassical facade, across the square once occupied by the Roman Forum. The Ajuntament is a rich repository of sculpture and painting by the great Catalan masters, from Marès to Gargallo to Clarà, from Subirachs to Miró and Llimona. Inside is the famous Saló de Cent, from which the Consell de Cent, Europe's oldest democratic parliament, governed Barcelona between 1373 and 1714. The Saló de les Croniques (Hall of Chronicles) is decorated with Josep Maria Sert's immense black-and-burnished-gold murals (1928) depicting the early-14th-century Catalan campaign in Byzantium and Greece under the command of Roger de Flor. Sert's perspective technique makes the paintings seem to follow you around the room. The city hall is open (admission-free) to visitors on Sunday morning, with guided visits in English at 11; on local holidays; and for occasional concerts or events in the Saló de Cent. ✉ *Pl. Sant Jaume 1, Barri Gòtic* ☎ *93/402–7000* 🌐 *www.bcn.es* ⏲ *Sun. 10–1:30; Feb. 12, Apr. 23 and May 30, 10–8* Ⓜ *Jaume I, Liceu.*

Fodor's Choice ★ **Catedral de la Seu.** Barcelona's cathedral is a repository of centuries of the city's history and legend—although as a work of architecture visitors might find it a bit of a disappointment, compared to the Mediterranean Gothic Santa Maria del Mar and Gaudí's Moderniste Sagrada Família. It was built between 1298 and 1450; work on the spire and neo-Gothic facade began in 1892 and was not completed until 1913. Historians are not sure about the identity of the architect: one name often proposed is Jaume Fabre, a native of Majorca. The plan of the church is cruciform, with transepts standing in as bases for the great tower—a design also seen in England's Exeter Cathedral. The building is perhaps most impresssive at night, floodlit with the stained-glass windows illuminated from inside; book a room with a balcony at the Hotel Colon, facing the Cathedral square, and make the most of it.

GETTING ORIENTED

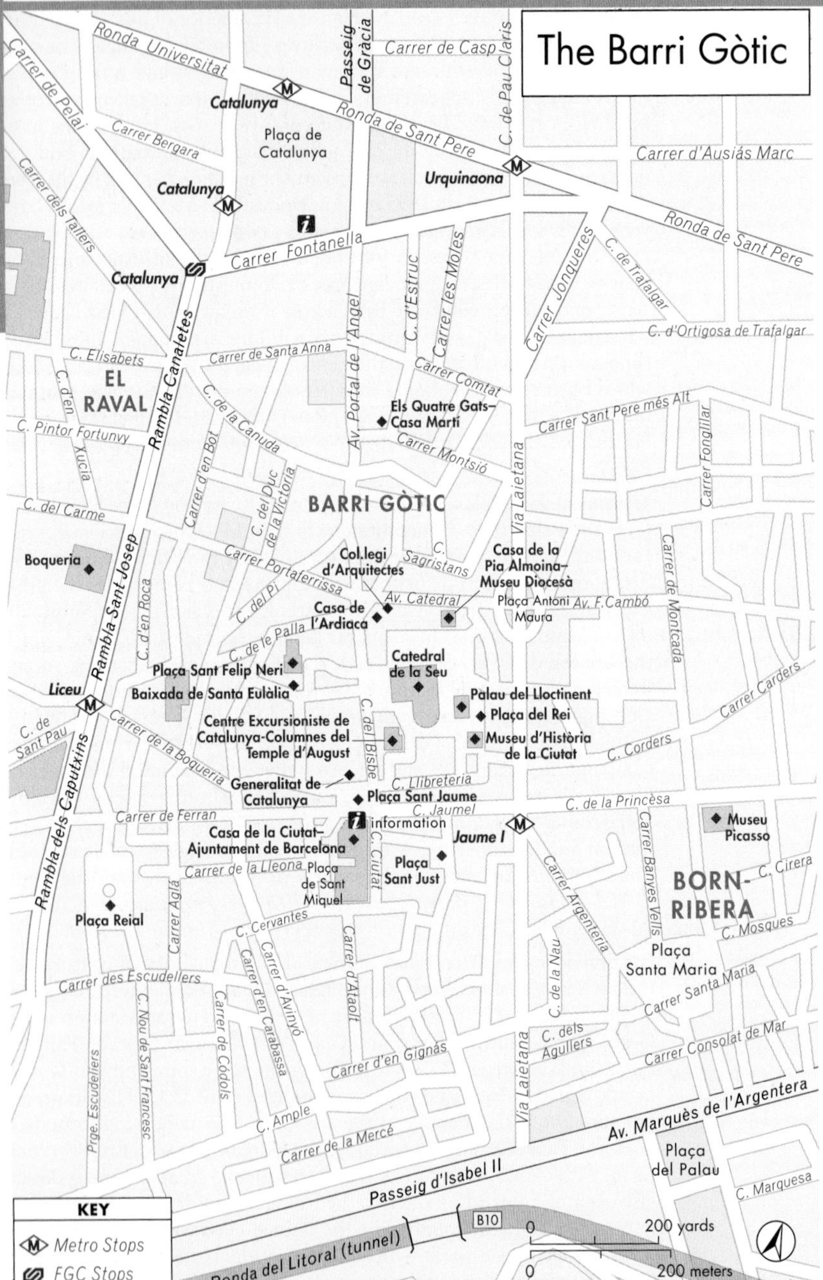

TIMING

Exploring the Barri Gòtic should take about three hours, depending on how often you stop and how long you linger. Allow another hour or two for the Museum of the History of the City. Plan to visit before 1:30 or after 4:30, or you'll miss a lot of street life; some churches are closed midafternoon as well.

GETTING HERE

The best way to get to the Barri Gòtic and the cathedral is to start down La Rambla from the Plaça de Catalunya metro stop. Take your first left on Carrer Canuda and walk past Barcelona's Ateneu Barcelonès at No. 6, through Plaça Villa de Madrid and its Roman tombstones, then through Passatge and Carrer Duc de la Victoria and out Carrer Boters (where the boot makers were located in medieval times) to Plaça Nova.

QUICK BITES

Café de l'Acadèmia. Government workers from nearby Pl. Sant Jaume fill Café de l'Acadèmia at lunchtime. ✉ *Carrer Lledó 18, Barri Gòtic* ☎ *93/319–8253.*

El Gallo Quirico. Take a breather at this restaurant in the heart of the Barri Gòtic, just a block west of Plaça Sant Jaume, where you can get a table between two 4th-century Roman watchtowers. ✉ *Carrer d'Avinyó 19, Barri Gòtic* ☎ *93/301–0280.*

Mesón del Café. If a coffee is all you need, look for the Mesón del Café, where a deep breath is nearly as strengthening as a cappuccino. ✉ *Carrer Llibreteria 16, Barri Gòtic* ☎ *93/315–0754.*

TOP ATTRACTIONS

Catedral de la Seu

Els Quatre Gats–Casa Martí

Museu d'Història de la Ciutat

Plaça Sant Felip Neri

Plaça Sant Jaume

Roman columns of the Temple of 'Augustus

TOP EXPERIENCES

Exploring the Casa de l'Ardiaca and its' 4th-century Roman walls

Wandering through El Call, the Jewish Quarter

Listening to a guitarist behind the cathedral

Lingering over a coffee at the historic Els Quatre Gats–Casa Martí

Watching *sardanas* in the Plaça de la Catedral

WHERE TO EAT (⇨ CH. 3)

ATN Restaurant

Agut

Café de l'Acadèmia

Cometacinc

Cuines Santa Caterina

La Palma

Nonell

Shunka

Taller de Tapas

This is reputedly the darkest of all the world's great cathedrals—even at high noon the nave is enveloped in shadows, which give it magically much larger dimensions than it actually has—so it takes a while for your eyes to adjust to the rich, velvety pitch of the interior. Don't miss the beautifully carved choir stalls of the Knights of the Golden Fleece; the intricately and elaborately sculpted organ loft over the door out to Plaça Sant Iu (with its celebrated *Saracen's Head* sculpture); the series of 60-odd wood sculptures of evangelical figures along the exterior lateral walls of the choir; the cloister with its fountain and geese in the pond; and, in the crypt, the tomb of Santa Eulàlia.

St. Eulàlia, originally interred at Santa Maria del Mar—then known as Santa Maria de les Arenes (St. Mary of the Sands)—was moved to the cathedral in 1339, and venerated here as its patron and protector. *Eulalistas* (St. Eulàlia devotees, rivals of a sort to the followers of La Mercé, or Our Lady of Mercy) celebrate the fiesta of La Laia (the nickname for Eulàlia) February 9–15, and would like to see the cathedral named for her, but for the moment it is known simply as La Catedral, or in Catalan "La Seu" ("the See," or seat of the bishopric).

Enter from the front portal (there are also entrances through the cloister and from Carrer Comtes down the left side of the apse), and the first thing you see are the high-relief sculptures of the **story of St. Eulàlia,** on the near side of the choir stalls. The first scene, on the left, shows St. Eulàlia in front of Roman Consul Decius with her left hand on her heart and her outstretched right hand pointing at a cross in the distance. In the next, she is tied to a column and being whipped by the Consol's thugs. To the right of the door into the choir the unconscious Eulàlia is being hauled away, and in the final scene on the right she is being lashed to the X-shaped cross upon which she was crucified mid-February in the year 303. To the right of this high relief is a sculpture of the martyred heroine, resurrected as a living saint.

Among the two dozen ornate and gilded chapels in the basilica, pay due attention to the **Capilla de Lepanto,** dedicated to Santo Cristo de Lepanto, in the far right corner as you enter through the front door. According to legend, the 15th-century polychrome wood sculpture of a battle-scarred, dark-skinned Christ, visible on the altar of this 100-seat chapel behind a black-clad Mare de Deu dels Dolors (Our Lady of the Sorrows), was the bowsprit of the flagship Spanish galley at the battle fought between Christian and Ottoman fleets on October 7, 1571. (A plaque next to the alms box of the chapel notes that, though Juan de Austria was the commander in chief, the captain who led the fleet into battle was Lluís de Requesens, a Catalan aristocrat and prominent Spanish general during the reign of Felipe II.

Outside the main nave of the cathedral to the right, you'll find the leafy, palm tree–shaded **cloister** surrounding a tropical garden, and a pool populated by 13 snow-white geese, one for each of the tortures inflicted upon St. Eulàlia in an effort to break her faith. Legend has it that they are descendants of the flock of geese from Rome's Capitoline Hill, whose honking alarms roused the city to repel invaders during the days of the Roman Republic. Don't miss the fountain with the bronze

CLOSE UP

El Call: The Jewish Quarter

Barcelona's Jewish Quarter, the Call (a name derived from the Hebrew word *qahal, or* "meeting place"), is just to the Rambla side of the Palau de la Generalitat. Carrer del Call, Carrer de Sant Domènec del Call, Carrer Marlet, and Arc de Sant Ramón del Call mark the heart of the medieval ghetto. Confined by law to this area at the end of the 7th century (one reason the streets in Calls or Aljamas were so narrow was that their inhabitants could only build into the streets for more space), Barcelona's Jews were the private bankers to Catalonia's sovereign counts (only Jews could legally lend money). The Jewish community also produced many leading physicians, translators, and scholars in medieval Barcelona, largely because the Jewish faith rested on extensive Talmudic and textual study, thus promoting a high degree of literacy. The reproduction of a plaque bearing Hebrew text on the corner of Carrer Marlet and Arc de Sant Ramón del Call was the only physical reminder of the Jewish presence here until the medieval synagogue reopened in 2003.

The **Sinagoga Major de Barcelona** (✉ *Carrer Marlet 2, Barri Gòtic* 🌐 *www.calldebarcelona.org* 🎫 *€2.50* 🕓 *Tues.–Sat. 11–2, Sun. 4–7*), the restored original synagogue at the corner of Marlet and Sant Domènec del Call, is virtually all that survives of the Jewish presence in medieval Barcelona. Tours are given in English, Hebrew, and Spanish, and a booklet in English (€5) explains the history of the community.

The story of Barcelona's Jewish community came to a bloody end in August 1391, when during a time of famine and pestilence a nationwide outbreak of anti-Semitic violence reached Barcelona, with catastrophic results: nearly the entire Jewish population was murdered or forced to convert to Christianity.

sculpture of an equestrian St. George, hacking away at his perennial foe, the dragon, on the eastern corner of the cloister. On the day of Corpus Christi, this fountain is one of the more spectacular displays of the traditional *ou com balla* (dancing egg). The intimate **Santa Llúcia chapel** is at the front right corner of the block (reached by a separate entrance or from the cloister). Another Decius victim, St. Llúcia allegedly plucked out her own eyes to dampen the Roman consul's ardor, whereupon she miraculously generated new ones. Patron saint of seamstresses, of the blind, and of the light of human understanding, St. Llúcia is portrayed over the altar in the act of presenting her plucked-out eyes, sunny-side up on a plate, to an impassive Decius.

In front of the cathedral is the grand square of **Plaça de la Seu,** where on Saturday from 6 pm to 8 pm, Sunday morning, and occasional evenings, barcelonins gather to dance the *sardana,* the circular folk dance performed for centuries as a symbol-in-motion of Catalan identity and the solidarity of the Catalan people. Nimble-footed oldsters share the space with young *esbarts* (dance troupes), coats and bags piled in the center of the ring, all dancing together to the reedy music of the *cobla* (band) in smooth, deceptively simple, heel-and-toe sequences of steps.

The ornate Gothic interior of the Catedral de la Seu is always enclosed in shadows, even at high noon.

No tourist attraction, this: Catalans dance the *sardana* for themselves, for the pleasure of it. Also check out the leisure magazine listings for the annual series of evening organ concerts held in the cathedral. ✉ *Pl. de la Seu s/n, Barri Gòtic* ☎ *93/315–1554* 🌐 *www.catedralbcn.org* 🎟 *Free 8–12:45 and 5:15–7:30, €6 1–5* ⏲ *Daily 8–7:30* Ⓜ *Jaume I.*

Columnes del Temple d'August (*Columns of the Temple of Augustus*). The highest point in Roman Barcelona is marked with a circular millstone at the entrance to the Centre Excursioniste de Catalunya, a club dedicated to exploring the mountains and highlands of Catalonia on foot and on skis. Inside the entryway on the right are some of the best-preserved 1st- and 2nd-century Corinthian Roman columns in Europe. Massive, fluted, and crowned with the typical Corinthian acanthus leaves in two distinct rows under eight fluted sheaths, these columns remain only because Barcelona's early Christians elected, atypically, not to build their cathedral over the site of the previous temple. The Temple of Augustus, dedicated to the Roman emperor, occupied the northwest corner of the Roman Forum, which coincided approximately with today's Plaça Sant Jaume. ✉ *Centre Excursioniste de Catalunya, Carrer Paradís 10, Barri Gòtic* ☎ *93/315–2311, 93/256–2122* ⏲ *Mon. 10–2, Tues.–Sat. 10–7, Sun. 10–8* Ⓜ *Jaume I.*

Els Quatre Gats–Casa Martí. Built by Josep Puig i Cadafalch for the Martí family, this Art Nouveau house, a three-minute walk from the cathedral, was the fountainhead of Bohemianism in Barcelona. It was here in 1897 that four friends, notable dandies all—Ramon Casas, Pere Romeu, Santiago Russinyol and Miguel Utrillo—started a café-restaurant called the Els Quatre Gats (The Four Cats), meaning to make it *the* place for artists and art lovers to gather and shoot the breeze, in the best Left Bank tradition. (One of their wisest decisions was to mount a show, in February 1900, for an up-and-coming young painter named Pablo Picasso, who had done the illustration for the cover of the menu.) The exterior was decorated with figures by sculptor Eusebi Arnau (1864–1934), a darling of the Moderniste movement—notice the wrought-iron St. George and the dragon, which no Puig i Cadafalch project ever failed to include, over the door. Inside, the Four Cats hasn't changed an iota: the tile and stained glass are as they were; the bar is at it was; the walls are hung with copies of work by the original owners and their circle. (Pride of place goes to the Casas self-portait, smoking his pipe, comedically teamed up on a tandem bicycle with Romeu.) Drop in for a break: Who knows? You might be taking your café au lait in Picasso's chair. Have a quick look as well at the dining room in back, with its unusual gallery seating upstairs; the room (where Miró used to produce puppet theater) is charming, but the food, unfortunately, is so-so at best. *Quatre gats* ("four cats") is a Catalan euphemism for "hardly anybody," but the four founders were all definitely somebodies. ✉ *Carrer Montsió 3 bis, Barri Gòtic* ☎ *93/302–4140* 🌐 *www.4gats.com* ⏲ *Daily 10 am–1 am* Ⓜ *Pl. de Catalunya.*

BARCELONA'S DANCING EGG

Barcelona's early June Corpus Christi celebration is a day to visit the city's medieval courtyards to see fountains, when the *ou com balla* (dancing eggs) are bobbing miraculously atop the jets of water. The egg, in Christian ritual a symbol of fertility, represents the rebirth of life after Easter's tragic events. In the Mediterranean's megalithic religions that preceded Christianity, the dancing egg augured a successful growing season as spring turned to summer.

Generalitat de Catalunya. Opposite city hall, the Palau de la Generalitat is the seat of the autonomous Catalan government. Seen through the front windows of this ornate 15th-century palace, the gilded ceiling of the Saló de Sant Jordi (St. George's Hall), named for Catalonia's dragon-slaying patron saint, gives an idea of the lavish decor within. Carrer del Bisbe, running along the right side of the building from the square to the Cathedral, offers a favorite photo op: the ornate gargoyle-bedecked Gothic bridge overhead, connecting the Generalitat to the building across the street. The Generalitat opens to the public on the second and fourth Saturdays of the month, on Día de Sant Jordi (St. George's Day: April 23), during the Fiesta de la Mercé in late September, and on various other city or Catalonian holidays. There are carillon concerts here on Sunday at noon, another opportunity to see the inside of the building. ✉ *Pl. de Sant Jaume 4, Barri Gòtic* ☎ *93/402–4600* 🌐 *www.gencat.net* ⏲ *2nd and 4th Sat. of every month and some holidays. Check with protocol office through main telephone number* Ⓜ *Jaume I.*

BATS IN THE BELFRY

Spain, like the United States, chose the eagle as its national bird, but Catalonia's aerial mascot, oddly enough, is the bat—allegedly because King Jaume I was a fan, ever since bats alerted his troops to repel a dawn attack during his Balearic campaign. Barcelona bats hang from the chandeliers in the City Hall's Saló de Cent, are sculpted into the Triumphal Arch on Passeig Lluís Companys, and preside over the main Carrer Hospital entrance to the medieval hospital.

Fodor'sChoice ★ **Museu d'Història de la Ciutat** (*Museum of the History of the City*). This fascinating museum (MUHBA for short) just off Plaça del Rei traces Barcelona's evolution from its first Iberian settlement through its Roman and Visigothic ages and beyond. Antiquity is the focus here: the Romans took the city during the Punic Wars, and the striking underground remains of their Colonia Favencia Julia Augusta Paterna Barcino (Favored Colony of the Father Julius Augustus Barcino), through which you can roam on metal walkways, are the museum's main treasure. Archaeological finds include the walls of houses, mosaics and fluted columns, and workshops (for pressing olive oil and salted fish paste), marble busts, and funerary urns. Especially fascinating is to see how the Visgoths and their descendents built the early medieval walls on top of these ruins, recycling whatever came to hand: chunks of Roman stone and concrete, bits of columns—even headstones. The price of admission to the museum includes entry to the other treasures of the **Plaça del Rei,** including the **Palau Reial Major,** the splendid **Saló del Tinell,** and the chapel of **Santa Àgata.** ✉ *Palau Padellàs, Carrer del Veguer 2, Barri Gòtic* ☎ *93/256–2122* 🌐 *www.museuhistoria.bcn.cat* 🎫 *€7 (includes admission to Monestir de Pedralbes, Centre d'Interpretació del Park Güell, Centre d'Interpretació del Call, Centre d'Interpretació Històrica, Refugi 307, and Museu-Casa Verdaguer). Free with the Barcelona Card, and Sun. after 3* ⏲ *Tues.–Sat. 10–7, Sun. 10–8* Ⓜ *Pl. de Catalunya, Liceu, Jaume I.*

Fodor'sChoice ★ **Plaça del Rei.** This little square is as compact a nexus of history as anything the Barri Gòtic has to offer. Long held to be the scene of Columbus's triumphal return from his first voyage to the New World—the precise spot where Ferdinand and Isabella received him is purportedly on the stairs fanning out from the corner of the square (though evidence indicates that the Catholic monarchs were at a summer residence in the Empordá)—the **Palau Reial Major** was the official royal residence in Barcelona. The main room is the **Saló del Tinell,** a magnificent banquet hall built in 1362. To the left is the **Palau del Lloctinent** (Lieutenant's Palace); towering overhead in the corner is the dark 15th-century **Torre Mirador del Rei Martí** (King Martin's Watchtower). The 14th-century **Capilla Reial de Santa Àgueda** (Royal Chapel of St. Agatha) is on the right side of the stairway, and behind and to the right as you face the stairs is the **Palau Clariana-Padellàs,** moved to this spot stone by stone from Carrer Mercaders in the early 20th century and now the entrance to the **Museu d'Història de la Ciutat.** ✉ *Pl. del Rei, Barri Gòtic* Ⓜ *Liceu, Jaume I.*

Plaça Sant Felip Neri. A tiny square just behind **Plaça de Garriga Bachs** off the side of the cloister of the Catedral de la Seu, this was once a burial ground for Barcelona's executed heroes and villains, before all church graveyards were moved to the south side of Montjuïc, the present site of the municipal cemetery. The church of San Felip Neri here is a frequent venue for classical concerts. Fragments of a bomb that exploded in the square during the Civil War made the pockmarks on the walls of the church. ✉ *Pl. Sant Felip Neri, Barri Gòtic* Ⓜ *Liceu, Jaume I.*

Plaça Sant Jaume. Facing each other across this oldest epicenter of Barcelona (and often politically on opposite sides as well) are the seat of Catalonia's regional government, the Generalitat de Catalunya, in the **Palau de La Generalitat,** and the City Hall, the Ayuntamiento de Barcelona, in the **Casa de la Ciutat.** Just east of the Cathedral, this square was the site of the Roman forum 2,000 years ago, though subsequent construction filled the space with buildings. The square was cleared in the 1840s; the two imposing government buildings facing each other across it are much older: the Ayuntamiento dates to the 14th century; the Generalitat was built between the 15th and mid-17th centuries. ✉ *Pl. Sant Jaume, Barri Gòtic* 🌐 *www.bcn.es* ⏲ *Tours of the Ayuntamiento in English, weekends at 11; tours of the Generalitat, 2nd and 4th weekends every month 10:30–1, by reservation only.* Ⓜ *Jaume I.*

Santa Maria del Pi (*St. Mary of the Pine*). Sister church to Santa Maria del Mar and to Santa Maria de Pedralbes, this early Catalan Gothic structure is perhaps the most fortresslike of all three: hulking, dark, and massive, and perforated only by the main entryway and the mammoth rose window, said to be the world's largest. Try to see the window from inside in the late afternoon to get the best view of the colors. The church was named for the lone *pi* (pine tree) that stood in what was a marshy lowland outside the 4th-century Roman walls. An early church dating back to the 10th century preceded the present Santa Maria del Pi, which was begun in 1322 and finally consecrated in 1453. The interior compares poorly with the clean and lofty lightness of Santa Maria del Mar, but there are two interesting things to see: the original wooden choir loft, and the Ramón Amadeu painting, "La Mare de Deu dels Desamparats" (Our Lady of the Helpless), in which the artist reportedly used his wife and children as models for the Virgin and children. The lateral facade of the church, around to the left in Plaça Sant Josep Oriol, bears a plaque dedicated to the April 6, 1806, fall of the portly parish priest José Mestres, who slipped off the narrow catwalk circling the outside of the apse. He survived the fall unhurt, and the event was considered a minor miracle commemorated with the plaque. The church is a regular venue for classical guitar concerts by well-known soloists. Tours of the basilica are not conducted in English.

The adjoining squares, **Plaça del Pi** and **Plaça de Sant Josep Oriol,** are two of the liveliest and most appealing spaces in the Old Quarter, filled with much-frequented outdoor cafés and used as a venue for markets selling natural products or paintings, or as an impromptu concert hall for musicians. The handsome entryway and courtyard at Plaça de Sant

Josep Oriol 4 across from the lateral facade of Santa Maria del Pi is the **Palau Fivaller,** now seat of the Agricultural Institute, an interesting patio to have a look through. From Placeta del Pi, tucked in behind the church, you can see the bell tower and the sunny facades of the apartment buildings on the north side of Plaça Sant Josep Oriol. Placeta del Pi was once the cemetery for the blind, hence the name of the little street leading in: Carrer Cecs de la Boqueria (Blind of the Boqueria). This little space with its outdoor tables is a convenient place for a coffee or tapas, at El Taller de Tapas. ✉ *Pl. del Pi 7, Barri Gòtic* ☎ *93/318–4743* 🎫 *€3 (basilica only, free 9:30–11 and 6–8:30)* ⏲ *Museum and basilica weekdays 11–6, Sat. 11–3, Sun. 4–8* Ⓜ *Liceu.*

WORTH NOTING

Casa de la Pia Almoina–Museu Diocesà (*Diocesan Museum*). This 11th-century Gothic building, now a museum, once served soup to the city's poor; hence its popular name, the "House of Pious Alms". The museum houses a permanent collection of religious sculpture and liturgical paraphernalia, from monstrances to chalices to the 12th-century paintings from the apse of the Sant Salvador de Polinyà chapel; there are also occasional temporary art exhibits. Anyone contemplating a tour of the Roman walls should consult the excellent relief map/scale model of Roman Barcelona in the vestibule (copies of the map and model are for sale in the nearby **Museu d'Història de la Ciutat,** the Museum of the History of the City). Inside, Roman stones are clearly visible in this much-restored structure, the only octagonal tower of the 82 that ringed 4th-century Barcino. Look for the Romanesque *Mares de Deu* (Mothers of God) wood sculptures, such as the one from Sant Pau del Camp church in Barcelona's Raval. The museum is behind the massive floral iron grate in the octagonal Roman watchtower to the left of the stairs of the Catedral de la Seu. ✉ *Av. de la Catedral 4, Barri Gòtic* ☎ *93/315–2213* 🎫 *€6* ⏲ *Tues.–Sat. 10–2 and 5–8, Sun. 11–2* Ⓜ *Jaume I.*

Col.legi d'Arquitectes. Barcelona's College of Architects, constructed in 1961 by Xavier Busquets, houses three important gems: a superb library (across the street), where for a small fee the college's bibliographical resources are at your disposal for research; a bookstore specializing in architecture, design, and drafting supplies; and an excellent restaurant (one of the city's great secrets). The Picasso friezes on the facade of the building were designed by the artist in 1960; inside are two more, one a vision of Barcelona and the other dedicated to the *sardana,* Catalonia's traditional folk dance. The glass-and-concrete modernity of the building itself raises hackles: how could *architects*, of all people, be so blithely unconcerned—even contemptuous—about the aesthetics of accommodation to the Gothic setting around it? (For English on the website, click under Idioma.) ✉ *Pl. Nova 5, Barri Gòtic* ☎ *93/301–5000* 🌐 *www.coac.net* ⏲ *Mon.–Sat. 10–8* Ⓜ *Jaume I.*

Palau del Lloctinent (*Lieutenant's Palace*). The three facades of the Palau face Carrer dels Comtes de Barcelona on the cathedral side, the Baixada de Santa Clara, and Plaça del Rei. Typical of late Gothic–early Renaissance Catalan design, it was constructed by Antoni Carbonell between 1549 and 1557, and remains one of the Barri Gòtic's most graceful buildings. The heavy stone arches over the entry, the central patio,

DID YOU KNOW?

The Barri Gòtic actually sits on top of the first Roman settlement. Roman walls are visible around the edges of the neighborhood.

and the intricately coffered wooden roof over the stairs are all good examples of noble 16th-century architecture. The door on the stairway is a 1975 Josep Maria Subirachs work portraying scenes from the life of Sant Jordi and the history of Catalonia. The Palau del Lloctinent was inhabited by the king's official emissary or viceroy to Barcelona during the 16th and 17th centuries, and now offers an excellent exhibit on the life and times of Jaume I, one of early Catalonia's most important figures. The patio also occasionally hosts early music concerts, and during the Corpus Christi celebration is one of the main venues for the *ou com balla,* when an egg "dances" on the fountain amid an elaborate floral display. ⊠ *Carrer dels Comtes de Barcelona 2, Barri Gòtic* ☏ *93/315–0211* Ⓜ *Jaume I.*

Plaça Sant Just. Off to the left side of city hall down Carrer Hèrcules (named for the mythical founder of Barcelona) are this square and the site of the Església de Sant Just i Pastor, one of the city's oldest Christian churches. Unfortunately, nothing remains of the original church, founded in 801 by King Louis the Pious; the present structure dates to 1342. Christian catacombs are reported to have been found beneath Plaça. The Gothic fountain was built in 1367 by the patrician Joan Fiveller, then Chief Minister of the city administration. (Fiveller's major claim to fame was to have discovered a spring in the Collserola hills, and had the water piped straight to Barcelona.) The fountain in the square bears an image of St. Just, and the city and sovereign count-kings' coats of arms, along with a pair of falcons. The excellent entryway and courtyard to the left of Carrer Bisbe Caçador is the Palau Moixó, the town house of an important early Barcelona family; down Carrer Bisbe Caçador is the Acadèmia de Bones Lletres, the Catalan Academy of Arts and Letters. The church is dedicated to the boy martyrs Just and Pastor; the Latin inscription over the door translates into English as "Our pious patron is the black and beautiful Virgin, together with the sainted children Just and Pastore." ⊠ *Pl. Sant Just, Barri Gòtic* Ⓜ *Jaume I.*

EL RAVAL

Sightseeing ★★★★☆
Nightlife ★★★☆☆
Dining ★★★☆☆
Lodging ★★☆☆☆
Shopping ★★★☆☆

El Raval (from *arrabal,* meaning "suburb" or "slum") is the area to the west of La Rambla, on the right as you walk toward the port. Originally a rough quarter outside the second set of city walls that ran down the left side of La Rambla, El Raval used to be notorious for its Barri Xinès (or Barrio Chino) red-light district, the lurid attractions of which are known to have fascinated the young Pablo Picasso.

Gypsies, acrobats, prostitutes, and *saltimbanques* (clowns and circus performers) who made this area their home soon found immortality in the many canvases Picasso painted of them during his Blue Period. It was the ladies of the night on Carrer Avinyó, not far from the Barri Xinès, who inspired one of the 20th-century's most famous paintings, Picasso's *Les Demoiselles d'Avignon,* an important milestone on the road to Cubism. Not bad for a city slum.

El Raval, though still rough and tumble, has been gentrified and much improved since 1980, largely as a result of the construction of the Museu d'Art Contemporani de Barcelona (MACBA) and other cultural institutions nearby, such as the Centre de Cultura Contemporània (CCCB) and the Convent dels Àngels. La Rambla del Raval has been opened up between Carrer de l'Hospital and Drassanes, bringing light and air into the streets of the Raval for the first time in a thousand years. The medieval Hospital de la Santa Creu, Plaça del Pedró, the Mercat de Sant Antoni, and Sant Pau del Camp are highlights of this helter-skelter, rough-and-tumble part of Barcelona. The only area to consider avoiding is the lower part between Carrer de Sant Pau and the back of the Drassanes Reials shipyards on Carrer del Portal Santa Madrona.

GETTING ORIENTED

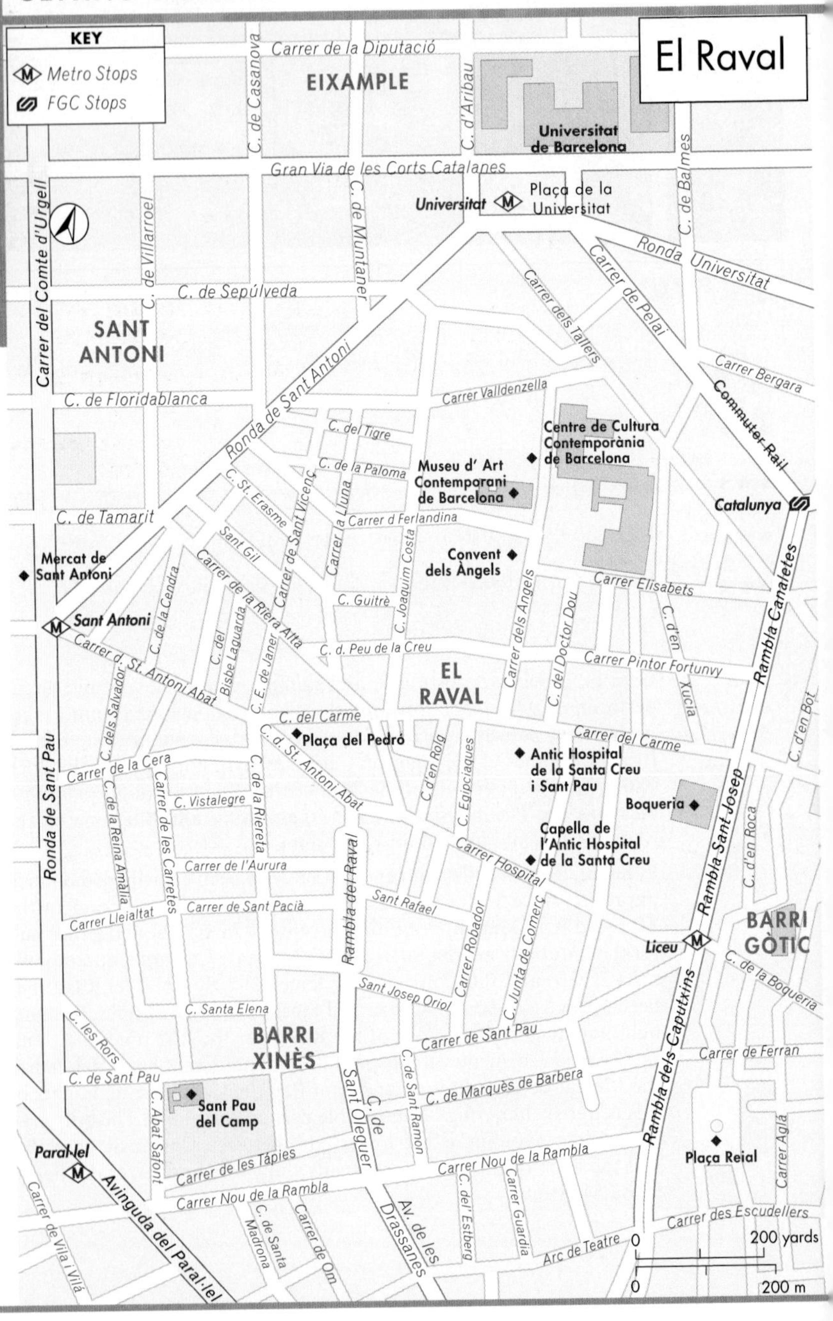

TIMING

The Raval covers a lot of ground. Plan on a four-hour walk or break your exploration into two two-hour hikes. The cloister of Sant Pau del Camp, not to be missed, is closed Monday morning, Saturday afternoon, and all day Sunday except for mass.

GETTING HERE

Begin at Plaça de Catalunya, with its convenient metro stop. Walk down La Rambla and take your first right into Carrer Tallers, working your way through to the MACBA.

QUICK BITES

Bar Castells. Enjoy tapas, coffee, and other light items at Bar Castells, which has a lovely marble counter and a gorgeous wood-framed mirror behind the bar. ✉ *Pl. Bonsuccés 1, El Raval* ☎ *93/302–1054* Ⓜ *Pl. de Catalunya, Liceu.*

Buenas Migas. A leafy terrace a block in from La Rambla, Buenas Migas serves good sandwiches (*migas* means crumbs and the expression *hacer buenas migas* refers to new friends hitting it off). ✉ *Pl. Bonsuccés 8, El Raval* ☎ *93/318–3708* Ⓜ *Pl. de Catalunya, Liceu.*

El Jardí. In a corner of the medieval hospital courtyard El Jardí serves tapas and salads. ✉ *Hospital 56, El Raval* ☎ *93/329–1550* Ⓜ *Pl. de Catalunya, Liceu.*

TOP ATTRACTIONS

Antic Hospital de la Santa Creu i Sant Pau

Museu d'Art Contemporani de Barcelona

Sant Pau del Camp

TOP EXPERIENCES

Exploring the medieval Antic Hospital de la Santa Creu

Lingering by the fountain in the Sant Pau del Camp cloister

Stroking Botero's bronze cat on La Rambla del Raval

Watching the skateboarders strut their stuff in the courtyard of the MACBA

WHERE TO EAT (⇨ CH. 3)

Ca l'Estevet

Ca l'Isidre

Casa Leopoldo

El Cafetí

Quimet-Quimet

HAPPENING NIGHTLIFE (⇨ CH. 5)

Bar Muy Buenas

Caravan

Jazz sí Club

L'Ovella Negra

La Paloma

London Bar

Skateboarders enjoy practicing in front of the Museu d'Art Contemporani de Barcelona.

TOP ATTRACTIONS

Fodor's Choice ★ **Antic Hospital de la Santa Creu i Sant Pau.** Founded in the 10th century, this is one of Europe's earliest medical complexes, and contains some of Barcelona's most impressive Gothic architecture. The buildings that survive today date mainly to the 15th and 16th centuries; the first stone for the hospital was laid by King Martí el Humà (Martin the Humane) in 1401. From the entrance on Carrer del Carme, the first building on the left is the 18th-century **Reial Acadèmia de Cirurgia i Medecina** (Royal Academy of Surgery and Medicine); the amphitheater is kept just as it was in the days when students learned by observing dissections. (One assumes that the paupers' hospital next door was always ready to oblige with cadavers.) The Academy is open to the public on Wednesday from 10 to 1. For guided tours by appointment call ☎ *93/317–1686*.) Across the way on the right is the gateway into the patio of the **Casa de la Convalescència,** where patients who survived their treatment in the hospital were moved for recuperation; it now houses the Institute for Catalan Studies. The walls of the forecourt are covered with brightly decorated scenes of the life of St. Paul in blue-and-yellow ceramic tiles; the story begins with the image to the left of the door to the inner courtyard, recounting the moment of the saint's conversion: "*Savle, Savle, quid me persegueris?*" ("Saul, Saul, why do you persecute me?"). The ceramicist, Llorenç Passolas, also designed the late 17th-century tiles around the inner patio. The image of St. Paul in the center of the pillared courtyard, over what was once a well, pays homage to the building's first benefactor, Pau Ferran. Look for the horseshoes, two of them around the keyholes, on the double wooden doors in the entryway: tokens of good luck for the afflicted who came here to recover—again, in reference to benefactor Ferran, from *ferro* (iron), as in *ferradura* (horseshoe).

Through a gate to the left of the Casa de Convalescència is the garden-courtyard of the hospital complex, the **Jardins de Rubió i Lluc,** centered on a baroque cross and lined with orange trees. On the right is the **Biblioteca de Catalunya** (✉ *Carrer de l'Hospital 56* ☎ *93/270–2300* 🌐 *www.bnc.cat* ⏲ *Weekdays 9–8, Sat. 9–2*), Catalonia's national library and—with some 2 million volumes in its collection—second only to Madrid's Biblioteca Nacional. The stairway under the arch, leading up to the library, was built in the 16th century; the Gothic well to the left of the arch is from the 15th century, as is the little Romeo-and-Juliet balcony in the corner to the left of the doors to the Escola Massana academy of design. The library itself is spectacular: two parallel halls—once the core of the hospital—70 meters (230 feet) long, with towering Gothic arches and vaulted ceilings, designed in the 15th century by the architect of the church of Santa Maria del Pi, Guillem Abiell. This was the hospital where Antoni Gaudí was taken, unrecognized and assumed to be a pauper, after he was struck by a trolley on June 7, 1926. Among the library's collections are archives recording Gaudí's admittance and photographs of the infirmary and the private room where he died. The staggering antiquarian resources here go back to the earliest history of printing, and range from silver medieval book covers to illuminated manuscripts from the *Llibre Vermell* (*Red Book*) of medieval Catalonian liturgical music, to rare editions of Cervantes. (For free guided tours by appointment, contact Sr. Sergi Font at ☎ *93/270–2300, ext. 2123* or by email at ✉ *sfont@bcn.cat.*)

Leave the complex through the heavy wooden doors to Carrer Hospital, and turn left, towards La Rambla. The next set of doors leads to the **Capella** (Chapel) of the Hospital, an interesting art space well worth a visit. Built in the early 15th century, on the site of what had been the old Hospital de Colom (founded in 1219), it is now a showcase for promising young artists, chosen by a jury of prominent museum directors and given this impressive space, with its Romanesque tunnel vault and medieval arches, to exhibit their work (🌐 *www.bnc.cat/lacapella* ⏲ *Tues.–Sat. 12–2 and 4–8, Sun. 11–2*).

In 1587 King Felipe II granted the Hospital de Santa Creu i Sant Pau the privilege of mounting theatrical performances, the proceeds to be used to support its charitable work. In the early 17th century the Hospital built its own theater for this purpose (variously called the Casa de Comèdias or the Teatre de la Santa Creu); it was the city's sole venue for itinerant theater and opera companies until it burned down in 1787. Rebuilt, it kept its royal monopoly on entertainment in Barcelona until 1844, when Queen Isable II gave the Societat del Liceu permission to build a bigger, grander opera house on La Rambla. The Teatre de la Santa Creu became the Teatre Principal, and remained a rival to the Licea until it, too, burned down in 1915. ✉ *Carrer Hospital 56 (or Carrer del Carme 45), El Raval* ☎ *93/270–2300* Ⓜ *Liceu.*

Centre de Cultura Contemporània de Barcelona (*CCCB*). Just next door to the MACBA, this multidisciplinary gallery, lecture hall, and concert and exhibition space offers a year-round program of cultural events and projects, well worth checking out. The center also has a remarkable film archive of historic shorts and documentaries, free to the public. Housed in the restored and renovated Casa de la Caritat, a former medieval convent and hospital, the CCCB is, like the Palau de la Música Catalana, one of Barcelona's shining examples of how a much-needed contemporary addition can be wedded to traditional architecture and design. A smoked-glass wall on the right side of the patio, designed by architects Albert Villaplana and Helio Piñon, reflects out over the rooftops of El Raval to Montjuïc and the Mediterranean beyond. ✉ *Montalegre 5, El Raval* ☎ *93/306–4100* 🌐 *www.cccb.org* 🎫 *Occasional special exhibitions €6–€8; otherwise free* ⏲ *Tues.–Sun. 11–8* Ⓜ *Pl. de Catalunya.*

MAY 11 IN RAVAL

El Raval's big day is May 11, when Carrer Hospital celebrates the Fira de Sant Ponç, a beloved Barcelona holiday. The feast day of Sant Ponç, patron saint of herbalists and beekeepers, brings Catalonia's *pagesos* (country folk) to Barcelona laden with every natural product they can haul. Everything from bees in glass cases to chamomile, rosemary, thyme, lavender, basil, pollens, mint, candied fruits, snake oil, headache remedies, and aphrodisiacs, and every imaginable condiment and savory takes over the city's streets and, more importantly, the air.

Fodor's Choice ★ **Museu d'Art Contemporani de Barcelona** (*Barcelona Museum of Contemporary Art, MACBA*). Designed by American architect Richard Meier in 1992, this gleaming explosion of light and geometry in the darkest corner of El Raval houses a permanent collection of contemporary art, and regularly mounts special thematic exhibitions of works on loan. Meier gives a nod to Gaudí (with the Pedrera-like wave on one end of the main facade), but his minimalist building otherwise looks a bit like the scaffolding hadn't been taken down yet. That said, the MACBA is unarguably an important addition to the cultural capital of this once-shabby neighborhood. Skateboarders weave in and out around Basque sculptor Jorge Oteiza's massive black, blocky *La Ola* (*The Wave*) in the courtyard; the late Eduardo Chillida's *Barcelona* (donated by the Sara Lee Corporation!) covers half the wall in the little square off Calle Ferlandina, on the left of the museum, in the sculptor's signature primitive black geometrical patterns. The MACBA's 20th-century art collection (Calder, Rauschenberg, Oteiza, Chillida, Tàpies) is excellent, as is the guided tour: a useful introduction to the philosophical foundations of contemporary art as well as the pieces themselves. ✉ *Pl. dels Àngels s/n, El Raval* ☎ *93/412–0810* 🌐 *www.macba.es* 🎫 *€9* ⏲ *Mon. and Wed.–Fri. 11–7:30, Sat. 10–9, Sun. 10–3; free guided tours daily at 4 (Mon. at 4 and 6)* Ⓜ *Pl. de Catalunya.*

Sant Agustí. This unfinished church is one of Barcelona's most unusual structures, with jagged stone sections projecting down the left side, and the upper part of the front entrance on Plaça Sant Agustí waiting to be covered with a facade. The church has had an unhappy history.

One of the earliest medical complexes in Europe is the Antic Hospital de la Santa Creu i Sant Pau.

Begun in 1728, it was abandoned 20 years later, burned in the anti-religious riots of 1825, when the cloisters were demolished, restored, then looted and torched again in the closing days of the Civil War. Sant Agustí comes alive on May 22, feast day of Santa Rita, patron saint of "*los imposibles*"—that is, lost causes. Unhappily married women, unrequited lovers, and all-but-hopeless sufferers of every stripe and spot form long lines through the square and down Carrer Hospital. Each carries a rose that will be blessed at the chapel of Santa Rita on the right side of the altar. ✉ *Pl. Sant Agustí s/n, El Raval* ☎ *93/318–6231, 93/368–9700* Ⓜ *Liceu.*

Fodor's Choice ★ **Sant Pau del Camp.** Barcelona's oldest church was originally outside the city walls (*del camp* means "in the fields") and was a Roman cemetery as far back as the 2nd century, according to archaeological evidence. A Visigothic belt buckle found in the 20th century confirmed that Visigoths used the site as a cemetery between the 2nd and 7th centuries. What you see now was built in 1127 and is the earliest Romanesque structure in Barcelona. Elements of the church—the classical marble capitals atop the columns in the main entry—are thought to be from the 6th and 7th centuries. Sant Pau is bulky and solid, featureless (except for what may be the smallest stained-glass window in Europe, high on the facade facing Carrer Sant Pau), with stone walls three feet thick and more; medieval Catalan churches and monasteries were built to be refuges for the body as well as the soul, bulwarks of last resort against Moorish invasions—or mauraders of any persuasion. Check local events listings carefully for musical performances here; the church is an acoustical gem. (Rebecca Ryan's Mercyhurst Madrigal Singers sang

American composer Horatio Parker's "Lord We Beseech Thee" here in 2009.) The tiny cloister is Sant Pau del Camp's best feature, and one of Barcelona's hidden treasures. Look carefully at the capitals that support the Moorish-influenced Mudejar arches, carved with biblical scenes and exhortations to prayer. This penumbral sanctuary, barely a block from the heavily-trafficked Avinguda del Paral.lel, is a gift from time. ✉ *Sant Pau 99, El Raval* ☎ *93/441–0001* 🎫 *Cloister €3* ⏲ *Cloister Mon.–Sat. 10–1:30 and 4–7, Sun. mass at 10:30, 12:30, and 8* Ⓜ *Paral.lel.*

WORTH NOTING

Convent dels Àngels. This former Augustinian convent directly across from the main entrance to the MACBA, built by Bartolomeu Roig in the middle of the 16th century, has been converted into a general cultural center with an exhibition hall (El Fòrum dels Àngels), a bookstore, a 150-seat auditorium, and a restaurant and bar. The Foment de les Arts i del Desseny (FAD) now operates this handsome Raval resource. The Fòrum dels Àngels is an impressive space, with beautifully carved and restored sculptures of angels in the corners and at the top of the walls. ✉ *Pl. dels Àngels, El Raval* ☎ *93/4437520* 🌐 *www.fad.cat* ⏲ *Mon.–Sat. 9–9, Sun. 10–2* Ⓜ *Pl. de Catalunya.*

Hotel España. Just off La Rambla behind the Liceu Opera House on Carrer Sant Pau is the Hotel España, remodeled in 1904 by Lluís Domènech i Montaner, architect of the Moderniste flagship Palau de la Música Catalana. Completely refurbished in 2010, the interior is notable for its Art Nouveau decor. The sculpted marble Eusebi Arnau fireplace in the bar, the Ramon Casas undersea murals in the salon (mermaids singing each to each), and the lushly ornate dining room, are the hotel's best artistic features. The España is so proud of its place in the cultural history of the city—and justly so—it opens to the public for 40-minute guided tours, weekdays at 12:15 and 4:30. (Note that tours are normally in Spanish, but English can be requested.) ✉ *Carrer Sant Pau 9–11, El Raval* ☎ *93/550–0000* 🌐 *www.hotelespanya.com* Ⓜ *Liceu.*

Mercat de Sant Antoni. Now undergoing a vast restoration project, this fascinating and multifaceted market was scheduled to reopen, in all its former glory, in 2013, but the date has been pushed forward to 2016—mainly to allow for changes in the design to incorporate archaelogical remains of medieval Barcelona that were discovered underneath. Directors of the makeover project have vowed to maintain the market's character. Meanwhile, it's business as usual, under a large marquis on Carrer Tamarit: a combination food, clothing, and flea market—with a book, stamp, and coin market on the north end, on Carrer d'Urgell between Carrer Tamarit and Carrer Floridablanca, on Sunday morning. The Sant Antoni market is a mammoth steel hangar at the junction of Ronda de Sant Antoni and Comte d'Urgell designed in 1882 by Antoni Rovira i Trias, the winner of the competition for the planning of Barcelona's Eixample. Considered the city's greatest masterpiece of ironwork architecture, the Greek cross–shape market covers an entire block on the edge of the Eixample. Some of the best Moderniste stall facades in Barcelona distinguish this exceptional space. ✉ *Carrer Comte d'Urgell s/n, El Raval* ☎ *93/443–7520, 93/426–3521* ⏲ *Mon.–Sat. 7 am–8:30 pm, Sun. 10–2* Ⓜ *Sant Antoni.*

Plaça del Pedró. This landmark in medieval Barcelona was the dividing point where ecclesiastical and secular paths parted. The high road, Carrer del Carme, leads to the cathedral and the seat of the bishopric; the low road, Carrer de l'Hospital, heads down to the medieval hospital and the Boqueria market, a clear choice between body and soul. Named for a stone pillar, or *pedró* (large stone), marking the fork in the road, the square became a cherished landmark for Barcelona Christians after Santa Eulàlia, co-patron of Barcelona, was crucified there in the 4th century after suffering the legendary 13 ordeals designed to persuade her to renounce her faith—which of course, she heroically refused to do. As the story goes, an overnight snowfall chastely covered her nakedness with virgin snow. The present version of Eulàlia and her cross was sculpted by Barcelona artist Frederic Marès and erected in 1951. The bell tower and vacant alcove at the base of the triangular square are the **Sant Llàtzer** church, originally built in the open fields in the mid-12th century and used as a leper hospital and place of worship after the 15th century when Sant Llàtzer (Saint Lazarus) was officially named patron saint of lepers. Presently in the process of being rescued from the surrounding buildings that once completely obscured the church, the Sant Llàtzer chapel has a tiny antique patio and apse visible from the short Carrer de Sant Llàtzer, which cuts behind the church between Carrer del Carme and Carrer Hospital. ✉ *Pl. del Pedró, El Raval* Ⓜ *Sant Antoni.*

SANT PERE AND LA RIBERA

Sightseeing ★★★★★
Nightlife ★★★★★
Dining ★★★★★
Lodging ★★★★☆
Shopping ★★★★★

The textile and waterfront neighborhoods are home to some of the city's most iconic buildings, from the Gothic 14th-century basilica of Santa Maria del Mar to the over-the-top Moderniste Palau de la Música Catalana. At the Museu Picasso, works of the 20th-century master are displayed in five adjoining Renaissance palaces.

Sant Pere, Barcelona's old textile neighborhood, is centered on the church of Sant Pere. A half-mile closer to the port, the Barri de la Ribera and the former market of El Born, now known as the Born-Ribera district, were at the center of Catalonia's great maritime and economic expansion of the 13th and 14th centuries. Surrounding the basilica of Santa Maria del Mar, the Born-Ribera area includes Carrer Montcada, lined with 14th- to 18th-century Renaissance palaces; Passeig del Born, where medieval jousts were held; Carrer Flassaders and the area around the early mint; the shop- and restaurant-rich Carrer Banys Vells; Plaça de les Olles; and Pla del Palau, where La Llotja, Barcelona's early maritime exchange, housed the fine-arts school where Picasso, Gaudí, and Domènech i Montaner all studied, as did many more of Barcelona's most important artists and architects.

Long a depressed neighborhood, La Ribera began to experience a revival in the 1980s; liberally endowed now with intimate bars, cafés, and trendy boutiques, it continues to enjoy the blessings of gentrification. An open excavation in the center of El Born, the onetime market restored as a multipurpose cultural center, offers a fascinating view of pre-1714 Barcelona, dismantled by the victorious troops of Felipe V at the end of the War of the Spanish Succession. The Passeig del Born, La Rambla of medieval Barcelona, is once again a pleasant leafy promenade.

TOP ATTRACTIONS

Fossar de les Moreres (*Cemetery of the Mulberry Trees*). This low marble monument runs across the eastern side of the church of Santa Maria del Mar. It honors defenders of Barcelona who gave their lives in the final siege that ended the War of the Spanish Succession on September 11, 1714. The inscription (in English: "In the cemetery of the mulberry trees no traitor lies") refers to the graveyard keeper's story. He refused to bury those on the invading side, even when one turned out to be his son. This is the traditional gathering place for the most radical elements of Catalonia's nationalist (separatist) movement, on the National Day of Catalonia, which celebrates the heroic defeat.

From the cemetery, look back at Santa Maria del Mar. The lighter-color stone on the lateral facade was left by the 17th-century Pont del Palau (Palace Bridge), erected to connect the Royal Palace in the nearby Pla del Palau with the Tribuna Real (Royal Box) over the right side of the Santa Maria del Mar altar, so that nobles and occupying military officials could get to mass without the risk of walking in the streets. The bridge, regarded as a symbol of imperialist oppression, was finally dismantled in 1987. The steel arch with its eternal flame was erected in 2002. ✉ *Pl. de Santa Maria, Born-Ribera* Ⓜ *Jaume I.*

La Llotja (*Maritime Exchange*). Barcelona's maritime trade center was designed to be the city's finest example of civil (nonecclesiastic) architecture. Originally little more than a roof, Barcelona's present maritime exchange was constructed in the Catalan Gothic style between 1380 and 1392. At the end of the 18th century the facades were (tragically) covered in the neoclassical uniformity of the time, but the interior, the great Saló Gòtic (Gothic Hall), remained unaltered, and was a grand venue for balls and celebrations throughout the 19th century. The Gothic Hall was used as the Barcelona stock exchange until 1975, and until late 2001 as the grain exchange. The hall has now been brilliantly restored and though public visits have not been formally established, any chance to see the inside of this historic hall will reveal Gothic arches and columns and a marble floor made of light Carrara and dark Genovese marble.

The Escola de Belles Arts (School of Fine Arts) occupied the southwestern corner of the Llotja from 1849 until 1960. Many illustrious Barcelona artists studied here, including Gaudí, Miró, and Picasso. The **Reial Acadèmia Catalana de Belles Arts de Sant Jordi** (Royal Catalan Academy of Fine Arts of St. George) still has its seat in the Llotja, and its museum is one of Barcelona's semisecret collections of art, from medieval paintings by unknown artists to modern works by members of the Academy itself. **TIP→ To slip into the Saló Gòti, walk down the stairs from the museum to the second floor, then take the marble staircase down and turn right.** ✉ *Casa Llotja, Passeig d'Isabel II 1, Born-Ribera* ☎ *93/319–2432 for museum, 670/466260 for guided visits to the museum* 🌐 *www.racba.org* 🎫 *Museum free* ⏲ *Museum weekdays 10–2* Ⓜ *Jaume I.*

GETTING ORIENTED

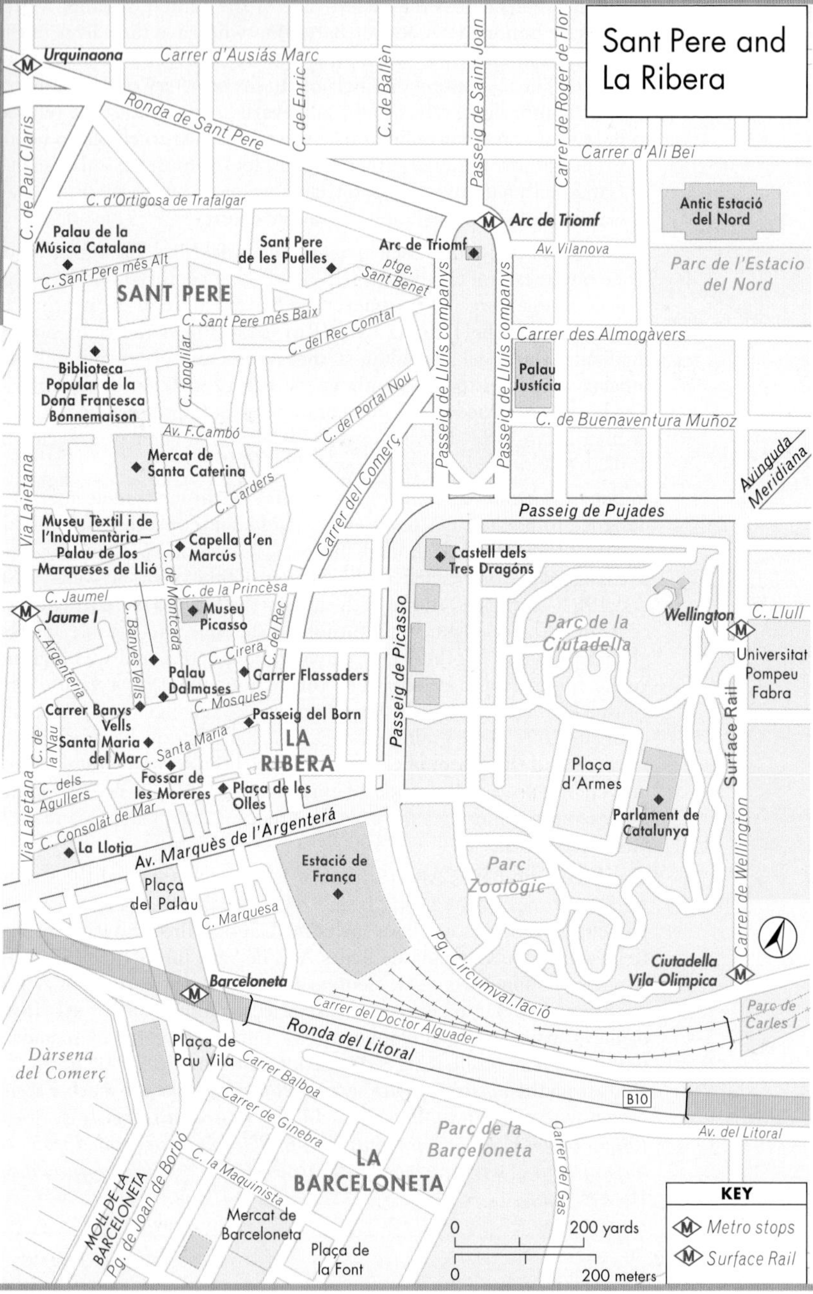
Sant Pere and La Ribera
Urquinaona
Carrer d'Ausiás Marc
Ronda de Sant Pere
C. de Enric
C. de Ballèn
Passeig de Saint Joan
Carrer de Roger de Flor
Carrer d'Ali Bei
C. de Pau Claris
C. d'Ortigosa de Trafalgar
Arc de Triomf
Antic Estació del Nord
Palau de la Música Catalana
Sant Pere de les Puelles
Av. Vilanova
Parc de l'Estacio del Nord
C. Sant Pere més Alt
ptge. Sant Benet
SANT PERE
C. Sant Pere més Baix
C. del Rec Comtal
Carrer des Almogàvers
Biblioteca Popular de la Dona Francesca Bonnemaison
C. Jonqilar
Passeig de Lluís companys
Palau Justícia
C. del Portal Nou
C. de Buenaventura Muñoz
Av. F.Cambó
Mercat de Santa Caterina
Avinguda Meridiana
Via Laietana
C. Carders
Carrer del Comerç
Passeig de Pujades
Museu Tèxtil i de l'Indumentària—Palau de los Marqueses de Llió
Capella d'en Marcús
Castell dels Tres Dragóns
C. de la Princèsa
C. Jaumel
C. de Montcada
Jaume I
Museu Picasso
C. del Rec
Wellington
C. Llull
C. Argenteria
C. Banyes Vells
Parc de la Ciutadella
Passeig de Picasso
Universitat Pompeu Fabra
C. Cirera
Palau Dalmases
Carrer Flassaders
C. Mosques
Carrer Banys Vells
Passeig del Born
Surface Rail
C. de la Nau
Santa Maria del Mar
C. Santa Maria
LA RIBERA
Fossar de les Moreres
Plaça de les Olles
Plaça d'Armes
C. dels Agullers
Parlament de Catalunya
C. Consolat de Mar
Av. Marquès de l'Argenterá
La Llotja
Estació de França
Parc Zoològic
Carrer de Wellington
Plaça del Palau
C. Marquesa
Pg. Circumval.lació
Ciutadella Vila Olimpica
Barceloneta
Carrer del Doctor Aiguader
Parc de Carles I
Ronda del Litoral
Dàrsena del Comerç
Plaça de Pau Vila
Carrer Balboa
B10
Carrer de Ginebra
Parc de la Barceloneta
Av. del Litoral
Carrer del Gas
C. la Maquinista
LA BARCELONETA
MOLL DE LA BARCELONETA
Pg. de Joan de Borbó
Mercat de Barceloneta
Plaça de la Font
0
200 yards
0
200 meters
KEY
Metro stops
Surface Rail

TIMING

Depending on the number of museum visits and stops, exploring these neighborhoods can take a full day. Count on at least four hours of actual walking time. Catching Santa Maria del Mar open is key (it's closed daily 1:30–4:30). If you make it to Cal Pep for tapas before 1:30, you might get a place at the bar; if you don't, it's well worth the wait. The Picasso Museum is at least a two-hour visit.

GETTING HERE

From the central Plaça de Catalunya metro hub, it's a 10-minute walk over and down to the Palau de la Música Catalana for the beginning of this tour. The yellow L4 metro stop at Jaume I is closer to Santa Maria del Mar, but it's a hassle if you have to change trains; Plaça de Catalunya is close enough, and makes for a pleasant stroll.

QUICK BITES

La Vinya del Senyor. The patio of La Vinya del Senyor serves top wines from around the world by the glass, along with light tapas: try the Ibérico ham. ✉ *Pl. de Santa Maria 1, Born-Ribera* ☎ *93/310–3379.*

TOP ATTRACTIONS

Museu Picasso

Palau de la Música Catalana

Santa Maria del Mar

TOP EXPERIENCES

Grazing on counter food at Cal Pep

Feasting your eyes at the Mercat de Santa Caterina

Going to a concert in the Palau de la Musica Caterina

Browsing for exotic foodstuffs at the 150-year-old Casa Gispert

Attending a requiem mass in Santa Maria del Mar

WHERE TO EAT (⇨ CH. 3)

Cal Pep

Comerç 24

El Foro

El Passadís d'en Pep

El Pebre Blau

La Báscula

Mundial Bar

Sagardi

HAPPENING NIGHTLIFE (⇨ CH. 5)

El Born

El Copetín

La Taverna del Palau

Miramelindo

MUSEU PICASSO

✉ *Carrer Montcada 15–19, Born-Ribera* ☎ *93/319–6310* 🌐 *www.museupicasso.bcn.cat* 🎫 *€11 (free Sun. 3–8 and 1st Sun. of month)* 🕓 *Tues.–Sun. 10–8* Ⓜ *Jaume I.*

TIPS

■ Diumenges al Picasso (Sundays at the Picasso Museum) offers Sunday morning performances in the museum, ranging from classical music to clowns.

■ When the museum offers free admission, expect long lines and crowds, so arrive extra early.

■ For a light Mediterranean meal, the terrace café and restaurant provides a good resting point and breaks up your visit into manageable portions.

This museum focused on the works of famous Spanish artist Pablo Picasso is housed in five adjoining palaces on Carrer Montcada, a street known for Barcelona's most elegant medieval palaces. Picasso spent his key formative years in Barcelona (1895–1904), and this collection, while it does not include a significant number of his best paintings, is particularly strong on his early work. The museum was begun in 1962 on the suggestion of Picasso's crony Jaume Sabartés, and the initial donation was from the Sabartés collection. Later Picasso donated his early works, and in 1981 his widow, Jaqueline Roque, added 141 pieces.

Highlights

Displays include childhood sketches, works from the artist's Rose and Blue periods, and the famous 1950s Cubist variations on Velázquez's *Las Meninas* (in Rooms 22–26). The lower-floor sketches, oils, and schoolboy caricatures and drawings from Picasso's early years in La Coruña are perhaps the most fascinating part of the whole museum, showing the facility the artist seemed to possess almost from the cradle. His *La Primera Communión* (*First Communion*), painted at the age of 16, gives an idea of his early accomplishment. On the second floor you see the beginnings of the mature Picasso and his Blue Period in Paris, a time of loneliness, cold, and hunger for the artist.

SANTA MARIA DEL MAR

Pl. de Santa Maria, Born-Ribera ☎ *93/310–2390* ⏲ *Mon.–Sat. 9–1:30 and 4:30–8; Sun. 10:30–1:30 and 4:30–8* Ⓜ *Jaume I.*

DETAILS

- The paintings in the keystones overhead represent, from the front, the Coronation of the Virgin, the Nativity, the Annunciation, the equestrian figure of the father of Pedro IV, King Alfons, and the Barcelona coat of arms.
- The 34 lateral chapels are dedicated to saints and images. The first chapel to the left of the altar (No. 20) is the Capella del Santo Cristo (Chapel of the Holy Christ), its stained-glass window an allegory of Barcelona's 1992 Olympic Games.
- An engraved stone riser to the left of the side door onto Carrer Sombrerers marks the spot where San Ignacio de Loyola, founder of the Jesuit Order, begged for alms in 1524.

TIPS

- Set aside half an hour to see Santa Maria del Mar. La Catedral del Mar (the Cathedral of the Sea) by Ildefonso Falcons chronicles the construction of the basilica and 14th-century life in Barcelona.
- Check weekly listings magazines for concerts in the basilica; the setting and acoustics make performances here an unforgettable experience.

The most beautiful example of early Catalan Gothic architecture, Santa Maria del Mar is extraordinary for its unbroken lines and elegance. The lightness of the interior is especially surprising considering the blocky exterior. The site, originally outside the 1st- to 4th-century Roman walls at what was then the water's edge, was home to a Christian cult from the late 3rd century. Built by stonemasons who chose, fitted, and carved each stone hauled down from the same Montjuïc quarry that provided the sandstone for the 4th-century Roman walls, Santa Maria del Mar is breathtakingly and nearly hypnotically symmetrical. The medieval numerological symbol for the Virgin Mary—the number eight (or multiples thereof)—runs through every element of the basilica: The 16 octagonal pillars are 2 meters in diameter and spread out into rib vaulting arches at a height of 16 meters. The painted keystones at the apex of the arches are 32 meters from the floor. The central nave is twice as wide as the lateral naves (8 meters each); their width equals the difference (8 meters) between their height and that of the central nave. The result of all this proportional balance and harmony is a sense of uplift that, especially in baroque and Moderniste Barcelona, is both exhilarating and soothing.

Ironically, the church owes its present form to the anticlerical fury of anarchists who, on July 18, 1936, burned nearly all of Barcelona's churches as a reprisal against the alliance of army, church, and oligarchy during the military rebellion. The basilica, filled with ornate side chapels and choir stalls, burned for 11 days, and nearly crumbled as a result of the heat. Restored after the end of the Civil War by a series of Bauhaus-trained architects, Santa Maria del Mar has become one of the city's most universally admired architectural gems.

DID YOU KNOW?

The Palau de la Música Catalana was created to encourage musical knowledge at a popular level, as opposed to the Liceu opera house, which identified with Catalan aristocracy.

Mercat de Santa Caterina. This marketplace, a splendid carnival of colors with a roller-coaster rooftop, was restored by the late Enric Miralles, whose widow Benedetta Tagliabue finished the project in 2005. Undulating wood and colored-ceramic mosaic ceilings redolent of both Gaudí and Miró cover a bustling and dramatically illuminated market with an excellent restaurant, Cuines de Santa Caterina (☎ *93/268–9918*), and several good bars and cafés. The archeological section of the building is at the eastern end, showing Visigothic remains and sections of the 13th-century church and convent that stood here until the early 18th century. ✉ *Av. Francesc Cambó s/n, Born-Ribera* 🌐 *www.mercatsantacaterina.com* Ⓜ *Jaume I, Urquinaona.*

Palau Dalmases. If you can get through the massive wooden gates that open onto Carrer Montcada (at the moment, the only opportunity is when the first-floor Café Espai Barroc is open) you'll find yourself in Barcelona's best 17th-century Renaissance courtyard, built into a former 15th-century Gothic palace. Note the doorknockers up at horseback level; then take a careful look at the frieze of "The Rape of Europa" running up the stone railing of the elegant stairway at the end of the patio. It's a festive abduction: Neptune's chariot, cherubs, naiads, dancers, tritons, and musicians accompany Zeus, in the form of a bull, as he carries poor Europa up the stairs and off to Crete. The stone carvings in the courtyard, the 15th-century Gothic chapel, with its reliefs of angelic musicians, and the vaulting in the reception hall and salon, are all that remain of the original 15th-century palace. Espai Barroc, on the ground floor, is a café with baroque-era flourishes, period furniture, and musical performances. ✉ *Carrer Montcada 20, Born-Ribera* ☎ *93/310–0673 for Café Espai Barroc* 🎫 *Free* ⏲ *Café Tues.–Sun. 7 pm–2 am* Ⓜ *Jaume I.*

Fodor's Choice ★ **Palau de la Música Catalana.** On Carrer Amadeus Vives, just off Via Laietana, a 10-minute walk from Plaça de Catalunya, is one of the world's most extraordinary music halls. From its polychrome ceramic tile ticket windows on Carrer de Sant Pere Més Alt side to the row overhead of busts of (from left to right) Palestrina, Bach, Beethoven, and—around the corner on Carrer Amadeus Vives—Wagner, the Palau is a flamboyant tour de force, a riot of color and form designed in 1908 by Lluís Domènech i Montaner. It was meant by its sponsors, the Orfeó Català musical society, to celebrate the importance of music in Catalan culture and the life of its ordinary people (as opposed to the Liceu opera house, with its Castilian-speaking, monarchist upper-class patrons, and its music from elsewhere), but the Palau turned out to be anything but commonplace; it and the Liceu were for many decades opposing cross-town forces in Barcelona's musical as well as philosophical discourse. If you can't fit a performance into your itinerary, you owe it to yourself to at least take a tour of this amazing building.

The exterior is remarkable. The Miquel Blay sculptural group over the corner of Amadeu Vives and Sant Pere Més Alt is a hymn in stone to Catalonia's popular traditions, with hardly a note left unsung: St. George the dragon slayer (at the top), women and children at play and work, fishermen with oars over their shoulders—a panoply of everyday life. (The glass facade over the present ticket-window entrance is one of

A wooden door leads to Barcelona's best 17th-century patio in the Palau Dalmases.

the city's best examples of nonintrusive modern construction wedded to heritage from the past.) Inside, the decor of the Palau assaults your senses before the first note of music is ever heard. Wagner's Valkyrie burst from the right side of the stage over a heavy-browed bust of Beethoven; Catalonia's popular music is represented by the graceful maidens of Lluís Millet's song "Flors de Maig" ("Flowers of May") on the left. Overhead, an inverted stained-glass cupola seems to channel the divine gift of music straight from heaven; painted rosettes and giant peacock feathers adorn the walls and columns; across the entire back wall of the stage is a relief of muse-like Art Nouveau musicians in costume. The visuals alone make music sound different here, be it a chamber orchestra, a renowned piano soloist, a gospel choir, or an Afro-Cuban combo. ✉ *Carrer Sant Pere Més Alt 4–6, Born-Ribera* ☎ *93/295–7200* 🌐 *www.palaumusica.org* 🎫 *Tour €17* ⏲ *Sept.–June, daily 10–3:30; July and Aug., daily 10–7. Tours every 30 mins* Ⓜ *Urquinaona.*

Passeig del Born. Once the site of medieval jousts and Inquisitional autos-da-fé, the passeig, at the end of Carrer Montcada behind the church of Santa Maria del Mar, was early Barcelona's most important square. Late-night cocktail bars and miniature restaurants with tiny spiral stairways now line the narrow, elongated plaza. The numbered cannonballs under the public benches are the work of the "poet of space"—a 20th-century specialist in combinations of letters, words, and sculpture—the late Joan Brossa. The cannonballs evoke the 1714 siege of Barcelona that concluded the 14-year War of the Spanish Succession, when Felipe V's conquering Castilian and French troops attacked the city ramparts at their lowest, flattest flank. After their victory, the Bourbon forces obliged residents of the Barri de la Ribera (Waterfront District) to tear down nearly a thousand of their own houses, some 20% of Barcelona at that time, to create fields of fire so that the occupying army of Felipe V could better train its batteries of cannon on the conquered populace and discourage any nationalist uprisings. Thus began Barcelona's "internal exile" as an official enemy of the Spanish state.

Walk down to the Born itself—a great iron hangar, once a produce market designed by Josep Fontseré. The initial stages of the construction of a public library in the Born uncovered the remains of the lost city of 1714, complete with blackened fireplaces, taverns, wells, and the canal that brought water into the city. The Museu d'Història de la Ciutat opened a museum here in September 2013, kicking off a year of events concluding with the September 11, 2014 commemoration of Barcelona's defeat. The streets of the 14th- to 18th-century Born-Ribera lie open in the sunken central square of the old market; around it, on the ground level, are a number of new multifunctional exhibition and performance spaces; these give the city one of its newest and liveliest cultural subcenters. ✉ *Passeig del Born, Born-Ribera* Ⓜ *Jaume I.*

WORTH NOTING

Biblioteca Popular de la Dona Francesca Bonnemaison (*Women's Public Library*). Barcelona's (and probably the world's) first library established exclusively for women, this lovely spot was founded in 1909 as a female sanctuary, evidence of the city's early-20th-century progressive attitudes and tendencies. Over the opulently coffered main reading room, the stained-glass skylight reads, "*Tota dona val mes quan letra apren*" ("Any woman's worth more when she learns how to read"), the first line of a ballad by the 13th-century Catalan troubadour Severí de Girona. Once Franco's Spain composed of church, army, and oligarchy had restored law and order after the Spanish civil war, the center was taken over by Spain's one legal political party, the Falange, and women's activities were reoriented toward more domestic pursuits such as sewing and cooking. Today the library complex includes a small theater and offers a lively program of theatrical and cultural events. (Website is in Catalan only.) ✉ *Sant Pere Més Baix 7, Sant Pere* ☎ *93/268–7360* 🌐 *www.bonnemaison-ccd.org* ⏲ *Tues.–Fri. 10–2 and 4–9, Sat. 10–2* Ⓜ *Jaume I, Urquinaona.*

Capella d'en Marcús (*Marcús Chapel*). This Romanesque hermitage looks as if it had been left behind by some remote order of hermit-monks who meant to take it on a picnic in the Pyrenees. The tiny chapel, possibly—along with Sant Llàtzer—Barcelona's smallest religious structure, was originally built in the 12th century on the main Roman road into Barcelona, the one that would become Cardo Maximo just a few hundred yards away as it passed through the walls at Portal de l'Àngel. Bernat Marcús, a wealthy merchant concerned with public welfare and social issues, built a hospital here for the poor. The chapel today known by his name was built as the hospital chapel and dedicated to the Mare de Déu de la Guia (Our Lady of the Guide). As a result of its affiliation, combined with its location on the edge of town, the chapel became linked with the Confraria del Correus a Cavall (Brotherhood of the Pony Express), also known as the *troters*

CLOSE UP

Picasso's Barcelona

The city's claim to Pablo Picasso (1881–1973) has been contested by Málaga (the painter's birthplace), as well as by Madrid, where *La Guernica* hangs, and by the town of Gernika, victim of the 1937 Luftwaffe saturation bombing that inspired the famous canvas. Fervently anti-Franco, Picasso refused to return to Spain after the Civil War; in turn, the regime allowed no public display of his work until 1961, when the artist's *Sardana* frieze on Barcelona's Architects' Guild building was unveiled. Picasso never set foot on Spanish soil for his last 39 years.

Picasso spent a sporadic but formative period of his youth in Barcelona between 1895 and 1904, after which he moved to Paris. His father was an art professor at the Reial Acadèmia de Belles Arts in La Llotja—where his son, a precocious draftsman, began advanced classes at the age of 15. The 19-year-old Picasso first exhibited at Els Quatre Gats, a tavern on Carrer Montsió that looks today much as it did then. His early Cubist painting *Les Demoiselles d'Avignon* was inspired not by the French town but by the Barcelona street Carrer d'Avinyó, then infamous for its brothels. After moving to Paris, Picasso returned occasionally to Barcelona until his last visit in 1934. Considering the artist's off-and-on tenure, it is remarkable that the city and Picasso should be so intertwined in the world's perception. The Picasso Museum, deservedly high on the list of the city's must-see attractions, is perhaps fourth (after the Miró, the MNAC, and the MACBA) on any connoisseur's roster of Barcelona art collections.

Iconoserveis Culturals (✉ *Av. Portal de l'Àngel 38, 4°–2ª, Born-Ribera* ☎ *93/410–1405* 🌐 *www.iconoserveis.com*) gives walking tours through the key spots in Picasso's Barcelona life, covering studios, galleries, family apartments, and the painter's favorite haunts and hangouts. 🎟 *Groups up to 20: Weekdays €220, weekends €265.*

(trotters), and for two centuries (13th and 14th) made Barcelona the key link in overland mail between the Iberian Peninsula and France. ✉ *Carrer Carders 2 (Placeta d'en Marcús), Born-Ribera* ⏲ *Mass only, daily at 10 am.* Ⓜ *Jaume I.*

Carrer Banys Vells. This little pedestrian-only alleyway paralleling Carrer Montcada just gets better and better. Exploring Banys Vells is a delight, from the beautifully appointed Teresa Ferri restaurant **El Pebre Blau** all the way down the street to the **Tarannà** shop (original jewelry, lamps, household doodads) on the corner at Carrer Barra de Ferro 4. Banys Vells means "old baths," referring to the site of the early public baths. Later baths were on the street Banys Nous (New Baths) in the Barri Gòtic near the cathedral. ✉ *Carrer Banys Vells, Born-Ribera* Ⓜ *Jaume I.*

Carrer Flassaders. Named for the weavers and blanket makers whose street this was in medieval times, Carrer Flassaders begins on Carrer Montcada opposite La Xampanyet, one of La Ribera's most popular bars for tapas and Cava. Duck into the short, dark Carrer Arc de Sant Vicenç; at the end you'll find yourself face to face with **La Seca,** the Royal Mint (officially, the *Reial Fàbrica de la Moneda de la Corona d'Aragó*), where money was manufactured until the mid-19th century.

Coins bearing the inscription, in Castilian, "Principado de Cataluña" (Principality of Catalonia) were minted here as late as 1836. La Seca has been exquisitely restored, with the original wooden beams, pillars, and brickwork intact; it's home now to a small avant-garde repertory theater company called Espai Brossa. Adjacent is the studio and showroom of internationally acclaimed sculptor Manel Àlvarez.

Moving left to Carrer de la Cirera, look overhead to the left for the niche with the image of **Santa Maria de Cervelló,** one of the patron saints of the Catalan fleet, on the back side of the Palau Cervelló on Carrer Montcada. Moving down to the right on Carrer de la Cirera past the Otman shop and tearoom, you arrive at the corner of **Carrer dels Flassaders.** Walk left past several shops—**Re-Born** at No. 23; cozy **La Báscula** café in the former candy factory at No. 30; the restaurant and design store **Café de la Princesa** at the corner of Carrer Sabateret; and the gourmet **Montiel** restaurant at No. 19. Then turn back down Flassaders through a gauntlet of elegant clothing, furnishings, and jewelry boutiques past the main entry to La Seca at No. 40, with the gigantic royal Bourbon coat of arms over the archway. At No. 42 is **Loisaida** (vintage clothing and curios: the name is Spanglish for the Lower East Side in New York City). The stylish Cortana clothing store is across the street. Look up to your right at the corner of the gated Carrer de les Mosques, famous as Barcelona's narrowest street. The mustachioed countenance peering down at you was once a medieval advertisement for a brothel. **Hofmann,** at No. 44, is the excellent pastry store of famous Barcelona chef Mey Hofmann, whose cooking school is on nearby Carrer Argenteria. A right on Passeig del Born will take you back to Santa Maria del Mar. ✉ *Carrer Flassaders, Born-Ribera* Ⓜ *Jaume I.*

Disseny Hub. This new center of activity represents the efforts of Barcelona's urban planners to put all the city's designer eggs in one basket and to plant an eye-catching architectural anchor in the long-delayed renewal project on Plaça de les Glories. The new building is home to the **Museu Tèxtil i d'Indumentària** collection of textiles, embroidery, and accessories from the 16th century to the present; it's also home to the **Museu de Ceràmica** and the **Museu del Disseny** collections of decorative and graphic arts. The DHUB store has a fine selection of books on design as well as reproductions that make great gifts. ✉ *Edific DHUB, Pl. de les Glòries Catalans 37–8, Eixample* ☎ *93/256–3465* 🌐 *www.museudeldisseny.cat* ⏲ *Tues.–Sun. 10–6* Ⓜ *Glories.*

Plaça de les Olles. This pretty little square named for the makers of *olles,* or pots, has been known to host everything from topless sunbathers to elegant Viennese waltzers to the overflow from popular nearby tapas bar Cal Pep. Notice the balconies at No. 6 over Café de la Ribera, oddly with colorful blue and yellow tile on the second and top floors. The house with the turret over the street on the right at the corner leading out to Pla del Palau (at Plaça de les Olles 2) is another of Enric Sagnier i Villavecchia's retro-Moderniste works. ✉ *Plaça de les Olles, Born-Ribera* Ⓜ *Jaume I.*

LA CIUTADELLA AND BARCELONETA

Sightseeing ★★★★★
Nightlife ★★★☆☆
Dining ★★★★★
Lodging ★★★☆☆
Shopping ☆☆☆☆☆

Now Barcelona's central downtown park, La Ciutadella was originally the site of a fortress built by the conquering troops of the Bourbon monarch Felipe V after the fall of Barcelona in the 1700–14 War of the Spanish Succession. Barceloneta has always been a little seedy: the people who live here hang their washing out over the narrow streets; they will cheerfully direct you to the nearest tattoo parlor, or the funky bar around the corner that serves a great paella; they thumb their noses a bit at the fancy yachts in the marina across the Passeig Joan de Borbó—but like the folks in the Born, they are not immune to the recent siren song of gentrification.

Barceloneta and La Ciutadella make a historical fit. In the early 18th century, some 1,000 houses in the Barrio de la Ribera, then the waterfront neighborhood around Plaça del Born, were ordered torn down, to create fields of fire for the cannon of La Ciutadella, the newly built fortress that kept watch over the rebellious Catalans. Barceloneta, then a marshy wetland, was filled in and developed almost four decades later, in 1753, to house the families who had lost homes in La Ribera.

Open water in Roman times and gradually silted in only after the 15th-century construction of the port, it became Barcelona's fishermen's and stevedores' quarter. Originally composed of 15 longitudinal and three cross streets and 329 two-story houses, this was Europe's earliest planned urban development, built by the military engineer Juan Martin Cermeño under the command of El Marquès de la Mina, Juan Miguel de Guzmán Dávalos Spinola (1690–1767). Barceloneta was always sort of a safety valve, a little fishing village next door where barcelonins could go to escape the formalities and constraints of city life, for a Sunday seafood lunch on the beach and a stroll through what felt like a freer world. With its tiny original apartment blocks, and its history of seafarers and gypsies, Barceloneta even now maintains its spontaneous, carefree flavor.

TOP ATTRACTIONS

Carrer Sant Carles No. 6. The last Barceloneta house left standing in its original 1755 two-story entirety, this low, boxlike structure was planned as a single-family dwelling with shop and storage space on the ground floor and the living space above. Overcrowding soon produced split houses and even quartered houses, with workers and their families living in tiny spaces. After nearly a century of living under Madrid-based military jurisdiction, Barceloneta homeowners were given permission to expand vertically, and houses of as many as five stories began to tower over the lowly original dwellings. The house is not open to the public. ✉ *Carrer Sant Carles 6, Barceloneta* Ⓜ *Barceloneta.*

OFF THE BEATEN PATH

Dipòsit de les Aigües–Universitat Pompeu Fabra. The Ciutadella campus of Barcelona's private Universitat Pompeu Fabra contains a contemporary architectural gem worth seeking out. It's two blocks up from the Ciutadella–Vil.la Olímpica metro stop, just beyond where the tramline out to the Fòrum begins. Once the hydraulic cistern for the Ciutadella waterworks, built in 1880 by Josep Fontseré, the Dipòsit de les Aigües was converted to the school's Central Library in 1999 by the design team of Lluís Clotet and Ignacio Paricio. The massive, 3-foot-thick walls, perforated and crowned with tall brick arches, are striking; the trompe-l'oeil connecting corridor between the reading rooms is a brilliant touch. Even in humble Barceloneta, there are opportunities for really gifted architects to take a historical property in hand, and work magic. ✉ *Ramon Trias Fargas 25–27, La Ciutadella* ☎ *93/542–1709* *Free* ⏲ *Weekdays 8–1:30 am, weekends 10–9* Ⓜ *Ciutadella–Vil.la Olímpica.*

Estació de França. Barcelona's main railroad station until about 1980 and still in use, the elegant Estació de França is outside the west gate of the Ciutadella. Rebuilt in 1929 for the International Exhibition, restored in 1992 for the Olympics, this mid-19th-century building ill-deserves the reduction in traffic it has suffered since Estació de Sants became the city's main intercity and international terminus: the marble and bronze, the Moderniste decorative details, and the delicate tracery of its wrought-iron roof girders make this one of the most beautiful buildings of its kind anywhere. Stop in for a sense of the bygone romance of European travel. ✉ *Marquès de l'Argentera s/n, Born-Ribera* ☎ *93/496–3464, 902/240202* Ⓜ *Barceloneta.*

Museu d'Història de Catalunya. Established in what used to be a port warehouse, this state-of-the-art interactive museum makes you part of Catalonian history from prehistoric times through more than 3,000 years and into the contemporary democratic era. After centuries of "official" Catalan history dictated from Madrid (from 1714 until the mid-19th century Renaixença, and from 1939 to 1975), this offers an opportunity to revisit Catalonia's autobiography. Explanations of the exhibits appear in Catalan, Castilian, and English. Guided tours are

GETTING ORIENTED

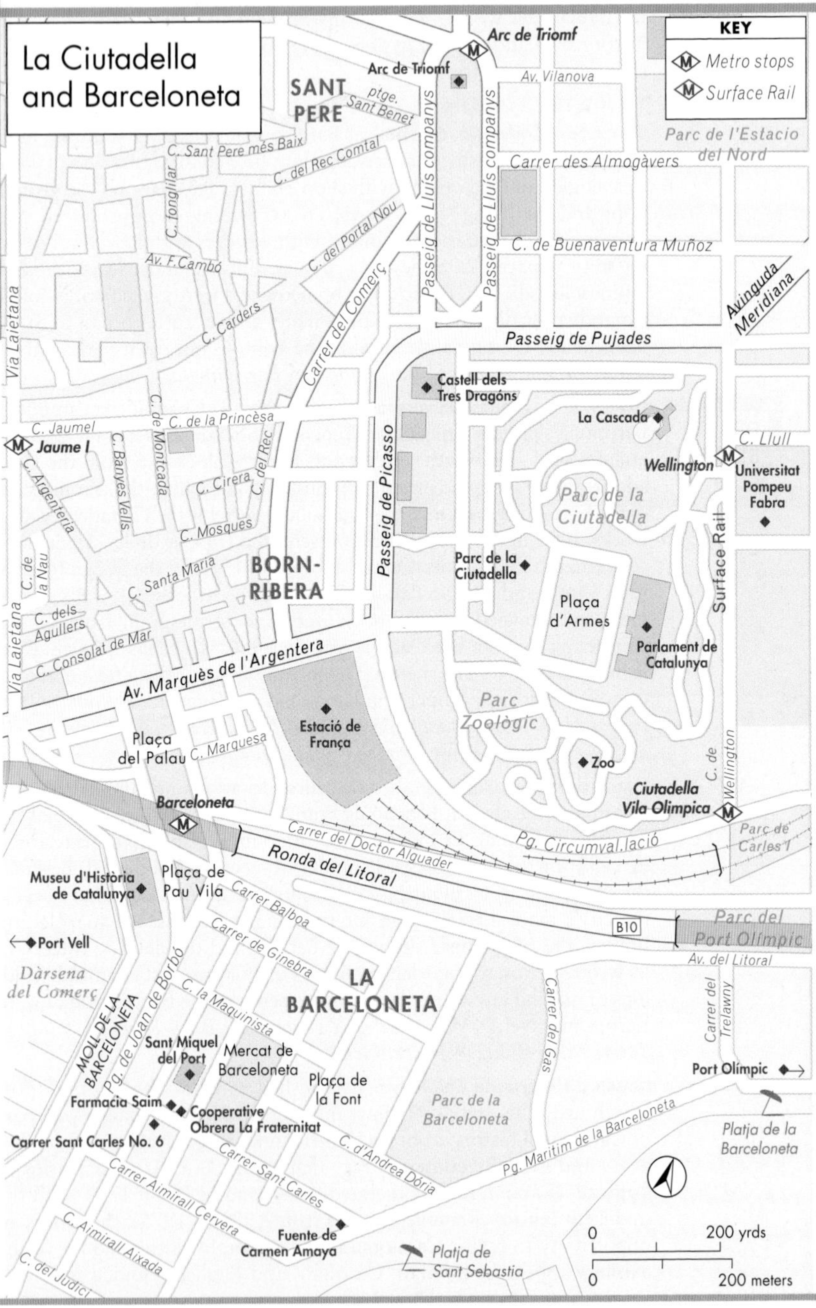
La Ciutadella and Barceloneta
KEY
Metro stops
Surface Rail
Arc de Triomf
Av. Vilanova
SANT PERE
ptge. Sant Benet
Passeig de Lluís companys
Parc de l'Estacio del Nord
C. Sant Pere més Baix
C. del Rec Comtal
Carrer des Almogàvers
C. fonollar
C. del Portal Nou
C. de Buenaventura Muñoz
Av. F.Cambó
Avinguda Meridiana
C. Carders
Carrer del Comerç
Via Laietana
Passeig de Pujades
Castell dels Tres Dragóns
La Cascada
C. de Montcada
C. de la Princèsa
C. Jaumel
Jaume I
C. Banyes Vells
C. Argenteria
C. Cirera
C. del Rec
C. Mosques
Passeig de Picasso
C. Llull
Wellington
Universitat Pompeu Fabra
Parc de la Ciutadella
Surface Rail
C. de la Nau
C. Santa Maria
BORN-RIBERA
Plaça d'Armes
Parlament de Catalunya
C. dels Agullers
C. Consolat de Mar
Av. Marquès de l'Argentera
Parc Zoològic
Plaça del Palau
C. Marquesa
Estació de França
Zoo
C. de Wellington
Ciutadella Vila Olimpica
Barceloneta
Carrer del Doctor Alguader
Pg. Circumval.lació
Parc de Carles I
Ronda del Litoral
Museu d'Història de Catalunya
Plaça de Pau Vila
Carrer Balboa
B10
Parc del Port Olímpic
Port Vell
Carrer de Ginebra
Av. del Litoral
Dàrsena del Comerç
LA BARCELONETA
MOLL DE LA BARCELONETA
Pg. de Joan de Borbó
C. la Maquinista
Carrer del Gas
Carrer del Trelawny
Sant Miquel del Port
Mercat de Barceloneta
Port Olímpic
Plaça de la Font
Farmacia Saim
Cooperative Obrera La Fraternitat
Parc de la Barceloneta
Platja de la Barceloneta
Pg. Marítim de la Barceloneta
Carrer Sant Carles No. 6
C. d'Andrea Dória
Carrer Sant Carles
Carrer Aimirall Cervera
Fuente de Carmen Amaya
Platja de Sant Sebastia
C. Aimirall Aixada
C. del Judici
0
200 yrds
0
200 meters

TIMING

Exploring Ciutadella Park and Barceloneta can take from three to four hours. Add at least another hour if you're stopping for lunch. Try to time your arrival in Barceloneta so you catch the local market in full swing at midday (until 3) and work your way through the neighborhood to a beachside table for paella. Can Manel la Puda serves paella until 4 in the afternoon.

GETTING HERE

The Barceloneta stop on the metro's yellow line (L4) is the closest subway stop; there's lots to see on a walk to the beach through the Barri Gòtic from Plaça de Catalunya, but it could leave you a little footsore. For La Ciutadella, the Arc de Triomf stop on the red line (L1) is closest.

QUICK BITES

El Vaso de Oro. Friendly El Vaso de Oro is a famous tapas specialist, always full of grazers, local and otherwise. ✉ *Balboa 6, Barceloneta* ☎ *93/319–3098* Ⓜ *Barceloneta.*

Els Fogons de La Barceloneta. The welcoming Els Fogons de La Barceloneta serves traditional Barceloneta tapas next to the market. ✉ *Pl. de la Font s/n, Barceloneta* ☎ *93/224–2626* Ⓜ *Barceloneta.*

TOP ATTRACTIONS

Carrer Sant Carles No. 6

Estació de França

Museu d'Història de Catalunya

Sant Miquel del Port church

TOP EXPERIENCES

Dining at the edge of the sand

Joining a Sunday drum fest in Ciutadella Park

Renting a windsurfer and catching a breeze

Walking the beachfront from W Hotel Barcelona to the Hotel Arts

WHERE TO EAT (⇨ CH. 3)

Agua

Antiga Casa Solé

Barceloneta

Can Majó

Can Manel la Puda

CDLC

El Lobito

El Vaso de Oro

Suquet de l'Almirall

Torre d'Alta Mar

HAPPENING NIGHTLIFE (⇨ CH. 5)

Shôko

City strollers hit the beach on summer days.

available on Sunday at noon and 1. The rooftop restaurant has excellent views over the harbor and is open to the public (whether or not you visit the museum itself) during museum hours. ✉ *Pl. Pau Vila 3, Barceloneta* ☎ *93/225–4700* 🌐 *www.mhcat.net* 🎫 *€4 (free 1st Sun. of month)* 🕓 *Tues. and Thurs.–Sat. 10–7, Wed. 10–8, Sun. 10–2:30* Ⓜ *Barceloneta.*

WORTH NOTING

Arc del Triomf. This imposing, exposed-redbrick arch was built by Josep Vilaseca as the grand entrance for the 1888 Universal Exhibition. Similar in size and sense to the traditional triumphal arches of ancient Rome, this one refers to no specific military triumph anyone can recall. In fact, Catalonia's last military triumph of note may have been Jaume I el Conqueridor's 1229 conquest of the Moors in Mallorca—as suggested by the bats (always part of Jaume I's coat of arms) on either side of the arch itself. The Josep Reynés sculptures adorning the structure represent Barcelona hosting visitors to the exhibition on the west (front) side, while the Josep Llimona sculptures on the east side depict the prizes being given to its outstanding contributors. ✉ *Passeig de Sant Joan, La Ciutadella* Ⓜ *Arc de Triomf.*

El Transbordador Aeri del Port (*cable car*). This hair-raising cable-car ride over the Barcelona harbor from Barceloneta to Montjuïc (with a midway stop in the port) is spectacular—an adrenaline rush with a view. The rush comes from being packed in with 18 other people, standing room only, in a tiny gondola swaying a hundred feet or so above the Mediterranean. The cable car leaves from the tower at the end of Passeig Joan de Borbó and connects the Torre de San Sebastián on the Moll de Barceloneta, the tower of Jaume I in the port boat terminal, and the

Torre de Miramar on Montjuïc. Critics maintain, not without reason, that the ride is expensive, not very cool, and actually pretty scary. On the positive side, this is undoubtedly the slickest way to connect Barceloneta and Montjuïc, and the Torre de Altamar restaurant in the tower at the Barceloneta end serves excellent food and wine. ✉ *Passeig Joan de Borbó s/n, Barceloneta* ☎ *93/225–2718, 93/430–4716* 🎫 *€16.50 round-trip, €11 one-way* ⏲ *Sep.–June, daily 11–7; Jul. and Aug., daily 11–8* Ⓜ *Barceloneta.*

Fuente de Carmen Amaya (*Carmen Amaya Fountain*). Down at the eastern end of Carrer Sant Carles, where Barceloneta joins the beach, is the monument to the famous Gypsy flamenco dancer Carmen Amaya (1913–63), born in the Gypsy settlement known as Somorrostro, part of Barceloneta until 1920, when development sent the gypsies farther east to what is now the Fòrum grounds (from which they were again displaced in 2003). Amaya achieved universal fame at the age of 16, in 1929, when she performed at Barcelona's International Exposition. Amaya made triumphal tours of the Americas and starred in films such as *La hija de Juan Simón* (1934) and *Los Tarantos* (1962). The fountain, and its high-relief representations of cherubic children as flamenco performers (two guitarists, three dancers—in the nude, unlike real flamenco dancers), has been poorly maintained since it was placed here in 1959, but it remains an important reminder of Barceloneta's roots as a rough-and-tumble, romantic enclave of free-living sailors, stevedores, Gypsies, and fishermen. This Gypsy ambience all but disappeared when the last of the *chiringuitos* (ramshackle beach restaurants specializing in fish and rice dishes) fell to the wreckers' ball shortly after the 1992 Olympics. ✉ *Carrer Sant Carles s/n, Barceloneta* Ⓜ *Barceloneta.*

La Cascada. The sights and sounds of Barcelona seem far away when you stand near this monumental, slightly overdramatized creation by Josep Fontseré, presented as part of the 1888 Universal Exhibition. The waterfall's somewhat overwrought rocks were the work of a young architecture student named Antoni Gaudí—his first public work, appropriately natural and organic, and certainly a hint of things to come. ✉ *Parc de la Ciutadella, La Ciutadella* Ⓜ *Arc de Triomf.*

FAMILY **Parc de la Ciutadella** (*Citadel Park*). Once a fortress designed to consolidate Madrid's military occupation of Barcelona, the Ciutadella is now the city's main downtown park. The clearing dates from shortly after the War of the Spanish Succession in the early 18th century, when Felipe V demolished some 1,000 houses in what was then the Barri de la Ribera to build a fortress and barracks for his soldiers and a *glacis,* or open space, between rebellious Barcelona and his artillery positions. The fortress walls were pulled down in 1868 and replaced by gardens laid out by Josep Fontseré. In 1888 the park was the site of the Universal Exposition that put Barcelona on the map as a truly European city; today it is home to the Castell dels Tres Dragons, built by architect Lluís Domènech i Montaner as the café and restaurant for the exposition (the only building to survive that project, now a botanical research center), the Catalan parliament, and the city zoo. ✉ *La Ciutadella* Ⓜ *Barceloneta, Arc de Triomf, Ciutadella/Vila Olimpica.*

Downtown's main park, the Parc de la Ciutadella

Parlament de Catalunya. Once the arsenal for the Ciutadella—as evidenced by the thickness of the building's walls—this is the only surviving remnant of Felipe V's fortress. It now houses the Catalan Parliament. ✉ *Pas de l'Institut Escola, Parc de la Ciutadella, La Ciutadella* ☎ *93/304–6500, 93/304–6645 for guided visits* 🎫 *Free* ⏲ *Sat. 10–7, Sun. 10–2* Ⓜ *Ciutadella/Vila Olímpica.*

Port Olímpic. Choked with yachts, restaurants, tapas bars, and mega-restaurants serving reasonably decent fare continuously 1 pm to 1 am, the Olympic Port is 2 km (1 mile) up the beach from Barceloneta, marked by the mammoth shimmering goldfish sculpture by starchitect Frank Gehry, who designed the Guggenheim Museum in Bilbao (Bilbao got a leviathan; Barcelona got a goldfish). In the shadow of Barcelona's first real skyscraper, the Hotel Arts, the Olympic Port draws hundreds—nay, thousands—of young people of all nationalities on Friday and Saturday nights, especially in summer, on the beach at Nova Icària, generating a buzz redolent of spring break in Cancún. ✉ *Port Olímpic* Ⓜ *Ciutadella/Vila Olímpica.*

Port Vell (*Old Port*). From Pla del Palau, cross to the edge of the port, where the Moll d'Espanya, the Moll de la Fusta, and the Moll de Barceloneta meet. (*Moll* means docks.) Just beyond the colorful Roy Lichtenstein sculpture in front of the post office, the modern Port Vell complex—an IMAX theater, aquarium, and Maremagnum shopping mall—looms seaward on the Moll d'Espanya. The Palau de Mar, with its five somewhat pricey and impersonal quayside terrace restaurants, stretches down along the Moll de Barceloneta (try Llevataps or the Merendero de la Mari; even better is El Magatzem, by the entrance to the Museu de Història de Catalunya in the Palau de Mar). Key points in the Maremagnum complex are the grassy hillside (for lovers, especially, on April 23, Sant Jordi's Day, Barcelona's variant of Valentine's Day); and the *Ictineo II* replica of the submarine created by Narcis Monturiol (1819–85)—the world's first, launched in the Barcelona port in 1862. ✉ *Port Vell, Barceloneta* Ⓜ *Barceloneta.*

Sant Miquel del Port. Have a close look at this baroque church with its modern (1992), pseudo-bodybuilder version of the winged archangel Michael himself, complete with sword and chain, in the alcove on the facade. One of the first buildings to be completed in Barceloneta, Sant Miquel del Port was begun in 1753 and finished by 1755 under the direction of architect Damià Ribes. Due to strict orders to keep Barceloneta low enough to fire La Ciutadella's cannon over, Sant Miquel del Port had no bell tower and only a small cupola until Elies Rogent added a new one in 1853. Interesting to note are the metopes, palm-size, gilt bas-relief sculptures around the interior cornice and repeated outside at the top of the facade. These 74 Latin-inscribed allegories each allude to different attributes of St. Michael: for example, the image of a boat and the Latin inscription "*iam in tuto*" ("finally safe"), alluding to the saint's protection against the perils of the sea. To the right of Sant Miquel del Port at Carrer de Sant Miquel 41 is a house decorated by seven strips of floral *sgraffiti* and a plaque commemorating Fernando de Lesseps, the engineer who built the Suez Canal, who lived in the house while serving as French consul to Barcelona. In the square by the church, take a close look at the fountain, with its Barcelona coat of arms, and Can Ganassa, on the east side, a worthy tapas bar. ✉ *Pl. de la Barceloneta s/n, Barceloneta* Ⓜ *Barceloneta.*

FAMILY **Zoo.** Barcelona's excellent zoo occupies the whole eastern end of the Parc de la Ciutadella. There's a superb reptile house and a full assortment of African animals. The dolphin show usually plays to a packed house. ✉ *Parc de la Ciutadella, Ciutadella* ☎ *93/225–6780* 🌐 *www.zoobarcelona.cat* 🎟 *€19.60* ⏲ *Winter, daily 10–5:30; summer, daily 10–8* Ⓜ *Ciutadella/Vila Olímpica, Barceloneta.*

THE EIXAMPLE

Sightseeing ★★★★★
Nightlife ★★★★★
Dining ★★★★★
Lodging ★★★★★
Shopping ★★★★★

Barcelona's most famous neighborhood, this late 19th-century urban development is known for its dazzling Art Nouveau architecture. Called the "Expansion" in Catalan, the district appears on the map as a geometric grid laid out north above the Plaça de Catalunya. The upscale shops, the art galleries, the facades of the Moderniste townhouses, and the venues for some of the city's finest cuisine, are the attractions here for visitors and barcelonins alike.

The Eixample (ay-shompla) is an open-air Moderniste museum. Designed as a grid, in the best Cartesian tradition, the Eixample is oddly difficult to find your way around in; the builders neglected to number the buildings or alphabetize the streets, and even Barcelona residents can get lost in it. The easiest orientation to grasp is the basic division between the well-to-do Dreta, to the right of Rambla Catalunya looking inland, and the more working-class Ezquerra to the left. Eixample locations are also either *mar* (on the ocean side of the street) or *muntanya* (facing the mountains).

The Eixample was created when the Ciutat Vella's city walls were demolished in 1860, and Barcelona embarked on a vast expansion, financed by the return of rich colonials from the Americas, aristocrats who had sold their country estates, and the city's industrial magnates. They expected their investment to trumpet not only their own wealth and influence, but also the resurgence of Barcelona itself and its unique cultural heritage—not Spanish, but Catalan, and modern European. The grid was the work of engineer Ildefons Cerdà, and much of the construction was done in the peak years of the Moderniste movement by a who's who of Art Nouveau architects, starring Gaudí, Domènech i Montaner, and Puig i Cadafalch; rising above it all is Gaudí's Sagrada Família church. The Eixample's principal thoroughfares are La Rambla de Catalunya and the Passeig de Gràcia, where many of the city's most elegant shops occupy the ground floors of the most interesting Art Nouveau buildings.

TOP ATTRACTIONS

Fodor's Choice ★ **Casa Milà.** Usually referred to as **La Pedrera** (The Stone Quarry), this building, with its wavy, curving stone facade undulating around the corner of the block, is one of Gaudí's most celebrated yet initially reviled designs. Topped by chimneys so eerie they were nicknamed *espantabruxes* (witch scarers), the Casa Milà was unveiled in 1910 to the horror of local residents. The sudden appearance of this strange facade on the city's most fashionable street led to the immediate coining of unflattering descriptions; newspapers called it the "Rock Pile," and made unflattering references to the gypsy cave dwellings in Granada's Sacromonte. The exterior has no straight lines; the curlicues and wrought-iron foliage of the balconies, sculpted by Josep Maria Jujol, and the rippling, undressed stone, made you feel, as one critic put it, "as though you are on board a ship in an angry sea."

The building was originally meant to be dedicated to the Mother of God and crowned with a sculpture of the Virgin Mary. The initial design was altered by owner Pere Milà i Camps, who, after the anticlerical violence of the Setmana Tràgica (Tragic Week) of 1909, decided that the religious theme would be an invitation to a new outbreak of mayhem. Gaudí's rooftop chimney park, alternately interpreted as veiled Saharan women or helmeted warriors, is as spectacular as anything in Barcelona, especially in late afternoon, when the sunlight slants over the city into the Mediterranean. Inside, the handsome **Espai Gaudí** (Gaudí Space) in the attic has excellent critical displays of Gaudí's works from all over Spain, as well as explanations of theories and techniques, including an upside-down model (a reproduction of the original in the Sagrada Família museum) of the Güell family crypt at Santa Coloma, made of weighted hanging strings. This hanging model is based on the theory of the reversion of the catenary, which says that a chain suspended from two points will spontaneously hang in the exact shape of the inverted arch required to convert the stress to compression, thus providing structural support. The **Pis de la Pedrera** apartment is an interesting look into the life of a family that lived in La Pedrera in the early 20th century. Everything from the bathroom to the kitchen is filled with reminders of how comprehensively life has changed in the last century. People still live in the other apartments.

In the summer high season the lines of visitors waiting to see the Pedrera can stretch a block or more; if you can, sign up for a Pedrera Secreta (Secret Pedrera) private guided tour of the building by night, offered with or without dinner (☎ *902/202138 for reservations [essential]* ✉ *reserves@lapedrera.com for reservations* ⏲ *Mar.–Oct., daily 8:15 pm–midnight; Nov.–Feb., Wed.–Sat. 7:15–11*). There are also guided tours in various languages (☎ *902/202138 for reservations/info* ✉ *grupslapedrera@oscatalunyacaixa.com for reservations/info* ⏲ *Weekdays at 6 pm, weekends at 11 am*). On Nits d'Estiu (Summer nights: Thurs., Fri., and Sat., Jun. 20–Sept. 7) the Espai Gaudí and the roof terrace are open for drinks and jazz concerts; the doors open at 9:45 pm and concerts begin at 10:30. Admission is €27. ✉ *Passeig de Gràcia 92, Eixample* ☎ *902/202138* 🎟 *€16.50; Pedrera Secreta tours €30/€49* ⏲ *Daily, Nov.–Feb., 9–6:30; Mar.–Oct., 9–8* Ⓜ *Diagonal, Provença.*

GETTING ORIENTED

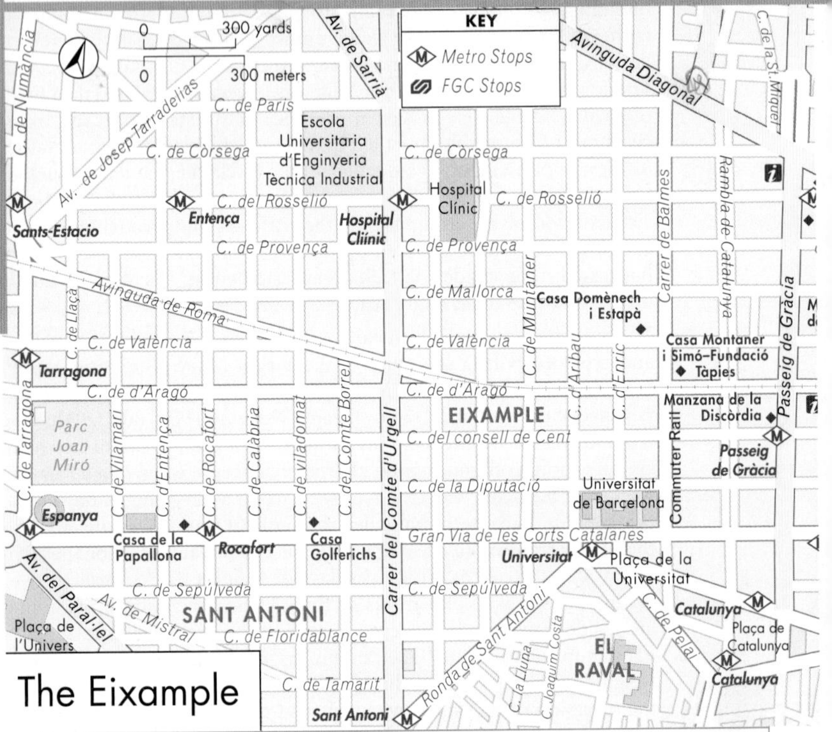

The Eixample

TIMING	GETTING HERE AND AROUND
Exploring the Eixample can take days, but three hours will be enough to cover the most important sites. Add another two or three hours (including the wait in line) for the Sagrada Família. Look for the *passatges* (passageways) through some of the Eixample blocks; Passatge Permanyer, Passatge de la Concepció, and Passatge Mendez Vigo are three of the best. Beware of the tapas emporia on Passeig de Gràcia; almost all of them microwave previously prepared bits and are not the best.	The metro stops at Plaça de Catalunya and Provença nicely bracket this quintessential Barcelona neighborhood; the Diagonal and Passeig de Gràcia stations are right in the center. Barcelona's unnumbered Eixample (Expansion), the post-1860 grid, is a perfect place to get lost, but fear not: the Eixample is vertebrate. Carrer Balmes divides the working-class *Esquerra* (left, looking uphill) from its bourgeois *Dreta* (right). Even the blocks are divided by flats *davant* (front) or *darrera* (behind). The sides of the streets are either *mar* (seaward) or *muntanya* (facing the mountain).

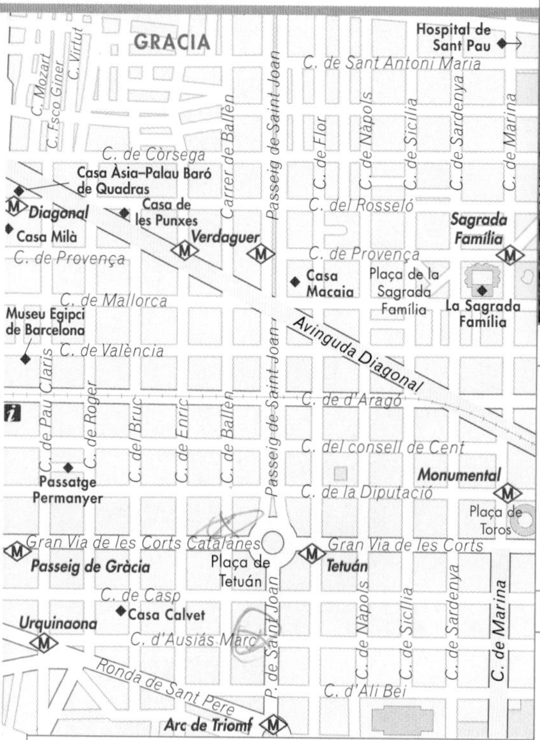

DISCOUNT TICKETS

The Ruta del Modernisme (Moderniste Route) ticket offers coupon booklets, including discounted visits, to more than 100 Moderniste buildings in and around Barcelona. For €18, a manual published in various languages allows you to self-guide through the city's Art Nouveau architecture. Inquire at your hotel or the nearest tourist office, or purchase tickets directly at the **Modernisme Centre** (✉ *Pl. de Catalunya 17, Eixample* ☎ *93/317–7652* 🌐 *www.rutadelmodernisme.com* 🕒 *Mon.–Sat. 10–7, Sun. 10–2*), which is part of the Barcelona Tourist Information Center. You can also purchase tickets at the Pavellons de la Finca Güell (✉ *Av.de Pedralbes 7*) or at the Hospital de la Santa Creu i de Sant Pau (✉ *Sant Antoni Maria Claret 167*).

TOP ATTRACTIONS

Casa Milà

Casa Montaner i Simó–Fundació Tàpies

Manzana de la Discòrdia

Temple Expiatori de la Sagrada Família

TOP EXPERIENCES

Exploring the art galleries on Consell de Cent

Strolling down the leafy promenade of La Rambla de Catalunya

Walking the rooftop of Casa Milà

WHERE TO EAT (⇨ CH. 3)

Alkimia

Bar Mut

Café Paris

Can Gaig

Casa Calvet

Cinc Sentits

L'Olivé

Tragaluz

Ya Ya Amelia

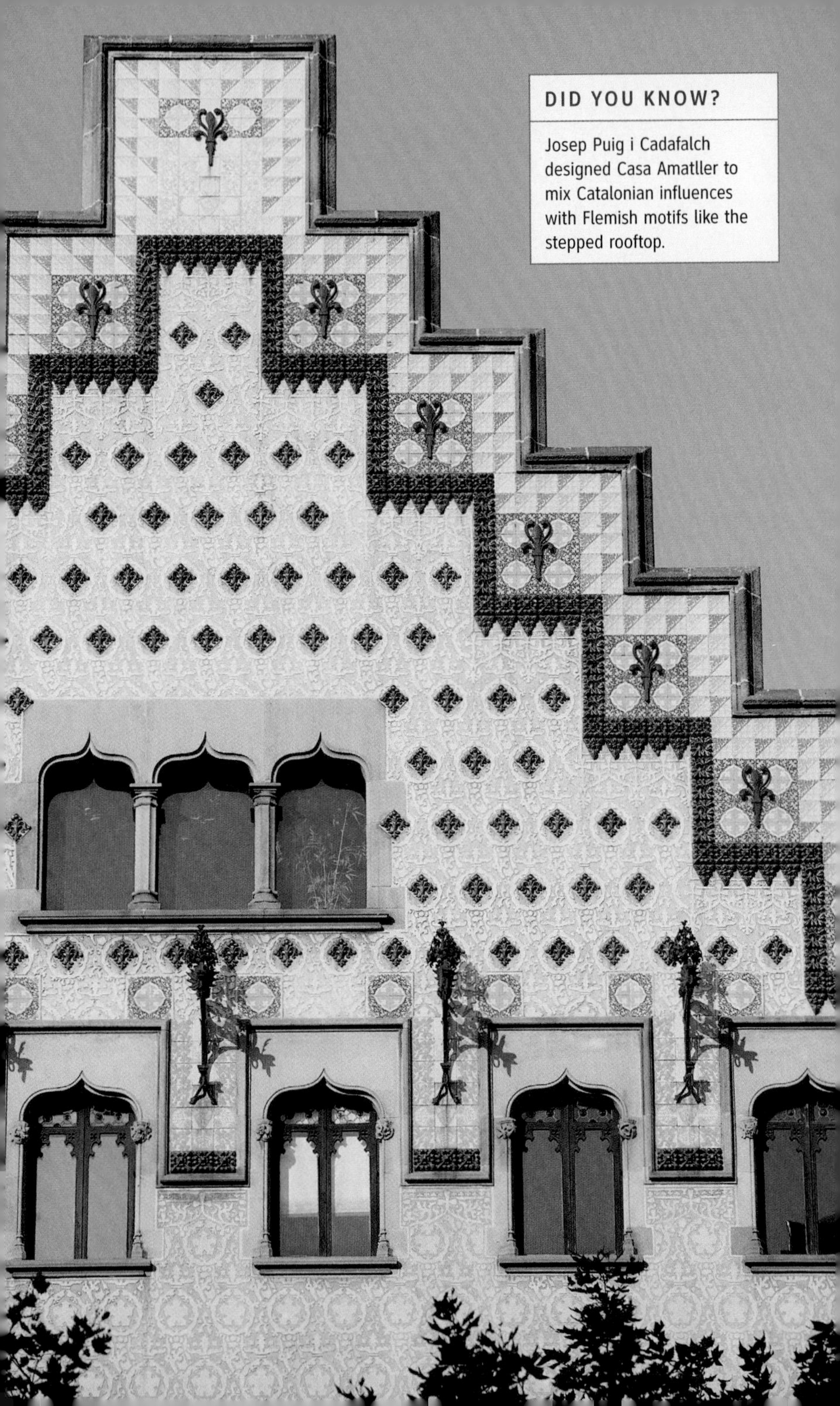

DID YOU KNOW?

Josep Puig i Cadafalch designed Casa Amatller to mix Catalonian influences with Flemish motifs like the stepped rooftop.

Fodor's Choice ★ **Manzana de la Discòrdia.** The name is a pun on the Spanish word *manzana,* which means both apple and city block, alluding to the three-way architectural counterpoint on this street and to the classical myth of the Apple of Discord (which played a part in that legendary tale about the Judgment of Paris and the subsequent Trojan War). The houses here are spectacular and encompass three monuments of Modernisme—Casa Lleó Morera, Casa Amatller, and Casa Batlló. Of the three contrasting buildings (four if you count Sagnier i Villavecchia's comparatively tame 1910 Casa Mulleras at No. 37), Casa Batlló is clearly the star attraction and the only one of the three offering visits to the interior. ✉ *Passeig de Gràcia 35–43, Eixample* Ⓜ *Passeig de Gracia.*

Casa Amatller. The neo-Gothic Casa Amatller was built by Josep Puig i Cadafalch in 1900, when the architect was 33 years old. Eighteen years younger than Domènech i Montaner and 15 years younger than Gaudí, Puig i Cadafalch was one of the leading statesmen of his generation, mayor of Barcelona and, in 1917, president of Catalonia's first home-rule government since 1714, the Mancomunitat de Catalunya. Puig i Cadafalch's architectural historicism sought to recover Catalonia's proud past, in combination with eclectic elements from Flemish and Dutch architectural motifs. Note the Eusebi Arnau sculptures—especially his St. George and the dragon, and the figures of a drummer with his dancing bear. The flowing-haired "Princesa" is thought to be Amatller's daughter; the animals above the motif are depicted pouring chocolate, a reference to the source of the Amatller family fortune. The upper floors are generally closed to the public, although the Fundació Institut Amatller d'Art Hispànic holds occasional cultural events upstairs. The small gallery on the first floor, which mounts various exhibitions related to Modernisme, is open to the public free of charge; a quick visit will give you a sense of what the rest of the building is like—and a chance to buy some chocolate *de la casa* at the boutique. ✉ *Passeig de Gràcia 41, Eixample* ☎ *93/487–7217* 🌐 *www.amatller.org.*

Casa Batlló. Gaudí at his most spectacular, the Casa Batlló is actually a makeover: it was originally built in 1877 by Emili Sala Cortés, one of Gaudí's teachers, and acquired by the Batlló family in 1900. Batlló wanted to tear down the undistinguished Sala building and start over, but let Gaudí persuade him to remodel the facade and the interior instead. The result is astonishing: the facade, with its rainbow of colored glass and *trencadís* polychromatic tile fragments, and the toothy masks of the wrought-iron balconies projecting outward toward the street, is an irresistible photo op. Nationalist symbolism is at work here: the scaly roof line represents the Dragon of Evil impaled on St. George's cross, and the skulls and bones on the balconies are the dragon's victims—allusions to medieval Catalonia's code of chivalry and religious piety. Gaudí is said to have directed the composition of the facade from the middle of Passeig de Gràcia, calling instructions to workmen on the scaffolding, about how to place the trencadís. Inside, the translucent windows on the landings of the central staircase light up the maritime motif and the details of the building, all whorls and spirals and curves: here, as everywhere in his oeuvre, Gaudí opted for natural shapes and rejected straight lines.

Budget-conscious visitors will content themselves with the outside view of the Casa Batlló; the admission fee is ridiculously high, and you won't see much inside that you can`t also see in the Casa Milà, up the Passeig de Gràcia on the opposite side. ✉ *Passeig de Gràcia 43, Eixample* ☎ *93/216–0306* 🌐 *www.casabatllo.es* 🎟 *€20.35* ⏲ *Daily 9–9 (hrs vary).*

Casa Lleó Morera. The ornate Casa Lleó Morera was extensively rebuilt from 1902 to 1906 by Palau de la Música Catalana architect Domènech i Montaner and is a treasure house of Catalan Modernisme. The facade is covered with ornamentation and sculptures depicting female figures using the modern inventions of the age: the telephone, the telegraph, the camera, and the Victrola. The inside, presently closed to the public, is even more astounding, another anthology of Art Nouveau techniques assembled by the same team of glaziers, sculptors, and mosaicists Domènech i Montaner directed in the construction of the Palau de la Música Catalana. The Eusebi Arnau sculptures around the top of the walls on the main floor are based on the Catalan lullaby "La Dida de l'Infant del Rei" (The Nurse of the King's Baby); while the stained-glass scenes in the old dining room, of Lleó Morera family picnics, resemble Moderniste versions of impressionist paintings. (Though Casa Lleó Morera is not open to the public at this writing, check the current status with the Modernisme Centre [☎ *93/317–7652*] and ask how to arrange a visit.) ✉ *Passeig de Gracia 35, Eixample.*

Palau Baró de Quadras. The neo-Gothic and Plateresque (intricately carved in silversmith-like detail) facade of this house built in 1904 for Baron Quadras has one of the most spectacular collections of Eusebi Arnau sculptures in town (other Arnau sites include the Palau de la Música Catalana, Els Quatre Gats–Casa Martí, Casa Amatller, and Casa Lleó Morera). Look for the theme of St. George slaying the dragon once again, this one in a spectacularly vertiginous rush of movement down the facade. Don't miss the intimate-looking row of alpine chalet–like windows across the top floor. The Palau currently houses the Institut Ramon Llull, a nonprofit organization dedicated to spreading the knowledge of Catalan culture worldwide. ✉ *Av. Diagonal 373, Eixample* ☎ *93/467–8000* 🌐 *www.llull.cat* 🎟 *Free* ⏲ *Tues.–Sat. 10–8, Sun. 10–2* Ⓜ *Diagonal.*

Plaça de Catalunya. Barcelona's main bus-and-metro hub is the frontier between the Ciutat Vella and the post-1860 Eixample. Fountains and statuary, along with pigeons and backpackers in roughly equal numbers, make the Plaça de Catalunya an open space to scurry across on your way to somewhere quieter, shadier, and gentler on the senses. Across the street on the west side is **Café Zurich**, the classic Barcelona rendezvous point at the top of La Rambla, by the steps down to the metro. The block behind the Zurich, known as El Triangle, houses a collection of megastores, including FNAC (for electronics, books, and music) and Habitat (for designer furniture and household fixtures). El Corte Inglés, the department store on the northeast side of the square, offers quality Spanish goods at decent prices—if you can get the attention of one of their famously indifferent salespeople.

The works of sculpture ringing the square provide a study in contrasts. Marvel first at the eyesore prize, in the corner nearest the top of La

Rambla: the monumentally banal stone stepladder by Josep Maria Subirachs, offered up as a monument to Francesc Macià, president of the Generalitat (the autonomous Catalan government) from 1934 to 1936. In the center of the reflecting pool is Josep Clarà's stunning marble *Déesse* (*Goddess*), kneeling gracefully in water. (The figure is actually a copy of the original, moved to the Generalitat building in Plaça Sant Jaume to protect it from the elements.) At the northwest corner is Pau Gargallo's heroic bronze rendition of the grape harvest, an allegorical reference to Girona, one of the provinces of Catalunya celebrated for its agriculture. And at the northeast corner, across from El Corte Inglés, is the Federic Marès bronze of a buxom maiden on horseback holding a model of the ship Columbus used in his historic voyage.

TIP→ The underground Tourist Information Office on the northeast corner is the place to pick up maps and brochures, download free apps for exploring the city to your mobile device, and check on walking tours, some in English, that originate there. ✉ *Pl. de Catalunya, Eixample* Ⓜ *Pl. de Catalunya.*

Fodor's Choice ★ **Recinte Modernista de Sant Pau.** Among the more recent tourist attractions in Barcelona, the Recinte Modernista (Modernist Complex) is set in what was surely one of the most beautiful public projects in the world: the Hospital de Sant Pau. A World Heritage site, the complex is extraordinary in its setting and style, and in the idea that inspired it. Architect Lluis Domènech i Montaner believed that trees and flowers and fresh air were likely to help people recover from what ailed them more than anything doctors could do in emotionally sterile surroundings. The hospital wards were set among gardens, their brick facades topped with polychrome ceramic tile roofs in extravagant shapes and details. Domènech also believed in the therapeutic properties of form and color, and decorated the hospital with Pau Gargallo sculptures and colorful mosaics, replete with motifs of hope and healing and healthy growth. Begun in 1900, this monumental production won Domènech i Montaner his third Barcelona "Best Building" award in 1912. (His previous two prizes were for the Palau de la Música Catalana and Casa Lleó Morera.)

No longer a functioning hospital (the new Sant Pau—comparatively soulless but fully functional and state-of-the-art—is uphill from the complex), many of the buildings have been taken over for other purposes. The Sant Manuel Pavillion, for example, now houses the **Casa Àsia,** a comprehensive resource for cultural and business-related research on all the countries of Asia, with library holdings of books, films, and music from each of them. Tours of the Complex are offered in English daily at 10, 11, 12 and 1. ✉ *Carrer Sant Antoni Maria Claret 167, Eixample* ☎ *93/553–7801, 93/269–2444* 🌐 *www.santpaubarcelona.org* 🎫 *Tour €10* Ⓜ *Hospital de Sant Pau.*

WORTH NOTING

Casa Calvet. This exquisite but more conventional townhouse (for Gaudí, anyway) was the architect's first commission in the Eixample (the second was the dragonlike Casa Batlló, and the third and last—he was never asked to do another—was the stone quarry–esque Casa Milà). Peaked with baroque scroll gables over the unadorned (no ceramics, no color, no sculpted ripples) Montjuïc sandstone facade, Casa Calvet compensates for its structural conservatism with its Art Nouveau details, from the door handles to the benches, chairs, vestibule, and spectacular glass-and-wood elevator. Built in 1900 for the textile baron Pere Calvet, the house includes symbolic elements on the facade, ranging from the owner's stylized letter "C" over the door to the cypress, symbol of hospitality, above. The wild mushrooms on the main (second) floor reflect Pere Calvet's (and perhaps Gaudí's) passion for mycology, while the busts at the top of the facade represent St. Peter, the owner's patron saint; and St. Genis of Arles and St. Genis of Rome, patron saints of Vilassar, the Calvet family's hometown in the coastal Maresme north of Barcelona. For an even more sensorial taste of Gaudí, dine in the building's **Casa Calvet** restaurant, originally the suite of offices for Calvet's textile company, with its exuberant Moderniste decor. ✉ *Carrer Casp 48, Eixample* Ⓜ *Urquinaona.*

Casa de la Papallona. This extraordinary apartment house crowned with an enormous yellow butterfly (*papallona*) made of *trencadís* (broken ceramic chips used by the Modernistes to add color to curved surfaces) was built in 1912 by Josep Graner i Prat. Next to Plaça de Espanya, directly overlooking the Arenes de Barcelona (the former bullring, now a multilevel shopping mall), the building displays lines of a routine, late-19th-century design—that is, until you reach the top of the facade. ✉ *Llançà 20, Eixample* Ⓜ *Rocafort.*

Casa de les Punxes (*House of the Spikes*). Also known as Casa Terrades for the family that owned the house and commissioned Puig i Cadafalch to build it, this extraordinary cluster of six conical towers ending in impossibly sharp needles is another of Puig i Cadafalch's northern European inspirations, this one rooted in the Gothic architecture of Nordic countries. One of the few freestanding Eixample buildings, visible from 360 degrees, this ersatz-Bavarian or Danish castle in downtown Barcelona is composed entirely of private apartments. Some of them are built into the conical towers themselves and consist of three circular levels connected by spiral stairways, about right for a couple or a very small family. Interestingly, Puig i Cadafalch also designed the Terrades family mausoleum, albeit in a much more sober and respectful style. ✉ *Av. Diagonal 416–420, Eixample* Ⓜ *Diagonal.*

Casa Domènech i Estapà. This less radical example of Eixample Art Nouveau architecture is interesting for its balconies and curved lines on the facade, for its handsome doors and vestibule, and for the lovely etched designs on the glass of the entryway. Built by and for the architect Domènech i Estapà in 1908–09, eight years before his death, this building represents a more conservative interpretation of the aesthetic canons of the epoch, revealing the architect's hostility to the Art Nouveau movement. Domènech i Estapà built more civil projects than any other architect of his time (Reial Acadèmia de Ciències y Artes, Palacio de Justicia, Sociedad Catalana de Gas y Electricidad, Hospital Clínico, Observatorio Fabra) and was the creator of the Carcel Modelo (Model Prison), considered a state-of-the-art example of penitentiary design when it was built in 1913. ✉ *Valencia 241, Eixample* Ⓜ *Passeig de Gràcia.*

Continued on page 109

DID YOU KNOW?

Casa de les Punxes (aka House of the Spikes) is one of the only freestanding buildings in the Moderniste Eixample neighborhood, visible from 360 degrees.

TEMPLE EXPIATORI DE LA SAGRADA FAMÍLIA

Antoni Gaudí's striking and surreal masterpiece was conceived as nothing short of a Bible in stone, an arresting representation of the history of Christianity. Today this Roman Catholic church is Barcelona's most emblematic architectural icon. Looming over Barcelona like a mid-city massif of grottoes and peaks, the Sagrada Família strains skyward in piles of stalagmites. Construction is ongoing and continues to stretch toward the heavens.

CONSTRUCTION, PAST AND PRESENT

"My client is not in a hurry," was Gaudí's reply to anyone curious about his project's timetable . . . good thing, too, because the Sagrada Família was begun in 1882 under architect Francesc Villar, passed on in 1891 to Gaudí, and is still thought to be more than a decade from completion. Gaudí added Art Nouveau touches to the crypt and in 1893 started the Nativity facade. Conceived as a symbolic construct encompassing the complete story and scope of the Christian faith, the church was intended by Gaudí to impress the viewer with the full sweep and force of the Gospel. At the time of his death in 1926 only one tower of the Nativity facade had been completed.

By 2026, the 100th anniversary of Gaudí's death, after 144 years of construction in the tradition of the great medieval and Renaissance cathedrals of Europe, the Sagrada Família may well be complete enough to call finished. Architect Jordi Bonet continues in the footsteps of his father, architect Lluís Bonet, to make Gaudí's vision complete as he has since the 1980s.

(left) Twilight at the Sagrada Família, still under construction today. (top) Shepherds gather to witness the birth of Christ in the Nativity facade.

BIBLE STUDIES IN STONE: THE FACADES

Gaudí's plans called for three immense facades. The northeast-facing **Nativity facade** and the southwest-facing **Passion facade** are complete. The much larger southeast-facing **Glory facade**, the building's main entry, is still under construction. The final church will have **eighteen towers**: The four **bell towers** over each facade represent the twelve apostles; the four **larger towers** represent the evangelists Mark, Matthew, John, and Luke; the **second-highest tower** in the reredos behind the altar honors the Virgin Mary; and in the center the **Torre del Salvador** (Tower of the Savior) will soar to a height of 564 feet.

THE NATIVITY FACADE

Built during Gaudí's lifetime, this facade displays his vision and sculptural style, the organic or so-called "melting wax" look that has become his signature. The facade is crowned by **four bell towers**, representing the apostles Barnabas, Jude, Simon, and Matthew and divided into three sections around the doors of **Charity** in the center, **Faith** on the right, and **Hope** on the left.

(left) The ornamental Nativity facade. (above, top right) A figure in the Portal of Faith. (above, center right) The spiraling staircase. (above, bottom right) A decorative cross.

The focal point in the Nativity facade: Joseph and Mary presenting the infant Jesus.

Over the central **Portal of Charity** is the birth of Christ, with a representation of the Annunciation overhead in an ice grotto, another natural element. Above that are the signs of the zodiac for the Christmas sky at Bethlehem, with two babies representing the Gemini, and the horns of a bull for Taurus. The evergreen cypress tree rising above symbolizes eternity, with the white doves as souls seeking life everlasting.

The **Portal of Faith** on the right shows Christ preaching as a youth. Higher up are the Eucharistic symbols of grapes and wheat, and a hand and eye, symbols of divine Providence.

The **Portal of Hope** on the left shows a series of biblical scenes including the slaughter of the innocents, the flight into Egypt, Joseph surrounded by his carpenter's tools looking down at his infant son, and the marriage of Joseph and Mary with Mary's parents, Joaquin and Anna, looking on. Above is a boat, representing the Church, piloted by Joseph, with the Holy Spirit represented as a dove.

THE PASSION FACADE

On the **Passion facade**, Gaudí intended to dramatize the abyss between the birth of a child and the death of a man. In 1986 Josep Maria Subirachs, an artist known for his atheism and his hard-edged and geometrical sculptural style, was commissioned to finish the Passion facade. The contrast is sharp, in content and in sculptural style, between this facade and the Nativity facade. Framed by leaning columns of tibia-like bones, the Passion facade illustrates the last days of Christ and his Resurrection. The scenes are laid out chronologically in an S-shape path beginning at the bottom left and ending at the upper right.

At bottom left is the **Last Supper**, the disciples' faces contorted in confusion and anguish, most of all Judas clutching his bag of money behind his back over a reclining hound, the contrasting symbol of fidelity. To the right is the Garden of Gethsemane and Peter awakening, followed by the **Kiss of Judas**. To the right of the door is **Peter's Third Denial** of

Judas kissing Jesus while a cryptogram behind contains a numerical combination adding up to 33, the age of Christ's death.

The stark, geometric Passion facade.

Christ "ere the cock crows." Farther to the right are **Pontius Pilate and Jesus** with the crown of thorns.

Above on the second tier are the **Three Marys** and Simon helping Jesus lift the cross. Over the center, **Jesus carries the cross.** To the left, Gaudí himself is portrayed, pencil in hand, the evangelist in stone, while farther left a **mounted centurion** pierces the side of the church with his spear, the church representing the body of Christ. At the top left, **soldiers gamble for Christ's clothing** while at the top center is the **crucifixion**, featuring Subirachs's controversial (in 1971 when it was unveiled) naked and anatomically complete Christ. Finally to the right, Peter and Mary grieve at **Christ's entombment**, an egg overhead symbolizing rebirth and the resurrection. At a height of 148 feet are the four Apostles on their bell towers. Bartholomew, on the left, looks upward toward the 26-foot risen Christ between the four bell towers at a height of 198 feet.

THE GLORY FACADE

The Glory facade, still under construction, will have a wide stairway and esplanade or porch leading up to three portals dedicated, as in the other facades, to Charity, Faith, and Hope. The doors are inscribed with the Lord's Prayer in bronze in fifty different languages with the Catalan version in the center in relief. Carrer Mallorca will be routed underground and the entire city block across the street will be razed to make space for the esplanade and park. Present predictions are between 2026 and 2030 for the completion of this phase.

A new element in the Sagrada Família: the bronze doorway of the Glory facade.

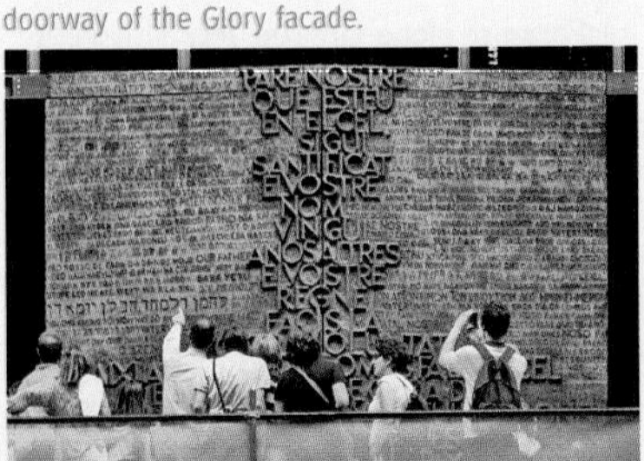

THE INTERIOR: "TEMPLE OF HARMONIOUS LIGHT"

(top) Above the altar, supporting columns form a canopy of light. (below) Towering columns and stained-glass windows keep the interior bright.

Until 2010, The Sagrada Família was able to be adequately appreciated without going inside. But since the interior was completed for the Papal consecration, it's become Barcelona's most stunning space, comparable to the breathtaking upsweep of the finest soaring Gothic architecture but higher, brighter, and carved in a dazzling fusion of hard-edged Subirachs over organic Gaudí.

DESIGN

The floor plan for the church is laid out in the form of a **Latin cross** with five longitudinal naves intersected by three transepts. The **apse** has space for 15,000 people, a choir loft for 1,500, and is large enough to encompass the entire Santa Maria del Mar basilica. From the Glory Façade, the Baptistry Chapel is to the left and the Chapel of the Sacrament and Penitence is to the right. The Chapel of the Assumption is at the back of the apse. Over the main altar is the figure of the crucified Christ, suspended in mid-air under a diaphanous canopy.

LIGHT

The main nave and the apse of the basilica create an immense and immaculate space culminated by the highest point: the hyperboloid skylight over the main altar 75 meters (247.5 ft) above the floor. The vaulting is perforated with 288 skylights admitting abundant light. The sharp-edged, tree-like leaning columns shape the interior spaces and will support the six towers being built above them. Vaults are decorated with green and gold Venetian mosaics that diffuse the light as if they were leaves in a forest, making the basilica, in the words of Gaudí, "the temple of harmonious light."

DETAILS TO DISCOVER: THE EXTERIOR

GAUDÍ IN THE PASSION FACADE

Subirachs pays double homage to the great Moderniste master in the Passion facade: Gaudí himself appears over the left side of the main entry making notes or drawings, the evangelist in stone, while the Roman soldiers are modeled on Gaudí's helmeted, Star Wars–like warriors from the roof of La Pedrera.

TOWER TOPS

Break out the binoculars and have a close look at the pinnacles and peaks of the Sagrada Família's towers. Sculpted by Japanese artist Etsuro Sotoo, these clusters of grapes and different kinds of fruit are symbols of fertility, of rebirth, and of the Resurrection of Christ.

SUBIRACHS IN THE PASSION FACADE

At Christ's feet in the entombment sculpture is a blocky figure with a furrowed brow, thought to be a portrayal of the agnostic's anguished search for certainty. This figure is generally taken as a self-portrait of Subirachs, characterized by the sculptor's giant hand and an "S" on his massive right arm.

DONKEY ON THE NATIVITY FACADE

On the left side of the Nativity facade over the Portal of Hope is a *burro*, a small donkey, known to have been modeled from a donkey that Gaudí saw near the work site. The *ruc català* (Catalan donkey) is a beloved and iconic symbol of Catalonia, often displayed on Catalonian bumpers as a response to the Spanish fighting bull.

THE ROSE TREE DOOR

The richly sculpted Rose Tree Door, between the Nativity facade and the cloisters, portrays Our Lady of the Rose Tree with the infant Jesus in her arms, St. Dominic and St. Catherine of Siena in prayer, with three angels dancing overhead. The sculptural group on the wall known as "The Death of the Just" portrays the Virgin and child comforting a moribund old man, the Spanish prayer "Jesús, José, y María, asistidme en mi última agonía" (Jesus, Joseph, and María, help me in my final agony). The accompanying inscriptions in English, "Pray for us sinners now and at the hour of our death, Amen" are the final words of the Ave María prayer.

Gaudí in the Passion facade

Sotoo's ornamental fruit

The donkey in the Nativity facade

The heavily embelished Rose door

COLUMN FROM THE PORTAL OF CHARITY

The column, dead center in the Portal of Charity, is covered with the genealogy of Christ going back through the House of David to Abraham. At the bottom of the column is the snake of evil, complete with the apple of temptation in his mouth, closed in behind an iron grate, symbolic of Christianity's mission of neutralizing the sin of selfishness.

FACELESS ST. VERONICA

Because her story is considered legendary, not historical fact, St. Veronica appears faceless in the Passion facade. Also shown is the veil she gave Christ to wipe his face with on the way to Calvary that was said to be miraculously imprinted with his likeness. The veil is torn in two overhead and covers a mosaic that Subirachs allegedly disliked and elected to conceal.

STAINED-GLASS WINDOWS

The stained-glass windows of the Sagrada Família are work of Joan Vila-Grau. The windows in the west central part of the nave represent the light of Jesus and a bubbling fountain in a bright chromatic patchwork of shades of blue with green and yellow reflections. The main window on the Passion facade represents the Resurrection. Gaudí left express instructions that the windows of the central nave have no color so as not to alter the colors of the tiles and trencadis (mosaics of broken tile) in green and gold representing palm leaves. These windows will be clear or translucent, as a symbol of purity and to admit as much light as possible.

TORTOISES AND TURTLES

Nature lover Gaudí used as many elements of the natural world as he could in his stone Bible. The sea tortoise beneath the column on the Mediterranean side of the Portal of Hope and the land turtle supporting the inland Portal of Faith symbolize the slow and steady stability of the cosmos and of the church.

SAINT THOMAS IN THE BELL TOWER

Above the Passion facade, St. Thomas demanding proof of Christ's resurrection (thus the expression "doubting Thomas") and perched on the bell tower is pointing to the palm of his hand asking to inspect Christ's wounds.

CHRIST RESURRECTED ABOVE PASSION FACADE

High above the Passion facade, a gilded Christ sits resurrected, perched between two towers.

The column in the Portal of Charity

St. Veronica with the veil

Stained-glass windows

Christ resurrected

MAKING THE MOST OF YOUR TRIP

The Nativity facade

WHEN TO VISIT

To avoid crowds, come first thing in the morning. And save your trip for a sunny day so you can admire the facades at length.

WHAT TO WEAR AND BRING

Keep in mind that you're visiting a church: don't wear shorts and cover bare shoulders. It's a good idea to bring binoculars to absorb details all the way up.

TIMING

If you're just walking around the exterior, an hour or two should cover it. If you'd like to go inside to the crypt, visit the museum, and take the elevator up the towers and walk down the spiraling stairway, you'll need three to four hours.

HIGHLIGHTS

The Passion facade, the Nativity facade, the Portal of Faith, the Portal of Hope, and the main altar.

BONUS FEATURES

The museum displays Gaudí's scale models and shows photographs of the construction. The crypt holds Gaudí's remains. For €2 (and a 45-minute wait in line), you can take an elevator to the top of the bell towers for spectacular views.

TOURS

English-language tours are given daily at 11 AM, 1 PM, 3 PM, and 5 PM and cost €4.

VISITOR INFORMATION

✉ Pl. de la Sagrada Família, Eixample ☎ 93/207–3031 🌐 www.sagradafamilia.org 🎟 €11, bell tower elevator €2, audio guides €4 ⏲ Oct.–Mar., daily 9–6; Apr.–Sept., daily 9–8 Ⓜ Sagrada Família.

TOWERS

Climbing the towers is no longer permitted, and lines for the elevator are long. Only the Passion Facade may be descended on foot, which is highly recommended for a close look at some of the figures, including that of Gaudí himself.

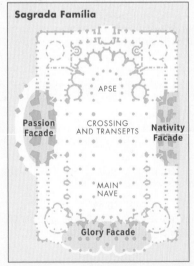

Sagrada Família

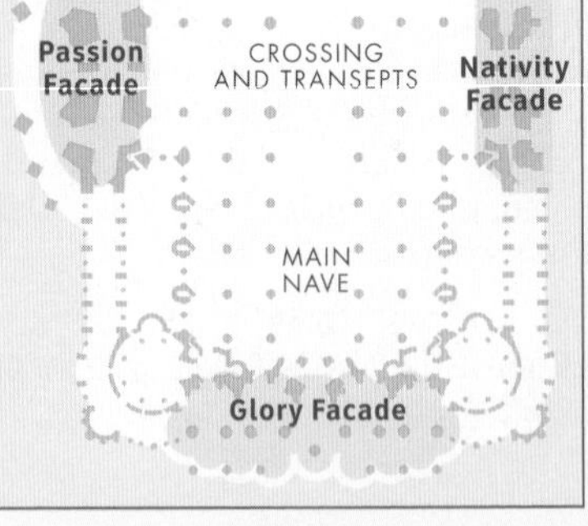

Casa Golferichs. Gaudí disciple Joan Rubió i Bellver built this extraordinary house, known as El Xalet (The Chalet), for the Golferichs family when he was not yet 30. The rambling wooden eaves and gables of the exterior enclose a cozy and comfortable dark-wood-lined interior with a pronounced verticality. The top floor, with its rich wood beams and cerulean walls, is often used for intimate concerts; the ground floor exhibits paintings and photographs. The building serves now as the quarters of the Golferichs Centre Civic, which offers local residents a range of adult education courses, and organizes various thematic walking tours of the city. (The website is in Catalan only.) ✉ *Gran Via 491, Eixample* ☎ *93/323–7790* 🌐 *www.golferichs.org* 🕑 *Weekdays 10–2 and 4–8, Sat. 10–2* Ⓜ *Rocafort, Urgell.*

Casa Macaya. This graceful Puig i Cadafalch building constructed in 1901 was the former seat of the Centre Cultural Fundació "La Caixa," a deep-pocketed, far-reaching cultural social-welfare organization funded by the Caixa Catalana (Catalan Savings Bank). Look for the Eusebi Arnau sculptures over the door depicting, somewhat cryptically, a man mounted on a donkey and another on a bicycle, reminiscent of the similar Arnau sculptures on the facade of Puig i Cadafalch's Casa Amatller on Passeig de Gràcia. ✉ *Passeig de Sant Joan 108, Eixample* Ⓜ *Verdaguer.*

Casa Montaner i Simó–Fundació Tàpies. This former publishing house—and the city's first building to incorporate iron supports, built in 1880—has been handsomely converted to hold the work of preeminent contemporary Catalan painter Antoni Tàpies, as well as temporary exhibits. Tàpies, who died in 2012, was an abstract painter, although influenced by surrealism, which may account for the sculpture atop the structure—a tangle of metal titled *Núvol i cadira* (*Cloud and Chair*). The modern, airy split-level gallery also has a bookstore that's strong on Tàpies, Asian art, and Barcelona art and architecture. ✉ *Carrer Aragó 255, Eixample* ☎ *93/487–0315* 🌐 *www.fundaciotapies.org* 🎫 *€7* 🕑 *Tues.–Sun. 10–8* Ⓜ *Passeig de Gràcia.*

OFF THE BEATEN PATH

Museu Egipci de Barcelona. Presumably you came to Barcelona to learn about Catalonia, not ancient Egypt, but you might be making a mistake by skipping this major collection of art and artifacts. Housing what is probably Spain's most comprehensive exhibition on Egypt, this excellent museum takes advantage of state-of-the-art curatorial techniques that are nearly as interesting as the subject matter, which ranges from mummies to exhibits on what the ancient Egyptian had for dinner. ✉ *Fundació Arqueòlogica Clos, Valencia 284, Eixample* ☎ *93/488–0188* 🌐 *www.museuegipci.com* 🎫 *€11* 🕑 *Mon.–Sat. 10–8, Sun. 10–2; guided tour with Egyptologists Sat. at noon and 2; night visits with actors and theatrical scenes Fri. and Sat. 9:30–11 by reservation; tours in English Fri. at 5 or by reservation* Ⓜ *Passeig de Gràcia.*

Passatge Permanyer. Cutting through the middle of the block bordered by Pau Claris, Roger de Llúria, Consell de Cent, and Diputació, this charming, leafy mid-Eixample sanctuary is one of 46 *passatges* (alleys or passageways) that cut through the blocks of this gridlike area. Inspired by John Nash's neoclassical Regent's Park terraces in London (with their formal and separate town houses), Ildefons Cerdà originally envisioned many more of these utopian mid-block gardens, but Barcelona never endorsed his vision. Once an aristocratic enclave and hideaway for pianist Carles Vidiella and poet, musician, and illustrator Apel.les Mestre, Passatge Permanyer is, along with the nearby Passatge Méndez Vigo, the best of these through-the-looking-glass downtown Barcelona alleyways. ✉ *Passatge Permanyer, Eixample* Ⓜ *Passeig de Gràcia.*

POBLENOU

Converted loft spaces and cutting-edge architecture collide with handsome 19th-century residences in Poblenou. This sizeable neighborhood faces the sea, and is considered to be one of Barcelona's up-and-coming (and most underrated) neighborhoods. The most appealing place for a stroll is the **Rambla de Poblenou.**

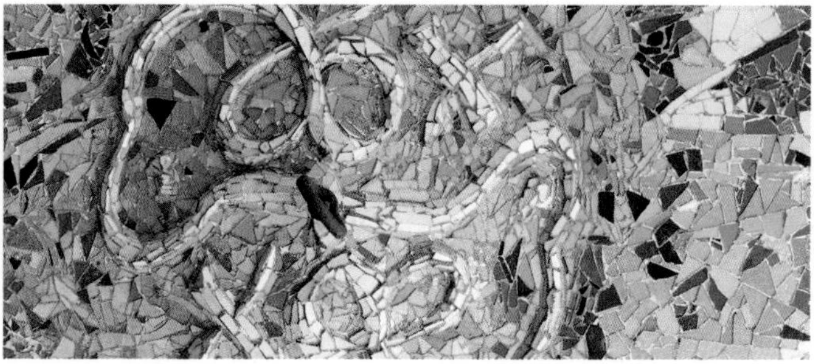

2

GRÀCIA

Sightseeing ★★★☆☆
Nightlife ★★★★☆
Dining ★★★★☆
Lodging ★★☆☆☆
Shopping ★★☆☆☆

Gràcia is a state of mind. More than a neighborhood, it is a village republic that has periodically risen in armed rebellion against city, state, and country; its jumble of streets have names (Llibertat, Fraternitat, Progrès) that invoke the ideological history of this fierce little progressive, working-class enclave.

The site of Barcelona's first factory collectives, it was fertile ground for all sorts of radical reform movements, as workers organized and developed into groups ranging from anarchists to feminists to Esperantists. Once an independent village that joined the municipality of Barcelona only under duress, Gràcia attempted to secede from the Spanish state in 1856, 1870, 1873, and 1909.

Lying above the Diagonal from Carrer de Còrsega all the way up to Park Güell, Gràcia is bound by Via Augusta and Carrer Balmes to the west and Carrer de l'Escorial and Passeig de Sant Joan to the east. Today the area is filled with hip little bars and trendy restaurants, movie theaters, outdoor cafés, gourmet shops and designer boutiques, and the studios of struggling artists: this is where Barcelona's young cohort want to live and come to party. Mercé Rodoreda's novel *La Plaça del Diamant* (translated by the late David Rosenthal as *The Time of the Doves*) begins and ends in Gràcia during the August Festa Major, a festival that fills the streets with the rank-and-file residents of this always lively, intimate little pocket of general resistance to Organized Life.

TOP ATTRACTIONS

Casa Vicens. Antoni Gaudí's first important commission as a young architect began in 1883 and finished in 1885. For this house Gaudí still used his traditional architect's tools, particularly the T square. The historical eclecticism (that is, borrowing freely from past architectural styles around the world) of the early Art Nouveau movement is evident in the Orientalist themes and Mudejar motifs lavished throughout the facade. The fact that the house was commissioned by a ceramics

GETTING ORIENTED

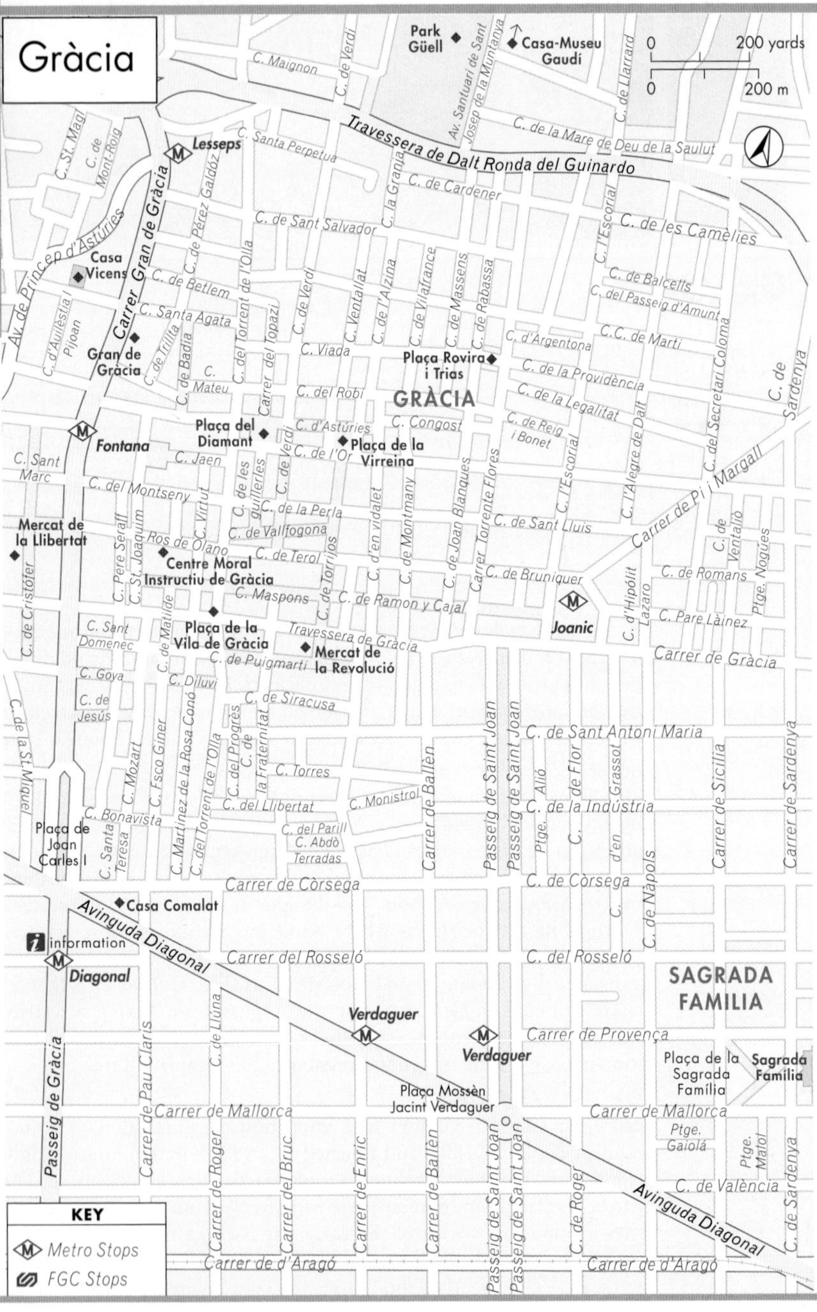

TIMING

Exploring Gràcia is a three- to four-hour outing that could take five with lunch included—or an entire day to really get the full feel of the neighborhood. Evening sessions at the popular Verdi cinema (showing films in their original languages) usually get out just in time for a late-night supper in any of a number of bars and restaurants, including Botafumeiro, which closes at 1 am. Park Güell is best in the afternoon, when the sun spotlights the view east over the Mediterranean. Exploring Gràcia when the Llibertat and Revolució markets are closed would be a major loss, so plan to get here before 2 pm.

GETTING HERE

By metro, the Gràcia stop on the FGC (Ferrocarril de la Generalitat de Catalunya) trains that connect Sarrià, Sabadell, Terrassa, and Sant Cugat with Plaça de Catalunya is your best option. The metro's green line (L3) stations at Fontana and Lesseps put you in the heart of Gràcia and in hiking distance of Park Güell, respectively. The yellow line (L4) stop at Joanic is a short walk from Gràcia's northeast side.

QUICK BITES

Nou Candanchú. A refreshing stop, this bar runs tables inside and out until early morning, serving a variety of tapas, sandwiches, salads, and seafood dishes. ✉ *Pl. de la Vila de Gràcia 9, Gràcia* ☎ *93/237–7362* Ⓜ *Gràcia.*

Botafumeiro. For an upscale treat, Botafumeiro never disappoints; the counter is the place to be for an icy albariño and *pop a feira* (octopus on potato slices with smoked paprika), a Galician favorite. ✉ *Gran de Gràcia 81, Gràcia* ☎ *93/218–4230* Ⓜ *Gràcia.*

TOP ATTRACTIONS

Casa Vicens

Gran de Gràcia

Mercat de la Llibertat

Park Güell

Plaça de la Vila de Gràcia

TOP EXPERIENCES

Browsing the Mercat de la Llibertat

Doing the classic "cinema night out," Barcelona-style, with the movie first and a late supper after

Taking in the Moderniste buildings on Gran de Gràcia

Relaxing at an outdoor café terrace in Plaça del Sol

Walking down through Gràcia from Park Güell

WHERE TO EAT (⇨ CH. 3)

Adarra

Amrit

Bilbao

Botafumeiro

Hofmann

Ipar-Txoko

L'Arrosseria Xàtiva

Roig Robí

merchant may explain the use of the green ceramic tiles that turn the facade into a striking checkerboard. Casa Vicens was the first polychromatic facade to appear in Barcelona. The chemaro palm leaves decorating the gate and surrounding fence are thought to be the work of Gaudí's assistant Francesc Berenguer, while the comic iron lizards and bats oozing off the facade are Gaudí's playful version of the Gothic gargoyle. The interior (which you can't see except on the off chance that the owners open the house to the public) is even more surprising than the outside, with its trompe-l'oeil birds painted on the walls of the salon and the intricately Mocarabe, or Moorish-style, carved ceiling in the smoking room. Gaudi's second commission, built in 1885, was in the little town of Comillas in Santander, for the Marquès de Comillas, Antonio López y López, a shipping magnate and the most powerful man of his time. Not surprisingly, the two houses bear a striking resemblance to each other. ✉ *Carrer de les Carolines 24–26, Gràcia* Ⓜ *Fontana.*

Gran de Gràcia. This central artery up through Gràcia would be a lovely stroll if the car and (worse) motorcycle din weren't so overpowering. (A tunnel would do the trick nicely.) However, many of the buildings along Gran de Gràcia are of great artistic and architectural interest, beginning with **Can Fuster,** at the bottom of Gran de Gràcia 2–4. Built between 1908 and 1911 by Palau de la Música Catalana architect Lluís Domènech i Montaner in collaboration with his son Pere Domènech i Roure, the building shows a clear move away from the chromatically effusive heights of Art Nouveau. More powerful, and somehow less superficial, than much of that style of architecture, it uses the winged supports under the balconies and the floral base under the corner tower as important structural elements instead of as pure ornamentation, as Domènech i Montaner the elder might have. As you move up Gran de Gràcia, probable Francesc Berenguer buildings can be identified at No. 15; No. 23, with its scrolled cornice; and Nos. 35, 49, 51, 61, and 77. Officially attributed to a series of architects—since Berenguer lacked a formal degree (having left architecture school to become Gaudí's "right hand")—these Moderniste masterworks have long inspired debate over Berenguer's role. ✉ *Gran de Gràcia, Gràcia* Ⓜ *Fontana, Gràcia.*

Mercat de la Llibertat. This uptown version of La Rambla's Boqueria market is one of Gràcia's coziest spaces, a food market big enough to roam in and small enough to make you feel at home. Built by Francesc Berenguer between 1888 and 1893, the Llibertat market reflects, in its name alone, the revolutionary and democratic sentiment strong in Gràcia's traditionally blue-collar residents. Look for Berenguer's decorative swans swimming along the roofline and the snails surrounding Gràcia's coat of arms. ✉ *Pl. Llibertat 27, Gràcia* ☎ *93/217–0995* 🌐 *www.bcn.es/mercatsmunicipals* ⏲ *Daily 7–3* Ⓜ *Gràcia.*

Mercat de la Revolució. Officially the Abaceria Central, the market got its early name from the nearby Plaça de la Revolució de Setembre de 1868 just a block away up Carrer dels Desamparats. Browse your way through, and consider having something delicious such as a plate of wild mushrooms or a *tortilla de patatas* (potato omelet) at the very good bar and restaurant at the far corner on the lower east side. ✉ *Travessera de Gràcia 186, Gràcia* ☎ *93/213–6286* 🌐 *www.bcn.es/mercatsmunicipals* ⏲ *Daily 7–3* Ⓜ *Joanic.*

FAMILY Fodor's Choice ★ **Park Güell.** This park is one of Gaudí's, and Barcelona's, most visited attractions. Named for and commissioned by Gaudí's steadfast patron, Count Eusebi Güell, it was originally intended as a gated residential community based on the English Garden City model, centered on a public square, where impromptu dances and plays could be performed, built over a covered marketplace. Only two of the houses were ever built (one of which, designed by Gaudí's assistant Francesc Berenguer, became Gaudí's home from 1906 to 1926 and now houses the **Casa-Museu Gaudí** museum of memorabilia). Ultimately, as Barcelona's bourgeoisie seemed happier living closer to "town," the Güell family turned the area over to the city as a public park—which it still is, for local residents; as of September 2013, visitors are assessed an entrance fee.

An Art Nouveau extravaganza with gingerbread gatehouses, Park Güell is a perfect place to visit on a sunny afternoon, when the blue of the Mediterranean is best illuminated by the western sun. The gatehouse on the right, topped with a rendition in ceramic tile of the hallucinogenic red-and-white fly ammanite wild mushroom (rumored to have been a Gaudí favorite) houses the Center for the Interpretation and Welcome to Park Güell. The center has plans, scale models, photos, and suggested routes analyzing the park in detail. Atop the gatehouse on the left sits the *phallus impudicus* (no translation necessary). Other Gaudí highlights include the Room of a Hundred Columns—a covered market supported by tilted Doric-style columns and mosaic medallions; the double set of stairs; and the iconic lizard guarding the fountain between them. There's also the fabulous serpentine, polychrome bench enclosing the square. The bench is one of Gaudí assistant Josep Maria Jujol's most memorable creations, and one of Barcelona's best examples of the *trencadís* technique of making colorful mosaics with broken bits of tile. From the metro at Plaça de Lesseps, or the Bus Turistic stop on Travessera de Dalt, take Bus No. 24 to the park entrance, or make the steep 10-minute climb uphill on Carrer de Lallard. ✉ *Carrer d'Olot s/n, Gràcia* 🌐 *www.parkguell.es* 🎫 *€8 (€7 online)* ⏲ *Jan.–Oct., daily 8–9:30; Nov. and Dec., daily 8:30–6* Ⓜ *Lesseps.*

Plaça de la Vila de Gràcia. Originally named (until 2009) for the memorable Gràcia mayor Francesc Rius i Taulet, this is the town's most emblematic and historic square, marked by the handsome clock tower in its center. The tower, built in 1862, is just over 110 feet tall. It has water fountains around its base, royal Bourbon crests over the fountains, and an iron balustrade atop the octagonal brick shaft stretching up to the clock and belfry. The symbol of Gràcia, the clock tower was bombarded by federal troops when Gràcia attempted to secede from the Spanish state during the 1870s. Always a workers' neighborhood and prone to social solidarity, Gràcia was mobilized by mothers who refused to send their sons off as conscripts to fight for the crumbling Spanish Imperial forces during the late 19th century, thus requiring a full-scale assault by Spanish troops to reestablish law and order. Today sidewalk cafés prosper under the leafy canopy here. The Gràcia Casa de la Vila (Town Hall) at the lower end of the square is yet another Francesc Berenguer opus. ✉ *Pl. de la Vila de Gràcia, Gràcia* Ⓜ *Fontana; Gràcia (FGC).*

DID YOU KNOW?

Park Güell was originally built to be a private garden community. One of the houses built here became Gaudí's residence from 1906 to 1926.

WORTH NOTING

Casa Comalat. At the bottom of Gràcia between the Diagonal and Carrer Còrsega, this often-overlooked Moderniste house (not open to the public) built in 1911 is a good one to add to your collection. For a look at the best side of this lower Gràcia Art Nouveau gem, cut down past Casa Fuster at the bottom of Gran de Gràcia, take a left on Bonavista, then a right on Santa Teresa down to Casa Comalat just across Carrer Còrsega. This Salvador Valeri i Pupurull creation is one of Barcelona's most interesting Moderniste houses, especially this side of it, with its bulging polychrome ceramic balconies and its melted wax–like underpinnings. Look for the curious wooden galleries, and don't miss a look into the excellent Bar Mut at Pau Claris 192 just across the street. ✉ *Carrer de Còrsega 316, Gràcia* Ⓜ *Diagonal.*

Casa-Museu Gaudí. Up the steps of **Park Güell** and to the right, the museum is the Alice-in-Wonderland house where Gaudí lived with his niece from 1906 to his death in 1926. Exhibits include Gaudí-designed furniture and decorations, drawings, and portraits and busts of the architect. ✉ *Park Güell, Gràcia* ☎ *93/219–3811* 🌐 *www.casamuseugaudi.org* 🎫 *€5.50* 🕘 *Daily 10–6* Ⓜ *Lesseps, Vallcarca.*

Centre Moral Instructiu de Gràcia. Another creation by Gaudí's assistant Francesc Berenguer (Gràcia is Berenguer country), this building is one of the few in Barcelona with an exposed-brick Mudejar facade. The Centre Moral Instructiu was built in 1904 and still functions as a cultural institution; its wide range of programs—founded, it would seem, on the premise that recreation and sport are morally uplifting—includes chess and table tennis tournaments, craft workshops, language courses, and childrens' theater performances. Berenguer himself was its president at one time. ✉ *Carrer Ros de Olano 9, Gràcia* ☎ *93/218–1964* Ⓜ *Gràcia.*

Plaça de la Virreina. The much-damaged and oft-restored church of Sant Joan de Gràcia in this square stands where the Palau de la Virreina once stood, the mansion of the same *virreina* (wife—in this case widow—of a viceroy) whose 18th-century palace, the Palau de la Virreina, stands on La Rambla. (The Palau is now a prominent municipal museum and art gallery.) The story of La Virreina, a young noblewoman widowed at an early age by the death of the elderly viceroy of Peru, is symbolized in the bronze sculpture in the center of the square: it portrays Ruth of the Old Testament, represented carrying the sheaves of wheat she was gathering when she learned of the death of her husband, Boaz. Ruth is the Old Testament paradigm of wifely fidelity to her husband's clan, a parallel to La Virreina—who spent her life doing good deeds with her husband's fortune.

The rectorial residence at the back of the church is the work of Gaudí's perennial assistant and right-hand man Francesc Berenguer. Just across the street, the house at Carrer de l'Or 44 was built in 1909, also by Berenguer. Giddily vertical and tightly packed into its narrow slot, it demonstrates one of his best tricks: putting up townhouses that share walls with adjacent buildings. ✉ *Pl. de la Virreina, Gràcia* Ⓜ *Fontana.*

BERENGUER: GAUDÍ'S RIGHT HAND

Francesc Berenguer's role in Gaudí's work and the Moderniste movement, despite his leaving architecture school prematurely to work for Gaudí, was significant (if not decisive), and has been much debated by architects and Art Nouveau scholars. If Barcelona was Gaudí's grand canvas, Gràcia was Berenguer's. Though he was not legally licensed to sign his projects, Berenguer is known to have designed nearly every major building in Gràcia, including the Mercat de la Llibertat. The house at Carrer de l'Or 44 remains one of his greatest achievements, a vertical tour de force with pinnacles at the stress lines over rich stacks of wrought-iron balconies. The Gràcia Town Hall in Plaça Rius i Taulet and the Centre Moral Instructiu de Gràcia at Carrer Ros de Olano 9 are confirmed as his; the buildings on Carrer Gran de Gràcia at Nos. 15, 23, 35, 49, 51, 61, 77, and 81 are all either confirmed or suspected Berenguer designs. Even Gaudí's first domestic commission, Casa Vicens, owes its palm-leaf iron fence to Berenguer. When Berenguer died young in 1914, at the age of 47, Gaudí said he had "lost his right hand." Indeed, in his last 12 years, Gaudí worked on nothing but the Sagrada Família and, in fact, made little progress there.

Plaça del Diamant. This little square is of enormous sentimental importance in Barcelona as the site of the opening and closing scenes of 20th-century Catalan writer Mercé Rodoreda's famous 1962 novel *La Plaça del Diamant*. Translated by the late American poet David Rosenthal as *The Time of the Doves*, it is the most widely translated and published Catalan novel of all time: a tender yet brutal story of a young woman devoured by the Spanish Civil War and, in a larger sense, by life itself. A bronze statue in the square portrays Colometa, the novel's protagonist, caught in the middle of her climactic scream. The bronze birds represent the pigeons that Colometa spent her life obsessively breeding; the male figure on the left pierced by bolts of steel is Quimet, her first love and husband, whom she met at a dance in this square and later lost in the war. ⊠ *Pl. del Diamant* Ⓜ *Fontana*.

Plaça Rovira i Trias. This charming little square and the story of Antoni Rovira i Trias shed much light on the true nature of Barcelona's eternal struggle with Madrid and Spanish central authority. Take a careful look at the map of Barcelona positioned at the feet of the bronze effigy of the architect and urban planners near the center of the square and you will see a vision of what the city might have looked like if Madrid's (and the Spanish army's) candidate for the design of the Eixample in 1860, Ildefons Cerdà, had not been imposed over the plan devised by Rovira i Trias, initial and legitimate winner of the open competition for the commission. Rovira i Trias's plan shows an astral design radiating out from a central Eixample square that military minds saw as avenues of approach; Cerdà's design, on the other hand, made the Diagonal into a natural barrier. ⊠ *Pl. Rovira i Trias, Gràcia* Ⓜ *Lesseps, Joanic*.

2

UPPER BARCELONA: SARRIÀ AND PEDRALBES

Sightseeing ★★★☆☆
Nightlife ★★☆☆☆
Dining ★★★★☆
Lodging ★★★☆☆
Shopping ★★★☆☆

Sarrià was originally a country village, overlooking Barcelona from the foothills of the Collserola. Eventually absorbed by the westward-expanding city, the village, 15 minutes by FGC commuter train from Plaça de Catalunya, has become a unique neighborhood with at least four distinct populations: the old-timers, who speak only Catalan among themselves, and talk of "going down to Barcelona" to shop; writers, artists and designers, and people in publishing and advertising, drawn here in the 1970s and 1980s by the creative vibe; yuppie starter families, who largely support Sarriá's gourmet shops and upscale restaurants; and a cadre of expats, who prize the neighborhood for its proximity to the international schools. Sarriá and environs, in fact, have perhaps more schools than any single postal code in Europe, many of them occupying what were once the palatial Moderniste summer homes of the city's financial and industrial moguls.

Did we mention gourmet shops? J. V. Foix, the famous Catalan poet, was a native son of Sarrià; his father founded what is arguably the best patisserie in Barcelona, and his descendants still run the quintessential Sarrià family business. On Sundays, barcelonins come to the village from all over town; Sunday just wouldn't be Sunday without a cake from Foix to take to grandma's. Cross Avinguda Foix from Sarriá

GETTING ORIENTED

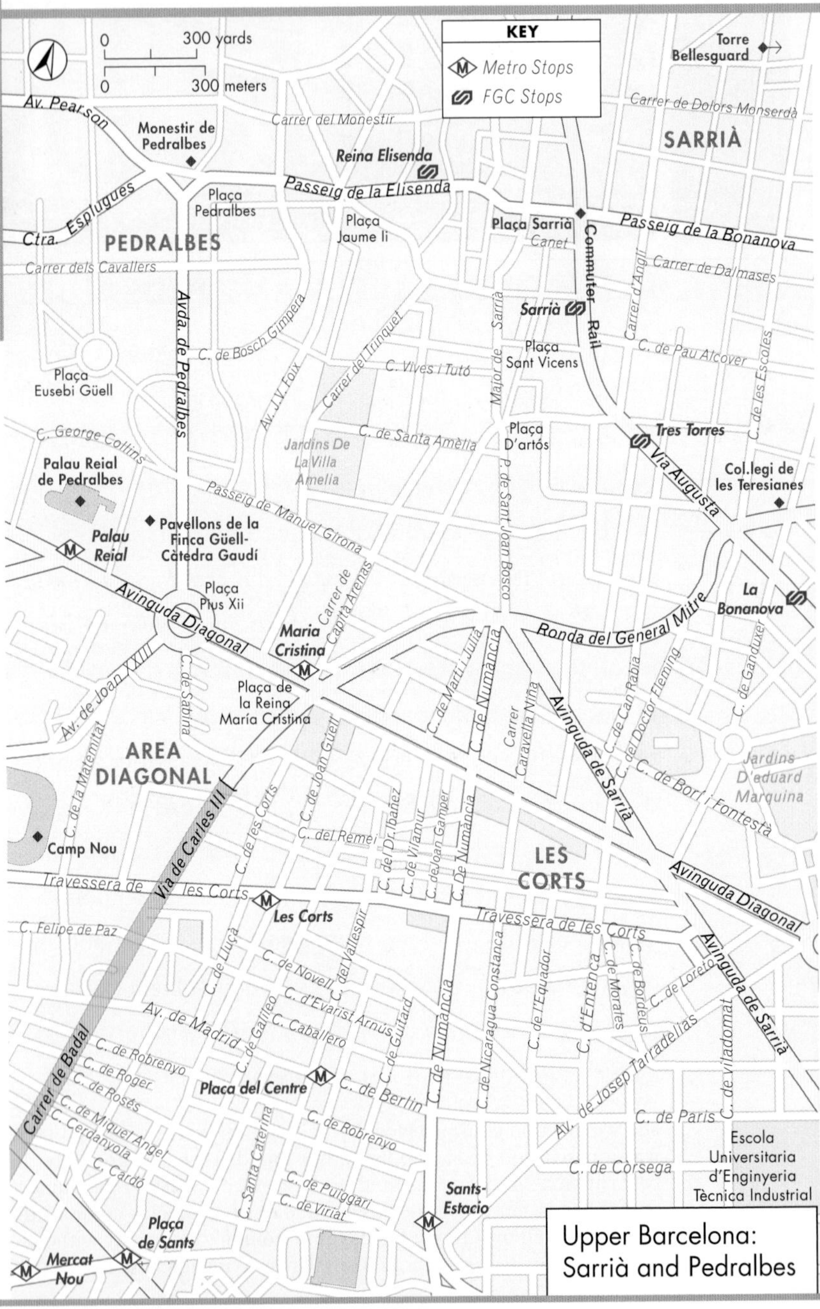

TIMING

An exploration of Sarrià and Pedralbes is a three- to four-hour jaunt, including at least an hour in the monastery. Count four or five with lunch included. Plan to visit the monastery in the morning. Bar Tomás serves its famous potatoes with *allioli* (spicy garlic mayonnaise) 1–4 and 7–10, another key timing consideration, while the Foix de Sarrià pastry emporium (⇨ *see Sarrià)* is open until 9.

GETTING HERE

Sarrià is best reached on the FGC (Ferrocarril de la Generalitat de Catalunya) line, which is part of the city metro system, though a cut above. From Plaça de Catalunya, all the FGC trains (except those bound for Tibidabo) stop at Sarrià; only local trains branch off from there to the terminus at Reina Elisenda. The trip uptown takes about 15 minutes. By bus, you can take the V7, which runs from Plaça d'Espanya to Sarrià, or the No. 64, which takes a somewhat roundabout route from Barceloneta to Pedralbes, with a stop at Plaça Sarriá.

QUICK BITES

Bar Tomás. On the corner of Jaume Piquet, Bar Tomás is a Barcelona institution, home of the finest *patatas bravas* (fried potatoes) in town—a cynosure so prosperous it can afford to shut for the night at 10 pm. Order the famous *doble mixta* of potatoes with allioli and hot sauce, and a draft beer (ask for a *caña*) to sluice them down. ✉ *Major de Sarrià 49, Sarrià* ☎ *93/203–1077* Ⓜ *Sarrià (FCG).*

TOP ATTRACTIONS

Monestir de Pedralbes

Plaça de Sarrià

Torre Bellesguard

TOP EXPERIENCES

Browsing through the Sarrià market

Stocking up on calories at Pasteleria Foix

Hiking up to the Torre de Bellesguard

Meditating in the cloister of the Pedralbes Monastery

Scarfing patatas allioli at Bar Tomás

Wandering the village streets

WHERE TO EAT (⇨ CH. 3)

Acontraluz

Bar Tomás

Dole Café

El Mató de Pedralbes

Fishhh!

Freixa Tradició

Gouthier

Icho

Le Quattro Stagioni

Tram-Tram

Vivanda

and you're in Pedralbes—the wealthiest residential neighborhood in the city. (Fútbol superstar Leo Messi has his multimillion-Euro home here; the exclusive Real Club de Tenis de Barcelona is not far off.) The centerpiece of this district is the 14th-century Monestir (Monastery) de Pedralbes; other points of interest include Gaudí's Pavellons de la Finca Güell on Avinguda de Pedralbes, and the gardens of the Palau Reial de Pedralbes, a 20-minute walk downhill from the monastery. The Futbol Club Barcelona's 98,000-seat Camp Nou stadium and museum are another 20 minutes' walk, down below the Diagonal.

TOP ATTRACTIONS

Camp Nou. If you're in Barcelona between September and June, a chance to witness the celebrated FC Barcelona play soccer (preferably against Real Madrid, if you can get in) at Barcelona's gigantic stadium is a seminal Barcelona experience. Just the walk down to the field from the Diagonal with another hundred thousand fans walking fast and hushed in electric anticipation is unforgettable. Games are played Saturday night at 9 or Sunday afternoon at 5, though there may be international Champions League games on Tuesday or Wednesday evenings as well. A worthwhile alternative to seeing a game is the guided tour of the FC Barcelona museum—the city's most-visited tourist attraction—and facilities. ✉ *Arístides Maillol 12–18, Les Corts* ☎ *93/496–3600 for museum, 902/189900 for club office* 🌐 *www.fcbarcelona.cat* 🎫 *Museum €23 (combined ticket including tour of museum, field, and sports complex)* ⏲ *Museum Mon.–Sat. 10–6:30 (Apr.–Oct. till 8), Sun. 10–2:30. On match days, the museum closes 3 hrs early, and stadium tours are not available.* Ⓜ *Collblanc, Palau Reial.*

OFF THE BEATEN PATH

CosmoCaixa–Museu de la Ciència Fundació "La Caixa". Young scientific minds work overtime in this interactive science museum, just below Tibidabo. Among the many displays designed for children 7 and up are the Geological Wall, a history of rocks and rock formations; and the Underwater Forest, showcasing a slice of the Amazonian rain forest in a large greenhouse. ✉ *Teodor Roviralta 47–51, Sant Gervasi* ☎ *93/212–6050* 🌐 *obrasocial.lacaixa.es/laCaixaFoundation/home_en.html* 🎫 *€4 (plus €2 per interactive activity inside); free 1st Sun. of the month* ⏲ *Tues.–Sun. 10–8* Ⓜ *Av. Tibidabo (FGC), then Tramvía Blau.*

Fodor's Choice ★

Monestir de Pedralbes. This marvel of a monastery, named for its original white stones (*pedres albes*), is really a convent, founded in 1326 for the Franciscan order of Poor Clares by Reina (Queen) Elisenda. The three-story Gothic cloister, one of the finest in Europe, surrounds a lush garden. The day cells, where the nuns spend their mornings praying, sewing, and studying, circle the arcaded courtyard. The queen's own cell, the Capella de Sant Miquel, just to the right of the entrance, has murals painted in 1346 by Catalan master Ferrer Bassa. Look for the letters spelling out "*Joan no m'oblides*" ("John, do not forget me.") scratched between the figures of St. Francis and St. Clare (with book and quill), written by a brokenhearted novice. Farther along, inscriptions over the tombs of nuns who died here can be seen through the paving grates. The nuns' upstairs dormitory contains the convent's treasures: paintings, liturgical objects, and seven centuries of artistic and cultural patrimony. Temporary exhibits are displayed in this space. The refectory where the Poor Clares dined in silence has a pulpit used for readings, while wall inscriptions exhort *"Silentium"* ("Silence"), *"Audi tacens"* ("Listening makes you wise."), and *"Considera morientem"* ("Consider, we are dying."). Notice the fading mural in the corner, and the paving tiles broken by heavy cannon positioned here during the 1809 Napoleonic occupation. Your ticket also includes admission to Museu d'Història de la Ciutat, Centre d'Interpretació del Park Güell, Centre d'Interpretació del Call, Centre d'Interpretació Històrica, Refugi 307, and Museu-Casa Verdaguer. ✉ *Baixada Monestir 9, Pedralbes* ☎ *93/256–3434* 🌐 *www.bcn.cat/monestirpedralbes* 🎫 *€7 (free Sun. after 3)* ⏲ *Oct.–Mar., Tues.–Fri. 10–2, weekends 10–5; Apr.–Sept., Tues.–Fri. 10–5, Sat. 10–7, Sun. 10–8* Ⓜ *Reina Elisenda (FGC).*

Pavellons de la Finca Güell–Càtedra Gaudí. Work on the Finca began in 1883 as an extension of the Count Eusabi Güell's family estate. Gaudí, the count's architect of choice, was commissioned to do the gardens and the two entrance pavillions (1884-87); the rest of the project was never finished. The pavillions now belong to the University of Barcelona; the one on the right houses the Càtedra Gaudí, a Gaudí library and study center. The fierce wrought-iron dragon gate is Gaudí's reference to the Garden of the Hesperides, as described by national poet Jacint Verdaguer's epic poem *L'Atlàntida*—the *Iliad* of Catalonia's historic/mythic origins—published in 1877. The property is open for guided tours in English on Saturdays and Sundays at 10:15 and 12:15. Admission is limited to 25 visitors: call ahead, or book on the Ruta del Modernisme website. (The Ruta is a walking tour covering 115 masterworks of the Moderniste period, including Gaudí, Domènech i Montaner, and Puig i Cadafalch. Pick up a guide—which includes a map and discounts for admission to many of the sites—here at the Pavellons or at the **Turisme de Barcelona** office in the Plaça de Catalunya.) ✉ *Av. Pedralbes 7, Pedralbes* ☎ *93/317–7652* 🌐 *www.rutadelmodernisme.com* Ⓜ *Palau Reial.*

Sarrià. The village of Sarrià was originally a cluster of farms and country houses overlooking Barcelona from the hills. Once dismissively described as nothing but "winds, brooks, and convents," this quiet enclave is now a haven at the upper edge of the city. Start an exploration at the square—the locus, at various times, of antique and bric-a-brac markets, book fairs, artisanal food and wine fairs, sardana dances (Sunday morning), concerts and Christmas pageants. The 10th-century Romanesque **Church of Sant Vicenç** dominates the square; the bell tower, illuminated on weekend nights, is truly impressive. Across Passeig de la Reina Elisenda from the church (50 yards to the left) is the 100-year-old Moderniste **Mercat** (Market) **de Sarriá.**

From the square, cut through the Placeta del Roser to the left of the church to the elegant **town hall** (1896) in the Plaça de la Vila; note the buxom bronze sculpture of **Pomona,** goddess of fruit, by famed Sarrià sculptor Josep Clarà (1878–1958). Follow the tiny Carrer dels Paletes, to the left of the Town Hall (the saint enshrined in the niche is Sant Antoni, patron saint of *paletes,* or bricklayers), and right on Major de Sarrià, the High Street of the village. **TIP→ Lunch time? Try Casa Raphael, on the right as you walk down—in business (and virtually unchanged) since 1873.** Further on, turn left into **Carrer Canet.**

The two-story row houses on the right were first built for workers on the village estates; these, and the houses opposite at Nos. 15, 21, and 23, are among the few remaining original village homes in Sarrià. Turn right at the first corner on Carrer Cornet i Mas and walk two blocks down to Carrer Jaume Piquet.

On the left is No. 30, Barcelona's most perfect small-format **Moderniste house,** thought to be the work of architect Domènech i Montaner, complete with faux-medieval upper windows, wrought-iron grillwork, floral and fruited ornamentation, and organically curved and carved wooden doors either by or inspired by Gaudí himself. The next stop down Cornet i Mas is Sarrià's prettiest square, **Plaça Sant Vicenç,** a leafy space ringed by old Sarrià houses and centered on a statue of Sarrià's patron, St. Vicenç, portrayed, as always, beside the millstone used to sink him to the bottom of the Mediterranean after he was martyred in Valencia in 302. **Can Pau,** the café on the lower corner with Carrer Mañé i Flaquer, is the local hangout, a good place for coffee and once a haven for authors Gabriel García Marquez and Mario Vargas Llosa, who lived in Sarrià in the late 1960s and early 1970s.

Other Sarrià landmarks to look for include the two **Foix** pastry stores, one at Plaça Sarrià 9–10 and the other at Major de Sarrià 57, above Bar Tomás. The late J. V. Foix (1893–1987), son of the store's founders, was one of the great Catalan poets of the 20th century, a key player in keeping the Catalan language alive during the 40-year Franco regime. The shop on Major de Sarrià has a bronze plaque identifying the house as the poet's birthplace and inscribed with one of his most memorable verses, translated as, "Every love is latent in the other love/ every language is the juice of a common tongue/every country touches the fatherland of all/every faith will be the lifeblood of a higher faith." ⊠ *Pl. Sarrià, Sarrià* Ⓜ *Sarrià; Reina Elisenda (FGC).*

Torre Bellesguard. For a Gaudí experience to the last drop, climb up above Plaça de la Bonanova to this private residence built between 1900 and 1909 over the ruins of the summer palace of the last of the sovereign count-kings of the Catalan-Aragonese realm, Martí I l'Humà (Martin I the Humane), whose reign ended in 1410. In homage to this medieval history, Gaudí endowed the house with a tower, gargoyles, and crenellated battlements; the rest—the catenary arches, the *trencadís* (broken bits of polychromatic ceramic tile) of the facade, the stained-glass windows—is pure Art Nouveau. Look for the red and gold Catalan *senyera* (banner) on the tower, topped by the four-armed Greek cross Gaudí often used. Over the front door is the inscription *sens pecat fou concebuda* (without sin was she conceived) referring to the Immaculate Conception of the Virgin Mary; on either side of the front door are benches with trencadís mosaics of playful fish bearing the crimson *quatre barres* (four bars) of the Catalan flag as well as the Corona d'Aragó (Crown of Aragón).

Still a private home and long closed to visitors, the Torre Bellesguard is now accessible to small groups. **■ TIP→ Sign up (✉ reserva@bellesguardgaudi.com) for a guided tour: this is a treat not to be missed.** ⊠ *Bellesguard 16–20, Sant Gervasi* ☎ *93/250–4093, 646/800127*

A quiet space for reflection: the courtyard of the Monestir de Pedralbes

www.bellesguardgaudi.com *Full tour €16 (reservations required), grounds only €7 (with audio guide)* *Guided 1-hr tour of house and grounds in English (maximum 15 persons) weekdays at 11; open visits to grounds Nov.–Mar., weekdays 10–≠3; Apr.–Oct., weekdays 10–7:30* M *Sarrià.*

OFF THE BEATEN PATH

Vallvidrera. This perched village is a quiet respite from Barcelona's headlong race. Oddly, there's nothing exclusive or upmarket—for now—about Vallvidrera, as most well-off barcelonins prefer to be closer to the center. From **Plaça Pep Ventura,** in front of the Moderniste funicular station, there are superb views over the Vallvidrera houses and the Montserrat. Vallvidrera can be reached from the Peu del Funicular suburban-rail stop, then the Funicular de Vallvidrera; by road; or on foot from Tibidabo or Vil.la Joana. The cozy Can Trampa at the center of town in Plaça de Vallvidrera, and Can Martí down below are fine spots for a meal. M *Peu del Funicular (FGC).*

WORTH NOTING

Col.legi de les Teresianes. Built in 1889 for the Reverend Mothers of St. Theresa, when Gaudí was still occasionally using straight lines, this building, an operating school, showcases upper floors reminiscent of those in Berenguer's apartment house at Carrer de l'Or 44, with its steep peaks and verticality. Hired to finish a job begun by another architect, Gaudí found his freedom of movement somewhat limited in this project. The dominant theme here is the architect's use of steep, narrow catenary arches and Mudejar exposed-brick pillars. The most striking effects are on the second floor, where two rows of a dozen catenary arches run the width of the building, each of them unique because, as

Gaudí explained, no two things in nature are identical. The brick columns are crowned with T-shape brick capitals (for St. Theresa). Look down at the marble doorstep for the inscription by mystic writer and poet Santa Teresa de Avila (1515–82), the much-quoted "*Todo se pasa*" ("All things pass"). For visits, consult the **Ruta del Modernisme** (☎ *93/317–7652, 902/076621 within Spain* 🌐 *www.rutadelmodernisme.com*). ✉ *Ganduxer 85, Sant Gervasi* ☎ *93/254–1670* Ⓜ *Les Tres Torres.*

Palau Reial de Pedralbes (*Royal Palace of Pedralbes*). Built in the 1920s as the palatial estate of Count Eusebi Güell—one of Gaudí's most important patrons—this mansion was transformed into a royal palace by architect Eusebi Bona i Puig and completed in 1929. King Alfonso XIII, grandfather of Spanish king Juan Carlos I, visited the palace in the mid-1920s before its completion. In 1931, during the Second Spanish Republic, the palace became the property of the municipal government, and it was converted to a decorative arts museum in 1932. In 1936 the rambling, elegant country-manor-house palace was used as the official residence of Manuel Azaña, last president of the Spanish Republic. It is not open to the public. ✉ *Av. Diagonal 686, Pedralbes* Ⓜ *Palau Reial.*

OFF THE BEATEN PATH

Tibidabo. One of Barcelona's two promontories, this hill bears a distinctive name, generally translated as "To Thee I Will Give"—referring to the Catalan legend that this was the spot from which Satan tempted Christ with all the riches of the earth below (namely, Barcelona). On a clear day, the views from this 1,789-foot peak are legendary. Tibidabo's skyline is marked by a neo-Gothic church, the work of Enric Sagnier in 1902, and—off to one side, near the village of Vallvidrera—the 854-foot communications tower, the **Torre de Collserola,** designed by Sir Norman Foster. Do you have youngsters in tow? Take the cute little San Francisco–style Tramvía Blau (Blue Trolley) cable car from Plaça Kennedy to the overlook at the top, and transfer to the funicular to the 100-year-old **Amusement Park** at the summit. ✉ *Pl. Tibidabo 3–4, Tibidabo* ☎ *93/211–7942* 🌐 *www.tibidabo.cat* 🎫 *Amusement Park €28.50* ⏲ *Noon to 7* Ⓜ *Av. Tibidabo (FGC).*

El Mirador de la Venta. You may come here for the great views, but El Mirador de la Venta has good contemporary cuisine to accompany them. ✉ *Pl. Doctor Andreu s/n* ☎ *93/212–6455.*

Mirablau. This bar overlooks the city lights and is a popular late-night hangout. ✉ *Pl. Doctor Andreu s/n* ☎ *93/418–5879.*

OFF THE BEATEN PATH

Torre de Collserola. The Collserola Tower was designed by Norman Foster for the 1992 Olympics, amid controversy over defacement of the traditional skyline. A vertigo-inducing elevator ride takes you to the observation deck. Take the FGC S1, S2, or S5 line to Peu del Funicular, then the funicular up to Vallvidrera; from the village of Vallvidrera it's a pleasant walk to the tower. ✉ *Av. de Vallvidrera* ☎ *93/211–7942* 🌐 *www.torredecollserola.com* 🎫 *€5.60* ⏲ *Weekends noon–2 and 3:30–6* Ⓜ *Av. Tibidabo (FGC).*

MONTJUÏC

Sightseeing
★★★★★
Nightlife
★★★☆☆
Dining
★★★☆☆
Lodging
☆☆☆☆☆
Shopping
★★★☆☆

This hill overlooking the south side of the port is said to have originally been named Mont Juif for the Jewish cemetery once on its slopes, though a 3rd-century Roman document referring to the construction of a road between Mons Taber (around the cathedral) and Mons Jovis (Mount of Jove) suggests that in fact the name may derive from the Roman deity Jupiter. Either way, Montjuïc is now Barcelona's largest and lushest public space, a vast complex of museums and exhibition halls, gardens and picnic grounds, sports facilities—and even a Greek-style amphitheater.

A bit remote from the hustle and bustle of Barcelona street life, Montjuïc more than justifies a day or two of exploring. The Miró Foundation, the Museu Nacional d'Art de Catalunya, the minimalist Mies van der Rohe Pavilion, the lush Jardins de Mossèn Cinto Verdaguer, and the gallery and auditorium of the CaixaFòrum (the former Casaramona textile factory) are all undoubtedly among Barcelona's must-see sights. The Museu Nacional d'Art de Catalunya, especially, contains what is considered the world's best collection of Romanesque frescoes, removed for restoration from Pyrenean chapels in the 1930s and ingeniously restored with their original contours. The MNAC also houses an especially fine collection of impressionist and Moderniste painters, and another of Gothic art. Other Montjuïc attractions include the fortress, the Olympic stadium, the Palau Sant Jordi, and the Poble Espanyol. There are buses within Montjuïc that visitors can take from sight to sight.

GETTING ORIENTED

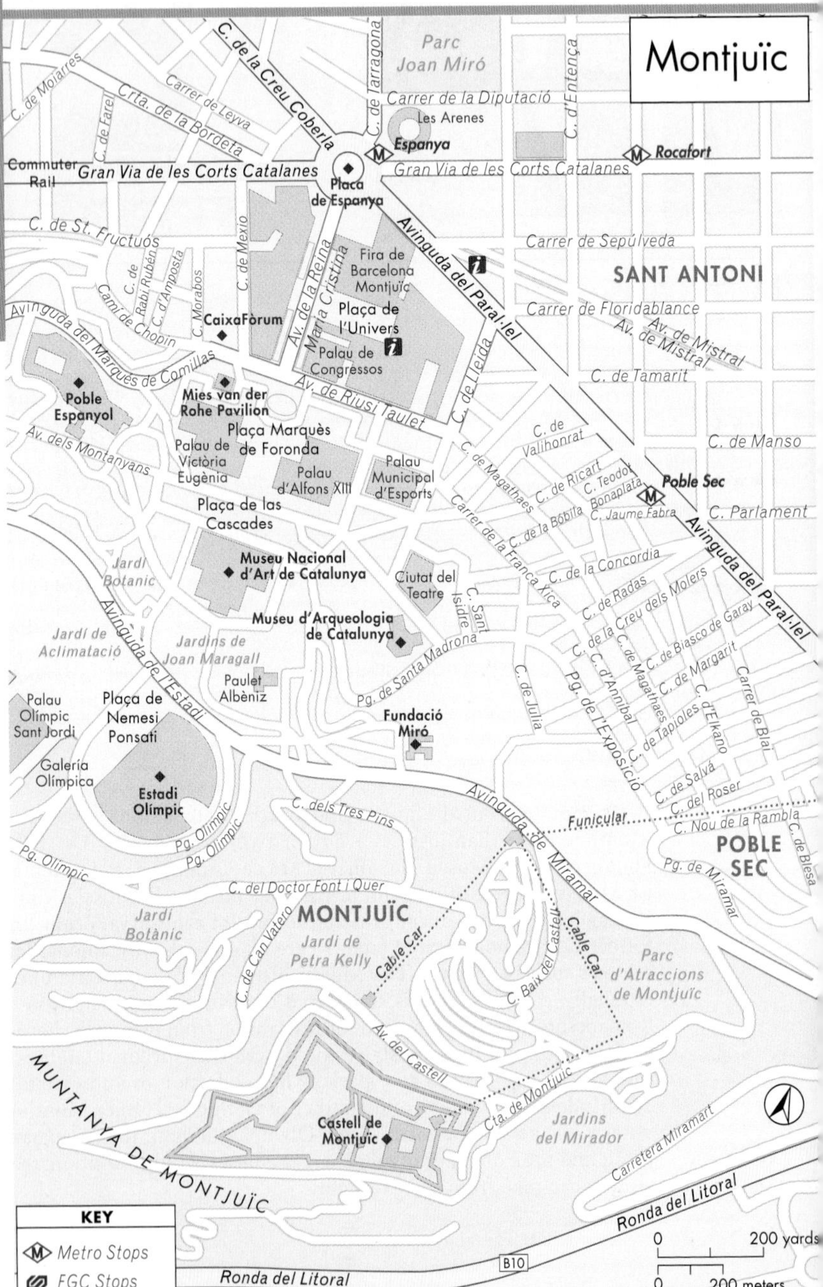
Montjuïc
Parc Joan Miró
C. de la Creu Coberta
C. de Tarragona
C. d'Entença
Carrer de la Diputació
Les Arenes
Espanya
Rocafort
C. de Molarres
Carrer de Leyva
Crta. de la Bordeta
C. de Farel
Commuter Rail
Gran Via de les Corts Catalanes
Plaça de Espanya
C. de St. Fructuós
C. de Mexic
Av. de la Reina Maria Cristina
Fira de Barcelona Montjuïc
Avinguda del Paral·lel
Carrer de Sepúlveda
SANT ANTONI
C. de Rabí Rubén
C. d'Amposta
C. Morabos
Camí de Chopin
CaixaFòrum
Plaça de l'Univers
Palau de Congressos
Carrer de Floridablanca
Av. de Mistral
C. de Tamarit
Avinguda del Marquès de Comillas
Poble Espanyol
Mies van der Rohe Pavilion
Av. de Rius i Taulet
C. de Lleida
Plaça Marquès de Foronda
Palau de Victòria Eugènia
Av. dels Montanyans
Palau d'Alfons XIII
Palau Municipal d'Esports
C. de Valihonrat
C. de Manso
C. de Magalhaes
C. de Ricart
C. Teodor Bonaplata
Poble Sec
C. Jaume Fabra
C. Parlament
Plaça de las Cascades
Carrer de la França Xica
C. de la Bòbila
C. de la Concordia
Jardí Botanic
Museu Nacional d'Art de Catalunya
Ciutat del Teatre
C. Sant Isidre
C. de Radas
C. de la Creu dels Molers
Avinguda de l'Estadi
Museu d'Arqueologia de Catalunya
Jardí de Aclimatació
Jardins de Joan Maragall
Pg. de Santa Madrona
C. de Blasco de Garay
C. de Margarit
C. de Julià
Pg. de l'Exposició
C. d'Annibal
C. de Tapioles
C. d'Elkano
Carrer de Blai
Paulet Albèniz
Palau Olímpic Sant Jordi
Plaça de Nemesi Ponsati
Fundació Miró
Galería Olímpica
Estadi Olímpic
C. de Salvà
C. del Roser
C. dels Tres Pins
Avinguda de Miramar
Funicular
C. Nou de la Rambla
POBLE SEC
C. de Blesa
Pg. Olímpic
Pg. de Miramar
C. del Doctor Font i Quer
MONTJUÏC
Jardí Botànic
C. de Can Valero
Jardí de Petra Kelly
Cable Car
C. Baix del Castell
Parc d'Atraccions de Montjuïc
Av. del Castell
MUNTANYA DE MONTJUÏC
Cta. de Montjuïc
Castell de Montjuïc
Jardins del Mirador
Carretera Miramart
Ronda del Litoral
B10
KEY
Metro Stops
FGC Stops
0
200 yards
0
200 meters

TIMING

With unhurried visits to the Miró Foundation and any or all of the Museu Nacional d'Art de Catalunya collections in the Palau Nacional, this is a four- to five-hour excursion, if not a full day. Have lunch afterward in the Poble Espanyol, just up from Mies van der Rohe's Barcelona Pavilion or in the cafeteria-restaurant at the Fundació Miró.

GETTING HERE

The most dramatic approach to Montjuïc is the cross-harbor cable car (Transbordador Aeri) from Barceloneta or from the mid-station in the port. You can also take a taxi or Bus No. 61 (or walk) from Plaça d'Espanya; yet another option is the funicular from the Paral.lel (Paral.lel metro stop, L3). The Telefèric de Montjuïc from the funicular stop to the Castell de Montjuïc is the final leg to the top.

WORD OF MOUTH

"We took the metro to Parel.el stop and connected to the free funicular up Montjuïc. This is where one would exit for the Fundació Miró and other museums. We opted for the cable car, Telefèric de Montjuïc, which continues up the mountain. It isn't a very long ride, but it offers a lovely view of the city and ocean." —yk

TOP ATTRACTIONS

CaixaFòrum

Fundació Miró

Mies van der Rohe Pavilion

Museu Nacional d'Art de Catalunya

TOP EXPERIENCES

Contemplating the ingenious display of frescoes at the MNAC

Discovering how less is more at the Mies van der Rohe Pavilion

Attending a concert at the CaixaFòrum

Shopping for traditional crafts' in Poble Espanyol

Exploring the Fundació Miró

Watching the sunset from the top of the MNAC stairs

WHERE TO EAT (⇨ CH. 3)

Fundació Miró Café

Oleum (in MNAC)

AREA SHOPS

CaixaFòrum gift shop

Fundació Miró gift shop

Mies van der Rohe Pavilion shop

MNAC gift shop

Poble Espanyol studios and shops

DID YOU KNOW?

The Museu Nacional d'Art de Catalunya embraces art from multiple mediums, including drawings, engravings, sculpture, paintings, photography, coinage, and objets d'art from the Romanesque era to the 20th century.

TOP ATTRACTIONS

CaixaForum (*Casaramona*). This redbrick, neo-Mudejar Art Nouveau fortress, built to house a factory in 1911 by Josep Puig i Cadafalch (architect of Casa de les Punxes, Casa Amatller, Casa Martí, and Casa Quadras), now CaixaForum, is a center for art exhibits, concerts, lectures, and cultural events. Well worth keeping an eye on in newspaper and magazine leisure listings, for special exhibitions. The restoration is a brilliant example of the fusion of ultramodern design techniques with traditional (even Art Nouveau) architecture. The entryway was designed by Japanese architect Arata Isozaki, author of the nearby Palau Sant Jordi. ✉ *Av. Francesc Ferrer i Guàrdia 6–8, Montjuïc* ☎ *93/476–8600* 🌐 *obrasocial.lacaixa.es/laCaixaFoundation/culture_en.html* 🎟 *Free; charge for evening concerts and €4 for special exhibitions* ⏲ *Weekdays 10–8, weekends 10–9; later for concerts* Ⓜ *Espanya.*

Fodor's Choice ★ **Fundació Miró.** The Miró Foundation, a gift from the artist Joan Miró to his native city, is one of Barcelona's most exciting showcases of contemporary art. The airy, white building, with panoramic views north over Barcelona, was designed by the artist's close friend and collaborator Josep Lluís Sert and opened in 1975; an extension was added by Sert's pupil Jaume Freixa in 1988. Miró's playful and colorful style, filled with Mediterranean light and humor, seems a perfect match for its surroundings, and the exhibits and retrospectives that open here tend to be progressive and provocative. Look for Alexander Calder's fountain of moving mercury. Miró himself rests in the cemetery on Montjuïc's southern slopes. During the Franco regime, which he strongly opposed, Miró first lived in self-imposed exile in Paris, then moved to Majorca in 1956. When he died in 1983, the Catalans gave him a send-off amounting to a state funeral. ✉ *Av. Miramar 71, Montjuïc* ☎ *93/443–9470* 🌐 *www.fundaciomiro-bcn.org* 🎟 *€11* ⏲ *Tues., Wed., Fri., and Sat. 10–7, Thurs. 10–9:30, Sun. 10–2:30.*

Mies van der Rohe Pavilion. One of the masterpieces of the Bauhaus School, the legendary Pavelló Mies van der Rohe—the German contribution to the 1929 International Exhibition, reassembled between 1983 and 1986—remains a stunning "less is more" study in interlocking planes of white marble, green onyx, and glass. In effect, it is Barcelona's aesthetic antonym (possibly in company with Richard Meier's Museu d'Art Contemporani and Rafael Moneo's Auditori) to the flamboyant Art Nouveau—the city's signature Modernisme—of Gaudí and his contemporaries. Don't fail to note the mirror play of the black carpet inside the pavilion with the reflecting pool outside, or the iconic Barcelona chair designed by Mies van der Rohe (1886–1969); reproductions of the chair have graced modern interiors around the world for decades. A free guided tour in English is offered on Saturday at 10 am. ✉ *Av. Francesc Ferrer i Guàrdia 7, Montjuïc* ☎ *93/423–4016* 🌐 *www.miesbcn.com* 🎟 *€5* ⏲ *Daily 10–8; guided tours Sat. at 10.* Ⓜ *Espanya.*

Fodor's Choice ★ **Museu Nacional d'Art de Catalunya** (*Catalonian National Museum of Art, MNAC*). Housed in the imposingly domed, towered, frescoed, and columned **Palau Nacional,** built in 1929 as the centerpiece of the International Exposition, this superb museum was renovated in 1995 by Gae Aulenti, architect of the Musée d'Orsay in Paris. In 2004 the museum's

Architect Arata Isozaki designed the futuristic Palau Sant Jordi Sports Palace.

three holdings—Romanesque, Gothic, and the Cambó Collection—an eclectic trove, including a Goya, donated by Francesc Cambó—were joined by the 19th- and 20th-century collection of Catalan impressionist and Moderniste painters. Also now on display is the Thyssen-Bornemisza collection of early masters, with works by Zurbarán, Rubens, Tintoretto, Velázquez, and others. With this influx of artistic treasure, the MNAC becomes Catalonia's grand central museum. Pride of place goes to the Romanesque exhibition, the world's finest collection of Romanesque frescoes, altarpieces, and wood carvings, most of them rescued from chapels in the Pyrenees during the 1920s to save them from deterioration, theft, and art dealers. Many, such as the famous *Cristo de Taüll* fresco (from the church of Sant Climent de Taüll in Taüll), have been painstakingly removed from crumbling walls of abandoned sites and remounted on ingenious frames that exactly reproduce the contours of their original settings. The central hall of the museum, with its enormous pillared and frescoed cupola, is stunning. ✉ *Palau Nacional, Montjuïc* ☎ *93/622–0376* 🌐 *www.mnac.cat* 🎫 *€12 (valid for day of purchase and one other day in same month); free Sat. 3–6 and 1st Sun. of the month* ⏲ *Jun.–Sept., Tues.–Sat. 10–8, Sun. 10–3; Oct.–May, Tues.–Sat. 10–6, Sun. 10–3* Ⓜ *Espanya.*

WORTH NOTING

Castell de Montjuïc. Built in 1640 by rebels against Felipe IV, the castle has had a dark history as a symbol of Barcelona's military domination by foreign powers, usually the Spanish army. The fortress was stormed several times, most famously in 1705 by Lord Peterborough for Archduke Carlos of Austria. In 1808, during the Peninsular War, it was seized by the French under General Dufresne. Later, during an 1842 civil disturbance, Barcelona was bombed from its heights by a Spanish artillery battery. After the 1936–39 Civil War, the castle was used as a dungeon for political prisoners. Lluís Companys, president of the Generalitat de Catalunya during the civil war, was executed by firing squad here on October 14, 1940. In 2007 the fortress was formally ceded back to Barcelona. The present uses of the space include a Interpretation Center for Peace, a Space for Historical Memory, and a Montjuïc Interpretation Center, along with cultural and educational events and activities. A popular weekend park and picnic area, the moat contains attractive gardens, with one side given over to an archery range, and the various terraces have panoramic views over the city and out to sea. ✉ *Ctra. de Montjuïc 66, Montjuïc* ☎ *93/329–8613* 🎫 *Free* ⏲ *Tues.–Sun. 9–7.*

Estadi Olímpic (*Olympic Stadium*). Open for visitors, the Olympic Stadium was originally built for the International Exhibition of 1929, with the idea that Barcelona would then host the 1936 Olympics (ultimately staged in Hitler's Berlin). After failing twice to win the nomination, the city celebrated the attainment of its long-cherished goal by renovating the semiderelict stadium in time for 1992, providing seating for 70,000. The **Galeria Olímpica,** a museum about the Olympic movement in Barcelona, displays objects and shows audiovisual replays from the 1992 Olympics. An information center traces the history of the modern Olympics from Athens in 1896 to the present. Next door and just downhill stands the futuristic **Palau Sant Jordi Sports Palace,** designed by the noted Japanese architect Arata Isozaki. The Isozaki structure has no pillars or beams to obstruct the view, and was built from the roof down—the roof was built first, then hydraulically lifted into place. ✉ *Av. de l'Estadi s/n, Montjuïc* ☎ *93/4262089* 🌐 *www.fundaciobarcelonaolimpica.es* 🎫 *Free* ⏲ *Daily 10–2 and 4–7* Ⓜ *Espanya.*

Museu d'Arqueologia de Catalunya. Just downhill to the right of the Palau Nacional, the Museum of Archaeology holds important finds from the Greek ruins at Empúries, on the Costa Brava. These are shown alongside fascinating objects from, and explanations of, megalithic Spain. ✉ *Passeig Santa Madrona 39–41, Montjuïc* ☎ *93/4232149* 🌐 *www.mac.es* 🎫 *€3; last Sun. of the month free* ⏲ *Tues.–Sat. 9:30–7, Sun. 10–2:30.*

Plaça d'Espanya. This busy circle is a good place to avoid, but sooner or later you'll probably need to cross it to go to the convention center or to the Palau Nacional. It's dominated by the so-called Venetian Towers (they're actually Tuscan) built in 1927 as the grand entrance to the 1929 International Exposition. The fountain in the center is the work of Josep Maria Jujol, the Gaudí collaborator who designed the curvy and colorful benches in Park Güell. The sculptures are by Miquel Blay, one of the master artists and craftsmen who put together the Palau de la Música. The neo-Mudejar bullring, Les Arenes, is now a multi-level shopping mall. On the corner of Carrer Llançà, just down to the right looking at the bullring, you can just get a glimpse of the kaleidoscopic lepidopteran atop the Art Nouveau Casa de la Papallona (House of the Butterfly). From the plaza, you can take the metro or Bus No. 38 back to the Plaça de Catalunya. ✉ *Plaça d'Espanya, Sants.*

FAMILY **Poble Espanyol.** Created for the 1929 International Exhibition as a sort of artificial Spain-in-a-bottle, with faithful reproductions of Spain's various architectural styles punctuated with boutiques, workshops, and studios, the Spanish Village takes you from the walls of Ávila to the wine cellars of Jerez de la Frontera. The liveliest time to come is at night, and a reservation at one of the half-dozen restaurants gets you in for free, as does the purchase of a ticket for either of the two discos or the Tablao del Carmen flamenco club. ✉ *Av. Francesc Ferrer i Guàrdia 13, Montjuïc* ☎ *93/508–6300* 🌐 *www.poble-espanyol.com* 🎫 *€11 (€6.50 after 8* 🕐 *Mon. 9–8, Tues.–Thurs. and Sun. 9 am–midnight, Fri. 9 am–3 am, Sat. 9 am–4 am. Shops daily 10–6.*

WHERE TO EAT

By Steve Tallantyre

Barcelona's restaurant scene is an ongoing adventure. Between avant-garde culinary innovation and the more rustic dishes of traditional Catalan fare, there is a fleet of brilliant classical chefs producing some of Europe's finest Mediterranean cuisine.

Catalans are legendary lovers of fish, vegetables, rabbit, duck, lamb, game, and natural ingredients from the Pyrenees or the Mediterranean. The *mar i muntanya* (literally, "sea and mountain"—that is, surf and turf) is a standard. Combining salty and sweet tastes—a Moorish legacy—is another common theme.

The Mediterranean diet—based on olive oil, seafood, fibrous vegetables, onions, garlic, and red wine—is at home in Barcelona, embellished by Catalonia's four basic sauces: *allioli* (whipped garlic and olive oil), *romesco* (almonds, nyora peppers, hazelnuts, tomato, garlic, and olive oil), *sofregit* (fried onion, tomato, and garlic), and *samfaina* (a ratatouille-like vegetable mixture).

Typical entrées include *fabes a la catalana* (a spicy broad-bean stew), *arròs caldós* (a rice dish more typical of Catalonia than paella, often made with lobster), and *espinaques a la catalana* (spinach cooked with oil, garlic, pine nuts, raisins, and cured ham). Toasted bread is often doused with olive oil and rubbed with squeezed tomato to make *pa amb tomaquet*—delicious on its own or as a side order.

Beware of the advice of hotel concierges and taxi drivers, who have been known to warn that the place you are going is either closed or no good anymore, and to recommend places where they get kickbacks.

Aside from restaurants, Barcelona may have more bars and cafés per capita than any other place in the world. Cafés serve an important function: outdoor living room, meeting place, and giant cocktail party to which everyone is invited. Be advised: the sidewalk cafés along La Rambla are noisy, dusty, overpriced, and exposed to pickpockets.

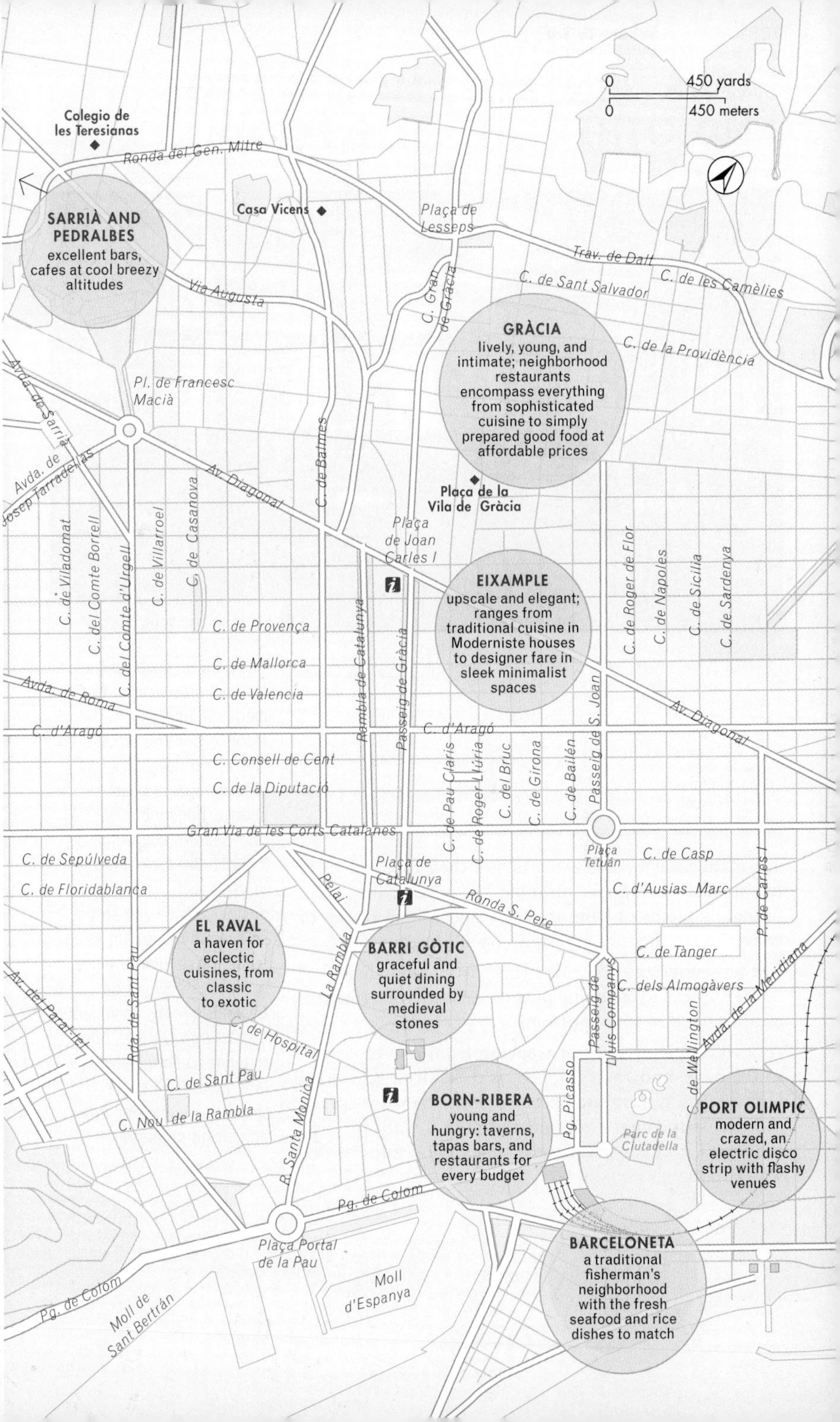
0 450 yards
0 450 meters
Colegio de les Teresianas
Ronda del Gen. Mitre
Casa Vicens
Plaça de Lesseps
Trav. de Dalt
C. de les Camèlies
C. de Sant Salvador
SARRIÀ AND PEDRALBES
excellent bars, cafes at cool breezy altitudes
Via Augusta
C. Gran de Gràcia
GRÀCIA
lively, young, and intimate; neighborhood restaurants encompass everything from sophisticated cuisine to simply prepared good food at affordable prices
C. de la Providència
Pl. de Francesc Macià
Avda. de Sarrià
Avda. de Josep Tarradellas
Av. Diagonal
C. de Balmes
Plaça de la Vila de Gràcia
Plaça de Joan Carles I
C. de Viladomat
C. del Comte Borrell
C. del Comte d'Urgell
C. de Villarroel
C. de Casanova
EIXAMPLE
upscale and elegant; ranges from traditional cuisine in Moderniste houses to designer fare in sleek minimalist spaces
C. de Roger de Flor
C. de Napoles
C. de Sicília
C. de Sardenya
C. de Provença
C. de Mallorca
C. de Valencia
Avda. de Roma
Rambla de Catalunya
Passeig de Gràcia
Av. Diagonal
Passeig de S. Joan
C. d'Aragó
C. d'Aragó
C. Consell de Cent
C. de la Diputació
C. de Pau Claris
C. de Roger Llúria
C. del Bruc
C. de Girona
C. de Bailén
Gran Via de les Corts Catalanes
C. de Sepúlveda
C. de Floridablanca
Plaça de Catalunya
Plaça Tetuán
C. de Casp
C. d'Ausias Marc
Pelai
Ronda S. Pere
P. de Carles I
EL RAVAL
a haven for eclectic cuisines, from classic to exotic
BARRI GÒTIC
graceful and quiet dining surrounded by medieval stones
La Rambla
C. de Tànger
C. dels Almogàvers
Av. del Paral·lel
Rda. de Sant Pau
C. de Hospital
Passeig de Lluis Companys
C. de Wellington
Avda. de la Meridiana
C. de Sant Pau
C. Nou de la Rambla
R. Santa Monica
BORN-RIBERA
young and hungry: taverns, tapas bars, and restaurants for every budget
Pg. Picasso
Parc de la Ciutadella
PORT OLIMPIC
modern and crazed, an electric disco strip with flashy venues
Pg. de Colom
Plaça Portal de la Pau
BARCELONETA
a traditional fisherman's neighborhood with the fresh seafood and rice dishes to match
Moll d'Espanya
Pg. de Colom
Moll de Sant Bertrán

TAPAS, PINTXOS, MONTADITOS, AND OTHER BITE-SIZE FOOD

Barcelona arrived late on the tapas scene, which originated in Andalusia and flourished in the Basque Country, but Catalan restaurateurs eventually embraced tapas with abandon.

Tapas themselves, small snacks, got their moniker from the Spanish verb *tapar*, meaning "to cover"; they were originally pieces of ham or cheese laid across glasses of wine to keep flies out and stagecoach drivers sober.

The term now covers a wide variety, from individual bites on toothpicks to steaming pots of stick-to-your-ribs creations served in small portions.

A Seville-style evening of weaving from one tapas bar to the next, known as a *tapeo*, is difficult in Barcelona because while there are excellent spots they are spread out across the city. Find one and take a walk through the menu instead: select what looks good and ask for wines to match.

A BRIEF HISTORY

Tapas owes much to the Moorish presence on the Iberian Peninsula. The Moorish taste for small and varied delicacies has become Spain's best-known culinary innovation. Spanish king Alfonso X (1221–84) took small morsels with wine on his doctor's advice and so enjoyed the cure that he made it a regular practice in his court. Miguel de Cervantes, in his universal classic, *Don Quixote*, refers to tapas as *llamativos* (attention getters), for their stimulating appetite-enhancing properties.

TAPAS 101

Belly up to the bar, order a drink, and dig in. You'll receive a plate for staging your tapas and collecting your toothpicks, which is sometimes how the bartender tallies up your bill. If you're sitting at a table, the waiter will keep track of the dishes you've ordered and bring them to you in rapid succession.

The term *tapas* covers various forms of nibbling. *Tentempiés* are "keep you on your feet" snacks. *Pintxos* are bite-size offerings on toothpicks; *banderillas* are wrapped in colorful paper resembling the batons used in bullfights. *Montaditos* are canapés, delicacies "mounted" on toast; *raciones* (rations) are hot tapas served in small casseroles.

A few tapas to try: *calamares* (fried cuttlefish, often mistaken for onion rings), *pulpo a feira* (aka *pulpo gallego*, octopus on slices of potato), *chipirones* (baby cuttlefish), *chistorra* (fried spicy Basque sausage), *champiñones* (mushrooms), *setas* (wild mushrooms), *gambas al ajillo* (shrimp cooked in parsley, oil, and garlic), *langostinos* (jumbo shrimp or prawns), *patatas bravas* (potatoes in spicy sauce), *pimientos de Padrón* (peppers from the Galician town of Padrón), and *almendras* (almonds fried and sprinkled with salt).

Some of the tastiest tapas often sound unappealing, so be bold and take chances. *Caracoles* (snails) are

usually served in a rich, meaty sauce, best mopped up with crusty bread after you've tackled the snails with a toothpick.

Many skeptics have been won over by *callos* (tripe), a hearty dish served in a spicy tomato sauce. *Morro* (pork rinds) is the perfect snack to enjoy with cold beer, as is *oreja* (fried pig's ear). *Anchoas* (salt-cured anchovies) are good, but even those who dislike them may enjoy *boquerones en vinagre* (anchovies marinated in vinegar and oil).

BARCELONA DINING PLANNER

EATING-OUT STRATEGY

The selection here represents the best this city has to offer—from tapas bars to haute cuisine. Search "Best Bets" for top recommendations by price, cuisine, and experience. Or find a review quickly in the alphabetical listings by neighborhood.

HOURS

Barcelona dines late. Lunch is served 2–4 and dinner 9–11. If you arrive a half-hour early, you may score a table but miss the life and fun of the place. The city is slowly adapting, however, to the imported eating timetables of tourists, and a number of decent restaurants now offer all-day and late-night hours. Hunger attacks between meals are easily resolved in the city's numerous cafés and tapas bars.

PRICES

Barcelona is no longer a bargain. Whereas low-end fixed-price lunch menus can be found for as little as €10, most good restaurants cost closer to €40 or €50 for a full meal, when ordering à la carte. For serious evening dining, plan on spending €55–€80 per person, the most expensive places costing even more. ■ **TIP→ Barcelona restaurants, even many of the pricey establishments, offer a daily lunchtime menu (menú del día) consisting of two courses plus wine, coffee, or dessert.**

Prices in the restaurant reviews are the average cost of a main course at dinner or, if dinner is not served, at lunch.

TIPPING AND TAXES

Tipping, though common, is not required; the gratuity is included in the check. If you do tip as an extra courtesy, anywhere from 5% to 10% is perfectly acceptable. No one seems to care much about tipping, though all parties seem to end up happier if a small gratuity is left.

The 7% Value-Added Tax (IVA) will not appear on the menu, but is tacked on to the final tally on your check.

RESERVATIONS

Nearly all of Barcelona's best restaurants require reservations. As the city has grown in popularity, more and more receptionists are able to take your reservations in English. Your hotel concierge will also be happy to call and reserve you a table. Beware of taxi drivers and hotel receptionists who try to send you to other restaurants they claim are better.

USING THE MAPS

Throughout the chapter, you'll see mapping symbols and coordinates (✣ F:2) at the end of the reviews that correspond to the atlas at the end of this chapter. The letter and number after the ✣ symbol indicate the property's coordinates on the map grid.

RESTAURANT REVIEWS

Listed alphabetically within neighborhoods.

CIUTAT VELLA (OLD CITY)

Ciutat Vella includes La Rambla, Barri Gòtic, Born-Ribera, and El Raval districts between Plaça de Catalunya and the port. Chic new restaurants and cafés seem to open daily in Barcelona's Ciutat Vella, but classic, family-owned eateries still offer generations of accumulated culinary expertise.

BARRI GÒTIC

$$ CATALAN **Agut.** Wainscoting and 1950s' canvases are the background for the mostly Catalan crowd in this homey restaurant in the lower reaches of the Barri Gòtic. Agut was founded in 1924, and its popularity has never waned—after all, hearty Catalan fare at a fantastic value is always in demand. In season (September–May), try the *pato silvestre agridulce* (sweet-and-sour wild duck). There's a good selection of wine, but no frills such as coffee or liqueur. *Average main: €16* *Gignàs 16, Barri Gòtic* *93/315–1709* *www.restaurantagut.com* *Closed Mon., and 2 wks in Aug. No dinner Sun.* *Jaume I* *I:13.*

$$ CATALAN **ATN Restaurant.** Specializing in country cuisine from northern Catalonia's volcanic Garrotxa region, this restaurant, in the entryway to Barcelona's Ateneu (the cultural and literary club), is a find. The clean-lined dining room stresses glass and wood and the kitchen produces traditional recipes based on duck, goose, rabbit, and lamb. The location overlooks Plaça Vila de Madrid, is near the top of the Rambla, and is great for anyone looking to rest after the promenade's crowds. *Average main: €16* *Canuda 6, Barri Gòtic* *93/318–5238* *www.atnrestaurant.cat* *Closed Sun. No dinner Mon.* *Pl. de Catalunya* *H:12.*

$$ CATALAN **Café de l'Acadèmia.** With wicker chairs, stone walls, and classical music playing, this place is sophisticated-rustic, and the excellent contemporary Mediterranean cuisine specialties such as *timbal d'escalibada amb formatge de cabra* (roast vegetable salad with goat cheese) or *crema de pastanaga amb gambes i virutes de parmesá* (cream of carrot soup with shrimp and Parmesan cheese shavings) make it more than a mere café. Politicians and functionaries from the nearby Generalitat frequent this dining room, which is always boiling with life. Be sure to reserve a table at lunchtime. *Average main: €18* *Lledó 1, Barri Gòtic* *93/319–8253* *Closed weekends and 2 wks in Aug.* *Jaume I* *I:13.*

$$ CATALAN **Cometacinc.** In an increasingly chic neighborhood of artisans and antiquers, this stylish place in the Barri Gòtic is a fine example of Barcelona's new-over-old architecture and interior-design panache. Although the 30-foot, floor-to-ceiling, wooden shutters are already a visual feast, the carefully prepared interpretations of old standards such as the *xai al forn* (roast lamb) or the more surprising *raviolis de vieiras* (scallop raviolis) awaken the palate brilliantly. The separate dining room, for a dozen to two-dozen diners, is a perfect place for a private party. *Average main: €17* *Carrer Cometa 5, Barri Gòtic* *93/310–1558* *www.cometacinc.com* *No lunch* *Jaume I* *I:13.*

BEST BETS FOR FOR BARCELONA DINING

Need a cheat sheet for Barcelona's thousands of restaurants? Our Fodor's writer has selected some of his favorites by price, cuisine, and experience in the lists shown here. You can also search by neighborhood or find specific details about a restaurant in our full reviews—just peruse the following pages. Happy dining in Catalonia's capital by the sea. *¡Bon profit!*

Fodor's Choice ★

Ca l'Isidre, $$$$, p. 152
Casa Leopoldo, $$$$, p. 152
Cinc Sentits, $$$$, p. 159
El Vaso de Oro, $, p. 155
Embat, $$, p. 160
Enoteca, $$$$, p. 156
Gelonch, $$$, p. 160
Gresca, $$, p. 161
La Mar Salada, $$, p. 156
La Pastisseria Barcelona, $, p. 162
La Taverna del Clinic, $$$, p. 162
Manairó, $$, p. 163
Quimet I Quimet, $, p. 154
Roca Moo, $$$, p. 164
Sant Pau, $$$$, p. 180
Silvestre, $$, p. 178
Tram-Tram, $$$, p. 178
Via Veneto, $$$$, p. 178

By Price

$

Bambarol, p. 176
Ca l'Estevet, p. 152
Cera 23, p. 152
El Vaso de Oro, p. 155
Irati Taverna Basca, p. 144
La Pastisseria Barcelona, p. 162
Vivanda, p. 178

$$

Café de l'Acadèmia, p. 141
Cometacinc, p. 141
Embat, p. 160
Gresca, p. 161
La Mar Salada, p. 156
Manairó, p. 163
Silvestre, p. 178

$$$

Espai Sucre, p. 149
Gelonch, p. 160
Ipar-Txoko, p. 174
La Taverna Del Clinic, p. 162
Roca Moo, p. 164
Tram-Tram, p. 178

$$$$

Ca l'Isidre, p. 152
Casa Leopoldo, p. 152
Cinc Sentits, p. 159
Enoteca, p. 156
Sant Pau, p. 180
Via Veneto, p. 178

By Cuisine

BASQUE

Ipar-Txoko, p. 174
Taktika Berri, p. 172

CAFÉS

Bar Paris, p. 157
Dole Café, p. 176
La Cerería, p. 144
La Pastisseria Barcelona, p. 162
Mercat Princesa, p. 150

CONTEMPORARY CATALAN

ABaC, p. 179
Embat, p. 160
L'Olivé, p. 163
Sant Pau, p. 180
Saüc, p. 146
Via Veneto, p. 178

LA NUEVA COCINA/ EXPERIMENTAL CUISINE

Alkimia, p. 157
Cinc Sentits, p. 159
Comerç 24, p. 148
Gelonch, p. 160
Gresca, p. 161
Manairó, p. 163
Roca Moo, p. 164
Tickets & 41°, p. 154

MEDITERRANEAN

Ca l'Isidre, p. 152
Caldeni, p. 158
Cinc Sentits, p. 159
Llamber, p. 150
Neichel, p. 177
Sant Pau, p. 180

By Experience

$$$ ECLECTIC ✕ **Cuines Santa Caterina.** A lovingly restored market designed by the late Enric Miralles and completed by his widow Benedetta Tagliabue provides a spectacular setting for one of the city's most original dining operations. Under the undulating wooden superstructure of the market, the breakfast and tapas bar, open from dawn to midnight, offers a variety of culinary specialties cross-referenced by different cuisines (Mediterranean, Asian, vegetarian) and products (pasta, rice, fish, meat), all served on sleek counters and long wooden tables. *$ Average main: €22 ✉ Av. Francesc Cambó 16, Barri Gòtic ☎ 93/268–9918 ⊕ www.cuinessantacaterina.com M Urquinaona, Jaume I ✥ J:12.*

$ CATALAN ✕ **El Bitxo.** An original wine list and ever-rotating choices of interesting cava selections accompany creative tapas and small dishes from *foie* (duck or goose liver) to Ibérico hams and cheeses, all in a rustic wooden setting 50 yards from the Palau de la Música, close enough for intermissions. *$ Average main: €10 ✉ Carrer Verdaguer i Callis, 9, Sant Pere ☎ 93/268–1708 ⏲ Tues.–Sat. 1–1, Mon. 7 pm–1 am ⏲ No lunch Mon. M Urquinaona ✥ I:12.*

$ TAPAS ✕ **Irati Taverna Basca.** There's only one drawback to this lively Basque bar between Plaça del Pi and the Rambla: it's narrow at the street end and harder to squeeze into than the Barcelona metro at rush hour. Try coming on the early side, either at 1 pm or 7:30 pm. The tapas—skip the ones on the bar and opt for the plates brought out piping hot from the kitchen—should be accompanied by a freezing and refreshing *txakolí*, the young Basque white wine with a spritzer. The dozen tables in the back are surprisingly relaxed and crowd-free, and serve excellent Basque cuisine. *$ Average main: €7 ✉ Cardenal Casañas 17, Barri Gòtic ☎ 902/520522 ⊕ www.iratitavernabasca.com ⏲ 10 am–midnight M Liceu ✥ H:12.*

$$$ JAPANESE ✕ **Koy Shunka.** Two blocks away from their mothership Shunka, partners Hideki Matsuhisa and Xu Changchao have done it again. This time, with more space to work with, the Japanese-Chinese team of master chefs has organized a tribute to Asian fusion cooking based on products from the Catalan larder. *Berberechos en salsa de sake* (cockles in sake sauce), *cerdo ibérico con ciruelas* (Ibérico pork with plums), and *ventresca de atun* (tuna belly with grated tomato and lemon) are several of the infinite variations on the Asia-meets-Catalonia theme in this sleek, contemporary setting. *$ Average main: €22 ✉ Copons 7, Barri Gòtic ☎ 93/412–7939 ⊕ www.koyshunka.com ⏲ Closed Mon. and 3 wks in August. No dinner Sun. M Urquinaona ✥ I:12.*

$ CAFÉ ✕ **La Cerería.** At the corner of Baixada de Sant Miquel and Passatge de Crèdit, this ramshackle little terrace and café has a charm all its own. The tables in the Passatge itself are shady and breezy in summer, and cuisine is light and Mediterranean. Try the vegetarian salads, *escalibada* (roasted vegetables), and rice dishes. Look for the plaque at No. 4 commemorating the birth there of Catalan painter Joan Miró (1893–1983). *$ Average main: €7 ✉ Baixada de Sant Miquel 3–5, Barri Gòtic ☎ 93/301–8510 ▭ No credit cards ⏲ Closed Mon. and Tues. No lunch M Liceu ✥ H:13.*

CLOSE UP

A Primer on Barcelona's Cuisine

Menus in Catalan are as musical as they are aromatic, with rare ingredients such as *salicornia* (seawort, or sea asparagus) with *bacalao* (cod), or fragrant wild mushrooms such as *rossinyols* (chanterelles) and *moixernons* (St. George's mushroom) accompanying dishes like *mandonguilles amb sepia* (meatballs with cuttlefish).

Four sauces grace the Catalan table: *sofregit* (fried onion, tomato, and garlic—a base for nearly everything); *samfaina* (a ratatouille-like sofregit with eggplant and sweet red peppers); *picada* (garlic, almonds, bread crumbs, olive oil, pine nuts, parsley, saffron, or chocolate); and *allioli* (pounded garlic and virgin olive oil).

The three e's deserve a place in any Catalan culinary anthology: *escalibada* (roasted red peppers, eggplants, and tomatoes served in garlic and olive oil); *esqueixada* (shredded salt-cod salad served raw with onions, peppers, olives, beans, olive oil, and vinegar); and *escudella* (a winter stew of meats and vegetables with noodles and beans).

Universal specialties are *pa amb tomaquet* (toasted bread with squeezed tomato and olive oil), *espinaques a la catalana* (spinach cooked with raisins, garlic, and pine nuts), and *botifarra amb mongetes* (pork sausage with white beans). The *mar i muntanya* (Catalan "surf 'n' turf") has been a standard since Roman times. Rice dishes are simply called *arròs,* and range from standard seafood paella to the *arròs a banda* (paella with shelled prawns, shrimp, and mussels), to *arròs negre* (paella cooked in cuttlefish ink) or *arròs caldós* (a brothy risotto-like dish often made with lobster). *Fideuà* is a paella made of vermicelli noodles, not rice.

Fresh fish such as *llobarro* (sea bass, *lubina* in Spanish) or *dorada* (gilthead bream) cooked *a la sal* (in a shell of salt) are standards, as are grilled *llenguado* (sole) and *rodaballo* (turbot). Duck, goose, chicken, and rabbit frequent Catalan menus, as do *cabrit* (kid or baby goat), *xai* (lamb), *porc* (pork), *vedella* (young beef), and *bou* (mature beef). Finally come the two Catalan classic desserts, *mel i mató* (honey and fresh cream cheese) and *crema catalana* (a crème brûlée–like custard with a caramelized glaze).

A typical session *à table* in Barcelona might begin with *pica-pica* (hors d'oeuvres), a variety of delicacies such as *jamón ibérico de bellota* (acorn-fed ham), *xipirones* (baby squid), *pimientos de Padrón* (green peppers, some spicy), or *bunyols de bacallà* (cod fritters or croquettes), and pa amb tomaquet (bread with tomato). From here you can order a starter such as *canelones* (cannelloni) or you can go straight to your main course.

$ CAFÉ **La Palma.** Behind the Plaça Sant Jaume's *ajuntament* (city hall), toward the post office, sits this cozy and ancient café with marble tables, wine barrels, sausages hanging from the ceiling, and newspapers to linger over. An old favorite of early-20th-century artists ranging from Salvador Dalí to Pablo Picasso, this rustic space staunchly retains its antique charm while the rest of the city relentlessly redesigns itself. *Average main: €7 ⊠ Palma Sant Just 7, Barri Gòtic ☎ 93/315–0656 ⊙ Closed Sun. No lunch in Aug. Ⓜ Jaume I ⊕ I:13.*

$$ SEAFOOD ✕ **MariscCO.** The only decent dining choice in the elegant Plaça Reial—a square filled with sunny cafés serving mediocre fare—this combo fish market and restaurant specializes in fresh fish and rice dishes at surprisingly competitive prices. The raw materials, often still alive, are just inside on ice: you choose your fish, order the number of grams you want, and the show kitchen prepares it while you watch. Another bonus: it's open continuously from morning until after midnight. *Average main: €18 Pl. Reial 8, Rambla 93/412–4536 www.mariscCO.com Daily 10 am–1 am Liceu H:8.*

$$ TAPAS ✕ **Ohla Gastrobar.** Downstairs from his illustrious Saüc restuarant in the swanky Ohla Hotel, chef Xavier Franco has turned his talents to the presentation of more humble fare in this simpler gastropub. A trendy international crowd packs this place, sampling creative tapas, such as the magnificent rice *socarrat of capipota* (a type of crispy-bottomed paella) with baby cuttlefish, and charcoal-grilled fresh mussels with tomato sauce. The stylish high-ceilinged space keeps noise levels under control, and huge windows allow both natural light and views of passing street life. Live jazz on Sunday adds to the laid-back, metropolitan atmosphere. With Wi-Fi, excellent service, and late hours, Gastrobar scores high marks for cuisine and convenience. *Average main: €15 Via Laietana 49, Barri Gòtic 93/341–5050 www.ohlahotel.com Daily 7–4 and 7:30–midnight Urquinaona I:12.*

$$ CATALAN ✕ **Pla.** Filled with young couples night after night, this combination music, drinking, and dining place is candlelit and sleekly designed in glass over ancient stone, brick, and wood. The cuisine is light and contemporary, featuring inventive salads and fresh seafood. Open until 3 am (kitchen open until 12:30 am) on Friday and Saturday, Pla is a good postconcert option. *Average main: €18 Carrer Bellafila 5, Barri Gòtic 93/412–6552 www.elpla.cat No lunch Jaume I I:13.*

$$$$ CATALAN ✕ **Saüc.** Saüc's location in the Hotel Ohla two steps from the Palau de la Música Catalana has catapaulted chef Xavi Franco's inventive culinary offerings to increasted acclaim. Named for the curative elderberry plant, Saüc's elegantly modern decor—wide wood-plank floors and softly draped tablecloths—sets the mood, and the avant-garde tabletop centerpiece is the first hint that the fare here is far from standard. This postmodern *cuina d'autor* (original cuisine) uses fine ingredients and combines them in flavorful surprises such as scallops with cod tripe and black sausage or monkfish with snails. The tasting menu is an unbroken series of unusual combinations of standard products, none of which fail to please. Try the *coulant de chocolate y maracuyá* (chocolate pudding with passion fruit) for dessert. *Average main: €34 Via Laietana 49, Barri Gòtic 93/321–0189 www.ohlahotel.com Reservations essential Daily 1:30–4 and 8:30–11 Urquinaona I:12.*

$ CAFÉ ✕ **Schilling.** Near Plaça Reial, Schilling always seems to be packed to the point where you might have some difficulty getting a table. Home to an international set of merry visitors and cruising barcelonins winding up for the club scene that officially begins after 1 am, this is a good place for coffee by day and drinks by night, but there are better options in the area for tapas. *Average main: €8 Ferran 23, Barri Gòtic 93/317–6787 www.cafeschilling.com Mon.–Sat. 10 am–3 am, Sun. noon–1:30 am Liceu H:13.*

CLOSE UP

Barcelona's Sweet Tooth

For a long time, desserts were the Achilles' heel of the Barcelona culinary scene. Diners groaning in anticipation after devouring their lovingly prepared starters and entrées often experienced disappointment when the final course arrived at the table—straight from the local supermarket's deep freeze. Occasionally, the waiter delivered a good, homemade *crema catalana* (crème brûlée), but the odds of a truly memorable ending to one's meal weren't favorable. To find Barcelona's sweet spot, you needed to skip the *postres* and head to the local *pastiseria.*

These neighborhood bakeries have always supplied Catalans with a cornucopia of seasonal treats. Some of the most beloved delectables include *xuixos* (pastries stuffed with, yes, crema catalana) and *pastissets de cabell d'àngel* (half-moon pastries). *Coques* are flatbreads, usually enjoyed around Easter, Christmas, or on Saint's days. They're often topped with pine nuts and candied fruit, or even some delicious sweet-and-savory combinations, such as pork crackling and sugar. *Panellets* are another local favorite, worth seeking out in autumn: balls of baked marzipan and pine nuts served with a sweet wine.

Fortunately, the standard of desserts in Barcelona's restaurants is now improving. The more acclaimed establishments have raised the bar, and local chefs are applying the lessons learned in prestigious Barcelona cooking schools. One of them, the dazzlingly innovative school-restaurant Espai Sucre (Sugar Space), specializes in all things sweet.

But for the best treats in town, check out the chocolate. Oriol Balaguer sells pure black magic at his two shops, which look more like exquisite jewelry stores than food retailers. Often rated among the world's top chocolatiers, he vies with Enric Rovira for the crown of Catalonia's best. Another contender is Cacao Sampaka, founded by Quim Capdevilla. Be prepared to have your mind—and your wallet—blown wide open should you visit any of these haute confectioners. Travelers with children should consider a trip to the Museu de la Xocolata (Chocolate Museum) in El Born, where they can enjoy some finger-licking fun in the workshops, and shop for delicious sweets in the museum shop.

3

$$ TAPAS **Taberna Les Tapes.** Proprietors and chefs Barbara and Santi offer a special 10-selection tapas anthology at this narrow, cozy, cheery place, just behind the town hall and just seaward of Plaça Sant Jaume. Barbara, originally from Worcestershire, England, takes especially good care of visitors from abroad. The 10-tapa medley for two (€12.75) with croquettes, squash omelet, wild mushrooms, patatas bravas, chistorra, pimientos de Padrón, and four more according to market and season is a popular choice here. *Average main: €15* ✉ *Pl. Regomir 4, Barri Gòtic* ☎ *93/302–4840* ⏲ *Mon.–Sat. 5–11:30* ⏲ *Closed Aug.* Ⓜ *Jaume I* ✣ *I:13.*

$ TAPAS

Taller de Tapas. The original location of what is now a chain of six of branches across the city is a safe if unremarkable bet for a bite to eat while out on the tourist trail. The classic Catalan and Spanish dishes here lack character, but they are always fresh, competently executed, and served by a cheerful staff. *Average main: €11 Pl. de Sant Josep Oriol 9, Barri Gòtic 93/301–8020 Liceu I:13.*

BORN-RIBERA

$$ TAPAS

Cal Pep. Cal Pep, a two-minute walk east from Santa Maria del Mar, has been in a permanent feeding frenzy for 30 years, intensified even further by the hordes of tourists who now flock here. Pep serves a selection of tapas, cooked and served hot over the counter. Generally avoid ordering the fish dishes (unless you're willing to part with an extra €35–€50), and stick with green peppers, fried artichokes, garbanzos and spinach, baby shrimp, the "*trifasic*" (mixed tiny fish fry), the nonpareil *tortilla de patatas* (potato omelet), and *botifarra trufada en reducción de Oporto* (truffled sausage in Port wine reduction sauce). The house wines are good, but the Torre la Moreira albariño perfectly complements Pep's offerings. Be prepared to wait for 20 minutes for a place at the counter. Reservations for the tables in the tiny back room are accepted, but reserve well in advance and know that you'll miss out on the lively counter scene. *Average main: €18 Pl. de les Olles 8, Born-Ribera 93/310–7961 www.calpep.com Closed Sun. No lunch Mon. No dinner Sat. Closed 3 wks in Aug. Jaume I, Barceloneta J:13.*

$$$$ CATALAN

Comerç 24. Artist, aesthete, and chef Carles Abellán playfully reinterprets traditional Catalan favorites and creates new ones at this artfully decorated dining spot on Carrer Comerç. Try the *arroz d'ànec amb foie* (rice with duck and foie gras). For dessert, don't miss the postmodern version of the traditional Spanish after-school snack of chocolate, olive oil, salt, and bread. Abellán trained under superstar Ferran Adrià and is as original as the master; the best way to experience his creativity is to throw budget to the winds and order one of the two tasting menus (€92 and €116, without wine). *Average main: €32 Carrer Comerç 24, Born-Ribera 93/319–2102 www.projectes24.com Reservations essential Closed Sun. and Mon. No lunch Arc de Triomf J:12.*

$$ ECLECTIC

El Foro. Near the Born, this hot spot is always full to the rafters with lively young and not-so-young people. Painting and photographic exhibits line the walls, and the menu is dominated by meat cooked over coals, pizzas, and salads. Flamenco and jazz performances downstairs are a good postdinner diversion. *Average main: €16 Princesa 53, Born-Ribera 93/310–1020 www.restauranteelforo.com Closed Mon. Jaume I J:13.*

$$$$ SEAFOOD

El Passadís d'en Pep. Hidden away at the end of a narrow unmarked passageway off the Pla del Palau, near the Santa Maria del Mar church, this restaurant is a favorite with local politicos and fat cats from the nearby stock exchange. Sit down, and waiters begin to serve a rapid-fire succession of delicious seafood starters, whatever's freshest that day in the market. Don't bother asking for a menu: there isn't one. At some point you may be asked to decide on a main course; if you're already full, feel free to pass—but you might well be missing a pièce de résistance. *Average main: €38* *Pl. del Palau 2, Born-Ribera* *93/310–1021* *www.passadis.com* *Mon.–Sat. 12:30–3:30 and 8:30–11:30* *Closed Sun. and 3 wks in Aug.* *Jaume I* *J:13.*

$ TAPAS **El Xampanyet.** Just down the street from the Picasso Museum, hanging *botas* (leather wineskins) announce one of Barcelona's liveliest and prettiest taverns, with marble-topped tables and walls decorated with colorful ceramic tiles; it's usually packed to the rafters with a rollicking mob of local and out-of-town celebrants. Avoid the oversweet house sparkling wine (go for draft beer, cava, or wine), but don't miss the pa amb tomaquet or the Ibérico ham. *Average main: €10* *Montcada 22, Born-Ribera* *93/319–7003* *Tues.–Sat. noon–3:30 and 7–11; Sun. noon–3:30* *Closed Mon. and Aug.* *Jaume I* *J:13.*

$$$ ECLECTIC **Espai Sucre.** The world's first dessert-only restaurant sounds like one of those terrible ideas that receives ridicule on reality TV shows, but Espai Sucre has been making a success of this distinctive concept since 2000. Attached to a creative and pioneering patisserie school that Willy Wonka would be proud of, this 30-seat restaurant serves multicourse tasting menus based around sweet-and-savory "desserts" that never fail to astonish and somehow never feel overwhelming. Consider goat "cheesecake" with raspberries, red pepper, and ginger; or squid rice with saffron custard and passion fruit. The innovation-for-innovation's-sake has been scaled back in recent years, but this is still a long way from a conventional dining experience—expect the unexpected. *Average main: €28* *Princesa 53, Born-Ribera* *93/268–1630* *www.espaisucre.com* *Reservations essential* *Closed Sun. and Mon. No lunch* *Arc de Triomf* *J:13.*

$$ BASQUE **Euskal Etxea.** An elbow-shaped, pine-panel space, this spot (one of the Sagardi group of Basque restaurants) is one of the better grazing destinations in the Barri Gòtic, with a colorful array of tapas and canapés on the bar ranging from the olive-pepper-anchovy on a toothpick to chunks of tortilla or *pimientos de piquillo* (red piquillo peppers) stuffed with codfish paste. An excellent and usually completely booked restaurant (don't miss the *Euskal Txerria* confit and crispy suckling pig with thistle and walnuts) and a Basque cultural circle and art gallery round out this social and gastronomical oasis. *Average main: €18* *Placeta de Montcada 1–3, Born-Ribera* *902/520522* *www.euskaletxeataberna.com* *Daily 11 am–midnight* *Jaume I* *J:13.*

$ VEGETARIAN **La Báscula.** On one of the Born area's most picturesque streets you'll find this cozy vegetarian café. Curiously, the building, the next over from the medieval mint (La Seca) at Carrer Flassaders 42, was the main candy factory in 19th- and early-20th-century Barcelona. Look up outside this artistic café and admire the sign still engraved into the concrete: "*Fábrica de dulces—caramelos–conservas–turrones–chocolates–grageas–peladillas*": the entire gamut of Barcelona bonbons. Sandwiches, cakes, pies, coffee, tea, and juices are served in this gracefully decorated, peaceful spot on the street behind Carrer Montcada and the Picasso Museum. *Average main: €8* *Carrer del Flassaders 30 bis, Born-Ribera* *93/319–9866* *No dinner Sun.* *Jaume I* *J:13.*

$$ CUBAN ✕ **La Habana Vieja.** If you have an itch for a taste of Old Havana—*ropa vieja* (shredded beef) or *moros y cristianos* (black beans and rice) with *mojitos* (a cocktail of rum, mint, and sugar), or a round of *plátanos a puñetazos* (punched plantains)—this is your Barcelona refuge. The upstairs tables overlooking the bar are cozy little crow's nests, and the neighborhood is filled with quirky dives and saloons for pre- and postdinner carousing. *Average main: €16 Banys Vells 2, Born-Ribera 93/268–2504 www.habanavieja.es No dinner Sun. Jaume I J:13.*

$ TAPAS FAMILY ✕ **Llamber.** Although it may look like one of the many stylish, tourist-trap tapas restaurants that have sprung up here in recent years, Llamber's culinary pedigree sets it apart from the competition. Chef Francisco Heras learned his chops in Spain's top restaurants before opening his own establishments in his home region of Asturias and then Llamber in Barcelona. Efficient and friendly, this dapper space attracts a mixed crowd of couples and families with its excellent wine list and well-crafted tapas based on classic Spanish and Catalan recipes. Consider the splendidly light eggplant with honey, and potatoes stuffed with *cabrales* cheese and hazelnut praline. Year-round late-night hours make it a handy option. *Average main: €11 Carrer de la Fusina 5, Born-Ribera 93/319–6250 www.llamberbarcelona.com Daily 12:30 pm–1:30 am Jaume 1 J:13.*

$ ASIAN FUSION ✕ **Mercat Princesa.** One street behind Carrer Montcada and the Picasso Museum, this little boutique, restaurant, and café is a unique space dedicated to design, crafts, books, and wine and food tastings. The ancient exposed-brick walls and cozy nooks in this lovely spot merit a visit. True to its name, the Princesa is laid out like a market, with different stalls offering a wide variety of market-fresh products and cuisines, including Japanese, Indonesian and Spanish. *Average main: €15 Flassaders 21, Born-Ribera 93/268–1518 www.mercatprincesa.com Mon.–Wed. and Sun. 9 am– midnight, Thur.–Sat. 9 am–12:30 am Jaume I J:13.*

$$ BASQUE ✕ **Sagardi.** An attractive wood-and-stone cider-house replica, Sagardi piles the counter with a dazzling variety of cold tapas; even better are the hot offerings straight from the kitchen. The restaurant in back serves Basque delicacies like veal sweetbreads with artichokes and *txuletas de buey* (beef steaks) grilled over coals. The other Sagardi branches at *Carrer Muntaner 70–72* and *Av. Diagonal 3* (in Diagonal Mar) are equally good. *Average main: €22 Carrer Argenteria 62, Born-Ribera 93/319–9993 www.sagardi.com Daily 1:30–3:30 and 8 to midnight Jaume I I:13.*

$ TAPAS ✕ **Taverna del Born.** Tapas and sandwiches are served at this terrace, bar, and restaurant overlooking the Born market and operating dawn until midnight. The tables outside manage to attract a pleasant breeze in summer and plenty of sunshine in winter, and the intersection is one of the Born area's liveliest. The slider-style minihamburgers are the pick of the fairly predictable menu, but the unexceptional food is trumped overall by the excellent location, which is ideal for watching the world go by. *Average main: €14 Passeig de Born 27–29, Born-Ribera 93/315–0964 www.tavernadelborn.es Daily 8 am–midnight Jaume I J:13.*

LA RAMBLA

$ CAFÉ ✕ **Café de l'Opera.** Directly across from the Liceu opera house, this high-ceilinged Art Nouveau–interior café has welcomed operagoers and performers for more than 100 years. It's a central point on the Rambla traffic pattern and a good place to run into unexpected friends and ex-lovers. But don't expect to fill up here, just catch a drink and take in the scene. *Average main: €7 La Rambla 74, Rambla 93/317–7585 www.cafeoperabcn.com Daily 8 am–2:30 am Liceu H:12.*

$ CAFÉ ✕ **Café Viena.** There are more than 40 Viena cafés in Catalonia, but this particular branch is always packed with international travelers trying what Mark Bittman of the *New York Times* once consecrated as "the best sandwich in the world." One wonders if it was the only one he'd ever eaten: the *flautas de jamón ibérico* (thin bread "flutes" of Ibérico ham anointed with tomato squeezings) here are perfectly adequate but no better than those served in any typical Spanish bar and, at €9, are considerably more expensive. Viena is a pleasant enough place to have a snack, especially when the pianist is playing on the balcony, but it doesn't live up to the hype. *Average main: €8 La Rambla 115, Rambla 93/317–1492 www.viena.es Daily 8 am–1:30 am Pl. de Catalunya H:11.*

$ CAFÉ ✕ **Café Zurich.** This traditional café at the top of La Rambla and directly astride the main metro and transport hub remains the city's prime meeting point. Prices are reasonable, considering the location, but the sandwiches and snacks could most charitably be described as ordinary. Forget the food and enjoy a beer or coffee at a table on the terrace, perhaps the best spot in the city to observe street life. Pickpockets are rife here, so watch your belongings as closely as you watch the passersby. *Average main: €5 Pl. de Catalunya 1, Rambla 93/317–9153 No credit cards Weekdays 8 am–11 pm, weekends 9 am–12 am Pl. de Catalunya H:11.*

$ CATALAN ✕ **Can Culleretes.** Just off La Rambla in the Barri Gòtic, this family-run restaurant founded in 1786 displays tradition in both decor and culinary offerings. Generations of the Manubens and Agut families have kept this unpretentious spot—Barcelona's oldest restaurant (listed in the *Guinness Book of Records*)—popular for more than two centuries. Wooden beams overhead and bright paintings of sea- and landscapes on the walls surround a jumble of tables. The cooking is solid rather than sophisticated, but traditional Catalan specialties such as spinach cannelloni with cod, wild boar stew, and white beans with botifarra sausage are competently presented. *Average main: €13 Calle Quintana 5, Rambla 93/317–3022 www.culleretes.com Closed Mon. and July. No dinner Sun. Liceu H:13.*

EL RAVAL

$$ TAPAS ✕ **Bar Cañete.** A superb tapas and *platillos* (small plates) emporium, this spot is just around the corner from the Liceu Opera House. The long bar overlooking the burners and part of the kitchen leads down to the 20-seat communal tasting table at the end of the room. Specialists in Ibérico products, you'll find obscure cuts of Ibérico pork served here, such as *pluma ibérica* and *secreto ibérico* (nuggets of meat found on the inside of the rib cage and much-prized by Ibérico fanatics). *Average main: €16 C/de la Unió 17, El Raval 93/270–3458 www.antiguobarorgia.com Closed Sun. Liceu G:13.*

$ CATALAN **Ca l'Estevet.** Journalists, students, and artists haunt this romantic little spot near the MACBA (contemporary art museum), across the street from Barcelona's journalism school, and around the block from the former offices of Barcelona's *La Vanguardia* daily newspaper. Estevet and family are charming, and the carefully elaborated Catalan cuisine sings, especially at these prices. Try the asparagus cooked over coals, the *chopitos gaditanos* (deep-fried baby octopus), or the *magret de pato* (duck breast). The house wine is inexpensive, light, and perfectly drinkable. *Average main: €14 Valldonzella 46, El Raval 93/302–4186 www.restaurantestevet.com No dinner Sun. Universitat G:11.*

$$$$ CATALAN Fodor's Choice ★ **Ca l'Isidre.** A throwback to an age before foams and food science took over the gastronomic world, this restaurant has elevated simplicity to the level of the spectacular since the early 1970s. Isidre and Montserrat share their encyclopedic knowledge of local cuisine with guests while their daughter, Núria, cooks traditional Catalan dishes to an extraordinarily high standard using fresh produce from the nearby Boqueria market. Ignore the menu—just follow their recommendations and order whatever's in season. The restaurant is decorated with original works by a slew of luminaries, including Miró and Dalí, both former patrons. Spain's King Juan Carlos celebrated his wedding anniversary here, and regular guests include politicians and visiting Hollywood celebrities. *Average main: €38 Les Flors 12, El Raval 93/441–1139 www.calisidre.com Reservations essential Closed Sun., Easter wk, and 1st 2 wks of Aug. Paral.lel F:13.*

$$$$ CATALAN Fodor's Choice ★ **Casa Leopoldo.** In a hard-to-find pocket of the Raval, west of the Rambla, this family-run restaurant serves fine seafood and Catalan fare. To get here, approach along Carrer Hospital, take a left through the Passatge Bernardí Martorell, and go 50 feet right on Sant Rafael to the front door. Try the *revuelto de ajos tiernos y gambas* (eggs scrambled with young garlic and shrimp) or the famous *cap-i-pota* (stewed head and hoof of pork). Albariños and Priorats are among owner Rosa Gil's favorite wines. The dining room, lined in blue-and-yellow tiles, has an appropriately Mediterranean feel. *Average main: €38 Sant Rafael 24, El Raval 93/441–3014 www.casaleopoldo.com Closed Mon. and late July–late Aug. No dinner Sun. Liceu G:12.*

$ SPANISH **Cera 23.** The pick of a crop of new restaurants putting the razzle back into the run-down Raval, Cera 23 offers a winning combination of great service and robust cooking in a fun, friendly setting. Stand at the bar and enjoy a blackberry mojito cocktail while you wait for your table. The open kitchen is in the dining area, so guests can watch the cooks creating contemporary presentations of traditional dishes. Try the Volcano of Black Rice, with seafood "rocks" and saffron-flavored "lava," and the homemade duck foie gras *mi-cuit* (cooked partly through). The reasonably priced restaurant is popular and usually packed until quite late, but the surrounding area can be intimidating at night; get a taxi to the end of the street. *Average main: €14 Carrer de la Cera 23, El Raval 93/442–0808 www.cera23.com No lunch Sant Antoni F:12.*

$$$ ECLECTIC **Dos Palillos.** After 10 years as the chief cook and favored disciple of the pioneering chef Ferran Adrià, Albert Raurich opened this Asian fusion restaurant with a Spanish-Mediterranean touch—and he's garnered a Michelin star for it. Past the typical Spanish bar in the front room, the

Café Zurich has been a popular meeting spot since the 1920s.

dining room inside is a canvas of rich black surfaces bordered with red chairs around the kitchen, where an international staff of Japanese, Chinese, Colombian, and Scottish cooks do cooking performances of Raurich's eclectic assortment of tastes and textures. Nippon burgers (beef, ginger, cucumber, and shiso on steamed bun), dumplings, dim sum, and tataki of 150-day-aged Galician beef vie for space on the €75 and €90 tasting menus. *Average main: €28* *Elisabets 9, Eixample* *93/304–0513* *www.dospalillos.com* *Reservations essential* *Closed Sun. and Mon. No lunch Tues. and Wed.* *Pl. de Catalunya, Universitat* *H:11.*

$$$ MEDITERRANEAN **El Cafetí.** Candlelit and romantic, this little hideaway at the end of the passageway in from Carrer Hospital is an intimate bistro with a menu encompassing various ingredients from foie gras to cod to game in season. Try the *ensalada tibia de queso de cabra* (warm goat-cheese salad) or the *solomillo de corzo al foie* (roebuck filet mignon with foie gras). *Average main: €24* *Hospital 99 (at end of Passatge Bernardí Martorell), El Raval* *93/329–2419* *www.elcafeti.com* *Closed Mon. and Aug. No dinner Sun.* *Liceu* *G:12.*

$$ BISTRO **En Ville.** With French-Mediterranean cuisine and reasonable prices, this attractive bistro 100 yards west of the Rambla in the MACBA section of the Raval is a keeper. The lunch menu for under €10 would be reason enough to try their *risotto de setas y esparragos trigueros* (wild mushroom risotto with wild asparagus), while à la carte choices are tempting and economical. Traditional marble tabletops, graceful lighting, and one country kitchen table for six or eight diners in the dining room add to the appeal. *Average main: €16* *Dr. Dou 14, El Raval* *93/302–8467* *www.envillebarcelona.es* *Reservations essential* *Closed Mon. No dinner Sun.* *Pl. de Catalunya, Liceu, Universitat* *H:11.*

$ TAPAS Fodor's Choice ★ **Quimet i Quimet.** A foodie haunt, this tiny place is hugely popular with locals and in-the-know visitors alike. If you come too late, you might not be able to get in. Come before 1:30 pm or 7:30 pm, and you will generally find a stand-up table. Fourth-generation chef-owner Quim and his family improvise ingenious canapés. All you have to do is orient them toward cheese, anchovies, or whatever it is you might crave, and they masterfully do the rest *and* recommend the wine to go with it. *Average main: €15 Poeta Cabanyes 25, Poble Sec 93/442–3142 Weekdays noon–4 and 7–10:30, Sat. noon–4 Closed Aug. Paral.lel E:13.*

$$$ TAPAS **Tickets & 41°.** Ferran Adrià of elBulli fame and his brother, Albert, opened these adjoining tapas and cocktail bars in early 2011 to much international fanfare and curiosity. Tickets offers contemporary tapas, which, coming from the creators of elBulli, means ice-cream cones of salmon eggs, egg yolk, soy sauce, and wasabi, or little plates with names such as Bloody Mary: crusty tomatoes with basil butter, virgin olive oil, caviar, and cheddar cheese cookies. Albert's new creations are lovely, but Ferran's old favorites from the now-closed elBulli are the main draws here. The cocktail bar, 41°, takes mixology and snacks just as seriously, with a €265 "experience" featuring 41 dishes and drinks for 16 lucky diners per night. Reservations for both venues are taken online only (not by phone), up to 60 days in advance. Check the calendar on the website for exact instructions. *Average main: €25 Av. Paral.lel 164, El Raval No phone en.bcn50.org Reservations essential Closed Mon. Poble Sec E:11.*

BARCELONETA AND THE PORT OLÍMPIC

Barceloneta and the Port Olímpic (Olympic Port) have little in common beyond their seaside location. Port Olímpic offers a somewhat massive-scaled and modern environment with a crazed disco strip, while Barceloneta has retained its traditional character as a blue-collar neighborhood, even if few fishermen now live here. Traditional family restaurants and tourist traps can look similar from the street; a telltale sign of unreliable establishments is the presence of hard-selling waiters outside, aggressively courting passing customers.

$$$ MEDITERRANEAN **Agua.** With views through gnarled and ancient olive trees over the beach into the Mediterranean, this sleek spot hidden "under the boardwalk" near Frank Gehry's gleaming goldfish may not be classical Barceloneta in decor or cuisine, but it's an exciting place to dine. Hit the terrace on warm summer nights and sunny winter days, or just catch rays inside the immense bay windows. Seafood is the main draw, but rice dishes, beef, and lamb are also equally available. Expect action, bustle, streamlined design surroundings, beautiful people, elevated prices, and good-if-not-spectacular fare at this very popular tourist favorite. Be sure to reserve in advance. *Average main: €26 Passeig Marítim de la Barceloneta 30 (Marina Village), Port Olímpic 93/225–1272 www.grupotragaluz.com/rest-agua.php Ciutadella/Vila Olímpica L:15.*

$$$ SEAFOOD **Barceloneta.** This restaurant, in an enormous riverboatlike building at the end of the yacht marina in Barceloneta, is definitely geared up for high-volume business. But the food is delicious, the service impeccable,

and the hundreds of fellow diners make the place feel like a cheerful New Year's Eve celebration. Rice and fish dishes are the house specialty, and the salads are excellent. *Average main: €24 L'Escar 22, Barceloneta 93/221–2111 www.restaurantbarceloneta.com Barceloneta I:15.*

$$$ SEAFOOD FAMILY **Can Majó.** One of Barcelona's best-known seafood restaurants lies at the edge of the beach in Barceloneta and specializes in such house favorites as *caldero de bogavante* (a cross between paella and lobster bouillabaisse) and *suquet* (fish stewed in its own juices), but the full range of typical Spanish rice and seafood dishes are also available. Can Majó doesn't consistently reach the standards that once made it famous, but the cooking is still a notch above most of the touristy haunts nearby. In summer, the terrace overlooking the Mediterranean is a pleasantly upscale version of the Barceloneta *chiringuitos* (shanty restaurants) that used to line the beach here. Even so, there's nothing "shanty" about the decor: a white-tablecloth experience with soft pendant lighting inside. *Average main: €26 Almirall Aixada 23, Barceloneta 93/221–5455 www.canmajo.es Closed Mon. No dinner Sun. Barceloneta J:15.*

$$$ SEAFOOD **Can Solé.** Just two blocks from Barceloneta's prettiest square, the charming Plaça de Sant Miquel, this traditional midday Sunday luncheon site occupies a typical waterfront house and serves fresh, well-prepared seafood. Whether it's *llenguado a la plancha* (grilled sole) or the exquisite *arròs negre amb sepia en su tinta* (black rice with squid in its ink), everything here comes loaded with taste. In winter try to get close to the open kitchen for the aromas, sights, sounds, and warmth. *Average main: €28 Sant Carles 4, Barceloneta 93/221–5012 www.restaurantcansole.com Closed Mon. and 2 wks of Aug. No dinner Sun. Barceloneta I:15.*

$$$ ECLECTIC **CDLC.** Carpe Diem Lounge Club is a combination restaurant, chill crash pad, and nightclub, with spectacular views over the beach and a continuously open kitchen from 1 pm until 1 am every day of the year. The cuisine is a hit-and-miss jumble of Asian fusion, with everything from the 120-piece sushi selection to Kobe beef from Japan to fiery Indian curry. *Average main: €26 Passeig Marítim del Port Olímpic 32, Barceloneta 93/224–0470 www.cdlcbarcelona.com Ciutadella/Vila Olímpica L:15.*

$ TAPAS Fodor's Choice ★ **El Vaso de Oro.** A favorite with gourmands from Barcelona and beyond, this often overcrowded little counter serves some of the best beer and tapas in town. The artisanal draught beer, specially brewed for this classic bar, is drawn and served with loving care, with just the right amount of foam and always at the correct temperature. The high rate of consumption ensures you will never encounter a stale keg. To eat, the *solomillo con foie y cebolla* (beef filet mignon with duck liver and onions) is an overwhelming favorite, but the fresh fish prepared *a la plancha* (on the grill) is also excellent. If you avoid peak local lunch and dinner hours (2–4 and 9–11) you will have better luck carving out a place to perch your food and drink. *Average main: €10 Balboa 6, Barceloneta 93/319–3098 www.vasodeoro.com Barceloneta J:14.*

3

$$$ SEAFOOD FAMILY

Els Pescadors. A kilometer northeast of Port Olímpic in the interesting Sant Martí neighborhood, this handsome late-19th-century bistro-style dining room has a lovely terrace on a little square shaded by immense ficus trees. Kids can play safely in the traffic-free square while their parents concentrate on well-prepared seafood specialties such as paella, fresh fish, or fideuá. *Average main: €26* *Pl. de Prim 1, Sant Martí* *93/225–2018* *www.elspescadors.com* *Poblenou* *L:15.*

LA BARCELONETA, LAND OF PAELLA

Paella is Valencian, not Catalan, but Sunday paella in La Barceloneta is a classic Barcelona family outing. *Paella marinera* is a seafood rice boiled in fish stock and seasoned with clams, mussels, prawns, and jumbo shrimp, while the more traditional paella valenciana omits seafood but includes chicken, rice, and snails. *Arròs negre* (black rice) is rice cooked in squid ink, and *arròs caldòs* is a soupier dish that often includes lobster. *Fideuá* is made with vermicelli noodles mixed with the standard ingredients. Paella is for a minimum of two diners—it's usually enough for three.

$$$$ CATALAN Fodor's Choice ★

Enoteca. Located in the Hotel Arts, Enoteca has established a reputation for creative and surprising cooking using peerless Mediterranean and Pyrenean products, from the finest wild-caught turbot to black trumpet wild mushrooms in season to spring lambs from Burgos. The gorgeous white-on-white dining room captures a fresh modern look. White rectangular shelving echoes the wall of windows that keeps things light. A 550-bottle wine list and the bottle theme in the decoration remind diners that this is, after all, an *enoteca* or wine library. *Average main: €40* *Hotel Arts, Marina 19, Port Olímpic* *93/483–8108* *www.hotelartsbarcelona.com* *Closed Sun.* *Ciutadella/Vila Olímpica* *L:15.*

$$ SEAFOOD FAMILY

Kaiku. You could easily pass by this undistinguished-looking little dining room on the edge of the beach at the end of Passeig Joan de Borbó. But seeking it out is worth your while; the seafood here is excellent and the value is ironclad. Rice dishes, mussels, sea anemones, fish soup are all hearty. Try the *arròs del xef,* a smoky rice with calamari, asparagus, and wild mushrooms. The wine list has some surprising choices at reasonable prices. *Average main: €16* *Pl. del Mar 1, Barceloneta* *93/221–9082* *www.restaurantkaiku.cat* *Reservations essential* *Closed Tues. No dinner mid-Sept.–mid-May* *Barceloneta* *I:16.*

$$ SEAFOOD Fodor's Choice ★

La Mar Salada. This restaurant stands out along a street of seafood specialists by offering creative twists on classic dishes at rock-bottom prices. Traditional favorites such as paella, black rice, fideuá, and simple fresh fish are invigorated by the cooking of Chef Marc Sengla—also consider the delicious creations of dessert chef Albert Enrich. The fixed-price lunch menu changes weekly and offers a budget-friendly way to try what's in season. Freshness is assured, as the main ingredients come directly from the *lonja* fish quay across the street, a lively auction where Barcelona's small fishing fleet sells its wares. You can't do much better for value and quality in Barceloneta. *Average main: €18* *Passeig Joan de Borbó 58, Barceloneta* *93/221–2127* *www.lamarsalada.cat* *Closed Tues.* *Barceloneta* *I:15.*

$$$$ MEDITERRANEAN **Torre d'Alta Mar.** Location, location, location: at a height of 250 feet over the Barcelona waterfront in the Eiffel-tower-like Sant Sebastià cable-car station over the far side of the port, this restaurant has spectacular 360-degree views of Barcelona as well as far out into the Mediterranean. Seafood of every stripe, spot, fin, and carapace emanates from the kitchen here, but the *mar i montanya* (sea and mountain) combination of pork and prawns adds a meaty twist for carnivores. *Average main: €33 Torre de San Sebastián, Passeig Joan de Borbó 88, Barceloneta 93/221–0007 www.torredealtamar.com Reservations essential Closed Mon. No lunch Sun. Barceloneta H:16.*

EIXAMPLE

The sprawling blocks of the Eixample contain Barcelona's finest selection of restaurants, from upscale and elegant traditional cuisine in Moderniste houses to high-concept fare in sleek minimalist-experimental spaces. Many chefs with experience in multistar kitchens have started their own businesses here, leading to the so-called "bistronomic" movement of tiny restaurants offering limited menus of humble ingredients cooked to exacting standards. These stellar experiences at budget prices are as close as you can still get to a bargain in Barcelona.

$$$$ CATALAN **Alkimia.** Chef Jordi Vilà is making news here with his inventive creations and tasting menus at €68 and €94 that still manage to pass for a bargain at the top end of Barcelona culinary culture even in this current economy. The €39 price tag on the midday menu is daunting, but well worth the outlay. The place is usually packed, but the white-on-white graphic decor, reminiscent of a Mondrian canvas, provides a sense of space. Vilà's deconstructed pa amb tomaquet served in a shot glass is just a culinary wink before things get deadly serious with raw tuna strips, baby squid, or turbot. A dark-meat course, venison or beef, brings the taste progression to a close before dessert provides a sweet ending. Alkimia, as its name suggests, is pure magic—alas, it's open only on weekdays. *Average main: €30 Indústria 79, Eixample 93/207–6115 www.alkimia.cat Reservations essential Closed weekends Sagrada Família, Joanic L:7.*

$$$ CATALAN **Bar Mut.** Just above Diagonal, this elegant retro space serves first-rate products ranging from wild sea bass to the best Ibérico hams. Crowded, noisy, chaotic, delicious: it's everything a great tapas bar or restaurant should be. The name is a play on the word *vermut* (vermouth), which, not so long ago, was about as close to tapas as Barcelona was apt to get. The wine selections and range of dishes proposed on the chalkboard behind the bar are creative and traditional. Don't let the friendly and casual feel of the place lull you into thinking that *la cuenta* (the check) will be anything but sobering. *Average main: €26 Pau Claris 192, Eixample 93/217–4338 www.barmut.com Diagonal I:8.*

$ CAFÉ **Bar París.** Always a popular place to hang out and watch barcelonins kill some time, this lively café has hosted everyone from Prince Felipe, heir to the Spanish throne, to poet and pundit James Townsend Pi Sunyer. Prices are on the high side, but the tapas are decent, the beer is fresh and cold, and this old-fashioned *bar de toda la vida* (everyday bar) with its long counter and jumble of tables is open 365 days a year. *Average main: €8 Carrer Paris 187, Eixample 93/209–8530 Weekdays 7 am–2 am, weekends 10 am–3 am Diagonal G:7.*

$$$ MEDITERRANEAN **Boca Grande.** Bursting onto the Barcelona restaurant scene with ebullience and panache, this three-floor design triumph by Spain's hottest interior decorator Lázaro Rosa Violán has captured the city's imagination from day one. Abandoning the post-Modernisme minimalism that has dominated Barcelona for the last decades, Boca Grande is a baroque celebration of colonial and safari chic from the second floor bar, Bocachica, with its enormous elephant tusks behind the counter, to the spectacular unisex restrooms downstairs. *Average main: €28 Passatge de la Concepció 12, Eixample 93/467–5149 www.bocagrande.cat Diagonal I:8.*

$$$ CATALAN **Caldeni.** This clean, simple place par excellence is the perfect antidote to the sensory overload of Gaudí's nearby Sagrada Familia. A past winner of the Chef of the Year award in the annual Fòrum Gastronòmic de Girona, Dani Lechuga produces streamlined cuisine that is invariably long on taste and short on cost, especially if you take advantage of the bargain lunch prix-fixe menu. A specialist in beef of all kinds (Wagyu, Kobe, Angus, Girona, Asturian oxen), Caldeni also does tapas, soups, and an assortment of tastings, making any stop here a gastronomical event. *Average main: €26 València 452, Eixample 93/232–5811 www.caldeni.com Closed Sun., Mon., and 3 wks in Aug. Sagrada Familia M:9.*

$$$ MEDITERRANEAN **Casa Calvet.** It's hard to pass up the opportunity to break bread in a Gaudí-designed building. Completed in 1900, the Art Nouveau Casa Calvet includes a graceful dining room decorated in Moderniste ornamentation, from looping parabolic door handles to polychrome stained glass, etched glass, and wood carved in floral and organic motifs. Popular with local business people who want to entertain guests in style, the restaurant exudes velvet-and-mahogany charm and also attracts couples seeking an intimate meal for two. Chef Miguel Ajita's Catalan and Mediterranean fare is light and contemporary, seasonal and market-inspired. *Average main: €28 Casp 48, Eixample 93/412–4012 www.casacalvet.es Closed Sun. Urquinaona J:11.*

$$$ TAPAS **Casa Lucio.** With preserved and fresh ingredients and original dishes flowing from the kitchen, this tiny but handsome (though not inexpensive) dazzler two blocks south of the Mercat de Sant Antoni is well worth tracking down. Lucio's wife, chef Maribel, is relentlessly inventive. Try the *tastum albarole* (cured sheep cheese from Umbria) or the *pochas negras con morcilla* (black beans with black sausage). *Average main: €24 Viladomat 59, Eixample 93/424–4401 Mon.–Sat. 1–4 and 8–11 Sant Antoni E:11.*

$$ TAPAS **Cerveseria la Catalana.** A bright and booming bar with a few tables on the sidewalk, this spot is always packed for a reason: excellent food at fair prices. Try the small *solomillos* (filet mignons), minimorsels that will take the edge off your carnivorous appetite without undue damage to your wallet, or the jumbo shrimp brochettes. *Average main: €15 Mallorca 236, Eixample 93/216–0368 Diagonal, Passeig de Gracia H:8.*

Casa Calvet restaurant offers the chance to dine inside a Moderniste masterpiece.

$$$$ CATALAN Fodor's Choice ★ **Cinc Sentits.** The engaging Artal clan—led by master chef Jordi—is a Catalan-Canadian family offering something unique in Barcelona: cutting-edge, contemporary cooking explained eloquently in English. There's no à la carte option, only tasting menus: *Essències* is the simplest and *Sensacions* is more creative, while the lunchtime-only *Gastronomic* is top-of-the-line, foodie nirvana. The wine pairings, like the food, are obsessively local and scrupulously selected. Expect to spend from €59 to a budget-busting €109, not including drinks, depending on the menu. It's worth going all out for a sensational experience in a restaurant that lives up to its name. *Average main: €36* *Aribau 58, Eixample* *93/323–9490* *cincsentits.com* *Reservations essential* *Closed Sun. and Mon.* *Provença* *G:9.*

$$ TAPAS **Ciudad Condal.** At the bottom of Ramba de Catalunya, this scaled-up tapas bar draws a throng of mostly international clients and has tables outside on the sidewalk virtually year-round. The *solomillo* (miniature beef filet) is a winner here, as is the *brocheta d'escamarlans* (brochette of jumbo shrimp). A good late-night or postconcert solution, there is usually room to squeeze in at the long wooden bar, though table reservations provide more comfort and space. *Average main: €20* *Rambla de Catalunya 18, Eixample* *93/318–1997* *Daily 7:30 am–1:30 am* *Passeig de Gràcia, Catalunya* *H:10.*

$$ TAPAS **Cornelia and Co.** A sort of Catalan Dean & Deluca—part deli, part bakery, part restaurant, part tapas bar—Cornelia and Co. is all the rage in Barcelona. The staff, all charismatic and smart, seems to be having such a good time that it's contagious. Prices are rock bottom and the variety of morsels, passed around on small plates and tasted, is endless. There's nothing not to love here—from steak tartare to salmon

sashimi to foie gras with fried eggs to artichokes in tempura. $ *Average main: €18 ✉ Carrer Valencia 225, Eixample ☎ 93/272–3956 🌐 www.corneliaandco.com ⏲ Daily noon–1 am M Passeig de Gràcia ⊕ H:9.*

$$$$ MEDITERRANEAN ✕ **Dos Cielos.** Twins Javier and Sergio Torres have leaped to the top of Barcelona's culinary charts as well as to the top tower of the Hotel ME. It only seems fitting that their restaurant be named Dos Cielos, *cielo* being Spanish for heaven. A panoramic dining room around a vast open kitchen offers dazzling 360-degree views of the city. The cuisine, combining Brazilian, French, and Valencian touches reflecting the twins' accumulated culinary experiences around the world, is no less brilliant: pasta with black olives and sun-dried tomatoes, steamed organic vegetables, and *crema de mandioquinha con caviar de sagú* (cream of Brazilian white carrot with pearls of sago palm). $ *Average main: €42 ✉ Pere IV 272–286, Eixample ☎ 93/367–2070 🌐 www.doscielos.com ✍ Reservations essential ⏲ Closed Sun. and Mon. M Poble Nou ⊕ L:12.*

$$ CATALAN Fodor's Choice ★ ✕ **Embat.** An embat is a puff of wind in Catalan, and this little "bistronomic" is a breath of fresh air in the swashbuckling Eixample. The highly affordable market cuisine is always impeccably fresh and freshly conceived, starring thoughtful combinations such as the *cazuelita de alcachofas con huevo poché y papada* (casserole of artichokes and poached egg with pork dewlap) or the *pichón con bizcocho de cacao y cebolla confitada* (wood pigeon with cacao biscuit and onion confit). The dining room is minimally decorated with off-white tiles and wooden tables matching the classic cuisine. $ *Average main: €18 ✉ Mallorca 304, Eixample ☎ 93/458–0885 🌐 www.restaurantembat.es ✍ Reservations essential ⏲ Closed Sun. and Mon. No dinner Tues. and Wed. M Verdaguer ⊕ J:8.*

$$ CATALAN ✕ **Restaurant Gaig.** A rustic interpretation of the traditional cuisine that has made the Gaig family culinary stars, this cozy split-level restaurant has made a name for itself in Barcelona's ever-changing dining scene. As passions cooled for molecular gastronomy, Carles Gaig and a growing number of top chefs have returned to simpler and more affordable models. Look for standards such as *botifarra amb mongetes de ganxet* (sausage with white beans) or *perdiu amb vinagreta calenta* (partridge withe warm vinagrette) or *tartar de llobarro i gamba* (sea bass and shrimp tartare). The ample dining room is, in contrast to the cuisine, stylishly contemporary, with comfortable armchairs à table. $ *Average main: €18 ✉ Còrsega 200, Eixample ☎ 93/453–2020, 93/429–1017 🌐 www.restaurantgaig.com ✍ Reservations essential ⏲ Closed Mon. and 2 wks in Aug. No dinner Sun. M Hospital Clínic ⊕ G:9.*

$$$ CATALAN Fodor's Choice ★ ✕ **Gelonch.** This gem of a restaurant is something of a secret sensation in Barcelona. Listed in few guides, it caters mainly to clued-in locals who have fallen in love with chef-owner Robert Gelonch's relentless creativity and pursuit of perfection. It's worth making the effort to join them—the restaurant is off the beaten tourist track but still near the center of the neighborhood. Once there, depending on how hungry you are, expect to be astonished by a procession of small dishes from the short (€56) or long (€74) tasting menu. If you just want to dip your toe in the water, choose individual dishes from the "Moments of Madness" list. Some you will love, others you may not, but it is impossible to

CLOSE UP

Dining with Children?

Barceloneta's beachfront paella specialists are great favorites for Sunday lunches, with children free to get up and run, skate, cycle, or generally race up and down the boardwalk while their parents linger over brandies and coffee. **Els Pescadors** (✉ *Pl. de Prim 1, Port Olímpic* ☎ *93/225–2018* ⊙ *Closed Mon.* Ⓜ *Poblenou*), a seafood restaurant, has a lovely terrace opening onto a little square that is handy for children letting off steam.

The miniature scale and finger-food aspect of tapas usually appeals, and children will happily munch on a variety of commonly found dishes, including croquettes, cured meats, toasted almonds, and fried squid rings.

Every café, bar, and terrace in town can whip up sandwiches on the go, served on fresh bread—an inexpensive and respectable snack—or the Catalan staple pa amb tomaquet. And for dessert, Barcelona's ubiquitous ice-cream parlors and vendors are another favorite. Try **Cremeria Toscana** (✉ *Carrer Muntaner 161 or Carrer Princesa 26*) for some of the city's best *gelat*.

3

remain unmoved by the inventiveness and sheer talent on display here. Ⓢ *Average main: €25* ✉ *Bailen 56, Eixample* ☎ *93/265–8298* 🌐 *www.gelonch.es* ✍ *Reservations essential* ⊙ *Closed Sun., Mon., and last wk in Aug.–1st wk in Sept. No lunch* Ⓜ *Tetuan, Girona* ✣ *K:10.*

$$ BASQUE ✕ **Gorría.** Named for founder Fermín Gorría, this is quite simply the best straightforward Basque-Navarran cooking in Barcelona. Everything from the stewed *pochas* (white beans) to the heroic *chuletón* (steak) is as clear and pure in flavor as the Navarran Pyrenees. The Castillo de Sajazarra reserva, a semisecret brick-red Rioja, provides the perfect accompaniment. Ⓢ *Average main: €22* ✉ *Diputació 421, Eixample* ☎ *93/245–1164* 🌐 *www.restaurantegorria.com* ⊙ *Closed Sun., Easter wk, and Aug. No dinner Mon.* Ⓜ *Monumental* ✣ *L:10.*

$$ CATALAN Fodor's Choice ★ ✕ **Gresca.** Figurehead of the so-called "bistronomic" movement in Barcelona, head chef and owner Rafa Peña aims to put the creativity and skill he learned in the world's most celebrated kitchens within the reach of those on less astronomical budgets. In his small, minimalist restaurant, he cranks out inventive dishes based on humble ingredients to a fervently loyal customer base of local foodies. Expect limited choice, a well-chosen but shallow wine list, and some of the most delightful dishes you can find in Barcelona. The tasting menu is the best way to sample what's on offer—forget about choosing and just sit back and enjoy the ride. Ⓢ *Average main: €20* ✉ *Provença 230, Eixample* ☎ *93/451–6193* 🌐 *www.gresca.net* ✍ *Reservations essential* ⊙ *Closed Sun. and last wk in Aug.–1st wk in Sept. No lunch Sat.* Ⓜ *Diagonal* ✣ *H:8.*

$$$$ MEDITERRANEAN ✕ **Jaume de Provença.** Chef Jaume Bargués is beloved by Barcelona haute-cuisine fans. His no-frills, straight-up, fine Catalan cuisine dining repertoire was thriving before and during the molecular cuisine craze and shows every sign of continuing to do so as it all winds down. Winning dishes include *lenguado relleno de setas* (sole stuffed with mushrooms) and the *lubina* (sea bass) soufflé. The traditionally designed restaurant,

pine-paneled and complete with a bar and a spacious-yet-intimate dining room, is in the Hospital Clinic part of the Eixample. *Average main: €32 Provença 88, Eixample 93/430–0029 www.jaumeprovenza.com Reservations essential Closed Mon., Aug., Easter wk, and Dec. 25 and 26. No dinner Sun. M Entença F:8.*

$ TAPAS **La Flauta.** The name of this boisterous restaurant refers to the staple flutelike loaves of slipper bread used for sandwiches here. There are also infinite numbers of tapas and small portions of everything from wild mushrooms in season to wild asparagus or *xipirones* (baby cuttlefish) served in this vast counter space flanked with dozens of tables. Try a *sobrassada flauta* (a thin sandwich with pork paste made with paprika from Majorca). Although the food is decent, service can be brusque bordering on rude—perhaps a result of the sheer number of customers. A second branch, widely considered to be superior, is at Carrer Aribau 23. *Average main: €12 Carrer Balmes 171, Eixample 93/415–5186 Mon.–Sat. 1–4 and 8–midnight Closed Sun. and Aug. M Diagonal G:10.*

$ BAKERY Fodor's Choice ★ **La Pastisseria Barcelona.** This stylish pastisseria looks more like a high-class jewelry store than a simple bakery. Rows of world-class cakes and pastries gleam temptingly in glass cases, ready to be taken away or enjoyed in-store with coffee or a glass of Cava. Owner Josep Rodríguez learned his craft in Michelin-starred kitchens before winning the 2011 world pastry chef of the year award for his *rosa dels vents* (rose of the winds) cake—the lofty standard is maintained here. Everything is made by hand with ingredients of the finest quality, but prices are reasonable, making extra helpings irresistible. It's open daily from morning till early afternoon and, except on Sunday, again in the early evenings. *Average main: €10 Aragó 228, Eixample 93/451–8401 www.lapastisseriabarcelona.com M Passeig de Gracia H:9.*

$$$ TAPAS Fodor's Choice ★ **La Taverna Del Clinic.** The Simoes brothers have earned a solid reputation with discerning locals for serving creative and contemporary tapas based on traditional Catalan and Galician flavors. Chef Antonio left his family's restaurant to study under masters, including the late Santi Santamaria, before launching La Taverna with his brother, Manuel, a sommelier. Their cramped bar spills out onto a sunny street terrace where customers can enjoy truffle canelones, oyster tartare, and an award-winning variation on patatas bravas, paired with selections from the excellent wine list. A recent expansion has added extra tables, thereby reducing the wait for a seat. *Average main: €25 Carrer Roselló 155, Eixample www.latavernadelclinic.com Closed Sun. M Hospital Clinic G:8.*

$ CAFÉ **Laie Pau Claris.** Much than a mere bookstore, the café and restaurant here serves dinner until 1 am. Readings, concerts, and book presentations round out an ample program of events. The Laie group also runs pleasant cafés and restaurants at the iconic, Gaudi-designed Pedrera and the MNAC National Catalan Museum of Art *Average main: €14 Pau Claris 85, Eixample 93/302–7310 www.laierestaurants.es/pau_claris Weekdays 9–9, Sat. 10–9 Closed Sun. M Passeig de Gracia I:10.*

$$$$ BASQUE **Lasarte.** Martin Berasategui, one of San Sebastián's fleet of master chefs, opened his Barcelona restaurant in early 2006 and triumphed from day one. Berasategui has placed his kitchen in the capable hands of Alex Garés, who trained with the best and serves an eclectic selection of Basque, Mediterranean, market, and personal interpretations and creations. Expect whimsical aperitifs and dishes with serious flavor such as foie and smoked eel or simple wood pigeon cooked to perfection. For a lighter, more economical Berasategui-directed experience, try Loidi restaurant, across the street in the Hotel Condes de Barcelona annex. *Average main: €40 Mallorca 259, Eixample 93/445–3242 www.restaurantlasarte.com Reservations essential Jacket required Closed Sun., Mon., and 2 wks in Aug. M Diagonal I:8.*

3

$$$ CATALAN **L'Olivé.** Streamlined but traditional Catalan cooking means this busy and attractive spot is always packed with clued-in diners having a great time. The crowd may be boisterous, but the dining room is seriously elegant, with crisp white tablecloths, leather chairs, and a loftlike wall of windows. Excellent hearty food, smart service, and some of the best pa amb tomaquet in town leaves you wanting to squeeze in, too. *Average main: €28 Balmes 47, Eixample 93/452–1990 www.restaurantlolive.com Reservations essential No dinner Sun. M Universitat, Passeig de Gracia H:9.*

$$ CATALAN Fodor's Choice ★ **Manairó.** A *manairó* is a mysterious Pyrenean elf and Jordi Herrera may be the culinary version. A demon with meat cooked *al clavo ardiente* (à la burning nail)—fillets warmed from within by red-hot spikes producing meat both rare and warm and never undercooked—Jordi also serves an unforgettable version of squid with blowtorch-fried eggs (*calamari de huevo frito*) and a palate-cleansing gin and tonic with liquid nitrogen, gin, and lime. The intimate and edgy design of the dining room is a perfect reflection of the cuisine. *Average main: €20 Diputació 424, Eixample 93/231–0057 www.manairo.com Reservations essential Closed Sun. and 1st wk of Jan. M Sagrada Familia M:10.*

$$ TAPAS **Mantequeria Can Ravell.** Lovers of exquisite wines, hams, cheeses, oils, whiskies, cigars, caviars, baby eels, anchovies, and any other delicacy you can think of—this is your spot. The backroom table open from mid-morning to early evening is first come, first served; complete strangers share tales, tastes, and textures at this foodie forum. The upstairs dining room serving lunch (and dinners Thursday and Friday), through the kitchen and up a spiral staircase, has a clandestine, *Through the Looking-Glass* vibe. *Average main: €15 Carrer Aragó 313, Eixample 93/457–5114 www.ravell.com Tues.–Sat. 10–9, Sun. 10–3 Closed Mon. M Girona J:9.*

$$$$ CATALAN **Moments.** Inside the ultrasleek and contemporary Hotel Mandarin Oriental Barcelona, this restaurant continues the glamour with mod white chairs and glinting goldleaf on the ceiling. The cuisine, directed by Raül Balam, son of Carme Ruscalleda of the Sant Pau restaurant, lives up to its pedigree. Peerless raw materials used in original preparations add up to superior dining, with signature dishes such as the *arròs caldos* (a soupy rice dish) or the *pichón deshuesado* (boneless squab)

at the forefront of the traditional yet innovative offerings. The Blanc Brasserie and Gastrobar in the same hotel is also worth checking out if you're seeking something simpler—and less expensive. *Average main: €48 ✉ Passeig de Gràcia 38–40, Eixample ☎ 93/151–8888 ⊕ www.mandarinoriental.com/barcelona ✍ Reservations essential ⊙ Closed Sun., Mon., and Aug. Ⓜ Passeig de Gràcia ✣ I:10.*

$ TAPAS **Paco Meralgo.** The name, a pun on *para comer algo* ("to eat something" with an Andalusian accent), may be only marginally amusing, but the tapas here are no joke at all, from the classical *calamares fritos* (fried cuttlefish rings) to the *pimientos de Padrón* (green peppers, some fiery, from the Galician town of Padrón.) Whether à table, at the counter, or in the private dining room upstairs, this modern space always rocks. *Average main: €12 ✉ Carrer Muntaner 171, Eixample ☎ 93/430–9027 ⊕ www.pacomeralgo.com ⊙ Mon.–Sat. 1–4 and 8–12:30 ⊙ Closed Sun. Ⓜ Hospital Clinic ✣ G:7.*

$ TAPAS **Piratas.** Named for Roman Polanski's film of the same name, this extraordinary little spot just a block away from the Auditori de Barcelona is an excellent choice for a pre- or post-concert taste of chef Luis Ortega's improvisational cuisine, all prepared behind the bar. Cheeses, hams, potatoes, foies, caviars, olives, anchovies, and tuna, as well as carefully selected wines and cavas, flow freely here. Space is limited, so reservations are essential. *Average main: €14 ✉ Carrer Ausiàs Marc 157, Eixample ☎ 93/245–7642 ⊕ www.piratasbarcelona.com ✍ Reservations essential ⊙ Weekdays 1–midnight. Closed Aug. Ⓜ Marina ✣ L:11.*

$$$ CATALAN Fodor's Choice ★ **Roca Moo.** In any space as spectacular as Roca Moo, located in the Hotel Omm, there's a real risk of the food playing second fiddle to the surroundings. Fortunately, head chef Felip Llufriu keeps the spotlight firmly on the menu designed by the world-renowned El Cellar de Can Roca team. From behind the counter of an open kitchen he cooks with a Zenlike precision that suits the restaurant's Tokyo vibe. The dishes, like the space, are stylish and creative but draw on deep wells of Spanish culinary traditions, elevating humble barroom snacks like Russian salad and pig-trotter carpaccio with prawns to dazzling heights. The Menu Joan Roca is the chef's favorite, a tour-de-force balancing act of gutsy flavors and contemporary techniques matched with impressive wine selections. *Average main: €28 ✉ Roselló 265, Eixample ☎ 93/445–4000 ⊕ www.hotelomm.es/en/roca-moo ⊙ Closed Sun., Mon., and Jan. 6–15 Ⓜ Diagonal ✣ I:8.*

$$ MEDITERRANEAN **Sense Pressa.** *Sense pressa* means "without hurry" or "no rush" in Catalan, and if you can score one of the coveted half-dozen tables here at the corner of Carrer Còrsega, you will want to linger as long as possible to enjoy this miniscule winner. *Risotto de ceps* (wild mushroom risotto), *garbanzos con espardenyas y huevos fritos* (chickpeas with sea cucumbers and fried eggs), or filet mignon of grass-fed Girona beef cooked to perfection are all good choices. A wall of racked winebottles dominates the rustic decor, perfectly appropriate for this intimate spot. *Average main: €22 ✉ Enric Granados 96, Eixample ☎ 93/218–1544 ⊕ sensepressarestaurant.com ✍ Reservations essential ⊙ Closed Sun. and 2 wks in Aug. No dinner Mon. Ⓜ Diagonal ✣ G:8.*

Continued on page 172

Vineyard in Rioja.

THE WINES OF SPAIN

After years of being in the shadows of other European wines, Spanish wines are finally gunning for the spotlight—and what has taken place is nothing short of a revolution. The wines of Spain, like its cuisine, are currently experiencing a firecracker explosion of both quality and variety that has brought a new level of interest, awareness, and recognition throughout the world, propelling them to superstar status. A generation of young, ambitious winemakers has jolted dormant areas awake, rediscovered long-forgotten local grapes, and introduced top international varieties. Even the most established regions have undergone makeovers in order to keep up with these dramatic changes and to compete in the global market.

THE ROAD TO GREAT WINE

Frank Gehry designed the visitor center for the Marqués de Riscal winery in Rioja.

Spain has a long wine history dating back to the time when the Phoenicians introduced viticulture, over 3,000 years ago. Some of the country's wines achieved fame in Roman times, and the Visigoths enacted early wine laws. But in the regions under Muslim rule, winemaking slowed down for centuries. Starting in the 16th century, wine trade expanded along with the Spanish Empire, and by the 18th and 19th centuries the Sherry region *bodegas* (wineries) were already established.

In the middle of the 19th century, seeds of change blossomed throughout the Spanish wine industry. In 1846, the estate that was to become Vega Sicilia, Spain's most revered winery, was set up in Castile. Three years later the famous Tío Pepe brand was established to produce the excellent dry fino wines. Marqués de Murrieta and the Marqués de Riscal wineries opened in the 1860s creating the modern Rioja region and clearing the way for many centenary wineries. *Cava*—Spain's white or pink sparkling wine—was created the following decade in Catalonia.

After this flurry of activity, Spanish wines languished for almost a century. Vines were hit hard by phylloxera, and then a civil war and a long dictatorship left the country stagnant and isolated. Just 30 short years ago, Spain's wines were split between the same dominant trio of Sherry, Rioja, and cava, and loads of cheap, watered-down wines made by local cooperatives with little gumption to improve and even less expertise.

Starting in the 1970s, however, a wave of innovation crashed through Rioja and emergent regions like Ribera del Duero and Penedés. In the 1990s, it turned into a revolution that spread all over the landscape—and is still going strong. Today, Spain is the third-largest wine producer in the world and the largest in terms of land area. Europe's debt crisis means domestic wine consumption is down and vintners are doubling their effort to appeal to export markets.

SPANISH WINE CATEGORIES BY AGE

A unique feature of Spanish wines is their indication of aging process on wine labels. DO wines (see "A *Vino* Primer" on following page) show this on mandatory back panels. Aging requirements are longer for reds, but also apply to white, rosé, and sparkling wines. For reds, the rules are as follows:

Vino Joven

A young wine that may or may not have spent some time aging in oak barrels before it was bottled. Some winemakers have begun to shun traditional regulations to produce cutting-edge wines in this category. An elevated price distinguishes the ambitious new reds from the easy-drinking *jóvenes.*

Crianza

A wine aged for at least 24 months, six of which are in barrels (12 in Rioja, Ribera del Duero, and Navarra). A great bargain in top vintages from the most reliable wineries and regions.

Reserva

A wine aged for a minimum of 36 months, at least 12 of which are in oak.

Gran Reserva

Traditionally the top of the Spanish wine hierarchy, and the pride of the historic Rioja wineries. A red wine aged for at least 24 months in oak, followed by 36 months in the bottle before release.

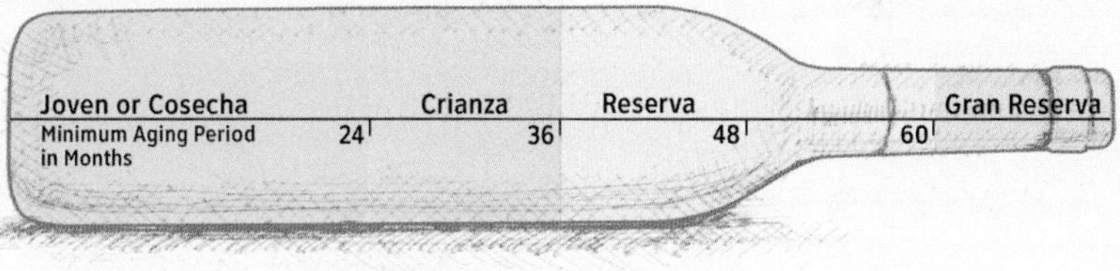

READING LABELS LIKE A PRO

A *VINO* PRIMER

Spain offers a daunting assortment of wine styles, regions, and varietals. But don't worry: a few pointers will help you understand unfamiliar names and terms. Most of Spain's quality wines come from designated regions called *Denominaciones de Origen* (Appellations of Origin), often abbreviated as DO. Spain has more than 60 of these areas, which are tightly regulated to protect the integrity and characteristics of the wines produced there. Beyond international varieties like Cabernet Sauvignon and Chardonnay, the country is home to several high-quality varietals, both indigenous and imported. Reds include Tempranillo, an early-ripening grape that blends and ages well, and Garnacha (the Spanish name for France's Grenache), a spicy, full-bodied red wine. The most popular white wines are the light, aromatic Albariño or Ruedas, and the full-bodied Verdejo.

Rioja wines

❶ The green and more humid areas of the Northwest deliver crisp, floral white albariños in Galicia's **Rías Biaxas.** In the **Bierzo** DO, the Mencía grape distills the essence of the schist slopes, where it grows into minerally infused red wines.

❷ Moving east, in the iron-rich riverbanks of the Duero, Tempranillo grapes, here called "Tinto Fino," produce complex and age-worthy **Ribera del Duero** reds and hefty **Toro** wines. Close by, the **Rueda** DO adds aromatic and grassy whites from local Verdejo and adopted Sauvignon Blanc.

❸ The **Rioja** region is a winemaker's paradise. Here a mild, nearly perfect vine-growing climate marries limestone and clay soils with Tempranillo, Spain's most noble grape, to deliver wines that possess the two main features of every great region: personality and quality. Tempranillo-based Riojas evolve from a young cherry color and aromas of strawberries and red fruits, to a brick hue, infused with scents of tobacco and leather. Whether medium or full-bodied, tannic or velvety, these reds are some of the most versatile and food-friendly wines, and have set the standard for the country for over a century.

Nearby, **Navarra** and three small DO's in Aragón deliver great wines made with the local Garnacha, Tempranillo, and international grape varieties.

❹ Southwest of Barcelona is the region of **Catalonia,** which encompasses the areas of Penedès and Priorat. Catalonia is best known as the heartland of *cava,*

Chardonnay vines in Navarra.

the typically dry, sparkling wine made from three indigenous Spanish varietals: Parellada, Xarel-lo, and Macabeo. The climatically varied Penedès—just an hour south of Barcelona—produces full-bodied reds like Garnacha on coastal plains, and cool-climate varietals like Riesling and Sauvignon Blanc in the mountains. Priorat is a region that has emerged into the international spotlight during the past decade, as innovative winemakers have transformed winemaking practices there. Now, traditional grapes like Garnacha and Cariñena are blended with Cabernet Sauvignon and Syrah to produce rich, concentrated reds with powerful tannins.

5 The region of **Valencia** is south of Catalonia on the Mediterranean coast. The wines of this area have improved markedly in recent years, with red wines from Jumilla and other appellations finding their way onto the international market. Tempranillo and Monastrell (France's Mourvèdre) are the most common reds. A local specialty of the area is Moscatel de Valencia, a highly aromatic sweet white wine.

6 In the **central plateau south of Madrid,** rapid investment, modernization, and replanting is resulting in medium bodied, easy drinking, and fairly priced wines made with Tempranillo (here called

Grapes harvested for Sherry

"Cencíbel"), Cabernet, Syrah, and even Petit Verdot, that are opening the doors to more ambitious endeavors.

7 In sun-drenched Andalusia, where the white albariza limestone soils reflect the powerful sunlight while trapping the scant humidity, the fortified **Jerez** (Sherry) and **Montilla** emerge. In all their different incarnations, from dry finos, Manzanillas, amontillados, palo cortados, and olorosos, to sweet creams and Pedro Ximénez, they are the most original wines of Spain.

JUST OFF THE VINE: NEW WINE DEVELOPMENTS

Beyond Tempranillo: The current wine revolution has recovered many native varieties. Albariño, Godello, and Verdejo among the whites, and Callet, Cariñena, Garnacha, Graciano, Mandó, Manto Negro, Mencía, and Monastrell among the reds, are gaining momentum and will likely become more recognized.

Cult Wines: For most of the past century, Vega Sicilia Unico was the only true cult wine from Spain. The current explosion has greatly expanded the roster: L'Ermita, Pingus, Clos Erasmus, Artadi, Cirsion, Terreus, and Termanthia are the leading names in a list that grows every year.

Vinos de Pagos: *Pago*, a word meaning plot or vineyard, is the new legal term chosen to create Spain's equivalent of a *Grand Cru* hierarchy, by protecting quality oriented wine producers that make wine from their own estates.

V.O.S. and V.O.R.S: Sherry's most dramatic change in over a century is the creation of the "Very Old Sherry" designation for wines over 20 years of age, and the addition of "Rare" for those over 30, to easier distinguish the best, oldest, and most complex wines.

Petit Verdot: Winemakers in Spain are discovering that Petit Verdot, the "little green" grape of Bordeaux, ripens much easier in warmer climates than in its birthplace. This is contributing to the rise of Petit Verdot in red blends, and even to the production of single varietal wines.

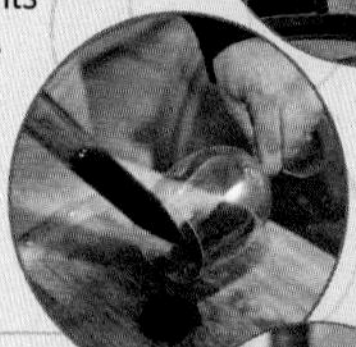

Innovative New Blends: A few wine regions have strict regulations concerning the varieties used in their wines, but most allow for experimentation. All over the country, *bodegas* are crafting wines with creative blends that involve local varieties, Tempranillo, and famous international grapes.

Andalusia's New Wines: For centuries, scorching southern Andalusia has offered world-class Sherry and Montilla wines. Now trailblazing winemakers are making serious inroads in the production of quality white, red, and new dessert wines, something deemed impossible a few years back.

Island Wines: In both the Balearic and Canary Islands the strong tourist industry helped to revive local winemaking. Although hard to find, the best Callet and Manto Negro based red wines of Majorca, and the sweet *malvasías* of Lanzarote will reward the adventurous drinker.

SPAIN'S SUPERSTAR WINEMAKERS

Mariano García

Peter Sisseck

Alvaro Palacios

Josep Lluís Pérez

The current wine revolution has made superstars out of a group of dynamic, innovative, and visionary winemakers. Here are some of the top names:

Mariano García. His 30 years as winemaker of Vega Sicilia made him a legend. Now García displays his deft touch in the Ribera del Duero and Bierzo through his four wineries: Aalto, Mauro, San Román, and Paixar.

Peter Sisseck. A Dane educated in Bordeaux, Sisseck found his calling in the old Ribera del Duero vineyards, where he crafted Pingus, Spain's most coveted cult wine.

Alvaro Palacios. In Priorat, Palacios created L'Ermita, a Garnacha wine that is one of Spain's most remarkable bottlings. Palacios also is a champion of the Bierzo region, where he produces wines from the ancient Mencía varietal, known for their vibrant berry flavors and stony minerality.

Josep Lluís Pérez. From his base in Priorat and through his work as a winemaker, researcher, teacher, and consultant, Pérez (along with his daughter Sara Pérez) has become the main driving force in shaping the modern Mediterranean wines of Spain.

MATCHMAKING KNOW-HOW

A pairing of wine with *jamón* and Spanish olives.

Spain has a great array of regional products and cuisines, and its avant-garde chefs are culinary world leaders. As a general rule, you should match local food with local wines—but Spanish wines can be matched very well with some of the most unexpected dishes.

Albariños and the white wines of Galicia are ideal partners for seafood and fish. Dry sherries complement Serrano and Iberico hams, *lomo, chorizo,* and *salchichón* (white dry saugage), as well as olives and nuts. Pale, light, and dry finos and Manzanillas are the perfect aperitif wines, and the ideal companion for fried fish. Fuller bodied amontillados, palo cortados, and olorosos go well with hearty soups. Ribera del Duero reds are the perfect match for the outstanding local lamb. Try Priorat and other Mediterranean reds with strong cheeses and barbecue meats. Traditional Rioja harmonizes well with fowl and game. But also take an adventure off the beaten path: manzanilla and fino are great with sushi and sashimi; Rioja *reserva* fit tuna steaks; and cream sherry will not be out of place with chocolate. *¡Salud!*

CLOSE UP

Barcelona's Must-Eat

Top priorities for a trip to Barcelona might just read: see great art and architecture, enjoy the nightlife, eat ham. In all seriousness, you shouldn't pass up the opportunity to eat Spain's exquisite artisanal ham—known in Catalan as *pernil* and in Spanish as *jamón*—made from acorn-fed native black pigs whose meat is salt-cured and then air-dried for two to four years. The best kind, *jamón ibérico de bellota,* comes from carefully managed and exercised pigs fed only acorns. This lengthy process results in a silky, slightly sweet and nutty meat that is contradictorily both light and intensely rich.

You can casually approach the quest for this delicacy at nearly any bar or restaurant across Barcelona, feasting on different qualities of hams, including jamón ibérico's lesser but still stellar cousin, *jamón serrano.*

Catalonia's love affair with cured pork isn't restricted to jamón. Sausages and other pork derivatives, known as *embutits* (*embutidos* in Spanish), are equally common sandwich-fillers, and are regularly served as starters in even high-end restaurants. For an authentic experience, try some with a cold glass of *vermut* (white vermouth) and a side of potato chips, ideally as a light snack on a terrace before a full lunch.

Chorizo is, of course, the best-known and most ubiquitous sausage in Spain. Pork and paprika are the two key ingredients, but styles and quality vary widely, ranging from cheap, mass-produced batons for stews to handmade *chorizo ibérico,* best savored in wafer-thin slices.

Local Catalan favorites include the chewy but tasty *llonganissa* cured sausages, and *fuet.* The latter can be almost inedibly tough or wonderfully delicious, depending on the quality, so don't rush to judgment after your first experience. *Bull* (pronounced, more or less, "boo-eey") comes in *blanc* (white) and *negre* (black) varieties—the latter is made with blood. Served cold in thin slices, bull is often served with salads.

Botifarra sausages are important components of Catalan cuisine. Most are served hot, typically with haricots vert, but cold *botifarra blanc* and *negre* are also common. A third variety, *botifarra d'ou,* includes eggs and has an unusual yellow hue. For a truly Catalan taste experience, look for *botifarra dolça*—this decidedly odd dessert sausage incorporates lemon and sugar.

$$ BASQUE **Taktika Berri.** Specializing in San Sebastián's favorite dishes, this Basque restaurant has only one drawback—a table is hard to score unless you call weeks in advance (an idea to consider before you travel). Your backup plan? The tapas served over the first-come, first-served bar: They're of such a high quality, you can barely do better à table. And the charming family that owns and runs this gem is the very definition of hospitality. *Average main: €20* *Valencia 169, Eixample* *93/453–4759* *Reservations essential* *Closed Sun. No dinner Sat.* *Hospital Clinic* *G:9.*

$ TAPAS **Tapas 24.** Celebrity chef Carles Abellán's irrepressibly creative Comerç 24 has been a hit for years, and his tapas emporium has followed suit. Here Abellán shows us how much he admires traditional Catalan and Spanish bar food, from patatas bravas to *croquetas de jamón ibérico* (croquettes made of Iberian ham). The counter can get crowded, but you can always take refuge on the terrace. *Average main: €14 Carrer Diputació 269, Eixample 93/488–0977 www.carlesabellan.es/restaurantes-tapas-24 Mon.–Sat. 8 am–midnight Closed Sun. Passeig de Gràcia ↔ I:10.*

$$$ MEDITERRANEAN **Tragaluz.** *Tragaluz* means skylight and this is an excellent choice if you're still on a design high from shopping at Vinçon or visiting Gaudí's Pedrera. The sliding roof opens to the stars in good weather, while the chairs, lamps, and fittings by Javier Mariscal (creator of 1992 Olympic mascot Cobi) reflect Barcelona's ongoing passion for playful design. The Mediterranean cuisine is traditional yet light and innovative. Luis de Buen's TragaFishh (an outpost from his restaurant Fishhh!) is the downstairs oyster bar. The redesigned main dining room upstairs is reached via the kitchen, and the top floor is an informal space for coffee or an after-dinner drink. *Average main: €28 Passatge de la Concepció 5, Eixample 93/487–0621 www.grupotragaluz.com Reservations essential Daily 1:30–4 and 8:30–11:30 Diagonal ↔ I:8.*

$ ECLECTIC **Woki Organic Market.** Just off Plaça de Catalunya, this combination ecological market and restaurant serves "ecotapas" and small plates composed of organically grown ingredients prepared using a variety of healthy techniques and traditions. The pasta station allows diners to combine woks of vegetables, noodles, sauces, and ingredients spontaneously. The beef is ecologically produced without the use of pesticides or synthetic fertilizers, the pastas are all made with ecologically pure flours, while the wines and vegetables are locally grown and carefully identified. The sustainability theme continues with the furniture and materials, all made of recycled items, adding to the lively, informal ambience redolent of London's indoor markets. *Average main: €12 Ronda Universitat 20, Eixample 93/302–5206 www.wokimarket.com Mon.–Thurs. 8 am–midnight, Fri.–Sat. 8 am–1 am, Sun. noon–midnight Pl. de Catalunya ↔ H:10.*

$$ CATALAN **Yaya Amelia.** Just two blocks uphill from Gaudí's Sagrada Família church, this kitchen serves lovingly prepared and clued-in dishes ranging from warm goat-cheese salad to foie to *chuleton de buey a la sal* (beef cooked in salt). The "Yaya" (an affectionate term for grandmother in Spanish) was apparently of Basque origin, as the cuisine here is a pleasantly schizoid medley of Basque and Catalan. Decidedly old-school, the interior is largely unchanged since the restaurant opened in 1976. Serving from noon to 6 and from 8 to midnight, the Yaya is a welcome relief for the ravenous and weary fresh from touring the Eixample sites. *Average main: €22 Sardenya 364, Eixample 93/456–4573 Closed Mon. Sagrada Família ↔ L:7.*

GRÀCIA

This lively and intimate neighborhood is home to many of Barcelona's artists, musicians, and actors. The bohemian atmosphere is reflected in an eclectic collection of restaurants encompassing everything from street food and affordable ethnic cuisine to thoroughly sophisticated dining.

$$$$ MEDITERRANEAN **Hofmann.** German-born, Catalonia-trained Mey Hofmann's locale, uptown just below Travessera de Gràcia, is a graceful designer space with a glassed-in kitchen as center stage. Hofmann's creative Mediterranean and international cuisine has been successful for more than two decades as a result of carefully selected raw materials and unrelenting quality in their preparation. Sardine tartare, foie gras in puff pastry, prawn risotto, wood pideon in two textures, and lovingly prepared baby vegetables are among the best choices at this carefully managed culinary tour de force. *Average main: €42 La Granada del Penedes 14–16, Gràcia 93/218–7165 www.hofmann-bcn.com Reservations essential Closed weekends, Easter wk, and Aug. Gràcia, Diagonal H:6.*

$$$ BASQUE **Ipar-Txoko.** This excellent little Basque enclave has managed to stay largely under the radar, and for that reason, among others (the cuisine is authentic, the prices are fair, and the service is personal and warm), it's a fantastic choice. A balanced menu offers San Sebastián specialties such as *txuleta de buey* (ox steak) or *besugo a la donostiarra* (sea bream covered with scales of crispy garlic and a vinegar sauce), flawlessly prepared, while the wine list presents classic Riojas and freezing Txomin Etxaniz txakolí (a dry sparkling white) straight from Getaria. *Average main: €24 Carrer Mozart 22, Gràcia 93/218–1954 www.ipar-txoko.com Reservations essential Closed Sun. and Aug. No dinner Mon. Gràcia, Diagonal I:7.*

$$$ SPANISH **L'Arrosseria Xàtiva.** This rustic dining room in Gràcia, a spinoff from the original in Les Corts, evokes the rice paddies and lowlands of Valencia and eastern Spain. Low lighting imparts a warm glow over exposed brick walls, beamed ceilings, and bentwood chairs. It's a great spot to savor some of Barcelona's finest paellas and rice dishes. Fish, seafood, and meats cooked over coals round out a complete menu prepared with loving care and using top ingredients. *Average main: €24 Torrent d'en Vidalet 26, Gràcia 93/284–8502 www.arrosseriaxativa.com Joanic J:6.*

$$$$ CATALAN **Roig Robí.** Rattan chairs and a garden terrace characterize this simple-yet-polished dining spot in the bottom corner of Gràcia just above the Diagonal (near Via Augusta). Rustic and relaxed, Roig Robí (ruby red in Catalan, as in the color of certain wines) maintains a high level of culinary excellence, serving traditional Catalan market cuisine with original touches directed by chef Mercé Navarro. A good example? The *arròs amb espardenyes i carxofes* (rice with sea cucumbers and artichokes). *Average main: €32 Seneca 20, Gràcia 93/218–9222 www.roigrobi.com Reservations essential Closed Sun. and Aug. No lunch Sat. Diagonal I:7.*

CLOSE UP

Ground Rules for Coffee

Coffee culture in Barcelona continues to focus on simplicity, in defiance of the near-infinite choices offered by certain barista-fronted international chains now moving into the city. A normal espresso, black coffee, is simply *un cafè*—a *café solo* in the rest of Spain. Add some extra water and it's a *cafè Americá*. In summer add ice for a *cafè amb gel*, and in winter add a dash of rum or brandy to make a *cigaló* (*carajillo* in Spanish). A *tallat*, from the Catalan verb *tallar* (to cut), is coffee with just a little milk (*café cortado* in Spanish), while *cafè amb llet* is Catalan for café con leche, or coffee mixed more evenly with milk. That's about as far as coffee menus stretch, but if you really want to see the waiter's eyes glaze over, order a *café descafeinado de maquina con leche desnatada natural* (decaffeinated coffee made in the espresso machine with skim milk applied at room temperature).

Finally, a word of warning to those who prefer their java on the run: coffee is still, for the most part, a sit-down or belly-up-to-the-bar affair. So take time to stop and smell the fresh roast.

POBLENOU

East of the Eixample and extending to the sea just beyond Port Olímpic, this formerly rough-around-the-edges neighborhood has lately seen an influx of edgy art studios, design shops, and even a few hip restaurants—many of these spaces are installed in converted warehouses and industrial concerns.

$$ TAPAS ✕ **Els Tres Porquets.** Somewhat off the beaten path (though handy to the Auditori and the Teatre Nacional de Catalunya and not that far from the Sagrada Familia), *Els Tres Porquets* (The Three Little Pigs) packs in foodies and bon vivants. A wide range of morsels, tapas, and small plates are the way to go here, with everything from Ibérico ham to *torta del Casar* cheeses and regional specialties from all around the Iberian Peninsula. *Average main: €16 ✉ Rambla del Poblenou 165, Poblenou ☎ 93/300–8750 🌐 www.elstresporquets.es ✍ Reservations essential ⏲ Mon.–Sat. 10–4 and 8:30–11 ⏲ Closed Sun. Ⓜ Glòries, Clot ✥ L:12.*

SARRIÀ, PEDRALBES, AND SANT GERVASI

Take an excursion to the upper reaches of town for an excellent selection of bars, cafés, and restaurants, along with cool summer evening breezes and a sense of well-heeled village life in Sarrià.

$$$ CATALAN ✕ **Acontraluz.** A stylish covered terrace in the leafy upper-Barcelona neighborhood of Tres Torres, Acontraluz, so named for its translucent ceiling, has a strenuously varied market-based menu ranging from game in season, such as *rable de liebre* (stewed hare) with chutney, to the more northern *pochas con almejas* (beans with clams). All dishes are prepared with care and talent, and the lunch menu is a bargain. *Average main: €26 ✉ Milanesat 19, Tres Torres ☎ 93/203–0658 🌐 www.acontraluz.com ✍ Reservations essential ⏲ Closed 2 wks in Aug. No dinner Sun. Ⓜ Les Tres Torres ✥ E:3.*

$ TAPAS ✕ **Bambarol.** The unpretentious nature of this new restaurant isn't what you might expect when looking at the galaxy of stars that chef-owners Ferran Maicas and Albert Ferrer have helped earn for some of Spain's most famous kitchens. The decor is simple, the names of dishes straightforward, and the cooking style entirely absent of palate-twisting molecular gastronomy. Despite—or perhaps because of—this, it's booked solid every night, with a growing waiting list of locals and in-the-know tourists. Friendly service and honest cooking executed to a very high standard for modest prices provides a winning combination. The menu is a mix of Catalan and Asian tapas—try the wonderful scallops with pork and wild mushrooms, and ask if they have the off-menu croquettes of foie gras, chicken, and mushrooms. *$ Average main: €13 ✉ Carrer Santaló 21, Tres Torres ☎ 93/250–7074 🌐 www.bambarol.cat ✍ Reservations essential ⏲ Closed Sun. No lunch Tues.–Fri. Ⓜ Gràcia ⊕ G:6.*

CALÇOTS FROM HEAVEN

Since the late 19th century, *calçots,* long-stemmed, twice-planted white onions cooked over grapevine clippings, have provided a favorite early-spring outing from Barcelona. Restaurants now serve calçots in the Collserola hills or on the beaches of Gavá and Castelldefells from November to April. Some in-town restaurants also serve calçots, always consumed with romescu sauce and accompanied by lamb chops, botifarra sausage, and copious quantities of young red wine poured from a long-spouted *porrón* held overhead. Wear dark (and preferably expendable) clothing.

$ TAPAS ✕ **Bar Tomás.** Famous for its *patatas bravas amb allioli* (potatoes with fiery hot sauce and allioli, an emulsion of crushed garlic, and olive oil), accompanied by freezing mugs of San Miguel beer, this old-fashioned Sarrià classic is worth seeking out as a contrast to the bland designer tapas bars that are becoming ubiquitous in Barcelona. You'll have to elbow your way to a tiny table and shout to be heard over the hubbub, but you'll get an authentic taste of local bar life. On Wednesday, when Bar Tomás is closed, its eager patrons crowd into Iborra (just behind it on Carrer d'Ivorra), which serves the same legendary fare. *$ Average main: €9 ✉ Major de Sarrià 49, Sarrià ☎ 93/203–1077 ⏲ Thurs.–Tues. 1–4 and 6–10 Ⓜ Sarrià ⊕ D:2.*

$$$$ MEDITERRANEAN ✕ **Coure.** *Cuina d'autor* is Catalan for creative or original cooking and that is what you get here in this slight sliver of a subterranean space on the intimate Passatge Marimón just above the Diagonal thoroughfare. Minimalist decor and culinary aesthetics pair well here: steak tartare, peerless tuna belly, ham, chicken croquettes, and a by-the-glass wine list catalog with interesting discoveries that change regularly. The bread and the expresso, seldom-failing bellwethers of quality, are excellent. *$ Average main: €32 ✉ Passatge Marimón 20, Sant Gervasi ☎ 93/200–7532 🌐 www.restaurantcoure.es ⏲ Closed Sun., Mon., and Aug. 1–21 Ⓜ Hospital Clinic, Gràcia ⊕ G:6.*

$ CAFÉ ✕ **Dole Café.** Little more than a slender slot on the corner of Capità Arenas and Manuel de Falla, this famous upper Barcelona café is absolutely vital to the Sarrià and Capità Arenas neighborhoods. Along with extraordinarily good coffee, sandwiches and pastries here are uncannily well made and tasty. A star attraction is the Popeye ("paw-pay-yay") a spinach, goat cheese, and Ibérico ham sandwich not to be missed. It's usually packed, so be prepared to wait. $ *Average main: €10* ✉ *Manuel de Falla 16–18, Sarrià* ☎ *93/204–1120* ⏲ *Weekdays 6–6, Sat. 6–1:30. Closed Sun.* Ⓜ *Maria Cristina; Sarriá (FGC)* ✣ *C:3.*

$$ CATALAN **El Mató de Pedralbes.** Named for the *mató* (cottage cheese) traditionally prepared by the Clarist nuns across the street in the Monestir de Pedralbes, this is a fine choice for a lunch stop after exploring the monastery. It also has one of the most authentically Catalan menus around at a great value. Look for *sopa de ceba gratinée* (onion soup), *trinxat* (chopped cabbage with bacon bits), or *truite de patata i ceba* (potato and onion omelet). $ *Average main: €16* ✉ *Bisbe Català 10, Pedralbes* ☎ *93/204–7962* ⏲ *No dinner Sun.* Ⓜ *Reina Elisenda* ✣ *B:1.*

$$$ MEDITERRANEAN **Fishhh!.** Everyone needs to go to a shopping mall sooner or later, and at L'Illa Diagonal, a mile west of Plaça Francesc Macià, you can shop *and* dine on some of Barcelona's best seafood at Lluís de Buen's first-rate fish emporium. Long a major seafood supplier of Barcelona's top restaurants (check out his seafood-central command post off the back left corner of the Boqueria market), Genaro and his staff have put together a lively and popular dining space that exudes Boqueria market-style excitement in the midst of a busy shopping venue. $ *Average main: €26* ✉ *Av. Diagonal 557, Sant Gervasi, Les Corts* ☎ *93/444–1139* 🌐 *www.fishhh.net* ⏲ *Closed Sun.* Ⓜ *Les Corts* ✣ *D:5.*

$$ CATALAN **Freixa Tradició.** When wunderkind molecular gastronomist Ramón Freixa turned the family restaurant back over to his father, Josep Maria Freixa, there was some speculation about the menu's headlong rush into the past. Now that the results are in, Barcelona food cognoscenti are coming in droves for the authentic Catalan fare that made El Racó d'en Freixa great before experimental cuisine took over the culinary landscape. Creamy rice with cuttlefish, monkfish with fried garlic, pig trotters with prunes and pine nuts and robust selection of local specialties are making the new-old Freixa better than ever. The dining room is all white-tablecloth elegance, but a witty installation of copper pots on the wall gives a wink to its traditional roots. $ *Average main: €21* ✉ *San Elies 22, Sant Gervasi* ☎ *93/209–7559* 🌐 *www.freixatradicio.com* ⏲ *Closed Mon., Easter wk, and Aug. No dinner Sun.* Ⓜ *Sant Gervasi* ✣ *G:5.*

$$$$ ITALIAN **Le Quattro Stagioni.** For excellent, streamlined Italian fare, this chic spot just down the street from the Tres Torres *ferrocarril* (FGC) stop is a winner. The dining room, filled with intriguing-looking bon vivants, mixes elegant touches like oversize mirrors with rustic nods such as woven chairs. The wine list includes some excellent Italian choices. In good weather, move to their garden which remains cool and fragrant on summer nights. $ *Average main: €36* ✉ *Dr. Roux 37, Sant Gervasi* ☎ *93/205–2279* 🌐 *www.4stagioni.com* ✍ *Reservations essential* ⏲ *No lunch Sun. and Mon.* Ⓜ *Les Tres Torres* ✣ *E:4.*

$$$ MEDITERRANEAN **Neichel.** Originally from Alsace, chef Jean-Louis Neichel skillfully manages a vast variety of exquisite ingredients such as foie gras, truffles, wild mushrooms, herbs, and the best seasonal vegetables. With his son Mario now at the burners, and his identical triplet daughters taking turns serving tables, Neichel is fully a family operation. His flawless Mediterranean

3

delicacies include *ensalada de gambas de Palamós al sésamo con puerros* (shrimp from Palamós with sesame seeds and leeks) and *espardenyes amb salicornia* (sea cucumbers with saltwort) on sundried tomato paste. The dining room is classically elegant with bold red accent walls and contrasting crisp white tablecloths. *Average main: €27* *Carrer Bertran i Rózpide 1, Pedralbes* *93/203–8408* *www.neichel.es* *Reservations essential* *Closed Sun., Mon., and Aug.* *Maria Cristina* *B:3.*

$$ MEDITERRANEAN Fodor's Choice ★

Silvestre. A graceful and easygoing mainstay in Barcelona's culinary galaxy, this restaurant serves modern cuisine to some of the city's most discerning and distinguished diners. Located just below Via Augusta, Silvestre's series of intimate dining rooms and cozy corners are carefully tended by chef Guillermo Casañé and his charming wife Marta Cabot, a fluent English–speaking maître d' and partner. Look for fresh market produce lovingly prepared in dishes such as tuna tartare, noodles and shrimp, or wood pigeon with duck liver. Willy's semisecret list of house wines is always surprising for its quality and value. *Average main: €20* *Santaló 101, Sant Gervasi* *93/241–4031* *www.restaurante-silvestre.com* *Closed Sun., 3 wks in Aug., and Easter wk. No lunch Sat.* *Muntaner* *G:5.*

$$$ CATALAN Fodor's Choice ★

Tram-Tram. At the end of the old tram line above the village of Sarrià, this restaurant offers one of Barcelona's finest culinary stops, with Isidre Soler and his wife Reyes at the helm. Try the *menú de degustació* and you might be lucky enough to get marinated tuna salad, cod medallions, and venison filet mignon, among other tasty creations. Perfectly sized portions and a streamlined, airy white space within this traditional Sarrià house add to the experience. In nice weather, request a table in the garden out back. *Average main: €22* *Major de Sarrià 121, Sarrià* *93/204–8518* *www.tram-tram.com* *Reservations essential* *Closed Sun., Mon., Easter wk, and 2 wks in Aug.* *Reina Elisenda* *D:1.*

$$$$ CATALAN Fodor's Choice ★

Via Veneto. Open since 1967, this family-owned temple of fine Catalan dining offers a contemporary menu punctuated by old-school classics. Elegant and stylish, the restaurant was a favorite of Salvador Dalí and now attracts local sports stars and politicians. Service is impeccable, and diners can safely place themselves in the hands of the expert staff to guide them through modern variations of regional specialities and a daunting 10,000-strong wine list. The starter of tagliolini pasta with free-range eggs cooked at a low temperature and served with Alba (Piedmont) white truffle threatens to be a showstopper, but the theatrical presentation of roast baby duck, deboned and pressed at the table, provides a memorable second act. *Average main: €38* *Ganduxer 10, Sarrià* *93/200–7244* *www.viavenetorestaurant.com* *Closed Sun. and Aug. 1–20. No lunch Sat.* *Hospital Clínic* *E:5.*

$ MEDITERRANEAN

Vivanda. Just above Plaça de Sarrià, Vivanda produces traditional Catalan miniatures, *para picar* (small morsels), *platillos* (little dishes), and half rations of meat and fish listed as *platillos de carne* and *platillos de pescado,* respectively, thanks to a redesigned menu by Alkimia's Jordi Vilà. The *coca de pa de vidre con tomate* (a delicate shell of bread with tomato and olive oil) and the venisonlike *presa de ibérico* (filet of Ibérico pig) are both exquisite. Weather permitting, book a table in the lush back garden for lunch. *Average main: €12* *Major de Sarrià 134, Sarrià* *93/203–1918* *No dinner Sun.* *Reina Elisenda* *D:1.*

TIBIDABO

From the Latin *tibi dabo* ("I will give to you"), the name of this mountain overlooking the city reflects the splendor of its views—the "kingdoms of the world" offered to Jesus by the devil, according to local legend. Restaurants here now offer some of Barcelona's best cuisine, often at prices as high as the mountain itself.

$$$$ CATALAN **ABaC.** Chef Jordi Cruz, the youngest chef ever to win a Michelin star and author of two books on his culinary philosophy and techniques, is known for his devotion to impeccable raw materials and his talent for combining creativity and tradition. The tasting menu is the only reasonable choice here: trust this chef to give you the best he has (and any attempt at economy is roughly analagous to quibbling about deck chairs on the Titanic). The hypercreative sampling has ranged from tartare of oysters with green-apple vinegar, fennel, and seawort to veal royal with concentrate of Pedro Ximénez sherry and textures of apples in cider. Connected to an exquisite five-star boutique hotel of the same name, the dining room, awash in beige and white linens with dark wooden floors in wide planks, delivers a suitably elegant backdrop. *Average main: €48* *Av. del Tibidabo 1–7, Tibidabo* *93/319–6600* *www.abacbarcelona.com* *Reservations essential* *Closed Sun. and Mon. No lunch.* *Tibidabo* *H:2.*

$$$$ SPANISH **El Asador de Aranda.** It's a hike to this immense palace a few-minutes walk above the Avenida Tibidabo metro station—but worth it if you're in upper Barcelona. The kitchen specializes in Castilian cooking, with *cordero lechal* (roast suckling lamb), *morcilla* (black sausage), and *pimientos de piquillo* (sweet red peppers) as star players. The Art Nouveau details here—carved-wood trim, stained-glass partitions, engraved glass, Moorish archways, and terra-cotta floors—belie the fact that this extravagantly beautiful building was originally a nunnery, funded by wealthy members of the Catalan industrial bourgeoisie as a place to stash their errant daughters. Other branches of the same chain across the city offer similar fare in less spectacular surroundings. *Average main: €46* *Av. del Tibidabo 31, Tibidabo* *93/417–0115* *www.asadordearanda.com* *Reservations essential* *No dinner Sun.* *Penitents, Vallcarca, Tibidabo* *H:1.*

OUTSKIRTS OF BARCELONA

With the many fine in-town dining options available in Barcelona, any out-of-town recommendations must logically rank somewhere in the uppermost stratosphere of gastronomic excellence. These three, all rated among the top five or six establishments below the Pyrenees, undoubtedly do.

$$$$ CATALAN **Hispania.** This famous pilgrimage—one of the best restaurants in Catalonia for the last 50 years—is 39 km (24 miles) up the beach north of Barcelona, easily reached by the Calella train from the RENFE station in Plaça de Catalunya. Sisters Francisca and Dolores Reixach continue to turn out the same line of classical Catalan cuisine that, despite the name Hispania, has characterized this spot from the start. *Faves amb botifarra negre* (fava beans with black sausage) ranks high

on the list of signature dishes here, but the fresh fish and seafood from the Arenys de Mar fish auction are invariably excellent. The dining room, a long glass rectangle surrounded by nature, adds to the elegant experience. $ *Average main: €35* ✉ *Camino Ral 54, Ctra. N II, 2 km south of Arenys de Mar* ☎ *93/791–0457* 🌐 *www.restauranthispania.com* ✍ *Reservations essential* ⊙ *Closed Tues. and 2 wks in Oct. No dinner Sun.* ✥ *L:15.*

$$$$ CATALAN Fodor's Choice ★ ✕ **Sant Pau.** One of the best restaurants below the Pyrenees, this Sant Pol de Mar treasure is a scenic 40-minute train ride along the beach from Plaça de Catalunya's RENFE station: the Calella train stops at the door. Inside are clean, spare lines and a garden overlooking the Mediterranean. Dishes change with the seasons, but picture *vieiras* (scallops) with crisped artichoke flakes on roast potato, or *lubina* (sea bass) on baby leeks and chard in *garnatxa* (sweet Catalan wine) sauce. If you're here for Sant Jordi, Barcelona's Lovers' Day on April 23, you might score a *misiva de amor* (love letter), a pastry envelope containing julienned berries and peaches. $ *Average main: €48* ✉ *Carrer Nou 10, Sant Pol de Mar* ☎ *93/760–0662* 🌐 *www.ruscalleda.com* ⊙ *Closed Sun., Mon., May 1–21, Nov. 1–21. No lunch Thurs.* ✥ *L:15.*

DINING AND LODGING ATLAS

KEY

- □ *Hotels*
- ■ *Restaurants*
- ■ *Restaurant in Hotel*
- Ⓜ *Métro Stations*
- ✥ *following dining and lodging reviews indicates a map-grid coordinate*

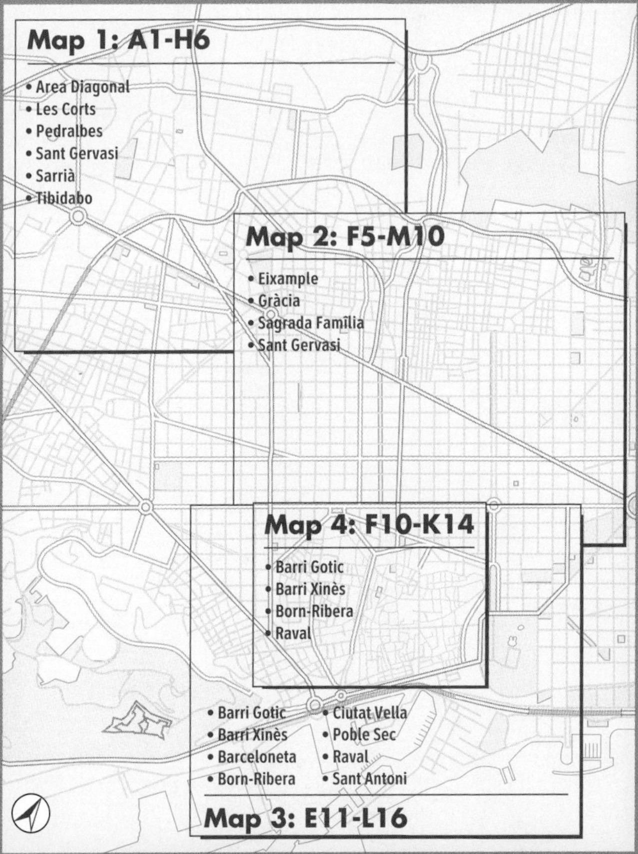

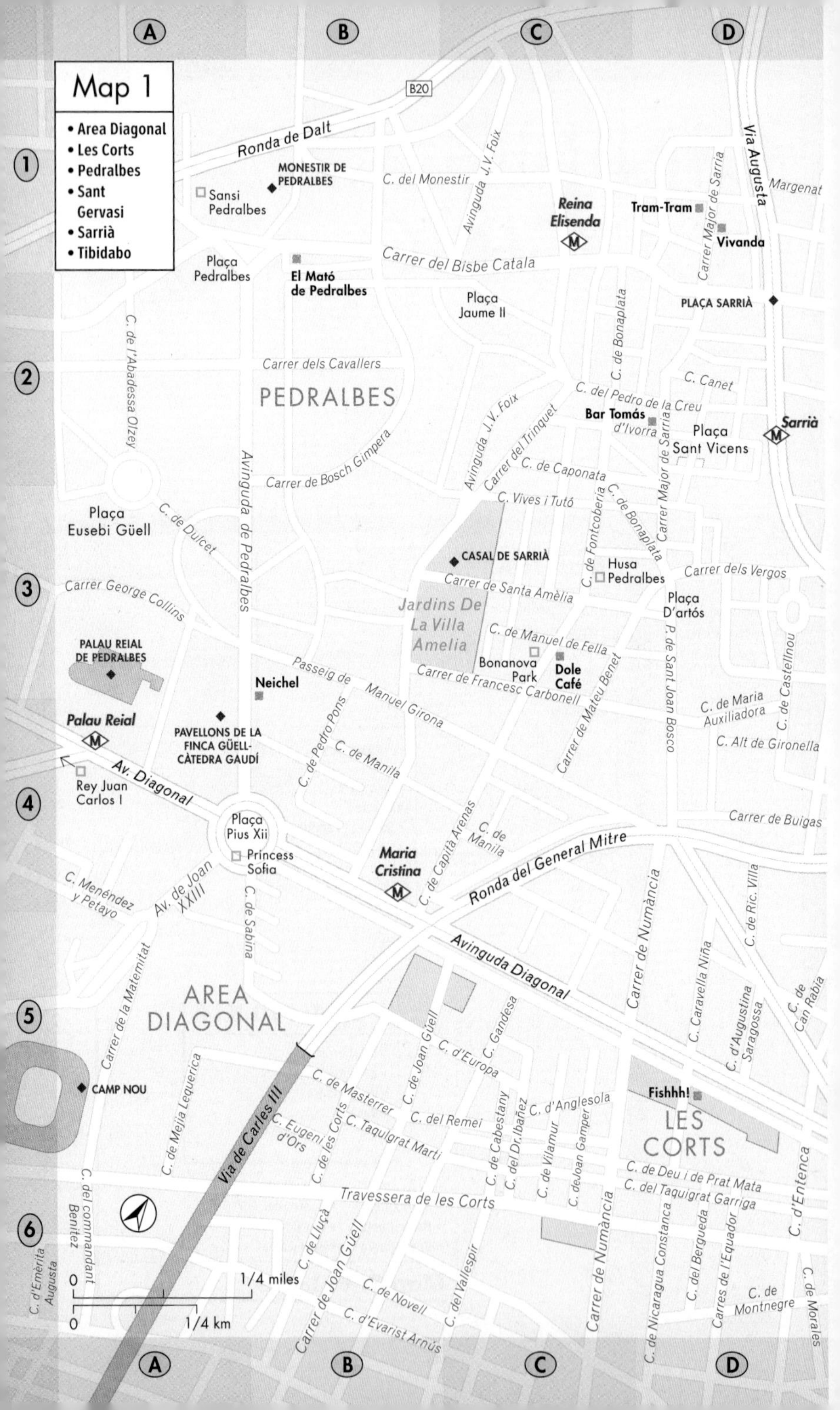
Map 1
• Area Diagonal
• Les Corts
• Pedralbes
• Sant Gervasi
• Sarrià
• Tibidabo
A
B
C
D
1
2
3
4
5
6
B20
Ronda de Dalt
MONESTIR DE PEDRALBES
Sansi Pedralbes
C. del Monestir
Avinguda J.V. Foix
Reina Elisenda
Tram-Tram
Vivanda
Via Augusta
Margenat
Carrer Major de Sarrià
Plaça Pedralbes
El Mató de Pedralbes
Carrer del Bisbe Catala
Plaça Jaume II
PLAÇA SARRIÀ
C. de l'Abadessa Olzey
Carrer dels Cavallers
PEDRALBES
C. de Bonaplata
C. Canet
C. del Pedro de la Creu
Bar Tomás
d'Ivorra
Plaça Sant Vicens
Sarrià
Carrer del Trinquet
C. de Caponata
Carrer de Bosch Gimpera
Avinguda de Pedralbes
C. Vives i Tutó
Plaça Eusebi Güell
C. de Dulcet
CASAL DE SARRIÀ
C. de Fontcoberia
Husa Pedralbes
Carrer dels Vergos
Carrer George Collins
Carrer de Santa Amèlia
Plaça D'artós
Jardins De La Villa Amelia
C. de Manuel de Fella
C. de Castellnou
PALAU REIAL DE PEDRALBES
Bonanova Park
Dole Café
Passeig de Manuel Girona
Carrer de Francesc Carbonell
Carrer de Mateu Benet
P. de Sant Joan Bosco
Neichel
C. de Maria Auxiliadora
Palau Reial
PAVELLONS DE LA FINCA GÜELL-CÀTEDRA GAUDÍ
C. de Pedro Pons
C. de Manila
C. Alt de Gironella
Rey Juan Carlos I
Av. Diagonal
Plaça Pius Xii
Princess Sofia
C. de Capità Arenas
C. de Manila
Carrer de Buigas
Maria Cristina
Ronda del General Mitre
C. Menéndez y Petayo
Av. de Joan XXIII
C. de Sabina
Avinguda Diagonal
Carrer de Numància
C. de Ric. Villa
AREA DIAGONAL
Carrer de la Maternitat
C. de Joan Güell
C. Gandesa
C. d'Europa
C. Caravella Niña
C. d'Augustina Saragossa
C. de Can Rabia
CAMP NOU
C. de Masterrer
C. del Remei
C. d'Anglesola
Fishhh!
LES CORTS
C. Eugeni d'Ors
C. de les Corts
C. Taquigrat Marti
C. de Mejia Lequerica
Via de Carles III
C. de Cabestany
C. del Dr. Ibañez
C. de Vilamur
C. deJoan Gamper
C. de Deu i de Prat Mata
C. del Taquigrat Garriga
C. d'Entenca
C. del commandant Benitez
Travessera de les Corts
C. de Lluçà
Carrer de Joan Güell
C. del Vallespir
Carrer de Numància
C. de Nicaragua Constanca
C. del Berguedà
Carres de l'Equador
C. de Montnegre
C. de Morales
C. d'Emèrita Augusta
0
1/4 miles
0
1/4 km
C. de Novell
C. d'Evarist Arnús

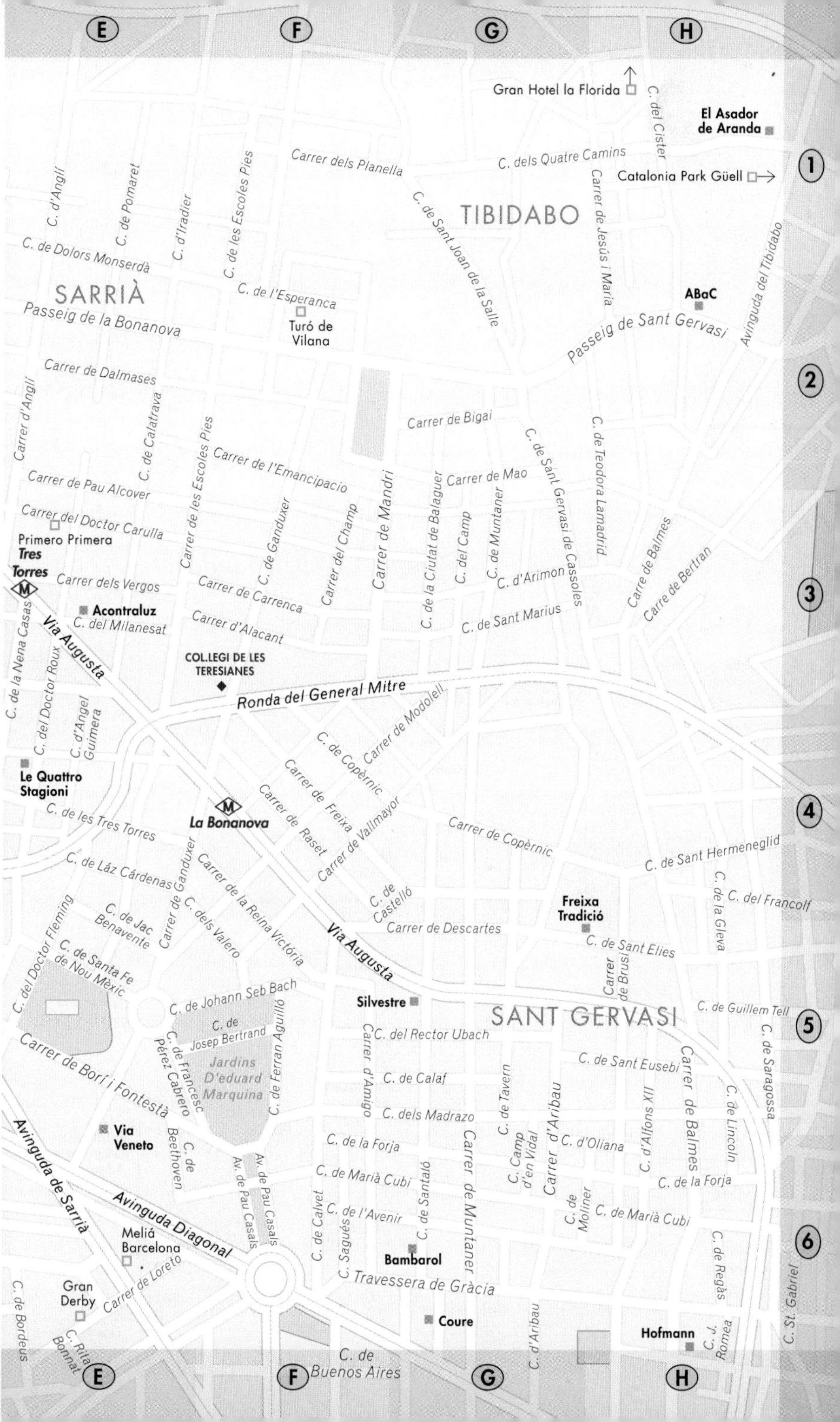
E
F
G
H
1
2
3
4
5
6
TIBIDABO
SARRIÀ
SANT GERVASI
Gran Hotel la Florida
El Asador de Aranda
Catalonia Park Güell
ABaC
Turó de Vilana
Primero Primera
Tres Torres
Acontraluz
COL.LEGI DE LES TERESIANES
Le Quattro Stagioni
La Bonanova
Freixa Tradició
Silvestre
Jardins D'eduard Marquina
Via Veneto
Meliá Barcelona
Gran Derby
Bambarol
Coure
Hofmann
C. del Cister
C. dels Quatre Camins
Carrer dels Planella
C. de Sant Joan de la Salle
Carrer de Jesús i Maria
Avinguda del Tibidabo
C. d'Anglí
C. de Pomaret
C. d'Iradier
C. de les Escoles Pies
C. de Dolors Monserdà
C. de l'Esperanca
Passeig de la Bonanova
Passeig de Sant Gervasi
Carrer de Dalmases
Carrer d'Anglí
C. de Calatrava
Carrer de Bigai
C. de Sant Gervasi de Cassoles
C. de Teodora Lamadrid
Carrer de les Escoles Pies
Carrer de l'Emancipacio
Carrer de Pau Alcover
Carrer del Doctor Carulla
C. de Ganduxer
Carrer del Champ
Carrer de Mandri
C. de la Ciutat de Balaguer
Carrer de Mao
C. del Camp
C. de Muntaner
Carre de Balmes
Carre de Bertran
C. d'Arimon
Carrer dels Vergos
Carrer de Carrenca
C. del Milanesat
Carrer d'Alacant
C. de Sant Marius
Via Augusta
C. de la Nena Casas
C. del Doctor Roux
C. d'Angel Guimera
Ronda del General Mitre
Carrer de Modolell
C. de Copèrnic
Carrer de Freixa
Carrer de Raset
Carrer de Vallmayor
Carrer de Copèrnic
C. de les Tres Torres
C. de Sant Hermeneglid
C. de Láz Cárdenas
Carrer de Ganduxer
Carrer de la Reina Victòria
C. dels Valero
C. de Castelló
C. de la Gleva
C. del Francolí
Carrer de Descartes
C. de Sant Elies
C. de Jac Benavente
C. del Doctor Fleming
C. de Santa Fe de Nou Mèxic
Carrer de Brusi
C. de Johann Seb Bach
C. de Guillem Tell
C. de Josep Bertrand
C. de Francesc Pérez Cabrero
C. de Ferran Agulló
C. del Rector Ubach
Carrer d'Amigo
C. de Saragossa
C. de Sant Eusebi
Carrer de Bori i Fontestà
C. de Calaf
C. de Tavern
Carrer d'Aribau
Carrer de Balmes
C. de Lincoln
C. d'Alfons XII
C. dels Madrazo
Carrer de Muntaner
C. d'Oliana
C. de Beethoven
C. de la Forja
C. Camp d'en Vidal
Avinguda de Sarrià
Av. de Pau Casals
C. de Marià Cubí
C. de Santaló
C. de Moliner
C. de l'Avenir
C. de Calvet
C. Sagués
Avinguda Diagonal
C. de Regàs
Carrer de Loreto
Travessera de Gràcia
C. St. Gabriel
C. de Bordeus
C. Rita Bonnat
C. d'Aribau
C. J. Romea
C. de Buenos Aires

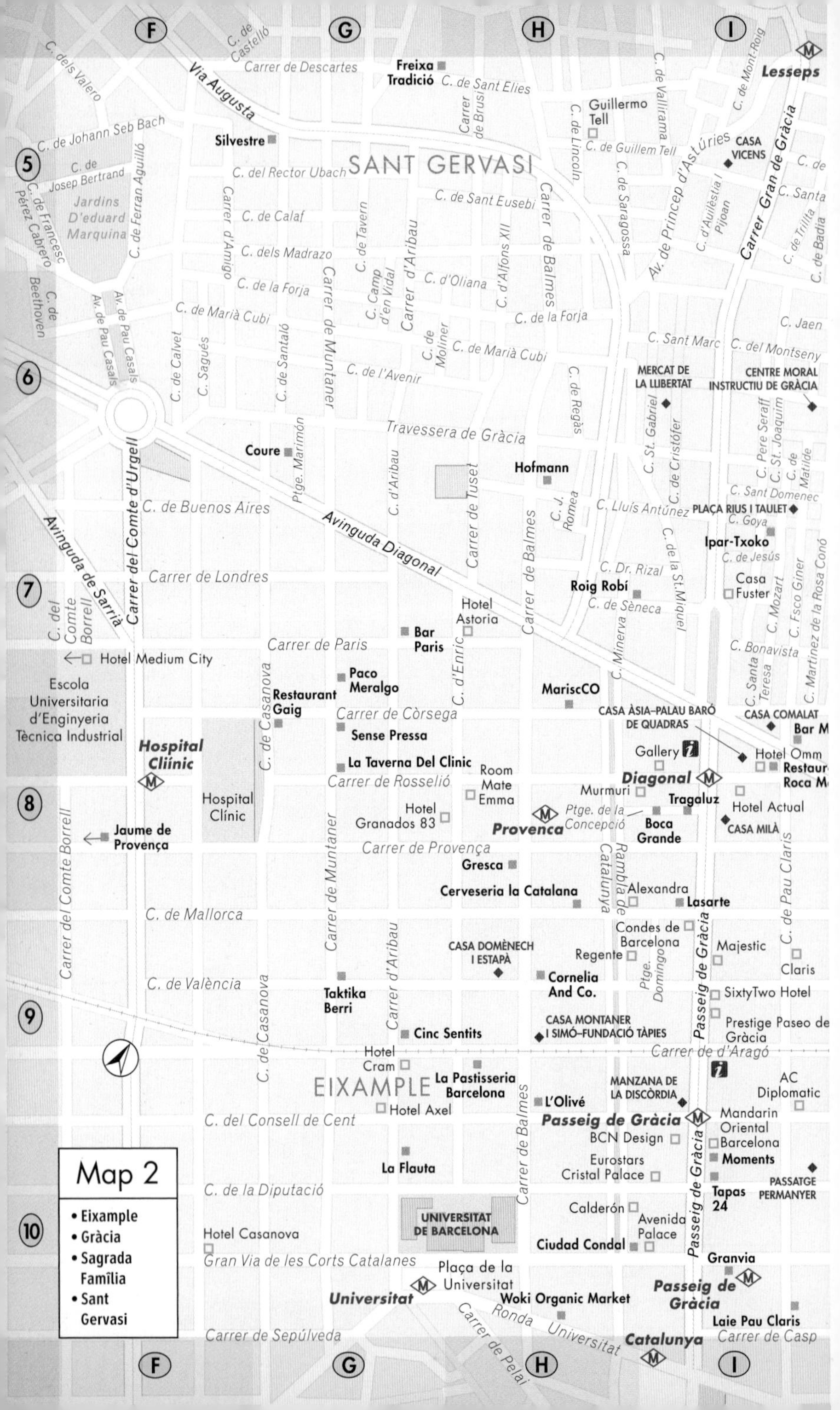
Map 2
• Eixample
• Gràcia
• Sagrada Família
• Sant Gervasi
F
G
H
I
5
6
7
8
9
10
SANT GERVASI
EIXAMPLE
C. dels Valero
C. de Castelló
Via Augusta
Carrer de Descartes
Freixa Tradició
C. de Sant Elies
Carrer de Brusi
C. de Vallirama
C. de Mont-Roig
Lesseps
C. de Johann Seb Bach
Silvestre
C. de Lincoln
Guillermo Tell
C. de Guillem Tell
Av. de Princep d'Astúries
CASA VICENS
Carrer Gran de Gràcia
C. de Josep Bertrand
C. del Rector Ubach
C. de Francesc Pérez Cabrero
Jardins D'eduard Marquina
C. de Ferran Agulló
Carrer d'Amigo
C. de Calaf
C. de Sant Eusebi
Carrer de Balmes
C. de Saragossa
C. d'Auilèstia i Pijoan
C. Santa
C. de Trillia
C. de Badia
C. dels Madrazo
C. de Tavern
Carrer d'Aribau
C. d'Alfons XII
C. de la Forja
C. d'Oliana
C. de Beethoven
Av. de Pau Casals
C. de Marià Cubi
C. Camp d'en Vidal
Carrer de Muntaner
C. de Moliner
C. Jaen
C. Sant Marc
C. del Montseny
C. de Calvet
C. Sagués
C. de Santaló
C. de l'Avenir
C. de Regàs
MERCAT DE LA LLIBERTAT
CENTRE MORAL INSTRUCTIU DE GRÀCIA
Travessera de Gràcia
Ptge. Marimón
Coure
C. d'Aribau
Hofmann
C. St. Gabriel
C. de Cristòfer
C. Pere Serafí
C. St. Joaquim
C. de Matilde
C. Sant Domenec
Carrer del Comte d'Urgell
C. de Buenos Aires
Avinguda Diagonal
Carrer de Tuset
C. J. Romea
C. Lluís Antúnez
PLAÇA RIUS I TAULET
C. Goya
Ipar-Txoko
C. de Jesús
C. de la St.Miquel
Avinguda de Sarrià
Carrer de Londres
C. Dr. Rizal
Roig Robí
Casa Fuster
C. Mozart
C. Fsco Giner
C. Martinez de la Rosa Conó
C. del Comte Borrell
Hotel Astoria
C. de Sèneca
Bar Paris
Carrer de Paris
C. d'Enric
C. Minerva
C. Bonavista
C. Santa Teresa
Hotel Medium City
Escola Universitaria d'Enginyeria Tècnica Industrial
C. de Casanova
Restaurant Gaig
Paco Meralgo
MariscCO
Carrer de Còrsega
CASA ÀSIA–PALAU BARÓ DE QUADRAS
CASA COMALAT
Bar M
Sense Pressa
Hospital Cliínic
Hospital Clínic
Gallery
Hotel Omm
Restaur
Roca M
La Taverna Del Clinic
Room Mate Emma
Carrer de Rosselló
Diagonal
Murmuri
Tragaluz
Hotel Actual
Hotel Granados 83
Ptge. de la Concepció
Boca Grande
CASA MILÀ
Provenca
Jaume de Provença
Carrer del Comte Borrell
Carrer de Provença
Rambla de Catalunya
Gresca
C. de Pau Claris
Cerveseria la Catalana
Alexandra
Lasarte
C. de Mallorca
Condes de Barcelona
Passeig de Gràcia
CASA DOMÈNECH I ESTAPÀ
Regente
Majestic
Claris
Ptge. Domingo
C. de València
Cornelia And Co.
Taktika Berri
SixtyTwo Hotel
CASA MONTANER I SIMÓ–FUNDACIÓ TÀPIES
Prestige Paseo de Gràcia
Cinc Sentits
Carrer de d'Aragó
Hotel Cram
La Pastisseria Barcelona
AC Diplomatic
MANZANA DE LA DISCÒRDIA
L'Olivé
Hotel Axel
C. del Consell de Cent
Passeig de Gràcia
Mandarin Oriental Barcelona
BCN Design
Moments
Eurostars Cristal Palace
La Flauta
PASSATGE PERMANYER
C. de la Diputació
Tapas 24
Calderón
UNIVERSITAT DE BARCELONA
Avenida Palace
Hotel Casanova
Ciudad Condal
Gran Via de les Corts Catalanes
Granvia
Plaça de la Universitat
Universitat
Woki Organic Market
Passeig de Gràcia
Ronda Universitat
Carrer de Pelai
Laie Pau Claris
Carrer de Sepúlveda
Catalunya
Carrer de Casp

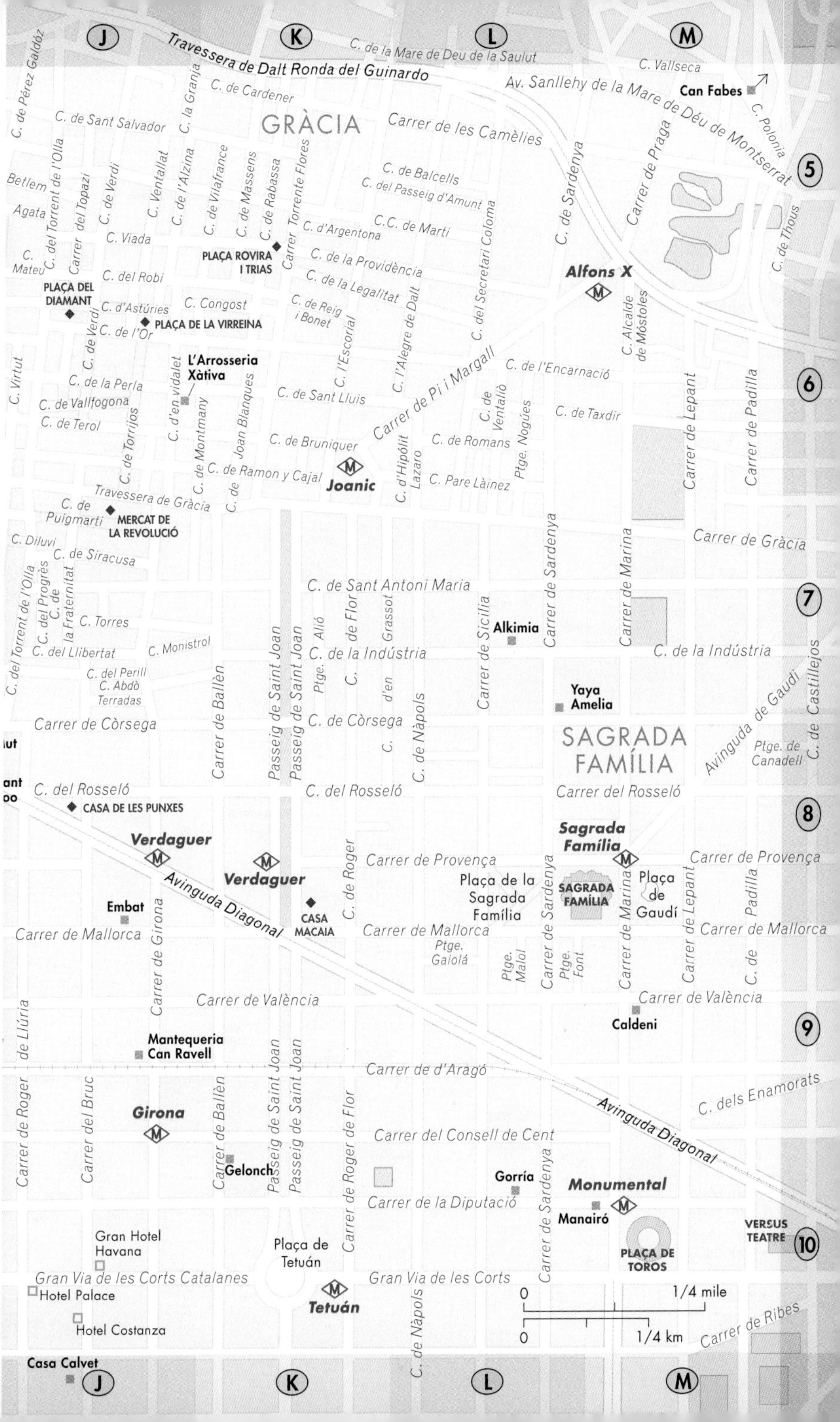

J
K
L
M
5
6
7
8
9
10
GRÀCIA
SAGRADA FAMÍLIA
Travessera de Dalt Ronda del Guinardo
C. de la Mare de Deu de la Saulut
C. Vallseca
Can Fabes
Av. Sanllehy de la Mare de Déu de Montserrat
C. Polonia
C. de Pérez Galdóz
C. de Sant Salvador
C. de Cardener
C. la Granja
Carrer de les Camèlies
C. de Sardenya
Carrer de Praga
C. de Thous
Betlem
Agata
C. Mateu
C. del Torrent de l'Olla
Carrer del Topazi
C. de Verdi
C. Ventallat
C. de l'Alzina
C. de Vilafrance
C. de Massens
C. de Rabassa
Carrer Torrente Flores
C. de Balcells
C. del Passeig d'Amunt
C.C. de Marti
C. del Secretari Coloma
C. Viada
C. d'Argentona
C. de la Providència
C. de la Legalitat
PLAÇA ROVIRA I TRIAS
C. del Robi
PLAÇA DEL DIAMANT
C. d'Astúries
C. Congost
C. de Reig i Bonet
C. de l'Or
PLAÇA DE LA VIRREINA
C. l'Escorial
C. l'Alegre de Dalt
Alfons X
C. Alcalde de Móstoles
C. Virtut
L'Arrosseria Xàtiva
C. d'en vidalet
C. de la Perla
C. de Vallfogona
C. de Terol
C. de Montmany
Joan Blanques
C. de Sant Lluis
Carrer de Pi i Margall
C. de l'Encarnació
C. de Ventalló
Ptge. Nogués
C. de Taxdir
Carrer de Lepant
Carrer de Padilla
C. de Torrijos
C. de Bruniquer
C. de Romans
C. de Ramon y Cajal
Joanic
C. d'Hipòlit Lazaro
C. Pare Làinez
Travessera de Gràcia
C. de Puigmarti
MERCAT DE LA REVOLUCIÓ
C. Diluvi
C. de Siracusa
Carrer de Gràcia
C. de Sant Antoni Maria
C. del Progrés
C. de la Fraternitat
C. Torres
C. del Llibertat
C. Monistrol
C. del Perill
C. Abdò Terradas
Ptge. Alió
C. de Flor
C. d'en Grassot
Carrer de Sicília
Alkimia
Carrer de Sardenya
Carrer de Marina
C. de la Indústria
Avinguda de Gaudí
C. de Castillejos
Yaya Amelia
Carrer de Còrsega
Carrer de Ballèn
Passeig de Saint Joan
C. de Còrsega
C. de Nàpols
Ptge. de Canadell
C. del Rosseló
Carrer del Rosseló
CASA DE LES PUNXES
Verdaguer
Sagrada Família
Carrer de Provença
Avinguda Diagonal
C. de Roger
Plaça de la Sagrada Família
SAGRADA FAMÍLIA
Plaça de Gaudí
Embat
CASA MACAIA
Carrer de Girona
Carrer de Mallorca
Ptge. Gaiolá
Ptge. Malol
Ptge. Font
Carrer de València
Caldeni
de Llúria
Mantequeria Can Ravell
Carrer de d'Aragó
C. dels Enamorats
Carrer de Roger
Carrer del Bruc
Girona
Carrer de Roger de Flor
Carrer del Consell de Cent
Gelonch
Gorría
Monumental
Carrer de la Diputació
Manairó
VERSUS TEATRE
PLAÇA DE TOROS
Gran Hotel Havana
Plaça de Tetuán
Gran Via de les Corts Catalanes
Gran Via de les Corts
Hotel Palace
Tetuán
Hotel Costanza
C. de Nàpols
0
1/4 mile
1/4 km
Carrer de Ribes
Casa Calvet

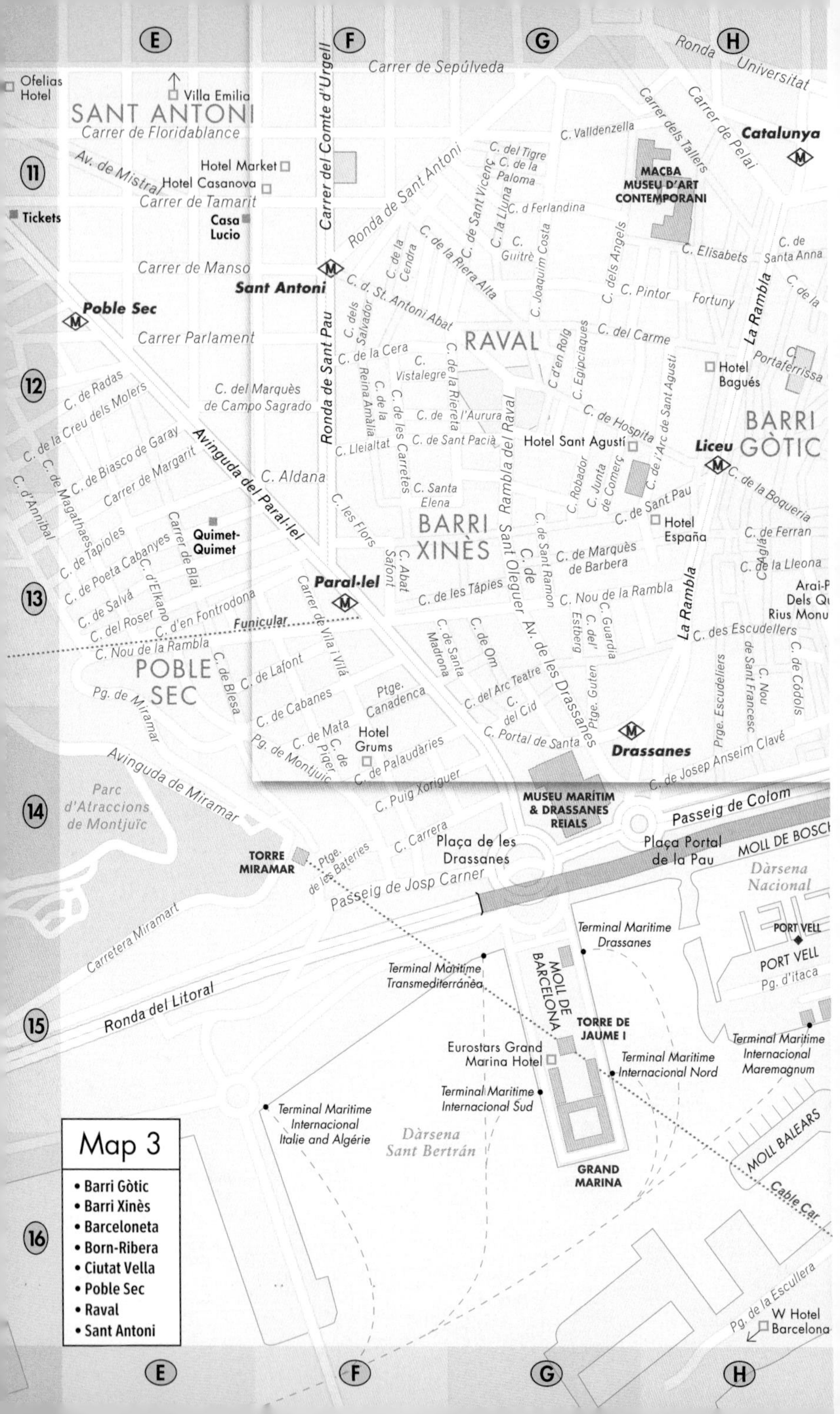
E
F
G
H
11
12
13
14
15
16
Map 3
• Barri Gòtic
• Barri Xinès
• Barceloneta
• Born-Ribera
• Ciutat Vella
• Poble Sec
• Raval
• Sant Antoni
SANT ANTONI
RAVAL
BARRI GÒTIC
BARRI XINÈS
POBLE SEC
Ofelias Hotel
Villa Emilia
Carrer de Sepúlveda
Ronda Universitat
Carrer de Floridablance
Av. de Mistral
Hotel Market
Hotel Casanova
Carrer de Tamarit
Tickets
Casa Lucio
Carrer de Manso
Sant Antoni
Poble Sec
Carrer Parlament
Carrer del Comte d'Urgell
Ronda de Sant Antoni
Ronda de Sant Pau
Catalunya
Carrer dels Tallers
Carrer de Pelai
C. Valldenzella
C. del Tigre
C. de la Paloma
C. de Sant Vicenç
C. la Lluna
C. d Ferlandina
MACBA MUSEU D'ART CONTEMPORANI
C. Elisabets
C. de Santa Anna
C. de la Cendra
C. de la Riera Alta
C. Guitrè
C. Joaquim Costa
C. dels Àngels
C. Pintor Fortuny
La Rambla
C. d. St. Antoni Abat
C. dels Salvador
C. de la Cera
C. Vistalegre
C. de la Riereta
C. del Carme
C. d'en Rolg
C. Egipciaques
C. de l'Arc de Sant Agustí
Hotel Bagués
C. Portaferrissa
C. del Marquès de Campo Sagrado
Reina Amàlia
C. de la
C. de les Carretes
C. de l'Aurura
C. de Sant Pacià
C. Lleialtat
Rambla del Raval
C. de Hospita
Hotel Sant Agustí
Liceu
C. de la Boqueria
C. de Radas
C. de la Creu dels Molers
C. de Biasco de Garay
Carrer de Margarit
Avinguda del Paral·lel
C. Aldana
C. Santa Elena
C. Robador
C. Junta de Comerç
C. de Sant Pau
Hotel España
C. de Ferran
C. d'Annibal
C. de Magathaes
C. de Tapioles
C. de Poeta Cabanyes
Carrer de Blai
Quimet-Quimet
C. les Flors
C. Abat Safont
Sant Oleguer
C. de Sant Ramon
C. de Marquès de Barbera
C. de la Lleona
C. Aglà
Arai-P Dels Q Rius Monu
C. de Salvá
C. d'Elkano
C. del Roser
C. d'en Fontrodona
Funicular
Carrer de Vila i Vilà
Paral·lel
C. de les Tàpies
C. Nou de la Rambla
C. Nou de la Rambla
C. de Santa Madrona
C. de Om
Av. de les Drassanes
C. dels Estberg
C. Guardia
C. des Escudellers
C. de Blesa
C. de Lafont
Pg. de Miramar
C. de Cabanes
Ptge. Canadenca
C. del Arc Teatre
C. del Cid
Ptge. Guten
Prge. Escudellers
C. Nou de Sant Francesc
C. de Còdols
C. de Mata
C. de Piqer
Hotel Grums
Pg. de Montjuïc
C. de Palaudàries
C. Portal de Santa
Drassanes
C. de Josep Anseim Clavé
Avinguda de Miramar
Parc d'Atraccions de Montjuïc
C. Puig Xoriguer
MUSEU MARÍTIM & DRASSANES REIALS
Passeig de Colom
C. Carrera
TORRE MIRAMAR
Ptge. de les Bateries
Plaça de les Drassanes
Plaça Portal de la Pau
MOLL DE BOSCH
Dàrsena Nacional
Passeig de Josp Carner
Carretera Miramart
Terminal Maritime Drassanes
PORT VELL
PORT VELL
Pg. d'itaca
Terminal Maritime Transmediterránea
MOLL DE BARCELONA
Ronda del Litoral
TORRE DE JAUME I
Terminal Maritime Internacional Maremagnum
Eurostars Grand Marina Hotel
Terminal Maritime Internacional Nord
Terminal Maritime Internacional Sud
Terminal Maritime Internacional Italie and Algérie
Dàrsena Sant Bertrán
GRAND MARINA
MOLL BALEARS
Cable Car
Pg. de la Escullera
W Hotel Barcelona

I
J
K
L
Carrer de Casp
Catalunya
Plaça de Catalunya
Urquinaona
Carrer d'Ausiás Marc
Carrer Fontanella
Ronda de Sant Pere
C. d'Ortigosa de Trafalgar
Av. Portal de l'Angel
C. Comtat
C. Sant Pere més Alt
Canuda
C. Montsió
C. Sagristans
Av. Catedral
Av. F.Cambó
C. Fonglilar
ptge. Sant Benet
C. del Rec Comtal
C. del Portal Nou
Carrer del Comerç
C. del Bisbe
CATEDRAL DE LA SEU
C. Carders
C. Corders
C. Llibreteria
C. Jaumel
Jaume I
C. de la Princèsa
MUSEU PICASSO
C. de Montcada
C. Banyes Vells
C. Argenteria
C. Ciutat
Palau Quatre ment
C. Cervantes
C. d'Ataolt
C. d'Avinyó
C. Mosques
Via Laietana
C. de la Nau
BORN-RIBERA
C. d'en Gignás
C. Ample
C. de la Mercé
Av. Marquès de l'Argenterá
Passeig d'Isabel II
ESTACIÓ DE FRANÇA
SEE DETAIL MAP 4
Passeig de Picasso
Passeig de Saint Joan
Carrer de Roger de Flor
C. de Nàpols
Carrer d'Ausiás Marc
Piratas
Carrer d'Ali Bei
Carrer de Sardenya
ANTIC ESTACIÓ DEL NORD
Arc de Triomf
Av. Vilanova
Passeig de Lluís companys
Parc de l'Estacio del Nord
Marina
Carrer des Almogàvers
ME Barcelona
C. de Buenaventura Muñoz
Avinguda Meridiana
Passeig de Pujades
Dos Cielos
Els Tres Porquets
Parc de la Ciutadella
Universitat Pompeu Fabra
Carrer de Ramon Trias Fargas
Carrer de Wellington
PARLAMENT DE CATALUNYA
Parc Zoològic
ZOO
Carrer de Marina
Ciutadella Vila Olimpica
Pg. Circumval.lació
Barceloneta
Carrer del Doctor Alguader
Ronda del Litoral
I ALSINA
MOLL D'ESPANYA
MUSEU D'HISTÒRIA DE CATALUNYA
Carrer Balboa
El Vaso de Oro
B10
Av. del Litoral
Carrer de Ginebra
Pg. de Joan de Borbó
MOLL DE LA BARCELONETA
Carrer la Maquinista
BARCELONETA
Carrer del Gas
Dàrsena del Comerç
AQUARIUM
FARMACIA SAIM
SANT MIQUEL DEL PORT
COOPERATIVE OBRERA LA FRATERNITAT
Can Solé
Carrer Sant Carles
C. d'Andrea Dória
Parc de la Barceloneta
Pg. Maritim de la Barceloneta
Hotel Arts
Enoteca
Can Roca
Els Pescadors
Hispania
Sant Pau
Agua
CDLC
Platja de la Barceloneta
Carrer Aimirall Cervera
Hotel 54
C. Aimirall Aixada
Barceloneta
La Mar Salada
Can Majó
FUENTE DE CARMEN AMAYA
C. Escar
C. del Judici
C. Drassana
Kaiku
Platja de Sant Sebastia
TORRE DE SANT SEBASTIÀ
Torre d'Alta Mar
Platja de Sant Miquel
0
1/4 miles
0
1/4 km
11
12
13
14
15
16

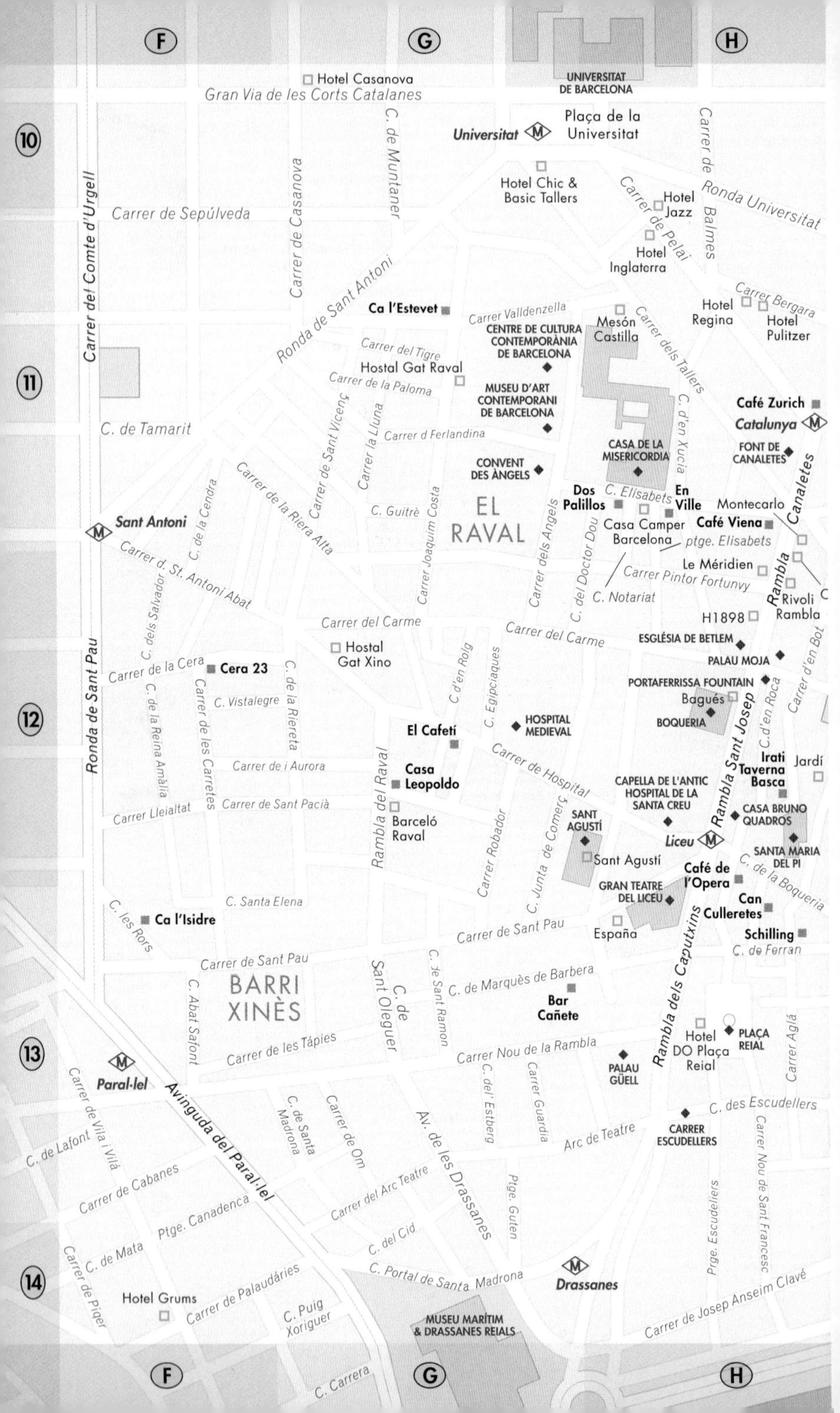

F
G
H
10
11
12
13
14
Hotel Casanova
Gran Via de les Corts Catalanes
UNIVERSITAT DE BARCELONA
Universitat
Plaça de la Universitat
Carrer de Balmes
Carrer de Ronda Universitat
Carrer del Comte d'Urgell
Carrer de Sepúlveda
Carrer de Casanova
C. de Muntaner
Hotel Chic & Basic Tallers
Hotel Jazz
Carrer de Pelai
Hotel Inglaterra
Ronda de Sant Antoni
Ca l'Estevet
Carrer Valldenzella
CENTRE DE CULTURA CONTEMPORÀNIA DE BARCELONA
Mesón Castilla
Carrer dels Tallers
Hotel Regina
Carrer Bergara
Hotel Pulitzer
Carrer del Tigre
Hostal Gat Raval
Carrer de la Paloma
MUSEU D'ART CONTEMPORANI DE BARCELONA
C. d'en Xucia
Café Zurich
Catalunya
C. de Tamarit
Carrer la Lluna
Carrer de Sant Vicenç
Carrer d Ferlandina
CASA DE LA MISERICORDIA
FONT DE CANALETES
CONVENT DES ÀNGELS
Canaletes
Carrer de la Riera Alta
C. de la Cendra
Carrer Joaquim Costa
EL RAVAL
Dos Palillos
C. Elisabets
En Ville
Montecarlo
Sant Antoni
C. Guitrè
Carrer dels Angels
C. del Doctor Dou
Casa Camper Barcelona
Café Viena
ptge. Elisabets
Rambla
Carrer d. St. Antoni Abat
C. dels Salvador
Le Méridien
Carrer Pintor Fortunvy
C. Notariat
Rivoli Rambla
H1898
Carrer del Carme
Carrer del Carme
ESGLÉSIA DE BETLEM
PALAU MOJA
Carrer d'en Bot
Hostal Gat Xino
Ronda de Sant Pau
Carrer de la Cera
Cera 23
C. de la Riereta
C. Vistalegre
C. de la Reina Amàlia
Carrer de les Carretes
C d'en Rolg
C. Egipciaques
PORTAFERRISSA FOUNTAIN
Bagués
BOQUERIA
C.d'en Roca
Rambla Sant Josep
HOSPITAL MEDIEVAL
El Cafetí
Carrer de Hospital
Carrer de i Aurora
Casa Leopoldo
Rambla del Raval
Irati Taverna Basca
Jardí
CAPELLA DE L'ANTIC HOSPITAL DE LA SANTA CREU
Carrer Lleialtat
Carrer de Sant Pacià
Barceló Raval
Carrer Robador
C. Junta de Comerç
SANT AGUSTÍ
CASA BRUNO QUADROS
Liceu
SANTA MARIA DEL PI
Sant Agustí
Café de l'Opera
C. de la Boqueria
C. Santa Elena
GRAN TEATRE DEL LICEU
C. les Rors
Ca l'Isidre
Can Culleretes
España
Carrer de Sant Pau
Schilling
C. de Ferran
Carrer de Sant Pau
BARRI XINÈS
C. Abat Safont
C. de Sant Oleguer
C. de Sant Ramon
C. de Marquès de Barbera
Bar Cañete
Rambla dels Caputxins
Hotel DO Plaça Reial
PLAÇA REIAL
Carrer Aglà
Carrer de les Tàpies
Carrer Nou de la Rambla
PALAU GÜELL
Paral·lel
Avinguda del Paral·lel
Carrer de Vila i Vilá
C. de Santa Madrona
Carrer de Om
C. del' Estberg
Carrer Guardia
Av. de les Drassanes
C. des Escudellers
CARRER ESCUDELLERS
C. de Lafont
Arc de Teatre
Carrer de Cabanes
Ptge. Canadenca
Carrer del Arc Teatre
Ptge. Guten
Ptge. Escudellers
Carrer Nou de Sant Francesc
C. de Mata
C. del Cid
Carrer de Piqer
C. Portal de Santa Madrona
Drassanes
Hotel Grums
Carrer de Palaudàries
C. Puig Xoriguer
MUSEU MARÍTIM & DRASSANES REIALS
Carrer de Josep Anseim Clavé
C. Carrera

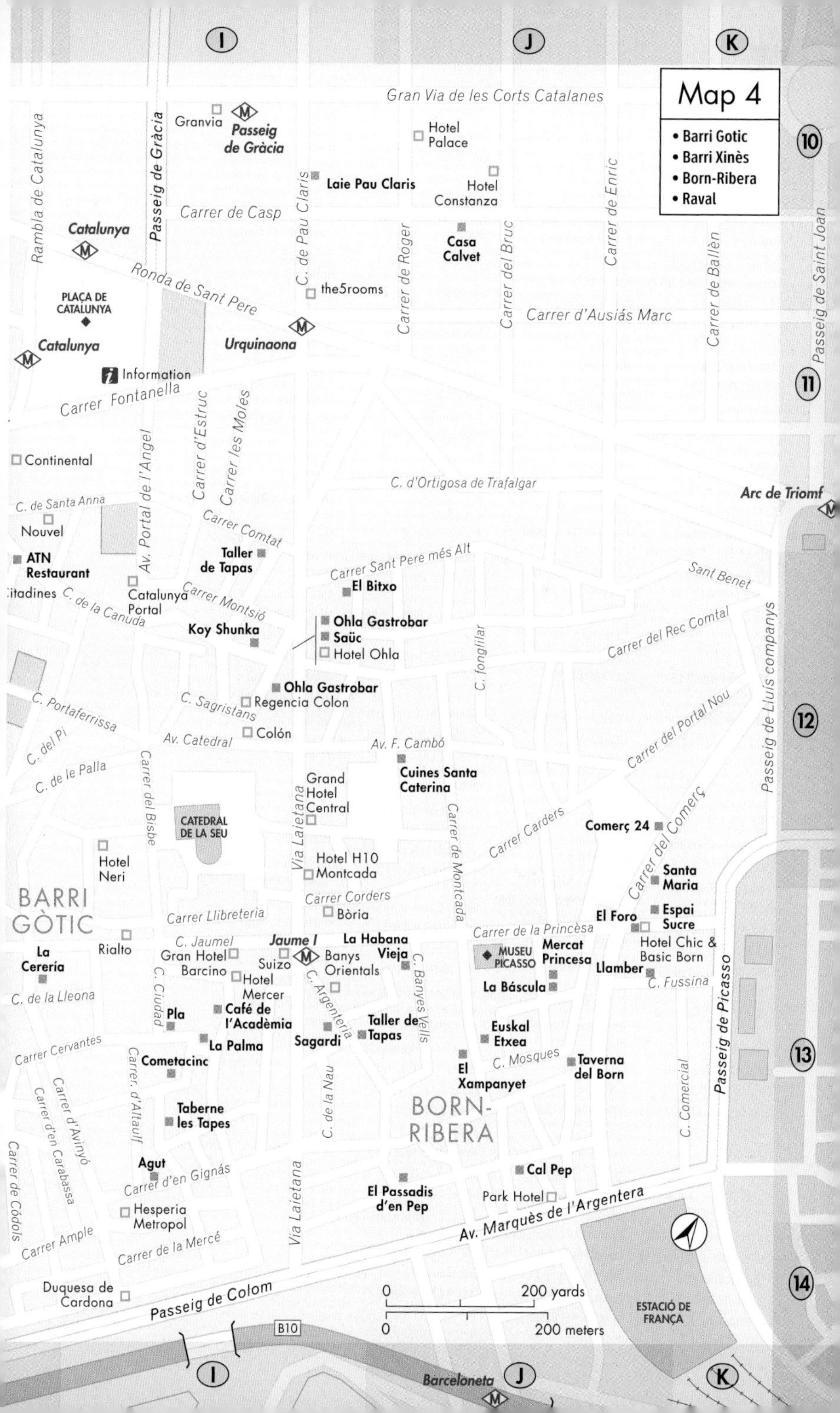

Map 4
• Barri Gotic
• Barri Xinès
• Born-Ribera
• Raval
I
J
K
10
11
12
13
14
Gran Via de les Corts Catalanes
Granvia
Passeig de Gràcia
Hotel Palace
Laie Pau Claris
Hotel Constanza
Rambla de Catalunya
Passeig de Gràcia
Carrer de Casp
C. de Pau Claris
Carrer de Roger
Carrer del Bruc
Carrer de Enric
Carrer de Ballèn
Passeig de Saint Joan
Catalunya
Casa Calvet
Ronda de Sant Pere
the5rooms
Carrer d'Ausiás Marc
PLAÇA DE CATALUNYA
Catalunya
Urquinaona
Information
Carrer Fontanella
Carrer d'Estruc
Carrer les Moles
Av. Portal de l'Angel
Continental
C. d'Ortigosa de Trafalgar
Arc de Triomf
C. de Santa Anna
Nouvel
Carrer Comtat
ATN Restaurant
Taller de Tapas
Carrer Sant Pere més Alt
Sant Benet
El Bitxo
Citadines
C. de la Canuda
Catalunya Portal
Carrer Montsió
Koy Shunka
Ohla Gastrobar
Saüc
Hotel Ohla
C. fonglilar
Carrer del Rec Comtal
Passeig de Lluís companys
Ohla Gastrobar
Regencia Colon
C. Sagristans
C. Portaferrissa
C. del Pi
Av. Catedral
Colón
Av. F. Cambó
Carrer del Portal Nou
C. de le Palla
Carrer del Bisbe
Grand Hotel Central
Cuines Santa Caterina
Via Laietana
CATEDRAL DE LA SEU
Carrer de Montcada
Carrer Carders
Comerç 24
Carrer del Comerç
Hotel Neri
Hotel H10 Montcada
Santa Maria
BARRI GÒTIC
Carrer Corders
Bòria
Carrer Llibreteria
El Foro
Espai Sucre
Carrer de la Princèsa
Rialto
C. Jaumel
Jaume I
La Habana Vieja
Mercat Princesa
MUSEU PICASSO
Hotel Chic & Basic Born
La Cerería
Gran Hotel Barcino
Suizo
Banys Orientals
C. Banyes Vells
Llamber
C. Fussina
Hotel Mercer
C. Argenteria
La Báscula
C. de la Lleona
C. Ciudad
Café de l'Acadèmia
Pla
Passeig de Picasso
Taller de Tapas
Euskal Etxea
Sagardi
La Palma
Carrer Cervantes
Cometacinc
El Xampanyet
C. Mosques
Taverna del Born
Carrer. d'Altaulf
Carrer d'en Carabassa
Carrer d'Aviñyó
Taberne les Tapes
C. de la Nau
BORN-RIBERA
C. Comercial
Carrer de Còdols
Agut
Carrer d'en Gignás
Cal Pep
El Passadis d'en Pep
Park Hotel
Hesperia Metropol
Via Laietana
Av. Marquès de l'Argentera
Carrer Ample
Carrer de la Mercé
Duquesa de Cardona
Passeig de Colom
0
200 yards
0
200 meters
ESTACIÓ DE FRANÇA
B10
Barceloneta

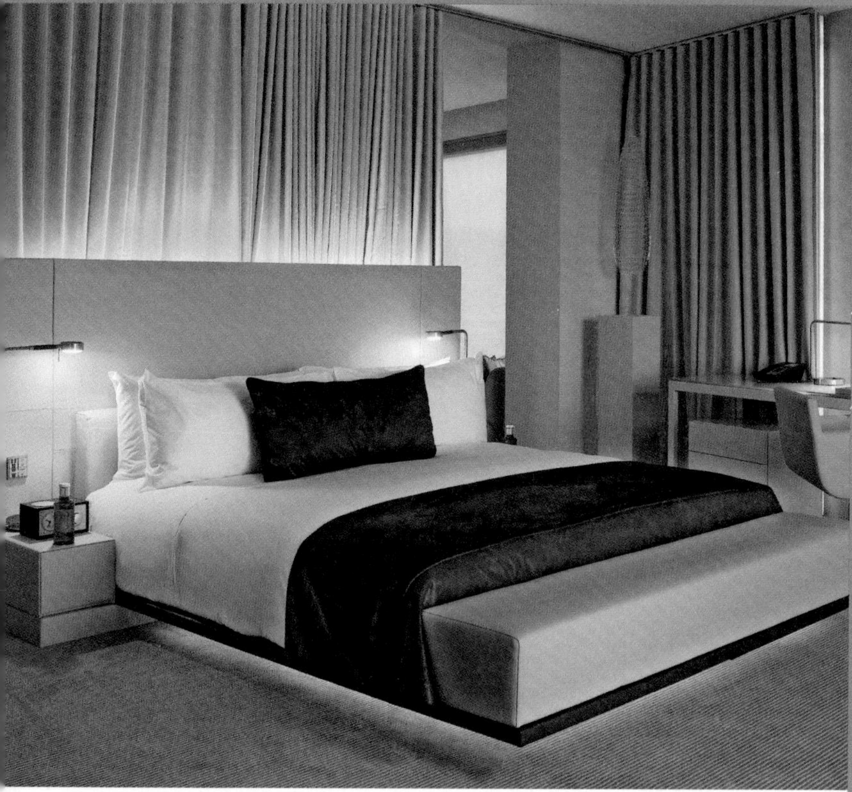

WHERE TO STAY

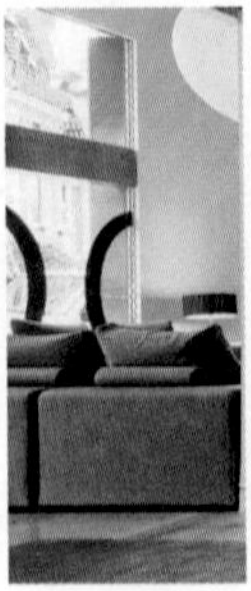

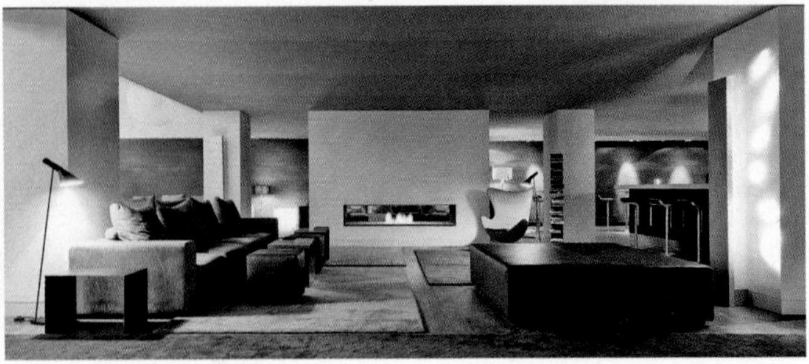

By Jared Lubarsky

Barcelona's hotel trade may be centuries removed from Miguel de Cervantes's 17th-century description of it as a "repository of courtesy, travelers' shelter," but in the 400 years or so since *Don Quijote* the city has never lost its talent for pampering and impressing visitors.

Barcelona's pre-Olympics hotel surge in the early 1990s was matched only by its post-Olympics hotel surge in the early 2000s. Barcelona is the premier tourist destination in Spain and the major cruise port in the Mediterranean. Starchitects like Ricardo Bofill and Rafael Moneo have changed the skyline with skyscraper hotels of eye-popping luxury; the Grand Hyatt group is about to add another, acquiring Jean Nouvel's emblematic Torre Agbar for the latest in it its collection. The real heroes of this story, however, are the architect-designer teams that take one after another of the city's historic properties and restore them with an astonishing tour de force of taste. Hotel restaurants, too—from the Arts's Enoteca to the Mandarin's Moments—are among the superstar attractions in the city's gastronomic scene.

Hotels in the Barri Gòtic and along La Rambla now compete for seasoned travelers with the newer lodgings in the Eixample or west along Diagonal; waterfront monoliths like the W Barcelona and the Eurostars Grand Marina, removed from the bustle of midtown, set the standard for upscale hospitality. Many Eixample hotels occupy restored late 19th- or early 20th-century town houses. The Claris, the Majestic Hotel & Spa, the Condes de Barcelona, the Hotel Neri, and the Colón mix style and luxury with a sense of place.

Small hotels in the Ciutat Vella, such as the Sant Agustí, Hotel Market, or Hotel Chic & Basic Born are less than half as expensive and more a part of city life. Overlooking Barcelona is the Gran Hotel la Florida for those who want to be out of the fray.

WHERE TO STAY?

	Neighborhood Vibe	Pros	Cons
Barri Gòtic and Born-Ribera	With gaslight-type lamps glowing in the corners of Roman and Gothic areas, this is a romantic part of town. The Picasso Museum and Santa Maria del Mar basilica are nearby.	The architecture of the Barri Gòtic is the great repository of the city's past. Plaça Sant Jaume, the cathedral, Plaça del Rei, and the Born-Ribera district are among the main reasons to visit the city.	It's easy to lose yourself in this labyrinth of narrow cobblestone streets. The Barri Gòtic can also be noisy, with echoes reverberating around this ancient sound chamber.
El Raval	El Raval has always been a rough-and-tumble part of town. But the nightlife is exciting and the diversity of the neighborhood is exemplary. Bonus: being steps from the Boqueria market.	For the closest thing to Marrakesh in Barcelona, El Raval has a buzz all its own. A contemporary art museum, the medieval hospital, and the Mercat de Sant Antoni offer plenty to explore.	El Raval can seem dangerous, and demands street-sense, especially at night. Pockets of it are the haunts of prostitutes, drug dealers, and other seamy characters.
La Rambla	A solid stream of humanity around the clock, La Rambla is a virtual anthology of Barcelona street life, shared equally by visitors, hucksters, café hoppers and local residents.	Boqueria market, flower stalls, the Liceu opera house, and Plaça Reial are all quintessential Barcelona sites.	The incessant crush of humanity can be overwhelming, especially if FC Barcelona wins a championship match and the entire city descends on La Rambla to celebrate.
Barceloneta and Port Olímpic	The onetime fishermen's quarter, Barceloneta retains its informal and working-class ambience, with sidewalk restaurants lining Passeig Joan de Borbó.	Near the beach, this part of town has a laid-back feel. Barceloneta is where you go for the best casual seafood restaurants in town.	Barceloneta offers few accommodations beyond the W Hotel; Port Olímpic's monolithic Hotel Arts is a bit isolated from the rest of town.
Eixample	Gaudí masterpieces Casa Milà and Casa Battló are here, on the Passeig de Gràcia; this Moderniste quarter boasts many of the city's top-tier hotels and restaurants. And then there's the shopping…	Art Nouveau architecture is everywhere in the Eixample, constantly rewarding to the eye. Gaudí's yet-unfinished masterpiece La Sagrada Família is within walking distance.	Too few buildings here have street numbers; for a neighborhood that was supposed to be structured as a grid, the Eixample can be difficult to navigate.
Pedralbes, Sarrià, and Upper Barcelona	Upper Barcelona is leafy and residential, where the air is always a little cooler and cleaner. Pedralbes is Barcelona's wealthiest residential quarter; Sarrià is the rustic little village next door.	A 15-minute train ride connects Sarrià with the middle of the Eixample and La Rambla.	Staying in upper Barcelona involves a 15-minute trip, at least, to the most important attractions. After midnight on weeknights this will require a taxi.

BARCELONA LODGING PLANNER

LODGING STRATEGY

Scan the "Best Bets" chart for top recommendations by price and experience. Or find a review quickly in the listings. Search by neighborhood, then alphabetically.

RESERVATIONS

Because of the annual summer onslaught of millions of tourists, you'll want to reserve well in advance from early April to late October. Note that high-season rates prevail also during the week before Easter and local fiestas. You should specify when reserving whether you prefer two beds or one double bed. Although single rooms (*habitacións sencillas*) are usually available, they are often on the small side, and you might prefer to pay a bit extra for single occupancy in a double room (*habitación doble uso individual*).

FACILITIES

Hotel entrances are marked with a plaque bearing the letter H and the number of stars. The letter R (standing for *residencia*) after the letter H indicates an establishment with no meal service. The designations *fonda* (F), *pensión* (P), and *hostal* (Hs) indicate budget accommodations—although a Spanish *hostal* can often be just as well-appointed and comfortable as a hotel.

Hotel ratings used by the Turisme de Barcelona are expressed in stars, with five stars as the highest category. The rating system, however, is essentially based on a checklist of facilities (pool, restaurant, concierge, etc.) more than an evaluation of quality; a hotel can lack one or more of the amenities on the list and still be a better choice than one in the next highest category.

PRICES

Barcelona's finer hotels are, alas, as expensive as those of any other major city—but rates can vary as widely (and mysteriously) as airline tickets. Prices are generally lower from October to June, when hotels have more availability, except when there are huge conventions in town or other special events.

Prices in the hotel reviews are the lowest cost of a standard double room in high season. Most prices include a V.A.T. (value-added tax) of 10%.

BEST BETS FOR BARCELONA LODGING

Fodor's offers a select listing of quality lodging experiences in every price range, from the city's best budget choice to its most sophisticated luxury hotel. Here we've compiled our top recommendations by price and experience. The very best properties—in other words, those that provide a particularly remarkable experience in their price range—are designated in the listings with the Fodor's Choice logo.

Fodor's Choice★

Arai-Palau, $$$, p. 196
Casa Fuster, $$$$, p. 209
Claris, $$$$, p. 203
Condes de Barcelona, $$, p. 204
Continental Palacete, $$, p. 204
H1898, $$$$, p. 200
Hotel Arts, $$$$, p. 201
Hotel España, $$$, p. 199
Hotel Granados 83, $$, p. 206
Hotel Murmuri, $$, p. 206
Hotel Neri, $$$, p. 197
Hotel Omm, $$$$, p. 206
Hotel SERHS Rivoli Rambla, $$$, p. 201
Jardí, $, p. 197
Le Méridien, $$$$, p. 200
Majestic Hotel & Spa, $$$, p. 207
Primero Primera, $$$, p. 210
Turó de Vilana, $, p. 210
W Barcelona, $$$$, p. 203

By Price

$

Banys Orientals, p. 198
Jardí, p. 197
Turó de Vilana, p. 210

$$

Hotel Murmuri, p. 206
Colón, p. 196
Condes de Barcelona, p. 204
Continental Palacete, p. 204
Duquesa de Cardona, p. 200
Hotel Granados 83, p. 206

$$$

Arai-Palau, p. 196
Hotel Jazz, p. 206
Majestic Hotel & Spa, p. 207
Hotel Neri, p. 197
Hotel Ohla, p. 197
Hotel Pulitzer, p. 207
Hotel SERHS Rivoli Rambla, p. 201
Primero Primera, p. 210

$$$$

Casa Fuster, p. 209
Claris, p. 203
H1898, p. 200
Hotel Arts, p. 201
Hotel DO Plaça Reial, p. 200
Hotel Omm, p. 206
Le Méridien, p. 200
Mandarin Oriental, p. 207
W Barcelona, p. 203

By Experience

BEST FOR HISTORY BUFFS

Arai-Palau, p. 196
Casa Fuster, p. 209
Colón, p. 196
Hotel España, p. 199
Sant Agustí, p. 199

BEST HOTEL RESTAURANT

Condes de Barcelona (Lasarte), p. 204
Hotel Cram (Can Gaig), p. 205
Hotel Ohla (Saüc), p. 197
Hotel Omm (Roca Moo), p. 206
Mandarin Oriental (Moments), p. 207

BEST VIEWS

Gran Hotel la Florida, p. 210
Hotel Arts, p. 201
W Barcelona, p. 203

CHILD-FRIENDLY

Casa Camper Barcelona, p. 198
Citadines, p. 200
Gran Hotel la Florida, p. 210
Gran Hotel Princesa Sofía, p. 209
Mandarin Oriental, p. 207
Primero Primera, p. 210

MOST ROMANTIC

Gran Hotel la Florida, p. 210
Hotel Mercer, p. 197
Hotel Neri, p. 197

4

HOTEL REVIEWS

Listed alphabetically within neighborhoods. Use the coordinate (✣ B:2) at the end of each review to locate a property on the corresponding map. For expanded reviews visit Fodors.com.

CIUTAT VELLA (OLD CITY)

The Ciutat Vella includes La Rambla, Barri Gòtic, Born-Ribera, and El Raval districts between Plaça de Catalunya and the port.

BARRI GÒTIC

$$$ HOTEL FAMILY Fodor's Choice ★ **Arai-Palau Dels Quatre Rius Monument.** You couldn't ask for a better location from which to explore Barcelona's Barri Gòtic—or for a bivouac more elegant—than one of the aparthotel suites in this stunning restoration. **Pros:** warm, attentive service; double shower heads in the bath; top-tier amenities; strategic location; superb soundproofing. **Cons:** pool on the rooftop terrace is tiny; no spa; no room service; rooms on the top floor lack some of the historic charm below. *Rooms from: €200 ✉ Avinyó 30, Barri Gòtic ☎ 93/320–3950 ⊕ www.hotelarai.com/#!en/home 30 rooms No meals ✣ I:13.*

$$$ HOTEL FAMILY **Bòria.** A sweet hideaway in a slightly scruffy neighborhood between the Santa Caterina market and the Picasso Museum, the Bòria has clean lines and design details which make it a welcome addition to the boutique hotel scene in Barcelona—and a boon for families. **Pros:** walking distance from nearly everything—Picasso, Palau de la Música, Santa Maria del Mar, La Rambla; pleasant rooftop terrace and solarium. **Cons:** no restaurant, bar, pool or room service; neighborhood can seem sketchy at night. *Rooms from: €180 ✉ Carrer de Bòria 24–26, Barri Gòtic ☎ 93/295–5893 ⊕ www.boriabcn.com 2 doubles, 7 suites, 2 lofts No meals Ⓜ Jaume I ✣ I:13.*

$ HOTEL **Catalunya Portal d'Angel.** Converted in 1998 from a historic stately home, the Catalunya Portal d'Angel beckons with its Neoclassic facade and original grand marble staircase. **Pros:** smooth professional service; babysitters on request; free walking tours of the Ciutat Vella and the Eixample; good value. **Cons:** rooms a bit small; lighting and soundproofing need improvement; small pool open only June through August. *Rooms from: €120 ✉ Av. Portal d'Angel 17, Barri Gòtic ☎ 93/318–4141 84 rooms No meals ✣ I:12.*

$$ HOTEL **Colón.** The Colón opened in 1951, and feels like it's been around forever: quiet, conservative, correct. **Pros:** walking distance from all of central Barcelona; pet-friendly; attentive staff. **Cons:** can feel a bid stodgy; pricey breakfast; undistinguished dining. *Rooms from: €150 ✉ Av. Catedral 7, Barri Gòtic ☎ 93/301–1404 ⊕ www.hotelcolon.es 15 singles, 121 doubles, 5 suites No meals Ⓜ Catalunya ✣ I:12.*

$$ HOTEL **Gran Hotel Barcino.** The Barcino (so named for the ancient Roman settlement that once comprised this part of the Barri Gòtic) is one of a group of hotels that markets itself mainly to the budget-conscious international traveler. **Pros:** central location; rooms on the 6th floor have small private terraces. **Cons:** less-than-effective lighting in the rooms; 75% of the rooms face the busy street Jaume I; no room service; no

gym, pool or spa. *$ Rooms from: €140 ✉ Jaume I, 6, Barri Gòtic ☎ 93/302–2012 🌐 www.hotelbarcino.com 68 rooms No meals M Jaume I ✣ I:13.*

$$$$ HOTEL **Grand Hotel Central.** At the edge of the Barri Gòtic, very near the Barcelona cathedral, this fashionable midtown hotel is popular with business and pleasure travelers alike. **Pros:** excellent location between the Barri Gòtic and the Born; attentive service; sleek look; good spa. **Cons:** for the price, rooms are small; no pets. *$ Rooms from: €270 ✉ Via Laietana 30, Barri Gòtic ☎ 93/295–7900 🌐 www.grandhotelcentral.com 125 rooms, 22 suites No meals M Jaume I ✣ I:12.*

$$ HOTEL **Hotel Gargallo Rialto.** With its glass-walled reception area on the corner of Pas de l'Ensenyança and Carrer Ferran, this spotless, well-lit place has standard rooms with wooden floorboards, patterned gray drapes and bedspreads, and solid walnut doors. **Pros:** central location; friendly staff; pets allowed. **Cons:** one of the busiest streets in the Ciutat Vella, rowdy at night; no room service; bed linens and drapes seem dated. *$ Rooms from: €168 ✉ Ferran 42, Barri Gòtic ☎ 93/318–5212 🌐 www.hotel-rialto.com 204 rooms, 1 suite Breakfast M Liceu, Catalunya ✣ I:13.*

$$$$ HOTEL **Hotel Mercer.** On a narrow side street near Plaça Sant Jaume, this romantic boutique hotel is among the latest examples of Barcelona's signature genius for the redesign and rebirth of historical properties. **Pros:** strategic location, minutes from anything you'd want to see in the Ciutat Vella; warm, professional hospitality; comfortable rooftop terrace with a plunge pool and (in season) a bar-café. **Cons:** hard on the budget; no gym or spa; no pets. *$ Rooms from: €370 ✉ Carrer dels Lledó 5, Barri Gòtic ☎ 93/310–7480 🌐 www.mercerbarcelona.com 19 rooms, 9 suites No meals M Jaume I ✣ I:13.*

$$$ HOTEL Fodor's Choice ★ **Hotel Neri.** Built into an 18th-century palace just steps from the Cathedral, this elegant upscale boutique hotel marries ancient and avant-garde design. **Pros:** central location; hip design; roof terrace for cocktails and breakfast. **Cons:** noise from adjacent Plaça Sant Filip Neri can be a problem on summer nights (and winter-morning school days); impractical hanging bed lights. *$ Rooms from: €200 ✉ Sant Sever 5, Barri Gòtic ☎ 93/304–0655 🌐 www.hotelneri.com 14 doubles, 8 suites No meals M Liceu, Catalunya ✣ I:12.*

$$$ HOTEL **Hotel Ohla.** One of Barcelona's top new design hotels, the Ohla's neoclassical exterior (not counting the goofy eyeballs stuck to the facade) belies its avant-garde interior, full of witty, design-conscious touches. **Pros:** strategic location, a two-minute walk from the Palau de la Música Catalana; attentive, professional staff. **Cons:** layout in some rooms sacrifices privacy to design; Via Laietana, just outside, is a nonstop noisy traffic artery. *$ Rooms from: €215 ✉ Via Laietana 49, Barri Gòtic ☎ 93/341–5050 🌐 www.ohlahotel.com 73 rooms, 1 suite No meals M Urquinaona ✣ I:12.*

$ HOTEL Fodor's Choice ★ **Jardí.** Facing charming Plaça del Pi and Plaça Sant Josep Oriol, this family-friendly little budget hotel couldn't be better situated for exploring La Rambla and the Barri Gòtic. **Pros:** central location; good value for price; impeccable bathrooms. **Cons:** no pets; no room service. *$ Rooms from: €95 ✉ Pl. Sant Josep Oriol 1, Barri Gòtic ☎ 93/301–5900 🌐 www.eljardi-barcelona.com 40 rooms No meals M Liceu, Catalunya ✣ H:12.*

4

BORN-RIBERA

$ HOTEL **Banys Orientals.** Despite its name, the "Oriental Baths" has, for the moment, no spa, but what it does have is chic high-contrast design, with dark stained wood and crisp white bedding, and strategic location at a reasonable price. **Pros:** central location; tasteful design; good value for price. **Cons:** no pets; no parking; no laundry service; communal fridge on each floor, but no room minibars. *Rooms from: €115 Argenteria 37, Born-Ribera 93/268–8460 www.hotelbanysorientals.com 43 rooms, 14 suites No meals Jaume I I:13.*

$$ HOTEL **Hotel Chic & Basic Born.** A revolutionary concept best illustrated by the middle-of-your-room glass shower stalls, the Chic & Basic chain is a hit with young hipsters looking for the combo package of splashy design with affordable prices. **Pros:** perfectly situated for Barcelona's hot Born-Ribera scene; clean-lined sleek design. **Cons:** tumultuous nightlife around the hotel requires closed windows on weekends; rooms and spaces are small. *Rooms from: €150 Carrer Princesa 50, Born-Ribera 93/295–4652 www.chicandbasic.com/hotel-barcelona-born/en 31 rooms No meals Jaume I J:13.*

$$ HOTEL **Hotel H10 Montcada.** Ultracontemporary, this hotel at the edge of the Barri Gòtic (part of the sleek H10 chain popping up all over Spain) is a sure bet for clean design and comfort. **Pros:** central location; attentive staff; family-friendly; good value for price. **Cons:** superior doubles are small and oddly laid-out; no room service; soundproofing barely copes with the traffic on Via Laietana. *Rooms from: €149 Via Laietana 24, Born-Ribera 93/268–8570 www.h10.es 87 rooms Breakfast Jaume I I:12.*

$$$ HOTEL **Park Hotel Barcelona.** Well situated for exploring some of Barcelona's prime art and architecture—and in a neighborhood blessed with wine and tapas bars—this mid-priced hotel has sleek rooms with espresso-color wood and punchy red accents. **Pros:** good location; cheerful, professional service. **Cons:** rooms a bit on the small side; no pool, gym or spa; no pets. *Rooms from: €178 Av. Marquès de l'Argentera 11, Born-Ribera 93/319–6000 www.parkhotelbarcelona.com 91 rooms No meals Barceloneta J:13.*

EL RAVAL

$$$ HOTEL **Barceló Raval.** For lodgings with an edgy, contemporary sense of design, at reasonable rates, in one of Barcelona's most colorful neighborhoods, this is an especially welcome addition to the city's hotel scene. **Pros:** central location five minutes from La Rambla; panoramic views over city; efficient staff. **Cons:** retro-modern design; mood lighting not to everyone's taste; soundproofing could be better; Rambla del Raval a bit dicey at night. *Rooms from: €185 Rambla del Raval 17–21, El Raval 93/320–1490 www.hotelbarceloraval.com 182 doubles, 4 suites No meals Liceu G:12.*

$$$ HOTEL **Casa Camper Barcelona.** A marriage between the Camper footwear empire and the Vinçon design store produced this brainchild, a 21st-century hotel halfway between La Rambla and the MACBA (Museum of Contemporary Art). **Pros:** handy mid-Raval location; just steps from MACBA and the Boqueria; hip, friendly staff. **Cons:** no pets; no way to get a car close to the hotel door; a bit pricey for what you

get. *Rooms from: €195* ✉ *C. Elisabets 11, El Raval* ☎ *93/342–6280* 🌐 *www.casacamper.com* *20 rooms, 5 suites* *Breakfast* Ⓜ *Catalunya* ✣ *H:11.*

$$$ HOTEL Fodor's Choice ★ **Hotel España.** This recently renovated Art Nouveau gem is among the oldest and best of Barcelona's smaller hotels. **Pros:** strategic location; steeped in artistic history; friendly staff; excellent restaurant ($$).**Cons:** the lower rooms on Carrer Sant Pau get some street noise despite the double-glazing; rooftop pool, spa, and gym only open Apr. 23–mid-Oct. *Rooms from: €180* ✉ *Sant Pau 9–11, El Raval* ☎ *93/550–0000* 🌐 *www.hotelespanya.com* *81 rooms, 1 suite* *No meals* Ⓜ *Liceu* ✣ *H:13.*

$ HOTEL **Hostal Chic & Basic Tallers.** A sleek budget choice in the upper Raval, this undertaking by the Chic & Basic group offers three sizes of rooms from medium to extra-large, all minimally decorated with crisp white bedding, graphic art on the walls, and red shower doors. **Pros:** a short walk to the center of town at Plaça de Catalunya; young and friendly staff. **Cons:** soundproofing not up to the noise from the streets in El Raval; en suite kitchen units make for a tight squeeze; no restaurant; no pets. *Rooms from: €80* ✉ *Carrer Tallers 82, El Raval* ☎ *93/302–5183* 🌐 *www.chicandbasic.com* *14 rooms* *Breakfast* Ⓜ *Catalunya, Universitat* ✣ *G:10.*

$ HOTEL **Hotel Inglaterra.** A welcoming Moderniste stairway in this neoclassical building leads to simple guest rooms decorated in blonde wood with Japanese characters as artwork. **Pros:** central location; modern facilities; near El Raval and the MACBA. **Cons:** noisy avenue in front of hotel; a bit pricey for the value; lacking high design or history to make it unique. *Rooms from: €124* ✉ *Pelai 14, El Raval* ☎ *93/505–1100* 🌐 *www.hotel-inglaterra.com* *58 rooms, 2 suites* *Breakfast* Ⓜ *Catalunya, Universitat* ✣ *H:11.*

$ HOTEL **Hotel Market.** Wallet-friendly and design-conscious, this boutique hotel is named for the Mercat de Sant Antoni a block away. **Pros:** well equipped, designed, and positioned for a low-cost Barcelona visit; young and friendly staff. **Cons:** rooms are a little cramped. *Rooms from: €69* ✉ *Carrer Comte Borrell 68, entrance on Passatge Sant Antoni Abat 10, El Raval* ☎ *93/325–1205* 🌐 *www.markethotel.com.es* *59 rooms* *No meals* Ⓜ *Sant Antoni* ✣ *F:11.*

$$ HOTEL **Sant Agustí.** In a leafy square just off La Rambla, the Sant Agustí bills itself as the oldest billet in Barcelona—built in 1720 as a convent and reborn as a hotel in 1840. **Pros:** central location near the Boqueria market, La Rambla and the Liceu opera house; traditional design with modern comfort; good value for price; family-friendly. **Cons:** Plaça Sant Agusti can be a homeless hangout; soundproofing less than best; so-so breakfast; service is hit-or-miss. *Rooms from: €135* ✉ *Pl. Sant Agustí 3, El Raval* ☎ *93/318–1658* 🌐 *www.hotelsa.com* *72 rooms, 8 suites* *Breakfast* Ⓜ *Liceu* ✣ *H:12.*

LA RAMBLA

$$$$ HOTEL **Bagués.** The luxury once confined to hotels in the Eixample has worked is way down to La Rambla—as this new boutique gem bears ample witness. **Pros:** warm, professional service; pet-friendly; steps from the opera house; view of the Cathedral and port from the rooftop terrace. **Cons:** rooms a bit small for the price; hard on the pocketbook;

tiny plunge pool on the terrace; bathrooms don't afford enough privacy. *Rooms from: €291* ✉ *La Rambla 105, Rambla* ☎ *93/343–5000* 🌐 *www.derbyhotels.com/en/hotel-bagues* *2 singles, 26 doubles, 3 suites* *No meals* Ⓜ *Pl. de Catalunya, Liceu* ✣ *H:12.*

$$$ HOTEL FAMILY **Citadines.** Located in two buildings at the upper end of La Rambla, Citadines is an excellent choice for families, groups of friends, or long-term visitors; the accommodations consist of apartments with sitting rooms and one-room studios with kitchenettes and small dining areas. **Pros:** central location; spacious rooms; free daily housekeeping. **Cons:** noisy neighborhood; no pool. *Rooms from: €180* ✉ *La Rambla 122, Rambla* ☎ *93/270–1111* 🌐 *www.citadines.com* *115 studios, 16 apartments* *No meals* Ⓜ *Catalunya* ✣ *H:12.*

$$ HOTEL **Duquesa de Cardona.** A refurbished 16th-century town house, this hotel on the port is a 10-minute walk from everything in the Barri Gòtic and Barceloneta, and no more than a 30-minute walk from the main Eixample attractions. **Pros:** great combination of traditional and contemporary; key spot near the port; ample roof terrace. **Cons:** rooms on the small side; no gym or spa; Passeig de Colom is a busy, noisy artery. *Rooms from: €150* ✉ *Passeig de Colom 12, Port* ☎ *93/268–9090* 🌐 *www.hduquesadecardona.com* *35 rooms, 5 junior suites* *No meals* Ⓜ *Drassanes* ✣ *I:14.*

$$$$ HOTEL Fodor's Choice ★ **H1898.** Overlooking La Rambla, this imposing mansion, once the headquarters of the Compañiá General de Tabacos de Filipinas, couldn't be better located—especially with the Liceu just around the corner, for opera fans. **Pros:** impeccable service; equally ideal for families and romantic couples. **Cons:** subway rumble discernible in lower rooms on La Rambla side. *Rooms from: €255* ✉ *La Rambla 109, Rambla* ☎ *93/552–9552* 🌐 *www.hotel1898.com* *166 rooms, 3 suites* *No meals* Ⓜ *Catalunya, Liceu* ✣ *H:12.*

$$$$ HOTEL **Hotel DO Plaça Reial.** Just at the entrance to the Neoclassic Plaça Reial, this 2012 addition to Barcelona's growing collection of boutique hotels—with its with two restaurants, La Terraza (under the arcades on the square) and La Cuina (downstairs under graceful brick vaulting)—is a find for foodies and lovers of tasteful design. **Pros:** walking distance from everything you will want to see in the old city center; perfect soundproofing; helpful multilingual staff. **Cons:** hard on the wallet; neighborhood can be rowdy at night. *Rooms from: €280* ✉ *Pl. Reial 1, Rambla* ☎ *93/481–3666* 🌐 *www.hoteldoreial.com* *18 rooms* *Breakfast* Ⓜ *Liceu* ✣ *H:13.*

$$$$ HOTEL Fodor's Choice ★ **Le Méridien Barcelona.** There's no dearth of hotels along La Rambla, in the heart of the city, but few rival the upscale Le Méridien. **Pros:** central location; spot-on professional service; gym open 24 hours. **Cons:** no pool; rooms just a tad small for the price; €55/day surcharge for pets. *Rooms from: €250* ✉ *La Rambla 111, Rambla* ☎ *93/318–6200* 🌐 *www.lemeridien.com/barcelona* *190 rooms, 40 suites* *No meals* Ⓜ *Catalunya* ✣ *H:12.*

$$$$ HOTEL **Montecarlo.** The Montecarlo makes a good first impression: an ornate, columned entrance takes you from La Rambla through a grand marble hall, to a sumptuous reception room with a dark-wood Art Nouveau ceiling. **Pros:** central location; not a venue for tour groups. **Cons:** noisy

neighborhood; correct but slightly impersonal service; no pool or spa; a bit pricey for what you get. *Rooms from: €240 La Rambla 124, Rambla 93/412–0404 www.montecarlobcn.com 50 rooms No meals Catalunya H:11.*

$$ HOTEL **Nouvel.** White marble, etched glass, and carved woodwork blend into a handsome Art Nouveau interior in this hotel. **Pros:** strategic location for exploring the Old Quarter; charming Moderniste details in public spaces. **Cons:** rooms on the small side; furniture and bedding look dated; surcharges for Wi-Fi and room safes; no pets. *Rooms from: €160 Carrer Santa Anna 18–20, Rambla 93/301–8274 www.hotelnouvel.es 71 rooms No meals Catalunya H:11.*

$$$ HOTEL Fodor's Choice ★ **Hotel SERHS Rivoli Rambla.** Behind this traditional upper-Rambla facade lies a surprisingly whimsical interior with marble floors and artwork by well-known Barcelona artist Perico Pastor on the columns and the ceiling. **Pros:** strategic location; pet-friendly; good value. **Cons:** no parking; no pool or spa; noisy neighborhood. *Rooms from: €205 La Rambla 128, Rambla 93/481–7676 www.hotelserhsrivolirambla.com 120 rooms, 6 suites No meals Catalunya H:12.*

4

BARCELONETA, PORT OLÍMPIC, AND FÒRUM

$$ HOTEL **Eurostars Grand Marina Hotel.** An alabaster cylindrical fortress built around a central patio, the Grand Marina offers a portside retreat two minutes from La Rambla, with stunning views of the city or the Mediterranean. **Pros:** close to the Ciutat Vella; great views out to sea; good restaurant. **Cons:** impersonal, high-rise-style construction and decor; not very family-friendly; facilities showing signs of age; cruise ship arrivals and departures can be very noisy; no pets. *Rooms from: €138 Moll de Barcelona s/n, Port Olímpic 93/603–9000 www.grandmarinahotel.com 291 rooms No meals Drassanes G:15.*

$$$$ HOTEL Fodor's Choice ★ **Hotel Arts.** This luxurious Ritz-Carlton-owned, 44-story skyscraper overlooks Barcelona from the Olympic Port, providing stunning views of the Mediterranean, the city, the Sagrada Família, and the mountains beyond. **Pros:** excellent views over Barcelona; impeccable service; fine restaurants; minutes from the beach; family-friendly. **Cons:** a 20-minute hike, at least, from central Barcelona; hard on the budget. *Rooms from: €535 Calle de la Marina 19–21, Port Olímpic 93/221–1000 www.hotelartsbarcelona.com 365 rooms, 44 suites, 28 apartments No meals Ciutadella–Vil.la Olímpica L:15.*

$ **Marina Folch.** A little hideaway in the pungent fishermen's quarter of Barceloneta, this hotel is surprisingly clean and crisp. Rooms are small, with pale blue walls and bedding, and equipped with somewhat matchstick furnishings, but most have views over the Barcelona harbor. Five minutes from the beach and with an excellent restaurant and a generous, caring family at the helm, it's a budget winner. **Pros:** great value; five minutes from the beach; surrounded by fine tapas and dining opportunities. **Cons:** bed frames somewhat light and flimsy; spaces cramped. *Rooms from: €95 Carrer Mar 16 entsol., Barceloneta 93/310–3709 www.hotelmarinafolchbcn.com 11 rooms No meals Barceloneta J:14.*

CLOSE UP

Lodging Alternatives

APARTMENT RENTALS

If you want a home base that's roomy enough for a family and comes with cooking facilities, consider a furnished rental. These can save you money, especially if you're traveling with a group. Apartment rentals are increasingly popular in Barcelona these days. Aparthotels rent apartments in residences subdivided into small living spaces at prices generally more economical than hotel rates. Rentals by the day or week can be arranged, though prices may rise for short stays. Prices range from €100 to €300 per day depending on the quality of the accommodations, but perfectly acceptable lodging for four can be found for around €150 per night. Apartment accommodations can be arranged through any of the agencies listed *below.*

LOCAL APARTMENT AGENCIES

Aparthotel Bertran ✉ *Bertran 150, Sant Gervasi* ☎ *93/212–7550* 🌐 *www.hotelbertran.com* Ⓜ *El Putxet.*

Aparthotel Bonanova ✉ *Bisbe Sivilla 7, San Gervasi* ☎ *93/253–1563* 🌐 *www.bonanovasuite.com* Ⓜ *El Putxet.*

Aparthotel Nàpols ✉ *Nàpols 116, Eixample* ☎ *93/246–4573* 🌐 *www.abapart.com* Ⓜ *Tetuan, Arc de Triomf.*

Apartment Barcelona ✉ *Paris 207, 5-2, Eixample* ☎ *93/481–3577* 🌐 *www.apartmentbarcelona.com* Ⓜ *Diagonal.*

Apartments Ramblas ☎ *93/301–7678* 🌐 *www.only-apartments.com/apartments-barcelona/html.*

Barcelona for Rent ✉ *Bailén 120, Eixample* ☎ *93/458–6340* 🌐 *www.barcelonaforrent.com* Ⓜ *Verdaguer.*

Barceloneta Suites ✉ *Grau i Torras 17, Barceloneta* ☎ *93/221–4225* 🌐 *www.barcelonetasuites.com* Ⓜ *Barceloneta.*

Feel Barcelona ✉ *Balmes 28, Eixample* ☎ *93/150–3176* 🌐 *www.localnomad.com* Ⓜ *Universitat.*

Flats By Days ✉ *Bellafila 5, Barri Gòtic* ☎ *93/342–6481* 🌐 *www.flatsbydays.com* Ⓜ *Jaume I.*

Friendly Rentals ✉ *Pasaje Sert 1–3, bajos, Eixample* ☎ *93/268–8051* 🌐 *www.friendlyrentals.com* Ⓜ *Urquinaona.*

Gobcn Apartments ✉ *Paral.lel 91, Poble Sec* ☎ *93/278–1156* 🌐 *www.gobcn.com* Ⓜ *Paral.lel, Poble Sec.*

Derby Hotels Collection ✉ *València 284, Eixample* ☎ *93/451–0402* 🌐 *www.barcelona-apartment.com* Ⓜ *Passeig de Gracia.*

Oh-Barcelona ✉ *Roger de Llúria 50, 1a, Eixample* ☎ *93/467–3779* 🌐 *www.gowithoh.com/vacation-barcelona-apartments* Ⓜ *Girona.*

Rent a Flat in Barcelona ✉ *Ronda Guinardó 2-4, bajos, Horta* ☎ *93/342–7300* 🌐 *www.rentaflatinbarcelona.com* Ⓜ *Urquinaona.*

HOME EXCHANGES

If you would like to exchange your home for someone else's, join a home-exchange organization, which will send you its updated listings of available exchanges for a year and will include your own listing in at least one of them. It's up to you to make specific arrangements. Home-exchange directories sometimes list rentals as well as exchanges.

$$$$ HOTEL Fodor's Choice ★ **W Barcelona.** This towering sail-shape monolith dominates the skyline on the Barcelona waterfront. **Pros:** unrivaled views and general design excitement and glamour; excellent restaurants; rooms are bright, clean-lined, with nonpareil views in all directions. **Cons:** the high-rise icon could seem garish to some; a good hike from the Barri Gòtic or the nearest public transportation. *Rooms from: €310 Pl. de la Rosa del Vents 1, Moll de Llevant, Barceloneta 93/295–2800 www.w-barcelona.com 406 rooms, 65 suites No meals Barceloneta H:16.*

EIXAMPLE

$$ B&B/INN FAMILY **the5rooms.** This charming little boutique B&B in the heart of the city has been recently expanded into a complex of nine spacious guest rooms and three apartment suites. **Pros:** a sense of home away from home; comfortable contemporary design; family-friendly; good value. **Cons:** no bar or restaurant; hot water can be iffy; Pau Claris a busy and noisy artery; no pets. *Rooms from: €145 Carrer Pau Claris 72, Eixample 93/342–7880 www.thefiverooms.com 9 rooms, 3 suites Breakfast Urquinaona, Catalunya I:11.*

$$ HOTEL **Alexandra Barcelona Doubletree by Hilton.** Behind a reconstructed Eixample facade, everything here is urban contemporary, with laquered surfaces, warm woods tables, and a cascade of chrome lights. **Pros:** central to the Eixample and a 20-minute walk from the port; tasteful contemporary decor. **Cons:** design doesn't reflect the Moderniste roots of the neighborhood; rooms could seem constricted after all the space in the lobby. *Rooms from: €150 Mallorca 251, Eixample 93/467–7166 www.hotel-alexandra.com 114 rooms, 2 suites No meals Provença I:8.*

$$$$ HOTEL **Avenida Palace.** A minute's walk from Plaça de Catalunya and the Passeig de Gràcia, this hotel earns top marks for location—and for nostalgia. **Pros:** prime location; excellent soundproofing; connected with most major-airline mileage plans. **Cons:** not for fans of minimalism or cutting-edge design; service can be a bit snooty. *Rooms from: €232 Gran Via 605–607, Eixample 93/301–9600 www.avenidapalace.com 137 rooms, 14 suites No meals Passeig de Gràcia I:10.*

$$ HOTEL **BCN Design.** This quirky property is what happens when design is allowed to triumph over utility. **Pros:** friendly, helpful staff; good breakfast. **Cons:** wardrobes have no drawers; washbasins and toiletry shelves poorly placed; no pets; no pool. *Rooms from: €145 Passeig de Gràcia 29–31, Eixample 93/344–4555 www.eurostarshotels.com 63 rooms, 2 suites No meals Passeig de Gràcia I:10.*

$$$$ HOTEL Fodor's Choice ★ **Claris.** Acclaimed as one of Barcelona's best hotels, the Claris is an artful icon of design and tradition, as is evident from the building itself: the glass-and-steel upper floors seem to have sprouted from the 19th-century town house below. **Pros:** elegant service and furnishings; central location for shopping and Moderniste sightseeing; spot-on friendly service. **Cons:** bathrooms are designer chic but a bit cramped; no spa. *Rooms from: €245 Carrer Pau Claris 150, Eixample 93/487–6262 www.hotelclaris.com 82 rooms, 42 suites No meals Passeig de Gràcia I:9.*

$$ HOTEL Fodor's Choice ★ **Condes de Barcelona.** One of Barcelona's most popular hotels, the Condes de Barcelona is perfectly placed for exploring the sights (and shops) of the city's most fashionable quarter, and—for the privileged location—offers exception value. **Pros:** elegant Moderniste building with subdued contemporary furnishings; prime spot in the middle of the Eixample. **Cons:** no spa; substantial surcharge (€45) for pets; restaurant Lasarte difficult to book. *Rooms from: €165 ✉ Passeig de Gràcia 73–75, Eixample ☎ 93/467–4780 www.condesdebarcelona.com 125 rooms, 1 suite No meals Ⓜ Passeig de Gràcia ↔ I:9.*

$$ HOTEL Fodor's Choice ★ **Continental Palacete.** This former palatial family home, or *palacete,* provides a splendid drawing room, a location nearly dead center for Barcelona's main attractions, views over leafy Rambla de Catalunya, and a 24-hour free buffet. **Pros:** family-friendly; attentive staff; ideal location; microwaves in all the rooms; good value for price. **Cons:** room decor is relentlessly pink and overdraped; bathrooms are a bit cramped and lack amenities. *Rooms from: €143 ✉ Rambla de Calatunya 30, crn. Diputació, Eixample ☎ 93/445–7657 www.hotelcontinental.com 20 rooms, 2 suites Breakfast Ⓜ Passeig de Gràcia ↔ I:10.*

$$ HOTEL **Gallery Hotel.** In the upper part of the Eixample below Diagonal, this contemporary hotel offers impeccable service and a central location for middle and upper Barcelona. **Pros:** privileged location; friendly personal service; gym and sauna; good value for price. **Cons:** breakfast area a bit small; no pets; rooftop deck with small plunge pool and no particular view. *Rooms from: €167 ✉ Roselló 249, Eixample ☎ 93/415–9911 www.galleryhotel.com/en 110 rooms, 5 suites No meals Ⓜ Diagonal; Provença (FGC) ↔ I:8.*

$$ HOTEL **HCC Hotel Regente.** The stained glass panels in the lobby and the bar demonstrate the Moderniste origins of this smallish, superbly located hotel. **Pros:** good value; the lively Rambla de Catalunya promenade is lined with upscale shops and casual restaurants. **Cons:** small public spaces; bathrooms (all with shower-in-bath) are a bit cramped, and lack makeup mirrors; no pets; no gym or spa. *Rooms from: €165 ✉ Rambla de Catalunya 76, Eixample ☎ 93/487–5989 www.hcchotels.com 79 rooms No meals Ⓜ Passeig de Gràcia; Provença (FGC) ↔ I:9.*

$$ HOTEL **Hotel Actual.** Situated between Passeig de Gràcia and Pau Claris, this hotel offers good value with tasteful contemporary design and a central Eixample location. **Pros:** a contemporary design triumph with smart public spaces; helpful and friendly service. **Cons:** rooms are small, and those on the street side can be noisy; no restaurant, pool or spa. *Rooms from: €150 ✉ Roselló 238, Eixample ☎ 93/552–0550 www.hotelactual.com 29 rooms, 4 suites No meals Ⓜ Diagonal ↔ I:8.*

$ HOTEL **Hotel Astoria.** Three blocks west of Rambla de Catalunya, near the upper middle of the Eixample, this renovated historic property is a trove for the budget-minded. **Pros:** prime location; friendly, professional staff; excellent value for price. **Cons:** tiny "gym" has only three machines and a claustrophobic sauna; rooms on the street side can be noisy. *Rooms from: €120 ✉ Carrer Paris 203, Eixample ☎ 93/209–8311 www.derbyhotels.com 112 rooms, 2 suites No meals Ⓜ Hospital Clínic ↔ H:7.*

$$ HOTEL **Hotel Axel.** In the heart of the more fashionable *Esquerra* (west, or "left" side) of the Eixample, this recently expanded and renovated hotel

caters primarily (but by no means exclusively) to gay travelers in an area dubbed by locals as "Gayxample." **Pros:** strategic location; friendly service. **Cons:** no pets; extra €2 charge for faster Wi-Fi; loud club music and advertising displays in the lobby ("Chocolate and Champagne" massage sessions at the Wellness Club 33, "Heterofriendly" briefs and tank tops) can be outside some guests' comfort zone. *Rooms from: €150 Aribau 33, Eixample 93/323–9393 www.axelhotels.com 101 rooms, 4 suites No meals Universitat G:9.*

$$ HOTEL **Hotel Constanza.** A few minutes' walk from the heart of the city at Plaça de Catalunya, this moderately priced boutique hotel has guest rooms restfully decorated in lush coffee and chocolate tones, offset with leather and wood textures. **Pros:** excellent value for price; friendly, professional staff; good grazing at restaurant Bruc 33 Tapas. **Cons:** no views; no pets; no room service; soundproofing not quite up to the noise on Carrer Bruc. *Rooms from: €150 Bruc 33, Eixample 93/270–1910 www.hotelconstanza.com 46 rooms No meals Urquinaona, Plaça de Catalunya J:10.*

$$$$ HOTEL **Hotel Cram.** A short walk from La Rambla, this Eixample design hotel offers impeccable mid-city accommodations with cheerful avant-garde decor and luxurious details. **Pros:** dazzlingly designed; strategic location; smart and friendly staff. **Cons:** Aribau is a major uptown artery, noisy at all hours; rooms are a bit small for the price; no gym or spa; no pets. *Rooms from: €228 Carrer Aribau 54, Eixample 93/216–7700 www.hotelcram.com 65 rooms, 2 suites No meals Universitat; Provença (FGC) G:9.*

$$$$ HOTEL **Hotel El Palace Barcelona.** Founded in 1919 by Caesar Ritz, this is the original Ritz, the grande dame of Barcelona hotels, renamed in 2005. **Pros:** equidistant from Barri Gòtic and central Eixample; excellent service; old-world elegance throughout. **Cons:** no pool; painfully pricey. *Rooms from: €575 Gran Via de les Corts Catalanes 668, Eixample 93/510–1130 www.hotelpalacebarcelona.com 119 rooms, 6 suites No meals Passeig de Gràcia J:10.*

$$ HOTEL **Hotel Eurostars Cristal Palace.** Just off Rambla de Catalunya and near the gardens of Barcelona's University, this modern hotel is in the middle of the art-gallery district and within walking distance of La Rambla, the Ciutat Vella, and the Moderniste architecture of the Eixample. **Pros:** well-located for exploring the Eixample or the Barri Gòtic; fair value for price. **Cons:** undistinguished modern building; maintenance and housekeeping need to up their game; service can be perfunctory; Carrer Diputació can be noisy. *Rooms from: €135 Diputació 257, Eixample 93/487–8778 www.eurostarshotels.com 147 rooms, 1 suite No meals Passeig de Gràcia I:10.*

$$$ HOTEL **Hotel Gran Derby Suite 4.** Clubby and comfortable, this Eixample hotel made up entirely of suites and duplexes with living rooms is ideal for groups. **Pros:** rooms and suites are spacious and tastefully hip; on a quiet side street; friendly service. **Cons:** far from the city's main attractions in an undistinguished neighborhood. *Rooms from: €190 Loreto 28, Eixample 93/322–2062 www.derbyhotels.es 43 suites No meals Muntaner, Hospital Clinic E:6.*

4

$$ HOTEL Fodor's Choice ★ **Hotel Granados 83.** Designed in the style of a New York City loft on a tree-shaded street in the heart of the Eixample, this hotel blends exposed brick, steel, and glass with Greek and Italian marble and Indonesian tamarind wood to achieve a downtown cool. **Pros:** quiet strategic location; polished professional service; wide variety of good casual restaurants nearby; excellent value for price. **Cons:** rooms a bit small; pricey buffet breakfast. *Rooms from: €170 Carrer Enric Granados 83, Eixample 93/492–9670 www.hotelgranados83.com 70 rooms, 7 suites No meals Provença H:8.*

$$ HOTEL **Hotel Granvía.** A 19th-century palatial home, with an Art Deco cupola in the entrance and a marble grand staircase, the Granvía dates as a hotel to 1935. **Pros:** strategic location, only a 15-minute walk from the Barri Gòtic; excellent value. **Cons:** no pool, gym or spa; no pets; most standard rooms have twin beds pushed together, rather than doubles. *Rooms from: €170 Gran Via 642, Eixample 93/318–1900 www.hotelgranvia.com 51 rooms, 7 suites Breakfast Passeig de Gràcia I:10.*

$$ HOTEL FAMILY **Hotel Grums.** Tucked off on a side street in Poble Sec, on the far side of El Raval, this recently opened small hotel lies within easy walking distance to the port and La Rambla—an especially convenient bivouac for cruise ship visitors. **Pros:** quiet location; family-friendly; good value for price. **Cons:** minimal amenities; poor bed lighting; inconvenient shelf-desk with small mirror for make-up; some rooms rather small. *Rooms from: €148 Palaudaries 26, Poble Sec 93/269–1126 www.hotelgrums.com 78 rooms No meals Paral.lel F:14.*

$$ HOTEL **Hotel H10 Casanova.** A chic, postmodern addition to Barcelona's top-end lodging options is hidden behind this traditional facade, which is a 15-minute walk from the top of La Rambla. **Pros:** good combination of comfort and style; strategic location; ample buffet breakfast. **Cons:** no pets; tiny plunge pool on rooftop terrace; room lighting could be better. *Rooms from: €170 Gran Via de les Corts Catalanes 559, Eixample 93/396–4800 www.casanovabcnhotel.com 113 rooms, 5 suites No meals Universitat, Urgell F:10.*

$$$ HOTEL **Hotel Jazz.** Bright colors, clean lines and contemporary artwork give this hotel a hip, fashionable feel. **Pros:** exciting, sleek lobby with punchy, urban decor; friendly, helpful staff. **Cons:** standard rooms have only twin beds; no pets; a bit pricey. *Rooms from: €187 Pelai 3, Eixample 93/552–9696 www.hoteljazz.com 96 rooms, 12 suites No meals Universitat; Catalunya (FGC) H:10.*

$$ HOTEL FAMILY Fodor's Choice ★ **Hotel Murmuri.** British designer Kelly Hoppen took this 19th-century townhouse on Rambla de Catalunya and transformed it in 2008 into a chic, intimate urban retreat. **Pros:** warm, professional service; strategic Eixample location; child-friendly; excellent value for price. **Cons:** no pool, gym or spa (though guest privileges at the nearby affiliated Hotel Majestic); no pets. *Rooms from: €169 Rambla de Catalunya 104, Eixample 93/550–0600 www.murmuri.com 51 rooms, 2 suites, 5 apartments No meals Diagonal; Provença (FGC) H:8.*

$$$$ HOTEL FAMILY Fodor's Choice ★ **Hotel Omm.** The lobby of this postmodern architectural stunner tells you what to expect throughout: perfect comfort, cutting-edge design, and meticulous attention to every detail. **Pros:** perfect location for the upper Eixample; spot-on, attentive service; oyster bar in the lobby; superb spa; family-friendly. **Cons:** small plunge pools; restaurant pricey

and a little precious; parking is expensive; no pets. *Rooms from: €330 Roselló 265, Eixample 93/445–4000 www.hotelomm.es 83 rooms, 8 suites No meals Diagonal; Provença (FGC) I:8.*

$$$ HOTEL **Hotel Pulitzer.** Built squarely over the metro's central hub and within walking distance of everything in town, this breezy clubhouse-hotel could not be better situated to take advantage of Barcelona's many attractions. **Pros:** surprisingly quiet for the central location; very pleasant lobby with bar, lots of sofas and library; breakfast room bright and cheery. **Cons:** standard rooms can be a bit narrow; soundproofing could be better; no pool or gym; no pets. *Rooms from: €200 Bergara 8, Eixample 93/481–6767 www.hotelpulitzer.es 90 rooms, 1 suite No meals Catalunya H:11.*

$$$ HOTEL **Hotel Regina.** What it lacks in the size of its standard guest rooms, this family-friendly little hotel makes up for in its matchless location—on a side street just steps from Plaça de Catalunya—and its relaxed contemporary décor. **Pros:** historic building; spot-on professional reception service. **Cons:** interior soundproofing needs improvement; no pool or gym. *Rooms from: €177 Calle Bergara 4, Eixample 93/301–3232 www.reginahotel.com/en 99 No meals H:11.*

$$$ HOTEL Fodor's Choice ★ **Majestic Hotel & Spa.** With an unbeatable location on Barcelona's most stylish boulevard, steps from Gaudí's Pedrera and a stone's throw to the boulevard's swankiest shops, this hotel is a near-perfect place to stay. **Pros:** very professional service; rooftop terrace with views of the ocean, Montjuïc and the Sagrada Família; 24-hour room service; good value for price. **Cons:** classic furniture a little dated; no pets; parking fees are a bit steep. *Rooms from: €189 Passeig de Gràcia 68, Eixample 93/488–1717 www.hotelmajestic.es 271 rooms, 32 suites No meals Passeig de Gràcia I:9.*

$$$$ HOTEL FAMILY **Mandarin Oriental Barcelona.** A carpeted ramp leading from the elegant Passeig de Gràcia (flanked by Tiffany and Brioni boutiques) lends this hotel the air of a privileged—and pricey—inner sanctum. **Pros:** central location; babysitters and/or parties for the kids, on demand. **Cons:** rooms fairly small for a 5-star accommodation; wardrobes lack drawer space; lighting a bit dim; very pricey breakfast. *Rooms from: €440 Passeig de Gràcia 38–40, Eixample 93/151–8888 www.mandarinoriental.com 120 rooms No meals Passeig de Gràcia, Diagonal; Provença (FGC) I:10.*

$$ HOTEL **Meliá Barcelona.** The lobby here has a waterfall that dominates the reception area and the piano bar (aptly christened Drinking in the Rain). **Pros:** relaxed atmosphere; ample sense of space; friendly and helpful staff. **Cons:** a bit far from most of Barcelona's main attractions; can be noisy when there's a major conference in town; billing system can be confusing; no pets. *Rooms from: €145 Av. de Sarrià 50, Eixample 93/410–6060, 902/144440 www.melia.com/es/hoteles/espana/barcelona/melia-barcelona/index.html 324 rooms, 9 suites No meals Provença, Maria Cristina E:6.*

$$ HOTEL **Meliá Barcelona Sky.** At a bit of a remove from the major tourist attractions, east along Diagonal from Plaça de les Glòries, the Meliá hotel group's Barcelona Sky gets much of its business from professional and trade conference organizers, but wins high marks as well from

recreational visitors for its luxurious appointments and lively design. **Pros:** handy to the Sagrada Família, the beach, and the Poble Nou nightlife scene; great views from the rooftop deck; good value for price. **Cons:** inconvenient to the Eixample and the Barri Gòtic; high-rise glass-and-concrete slab architecture; "open concept" bedroom/bathroom layout lacks privacy; some rooms need refurbishing; no pets. *Rooms from: €160 Pere IV 272--286, Eixample 93/367–2050 www.melia.com/en/hotels/spain/barcelona/melia-barcelona-sky/index.html 258 rooms No meals Poble Nou L:12.*

$$ HOTEL **NH Calderón.** On the chic and leafy Rambla de Catalunya, this modern high-rise has facilities normally found in hotels farther out of town. **Pros:** clean, contemporary design; ample public spaces; excellent buffet breakfast. **Cons:** Internet connection iffy; design somewhat generic; service can be a bit perfunctory. *Rooms from: €159 Rambla de Catalunya 26, Eixample 93/301–0000 www.nh-hoteles.com/nh/en/hotels/spain/barcelona/nh-calderon.html 235 rooms, 20 suites No meals Passeig de Gràcia H:10.*

$$$ HOTEL **Ofelias Hotel Barcelona.** Among the more recent crop of Barcelona's hip boutique hotels, the Ofelias rejoices in a strategic location: virtually around the corner from the Fira de Barcelona exposition grounds, the Las Arenas shopping center, and the airport shuttle bus stop in Plaça d'Espanya. **Pros:** friendly, multilingual staff; good buffet breakfast; free one-day bike hires. **Cons:** a bit removed from the tourist attractions of the Eixample and the Ciutat Vella; no pets. *Rooms from: €209 Llança 24, Eixample 93/423–3898, 93/769–0300 for reservations www.ofeliashotelbarcelona.com 44 rooms No meals Plaça d'Espanya, Rocafort E:11.*

$ HOTEL **Room Mate Emma.** The Emma's pivotal location allows easy walking to almost everything in Barcelona. **Pros:** strategic location; smart, hip staff; futuristic design. **Cons:** rooms on lower floors can be noisy; no pets; no pool or gym; no room service. *Rooms from: €119 Carrer Rosselló 205, Eixample 93/238–5606 www.room-matehotels.com 53 rooms No meals Provença (FGC) H:8.*

$$ HOTEL **Silken Gran Hotel Havana Barcelona.** Popular with cruise ship passengers who extend their vacations to savor the city, the Havana is about equidistant from the Moderniste sights of the Eixample and the Barri Gòtic. **Pros:** bright, lively public spaces; efficient service; good location. **Cons:** on a major crosstown artery, where traffic is heavy night and day; no gym or spa; undistinguished architecture and design; no pets. *Rooms from: €130 Gran Via 647, Eixample 93/412–1115 www.granhotelhavana.com 141 rooms, 4 suites No meals Passeig de Gràcia, Girona, Tetuan J:10.*

$$ HOTEL **SixtyTwo Hotel.** Across from Gaudí's Casa Batlló and just down Passeig de Gràcia from his Casa Milà (La Pedrera), this sleek boutique hotel, which opened in 2009, is surrounded by Barcelona's top shopping addresses and leading restaurants. **Pros:** ideal location; great value for price; friendly staff. **Cons:** bathrooms a bit small, with only basic amenities; no pool, gym or spa; no parking. *Rooms from: €129 Passeig de Gràcia 62, Eixample 93/272–4180 www.sixtytwohotel.com 45 rooms, 1 suite No meals Passeig de Gràcia I:9.*

$$$ HOTEL **Villa Emilia.** The Villa Emilia is a bit removed from the tourist attractions of the Eixample and the Ciutat Vella, but a mere five minutes' walk to the Fira de Barcelona exposition center, the Las Arenas shopping center, and the airport shuttle bus stop in Plaça d'Espanya. **Pros:** strategic location; good value. **Cons:** no pool, gym or spa; staff struggles a bit in English. *Rooms from: €175 ✉ Calàbria 115–117, Eixample ☎ 93/252–5285 www.hotelvillaemilia.com 53 rooms No meals Ⓜ Rocafort ✣ E:11.*

GRÀCIA

$$$$ HOTEL Fodor's Choice ★ **Casa Fuster.** This hotel offers one of two chances (the other is the Hotel España) to stay in an Art Nouveau building designed by Lluís Domènech i Montaner, architect of the sumptuous Palau de la Música Catalana. **Pros:** well placed for exploring both Gràcia and the Eixample; ample-sized rooms; polished professional service. **Cons:** rooms facing Passeig de Gràcia could use better soundproofing; no pets; hard on the budget, for what you get. *Rooms from: €500 ✉ Passeig de Gràcia 132, Gràcia ☎ 93/255–3000 www.hotelescenter.com/casafuster 86 rooms, 19 suites No meals Ⓜ Diagonal ✣ I:7.*

$ HOTEL **Hotel Medium City.** These clean, basic, budget-friendly accommodations are a bit removed from Barcelona's major attractions, but in hailing distance of the Sants railway station: a handy location for day-trips north to Girona and the Costa Brava, or south to Tarragona and beyond. **Pros:** friendly, helpful staff; good value for price. **Cons:** soundproofing could be better; undistinguished neighborhood; no pool or spa; no pets. *Rooms from: €120 ✉ Nicaragua 47, Sants ☎ 93/367–3474 www.mediumhoteles.com 80 rooms No meals Ⓜ Sants ✣ F:7.*

SARRIÀ, SANT GERVASI, PUTXET, AND PEDRALBES

$$ HOTEL FAMILY **Bonanova Park.** In upper Barcelona near Sarrià, this somewhat bare-bones hotel provides a break from the downtown crush at a moderate cost. **Pros:** good value; bargain breakfast; friendly, efficient staff. **Cons:** a bit of a walk to the nearest metro; no pets; no pool or spa; minimal amenities. *Rooms from: €125 ✉ Capità Arenas 51, Sarrià ☎ 93/204–0900 www.hotelbonanovapark.com 63 rooms No meals Ⓜ Maria Cristina, Sarrià (FGC) ✣ C:3.*

$$ **Husa Pedralbes.** The two best things about this simple little hotel are its location on the edge of leafy Sarrià (a 20-minute walk from the Monestir de Pedralbes, 15 minutes from the FC Barcelona soccer stadium, and 5 minutes from the Sarrià train stop) and its intimate, personal atmosphere. Rooms are contemporary with wood-panel walls and lots of beige upholstery; some can feel a bit cramped. **Pros:** intimate and friendly service; bright, clean, and simple. **Cons:** a long way (though just 15 minutes by subway) from the Barri Gòtic; rooms and public spaces can feel cramped. *Rooms from: €155 ✉ Fontcoberta 4, Sarrià ☎ 93/203–7112 www.husa.es 30 rooms No meals Ⓜ Sarrià, Maria Cristina ✣ C:3.*

$$ HOTEL **Gran Hotel Princesa Sofía.** Until the building boom touched off by the 1992 Olympics, this was one of a tiny handful of Barcelona's modern hotels de luxe; even now, it still offers a benchmark for classic comfort and elegance. **Pros:** excellent value for price; family-friendly; spot-on professional

service; the hotel's Aqua Diagonal spa has a 50-meter 6-lane pool and fully equipped gym. **Cons:** no pets; far from the Barri Gòtic and the Eixample; the patterned wall-to-wall carpeting can feel a little dated. *Rooms from: €154 Pl. Pius XII 4, Diagonal 93/508–1050 www.princesasofia.com 475 rooms, 25 suites Breakfast Maria Cristina A:4.*

$$$ HOTEL Fodor's Choice ★ **Primero Primera.** The Perez family converted their apartment building on a leafy sidestreet in the quiet upscale residential neighborhood of Tres Torres and opened it as an exquisitely designed, homey, boutique hotel in 2011. **Pros:** warm, professional service; family-friendly (baby-sitter service available); great value. **Cons:** bit of a distance from the action downtown. *Rooms from: €190 Doctor Carulla 25-29, Sant Gervasi 93/417–5600 www.primeroprimera.com 22 rooms, 8 suites Breakfast E:3.*

$$ HOTEL **Rey Juan Carlos I.** More of an urban resort and convention center than a mere hotel, with glass elevators gliding smoothly up and down a 15-story central atrium, the Rey Juan Carlos is a surprisingly affordable American-style ziggurat. **Pros:** 10 minutes from the airport; supremely comfortable and complete; polished and attentive service. **Cons:** considerably far from all of Barcelona's tourist attractions. *Rooms from: €135 Av. Diagonal 661–671, Diagonal 93/364–4040, 93/364–4223 www.hrjuancarlos.com 394 rooms, 38 suites No meals Zona Universitàri A:4.*

$$ HOTEL **Sansi Pedralbes.** A contemporary polished-marble-and-black-glass box, with Japanese overtones, a stone's throw from the gardens of the Monestir de Pedralbes, this hotel may be a bit removed from the action downtown, but there's a stop on the Bus Turistic just across the street, and the views up into the Collserola Hills above Barcelona are splendid. **Pros:** small and intimate; excellent and friendly service. **Cons:** the nearest subway stations, at Sarriá and Reina Elisenda, are 15 to 20 minutes away on foot; you'll need to budget for taxis. *Rooms from: €150 Av. Pearson 1–3, Pedralbes 93/206–3880 www.sansihotels.com 70 rooms No meals Reina Elisenda A:1.*

$ HOTEL Fodor's Choice ★ **Turó de Vilana.** In an upscale residential neighborhood above Passeig de la Bonanova, this boutique accommodation can make you forget you've come to a prime tourist destination in Spain. **Pros:** quiet surroundings; very good value. **Cons:** something of a trip (30 minutes in all) to the center of town; no pool or spa. *Rooms from: €115 Vilana 7, Sant Gervasi 93/434–0363 www.turodevilana.com 22 rooms Breakfast Sarrià F:2.*

TIBIDABO

$$$ HOTEL FAMILY **Gran Hotel la Florida.** Two qualities set this luxurious mountaintop retreat apart: its peace and privacy, and its stunning panoramic view. **Pros:** first-rate spa and fully equipped gym; Club Luna is the hotel's own jazz night spot; friendly and attentive front staff. **Cons:** old building with occasional maintenance problems; pricey food and beverage add-ons; pets accepted with an €80 surcharge; decor in the "Design Suites" a bit over-the-top. *Rooms from: €220 Ctra. Vallvidrera al Tibidabo 83–93, Tibidabo 93/259–3000 www.hotellaflorida.com 62 rooms, 8 suites No meals Tibidabo H:1.*

5

NIGHTLIFE AND THE ARTS

By Suzanne Wales

Barcelona's nocturnal roll call—from art openings and concerts to tapas bars, music bars, and clubbing—offers a wild mix of options. From the early-evening browsing and tapas-grazing through the area around the Born to stand-up howling and drinking at Bar Confitería and the Hotel Omm's Ommsession to late live and recorded music at Bikini, Shôko, CDLC, and Luz de Gas, Barcelona offers a thousand and one ways to make it through the night without resorting to slumber.

NIGHTLIFE AND THE ARTS PLANNER

HOURS

Daily events in the arts scene race headlong from 7 pm lectures and book presentations, *inauguraciones* and *vernissages* (art show openings), to 9 pm concerts and theater and dance performances. And then, sometime after 1 or 2 in the morning, the *real* nightlife kicks in.

SCORING TICKETS

Tickets for performances are available either at the theater (ticket offices generally open only in the evenings) or via web services such as TelEntrada (🌐 *www.telentrada.com*) and Ticketmaster (🌐 *www.ticketmaster.es*)—both have English-language options. After ordering your seats and giving credit-card information, you pick up tickets at the door of the venue or print them in advance. Ticketmaster uses the ATMs of local bank La Caixa, which print the tickets for you. If you want to do things the old-fashioned way, FNAC on Plaça de Catalunya has an office on the ground floor that sells tickets to many pop and rock performances.

TOP FIVE NIGHTLIFE EXPERIENCES

Concerts in the Palau de la Música Catalana followed by tapas at Cal Pep (⇨ *Ch. 2)*

Red-hot salsa at Antilla BCN Latin Club or Mojito Club

Movies at the Verdi multicine and hip dinners in Gràcia

Dinner and dancing until the wee hours above the beach at Shôko

The sun rising out of the Mediterranean as viewed from the bar Mirablau on Tibidabo

WHAT TO WEAR

Dress codes in Barcelona are eclectic, elastic, and casual, but never sloppy. Although there are rarely hard-and-fast rules at elegant restaurants or concert venues, tourists in shorts, tank tops, and baseball caps will feel out of place. Discos are another kettle of fish: uptown or at the seaside venues, autocratic bouncers may inspect aspiring clients carefully. (Read: The better you dress, the better your chance of getting in.) The Liceu Opera House often has black-tie evening galas, and although tourists are not expected to go out and rent tuxedos, a coat with lapels (necktie optional) blends better. The Palau de la Música Catalana and the Auditori are less formal than the Liceu, but a modicum of care with one's appearance is expected.

WHERE TO GET INFORMATION

To find out what's on, check "*agenda*" listings in Barcelona's leading daily newspapers, *La Vanguardia,* and *El Periódico de Catalunya,* or the weekly Catalan edition of *TimeOut,* available at newsstands all over town. Weekly online magazine *Le Cool* (🌐 *barcelona.lecool.com*) preselects noteworthy events and activities and is available in English. *Barcelona Metropolitan* magazine, published monthly in English, is given away free in English-language bookstores and hotel lobbies and also updates their online "what's on" section regularly (🌐 *www.barcelona-metropolitan.com*). Barcelona city hall's culture website (🌐 *barcelonacultura.bcn.cat*) also publishes complete listings and highlights and has an English edition. A nose and ear to the ground is the best way to find out about rock and pop gigs—look out for posters and flyers as you explore the city.

YEARLY FESTIVALS

Barcelona Acció Musical. Held over a week toward late September, this celebration forms part of the lively La Mercá festival, which honors Our Lady of Mercy, Barcelona's patron saint. It focuses on young and emerging talent (both national and international), with outdoor concerts in Plaça del Rei, Plaça de Catalunya, and other parks and squares. ☎ *93/301–7775* 🌐 *www.bcn.cat/bam.*

Barcelona Guitar Festival. Held between late March and early June, this festival features concerts in the Palau de la Música Catalana and other venues by master guitarists of all musical genres and styles. Folk, jazz, classical, and flamenco starring Spain's national instrument includes performances by guitar legends from Paco de Lucía to flamenco singer Niña Pastori. ☎ *93/301–7775* 🌐 *www.theproject.es.*

Fodor's Choice ★ **El Grec** (*Festival del Grec*). Barcelona's annual summer arts festival runs from late June to the end of July. Many of the concerts and theater and dance performances take place outdoors in such historic places as Plaça del Rei and the Teatre Grec on Montjuic, as well as in the Mercat de les Flors. ☎ *93/301–7775* 🌐 *www.bcn.es/grec.*

Festival Ciutat Flamenco. This festival, organized by the *Taller de Músics* (Musicians' Workshop) and held in the Mercat de les Flors in May, offers a chance to hear the real thing and skip the often disappointing tourist fare available at most of the formal flamenco dinner-and-show venues around town. ☎ *93/443–4346* 🌐 *www.ciutataflmenco.com.*

Festival de Música Antiga (*Early Music Festival*). This lively event brings the best early-music groups from all over Europe to town from late April to mid-May. Concerts are held in the city's principal concert halls, such as L'Auditori, the Liceu, and the Palau de la Música. ☎ *93/404–6000* 🌐 *barcelonacultura.bcn.cat.*

International Jazz Festival. One of Europe's oldest jazz festivals, this bustling gathering takes place from late October to early December, with concerts in illustrous venues like the Palau de la Musica and Luz de Gas. A chance to hear Latin-American jazz greats is always the highlight. ☎ *93/481–7040* 🌐 *www.theproject.es.*

Primavera Sound. From its modest beginnings in the Poble Espanyol, this event has evolved into one of the biggest and most exciting music festivals in Spain, attracting more than 100,000 visitors a year from all over Europe. Concerts are organized in small venues around the city during the weeks leading up to the event, but the main stint takes place for five days in late May or early June at the Parc del Fòrum. Everybody who's anybody, from Blur to Nick Cave, have played here, and you can rest assured that whoever is doing the big festival circuit this summer will pass through Primavera Sound. Full-festival tickets can be bought online. ✉ *Parc del Fòrum, Poblenou* 🌐 *www.primaverasound.com* Ⓜ *El Maresme Fòrum.*

Sónar. Over the past decade, Sónar has grown from a niche festival for electronic and dance music fans to one of Barcelona's largest and most celebrated happenings. Over three days in mid-June, thousands descend upon the city, turning Plaça d'Espanya—the site of the festival's principal venues—into a huge rave. The celebration is divided into "Day" and "Night" activities. Sónar by Day sees sets by international DJs, record fairs, and digital-art exhibits. Sónar by Night takes place in the Montjuïc 2 tradefair buildings, a temporary stage for concerts for the likes of Kraftwork, Die Antwoord, Massive Attack, or whoever is at the bleeding edge of the dance music scene. Tickets are best snapped up early via the festival website. 🌐 *www.sonar.es.*

NIGHTLIFE

Barcelona nights are long and as wild as you want, filling all of the hours of darkness and often rolling until dawn. Most of the best clubs don't even open until after midnight, but cafés and music bars serve as recruiting venues for the night's mission. The typical progression begins with drinks (wine or beer), tapas and dinner, a jazz or flamenco concert around 11 pm, then a pub or a music bar or two, and then—if the body can keep up with the spirit—dancing. Busting a move can be done in a variety of locales, from clubs to ballroom dance halls, and is apt to continue until the sun comes up. Late-night bars and early-morning cafés provide an all-important break to refresh and refuel.

New wine bars, cafés, music bars, and tiny live-music clubs are constantly scraping plaster from 500-year-old brick walls to expose medieval structural elements that offer striking backdrops for postmodern people and conversations. The most common closing time for Barcelona's nocturnal bars is 3 am, while clubs are open until 5 am.

BARRI GÒTIC

Small bars and bodegas proliferate all around the Barri Gótic, which on busy nights is thronged with people hopping from one to the next. The most lively scene is on Plaça Reial, Barcelona's traditional stage for nocturnal decadence.

BARS

Ateneu Gastronòmic. Across a square from Town Hall, this restaurant-*enoteca* (wine library) with an outdoor terrace in summer offers a wide selection of wines and fine food to go with them. ✉ *Pl. de Sant Miquel 2, Barri Gòtic* ☎ *93/302–1198* 🌐 *www.ateneugastronomic.com* ⏲ *Daily 1–4 and 8:15–10:30* Ⓜ *Liceu.*

Ginger. This serpentine two-story bar with plenty of cozy corners is principally designed to serve wine and tapas, but has a popular side business in the cocktail trade. The drinks, which range from Mojitos via Whisky Sour to White Russian, are as unpretentious and carefree as the atmosphere. If you come here, be prepared to settle in and stay. ✉ *Palma de Sant Just 1, Barri Gòtic* ☎ *93/310–5309* 🌐 *www.ginger.cat* ⏲ *Tues.–Sat. 8 pm–2:30 am (kitchen closes at 12.30 am).*

La Vinateria del Call. Just a block and a half from the cathedral cloister in the heart of the *Call,* Barcelona's medieval Jewish Quarter, this dark and candlelit spot serves a wide variety of well-thought-out wines and tapas and provides a chatty yet intimate ambience. ✉ *Sant Domènec del Call 9, Barri Gòtic* ☎ *93/302–6092* 🌐 *www.lavinateriadelcall.com* ⏲ *Mon.–Sat. 8:30 pm–1 am* Ⓜ *Liceu.*

Milk. Opened in 2005 by an Irish couple, this cozy lounge-bar tucked beside the main post office has become a favorite expat hangout. Plush sofas and gilt mirrors, attractively aged and worn, create a genial ambiance for cocktails and chatter, while during the day Milk is one of few places in Barcelona to serve a proper brunch, with eggs and bloody marys on the menu until 4:30 pm. ✉ *Gignas 21, Barri Gòtic* ☎ *93/268–0922* 🌐 *www.milkbarcelona.com* ⏲ *Daily 9 am–2 am* Ⓜ *Jaume I.*

DANCE CLUBS

Ocaña. When this swanky spot opened its doors to much fanfare in 2011, it injected some much-needed glamour into Plaça Reial. This astonishingly beautiful venue, situated in a trio of ancient mansions on the square's southern flank, is dedicated to Jose Peréz Ocaña, a cross-dressing artist, dedicated bohemian, and key figure of Barcelona's post-Franco *movida.* Accommodating a beautiful bar, café, cocktail lounge, and small club, the interior has been conceived as homage to his character, via a mise en scéne of decaying period elegance scattered with sumptuous antiques. Open from noon, it's a wonderful place for evening drinks on the terrace, before gliding inside for dinner and

NIGHTS OF WINE AND REVELRY

Wine-tasting (with cava-sipping on the side) has proliferated in Barcelona over the last decade. With light tapas for accompaniment, nomadic tippling is an unbeatable way to begin an evening.

A typical night out in Barcelona has several stages. Discos and music bars don't jump to life until after midnight, so the early part of the evening is a culinary and oenological prologue. The city is well equipped with opportunities to take advantage of this warm-up time; wine bars, specializing in light fare and new and interesting vintages, have become a popular part of Barcelona's nocturnal routine. Whether in Sarrià, the Eixample, or the Ciutat Vella, there are countless taverns to choose from. Wine served by the glass is usually chalked up on a blackboard, and selections change frequently. Walking between stops is important for the longevity of your nightlife plans; covering a couple of miles with short hops between *copas* is essential and will keep you clearheaded enough to last through the wee hours.

A GOOD WINE BAR CRAWL

Starting at **Terrabacus** (⌧ *Muntaner 185* ☎ *93/410–8633*), ask one of the fleet of sommeliers for suggestions. Next head to **Cata 1.81** (⌧ *Valencia 181* ☎ *93/323–6818*) a wine-tasting (*cata*) bar with creative fare. Five minutes east is **La Bodegueta Provença** (⌧ *Provença 245* ☎ *93/487–5221*), where an interesting selection of wines is detailed on the chalkboard. Nearby is the original **La Bodegueta** (⌧ *Rambla de Catalunya 100* ☎ *93/215–4894*), a charming dive—literally. Monvínic (⌧ *Diputació 249* ☎ *93/272–6187*) is the newest and smartest of the bunch.

SIPS TO SAMPLE

When you're eyeballing the wine list, keep a look out for these copas.

GRANS MURALLES

This Torres single-vineyard red wine will cost you well over a $100 a bottle, so this is one to look for sold by the glass at La Vinya del Senyor, Vinoteca Torres, or Cata 1.81. Made with ancient, pre-Phylloxera grapes (monastrell, garnacha tinto, carró, samsó, and cariñena), some of which are now extinct, this vineyard tucked in under the medieval walls of the Cistercian monastery of Poblet is a taste of history: dense, complex, peppery, tannic, and fruity.

JUVÉ I CAMPS RESERVA DE LA FAMILIA

A Barcelona favorite, this midrange cava made with the standard Penedès grape varieties of macabeu (40%), parellada (40%), and xarel.lo (20%) grapes is a tawny gold hue with feisty bubbles and a tart apple and citrus flavor. Crisp and fresh on the palate, the finish is balanced and clean as a whistle.

KRIPTA GRAN RESERVA

Agustí Torrelló, one of the fathers of Catalonia's cava, created this excellent gran reserva in homage to the Mediterranean winemaking tradition. The bottle is shaped like an amphora, requiring the use of an ice bucket à table. Made from old vines and aged for five years, the wine is a straw-color gold, intensely bubbly, and superbly crisp and refreshing. Complex on the palate, tastes range from chocolate to butter, with a solid mineral base.

TORRE LA MOREIRA

This full-bodied and acidic albariño from northwestern Spain's Rías Baixas wine region is a refreshing and fully satisfying accompaniment for seafood tapas at Cal Pep or Botafumeiro.

PAIR THAT WITH...

Start light with a few of Catalonia's own Arbequina olives. *Boquerones* (small, fresh, pickled, white anchovies) are another excellent and refreshing morsel to pair with an albariño or a flute of cava. A *ración* (portion) of regular anchovies wouldn't be a bad idea either. Beyond those preliminaries, *pimientos de Padrón,* lovely deep green peppers from the Galician village of Padrón, are always welcome additions at this point, as are *croquetas* (croquettes), small breaded fritters with a minced meat filling of ham or chicken. La Barceloneta has its own mega-croquetas called *bombas*—round, slightly-larger-than-golf-ball-size fritters filled with mashed potato and ham. *Chipirones* (baby octopi), cooked to a dry crisp, are delicious with white wines and cavas, while, as wines turn darker, a plate of *jamón ibérico de bellota* might be the perfect closer, unless a *ración de albóndigas* (serving of meatballs) or a sizzling *chistorra* (spicy sausage) proves irresistible.

cocktails in the downstairs Apotheke bar. ✉ *Pl. Reial 13–15, Barri Gòtic* ☎ *93/676–4814* 🌐 *www.ocana.cat* ⏲ *Mon.–Thurs. 5 pm–2:30 am, Fri. 5 pm–3 am, Sat. 11 am–3 am, Sun. 11 am–5 pm* Ⓜ *Drassanes.*

Sidecar Factory Club. A mainstay of the decadent nightlife centered around Plaça Reial, this long-running club has never fallen out of fashion—in fact, it just attracts new fans as the old ones retire. With a firm focus on giving an open mic to up-and-coming talent in music, theater, and performance, the venue offers something unexpected just about every night of the week. The Saturday-night anti-karaoke parties see Barcelona's night owls at their freakiest. ✉ *Pl. Reial 7, Barri Gòtic* ☎ *93/302–1586* 🌐 *www.sidecarfactoryclub.com* ⏲ *Mon.–Sat. doors at 8 pm. Most performances start at 10–10:30; club starts at 12:30 am.* Ⓜ *Drassanes.*

MUSIC CLUBS

Marula Café. A relatively new kid on the block, Marula Café opened with the express aim to bring what they consider "real music" back into the Barcelona nightlife. No electronic music will enter this slick venue with its backlighted glass walls: past the bouncer it's just funk, disco, and Latin peppered up with Afrofunk vibes. The crowd is a mix of hip locals who come dance and foreigners who've stumbled in from the tourist circuit off Plaça Reial. There are regular concerts, too; check the website for details. ✉ *Escudellers 49, Barri Gòtic* 🌐 *www.marulacafe.com* ⏲ *Daily 11 pm–5:30 am* Ⓜ *Liceu, Drassanes.*

MUSIC CLUBS: JAZZ AND BLUES

Harlem Jazz Club. This small but exciting live music venue is a five-minute walk from Plaça Reial. The name is a bit deceiving, everything from Senegalese song to gypsy soul can be heard here, too (check website for details). Most concerts start at 10 and finish around 1 am, with musos and aficionados hanging around till closing. ✉ *Comtessa de Sobradiel 8, Barri Gòtic* ☎ *93/310–0755* 🌐 *www.harlemjazzclub.es* ⏲ *Tues.–Sun. 8 pm–3 am* Ⓜ *Jaume I, Liceu.*

BORN-RIBERA

The übercool Born district has a plethora of cocktail bars and lounges centered on and around the Passeig del Born and Carrer Argentería. If you want to kick on, it's a short hop from here to the clubs of the Port Olímpic.

BARS

Cocktail Bar Juanra Falces. Formerly known as Gimlet, Cocktail Bar Juanra Falces is a little slice of Manhattan just off Passeig del Born. Small and discreet, this spot is taken up mostly by a wooden bar. Soft jazz floats through the air while formal, white-coated barmen (and women) go about their business, shaking up classic cocktails for a faithful clientele that includes middle-aged locals and informed blow-ins. Signature concoctions include a gimlet, all manner of martinis, and a knockout rum punch. ✉ *Rec 24, Born-Ribera* ☎ *93/310–1027* ⏲ *Tues.–Sat. 6 pm–2:30 am* Ⓜ *Jaume I.*

Singer-songwriters take the stage at Bar Pastis on Wednesday.

El Nus. Amid the trendsetting bars of the Born, the continued existence El Nus is comforting. This wooden, bottle-lined corner bar has provided late-night whiskeys and good conversation for decades—it's a cozy counterpoint to its designer-clad neighbors. It's best for couples, as loud groups are often given their marching orders. ✉ *Mirallers 5, Born-Ribera* ☎ *93/319–5355* ⏲ *Sun.–Thurs. 7:30 pm–2:30 am, Fri.–Sat. 7:30 pm–3 am* Ⓜ *Jaume I.*

La Vinya del Senyor. Ambitiously named "The Lord's Vineyard," this excellent wine bar directly across from the entrance to the lovely church of Santa Maria del Mar is etched into the ground floor of an ancient building. The best table is up a rickety ladder on the pint-sized mezzanine, or head outside on the terrace for people-watching. ✉ *Pl. de Santa Maria 5, Born-Ribera* ☎ *93/310–3379* 🌐 *www.lavinyadelsenyor.com* ⏲ *Tues.–Thurs. noon–1 am, Fri. and Sat. noon–2 am, Sun. noon–midnight* Ⓜ *Jaume I.*

MUSIC CLUBS

Sala Monasterio. This popular, pleasingly grungy basement venue just near the marina hosts live gigs most nights of the week, from headbanger to bluegrass, punk to electronica. The best thing about it is its intimate size, lending the gigs a "private party" feel—indeed, it's not unusual to see a guitarist's grandkids in the front row. ✉ *Paseig Isabel II 4, Born-Ribera* ⏲ *Most shows start at 10 pm* Ⓜ *Barceloneta.*

LA RAMBLA

The frenetic epicenter of the city's nightlife, La Rambla is best enjoyed early in the evening, when families are out for a stroll and the terraces offer a seat to enjoy the passing parade. Late in the evening, large clubs and loud drinking dens are there to appease the hangers-on.

BARS

Bar Pastis. In a tiny street off the bottom of La Rambla, this tiny hole-in-the-wall is a city treasure. Since 1947 Bar Pastis has provided a little slice of Paris deep in the Barrio Chino—the nicotine-stained walls, dusty shelves filled with ancient bottles, and bohemian patrons are all genuine. It holds acoustic gigs most nights of the week (generally starting around 10) of tango, cançon, soft jazz, or anything that fits with the bar's speakeasy groove. ✉ *Santa Mònica 4, La Rambla* ☎ *634/938422* 🌐 *www.barpastis.com* ⏲ *Daily 7:30 pm–2:30 am* Ⓜ *Drassanes.*

Boadas. Barcelona's oldest cocktail bar, Boadas opened its doors in 1933 and quickly gained a reputation as the only place to enjoy a genuine mojito. The faithful—who include a fair few of the city's luminaries—have been coming ever since, although Boadas is definitely more downbeat than its uptown *coctelería* cousins, despite the white-jacketed waiters and Art Deco surrounds. Its central location keeps it eternally buzzing. ✉ *Tallers 1, La Rambla* ☎ *93/318–9592* 🌐 *boadascocktails.com* ⏲ *Mon.–Thurs. noon–2 am, Fri. and Sat. noon–3 am* Ⓜ *Pl. de Catalunya.*

MUSIC CLUBS: JAZZ AND BLUES

Jamboree-Jazz and Dance-Club. This pivotal nightspot, another happy fiefdom of the imperial Mas siblings, is a center for jazz and blues and turns into a wild hip-hop and R&B dance club after performances. Local jazz greats Randy Greer, Jordi Rossy, Billy McHenry, Gorka Benítez, and Llibert Fortuny all perform here regularly, while on Monday night the popular WTF jam sessions hold sway. ✉ *Pl. Reial 17, La Rambla* ☎ *93/301–7564* 🌐 *www.masimas.com/jamboree* ⏲ *Daily 8 pm–5 am. Shows at 8 pm and 10 pm, club starts at midnight* Ⓜ *Liceu.*

EL RAVAL

A distinct hipster vibe and a slew of eclectic bars and intimate live music venues draw students and young creative types to El Raval after dark. If in doubt, just head to Rambla del Raval, a lively promenade packed with outdoor terraces.

BARS

Ambar. The clientele at this Raval watering hole is as colorful as the vintage furniture: young Erasmus students and bachelor parties rub shoulders with seasoned drinkers and locals warming up for a wild night. The interior is spacious, but always crowded, and the bar staff whip up long drinks and some simple cocktails. You either stop by Ambar for a drink on your way elsewhere, or come at the end of the night to occupy one of the sofas until the staff unceremoniously kick you out. ✉ *Sant Pau 77, El Raval* ⏲ *Daily 3 pm–3 am.*

Big Bang Bar. This classic-looking bar with its unassuming entrance on a Raval back street is one of the few in the old city that keeps the live music flag flying. Packed with people talking over gin-and-tonics, the back stage area is filled with couples giving it up to live funk and swing music, or witnessing a jazz jam session. Most gigs start at 10:30 or 11 pm. Check the website for details. ✉ *Botella 7, El Raval* 🌐 *www.bigbangbarcelona.com* ⏲ *Tues.–Sun. 10 pm–3 am* Ⓜ *Sant Antoni.*

Casa Almirall. The twisted wooden fronds framing the bar's mirror and Art Nouveau touches from curvy door handles to organic-shape table lamps to floral chair design make this one of the most authentic bars in Barcelona, and also the second-oldest, dating from 1860. (The oldest is the Marsella, another Raval favorite.) It's a good spot for evening drinks after hitting the nearby the MACBA (Museu d'Art Contemporani de Barcelona) or a prelunch vermut on weekends. ✉ *Joaquín Costa 33, El Raval* ☎ *93/318–9917* ⏲ *Mon.–Thurs. 6 pm–2 am, Fri. 6 pm–3 am, Sat. noon–3 am, Sun. noon–1 am* Ⓜ *Universitat.*

BARCELONA JAZZ

Barcelona has loved jazz ever since Sam Wooding and his Chocolate Kiddies triumphed here in 1929. Jack Hilton's visits in the early 1930s paved the way for Benny Carter and the Hot Club of Barcelona in 1935 and 1936. In the early years of the post–Spanish civil war Franco dictatorship, jazz was viewed as a dangerous influence from beyond, but by 1969 Duke Ellington's Sacred Concerts smuggled jazz into town under the protective umbrella of the same Catholic Church whose conservative elements cautioned the Franco regime against the perils of this "degenerate music."

La Confitería. In a former pastry shop, this bar conserves many of the "Modernisme" elements that were designed to invoke memories of Vienna coffeehouses. The bar in the front is usually packed with regulars and partygoers fueling up for the night, while the granite-and-metal tables in the back are popular with couples and small groups of friends enjoying a few beers or bottle of cava. The owner is a fan of flamenco, and shows are held on an ad hoc basis on Sundays. ✉ *Sant Pau 128, El Raval* ⏲ *Daily 7 pm–1 am* Ⓜ *Paral.lel.*

London Bar. The trapeze (often in use) suspended above the bar adds even more flair to this Art Nouveau circus haunt in the Barrio Chino. Stop in at least for a look, as this is one of the Raval's old standards, which has entertained generations of Barcelona visitors and locals with nightly gigs of jazz, blues, and occasionally a hairy head-banger outfit. Concerts start at 10:30. ✉ *Nou de la Rambla 34, El Raval* ☎ *93/318–5261* ⏲ *Weekdays 10 pm–3 am, weekends 6 pm–3:30 am* Ⓜ *Liceu, Drassanes.*

Manchester. There's no doubt about what the name of this laid-back Raval hangout pays tribute to: that of the early Haçienda years and the Madchester scene, of Joy Division and Happy Mondays and the Stone Roses, when rock and dance music shook an entire country. The sheer number of people (both locals and foreigners) crowding around the wood tables and dancing in the spaces in between suggest that a tribute is welcome. ✉ *Valldonzella 40, El Raval* ☎ *627/733081* 🌐 *www.manchesterbar.com* ⏲ *Daily 7 pm–3 am* Ⓜ *Pl. de Catalunya.*

Marsella. French poet and playwright Jean Genet was known to have been a regular here, and you can recognize scenes in his best-known work, *A Thief's Journal.* Marsella is pure history and decadence—the flaky walls, chipped-marble tables, and spidery chandeliers are as much a part of El Raval's urban history as the ladies of the night that tread the streets outside. Although popular with tourists downing shot glasses of absinthe, Marsella's bohemian credentials have never waivered. ✉ *Sant Pau 65, El Raval* ☎ *639/309759* ⏲ *Mon.–Thurs. 9 pm–2:30 am, Fri. and Sat. 9 pm–3 am* Ⓜ *Liceu.*

Negroni. This cocktail bar for the hip and sophisticated is characterized as much by its black interior as it is by its relative scarcity of seating (the row of leather stools is no match for the crowds that flock here on weekends). Yet while Negroni can sport a celebratory vibe, its original design is as classic as the drinks served: the customer on one side, the bartender on the other, with no menu between them, just knowledgeable recommendations. ✉ *Joaquin Costa 46, El Raval* 🌐 *www.negronicocktailbar.com* ⏲ *Mon.– Thurs. and Sun. 7 pm–2:30 am, Fri. and Sat. 7 pm–3 am* Ⓜ *Universitat.*

MUSIC CLUBS: JAZZ AND BLUES

Jazz Sí Club. Run by the Barcelona contemporary music school next door, this workshop and (during the day) café is a forum for musicians, teachers, and fans to listen and debate their art. There is jazz on Monday; pop, blues, and rock jam sessions on Tuesday; jazzmen jamming on Wednesday; Cuban salsa on Thursday; flamenco on Friday; and rock and pop on weekends. The small cover charge (€5–€9, depending on which night you visit) includes a drink; no cover charge Wednesday. Gigs start between 7:30 and 8:45 pm. ✉ *Requesens 2, El Raval* ☎ *93/329–0020* 🌐 *www.tallerdemusics.com* ⏲ *Daily 7 pm–11 pm* Ⓜ *Sant Antoni.*

BARCELONETA AND PORT OLÍMPIC

Away from the earshot of sleeping residents, the beaches of Barcelona have become the city's late, late-night pleasure ground. Chic lounges of the Port Olímpic and ad hoc *chiringuitos* (beach bars) provide plenty of opportunity to watch the sun come up over the Mediterranean.

BARS

Fodor's Choice ★ **Eclipse Bar.** On the 26th floor of the seaside W Hotel, Eclipse is undoubtedly the bar with the best view in all of Barcelona. Owned by a London hospitality group experienced in satisfying a demanding clientele, its slick interior design and roster of international DJs attract scores of beautiful people, Euro nighthawks, and local VIPs. Dress rules (i.e., your best glad rags) apply. ✉ *Pl. de la Rosa dels Vents 1, Barceloneta* ☎ *93/295–2800* 🌐 *www.w-barcelona.es* ⏲ *Mon. and Wed. 7 pm–2 am, Tues. and Thurs. 7 pm–3 am, Fri.–Sun. 7 pm–4 am.*

CASINOS

Gran Casino de Barcelona. Situated on the shore underneath the Hotel Arts, Barcelona's modern casino has everything from slot machines to roulette, plus restaurants, a bar, and a dance club. The casino regularly plays host to Texas hold 'em poker tournaments, which add an air of Vegas-style excitement. ✉ *Marina 19–21* ☎ *93/225–7878* 🌐 *www.casino-barcelona.com* ⏲ *Mon.–Sun. 9 am–5 am* Ⓜ *Ciutadella/Vila Olímpica.*

DANCE CLUBS

Shôko. The hottest of the glitterati spots below the Hotel Arts and the Frank Gehry fish, this is the place to see and be seen in Barcelona these days. The excellent restaurant morphs into a disco around midnight and continues until the wee hours of the morning, with all manner of local and international celebrities perfectly liable to make an appearance at one time or another. ✉ *Passeig Marítim de la Barceloneta 36, Port Olímpic–Barceloneta* ☎ *93/225–9200* 🌐 *www.shoko.biz* ⏲ *Restaurant daily noon–midnight. Club daily 12 am–3 am* Ⓜ *Ciutadella/Vila Olímpica.*

EIXAMPLE

Nocturnal partying in the Eixample is typified by stylish cocktail bars, often located in luxury hotels. A large swathe of the area's grid is occupied by the so-called Gayxample, Barcelona's hub of LGBT culture.

5

BARS

Banker's Bar. The super swish cocktail bar of Barcelona's Mandarin Oriental Hotel is actually situated in an old vault (the building itself spent its former life as a bank)—note the feature wall of original strong boxes. A treat at any time, especially when settled into an oversized mamasan chair with a ginger margarita in hand, the bar is especially fun on Wednesday "Gin and Live" nights, which see jazz and pop-tinged performances from noted national and local artists. ✉ *Hotel Mandarin Oriental, Passeig de Gràcia 38–40, Eixample* ☎ *93/151–8888* 🌐 *www.mandarinoriental.es* ⏲ *Mon.–Thurs. and Sun. 5–1, Fri. and Sat. 5–3* Ⓜ *Passeig de Gràcia.*

Bodega Sepúlveda. On a busy corner situated at the threshold of the increasingly trendy Sant Antoni district, this convivial bar has been a local favorite since 1936. Traditional, no-frills tapas (tortillas, patatas bravas, etc.) and decent house wine at friendly prices keep the punters happy and chatty, and the little marble tables inside full. ✉ *Sepúlveda 173 bis, Eixample* ☎ *93/323–5944* 🌐 *www.bodegasepulveda.net* ⏲ *Weekdays 8 am–1:30 and 8 pm–1 am, Sat. 8 pm–1 am* Ⓜ *Universitat.*

Cata 1.81. Wine tasting (*la cata*) in this contemporary design space comes with plenty of friendly advice about enology and some of the world's most exciting new vintages. Small delicacies such as macaroni with sobrassada (spiced pork pâté) make this streamlined sliver of a bar a gourmet haven as well. If you come in a group, be sure to reserve the table in the wine cellar in the back. ✉ *Valencia 181, Eixample* ☎ *93/323–6818* 🌐 *www.cata181.net* ⏲ *Mon.–Sat. 5:30 pm–midnight* Ⓜ *Provença.*

George and Dragon. Formerly one of Barcelona's most popular English pubs, the George and Dragon (named for the city's patron Saint Jordi, or George) remade itself as a hip *cerveseria* specializing in artisan beers, both bottled and draft, from all over the world. It's popular with expat workers who pour in for the evening happy hour. ✉ *Diputació 269, Eixample* ☎ *93/488–1765* ⏲ *Mon.–Thurs. 10 am–1 am, Fri. and Sat. 10 am–2:30 am* Ⓜ *Passeig de Gràcia.*

Harry's. This is Barcelona's version of Parisian favorite "sank roo-doe-noo" (5, rue Daunou) that intoxicated generations of American literati, faux, and otherwise, in Paris. Although the formal art of mixology remains somewhat alien to the Barcelona scene, those in need of a serious drink will find it here at Harry's. ✉ *Aribau 143, Eixample* ☎ *93/430–3423* ⏲ *Mon.–Sat. 5:30 pm–3 am* Ⓜ *Provença.*

La Vinoteca Torres. Miguel Torres of the Torres wine dynasty has finally given Passeig Gràcia a respectable address for tapas and wine, with more than 50 selections from Torres wineries around the world. The menu runs from selected Spanish olives to Ramón Peña seafood from the Rías de Galicia to stick-to-your-ribs *lentejas estofadas* (stewed lentils) or diced chunks of Galician beef with peppers from Gernika. ✉ *Passeig de Gràcia 78, Eixample* ☎ *93/272–6625* 🌐 *www.lavinotecatorres.com* ⏲ *Daily noon–4 and 7–1* Ⓜ *Passeig de Gràcia.*

Les Gens que J'aime. A Bohemian fantasy from a late-19th-century novel is reproduced in this time-warp salon. Neatly tucked under the sidewalk, this bar is saturated in the yellow glow of lighting and the deep reds and ochers of the sofas and armchairs, all suggesting a luxury smoking car on the *Orient Express*: perfect for an intimate tête-à-tête. ✉ *València 286 bajos, Eixample* ☎ *93/215–6879* 🌐 *www.lesgensquejaime.com* ⏲ *Mon.–Thurs. 6 pm–2:30 am, Fri. and Sat. 7 pm–3 am* Ⓜ *Passeig de Gràcia.*

Milano. Just off Plaça de Catalunya, this basement bar is an unexpected gem in an area dominated by student bars and tourist traps. Indeed, there's something naughty and exciting about stepping into Milano, as if by crossing the doorstep you were transported back to a Prohibition-era speakeasy of the more glamorous type: the large room with wooden floorboards and red velvet sofas, the waiters in white livery, and the large variety of whiskeys behind the bar. Live jazz and bebop most nights (generally starting at 8:30 pm) keeps the genial vibes flowing. ✉ *Ronda Universitat 35, Eixample* ☎ *93/112–7150* 🌐 *www.camparimilano.com* ⏲ *Daily noon–3 am* Ⓜ *Pl. de Catalunya.*

Fodor's Choice ★ **Monvínic.** "Wineworld" in Catalan, Monvínic offers 3,500 wines ranging in price from €10 to a mind-popping €5,000, ordered up from their wine cellar via a tablet or explained by the exceptionally friendly staff in a sleekly designed space, conceived by veteran local designer Alfons Tost. Small plates of perfect jamón and creative riffs on classical Catalan cuisine complement the vino, and full meals are available at the restaurant in back. ✉ *Diputació 249, Eixample* ☎ *93/272–6187* 🌐 *www.monvinic.com* ⏲ *Weekdays 1 pm–11 pm* Ⓜ *Passeig de Gràcia.*

Sala Be Cool. Independent but not grungy, cool but not bohemian, Sala Be Cool is the club for young middle-class music lovers who want to hear the latest in electronic and other contemporary genres in comfortable, clean surroundings. Since it opened in 2006, the Tennessee Three, the Unfinished Sympathy, and Jackmaster Funk have all graced the club's intimate stage. Once the gigs are over DJ sets keep the party rocking until 5 am. ✉ *Pl. de Joan Llongueras 5, Sant Gervasi* ☎ *93/362–0413* 🌐 *www.salabecool.com* ⏲ *Most shows start at 8:30 pm* Ⓜ *Hospital Clinic.*

A live orchestra encourages dancers to cut a rug at La Paloma.

Terrabacus. A sleek new tapas idea: combine an extensive wine list offering 250 different wines (50 served by the glass) with a wide variety of tapas from Catalonia, Spain, and beyond. Through the advice of a sommelier, various different wines are recommended for specific tapas, be they seafood, sashimi, or ibérico ham. The result is an exciting and different tapas and wine-tasting emporium with a happening young buzz. ✉ *Muntaner 185, Eixample* ☎ *93/410–8633* 🌐 *www.terrabacus.com* ⏲ *Weekdays 1:30 pm–4 pm and 9 pm–midnight, Sat. 9 pm–midnight* Ⓜ *Provença.*

Xampú Xampany. One of Barcelona's few authentic *xampanyerias*, specializing in cava—the Catalan sparkling wine similar to champagne (but much cheaper)—this spacious bar and delicatessen also offers fine Iberian hams, foies, and charcuterie. ✉ *Gran Via 702, Eixample* ☎ *93/265–0483* 🌐 *www.xampuxampany.com* ⏲ *Mon.–Sat. 8 am–1:30 am* Ⓜ *Tetuan.*

DANCE CLUBS

Antilla BCN Latin Club. This exuberantly Caribbean spot sizzles with salsa, son cubano, and merengue from the moment you step in the door. From 10 to 11 each night, enthusiastic dance instructors "teach you the secrets of the hips" for free. After that, the dancing begins and rarely stops to draw breath. This self-proclaimed "Caribbean cultural center" cranks out every variation of salsa ever invented. Thursday, see live concerts while on Friday and Saturday, the mike gives way to animated Latin DJs. ✉ *Aragó 141, Eixample* ☎ *93/451–2151* 🌐 *www.antillasalsa.com* ⏲ *Wed. 10 pm–5 am, Thurs. 11 pm–5 am, Fri. and Sat. 11 pm–5 am, Sun. 7 pm–5 am* Ⓜ *Urgell, Hospital Clinic.*

Bikini Barcelona. This sleek mega-club, which was reborn as part of L'Illa shopping center, boasts the best sound system in Barcelona. A smaller sala puts on concerts of emerging and cult artists—the Nigerian singer-songwriter Asa, local soulsters The Pepper Pots, and Gil Scott-Heron in one of his final performances are just some of the more memorable Bikini performances of recent years. When the gigs finish around midnight the walls roll back, and the space ingeniously turns into a sweaty nightclub for the post-grad crowd. ✉ *Diagonal 547, Eixample* ☎ *93/322–0800* 🌐 *www.bikinibcn.com* ⏲ *Club: Thurs.–Sat. midnight–6 am; show times vary* Ⓜ *Les Corts.*

City Hall. Wednesday-night Knockout parties starring electro house music and red-hot guest DJs from neighboring clubs guarantee dancing till you drop at this raging mid-city favorite. Deep, tech, groove, and microfunk are just some of the musical specialties you will experience, and a recent renovation has added a touch of sophistication to this party powder keg. ✉ *Rambla de Catalunya 2–4, Eixample* ☎ *93/233–3333* 🌐 *www.cityhallbarcelona.com* ⏲ *Wed.–Sat. 11:30 pm–5 am* Ⓜ *Pl. de Catalunya.*

Luz de Gas. This always-wired, faux–music hall hub of musical and general nightlife activity has something going on every night, from live performances to wild late-night dancing. Though the weekly schedule varies with the arrival of international names and special events, you can generally plan for world music and Latin sounds in the live sets, while the club music is focused on soul and standards. ✉ *Muntaner 246, Eixample* ☎ *93/209–7711* 🌐 *www.luzdegas.com* ⏲ *Club Tues.–Sun. midnight–5 am. Shows generally start around 9 pm* Ⓜ *Muntaner, Provença.*

Ommsession Club. The Hotel Omm attracts an army of the 35- to fortysomething crowd looking for excitement on Thursday, Friday, and Saturday nights. DJs and occasional live performances keep this well-groomed mob of young and not-so-young professionals clustered around the swish lobby bar with frequent dives down into the torrid dance floor downstairs. ✉ *Rosselló 265, Eixample* ☎ *93/445–400* 🌐 *www.hotelomm.es* ⏲ *Thurs.–Sat. 11 pm–4 am* Ⓜ *Diagonal.*

Otto Zutz. Just off Via Augusta, above Diagonal, this nightclub and disco is a perennial Barcelona favorite that keeps attracting a glitzy mix of Barcelona movers and shakers, models, ex-models, wannabe models, and the hoping-to-get-lucky mob that predictably follows this sort of pulchritude. Hip-hop, house, and Latino make up the standard soundtrack on the dance floor, with mellower notes upstairs and in the coveted Altos Club Privé (or "VIP section," to you and me). ✉ *Lincoln 15, Eixample* ☎ *93/238–0722* *www.ottozutz.com* ⏲ *Wed.–Sat. midnight–6 am* Ⓜ *Sant Gervasi, Plaça Molina.*

The Sutton Club. If there's anywhere you should dress up to get past the door, it's here. If the international "see and be seen" crowd converge around the seaside clubs below Hotel Arts, their local equivalents come to Sutton. The club is separated in several bars and dancing areas, playing R&B, hip hop, and house music. It's like a Vegas club in Barcelona: it may not be classy, but there's plenty of bling. ✉ *Tuset 13, Eixample* ☎ *93/414–4217* 🌐 *www.thesuttonclub.com* ⏲ *Wed. midnight–5 am, Thurs. midnight–5:30 am, Fri. and Sat. midnight–6 am, Sun. 10:30 pm–4:30 am* Ⓜ *Diagonal.*

GAY AND LESBIAN NIGHTLIFE

Arena Madre. The Arena Group is the queen of the club scene on the Gayxample (as this swath of the Eixample district is known), and Arena Madre is, well, the mother of them all. Pumping electronic and house music keep the dance floor sweaty and the punters streaming in until dawn. Although it's a gay club, all persuasions are welcome. ✉ *Balmes 32, Eixample* ☎ *93/487–8342* 🌐 *www.grupoarena.com* ⏲ *Daily 12:30 am–5 am* Ⓜ *Passeig de Gràcia.*

New Chaps. This off-Gayxample jeans-and-leather bar has steer horns mounted on the walls, myriad racy videos, and a labyrinthine dark room downstairs for a more mature gay crowd. ✉ *Av. Diagonal 365, Eixample* ☎ *93/215–5365* 🌐 *www.newchaps.com* ⏲ *Mon.–Thurs. and Sun. 9 pm–3 am, Fri. and Sat. 9 pm–3:30 am* Ⓜ *Diagonal, Verdaguer.*

La Penúltima. Situated in El Raval, this spot has a more mixed vibe than the sceney bars of the Gayxample. Early in the evening its rather serene, with people of all stripes nestled into aged leather sofas and old bentwood chairs sipping beers and unusually good-barreled wine to the soft din of house music. Come midnight, however, it becomes packed with pre-clubbers poised for a big night out. ✉ *Riera Alta 40, Eixample* ☎ *93/442–3508* ⏲ *Tues.–Sun. 9 pm–3 am* Ⓜ *Sant Antoni.*

5

GRÀCIA

Gràcia has always been a destination for intimate live-music bars (or *bares musicales*), and its growing cool factor has led a good many stylish coctelerías to open here as well. When the heat is on, Plaça de Sol buzzes with drinkers and partygoers.

BARS

Bonobo. The only item or furniture recalling the times when this Gràcia bar was a traditional *bodega* is the large wooden fridge behind the bar. As for the rest, the Catalan chansons have been replaced by funk and soul music and the occasional football match on the TV, the elderly men at the bar by cheerful thirtysomethings, the cheap wine by elaborate gin-tonics. What remains, however, is a distinctly local and honest atmosphere, rejecting all pretense of "see and be seen" and inviting everyone, regardless of age or nationality, to come in and have a good time. ✉ *Santa Rosa 14* ☎ *93/218–8796* ⏲ *Mon.–Sat. 4 pm–3 am* Ⓜ *Fontana.*

Fodor's Choice ★ **Viblioteca.** Viblioteca is the latest project of the owners of the bohemian Gràcia cocktail bar La Baignore, and here they've moved things up a notch. Dazzling white interiors, a large assortment of cured meats, cheeses, and salads, a few choice liquors—plus a selection of exquisite wines, each in limited supply, personally sourced and served together with the story behind it. Come for a quick glass at the bar or have a bottle or two at your table. It is best to reserve in advance since the small space fills up quickly. ✉ *Vallfogona 12* ☎ *93/284–4202* 🌐 *www.viblioteca.com* ⏲ *Weekdays 6 pm–1 am, Sat. 1–4 and 6–1, Sun. 1–4 and 7–midnight* Ⓜ *Fontana.*

SARRIÀ AND PEDRABLES

Not exactly brimming with nightlife, the well-heeled streets of Sarrià and neighboring Pedrables have bars that cater more to locals than out-of-towners. In Sarrià, revelers huddle around the Plaça de Sarrià, either perched on a terrace café or curled up in a wine bar.

BARS

La Cave. With 450 wines from around the world arranged by color and cost spectrums around a cool barrel-like wine cellar, this *enoteca* (wine library) is an oenophile's paradise. Selected small offerings from *magret de pato* (duck breast) to French cheeses ranging from Reblochon to Cabecou to Pont l'Éveque make this an ideal wine cellar for tastings and a light dinner. ✉ *Av. Josep Vicenç Foix 80* ☎ *93/206–3846* ⏲ *Tues.–Sat. 11–4:30 and 7–12:30* Ⓜ *Sarrià.*

DANCE CLUBS

Elephant. It could be a catwalk, with models showing off the latest fashions and strutting their stuff, or it could be a chalet-turned-Buddhist-Temple with well-dressed worshipers downing gin-tonics. But it's not—this club is uptown with a capital "U" in both location and style. Expect to rub shoulders with footballers and their wives, international business students, and other assorted wannabes tripping the night fantastic to safe and sultry dance music. ✉ *Passeig dels Til.lers 1, Pedralbes* ☎ *93/334–0258* 🌐 *www.elephantbcn.com* ⏲ *Thurs. 11:30 pm–4 am, Fri. and Sat. 11:30 pm–5 am* Ⓜ *Maria Cristina.*

POBLENOU

Once an industrial area, Poblenou abounds with large loft-like spaces that have become home to some of the city's wildest and loudest clubs and live-music venues. The daddy of them is Sala Razzmatazz, where live pop and rock is followed by all-night clubbing.

BARS

El Boo. What looks like a bright blue, beached submarine was for years a popular family diner. In 2011, a consortium of local personalities took it over to create an exclusive beach club and restaurant, far from the madding crowds that flock to the more central beach addresses. Situated on the northern swath of Poblenou beach, El Boo accommodates a restaurant, beach club, and cocktail lounge, plus a string of stylish parties during the high season. Isolated and clubby with a fitting Balearic decor, it's best to phone ahead in case the joint has been booked for a private party. ✉ *Espigó de Bac de Roda 1, Platja de la Nova Mar Bella, Poblenou* ☎ *93/225–0100* 🌐 *www.elboo.es* ⏲ *Daily 10 am–1:30 am* Ⓜ *Poblenou.*

DANCE CLUBS

The Loft. An offshoot of Sala Razzmatazz, this funky space dedicated to house and electronic music draws an edgy crowd of twenty- and thirtysomethings. The club opens at 1 am on Friday and Saturday, and the energy generated between then and dawn could provide electricity for the entire city if someone could figure out how to harness the stuff. ✉ *Pamplona 88, Poblenou* ☎ *93/320–8200* 🌐 *www.salarazzmatazz.com* Ⓜ *Marina, Bogatell.*

MUSIC CLUBS

Sala Razzmatazz. Razzmatazz stage weeknight concerts featuring international draws from James Taylor to Moriarty The small-format environment is extraordinarily intimate and beats out sports stadiums or the immense Palau Sant Jordi as a top venue for concerts. It shares its Friday and Saturday club madness with neighboring sister venture the Loft, around the corner, and has four other smaller *salas* where anything could happen, from an indie film shoot to Jarvis Cocker spinning discs at a private party. ✉ *Almogavers 122, Poblenou* ☎ *93/320–8200* 🌐 *www.salarazzmatazz.com* ⏲ *Shows generally start around 10 pm* Ⓜ *Marina, Bogatell.*

POBLE SEC

Whilst bustling Paral.lel avenue is the city's historic theater heartland, Carrer Blai has nurtured a cozy scene of tapas bars and bodegas. For diehards, the legendary Sala Apollo turns the beat around till dawn.

BARS

Rouge Bar. You'd be forgiven to think that Rouge Bar was originally part of the set to a college movie, specifically the heroine's apartment—complete with a selection of mismatched, threadbare furniture, posters of Impressionist paintings tacked to the wall, and the low light so effectively created by draping red pashmina shawls over lampshades. Luckily, that movie production's catering service included an excellent mixologist with a decent taste in lounge music who decided to stay behind. ✉ *Poeta Cabanyes 21, Poble Sec* ☎ *93/442–4985* 🌐 *rougebar-barcelona.blogspot.com.es* ⏲ *Wed.–Sun. 7 pm–3 am* Ⓜ *Paral.lel.*

MUSIC CLUBS

Sala Apolo. Once part of the music-hall scene along the Paral.lel, these days the beats come from an eclectic and varied program of international and local acts. Salif Keïta, Kitty, Daisy and Lewis, and Sharon Jones and the Dap-Kings are just a few that have taken the stage recently, though the offerings vary wildly from jazz and swing, to flamenco and hard rock. After the last encore, Sala Apollo converts to a hugely popular dance club—the Nasty Monday and Crappy Tuesday nights are particularly sinful ways to start the week. ✉ *Nou de la Rambla 113* ☎ *93/441–4001* 🌐 *www.sala-apolo.com* ⏲ *Dance club daily from midnight. Show times vary* Ⓜ *Paral.lel.*

BONANOVA AND SANT GERVASI

These leafy, residential neighborhoods north of Diagonal host a handful of destination venues tucked away in modern buildings. These areas are not well serviced by the metro system—a cab is your best way to get here.

Opiniao. In the upper reaches of Barcelona's Sant Gervasi district, this taste of Brazil above Via Augusta offers a low-key, quiet, and intimate sanctuary filled with booths and tables tucked into corners with occasional live performances for graduates and postgraduates still actively on the hunt. ✉ *Ciutat de Balaguer 67–69, Bonanova* ☎ *93/418–3399* 🌐 *www.opiniao.es* ⏲ *Daily 7 pm–3 am* Ⓜ *El Putxet.*

TIBIDABO

BARS

Mirablau. This bar is a popular hangout for evening drinks, but it's even more frequented as a romantic late-night vantage point for watching the city lights down below. Take the Tibidabo train (U-7) from Plaça de Catalunya or Buses 24 and 22 to Plaça Kennedy. At Avinguda Tibidabo, catch the Tramvía Blau (Blue Trolley), which connects with the funicular to the summit. ✉ *Plaça del Doctor Andreu s/n* ☎ *93/418–5879* 🌐 *www.mirablaubcn.com* 🕐 *Mon.–Thurs. 7 pm–2:30 am, Fri. 7 pm–3 am, Sun. 9 pm–3 am* Ⓜ *Av. Tibidabo.*

THE ARTS

A glance through the agenda pages of websites 🌐 *www.timeout.cat*, 🌐 *www.guiadelocio.com*, and 🌐 *www.barcelonacultura.bcn.cat* will remind you, every day, that it would be physically impossible to make it to all the art-exhibit openings, concerts, book presentations by famous authors, lectures, free films, and theatrical events that you would like to attend in Barcelona on any given day. Gallery events and book presentations alone, many of which serve drinks and canapés, could probably eliminate any need for a food or party budget in Barcelona's boiling cultural scene. Besides the above-mentioned sources, keep your eyes peeled for flyers and posters in shops, bars, and cafés for the latest cultural happenings.

ART GALLERIES

For art-gallery shopping, see Chapter 7.

Fodor's Choice ★ **CaixaFòrum.** The building itself, a restored textile factory, is well worth exploring (and is directly across from the Mies van der Rohe Pavillion on Montjuïc at the bottom of the steps up to the Palau Nacional). Temporary exhibits show the work of major artists from around the world, while the auditorium (and sometimes the outdoor area) hosts a regular program of world-music concerts, theater, and performance art. On most Sundays, a play for children is staged at midday, generally in Catalan but nearly always colorful and animated enough to be understood by all. ✉ *Av. Francesc Ferrer i Guàrdia 6–8, Montjuïc* ☎ *93/476–8600* 🌐 *www.fundacio.lacaixa.es* 🕐 *Weekdays 10–8, weekends 10–9. Event hrs vary* Ⓜ *Espanya.*

Centre Cultural Metropolità Tecla Sala. Some of the most avant-garde exhibits and installations that come through Barcelona find their way to this cultural powerhouse, a 15-minute metro ride away in the suburb of Hospitalet de Llobregat. (Note that the Josep Tarradellas address is not the in-town Barcelona street that runs between Estació de Sants and Plaça Francesc Macià). ✉ *Av. Josep Tarradellas 44, Hospitalet* ☎ *93/338–5771* 🌐 *www.teclasala.net* 🕐 *Tues.–Fri. 10–2 and 5–8, Sun. 11–2* Ⓜ *La Torrasa.*

Fundació Antoni Tàpies. This foundation created in 1984 by Catalonia's then-most-important living artist was closed for refurbishment for many

The Gran Teatre del Liceu hosts operas and concerts in an appropriately opulent setting.

years but reopened amid much excitement in 2010, still in its original Domènech i Montaner Modernisme building. Besides holding one of the most important collections of works by Tàpies, who died in 2012, the foundation holds challenging temporary exhibitions by other artists and art collectives, lecture series, film screenings, and an excellent library. ✉ *Aragó 255, Eixample* ☎ *93/487–0315* 🌐 *www.fundaciotapies.org* ⏲ *Tues.–Sun. 10–7* Ⓜ *Passeig de Gràcia.*

Fundació Miró. Sometimes used for outdoor concerts in the summer months, Joan Miró's sculpture garden at his foundation on Montjuïc is a surrealistic and enchanting place, and the permanent collection contains some of his most beautiful paintings. However, what makes this foundation truly stand out are the ambitious temporary exhibitions, often organized together with international museums, that can range from a showcase of leading mural artists to a masterpiece in the evolution of British art post–World War II. ✉ *Parc de Montjuïc, Montjuïc* ☎ *93/443–9470* 🌐 *www.fundaciomiro-bcn.org* ⏲ *Tues.–Sat. 10–7 (8 in summer), Sun. 10–2:30.*

La Capella de l'Antic Hospital de la Santa Creu. In this chapel, as in many Barcelona art galleries, the space itself is half the show. The choir loft, the inside of the cupola, and the vaulting in the side chapels are all lovely, while the exhibits and installations invariably have young artists showing experimental works. Opening times vary according to show and function, but generally they're held during the afternoon or early evening. ✉ *Hospital 56, El Raval* ☎ *93/442–7171* 🌐 *www.bcn.es/lacapella* Ⓜ *Liceu.*

Palau de la Virreina. With the Espai Xavier Miserachs showing photography, two other spaces and the patio available for other temporary exhibits, and lots of information available on the city's cultural happenings, this is an important Barcelona art hub, resource, and HQ of the Institut de Cultura. ✉ *La Rambla 99, Rambla* ☎ *93/316–1000* 🌐 *lavirreina.bcn.cat* ⏲ *Tues.–Sun. noon–8* Ⓜ *Pl. de Catalunya, Liceu.*

CONCERTS

For details on concerts throughout the year, check city hall's culture website (🌐 *barcelonacultura.bcn.cat*), buy the handy *Guia del Ocio* (published every Thursday), or stop by any of the tourist information offices scattered throughout town. Complete listings are also found online at 🌐 *www.ticketmaster.es,* where you can buy *entradas* often more cheaply than at the box office.

Barts (Arts on Stage). This new state-of-the-art theater on the Paral.lel—remodeled from the old Artèria Music Hall—has wildly diverse and interesting programming, accommodating everything from performances from the latest hipster musicians to musicals, magic shows, and cutting-edge theater. ✉ *Paral.lel 62, Poble Sec* ☎ *93/324–8492* 🌐 *www.barts.cat* ⏲ *Box office 6–9 pm* Ⓜ *Paral.lel.*

Fabra i Coats–Fàbrica de Creació. Opened in 2012, this exciting arts complex—remodeled from an old textile factory on the outer limits of the Poblenou district—has gotten off to a good start. A large part of the complex accommodates work spaces for resident artists and creative sorts, while the large performance areas are given over to dance troupes, events and concerts staged by local NGOs, game tournaments, visual-arts fests, and even the Three Kings at Christmas time. ✉ *Sant Adrià 20, Sant Andreu* ☎ *93/256–6150* 🌐 *fabraicoats.bcn.cat* Ⓜ *Sant Andreu.*

L'Auditori de Barcelona. Functional, sleek, and minimalist, the Rafael Moneo-designed Auditori schedules a full program of classical music—with regular forays into jazz, flamenco, and pop—near Plaça de les Glòries. Orchestras that perform here include the Orquestra Simfònica de Barcelona i Nacional de Catalunya (OBC) and the Orquestra Nacional de Cambra de Andorra. The excellent Museu de la Música is situated on the first floor. ✉ *Lepant 150, Eixample* ☎ *93/247–9300* 🌐 *www.auditori.cat* Ⓜ *Marina, Monumental.*

Fodor's Choice ★ **Palau de la Música Catalana.** Barcelona's most spectacular concert hall is a Moderniste masterpiece, largely regarded as Domènech i Montaner's best work, just off the bustling Via Laietana. Performances run year-round. While the focus is generally on classical (the Palau de la Música Catalana is the historic home of the Orfeó Catalá, or Catalan Choir), major music festivals—such as Barcelona's Jazz Festival and even Sónar—generally have a date or two on the Palau's magnificently ornate stage. A sensitive extension to the original building by local architect Oscar Tusquets accommodates the Petit Palau, a smaller venue for recitals and shows for children. Tickets for most classical and family concerts can be bought at the box office, where you can also book a guided tour of the building. ✉ *Carrera Sant Pere Més*

Alt 4–6, Urquinaona ☎ *902/442882* 🌐 *www.palaumusica.cat* ⏲ *Box office daily 9:30–3:30* Ⓜ *Urquinaona.*

Palau Sant Jordi. Arata Isozaki's huge venue, built for the 1992 Olympic Games, hosts massively attended pop concerts for stars like Bruce Springsteen or Justin Bieber, though occasional operas and other musical events are also presented here. ✉ *Palau Sant Jordi, Passeig Olímpic 5–7, Montjuïc* ☎ *93/426–2089* Ⓜ *Espanya.*

DANCE

Barcelona's dance scene has become more and more about flamenco, as this Andalusian art form has gained popularity in Catalonia over the last decade. Ballet troupes, both local and from abroad, perform at the Liceu Opera House with some regularity, while contemporary dance troupes such as those of Cesc Gelabert and Nacho Duato are often performing in a variety of theaters around town. The Mercat de les Flors theater is the city's main dance center. Most venues that host dance primarily feature theater productions.

5

El Mercat de les Flors. An old flower market converted into a modern performance space, theater, and dance school, the Mercat de Les Flors is the home of the Institut de Teatre and is set on lovely, expansive grounds at the foot of verdant Montjuïc. Modern dance is the mercat's raison d'être, but theater is also performed here as well, particularly during the summer Grec festival. Sunday is kids' day, with theater or musical concerts starting at midday. A great on-site café and plenty of wide, open space outside make it an excellent morning out for the family. ✉ *Lleida 59, Eixample* ☎ *93/426–1875* 🌐 *mercatflors.cat* Ⓜ *Espanya.*

FLAMENCO

Barcelona's flamenco scene is surprisingly vibrant for a culture so far removed from Andalusia. Los Tarantos, in Plaça Reial, regularly stages authentic flamenco performances.

El Cordobés. For about a half-century, this venerable dinner theater has thrived by catering to tour groups: visitors who may or may not know that flamenco is a cultural import here in Catalonia but relish a good show when they see one. El Cordobès maintains a high standard of professionalism, booking well-known and respected performers from all over Spain; the program changes regularly, and there are performances throughout the evening, from an early show with tapas to dinner presentations. ✉ *La Rambla 35, Rambla* ☎ *93/317–5711* 🌐 *www.tablaocordobes.com* Ⓜ *Drassanes.*

Los Tarantos. This small, basement boîte spotlights some of Andalusia's best flamenco in 30-minute shows of dance, percussion, and song. Think of them as flamenco "tapas" as opposed to a full-course meal of dance. At only €10 a pop, they're a good intro to the art and feel much less touristy than most standard flamenco fare. ✉ *Pl. Reial 17, Barri Gòtic* ☎ *93/304–1210* 🌐 *www.masimas.com/en/tarantos* ⏲ *Performances daily at 8:30, 9:30, and 10:30* Ⓜ *Liceu.*

Palacio del Flamenco. This Eixample music hall showcases some of the city's best flamenco at hefty prices starting from €40 for a drink and the show up to €55 to €90 for dinner and a show. Supper shows (late) are slightly cheaper. ✉ *Balmes 139, Eixample* ☎ *93/218–7237* 🌐 *www.palaciodelflamenco.com* Ⓜ *Provença, Diagonal.*

Bar La Lola. This sweet little Andaluz-style tavern buried in La Ribera district serves basic tapas, generous mixed drinks, and impromptu flamenco performances from local troupes on Thursday evening. The duende begins at 9, though its better to get there a bit early to nab a table. ✉ *Argenter 2, Born-Ribera* ☎ *93/328–3525* ⏲ *Jaume I* Ⓜ *Tues.–Sun. 6 pm–1 am.*

CATALAN FLAMENCO

Considered a foreign import from Andalusia, flamenco and Catalonia may sound incongruous, but Barcelona has a burgeoning and erudite flamenco audience. For the best flamenco available in Barcelona, consult listings and hotel concierges and don't be put off if the venue seems touristy—these venues often book the best artists. Barcelona-born *cantaors* include Mayte Martín and Miguel Poveda. Also watch the billboards for such names as Estrella Morente (daughter of the late, great Enrique Morente), Chano Domínguez (who often appears at the Barcelona Jazz Festival), and the legendary Paco de Lucía.

FILM

Although most foreign films here are dubbed, Barcelona has a full assortment of original-language cinema; look for listings marked "VOS" (*versión original subtitulada*). Yelmo Cineplex Icària near the Vila Olímpica is the main movie mill, showing more than a dozen films at any given time, all in VOS and most in 3D. Films in VOS are also shown at several other theaters.

Balmes Multicines. Barcelona's cine-aficionados were singing in the rain when this 12-screen complex opened its doors at the end of 2013. Screenings, which lean toward the latest Hollywood releases, are all in VOS. ✉ *Balmes 422–424, Sarrià* ☎ *902/510500* 🌐 *www.grupbalana.com* Ⓜ *El Putxet.*

Cines Verdi. Gràcia's movie center—and a great favorite for the pre- and postshow action in the bars and restaurants in the immediate vicinity—unfailingly screens recent releases (with a preference for serious-minded cinema) in their original-language versions. The sister cinema Verdi Park is just around the corner, and also shows films in VOS. ✉ *Verdi 32, Gràcia* ☎ *93/238–7990* 🌐 *www.cines-verdi.com* Ⓜ *Gràcia, Fontana.*

Filmoteca de Catalunya. After an endless production period, the new Filmoteca de Catalunya finally opened in the Raval in 2012 inside a Brutalist-style edifice designed by Josep Lluís Mateo. With plush seats, wide screens, and a state-of-the-art sound system, it's a film buff's paradise. Most movies are screened in VOS (though the original language is not always English) and are programmed in "cycles." The program is always serious and approached academically, whether the focus is musicals, film noir, or documentaries. ✉ *Pl. de Salvador Seguí 1, El Raval* ☎ *93/567–1070* 🌐 *www.filmoteca.cat* Ⓜ *Paral.lel.*

Icaria Yelmo. In a barren shopping mall, the Icaria Yelmo offers a solid mix of blockbusters and the latest releases in VOS, with many screenings in 3-D as well. ✉ *Salvador Espriu 61, Port Olímpic* ☎ *93/221–7585* 🌐 *www.yelmocines.es* Ⓜ *Ciutadella/Vila Olímpica.*

Renoir Floridablanca. A five-minute walk from the Plaça de la Universitat, this cinema is a good choice for recently released English-language features of all kinds, primarily of the indie ilk. ✉ *Floridablanca 135* ☎ *91/542–2702* 🌐 *www.cinesrenoir.com* Ⓜ *Universitat.*

Verdi Park. Part of the Cine Verdi complex around the corner, this cinema has three screens showing VOS films in the heart of buzzing Gràcia. Both venues offer reduced priced tickets Tuesdays to Thursdays. ✉ *Torrijos 49, Gràcia* ☎ *93/238–7990* 🌐 *www.cines-verdi.com* Ⓜ *Fontana, Joanic.*

OPERA

Fodor's Choice ★

Gran Teatre del Liceu. Barcelona's famous opera house on La Rambla—in all its gilt, stained-glass, and red plush glory—runs a full season September through June, combining the Liceu's own chorus and orchestra with first-tier, invited soloists. In addition, touring dance companies—ballet, flamenco, and modern dance—appear here. The downstairs foyer often holds early-evening recitals, while the Petit Liceu program sees child-friendly opera adaptations (though not always held in the Liceu itself). The Espai Liceu in the opera house annex includes an excellent café and a gift shop for music-related DVDs, CDs, books, instruments, and knickknacks. A tiny 50-seat theater projecting fragments of operas and a video of the history of the Liceu can be viewed as part of a tour of the building (tickets available online or in the Espai Liceu). Seats for performances can be expensive and hard to get; reserve well in advance. ✉ *La Rambla 51–59, La Rambla* ☎ *93/485–9900* 🌐 *www.liceubarcelona.cat* ⏲ *Tours daily at 10 am (subject to performances and rehearsals). Espai Liceu weekdays 11–8. Box office weekdays 1:30–8 and 1 hr before performances on weekends* Ⓜ *Liceu.*

THEATER

Most plays here are performed in Catalan, though some—especially the more lighthearted shows—are performed in Spanish. Barcelona is well known for avant-garde theater and for troupes that specialize in mime, large-scale performance art, and special effects (La Fura dels Baus, Els Joglars, and Els Comediants are among the most famous). Musicals are also popular, with most big-name productions like *Mama Mía* and *The Sound of Music* regularly making it over from Madrid.

El Molino. For most of the 20th century, this venue was the most legendary of all the cabaret theaters on Avinguda Paral.lel. Modeled after Paris's Moulin Rouge, it closed in the late 1990s as the building was becoming dangerously run-down. After an ambitious refurbishment, El Molino opened again in 2010 as one of the most stunning state-of-the-art cabaret theaters in Europe. The building now has five, instead of the original two, stories, with a bar and terrace on the third; the interior has been decked out with complex lighting systems that adapt to every change on the small stage. What has remained the same, however, is its essence—a contemporary version of burlesque, but bump-and-grind all the same. You can purchase tickets at the box office before performances, which start at 6:30 and 9:30. ✉ *Vilà i Vilà 99, Poble Sec* ☎ *93/205–5111* 🌐 *www.elmolinobcn.com* Ⓜ *Paral.lel.*

FAMILY **La Puntual Putxinel.lis de Barcelona.** The city's dedicated puppet (in Catalan, *putxinel.li*) theater is in the off-Born area just off Carrer del Comerç. Weekend matinee performances are major kid magnets and tend to sell out fast, so srrive early. ✉ *Allada-Vermell 15, Born-Ribera* ☎ *639/305353* 🌐 *www.lapuntual.info* Ⓜ *Jaume I.*

Sala Beckett. Tucked away in upper Gràcia, Sala Beckett—and the Obrador Internacional de Dramatúrgia (International Drama Workshop)—provides two intimate stages for some of Barcelona's most interesting, experimental, and thoughtful theater events. A second and larger Sala Beckett is situated in Poblenou (✉ *Carrer Batusta 15*) and is mainly used for courses but will possibly become the headquarters in the future. ✉ *Alegre de Dalt 55 bis, Gràcia* ☎ *93/284–5312* 🌐 *www.salabeckett.com* Ⓜ *Joanic.*

Teatre Nacional de Catalunya. Near Plaça de les Glòries, at the eastern end of the Diagonal, this grandiose glass-enclosed classical temple was designed by Ricardo Bofill, architect of Barcelona's airport. Programs cover everything from Shakespeare to avant-garde theater. Most productions, as the name suggests, are in Catalan. ✉ *Carrer l'Art 1* ☎ *93/306–5700* 🌐 *www.tnc.cat* Ⓜ *Glóries.*

Teatre Tívoli. One of the city's most beloved traditional theater and dance venues, the Tívoli has staged everything from the Ballet Nacional de Cuba to flamenco and teeny-bopper treats. ✉ *Casp 10* ☎ *902/332211* 🌐 *www.grupbalana.com* Ⓜ *Pl. de Catalunya.*

Teatre Victòria. This popular theater in the heart of Barcelona's show district is a historic venue for musicals and dance productions, from Swing to Bollywood. ✉ *Av. del Paral.lel 67–69, Poble Sec* ☎ *93/329–9189* 🌐 *www.teatrevictoria.com* Ⓜ *Paral.lel.*

SPORTS AND THE OUTDOORS

By Jared Lubarsky

"You've got to understand about us and Barça," said the barmaid at the little Catalan pub on the Costa Brava. "For all those years under Franco, Camp Nou (the Futbol Club Barcelona's 99,000-seat stadium) was the only place we could gather in numbers and shout out loud in our own language."

The FBC motto is "*Més que un club*" ("More than a club"); to its legion of fans, Barça is the symbol of their perennial itch for independence, the vessel of their pride in their decidedly un-Spanish Catalan identity. The way Barça plays the game embodies their sense of solidarity, their sense of style. Twice a year in La Liga (Spanish League) competition they take on archrival Real Madrid; the matches—*los clasicos*—are showdowns no less political than athletic. When Barça loses (which isn't often these days), it's a national day of mourning.

In 2009 Barça claimed a historic Triple Crown, winning La Liga, the Spanish King's Cup, and the European Champions League. Even the British press wrote that this might have been the greatest soccer team of all time. Since then Barça has gone on to consolidate that claim, winning the 2011 European FIFA Club World Cup and the UEFA Super Cup with even more grace and authority than in 2009. In 2012–13, they topped La Liga again, though dropping away in the King's Cup and Champions League in the semifinals—only to come back stronger than ever the following year.

Barcelona also boasts another first-division team, RCD (Reial Club Deportiu) Espanyol. Home ground for Espanyol is the 40,000-seat Estadi Cornellà-Prat, in the city's western suburb; tickets are easier to come by than for Barça matches, but the local fans are no less loyal.

Is fútbol not your spectator sport? Barcelona's Conde de Godó tournament brings the world's best tennis players here every April, while the Spanish Grand Prix at Mont Meló draws the top Formula One racing teams. Home court for the FC Barcelona basketball club, which has sent the likes of Pau and Marc Gasol to the NBA, is the Palau Blaugrana pavilion, next door to Camp Nou. As for keeping active yourself, there are diving, windsurfing, surfing, sailing, and water-sports activities in Barceloneta and all along the coast north and south of the city. Tennis and squash courts are available in various public and semiprivate clubs around town, and there are now nearly two dozen golf courses less than an hour away. Bicycle lanes run the length of Diagonal, and there are bike-rental agencies all over town.

BEACHES

See the illustrated feature for details on Barcelona's beaches.

BICYCLES AND IN-LINE SKATES

Exploring Barcelona on wheels, whether by bike or on skates, is a good way to see a lot, and to save on transport. Bicycle lanes run along most major arteries.

Barcelona By Bike. Gather at the meeting point next to the main entrance of the Barcelona Casino for a three-hour guided bike tour (€22 with a complimentary drink en route) of the Ciutat Vella and the Port. ✉ *Escullera de Poble Nou, Port Olímpic* ☎ *93/268–8107* 🌐 *www.barcelonabybike.com* Ⓜ *Ciutadella/Vila Olímpica.*

Bike Tours Barcelona. This company offers a three-hour bike tour (in English) for €22, with a drink included. Just look for the guide with a bike and a red flag at the northeast corner of the Town Hall in Plaça Sant Jaume, outside the Tourist Information Office. Tours depart daily from April 1 to September 15 at 11 am and 4:30 pm. The company will also organize private guided tours through the Barri Gòtic, Parks, Port Olímpic and Barceloneta, the Moderniste Route and other itineraries on request. ✉ *Carrer Esparteria 3, Barri Gòtic* ☎ *93/268–2105* 🌐 *www.biketoursbarcelona.com* Ⓜ *Jaume I.*

Classic Bikes. Just off pivotal Plaça de Catalunya, bicycles are available for rent here every day of the week from 9:30 to 8. The 24-hour rate is €15; take a bike in the morning and return it by closing time for €12; or ride for two hours for €6. ✉ *Tallers 45, El Raval* ☎ *93/317–1970* 🌐 *classicbikes.es* Ⓜ *Pl. de Catalunya.*

Fat Tire Bike Tours. Four-hour guided city tours with this company start in Plaça Sant Jaume daily at 11 am (and also at 4 pm, mid-April through mid-October), covering—with a lunch break—the usual suspects: the Barri Gòtic, Sagrada Família, Ciutadella Park, the Port, and Barceloneta. No reservations necessary, but call to confirm where to find the guide. ✉ *Sant Honorat 7, Barri Gòtic* ☎ *93/342–9275* 🌐 *www.fattirebiketours.com/barcelona* 🎟 *€24* Ⓜ *Jaume I.*

Steel Donkey Bike Tours. Groups up to 8 people can take four-hour "alternative" bike tours with this outfit, on Tuesday, Friday and Saturday mornings, meeting by the port at Drassanes at 10 am. The tours (€35, including bike and helmet rentals) are quirky, offering sights and experiences a bit off the beaten path from the standard itineraries. Call for reservations. ✉ *Escudellers 48, Barri Gòtic* ☎ *657/286854* 🌐 *www.steeldonkeybiketours.com* Ⓜ *Jaume I.*

6

BARCELONA'S BEST BEACHES

Over the last decade, Barcelona's *platjas* (beaches) have been improved, now stretching some 4 km (2½ miles) from Barceloneta's Platja de Sant Sebastià at the southwestern end, northward via the Platjas de Sant Miquel, Barceloneta, Passeig Marítim, Port Olímpic, Nova Icària, Bogatell, Mar Bella (the last bit of which is a nudist enclave), and La Nova Mar Bella to Llevant. The Barceloneta beach is the most popular stretch, easily accessible by several bus lines, notably the No. 64, and from the L4 metro stop at Barceloneta or at Ciutadella/Vila Olímpica. The best surfing is at the northeastern end of the Barceloneta beach, while the boardwalk offers miles of runway for walkers, cyclers, and joggers. Topless bathing is common on all beaches in and around Barcelona.

WORD OF MOUTH

"The beaches between Port Olimpic and Barceloneta [are] a bit more popular because you have small supermarkets a stone's throw away from the beach in case you need some food or drinks. Or [you can try] the beachfront restaurants and bars... take the metro to Barceloneta station and walk down Pg J. Borbo on the nice promenade along the old harbor. Several bus lines go down to the beach from many parts of the city. I'd try to avoid Sundays, because it gets really busy, and the beach bars (almost) double their prices." —Cowboy 1968

PLATJA DE LA BARCELONETA

Just to the left at the end of Passeig Joan de Borbó, this is the easiest beach to get to, hence the most crowded and the most fun for people-watching There are windsurfing and kite-surfing rentals to be found just up behind the beach at the edge of La Barceloneta. Rebecca Horn's sculpture L'Estel Ferit, a rusting stack of cubes, expresses nostalgia for the beach shack restaurants that lined the beach here until 1992. Surfers trying to catch a wave wait just off the breakwater in front of the excellent beachfront Agua restaurant.

PLATJA DE LA MAR BELLA

Closest to the Poblenou metro stop near the eastern end of the beaches, this is a thriving gay enclave and the unofficial nudist beach of Barcelona (suited bathers are welcome, too). The water sports center Base Nàutica de la Mar Bella rents equipment for sailing, surfing, and windsurfing. Outfitted with showers, safe drinking fountains, and a children's play area, La Mar Bella also has lifeguards who warn against swimming near the breakwater. The excellent Els Pescadors restaurant is just inland on Plaça Prim.

PLATJA DE LA NOVA ICÀRIA

One of Barcelona's most popular beaches, this strand is just east of the Port Olímpic with a full range of entertainment, restaurant, and refreshment venues close at hand. (Mango and El Chiringuito de Moncho are two of the most popular restaurants.) The beach is directly across from the area developed as the residential Vila Olímpica for the 1992 Games, an interesting housing project that has now become a popular residential neighborhood.

6

PLATJA DE SANT SEBASTIÀ

The landmark of Barceloneta's most southwestern beach (at the end of Passeig Joan de Borbó) now is the ultramodern W Barcelona Hotel, but Sant Sebastià is in fact the oldest of the city beaches, where 19th-century barcelonins cavorted in bloomers and bathing costumes. On the west end is the Club Natació de Barcelona, and there is a semiprivate feel that the beaches farther east seem to lack.

PLATJA DE GAVÀ-CASTELLDEFELS

A 15-minute train ride south of Barcelona (from the Estació de Sants) to Gavà brings you to the broad swath of clean golden sand at Gavà Mar, a popular outing for Barcelona families and beach party aficionados. Gavà Mar extends some 4 km (2½ miles) south to join the busier beach at Castelldefels; returning to Barcelona from Castelldefels allows for a hike down the beach to a variety of seaside shacks and restaurants serving local favorites like *calçots* (spring onions) and paella.

Un Cotxe Menys. "One Car Less" in Catalan—meaning one less automobile on the streets of Barcelona—organizes various kinds of guided tours (including some in English) and bicycle outings. ✉ *Esparteria 3, Born-Ribera* ☎ *93/268–2105.*

GOLF

Weekday golf outings to one of the 22 golf courses within an hour of Barcelona are a good way to exercise and see the Catalonian countryside. Midweek greens fees range from €50 to €85; weekend prices double. Midweek availability is excellent except during Easter vacation and August. Call ahead to confirm a tee time, and remember to bring proof of your USGA handicap or membership in a golf club or you may have trouble playing.

Club de Golf de Sant Cugat. This hilly 18-hole course, in the upscale Barcelona satellite of Sant Cugat, is one of the oldest—and most challenging—courses in the area. ✉ *Calle Villa 79, Sant Cugat del Vallès* ☎ *93/674–3908* 🌐 *www.golfsantcugat.cat* *18 holes. 5214 meters (5704 yds). Par 70. Greens fee €78/€100* ☞ *Facilities: Driving range, putting green, pitching area, golf carts, pull carts, rental clubs, pro-shop, restaurant, bar.*

Club de Golf Terramar. This breezy seaside course offers views and, though fairly gentle, it challenges with hazards such as lakes and a river. ✉ *Ctra. del Golf s/n, Sitges* ☎ *93/894–0580* 🌐 *www.golfterramar.com* *18 holes. 6054 meters (6623 yards). Par 71. Greens fee €75/€130* ☞ *Facilities: Driving range, putting green, pitching area, golf carts, pull carts, rental clubs, pro-shop, lessons, restaurant, bar.*

GYMS AND SPAS

Club Esportiu Femení Iradier. Just above the Passeig de la Bonanova in the upper part of Barcelona, this sleek, exclusive club for women offers Pilates, yoga, and original combinations of fitness programs, as well as squash, a gym, sauna, and pool. A day membership costs €30. ✉ *Carrer Iradier 18 bis, Sant Gervasi* ☎ *93/254–1717* 🌐 *www.iradier.com* Ⓜ *Sarriá (FGC).*

HIKING

The Collserola hills behind the city offer well-marked trails, fresh air, and lovely views. Take the San Cugat, Sabadell, or Terrassa FFCC train from Plaça de Catalunya and get off at Baixador de Vallvidrera; the information center, 10 minutes uphill next to Vil.la Joana (now the Jacint Verdaguer Museum), has maps of this mountain woodland just 20 minutes from downtown. The walk back into town can take two to five hours depending on your speed and the trails you choose. For longer treks, try the 15-km (9-mile) Sant Cugat–to–Barcelona hike, or take the train south to Sitges and make the three-day pilgrimage walk to the Monastery of Montserrat.

Associació Excursionista, Etnográfica i Folklore. Founded in 1945, the association advises lovers of *senderismo* (trekking) on nature walks and historical excursions throughout the region, and organizes outings of all kinds. Be aware: Catalan is the language spoken here. ✉ *Avinyó 19, Barri Gòtic* ☎ *93/302–2730* Ⓜ *Liceu, Jaume I.*

Centre Excursionista de Catalunya. The center has information on hiking throughout Catalonia and the Pyrenees, gives mountaineering courses, organizes excursions, and provides guides for groups. ✉ *Paradis 10, Barri Gòtic* ☎ *93/315–2311* Ⓜ *Jaume I.*

TOP 5 ACTIVITIES

- Watching European Champion Futbol Club Barcelona play in Camp Nou
- Playing the PGA Catalunya golf course in the Empordà
- Scuba diving in the Isles Medes off the Costa Brava
- Jogging the Carretera de les Aigües over Barcelona
- Cheering on Rafael Nadal in his next Conde de Godó championship

6

SAILING AND WINDSURFING

On any day of the week in Barcelona you can see midday regattas taking place off the Barceloneta beaches or beyond the *rompeolas* (breakwater) on the far side of the port. Believe it or not, Olympic-level sailors are being trained for competition just a stone's throw (or two) from La Rambla.

Reial Club Marítim de Barcelona. Barcelona's most exclusive and prestigious yacht club can advise visitors on maritime matters, from where to charter yachts and sailboats to how to sign up for sailing programs. ✉ *Moll d'Espanya 1, Port Vell* ☎ *93/221–4859* 🌐 *www.maritimbarcelona.org* Ⓜ *Drassanes.*

Ronáutica. Charter a yacth, sailboat, or power craft here. ✉ *Moll de la Marina 11, Port Olímpic* ☎ *93/221–8515, 93/221–0380* Ⓜ *Ciutadella/Vila Olímpica.*

SCUBA DIVING

The Costa Brava's Illes Medes nature preserve offers some of the Mediterranean's finest diving adventures. Seven tiny islands off the coastal town of L'Estartit are home to some 1,400 species of flora and fauna in an underwater wonderland of tunnels and caves. Other diving sites include the Illes Formigues off the coast of Palamós, Els Ullastres off Llafranc, and the Balfegó tuna pens off l'Ametlla de Mar, south of Tarragona.

Aquàtica–Centro de Buceo. Aquàtica–Centro de Buceo teaches diving, rents equipment, and organizes outings to the Illes Medes. With top safety-code requirements and certified instructors and biologists directing the programs in English, French, Catalan, or Spanish, this is one of Estartit's best diving opportunities. Aquàtica operates year-round, but winter excursions are suitable only for PADI-certified experienced divers. ✉ *Camping Rifort, L'Estartit* ☎ *972/750656* 🌐 *www.aquatica-sub.com/eng/home.*

SOCCER

Futbol Club Barcelona. Founded in 1899, the Futbol Club Barcelona attained its greatest glory in May 2009, when its victory over Manchester United in Rome sealed the club's third European Championship and Spain's first-ever *triplete* (triple), taking home all of the silverware: League, Cup, and European titles. Barça, as the club is affectionately known, is Real Madrid's perennial nemesis (and vice-versa) as well as a sociological and historical phenomenon of deep significance in Catalonia. Ticket windows at Access 14 to the stadium are open Monday though Saturday and game-day Sunday 10–2 and 5–8; you can also buy tickets at Servicaixa ATMs at Caixa de Catalunya banks, through ticket agencies, and directly online. ✉ *Camp Nou, Aristides Maillol 12, Les Corts* ☎ *93/496–3600, 902/189900* 🌐 *www.fcbarcelona.com* Ⓜ *Collblanc.*

Spain Ticket Bureau. This company can score seats for Barça home games, as well as other sporting events, concerts, and musicals, in Barcelona and elsewhere in Spain. Booking ahead online is a good idea, especially for headliner events, but expect to pay a healthy premium. ✉ *Rambla de Catalunya 89, Entl. A, Eixample* ☎ *93/488–2266, 902/903912* 🌐 *www.spainticketbureau.com* Ⓜ *Passeig de Gràcia, Catalunya.*

TENNIS AND SQUASH

Complejo Deportivo Can Caralleu (*Can Caralleu Sports Complex*). A 20-minute walk uphill from the Reina Elisenda subway stop, Can Caralleu has hard-surface tennis courts, a soccer pitch and running track, two pools, a fitness center—and even a climbing wall. A one-day membership (€13.25) provides unlimited court time (as available), and the use of all other facilities. ✉ *Carrer Esports 2–8, Pedralbes* ☎ *93/203–7874* 🌐 *www.cemcancaralleu.cat* ⏲ *Daily 8 am–11 pm* Ⓜ *Reina Elisenda (FGC).*

Trofeo Godó – Open Seat. Barcelona's main tennis tournament, held in late April, is a clay-court event long considered a French Open warm-up. For tickets to this event, consult with the Reial Club de Tenis de Barcelona or the tournament website beginning in late February. Tickets may also be obtained at 🌐 *www.servicaixa.com.* ✉ *Carrer de Bosch i Gimpera 21, Pedralbes* ☎ *93/203–7852* 🌐 *www.barcelonaopenbancsabadell.com.*

SHOPPING

By Suzanne Wales

Characterized by originality and relative affordability, shopping in Barcelona has developed into a jubilant fashion, design, craft, and gourmet-food fair. The fact that different parts of town provide distinct contexts for shopping makes exploring the city and browsing boutiques inclusive activities.

The Ciutat Vella, especially the Born-Ribera area, is rich in small-crafts shops, young designers, and an endless potpourri of artisans and merchants operating in restored medieval spaces that are often as dazzling as the wares on sale. Even the pharmacies and grocery stores of Barcelona are often sumptuous aesthetic feasts, filled with charming details.

Shopping for design objects and chic fashion in the Eixample is like buying art supplies at the Louvre: it's an Art Nouveau architecture theme park spinning off into dozens of sideshows—textiles, furnishings, curios, and knickknacks of every kind. Any specific shop or boutique will inevitably lead you past a dozen emporiums that you didn't know were there. Original and surprising yet wearable clothing items—what one shopper described as "elegant funk"—are Barcelona's signature contribution to fashion. Rather than copying the runways, Barcelona designers are relentlessly daring and innovative, combining fine materials with masterful workmanship.

Browsing through shops in this originality-obsessed metropolis feels more like museum-hopping than a shopping spree, although it can, of course, be both. Design shops like Vinçon and BD Ediciones de Diseño delight the eye and stimulate the imagination, while the area around the Passeig del Born is attracting hip young designers from all over the globe. Passeig de Gràcia has joined the ranks of Paris's Champs Elysées and Rome's Via Condotti as one of the great shopping avenues in the world, with the planet's fashion houses amply represented, from Armani to Zara. Exploring Barcelona's antiques district along Carrer Banys Nous and Carrer de la Palla is always an adventure. The shops opening daily around Santa Maria del Mar in the Born-Ribera district range from Catalan and international design retailers to shoe and leather-handbag designers, to T-shirt decorators, to dealers in nuts and spices or coffee emporiums. The megastores in Plaça de Catalunya, along Diagonal, and in L'Illa Diagonal farther west are commercial cornucopias selling fashions, furniture, furs, books, music, and everything else under the sun. The villagelike environments of Sarrià and Gràcia lend intimate warmth to antiques or clothes shopping, with friendly boutique owners adding a personal touch often lost in mainstream commerce.

SHOPPING PLANNER

BEST GOT-IT-IN-SPAIN PURCHASES

Saffron: the lightest, most aromatic, and best-value buy left in all of Spain—available in any supermarket or grocery

Rope-soled espadrilles from La Manual Alpargatera

Any items by Javier Mariscal or Miguel Milà, legendary local designers, at Vinçon

Custo Barcelona's ever-original tops

Ceramics from all over Spain at Art Escudellers

HOURS

Most stores are open Monday–Saturday 9–2 and 4:30–8. Virtually all stores close Sunday except during the Christmas season. Many top-end stores in the Eixample and in the malls, such as L'Illa Diagonal, stay open through the lunch hour. The big department stores such as El Corte Inglés and FNAC are open nonstop from 10 to 10. Designated pharmacies are open all night.

TAXES AND GUIDES

Food and basic necessities are taxed at the lowest rate, but most consumer goods are taxed at 16%. Non-EU citizens can request a Tax-Free Form on purchases of €90.15 and over in shops displaying the Tax-Free Shopping sticker. Refunds (either cash or credit) can be obtained at the airport. First get your forms stamped by the customs officer, then hand them to the refund counter in Terminal 1 or 2a (you can also mail them later). Remember that goods must be unused and unopened in order to get the refund. Global Blue Cheque users: you can also obtain a refund at the tourist office in Plaça de Catalunya, which can save you the stress of dealing with airport counters. For further information, plus tips on where to shop, check Turisme Barcelona's website (🌐 *www.barcelonashoppingline.com*).

BARRI GÒTIC

The Barri Gòtic was built on trade and cottage industries, and there are plenty of nimble fingers producing artisan goods in the old-world shops along its stone streets. Start at the Cathedral and work your way outward.

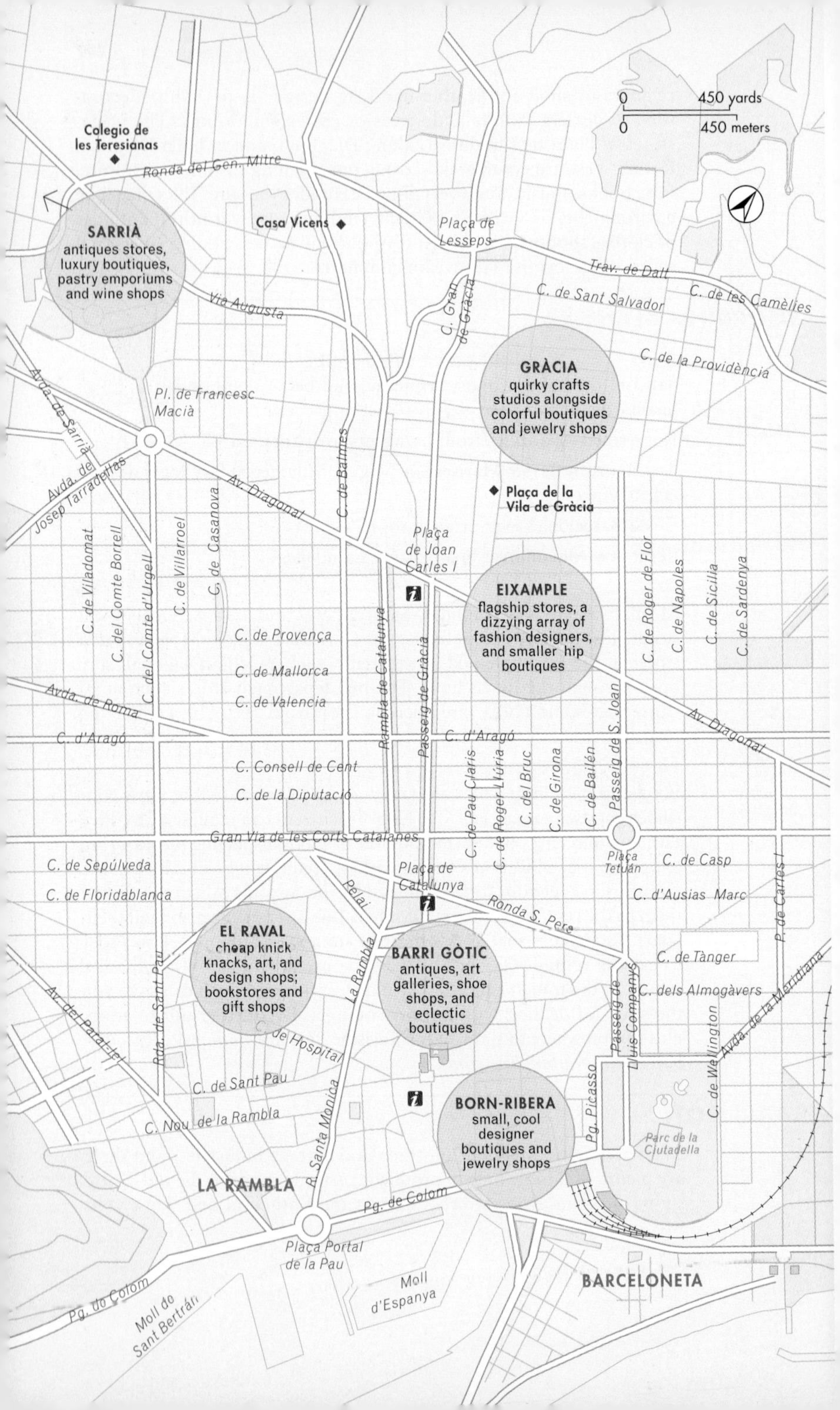

0 450 yards
0 450 meters
Colegio de les Teresianas
Ronda del Gen. Mitre
SARRIÀ
antiques stores, luxury boutiques, pastry emporiums and wine shops
Casa Vicens
Plaça de Lesseps
Trav. de Dalt
C. de Sant Salvador
C. de les Camèlies
Via Augusta
C. Gran de Gràcia
C. de la Providència
GRÀCIA
quirky crafts studios alongside colorful boutiques and jewelry shops
Pl. de Francesc Macià
Avda. de Sarrià
Avda. de Josep Tarradellas
Av. Diagonal
C. de Balmes
Plaça de la Vila de Gràcia
Plaça de Joan Carles I
EIXAMPLE
flagship stores, a dizzying array of fashion designers, and smaller hip boutiques
C. de Viladomat
C. del Comte Borrell
C. del Comte d'Urgell
C. de Villarroel
C. de Casanova
C. de Provença
C. de Mallorca
C. de Valencia
Rambla de Catalunya
Passeig de Gràcia
C. de Roger de Flor
C. de Napoles
C. de Sicilia
C. de Sardenya
Avda. de Roma
C. d'Aragó
C. d'Aragó
Av. Diagonal
C. Consell de Cent
C. de la Diputació
C. de Pau Claris
C. de Roger Llúria
C. del Bruc
C. de Girona
C. de Bailén
Passeig de S. Joan
Gran Via de les Corts Catalanes
C. de Sepúlveda
C. de Floridablanca
Plaça de Catalunya
Plaça Tetuán
C. de Casp
C. d'Ausias Marc
Pelai
Ronda S. Pere
P. de Carles I
EL RAVAL
cheap knick knacks, art, and design shops; bookstores and gift shops
BARRI GÒTIC
antiques, art galleries, shoe shops, and eclectic boutiques
C. de Tànger
C. dels Almogàvers
Av. del Paral·lel
Rda. de Sant Pau
La Rambla
C. de Hospital
Passeig de Lluís Companys
C. de Wellington
Avda. de la Meridiana
C. de Sant Pau
C. Nou de la Rambla
R. Santa Monica
BORN-RIBERA
small, cool designer boutiques and jewelry shops
Pg. Picasso
Parc de la Ciutadella
LA RAMBLA
Pg. de Colom
Plaça Portal de la Pau
Moll d'Espanya
BARCELONETA
Pg. de Colom
Moll de Sant Bertrán

ANTIQUES AND COLLECTIBLES

Antigüedades Fernández. Bric-a-brac is piled high in this workshop near the middle of this slender artery in the medieval Jewish Quarter. This master craftsman restores and sells antique furniture of all kinds. Stop by and stick your head in for the fragrance of the shellacs and wood shavings and a look at one of the last simple carpentry and woodworking shops you'll encounter in contemporary, design-mad, early-21st-century Barcelona. ✉ *Carrer Sant Domènec del Call 9* ☎ *93/301–0045* ⏲ *Mon.–Sat. 10–2 and 5–8* Ⓜ *Liceu, Jaume I.*

ART GALLERIES

Galeria Trama. Another Petritxol favorite, Trama, with occasional exceptions, tends to hang paintings that look as if they might be happier in low-price hostelry establishments, but the gallery merits a look if you find yourself on this picturesque little passageway. ✉ *Petritxol 5* ☎ *93/317–4877* 🌐 *www.galeriatrama.com* ⏲ *Tues.–Fri. 10:30–2 and 4–8, Sat. 10:30–2 and 4:30–8:30* Ⓜ *Liceu, Catalunya.*

Sala Parès. The dean of Barcelona's art galleries, this place opened in 1840 as an art-supplies shop; as a gallery, it dates to 1877, and has shown every Barcelona artist of note since then. Picasso and Miró showed here, as did Casas and Rossinyol before them. Nowadays, Catalan artists like Perico Pastor and Miquel Macaya get pride of place. ✉ *Petritxol 5* ☎ *93/318–7020* 🌐 *www.salapares.com* ⏲ *Mon. 4–8, Tues.–Fri. 10:30–2 and 4–8, Sat. 10:30–2 and 4:30–8:30, Sun. 11:30–2 (June–Oct. only)* Ⓜ *Liceu, Catalunya.*

BOOKS AND STATIONERY

Llibreria Quera. This is the bookstore to seek out if you're interested in the Pyrenees or in exploring any part of the Catalonian hinterlands. Maps, charts, and books detailing everything from Pyrenean ponds and lakes to Romanesque chapels are available in this diminutive giant of a resource. ✉ *Petritxol 2* ☎ *93/318–0743* 🌐 *www.llibreriaquera.com* ⏲ *Tues. 10–8, Wed.–Sat. 10–1:30 and 4:30–8* Ⓜ *Liceu.*

Papirum. Exquisite hand-printed papers, marbleized blank books, and writing implements await you and your muse at this tiny, medieval-tone shop. ✉ *Baixada de la Llibreteria 2* ☎ *93/310–5242* 🌐 *www.papirum-bcn.com* ⏲ *Weekdays 10–8:30, Sat. 10–2 and 5–8:30* Ⓜ *Jaume I.*

CERAMICS AND GLASSWARE

Art Escudellers. Ceramic pieces from all over Spain are on display at this large store across the street from the restaurant Los Caracoles; more than 140 different artisans are represented, with maps showing what part of Spain the work is from. Wine, cheese, and ham tastings are held downstairs, and you can even throw a pot yourself in the workshop. ✉ *Carrer Escudellers 23–25* ☎ *93/412–6801* 🌐 *www.escudellers-art.com* ⏲ *Daily 11–11* Ⓜ *Liceu, Drassanes.*

Caixa de Fang. Glazed tiles, glass objects, and colorful sets of cups and saucers are on sale at this little shop just off Plaça Sant Jaume. Translatable as "Box of Mud" in Catalan, Caixa de Fang shows handmade earthenware cooking vessels from all over Spain, as well as boxwood and olive-wood kitchen utensils. ✉ *Freneria 1* ☎ *93/315–1704* ⏲ *Mon.–Sat. 10–8, Sun. 11–2 and 3–8* Ⓜ *Jaume I.*

CLOTHING

Decathlon. Whether you're planning a trek through the Pyrenees or a beach yoga session, this mega–sports emporium should be your first port of call. From waterproof clothing to footballs to bike repairs, it caters to every conceivable sport and active hobby. Affordable and always busy, Decathlon is the best place to pick up practical travel clothing, such as that forgotten fleece jacket for a sudden cold snap. ✉ *Canuda 20* ☎ *93/342–6161* 🌐 *www.decathlon.es* ⏲ *Mon.–Sat. 9:30–9:30* Ⓜ *Catalunya.*

L'Arca de L'Àvia. As the name of the place ("grandmother's trunk") suggests, this is a miscellaneous potpourri of ancient goods of all kinds, especially period clothing, from shoes to gloves to hats and hairpins. Despite the found-object attitude and ambience of the place, they're not giving away these vintage baubles, so don't be surprised at the hefty price tags. ✉ *Banys Nous 20* ☎ *93/302–1598* 🌐 *www.larcadelavia.com* ⏲ *Weekdays 11–2 and 5–8, Sat. 11–2 and 5–8:30* Ⓜ *Liceu.*

Ojala!. Born in Madrid, based in Morocco, and with a shop in Barcelona, Paloma del Pozo is one of Spain's most original and creative fashion designers. Her perky, Audrey Herburn–ish coats, jackets, skirts, and dresses are realized in dashing, bold colors, luxurious fabrics (velvet is a favorite), and theatrical, Arabesque detailing. They are for women who want to make an entrance, and prices—given the level of quality—are extremely reasonable. ✉ *Ciutat 14* ☎ *93/601–1830* 🌐 *www.ojala.es* ⏲ *Mon.–Sat. 11–9:30* Ⓜ *Jaume I.*

FOOD

Caelum. At the corner of Carrer de la Palla and Banys Nous, this tearoom and coffee shop sells crafts and foods such as honey and preserves made in convents and monasteries all over Spain. The café and tearoom section extends neatly out into the intersection of Carrer Banys Nous (which means "new baths") and Carrer de la Palla, directly over the site of the medieval Jewish baths. ✉ *Carrer de la Palla 8* ☎ *93/302–6993* 🌐 *www.caelumbarcelona.com* ⏲ *Mon.–Thurs. 10:30–8:30, Fri.–Sat. 10:30 am–11 pm, Sun. 10:30–9* Ⓜ *Jaume I.*

Formatgeria La Seu. Scotswoman Katherine McLaughlin has put together the Barri Gòtic's most delightful cheese-tasting sanctuary on the site of an ancient buttery. (A 19th-century butter churn is visible in the back room.) A dozen artisanal cow, goat, and sheep cheeses from all over Spain, and olive oils can be tasted and taken home. La Seu is named for a combination of La Seu cathedral, as the "seat" of cheeses, and for cheese-rich La Seu d'Urgell in the Pyrenees. Katherine's wrapping paper, imaginatively chosen sheets of newspaper, give a final flourish to purchases. ✉ *Dagueria 16, Barri Gòtic* ☎ *93/412–6548* 🌐 *www.formatgerialaseu.com* ⏲ *Tues.–Thurs. 10–2 and 5–8, Fri. and Sat. 10–3:30 and 5–8* Ⓜ *Jaume I.*

La Casa del Bacalao. This cult store decorated with cod-fishing memorabilia specializes in salt cod and books of codfish recipes. Slabs of salt and dried cod, used in a wide range of Catalan recipes (such as *esqueixada*, in which shredded strips of raw salt cod are served in a marinade of oil and vinegar) can be vacuum-packed for portability. ✉ *Comtal 8, just off Porta de l'Àngel* ☎ *93/301–6539* ⏲ *Weekdays 9:30–2:30 and 4:30–8:30, Sat. 9:30–2:30* Ⓜ *Catalunya.*

GIFTS AND SOUVENIRS

Artesania Catalunya. In 2010 the Catalan government created the registered trademark Empremtes de Catalunya to represent Catalan artisans and to make sure that visitors get the real deal when buying what they believe to be genuine products. The official shop now sells jewelry re-created from eras dating back to pre-Roman times, Gaudí-inspired sculptures, traditional cava mugs, and some bravely avant-garde objects from young artisans—all officially sanctioned as fit to represent the city. ✉ *Banys Nous 11* ☎ *93/467–4660* 🌐 *www.artesania-catalunya.com* ⏲ *Mon.–Sat. 10–8, Sun. 10–2* Ⓜ *Jaume I, Liceu.*

Coses de Casa. The 19th-century windows of this lovely corner shop overlooking Plaça del Pi burst with all sorts of home textiles—from humble, superb-quality tea towels to country-chic patchwork quilts. If they don't stock the cushion cover you're after, it probably doesn't exist, although the most unique take-home item is a gingham bread bag—a sausage-shaped carrier for your morning baguette. ✉ *Pl. Sant Josep Oriol 5* ☎ *93/302–7328* 🌐 *www.cosesdecasa.com* Ⓜ *Liceu.*

Fodor's Choice ★ **Ganiveteria Roca.** Directly opposite the giant rose window of the Santa Maria del Pi church, the knife store (*ganivet* is Catalan for knife) beneath this lovely *sgraffito*-decorated facade takes cutlery culture to a new level. Knives, razors, scissors, hatchets, axes, swords, nail clippers, tweezers, and penknives are all displayed in this comprehensive cutting edge emporium. ✉ *Pl. del Pi 3* ☎ *93/302–1241* 🌐 *www.ganiveteriaroca.cat* ⏲ *Weekdays 9:45–1:30 and 4:15–8, Sat. 10–2 and 5–8* Ⓜ *Liceu.*

Guantería y Complementos Alonso. The storefront and interiors of this ancient little glove and accessory shop is well worth the visit. Lovely antique cabinets painstakingly stripped of centuries of paint display gloves, fans, shawls, mantillas, and a miscellany of textile crafts and small gifts. ✉ *Santa Ana 27* ☎ *93/317–6085* 🌐 *www.tiendacenter.com* ⏲ *Mon.–Sat. 10–8* Ⓜ *Catalunya.*

MARKETS

Mercat Gòtic. A browser's bonanza, this interesting if somewhat pricey Thursday market for antique clothing, jewelry, and art objects occupies the plaza in front of the cathedral. ✉ *Pl. de la Seu s/n* 🌐 *www.mercatgotic.com* Ⓜ *Jaume I, Urquinaona.*

Plaça del Pi. This little square fills with the interesting tastes and aromas of a natural-produce market (honeys, cheeses) throughout the month, while neighboring Plaça Sant Josep Oriol holds a painter's market every Sunday. ✉ *Pl. del Pi* ⏲ *1st and 3rd Fri., Sat., and Sun. of each month and some holidays, 10–9* Ⓜ *Catalunya, Liceu.*

SHOES, LUGGAGE, LEATHER GOODS, AND ACCESSORIES

Fodor's Choice ★ **La Manual Alpargatera.** If you appreciate old-school craftsmanship in footwear, visit this boutique just off Carrer Ferran. Handmade rope-sole sandals and espadrilles are the specialty, and this shop has sold them to everyone—including the Pope. The flat, beribboned espadrilles used for dancing the sardana are available, as are newly fashionable wedge heels with peep toes and comfy slippers. ✉ *Avinyó 7* ☎ *93/301–0172* 🌐 *www.lamanual.net* ⏲ *Mon.–Sat. 9:30–1:30 and 4:30–8* Ⓜ *Liceu, Jaume I.*

Vinçon sells a variety of hyperdesigned home goods in a space that was once painter Ramón Casas's studio.

S'avarca de Menorca. For a range of handmade leather sandals (often referred to as Abarcas or Menorcinas) with straps across the heels in infinite variations and colors, this is Barcelona's finest store for footwear from the Balearic Isles. Abarcas come with thicker soles for city walking or lighter ones for wearing around the house. ✉ *Capellans 2* ☎ *93/342–5738* 🌐 *www.savam.es* ⏲ *Mon.–Sat. 10–2 and 2:30–8:30* Ⓜ *Catalunya, Jaume I.*

L'Estanc de Laietana. Famous for its underground cave and humidor at sea level, this shrine to the Cuban cigar is unparalleled in Barcelona. In store for shoppers are cigarettes and rolling tobacco in an all-but-infinite variety of brands. ✉ *Via Laietana 4, Born-Ribera* ☎ *93/310–1034* ⏲ *Mon.–Sat. 10–7* Ⓜ *Jaume I.*

BORN-RIBERA

These two neighborhoods in the old waterfront district around the Santa Maria del Mar basilica seem continuously to breed new boutiques and retail establishments of all kinds, with design shops and clothiers the particular draw.

BOOKS AND STATIONERY

Papers Coma. On Barcelona's most artistic street, Papers Coma—a large warehouse-style shop—meets all your packaging and stationary needs, from bubble wrap to fancy envelopes. ✉ *Montcada 20* ☎ *93/319–7601* 🌐 *www.paperscoma.com* ⏲ *Weekdays 8:30–1:30 and 5–7:30, Sat. 9–1:30* Ⓜ *Jaume I.*

CERAMICS AND GLASSWARE

Baraka. Barcelona's prime purveyor of Moroccan goods, ceramics chief among them, Baraka is the city's general cultural commissar for matters relating to Spain's neighbor to the south. The prehaggled goods here are generally cheaper (and the quality better) than you could bring back from Morocco. ✉ *Canvis Vells 2* ☎ *93/268–4220* 🌐 *www.barakaweb.com* ⏲ *Weekdays 10–2 and 5–8:30, Sat. 11–2 and 5–8:30* Ⓜ *Jaume I.*

Helena Rohmer. In a small shop on a backstreet in the Born, Helena Rohmer is worth seeking out for its clean lines and minimal fuss—it's reminiscent of Gorg Jensen, whom she worked for in the past. Simple silver ring, earring, and pendent settings hold semiprecious stones and enamel disks in on-trend colors, conceived for accessorizing this season's wardrobe. ✉ *Espasseria 13* ☎ *93/319–8879* 🌐 *www.helenarohner.com* ⏲ *Mon.–Sat. 11–3 and 4:30–8:30* Ⓜ *Jaume I.*

CLOTHING

Coquette. Coquette specializes in the kind of understated, feminine beauty that Parisian women know to do so well. The now three shops (two in the Born, one uptown) present a small, careful selection of mainly French designers, like Isabel Marant, Vanessa Bruno, Laurence Doligé, and Chloé. Whether it's a romantic or a seductive look you're after, Coquette makes sure you'll feel both comfortable and irresistible. ✉ *Rec 65* ☎ *93/319–2976* 🌐 *www.coquettebcn.com* ⏲ *Weekdays 11–3 and 5–9, Sat 11:30–8:30* Ⓜ *Jaume I.*

Fodor's Choice ★ **Cortana.** A sleek and breezy Balearic Islands look for women is what this designer from Majorca brings to the fashion scene of urban Barcelona in a whitewashed shop reminiscent of an art gallery. Her dresses transmit a casual, minimalistic elegance and have graced many a red carpet in Madrid. ✉ *Flassaders 41* ☎ *93/310–1255* 🌐 *www.cortana.es* ⏲ *Mon. 3–8, Tues.–Sat. 11–2 and 3–8* Ⓜ *Jaume I.*

Custo Barcelona. Ever since Custido Dalmau and his brother David returned from a round-the-world motorcycle tour with visions of California surfing styles dancing in their heads, Custo Barcelona has been a runaway success doling out clingy cotton tops in bright and cheery hues. Now scattered all over Barcelona and the globe, Custo is scoring even more acclaim by expanding into coats, dresses, and kidswear. ✉ *Pl. de les Olles 7* ☎ *93/268–7893* 🌐 *www.custo-barcelona.com* ⏲ *Daily 10–9* Ⓜ *Jaume I.*

El Ganso. Who would have thought that two Madrid-born brothers could out-Brit the Brits? One of Spain's more recent fashion success stories, El Ganso makes very appealing preppy-inspired men's and women's wear—striped blazers, pleated skirts, and tailored suits made for upper-class frolics. ✉ *Vidrieria 7* ☎ *93/268–9257* 🌐 *www.elganso.com* ⏲ *Mon.–Sat. 11–9* Ⓜ *Jaume I.*

Kukuxumusu. As with more and more of Barcelona's boutiques, this one comes with a worldview. T-shirts, mugs, hats, pencils, notebooks, handkerchiefs, and just about anything you can apply a design to is decorated with Basque artist Mikel Urmeneta's zany zoological characters in the throes of love. ✉ *Argenteria 69* ☎ *93/310–3647* 🌐 *www.kukuxumusu.com* ⏲ *Mon.–Sat. 10–8* Ⓜ *Jaume I.*

FOOD

Fodor'sChoice ★ **Casa Gispert.** On the inland side of Santa Maria del Mar, this shop is one of the most aromatic and picturesque in Barcelona, bursting with teas, coffees, spices, saffron, chocolates, and nuts. The star element in this olfactory and aesthetic feast is an almond-roasting stove in the back of the store—purportedly the oldest in Europe, dating from 1851, like the store itself. But don't miss the acid engravings on the office windows or the ancient wooden back door before picking up a bag of freshly roasted nuts to take with you. ✉ *Sombrerers 23* ☎ *93/319–7547* 🌐 *www.casagispert.com* 🕑 *Tues.–Sat. 9:30–2 and 4–8:30, Sat. 10–2 and 5–8:30 (also Mon. late Oct.–Dec.)* Ⓜ *Jaume I.*

El Magnífico. This coffee emporium just up the street from Santa Maria del Mar is famous for its sacks of coffee beans from all over the globe. Coffee to go is also available—enjoy it on the little bench outside. ✉ *Carrer Argenteria 64* ☎ *93/319–3975* 🌐 *www.cafeselmagnifico.com* 🕑 *Mon.–Sat. 10–8* Ⓜ *Jaume I.*

Pastelería Hofmann. Mey Hofmann, a constellation in Barcelona's gourmet galaxy for the last three decades through her restaurant and cooking courses, has a sideline dedicated exclusively to pastry. Everything from the lightest, flakiest croissants to the cakes, tarts, and ice creams are about as good they get in this sweets emporium just off the Passeig del Born. ✉ *Flassaders 44* ☎ *93/268–8221* 🌐 *www.hofmann-bcn.com* 🕑 *Mon.–Wed 9–2 and 3:30–8, Thurs.–Sat. 9–2 and 3:30–8:30, Sun. 9–2:30* Ⓜ *Jaume I.*

La Botifarreria de Santa Maria. This busy emporium next to the church of Santa Maria del Mar stocks excellent cheeses, hams, pâtés, and homemade *sobrassadas* (pork pâté with paprika). *Botifarra,* a Catalan sausage, is the main item here, with a wide range of varieties, including egg sausage for meatless Lent and sausage stuffed with spinach, asparagus, cider, cinnamon, and Cabrales cheese. ✉ *Santa Maria 4* ☎ *93/319–9123* 🌐 *www.labotifarreria.com* 🕑 *Weekdays 8:30–2:30 and 5–8:30, Sat. 8:30–3* Ⓜ *Jaume I.*

Fodor'sChoice ★ **Vila Viniteca.** Near Santa Maria del Mar, this is perhaps the best wine treasury in Barcelona, with tastings, courses, and events meriting further investigation, including a hugely popular street party to welcome in new-harvest wines (usually late October or early November). The tiny family grocery store next door offers exquisite artisanal cheeses ranging from French goat cheese to Extremadura's famous Torta del Casar. ✉ *Carrer Agullers 7* ☎ *93/777–7017* 🌐 *www.vilaviniteca.es* 🕑 *Mon.–Sat. 8:30–8:30* Ⓜ *Jaume I.*

GIFTS AND SOUVENIRS

Natura. A gracefully decorated store in the Natura chain, this crafts specialist stocks a good selection of global trifles, including pieces from India and North Africa. Incense, clothing, tapestries, candles, furniture, and surprises of all kinds appear in this cross-cultural craft shop. ✉ *Argenteria 78* ☎ *93/268–2525* 🌐 *www.naturaselection.com* 🕑 *Mon.–Sat. 10–7* Ⓜ *Jaume I.*

HOUSEHOLD ITEMS AND FURNITURE

Doméstico Shop. This design shop off Carrer Calders offers the most striking contemporary design from Spain and beyond. It's chock-a-block with colorful, enticing, and often surprisingly affordable objects, furniture pieces, and gadgets from makers such as Tom Dixon, Hay, and local designer de jour Jaime Hayon. Doméstico also has a showroom in the Poblenou district at Almogávers 100 (by appointment only), which focuses on larger pieces—a good bet if you're looking to furnish the home of your dreams. ✉ *Pl. St. Agustí Vell 16* ☎ *93/310–4036* 🌐 *www.domesticoshop.com* ⌚ *Tues.–Fri. 10:30–2:30 and 4:30–8:30, Sat. 11:30–3 and 4–8:30* Ⓜ *Jaume I.*

Vitra. This dazzling two-story, glass-front showroom specializes in chairs and displays all you would expect from the referential Swiss design company—swoon-worthy Eames loungers, bright Panton chairs, and many more iconic pieces to park your derrière from the past 50 years of mod design. ✉ *Pl. Comercial 5* ☎ *93/268–7219* 🌐 *www.vitra.com* Ⓜ *Jaume I.*

JEWELRY AND ACCESSORIES

Galeria Alea. Enric Majoral's jewelry design takes inspiration from organic and natural shapes such as pea pods. With gold and pearl creations that seem to have sprouted from the forest floor, this collection makes even the most hard-core urbanite appreciate nature. ✉ *Carrer Argenteria 66* ☎ *93/310–1373* 🌐 *www.aleagaleria.com* ⌚ *Weekdays 10:30–8:30, Sat. 11–8:30* Ⓜ *Jaume I.*

7

MARKETS

Mercat de la Santa Caterina. Wide aisles, a calm and cool atmosphere, and stalls that value quality as much as presentation set this market apart from its more lively siblings. It stands out on the outside too, with its colorful waving roof—the work of local architect Benedetta Tagliabue—visible from the cathedral. ✉ *Av. Francesc Cambó 16* ☎ *93/319–5740* 🌐 *www.mercatsantacaterina.com* ⌚ *Mon. 7:30–2, Tues.–Thurs. and Sat. 7:30–3:30, Fri. 7:30 am–8:30 pm.*

TOBACCO

L'Estanc de Laietana. Famous for its underground cave and humidor at sea level, this shrine to the Cuban cigar is unparalleled in Barcelona. In store for shoppers are cigarettes and rolling tobacco in an all-but-infinite variety of brands. ✉ *Via Laietana 4, Born-Ribera* ☎ *93/310–1034* ⌚ *Mon.–Sat. 10–7* Ⓜ *Jaume I.*

LA RAMBLA

Although not exactly a shopping mecca—unless you're after a Sagrada Família snow globe from one of the dozens of tacky souvenir shops—La Rambla has a few establishments that make up with convenience what they may lack in style. The diamond in the rough is La Boqueria, one of the world's great food markets.

DEPARTMENT STORES AND MALLS

El Triangle. The Triangle d'Or or Golden Triangle at the top end of the Rambla on Plaça de Catalunya is a stylish and popular complex and home for, among other stores, FNAC, where afternoon book presentations and CD launches bring together crowds of literati and music lovers. ✉ *Pl. de Catalunya 1–4* ☎ *93/310–0108* 🌐 *www.eltriangle.es* 🕑 *Daily 10–9* Ⓜ *Catalunya.*

Maremàgnum. This modern shopping complex sits on an artificial "island" in the harbor and is accessed by Rambla del Mar, a wooden swing bridge. The shops inside are fairly run-of-the-mill, but this mall is one of the few places in Barcelona where you can shop on Sunday. On the first floor, there's a good food court with fine water views. ✉ *Moll d'Espanya, Port Vell* ☎ *93/225–8100* 🌐 *www.maremagnum.es* 🕑 *Daily 10–10* Ⓜ *Drassanes.*

MARKETS

Mercat de La Boqueria. The oldest of its kind in Europe, Barcelona's most colorful and bustling food market is a must-see for anybody interested in food, and especially Catalan cuisine. Predictably, the front stalls cater more to tourists with juices to go, bags of candy, and the like. Make your way to the center to the remarkable sea-creature stalls, bloody-offal sellers, and many stand-up bars where famous chefs on their daily sourcing missions sit cheek-by-jowl with banana vendors taking a break. Standout stalls include Petràs, the wild mushroom guru at the back of the market on Plaça de la Gardunya, and Juanito Bayen of the world-famous collection of bar stools known as Pinotxo. ✉ *La Rambla 91* ☎ *93/318–2017* 🌐 *www.boqueria.info* 🕑 *Mon.–Sat. 8–8* Ⓜ *Liceu, Catalunya.*

EL RAVAL

Shopping in the Raval reflects the district's multicultural and bohemian vibe. Around MACBA (Barcelona Museum of Contemporary Art) you'll find dozens of designer-run startups selling fashion, crafts, and housewares, while the southernmost, more edgy section has an abundance of curious establishments chockfull of ethnic foods (along Calles Hospital and Carme) and vintage clothing (on Calle Riera Baixa).

BOOKS

La Central del Raval. This luscious bookstore in the former chapel of the Casa de la Misericòrdia sells books amid stunning architecture and holds regular cultural events. ✉ *Elisabets 6* ☎ *902/884–990* 🌐 *www.lacentral.com* 🕑 *Weekdays 9:30–9, Sat. 10–9* Ⓜ *Catalunya.*

Loring Art. This independent art and design bookshop has always prided itself on being a pioneer in Spain. Having started out with a small selection of high-quality art editions, the shop now holds about 20,000 titles covering architecture, industrial design, fashion, photography, film and dance, among others. Whether you're looking for instructions or simple aesthetic entertainment, this shrine to beauty and creativity won't disappoint. ✉ *Gravina 8* ☎ *93/412–0108* 🌐 *www.loring-art.com* 🕑 *Mon.–Sat. 10–8:30.*

CLOTHING

Home on Earth. Housewares and children's clothing with a homespun sensibility are on offer in this charming store run by a Scandinavian couple. Bags made of Thai tapestries, wooden instruments, felt baskets, and handmade lampshades are among the accessories worth checking out here. ✉ *Hospital 76, El Raval* ☎ *93/000–2515* 🌐 *www.homeonearth.com* 🕒 *Mon.–Thurs. 9:30–9, Fri.–Sat. 9:30–9:30, Sun. 10:30–8:30.*

Medwinds. Made locally, this casual clothing for men and women is constructed with natural cotton and wool in loose silhouettes to create an effortlessly cool look loved by El Raval's armies of hipsters. Lovely, squishy leather bags and backbacks are available, too. ✉ *Elisabets 7, El Raval* ☎ *93/619–0179* 🌐 *www.medwinds.com* 🕒 *Mon.–Sat. 10–9.*

SHOES

Noel Barcelona. Cowboy boots of every imaginable style and color are on display at this stupendous surprise in midtown Barcelona. High heel, low heel, stilletto toe, round toe, higher, lower, hand-tooled or plain leather, this is said to be the finest collection of cowboy boots in Europe. Espadrilles and other kind of shoes are also available. ✉ *Pelai 48* ☎ *93/317–8638* 🕒 *Mon.–Sat. 10–9* Ⓜ *Catalunya.*

EIXAMPLE

7

As if attempting to compete with the Eixample's landmarks, the best boutiques in this gracious and quite stylish neighborhood are destination unto themselves. Vinçon and Nanimarquina display furnishings and objects in haute settings, while the luxe fashion flagships along the Passeig de Gràcia excel in eye-popping window displays. Ardent shoppers could easily lose themselves for a day—or even a full weekend—browsing in the Eixample.

ANTIQUES AND COLLECTIBLES

Acanto. This shop, in the pivotal Bulevard dels Antiquaris, is a major clearinghouse for buying and selling a wide range of items from paintings, furniture, silver, sculpture, and bronzes to wood carvings, marble, clocks, watches, tapestries, porcelain, and ceramics. ✉ *Passeig de Gràcia 55–57* ☎ *93/215–3297* 🕒 *Weekdays 11–2 and 5–8* Ⓜ *Passeig de Gràcia.*

Bulevard dels Antiquaris. Look carefully for the stairway leading one flight up to this 73-store mother ship of all antiques arcades off Passeig de Gràcia. You never know what you might find here in this eclectic serendipity: dolls, icons, Roman or Visigothic objects, paintings, furniture, cricket kits, fly rods, or toys from a century ago. Haggle? Of course—but Catalan antiques dealers are tough nuts to crack. ✉ *Passeig de Gràcia 55* ☎ *93/215–4499* 🌐 *www.bulevarddelsantiquaris.com* 🕒 *Daily 10–2 and 4–8* Ⓜ *Passeig de Gràcia.*

ART GALLERIES

Galeria Carles Taché. This well-established gallery and exhibition space with shows ranging from the "visual poems" of Joan Brossa to severe landscape paintings by Hugo Fontela, Carles Taché carries painting and photography by an extensive stable of noted artists. ✉ *Consell de Cent 290* ☎ *93/487–8836* 🌐 *www.carlestache.com* 🕒 *Mon.–Sat. 11–8* Ⓜ *Passeig de Gràcia.*

A cornucopia of produce is available at Barcelona's markets.

Galeria Joan Prats. "La Prats" has been one of the city's top galleries since the 1920s, showing international painters and sculptors from Henry Moore to Antoni Tàpies. Barcelona painter Joan Miró was a prime force in the founding of the gallery when he became friends with Joan Prats. The motifs of bonnets and derbies on the gallery's facade attest to the trade of Prats's father. José Maria Sicilia and Juan Ugalde have shown here, while Erick Beltrán, Hannah Collins, and Eulàlia Valldosera are among the regulars. ✉ *Rambla de Catalunya 54* ☎ *93/216–0920* 🌐 *www.galeriajoanprats.com* 🕑 *Tues.–Sat. 11–8* Ⓜ *Passeig de Gràcia.*

Galeria Toni Tàpies. After the prolific Catalan painter Antoni Tàpies died in 2012, his son Toni decided to change the direction of his successful gallery and, as a touching homage, only show his late father's work, which is now on show permanently. This is complemented by periodic smaller shows and events from other leading artists, sometimes of one single piece, which have been chosen to create a "dialogue" with the Tàpies oeuvre. ✉ *Consell de Cent 282* ☎ *93/487–6402* 🌐 *www.tonitapies.com* 🕑 *Tues.–Fri. 10–2 and 4–8, Sat. 11–2 and 3–7* Ⓜ *Catalunya.*

Joan Gaspar. One of Barcelona's most prestigious galleries, Joan Gaspart and his father before him brought Picasso and Miró back to Catalonia during the '50s and '60s, along with other artists considered politically taboo during the Franco regime. These days you'll find leading contemporary lights such as Joan Pere Viladecans, Rafols Casamada, or Susana Solano here. ✉ *Pl. Dr. Letamendi 1* ☎ *93/323–0748* 🌐 *www.galeriajoangaspar.com* 🕑 *Mon.–Sat. 10:30–1:30 and 4:30–8* Ⓜ *Universitat.*

Marlborough. This international giant occupies an important position in Barcelona's art-gallery galaxy with exhibits of major contemporary artists from around the world, as well as local stars. Recent shows featured works by the late Spanish abstract artist Xavier Escribà and the contemporary designer and painter Alberto Corazón. ✉ *València 284, No. 2A* ☎ *93/467–4454* 🌐 *www.galeriamarlborough.com* ⏲ *Weekdays 11–2 and 3–7, Sat. by appointment* Ⓜ *Passeig de Gràcia.*

N2. A relatively new kid on the block, the Galería N2 already has established its position as a beacon at the crossroads of tradition and modernity, of high- and low-brow art. The vanguard but careful selection of artists featured in six annual solo shows ranges from the street artist Sixeart to the Argentine surrealist Mauricio Vergara. Since N2 specializes in up-and-coming and mid-career artists, works are generally affordable yet safe to invest in, and browsing here makes for a lighthearted change from the Eixample's more serious art houses. ✉ *Enric Granados 61* ☎ *93/452–0592* 🌐 *www.n2galeria.com* ⏲ *Weekdays 10–2 and 5–8, Sat. by appointment.*

Projecte SD. This gallery, located in one of the Eixample's most beautiful little passages, doesn't go easy on its visitors. No show at Projecte SD can be grasped without a little explanatory booklet, no piece of art fully appreciated in isolation. The pieces exhibited and sold here are complex, philosophical, challenging, and bleedingly conceptual—anything but simply decorative. Projecte SD is really more of a museum than a gallery. That makes every visit an experience and a purchase an audacious act of faith. ✉ *Passatge Mercader 8, Baixos 1* ☎ *93/488–1360* 🌐 *www.projectesd.com* ⏲ *Tues.–Fri. 11–7; Sat. by appointment* Ⓜ *Diagonal, Provença.*

7

Senda. A vernissage at Senda is a see-and-be-seen fest of the young yet sophisticated Catalan bourgeoisie. While they have shown the odd Picasso, Senda's specialty is the representation of a small selection of contemporary international artists whose names tend to cause some excitement on the art circuit, like the Mexican painter Gino Rubert, the American photographer Roger Ballen, or the Chinese Gao Xingjian, famous for his abstract ink drawings. Whatever you see here, you can be sure it's a classic in the making. ✉ *Consell de Cent 337* ☎ *93/487–6759* 🌐 *www.galeriasenda.com* ⏲ *Tues.–Sat. 11–8; closed Aug.* Ⓜ *Passeig de Gràcia.*

BOOKS AND STATIONERY

Altaïr. Barcelona's premier travel and adventure bookstore stocks many titles in English. Book presentations and events scheduled here feature a wide range of interesting authors from Alpinists to Africanists. ✉ *Gran Via 616* ☎ *93/342–7171* 🌐 *www.altair.es* ⏲ *Mon.–Sat. 10–8:30* Ⓜ *Catalunya.*

Casa del Llibre. On Barcelona's most important shopping street, Casa del Llibre is a major book feast with a wide variety of English titles. ✉ *Passeig de Gràcia 62* ☎ *902/026–407* 🌐 *www.casadellibro.com* ⏲ *Mon.–Sat. 9:30–9:30* Ⓜ *Passeig de Gràcia.*

FNAC. For musical recordings and the latest book publications, this is one of Barcelona's most dependable and happening addresses. Regular concerts, presentations of new recordings, and art exhibits take place in FNAC. Much more than a bookstore, it's an important cultural resource. ✉ *Centre Comercial L'Illa, Av. Diagonal 555–559* ☎ *902/100–632* 🌐 *www.fnac.es* ⏲ *Mon.–Sat. 10–9:30* Ⓜ *Maria Cristina, Les Corts.*

Laie. Not overly stocked with English-language titles, this bookstore boasts a very pleasant café-restaurant upstairs; the space is often used for readings and other and cultural events. ✉ *Pau Claris 85* ☎ *93/318–1739* 🌐 *www.laie.es* ⏲ *Tues.–Sat. 9–9* Ⓜ *Catalunya.*

Pepa Paper. Barcelona's most famous paper and stationery store, Pepa Paper (Pepa is a nickname for Josefina and Paper, Catalan for—you guessed it—paper), carries a gorgeous selection of cards, paper, and myriad objects and paraphernalia related to correspondence. ✉ *París 167* ☎ *93/410–3754* 🌐 *www.pepapaper.com* Ⓜ *Hospital Clínic/Provença* ✉ *Balmes 50* ☎ *93/505–4510* Ⓜ *Passeig de Gràcia* ✉ *L'Illa shopping, Av. Diagonal 557–575* ☎ *93/405–2478* Ⓜ *Maria Cristina.*

CERAMICS AND GLASSWARE

Fodor's Choice ★ **Lladró.** This Valencia company is famed worldwide for the beauty and quality of its figures. Barcelona's only Lladró factory store, this location has exclusive pieces of work, custom-designed luxury items of gold and porcelain, and classic and original works. Watch for the cheeky figurines by Jaime Hayon, a young Spanish designer put in charge of injecting the 60-year old company with some colorful postmodernism. ✉ *Passeig de Gràcia 101* ☎ *93/270–1253* 🌐 *www.lladro.com* ⏲ *Mon.–Sat. 10–8:30* Ⓜ *Diagonal.*

CLOTHING

Adolfo Domínguez. One of Barcelona's longtime fashion giants, this is one of Spain's leading designers, with many locations around town. Famed as the creator of the Iberia Airlines uniforms, Adolfo Domínguez has been in the not-too-radical mainstream and forefront of Spanish clothes design for the last quarter century. ✉ *Passeig de Gràcia 32* ☎ *619/660–277* 🌐 *www.adolfodominguez.com* ⏲ *Mon.–Sat. 10–8:30* Ⓜ *Passeig De Grácia.*

Ágatha Ruiz de la Prada. An Eixample address not to miss, Ágatha Ruiz de la Prada is a Madrid-born, Barcelona-educated design Vesuvius whose bright-color motifs in men's, women's, and children's clothing as well as furniture, carpets, ceramics, lamps, pens, pencils, towels, sheets—even Band-Aids—are characterized by Miró-like stars, suns, moons, hearts, bright polka dots. The designer's Barcelona flagship is bathed in her signature fuchsia pink, which illuminates every nook and cranny. ✉ *Consell de Cent 314–316* ☎ *93/215–5288* 🌐 *www.agatharuizdelaprada.com* ⏲ *Mon.–Sat. 10:30–8:30* Ⓜ *Passeig de Gràcia.*

Antonio Miró. With his Miró jeans label making major inroads with the young and fashionably adventurous, classicist Toni Miró is known for the very upper stratosphere of Catalan haute couture, with clean lines fortified by blacks and dark grays for both men and women. Miró's look is, in fact, so unisex that couples of similar sizes could probably get away with sharing some androgynous looks and saving closet space. ✉ *Rambla de Catalunya 125* ☎ *93/238-9942* 🌐 *www.antoniomiro.es* ⏲ *Mon.–Sat. 10:30–8:30* Ⓜ *Diagonal.*

Carolina Herrera. Originally from Venezuela but professionally based in New York, Carolina Herrera and her international CH logo have become Barcelona mainstays. (Daughter Carolina Herrera Jr. is a Spain resident and married to former bullfighter Miguel Báez.) Fragrances for men and women and clothes with a simple, elegant line—a white blouse is the CH icon—are the staples here. Herrera's light ruffled dresses and edgy urban footwear add feminine flourishes. ✉ *Passeig de Gràcia 87* ☎ *93/272–1584* 🌐 *www.carolinaherrera.com* ⏲ *Mon.–Sat. 10–8:30* Ⓜ *Diagonal.*

Conti. A favorite men's fashion outlet (although women are catered to also), Conti stocks threads by top international designers. The company's shop in Ramblas Catalunya specializes in jeans, from Bikkembergs to G-Star to the more conservative Armani Jeans label. ✉ *Rambla de Catalunya 78* ☎ *93/215–3232* 🌐 *www.econti.com* ⏲ *Mon.–Sat. 10–9* Ⓜ *Diagonal.*

El Avant. Under her own label, Silvia Garcia Presas—the creator of El Avant—offers quietly elegant and effortlessly chic clothing for women in her simple, woody boutique at the top end of Enric Granados. Fabrics are 100% natural (organic cotton, alpaca wool, etc.), and the generous and easy cuts are transgenerational and flattering. A small room at the back displays handmade soaps, ceramic wares, and other gifty bits sourced from across Asia and the Americas. ✉ *Enric Granados 106* ☎ *93/300–7673* 🌐 *www.theavant.com* ⏲ *Weekdays 10–2 and 4–8, Sat. 11–2* Ⓜ *Diagonal.*

Erre de Raso. Popular with the uptown crowd, Erre de Raso makes clothes in bright and breezy shades and patterns. With colors ranging from electric fuchsias to bright indigo blues and materials ranging from satin (*raso*) to cottons and silks, the objective is to outfit stylish women in chameleonic outfits that look equally appropriate picking up the kids from school, dropping by an art gallery opening, and hitting a cocktail party in the same sortie. ✉ *Aribau 69* ☎ *93/452–3754* 🌐 *www.errederaso.com* Ⓜ *Provença.*

Furest. This centenary menswear star, with four stores in town and another at the airport, markets its own designs as well as selections from Armani Jeans, Ralph Lauren, Hugo Boss, and Brooksfield, as well as their own collection of dapper suits, shirts, and gentlemen's accessories. ✉ *Passeig de Gràcia 12–14* ☎ *93/301–2000* 🌐 *www.furest.com* ⏲ *Mon.–Sat. 10–8:30* Ⓜ *Catalunya.*

Jofré. What started out as a single fashion shop in Barcelona is now a family-run chain of 20 boutiques in Spain and Belgium, often taking over entire sections of a street. Jofré stock the cream of classic luxury brands (think Prada, Fendi, Gucci, and Dior). Those may offer few surprises, but the sheer lushness of the shops and the attentive staff make shopping here a memorable experience. The main store is on busy Passeig de Gràcia; for the six smaller uptown boutiques, check the website. ✉ *Passeig de Gràcia 104* ☎ *93/185–0000* 🌐 *www.jofre.es* Ⓜ *Diagonal.*

Josep Abril Studio. Josep Abril is one of the country's leading men's fashion designers; his unconventional suits and signature knitwear are a mainstay on Spanish catwalks. However, the best way to experience Josep Abril is through his bespoke tailoring, carried out at the impressive former industrial estate in the Eixample that now houses his studio. Even if you're not in for a suit, it's worth having a look. ✉ *Consell de Cent 159* ☎ *695/938–449* 🌐 *www.josepabril.com.*

Loewe. Occupying the ground floor of Lluís Domènech i Montaner's Casa Lleó Morera, Loewe is Spain's answer to Hermès, a classical clothing and leather emporium for men's and women's fashions and luxurious handbags that whisper status. Farther north along the Passeig de Grácia at No. 91, the Galería Loewe holds stylish, sporadic shows on fashion and costume. ✉ *Passeig de Gràcia 35* ☎ *93/216–0400* 🌐 *www.loewe.es* ⏲ *Mon.–Sat. 10–8:30* Ⓜ *Passeig de Gràcia.*

Purificación García. Known as a gifted fabric expert whose creations are invariably based on the qualities and characteristics of her raw materials, Galicia-born Purificación García enjoys solid prestige in Barcelona. Understated hues and subtle combinations of colors and shapes place this contemporary designer squarely in the camp of the less-is-more school, and although her women's range is larger and more diverse, she is one female designer who understands men's tailoring. ✉ *Provença 292* ☎ *93/496–1336* 🌐 *www.purificaciongarcia.com* ⏲ *Mon.–Sat. 10–8:30* Ⓜ *Diagonal* ✉ *Av. Pau Casals 4* ☎ *93/200–6089* 🌐 *www.purificaciongarcia.com* ⏲ *Mon.–Sat. 10:30–8:30* Ⓜ *Muntaner.*

Santa Eulalia. The history of this luxury fashion superstore, which moved into its 2,000-square-meter premises designed by William Sofield in 2011, goes back to 1843. That year Domingo Taberner Prims opened the first shop, which would soon evolve into one of the city's first and foremost haute couture tailoring houses. Today it's run by the fourth generation of the founding family and features one of the best luxury brand selections in the country. It also regularly teams up with designers and design schools to present special collections or awards. When you're done browsing everything from Agent Provocateur to Vera Wang, refresh with some tea and cake at the fabulous terrace café on the first floor, or head to the basement to see the in-house tailors at work on bespoke suits and men's shirts. ✉ *Passeig de Gràcia 93* ☎ *93/215–0674* 🌐 *www.santaeulalia.com* ⏲ *Mon.–Sat. 10–8:30* Ⓜ *Diagonal.*

Sita Murt. The local Catalan designer Sita Murt produces smart, grown-up women's wear under her own label in this minimalist space near Plaça Sant Jaume. Colorful chiffon dresses and light, gauzy tops and knits characterize this line of clothing popular with professional women and wedding go-ers. ✉ *Mallorca 242* ☎ *93/215–2231* 🌐 *www.sitamurt.com* ⏲ *Mon.–Sat. 10–8:30* Ⓜ *Passeig de Gràcia.*

Teresa Helbig. A regular at Madrid Fashion Week, Teresa Helbig designs feminine and elegant pret-a-porter women's collections. Yet she is better known—and worth visiting—for her bespoke bridalwear and evening gowns, timeless haute couture she concocts for her well-heeled clients at her Barcelona studio-showroom. It may not come cheap, but you'll be able to hand it down through generations. ✉ *Mallorca 184, Loft, Eixample* ☎ *93/451–5544* 🌐 *www.teresahelbig.com* ⏲ *Mon.–Sat. 10:30–7:30.*

DEPARTMENT STORES AND MALLS

Bulevard Rosa. The sun has set a bit on this fashionable L-shape arcade, but it still provides some welcome serenity from bustling Passeig de Gràcia. Worth seeking out is the deconstructed range of clothing from Lurdes Bergada (shops 41–42) or Bimba and Lola's sophisticated mid-couture (near the Passeig de Grácia entrance). Afterward, drop by the excellent Mary's Market (at the entrance on Carrer Valencia) to admire the enormous selection of gourmet goodies and light lunch fare. ✉ *Passeig de Gràcia 53–55* ☎ *93/378–9191* 🌐 *www.bulevardrosa.com* Ⓜ *Passeig de Gràcia.*

El Corte Inglés. This iconic and ubiquitous Spanish department store has its main Barcelona branch on Plaça de Catalunya, with an annex 100 yards away in Porta de l'Àngel. You can find just about anything here—clothing, shoes, perfumes, electrical gadgets—and there is a wonderful supermarket on the lower-ground floor. Although seemingly stuck in the 1970s in terms of merchandising and layout, El Corte has generally professional and helpful staffers. ✉ *Pl. de Catalunya 14* ☎ *93/306–3800* 🌐 *www.elcorteingles.es* 🕒 *Mon.–Sat. 9:30–9:30* Ⓜ *Catalunya* ✉ *Portal de l'Àngel 19–21, Barri Gòtic* ☎ *93/306–3800* Ⓜ *Catalunya* ✉ *Pl. Francesc Macià, Av. Diagonal 471* ☎ *93/419–2020* Ⓜ *La Bonanova* ✉ *Av. Diagonal 617, Diagonal/Les Corts* ☎ *93/419–2828* Ⓜ *Maria Cristina.*

L'Illa Diagonal. This rangy complex buzzes with shoppers swarming through more than 100 stores and shops, including food specialists, Decathlon sports gear, and Bang & Olufsen sound systems, plus FNAC, Zara, Benetton, and all the usual High Street suspects. ✉ *Av. Diagonal 557* ☎ *93/487–1699* 🌐 *www.lilla.com* 🕒 *Mon.–Sat. 10–9:30* Ⓜ *Maria Cristina.*

Pedralbes Centre. This multistory conglomeration just a few blocks west of L'Illa Diagonal and next to a branch of the ubiquitous El Corte Inglés has a good selection of local brands: Camper shoes, Beatriz Furest leather bags, and Zara Home for on-trend textiles and domestic frippery. ✉ *Av. Diagonal 609–615* ☎ *93/410–6821* 🌐 *www.pedralbescentre.com* Ⓜ *Maria Cristina.*

FOOD

Cacao Sampaka. This centrally located shop is perfect for chocolate addicts to stop and satisfy their cravings. While it's perfectly possible to dash in and fill your bags with boxes of Cacao Sampaka's exquisite cocoa creations to take home with you (or nibble on the way back to your hotel), consider setting aside 30 minutes to sit down in the pleasant in-store café and order an "Azteca" hot chocolate drink. Quite possibly the best hot chocolate in Spain, a sip of this thick, rich, heaven-in-a-cup is the highlight of any Barcelona shopping spree. ✉ *Carrer del Consell de Cent 292* ☎ *93/272–0833* 🌐 *www.cacaosampaka.com* 🕒 *Mon.–Sat. 9–9* Ⓜ *Passeig de Gracia.*

Fodor's Choice ★ **Mantequeria Can Ravell.** Can Ravell is one of Barcelona's best, and certainly most charming, fine food and wine emporiums. Open for the good part of a century, it is a cult favorite with local and visiting gourmands and has a superb selection of everything you ever might want to savor, from the finest anchovies from La Scala to the best cheese from

Idiazabal. Through the kitchen and up the tiny spiral staircase, the dining room offers a memorable if pricey lunch, while the tasting table downstairs operates on a first-come, first-served basis. ✉ *Aragó 313, Eixample* ☎ *93/457–5114* 🌐 *www.ravell.com* ⏲ *Tues.–Sat. 10–9, Sun. 10–3* Ⓜ *Girona.*

CUSTO GUSTO

Only Barcelona could come up with Custo, an idiosyncratic fashion line created by a couple of motorcycling brothers. Since their 1980s start, the brothers Dalmau—Custido and David—have parlayed their passion for colorful and original tops into an empire that now includes footwear, denims, handbags, knits, and more. With stores scattered around Barcelona and the world (30 countries and counting), Custo's quirky embroidery and metallic graphic prints have become nearly as iconic as Gaudí's organic stalagmites or Miró's colorful asteroids.

Oriol Balaguer. Owner Balaguer is surely running out of room to store all the "Spain's Best" trophies he's collected over the years. He's a consultant to some of the world's most famous restaurants, and the heart of his empire is this little shop of chocolate-making magic. Bring your credit card and prepare to have your mind blown. Some of the confectionary creations are so beautiful you'll feel bad about biting into them—at least until you taste them. Balaguer has a second—equally stunning—boutique at Travessera de les Corts 340 and a shop called Classic Line at Carrer Benet i Mateu 62. ✉ *Pl. de Sant Gregori Taumaturg 2, Eixample* ☎ *93/201–1846* 🌐 *www.oriolbalaguer.com* Ⓜ *La Bonanova.*

Queviures Murria. Founded in 1890, this historic Moderniste shop, its windows decorated with Ramón Casas paintings and posters, has a superb selection of some 200 cheeses, sausages, wines, and conserves from Spain, Catalonia, and beyond. The ceramic Casas reproductions lining the interior walls are eye candy, as are all the details in this work of art-cum-grocery-store (*queviures* means foodstuffs—literally, "things to keep you alive"). ✉ *Roger de Llúria 85, Eixample* ☎ *93/215–5789* 🌐 *www.murria.cat* ⏲ *Tues.–Thurs. 9–2 and 5–9, Fri. 9–9, Sat. 10–2 and 5–9* Ⓜ *Passeig de Grácia.*

Reserva Ibérica. Purveyor of fine hams in Spain and abroad for more than 30 years, Reserva Ibérica has a shop in the Eixample where it not only sells a selection of its best, all-acorn-fed products, but also offers the opportunity for customers to taste the hams, accompanied by a glass of wine. ✉ *Rambla de Catalunya 61, Eixample* ☎ *93/215–5230* 🌐 *www.reservaiberica.com* ⏲ *Weekdays 9:30–9, Sat. 10–9.*

GIFTS AND SOUVENIRS

L'Appartement. This bright and quirky design shop fits right in with this part of the Eixample, known for its abundance of gay bars. Oversized wall decals, bold '60s-inspired chairs, plastic knickknacks (some of them even useful), and sci-fi light fixtures set the tone. L'Appartement has a keen eye for emerging talent, often stocking their goodies well before the big design shops catch on. ✉ *Enric Granados 44, Eixample* ☎ *93/452–2904* 🌐 *www.lappartement.es* ⏲ *Mon.–Sat. 10:30–9* Ⓜ *Provença.*

Servició Estació. It's a hardware store, yes, but one like you've never seen before. For starters, Servicio Estació is situated in a rationalist-style landmark building dating from 1962. For decades it served the city's builders and handymen with tools and materials, but more recently the huge inventory has expanded to modern design and housewares—it feels more like a cool department store than a DIY. It's the first port of call for the city's creative set, mom's looking for material for school projects, and home outfitters, selling everything from ropes of string to designer shopping carts. ✉ *Aragó 270, Eixample* ☎ *93/393–2410* 🌐 *www.serveiestacio.com* ⏲ *Mon.–Sat. 9–9* Ⓜ *Passeig de Gràcia.*

Fodor's Choice ★ **Vinçon.** A design giant some 70 years old, Vinçon steadily expanded its stylish premises through a rambling Moderniste house that was once the home and studio of the Art Nouveau artist Ramón Casas. It stocks everything from letter openers to Eames furniture, and has an interesting front-of-house section for chic, locally made knickknacks. If you can tear your eyes away from all the design, seek out the spectacular Moderniste fireplace on the first floor (in reality the furniture department) designed in wild Art Nouveau exuberance with a gigantic hearth in the form of a stylized face. The back terrace, used as a setting for outdoor furniture, is a cool respite and a breath of fresh air with views up to the next-door rooftop warriors of Gaudí's Casa Milà. ✉ *Passeig de Gràcia 96, Eixample* ☎ *93/215–6050* 🌐 *www.vincon.com* ⏲ *Mon.–Sat. 10–8:30* Ⓜ *Diagonal.*

HOUSEHOLD ITEMS AND FURNITURE

Fins de Siècles. The third of the Fins de Siècles shops is, like its siblings in Brussels and Isle sur Sorgue, the product of the undying passion of its Belgian owners to rescue as much European design heritage from the 20th century as they can. Their particular fascination is with theArt Deco period ranging from the 1930s through the '50s, which they buy all over Europe and have restored and newly upholstered respecting traditional methods. Desks, sofas, vanities, and tables are shipped all over the world, but they also stock smaller (and more affordable) items like lamps, vases, rugs, and silverware. ✉ *Enric Granados 70* ☎ *93/511–7606* 🌐 *www.finsdesiecles-artdeco.com* ⏲ *Weekdays 11:30–2 and 4:30–8:30, Sat. noon–2 and 5–8:30* Ⓜ *Provença.*

Jaime Beriestain Concept Store. The concept store of one of the city's hottest interior designers provides mere mortals the chance to appreciate the Beriestain groove. Reflecting his projects for hotels and restaurants, the shop offers an exciting mixture of midcentury-modern classics and new design pieces, peppered with freshly cut flowers (also for sale), French candles, handmade stationery, and the latest international design and architecture magazines to dress up your coffee table. The in-store café is worth a visit. ✉ *Pau Claris 167, Eixample* ☎ *93/515–0779* 🌐 *www.beriestain.com* ⏲ *Mon.–Sat. 10–9* Ⓜ *Diagonal.*

Mar de Cava. This Aladdin's Cave of design, housewares, furniture, clothing and accessories bursts with creativity and color. The carefully edited range of items will have you dizzy with desire as you skip between vases from cult ceramics-maker Apparatu, cabinets rendered in technicolored lacquers, African bead necklaces, and tables covered in antique tiles. The emphasis is more on craftsmanship than the latest trends—just about every product has an intriguing backstory. ✉ *Valencia 293* ☎ *93/458–5333* 🌐 *www.mardecava.com* Ⓜ *Passeig de Gràcia.*

Nanimarquina. A lover of both traditional methods and exuberant design, Nani Marquina makes textural rugs that look just as good on a wall as on the floor. Some of her rugs re-create ancient Persian or Hindu styles, others are trendy compositions by designers like Javier Mariscal or the Bouroullec brothers, and still others represent essentially a bed of leaves or roses. The one thing they all have in common: They will dominate any room they are placed in. ✉ *Rosselló 256, Eixample* ☎ *93/487–1606* 🌐 *www.nanimarquina.com* ⏲ *Mon. 4–8 pm, Tues.–Sat. 10–2 and 4–8* Ⓜ *Diagonal.*

JEWELRY

Bagués Masriera. The Bagués dynasty has bejeweled Barcelonians since 1839. While they stock much that glitters, the Lluís Masriera line of original Art Nouveau pieces is truly unique; intricate flying nymphs, lifelike golden insects, and other easily recognizable motifs from the period take on a new depth of beauty when executed in the translucent enameling process that Masriera himself developed. The location in Moderniste architect Puig i Cadafalch's Casa Amatller in the famous Mansana de la Discòrdia on Passeig de Gràcia is worth the visit alone, although sadly, the interior of the shop bears little of the building's exuberance. ✉ *Passeig de Gràcia 41* ☎ *93/216–0174* 🌐 *www.masriera.es* ⏲ *Weekdays 10–8:30, Sat. 11–8* Ⓜ *Catalunya.*

Puig Doria. This popular jeweler sells a full range of personal accessories of great style and taste, from neckties and watches to fashionable baubles in silver and gold. ✉ *Rambla de Catalunya 88* ☎ *93/215–1090* 🌐 *www.puigdoria.es* ⏲ *Weekdays 10–8:30, Sat. 10–2 and 5–8:30* Ⓜ *Diagonal* ✉ *Diagonal 612* ☎ *93/201–2911* Ⓜ *Maria Cristina.*

Zapata Joyero. The Zapata family, with three stores around town, has been prominent in Barcelona jewelry design and retail for the last half century. With original designs of their own and a savvy selection of the most important Swiss and international watch designers, this family business is now in its second generation and makes a point of taking good care of clients with large or small jewelry needs. Their L'Illa store, for example, specializes in jewelry accessible to the budgets of younger clients. ✉ *Diagonal 557* ☎ *93/444–0063* 🌐 *www.zapatajoyeros.com* Ⓜ *Maria Cristina* ✉ *Mandri 20, Sant Gervasi* ☎ *93/211–6774* Ⓜ *Sarrià* ✉ *L'Illa, Diagonal 557 (store nos. 126 and 133), Diagonal* ☎ *93/444–0063* Ⓜ *Maria Cristina.*

MARKETS

Els Encants Vells. One of Europe's oldest flea markets, Els Encants has recently been gifted with a new home—a stunning, glittering metal canopy that protects the rag-and-bone merchants (and their keen customers) from the elements. Stalls, and a handful of standup bars, have become a bit more upmarket, too, although you'll still find plenty of oddities to barter over in the central plaza. Saturday is the busiest day—try going during the week for a more relaxed rummage around this fascinating slice of urban history. ✉ *Pl. de Les Glóries Catalans s/n* ☎ *93/246–3030* 🌐 *www.encantsbcn.com* ⏲ *Mon., Wed., Fri. and Sat. 9–8* Ⓜ *Glòries.*

SHOES

Camper. This internationally famous Spanish shoe emporium, which in Barcelona also comprises a 25-room boutique hotel of the same name, offers a comprehensive line of funky boots, heels, and shoes of all kinds. Both men's and women's shoes, all in line with the company's organic outdoor philosophy, are displayed against an undulating chrome-and-wood backdrop designed by architect Benedetta Tagliabue. ✉ *Passeig de Gràcia 2–4* ☎ *93/521–6250* 🌐 *www.camper.com* Ⓜ *Catalunya.*

Fodor's Choice ★ **Norman Vilalta.** Norman Vilalta was a lawyer in Buenos Aires before he decided to move to Florence, Italy, and do something rather unusual: learn the trade of a traditional cobbler. Today he is one of a handful of people in the world who produce artisanal bespoke shoes, which take three months to produce, come complete with a video showing the entire making of, and will set you back somewhere between €2,500 and €5,000. However, you will also join the ranks of the chef Ferran Adrià, the architect Oscar Tusquets and members of the Spanish royal family as owner of a pair of Norman Vilalta shoes. And since they fit like no other and last a lifetime, you might consider it a worthy investment. ✉ *Enric Granados 5* ☎ *93/323–4014* 🌐 *www.normanvilalta.com* Ⓜ *Universitat.*

Fodor's Choice ★ **The Outpost.** A shop dedicated exclusively to men's accessories of the finest kind, the Outpost was created by a former Prada buyer who considers it his mission to bring stylishness to Barcelona men with this little island of avant-garde. The constantly changing window displays are little works of art, providing a first taste of what's to be found inside: Christian Peau shoes, Albert Thurston suspenders, Roland Pineau belts, Yves Andrieux hats, Balenciaga ties. You enter the Outpost as a mere mortal, but leave it as a gentleman—provided you carry the necessary cash. ✉ *Rosselló 281 bis, Eixample* ☎ *93/457–7137* 🌐 *www.theoutpostbcn.com* ⏲ *Mon.–Sat. 10:30–2:30 and 4:30–8:30* Ⓜ *Diagonal.*

Tascón. International footwear designers and domestic shoemakers alike fill these stores with trendy urban footwear from brands such as Camper, United Nude, and Audrey, as well as more sturdy models from Timberland and the like. Models designed in-house and made locally offer high style at reasonable prices. ✉ *Passeig de Grácia 64* ☎ *93/487–9084* 🌐 *www.tascon.es* Ⓜ *Passeig de Grácia* ✉ *Passeig de Gràcia 64* ☎ *93/487–9084* Ⓜ *Passeig de Gràcia* ✉ *Passeig del Born 8, Born-Ribera* ☎ *93/268–7293* Ⓜ *Jaume I.*

7

GRÀCIA

Cute and cozy Gràcia is steadily evolving into Barcelona's most eclectic shopping destination—think Williamsburg, Brooklyn's cool factor, softened with Mediterranean nonchalance. The best place to start is the Carrer d'Astúries, followed by the Carrer Verdi and Carrer Torrent d'Olla.

ART GALLERIES

Eat Meat. As its name suggests, Eat Meat gallery likes to provoke and scandalize. The brainchild of the local painter Rai Escalé, this isn't principally a commercial gallery but a nonprofit cultural association designed to support the less conventional outgrowth of contemporary art (works are still for sale though). In short, Eat Meat deals with the darker corners of the human body and soul, illustrated aptly by the haunting works of young painters like Milos Koptak, Kinki Texas, or Eva Alonso. It caters to a narrowly defined taste, but if it's yours, there's no better place for a purchase. ✉ *l'Alzina 20* ☎ *93/284–2894* 🌐 *www.eatmeat.cat* 🕐 *Thurs. and Fri. 6–9, Sat. noon–2 and 6–9* Ⓜ *Fontana.*

BEAUTY

Herbolari del Cel. Gràcia's "Herbolarium from Heaven" is widely considered among the best in Barcelona for herbal remedies, teas, spices, oils, natural cures and treatments, and cosmetics of all kinds. A mere deep breath of air here will probably cure whatever ails you. ✉ *Travessera de Gràcia 120* ☎ *93/218–7331* 🌐 *www.herbolaridelcel.com* 🕐 *Mon.–Sat. 10–2 and 5–8:30* Ⓜ *Fontana.*

SHOES

BBB. Any shoe store that satisfies the legendary three B requirements—*bueno, bonito,* and *barato* (good, beautiful, and cheap)—is not to be missed. Shoes in many styles from sandals to stiletto heels pack this popular Gràcia shoe emporium. ✉ *Gran de Gràcia 233* ☎ *93/237–3514* Ⓜ *Fontana.*

Nagore. Yet another company of cobblers from Mallorca, Nagore carries eco-chic styles that are reminiscent of the early shoes from Camper, their larger and more famous rival. The brightly colored leathers stand out on this simple whitewashed shop interior that evokes the company's Balearic provenance. ✉ *Astúries 50* ☎ *93/368–8359* 🌐 *www.nagore.es* Ⓜ *Fontana.*

TOYS

FAMILY **Bateau Lune.** Crafts, disguises, puzzles, games, and a thousand things to make you want to be a kid again are on display in this creative child-oriented gift shop on one of Gràcia's most emblematic squares. ✉ *Pl. de la Virreina 7* ☎ *93/218–6907* 🌐 *www.bateaulune.com* 🕐 *Mon.–Sat. 10:30–2 and 5–8:30* Ⓜ *Fontana.*

SARRIÀ

Just like its residents, shops in Sarrià are smart and well heeled. Most are along the Major de Sarrià, the 'hood's main drag, and on the elegant Plaça de Sarrià. The emphasis is on kitchen gadgets and gourmet food, such as that you can pick up at the legendary Foix de Sarrià and a lively local fresh produce market.

BEAUTY

JC Apotecari. Downtown beauty junkies happily make the trip uptown for the hard-to-source cult products that fill the lab-like shelves of JC Apotecari. Skin and hair brands such as Australian botanical Aesop products and Dr. Jackson's are offered alongside perfumed candles from Diptyque and Tweezerman tweezers. ✉ *Major de Sarrià 96* ☎ *93/205–8734* 🌐 *www.jcapotecari.com* ⏲ *Weekdays 10:30–2 and 5–8:30, Sat. 10:30–2* Ⓜ *Sarrià.*

CERAMICS

Neo Cerámica. This is the store to visit if you need an order of handsome tiles for your kitchen back home. With some truly striking patterns and the shipping system to get them to you in one piece (each tile, that is), you can trust the Vidal-Quadras clan for care and quality. ✉ *Mandri 43* ☎ *93/211–8958* 🌐 *www.neoceramica.es* Ⓜ *Sarrià, El Putxet.*

FOOD

Foix de Sarrià. Pastry and poetry under the same roof merit a stop. The verses of J. V. Foix, a major Catalan poet who managed to survive the Franco regime with his art intact, are engraved in bronze on the outside wall of the Major de Sarrià location, where he was born. Excellent pastries, breads, wines, cheeses, and cavas, all available on Sunday, have made Foix de Sarrià a Barcelona landmark. There is a smaller branch nearby at Major de Sarrià 57. ✉ *Pl. Sarrià 12–13* ☎ *93/203–0473* 🌐 *www.foixdesarria.com* Ⓜ *Sarrià* ✉ *Major de Sarrià 57* ☎ *93/203–0714* 🌐 *www.foixdesarria.com* Ⓜ *Sarrià.*

Ískia. Good wine advice and a perennially renewing stock of new values to try make Iskia one of upper Barcelona's best wine emporiums. The proprietors speak English and are glad to talk about latest wine trends or explain their products at length. ✉ *Major de Sarrià 132* ☎ *93/205–0070* 🌐 *www.iskiavins.com* ⏲ *Tues.–Fri. 10–2 and 5–9, Sat. 10–2 and 6–9, Sun. 11–4* Ⓜ *Sarrià.*

7

La Cave. When in Sarrià, have a stop at this original wine cellar, tapas bar, and restaurant. With every bottle in this barrel-shape space color-coded by taste, price, and geography, you are brilliantly rescued from pandemic wine store bewilderment. La Cave also provides a printout of tasting notes and technical data for every bottle so that you not only know what you're getting, but what you've had and why. ✉ *Av. J. V. Foix 80* ☎ *93/206–3846* 🌐 *www.lacave.es* ⏲ *Tues.–Sat. 11 am–midnight, Sun. 11–4:30* Ⓜ *Sarrià.*

MARKETS

Sarrià. A small Sunday antiques market in Sarrià's town square provides another good reason to explore this charming onetime outlying village in the upper part of the city. On other days, the nearby produce market, a mini-Boqueria, is the place for picnic fare before or after a hike over to the Monestir de Pedralbes and back. ✉ *Pl. de Sarrià* ⏲ *Tues. 9–3* Ⓜ *Sarrià, Reina Elisenda.*

POBLENOU

For all its eye-turning architecture and creative energy, Poblenou has lacked notable retail offerings until recently. While mom-and-pop shops gather dust along Rambla de Poblenou, brave new businesses selling cutting-edge design and housewares are starting to brighten up this large, and in places gritty, district.

HOUSEHOLD ITEMS AND FURNITURE

bd. This spare, cutting-edge home-furnishings store has just moved into a former industrial building near the sea. "Barcelona Design" cofounder Oscar Tusquets, master designer and architect, gives contemporary design star Javier Mariscal plenty of space here, while past giants such as Gaudí with his Casa Calvet chair, or Salvador Dalí and his Gala love seat, are also available—if your pockets are deep enough. ✉ *Ramón Turró 126, Poblenou* ☎ *93/457–0052* 🌐 *www.bdbarcelona.com* ⏲ *Weekdays 9–6* Ⓜ *Llacuna, Bogatell.*

Noak Room. The sleek style of Scandinavian design has truly taken hold in Barcelona, as seen in the cafés and restaurants of the Born and Eixample. Started by a couple who are passionate about retro and vintage pieces from northern Europe, this large, loft-like locale stocks a large selection of upcycled and renovated lamps, sofas, chairs, and mirrors from the 1950s to the '70s. International shipping can be arranged. ✉ *Rec Boronat 69, Poblenou* ☎ *93/309–5300* 🌐 *www.noakroom.com* ⏲ *Tues.–Sat. 11–3 and 5–9.*

8

CATALONIA, VALENCIA, AND THE COSTA BLANCA

WELCOME TO CATALONIA, VALENCIA, AND THE COSTA BLANCA

TOP REASONS TO GO

★ **Pax Girona:** Explore a city where the monuments of Christian, Jewish, and Islamic cultures that coexisted for centuries are only steps apart.

★ **Valencia Reborn:** The past 20 years have seen a transformation of the River Turia into a treasure trove of museums, concert halls, parks, and architectural wonders.

★ **Bon Appetit:** Foodies argue that the fountainhead of creative gastronomy has moved from France to Spain—and in particular to the great restaurants of the Empordà and Costa Brava.

★ **Hello Dalí:** Surreal doesn't begin to describe the Dalí Museum in Figueres or the wild coast of the artist's home at Cap de Creus.

★ **Burning passion:** Valencia's Las Fallas, in mid-March, a week of fireworks and solemn processions and a finale of spectacular bonfires, is one of the best festivals in Europe.

GETTING ORIENTED

Year-round, Catalonia is the most visited of Spain's autonomous communities. The Pyrenees that separate it from France provide some of the country's best skiing, and the rugged Costa Brava in the north and the Costa Dorada to the south are havens for sunseekers. The interior is full of surprises, too: an expanding rural tourism industry and the region's growing international reputation for food and wine give Catalonia a broad-based appeal. Excellent rail, air, and highway connections link Catalonia to the beach resorts of Valencia, its neighbor to the south.

1 Northern Catalonia. Inland and westward from the towns of Girona and Figueres is perhaps the most dramatic and beautiful part of old Catalonia; it's a land of medieval villages and hilltop monasteries, volcanic landscapes, and lush green valleys. The ancient city of Girona, often ignored by people bound for the Costa Brava, is an easy and interesting day trip from Barcelona. The upland towns of Besalú and Ripoll are Catalonia at its most authentic.

2 Costa Brava. Native son Salvador Dalí put his mark on the northeasternmost corner of Catalonia, where the Costa Brava (literally "rugged coast") begins, especially in the fishing village of Cadaqués and the coast of Cap de Creus. From here, south and west toward Barcelona, lie the beaches, historical settlements, and picturesque towns like Sant Feliu de Guixols that draw millions of summer visitors to the region.

3 Valencia and environs. Spain's third-largest city, with a rich history and tradition, is now a cultural magnet for its modern-art museum and its space-age City of Arts and Sciences complex. The Albufera Nature Park, just to the south, is an important wetland and wildlife sanctuary.

4 Costa Blanca. Culturally and geographically diverse, the Costa Blanca's most populated coastal resorts stretch north from the provincial capital of Alicante to Dénia. Alicante, a historic center and vibrant nightlife scene, is the hub of a rich agricultural area punctuated by towns like Elche, a UNESCO World Heritage Site. Dénia, capital of the Marina Alta region and a port for ferries to the Balearic Islands, is a charming destination and has a well-deserved reputation for gastronomy.

EATING AND DRINKING WELL IN CATALONIA, VALENCIA, AND THE COSTA BLANCA

Catalonia and Valencia share the classic Mediterranean diet, and Catalans feel right at home with paella valenciana. Fish preparations are similar along the coast, though inland favorites vary from place to place.

Top left: Paella valenciana in a classic paella pan. Top right: Fresh calçots. Bottom left: Suquet of fish, potatoes, onions, and tomatoes.

The grassy inland meadows of Catalonia's northern Alt Empordà region put quality beef on local tables; from the Costa Brava comes fine seafood, such as anchovies from L'Estartit and *gambas* (jumbo shrimp) from Palamós, both deservedly famous. *Romescu*—a blend of almonds, peppers, garlic, and olive oil—is used as a fish and seafood sauce in Tarragona, especially during the *calçotadas* (spring onion feasts) in February. *Allioli*, garlicky mayonnaise, is another popular topping. The Ebro Delta is renowned for fresh fish and eels, as well as *rossejat* (fried rice in a fish broth). Valencia and the Mediterranean coast are the homeland of paella *valenciana*. *Arròs a banda* is a variant in which the fish and rice are cooked separately.

CALÇOTS

The winter calçotada is a beloved event in Catalonia. The *calçot* is a sweet spring onion developed by a 19th-century farmer who discovered how to extend the edible portion by packing soil around the base. On the last weekend of January, the town of Valls holds a calçotada where upward of 30,000 people gather for meals of onions, sausage, lamb chops, and red wine.

RICE

Paella valenciana (Valencian paella) is one of Spain's most famous gastronomic contributions. A simple country dish dating from the early 18th century, "paella" refers to the wide frying pan with short, sturdy handles that's used to cook the rice. Anything fresh from the fields that day, along with rice and olive oil, traditionally went into the pan but paella valenciana has particular ingredients: short-grained rice, chicken, rabbit, *garrofó* (a local legume), tomatoes, green beans, sweet peppers, olive oil, and saffron. Artichokes and peas are also included in season. *Paella marinera* (seafood paella) is a different story: rice, cuttlefish, squid, mussels, shrimp, prawns, lobster, clams, garlic, olive oil, sweet paprika, and saffron, all stewed in fish broth. Many other paella variations are possible, including paella *negra,* a black rice dish made with squid ink; *arròs a banda* made with peeled seafood; and *fideuá,* paella made with noodles in place of rice.

SEAFOOD STEWS

Sèpia amb pèsols is a vegetable and seafood *mar i muntanya* (surf and turf) beloved on the Costa Brava: cuttlefish and peas are stewed with potatoes, garlic, onions, tomatoes, and a splash of wine. The *picadillo*—the finishing touches of flavors and textures—includes parsley, black pepper, fried bread, pine nuts, olive oil, and salt. *Es niu* ("the nest") of game fowl, cod, tripe, cuttlefish, pork, and rabbit is another Costa Brava favorite. Stewed for a good five hours until the darkness of the onions and the ink of the cuttlefish have combined to impart a rich chocolate color to the stew, this is a much-celebrated wintertime classic. You'll also find *suquet de peix,* the Catalan fish stew, at restaurants along the Costa Brava.

FRUITS AND VEGETABLES

Valencia and the eastern Levante region have long been famous as Spain's *huerta,* or garden. The alluvial soil of the littoral produces an abundance of everything from tomatoes to asparagus, peppers, chard, spinach, onions, artichokes, cucumbers, and the whole range of Mediterranean bounty. Catalonia's Maresme and Empordà regions are also fruit and vegetable bowls, making this coastline a true cornucopia of fresh produce.

WINES

The Penedès wine region west of Barcelona has been joined by new wine Denominations of Origin from all over Catalonia. Alt Camp, Tarragona, Priorat, Montsant, Costers del Segre, Pla de Bages, Alella, and the Empordà all produce excellent reds and whites to join Catalonia's sparkling Cava on local wine lists; the rich, full-bodied reds of Montsant and the Priorat, especially, are among the best in Spain.

8

By Jared Lubarsky

The long curve of the Mediterranean from the French border to Cabo Cervera, below Alicante, encompasses the two autonomous communities of Catalonia and Valencia, with the country's second- and third-largest cities (Barcelona and Valencia, respectively). Rivals in many respects, the two communities share a language, history, and culture that set them clearly apart from the rest of Spain.

Girona is the gateway to Northern Catalonia and its attractions—the Pyrenees, the volcanic region of La Garrotxa, and the beaches of the rugged Costa Brava. Northern Catalonia is memorable for the soft, green hills of the Empordàn farm country and the Alberes mountain range at the eastern end of the Pyrenees. Sprinkled across the landscape are *masías* (farmhouses) with austere, staggered-stone roofs and square towers that make them look like fortresses. Even the tiniest village has its church, arcaded square, and *rambla,* where villagers take their evening *paseo* (stroll).

Artist Salvador Dalí's deep connection to the Costa Brava is literally enshrined in the Teatre-Museu Dalí, in Figueres: he's buried in the crypt beneath it. His former home, a castle in Púbol, is where his wife, Gala, is buried. His summer home in Port Lligat Bay, north of Cadaqués, is now a museum of the Surrealist's life and work.

The province of Valencia was incorporated into the Kingdom of Aragón, Catalonia's medieval Mediterranean empire, when it was conquered by Jaume I in the 13th century. Along with Catalonia, Valencia became part of the united Spanish state in the 15th century, but defenders of its separate cultural and linguistic identity still resent the centuries of Catalan domination. The Catalan language prevails in Tarragona, a city and province of Catalonia, but Valenciano—a dialect of Catalan—is spoken and used on street signs in the Valencian provinces.

The *huerta* (a fertile, irrigated coastal plain) is devoted mainly to citrus and vegetable farming, which lends color to the landscape and fragrance to the air. Arid mountains form a stark backdrop to the lush coast. Over the years these shores have entertained Phoenician, Greek, Carthaginian, and Roman visitors; the Romans stayed several centuries and left archaeological remains all the way down the coast, particularly in Tarragona, the capital of Rome's Spanish empire by 218 BC. Rome's dominion did not go uncontested, however; the most serious challenge came from the Carthaginians of North Africa. The three Punic Wars, fought over this territory between 264 and 146 BC, established the reputation of the Carthaginian general Hannibal.

The coastal farmland and beaches that attracted the ancients now call to modern-day tourists, though a chain of ugly developments has marred much of the shore. Inland, however, local culture survives intact. The rugged and beautiful territory is dotted with small fortified towns, several of which bear the name of Spain's 11th-century national hero, El Cid, commemorating the battles he fought here against the Moors some 900 years ago.

PLANNING

WHEN TO GO

Come for the beaches in the hot summer months, but expect crowds and serious heat—in some places up to 40°C (104°F). The Mediterranean coast is more comfortable in May and September.

February and March are the peak months for skiing in the Pyrenees. Winter traveling in the region has other advantages: Valencia still has plenty of sunshine, and if you're visiting villages and wineries in the countryside you might find you've got the run of the place! A word of warning: many restaurants outside the major towns may close on weekdays in winter, so call ahead. Museums and centers of interest tend to have shorter winter hours, many closing at 6 pm.

The Costa Blanca beach area gets hot and crowded in summer, and accommodations are at a premium. In contrast, spring is mild and an excellent time to tour the region, particularly the rural areas, where blossoms infuse the air with pleasant fragrances and wildflowers dazzle the landscape.

FESTIVALS

In Valencia, the **Las Fallas** fiestas begin March 1 and reach a climax between March 15 and El Día de San José (St. Joseph's Day) on March 19, which is Father's Day in Spain. Las Fallas originated from St. Joseph's role as patron saint of carpenters; in medieval times, carpenters' guilds celebrated the arrival of spring by cleaning out their shops and making bonfires with scraps of wood. These days it's a 19-day celebration ending with fireworks, floats, carnival processions, and bullfights. On March 19, huge wood and papier-mâché effigies, typically of political figures and other personalities, the result of a year's work by local community groups, are torched to end the fiestas.

GETTING HERE AND AROUND

AIR TRAVEL

El Prat de Llobregat in Barcelona is the main international airport for the Costa Brava; Girona is the closest airport to the region, with bus connections directly into the city and to Barcelona. Valencia has an international airport with direct flights to London, Paris, Brussels, Lisbon, Zurich, and Milan as well as regional flights from Barcelona, Madrid, Málaga, and other cities in Spain. There is a regional airport in Alicante serving the Valencian region and Murcia.

BOAT AND FERRY TRAVEL

Many short-cruise lines along the coast offer the chance to view the Costa Brava from the sea. Visit the port areas in the main towns *listed below* and you'll quickly spot several tourist cruise lines. Plan to spend around €15–€27, depending on the length of the cruise. Many longer cruises include a stop en route for a swim. The glass-keeled Nautilus boats for observation of the Islas Medes underwater park cost €19 and run daily between April and October and weekends between November and March.

The shortest ferry connections to the Balearic Islands originate in Dénia. Balearia sails from there to Ibiza, Formentera, and Mallorca.

Boat and Ferry Information **Balearia** ☎ *902/160180* 🌐 *www.balearia.com.* **Creuers Badia de Roses** ✉ *Carrer Gravina 4, Roses* ☎ *608/431762.* **Iscomar** ☎ *902/119128* 🌐 *www.iscomar.com.* **Nautilus** ✉ *Passeig Marítim 23, Toroella, L'Estartit* ☎ *972/751489* 🌐 *www.nautilus.es.* **Roses Serveis Marítims.** Two departures are scheduled daily, for diving excursions (€36 with equipment rental) to the Cap de Creus Natural Park. ✉ *Carrer Eugeni D'ors 15, Roses* ☎ *609/893389* 🌐 *www.rosesub.com.* **Viajes Marítimos** ✉ *Carrer de Sant Pere 5, Lloret de Mar* ☎ *972/369095.*

BUS TRAVEL

Bus travel is generally inexpensive and comfortable. Private companies run buses down the coast and from Madrid to Valencia, and to Alicante. Alsa is the main bus line in this region; local tourist offices can help with timetables. Sarfa operate buses from Barcelona to Blanes, Lloret, Sant Feliu de Guixols, Platja d'Aro, Palamos, Begur, Roses, and Cadaqués.

Contacts **Alsa** ☎ *902/422242* 🌐 *www.alsa.es.* **Barcelonabus** ☎ *902/130014, 93/593–1300* 🌐 *www.barcelonabus.com.* **Sagalés** ✉ *Passeig Sant Joan 52, Barcelona* ☎ *902/130014* 🌐 *www.sagales.com.* **Sarfa.** Sarfa buses connect the towns along the Costa Brava and the Empordà with Barcelona. ✉ *Estació del Nord, Alí Bei 80, Barcelona* ☎ *972/301293, 902/302025* 🌐 *www.sarfa.com* Ⓜ *Arc de Triomf.*

CAR TRAVEL

A car is a practical necessity for explorations inland, where much of the driving is smooth, uncrowded, and scenic. Catalonia and Valencia have excellent roads; the only drawbacks are the high cost of fuel and the high tolls on the *autopistas* (highways, usually designed with the letters AP). The coastal N340 can get clogged, however, so you're often better off on toll roads if your time is limited.

TRAIN TRAVEL

Most of the Costa Brava is *not* served directly by railroad. A local line runs up the coast from Barcelona but takes you only to Blanes; from there it turns inland and connects at Maçanet-Massanes with the main line up to France. Direct trains stop only at major connections, such as Girona, Flaçà, and Figueres. To visit one of the smaller towns in between, you can take a fast direct train from Barcelona to Girona, for instance, then get off and wait for a local to come by. The stop on the main line for the middle section of the Costa Brava is Flaçà, where you can take a bus or taxi to your final destination. Girona and Figueres are two other towns with major bus stations that feed out to the towns of the Costa Brava. The train serves the last three towns on the north end of the Costa Brava: Llançà, Colera, and Portbou.

Express intercity trains reach Valencia from all over Spain, arriving at the new Joaquin Sorolla station; from there, a shuttle bus takes you to the Estación del Norte, the terminus in the center of town, for local connections. From Barcelona there are 15 trains a day, including the fast train TALGO, which takes 3½ hours. There are 22 daily trains to Valencia from Madrid; the high-speed train takes about 1 hour 40 minutes.

For the Costa Blanca, the rail hub is Alicante; for southern Catalonia, make direct train connections to Tarragona from either Barcelona or Valencia.

BEACHES

The beaches on the Costa Brava range from stretches of fine white sand to rocky coves and inlets; summer vacationers flock to San Pol, Roses, and Palafrugell; in all but the busiest weeks of July and August, the tucked-away coves of Cap de Creus national park are oases of peace and privacy. Valencia has a long beach that's wonderful for sunning and a promenade lined with paella restaurants; for quieter surroundings, head farther south to El Saler.

The southeastern coastline of the Costa Blanca varies from the long stretches of sand dunes north of Dénia and south of Alicante to the coves and crescents in between. The benign climate permits lounging on the beach at least eight months of the year. Altea, popular with families, is busy and pebbly, but the old town has retained a traditional pueblo feel with narrow cobbled streets and attractive squares. Calpe's beaches have the scenic advantage of the sheer outcrop Peñón de Ifach (Cliff of Ifach), which stands guard over stretches of sand to either side. Dénia has family-friendly beaches to the north, where children paddle in relatively shallow waters, and rocky inlets to the south.

South of Tarragona, Salou has the best beaches, with a lively, palm-lined promenade.

PLANNING YOUR TIME

Not far from Barcelona, the beautiful towns of Vic, Ripoll, Girona, and Cadaqués are easily reachable from the city by bus or train in a couple of hours. Figueres is a must: its Dalí Museum is one of the most-visited sites in Spain. Girona makes an excellent base from which to explore La

Garrotxa; for that, you'll need to rent a car. Tarragona and its environs are definitely worth a few days; it's easily reached from Barcelona via RENFE; allow 1½ hours to get there by car, especially on weekends and in summer. If you're driving, a visit to the wineries in the Penedès region en route is well worth the detour. Most of Spain's cava comes from here. Tarragona's important Roman remains are best seen on foot at a leisurely pace, broken up with a meal at any of the fine seafood restaurants in the Serallo fishing quarter.

Valencia is 3½ hours by express train from Barcelona; if you have a flexible schedule, you might think about stopping in Tarragona on your way. From Tarragona it's a comfortable one-hour train ride to Valencia; by car, you have the option of stopping for a meal and a walkabout in one of the coastal towns like Peñiscola or Castellon. Historic Valencia and the Santiago Calatrava–designed City of Arts and Sciences buildings can be covered in two days, but you might well want one more to indulge in the city's food and explore the nightlife in the Barrio del Carmen.

A day trip to the nature reserve at Delta de l'Ebre, outside of Valencia, is also highly recommended.

On the Costa Blanca, Alicante's town hall and travel agencies arrange tours of the city and bus and train tours to Guadalest, the Algar waterfalls, the Peñón de Ifach (Calpe), and Elche.

TOURS

Bus tours from Barcelona to Girona and Figueres (including the Dalí Museum) are run by Julià Travel. Buses leave Barcelona Tuesday through Sunday at 8:30 and return around 6. The price is €71 per person. Pullmantur runs tours to several points on the Costa Brava.

Hiking, cycling, and walking tours around Valencia and the Costa Blanca are an alternative to relaxing at the beach. The Sierra Mariola and Sierra Aitana regions are both easily accessible from the Costa Blanca resorts, and many companies—including Ciclo Costa Blanca and Mountain Walks—plan itineraries with hotels included.

There are also riding schools in a number of towns in the region, which provide classes as well as trekking opportunities. Pick up brochures at the local tourist offices.

Water sports are widely available, and you can learn to sail in most of the major resorts. Kite surfing is becoming increasingly popular; the necessary gear is available for rent at many of the beaches, including Santa Pola, and the same applies to windsurfing. A wide range of companies offer scuba-diving excursions, and in the smaller coastal towns it's possible to dive in the protected waters of offshore nature reserves if you book ahead.

If pedal power is more your thing, several companies offer a range of cycling holidays: Ciclo Costa Blanca is a good place to start.

Contacts Abdet 🌐 *www.abdet.com.* **Ciclo Costa Blanca** ✉ *Comercio Enara 2, Camino Viejo de Altea 24, Alfaz del Pi, Alicante* ☎ *699/045475* 🌐 *www.ciclocostablanca.com.* **Julià Travel** ✉ *Ronda Universidad 5, Barcelona* ☎ *93/317–6454, 902/024443* 🌐 *www.juliatravel.com.* **Mountain Walks** ☎ *965/511044* 🌐 *www.mountainwalks.com.*

FARMHOUSE STAYS IN CATALONIA

Dotted throughout Catalonia are farmhouses (*casas rurales* in Spanish, and *cases de pagès* or *masies* in Catalan), where you can spend a weekend or longer. Accommodations vary from small, rustic homes to spacious, luxurious farmhouses with fireplaces and pools. Sometimes you stay in a guest room, as at a bed-and-breakfast; in other places you rent the entire house and do your own cooking. Most tourist offices, including the main Catalonia Tourist Office in Barcelona, have info and listings for the *cases de pagès* of the region. Several organizations in Spain have detailed listings and descriptions of Catalonia's farmhouses, and it's best to book through one of these.

Contacts **Confederació del Turisme Rural i l'Agroturisme de Catalunya** 🌐 *www.catalunyarural.info.* **Federació del Turisme Rural d'Unió de Pagesos de Catalunya** 🌐 *www.agroturisme.org.*

RESTAURANTS

Catalonia's eateries are deservedly famous. Girona's El Celler de Can Roca was voted the best restaurant in the world in 2013 in the annual critics' poll conducted by British magazine *Restaurant*, and a host of other first-rate establishments continue to offer inspiring fine dining in Catalonia, which began in the hinterlands at the legendary Hotel Empordà. You needn't go to an internationally acclaimed restaurant, however, to dine well. Superstar chef Ferran Adrià of the former foodie paradise elBulli dines regularly at dives in Roses, where straight-up fresh fish is the day-in, day-out attraction. Northern Catalonia's Empordà region is known not only for seafood, but also for a rich assortment of inland and upland products. Beef from Girona's verdant pastureland is prized throughout Catalonia, while wild mushrooms from the Pyrenees and game from the Alberes range offer seasonal depth and breadth to menus across the region. From a simple beachside paella or *llobarro* (sea bass) at a *chiringuito* (shack) with tables on the sand, to the splendor of a meal at Celler de Can Roca, playing culinary hopscotch through Catalonia is a good way to organize a tour.

Prices in dining reviews are the average cost of a main course at dinner or, if dinner is not served, at lunch.

HOTELS

Lodgings on the Costa Brava range from the finest hotels to spartan *pensions*. The better accommodations are usually well situated and have splendid views of the seascape. Many simple hotels provide a perfectly adequate stopover. If you plan to visit during the high season (July and August), be sure to book reservations well in advance at almost any hotel in this area, especially the Costa Brava, which remains one of the most popular summer resort areas in Spain. Many Costa Brava hotels close down in the winter season, between November and March.

Prices in lodging reviews are the lowest cost of a standard double room in high season.

NORTHERN CATALONIA

Northern Catalonia is for many *the* reason to visit Spain. The historic center of Girona, its principal city, is a labyrinth of climbing cobblestone streets and staircases, with remarkable Gothic and Romanesque buildings at every turn. El Call—the Jewish Quarter here—is one of the best preserved in Europe, and the Gothic cathedral is an architectural masterpiece. Streets in the modern part of the city are lined with smart shops and boutiques, and the overall quality of life in Girona is considered among the best in Spain.

The nearby towns of Besalú and Figueres couldn't be more different from each other. Figueres is an unexceptional town made exceptional by the Dalí Museum. Besalu is a picture-perfect Romanesque village on a bluff overlooking the River Fluvià, with at least one of the most prestigious restaurants in Catalonia. Less well known are the medieval towns in and around La Garrotxa: Ripoll, Rupit, and Olot boast arguably the best produce in the region.

GIRONA

97 km (60 miles) northeast of Barcelona.

At the confluence of four rivers, Girona (population: 96,000) keeps intact the magic of its historic past—with its brooding hilltop castle, soaring cathedral, and dreamy riverside setting, it resembles a vision from the Middle Ages. Today, as a university center, Girona combines past and vibrant present: art galleries, chic cafés, and trendy boutiques have set up shop in many of the restored buildings of the Old Quarter, known as the Força Vella (Old Fortress), which is on the east side of the River Onya. Built on the side of the mountain, it presents a tightly packed labyrinth of medieval buildings and monuments on narrow cobblestone streets with connecting stairways. You can still see vestiges of the Iberian and Roman walls in the cathedral square and in the patio of the old university. In the centermost quarter is El Call, one of Europe's best-preserved ancient (12th- to 15th-century) Jewish communities and an important center of cabalistic studies.

The main street of the Old Quarter is Carrer de la Força, which follows the old Via Augusta, the Roman road that connected Rome with its provinces.

The best way to get to know Girona is on foot. As you wander through the Força Vella you will be repeatedly surprised by new discoveries. One of Girona's treasures is its setting, high above where the Onyarmerges with the Ter; the latter flows from a mountain waterfall that can be glimpsed in a gorge above the town. Regardless of your approach, walk first along the west bank of the Onyar, between the train trestle and the Plaça de la Independència, to admire the classic view of the Old Town, with its pastel yellow, pink, and orange waterfront facades. Many of the windows and balconies—always draped with colorful drying laundry—are adorned with fretwork grilles of embossed wood or delicate iron tracery. Cross Pont de Sant Agustí over to the Old Quarter from under the arcades in the corner of Plaça de la Independència and find

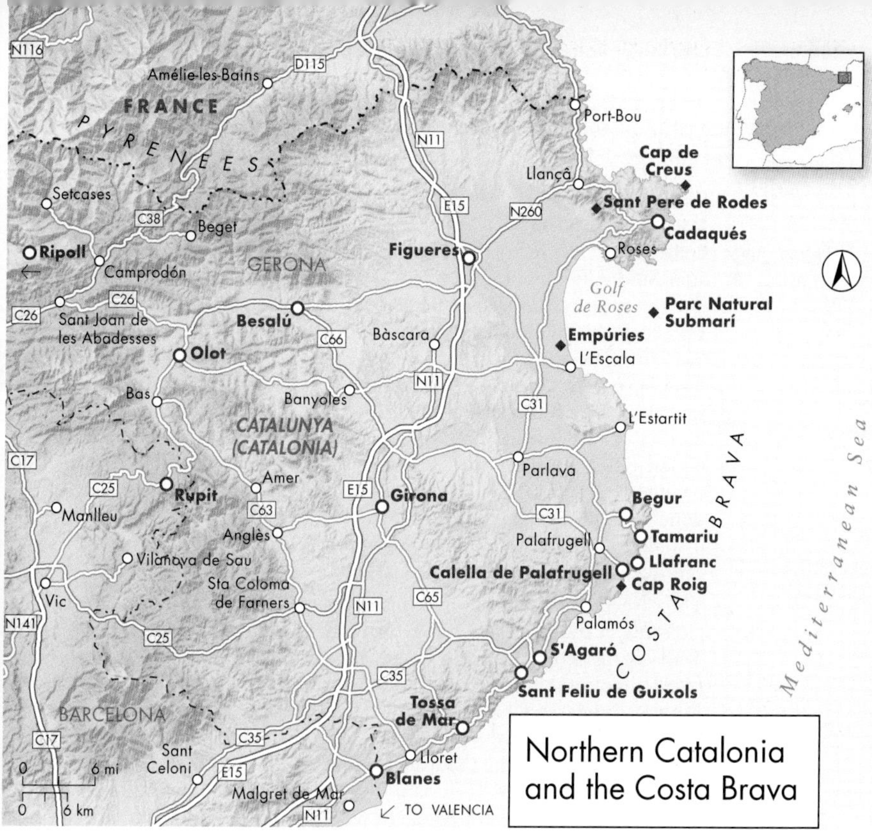

Northern Catalonia and the Costa Brava

your way to the Punt de Benvinguda tourist office, to the right at Rambla Llibertat 1. Then work your way up through the labyrinth of steep streets, using the cathedral's huge baroque facade as a guide.

The GironaMuseus card is good for discount admission to all the city's museums. **■TIP➔ Some are free on the first Sunday of every month.** Check with the tourist office or at the Punt de Benvinguda welcome center, which can also arrange guided tours.

Punt de Benvinguda. Look for this visitor information center—where you can also get help with hotel bookings—at the entrance to Girona from the town's main parking area on the right bank of the Onyar River. ✉ *Carrer Berenguer Carnisser 5* ☎ *972/211678.*

GETTING HERE AND AROUND

There are more than 20 daily trains from Barcelona to Girona (continuing on to the French border). Bus service to the city center is limited, but there are frequent Barcelonabus buses to Girona airport that take an average of 75 minutes and cost €12 one-way, €21 round-trip. Getting around the city is easiest on foot or by taxi; several bridges connect the historic old quarter with the more modern town across the river.

ESSENTIALS

Bus Information Barcelona Bus ✉ *Passeig de Sant Joan 52, Barcelona* ☎ *902/130014* 🌐 *www.barcelonabus.com.*

Visitor Information **Girona Office of Tourism** ✉ *Carrer Joan Maragall 1* ☎ *972/975975* 🌐 *www.girona.cat/turisme* ✉ *Rambla de la Llibertat 1* ☎ *972/226575.*

EXPLORING

TOP ATTRACTIONS

Fodor's Choice ★ **Cathedral.** At the heart of the Old City, the cathedral looms above 90 steps and is famous for its nave—at 75 feet, the widest in the world and the epitome of the spatial ideal of Catalan Gothic architects. Since Charlemagne founded the original church in the 8th century, it has been through many fires, changes, and renovations, so you are greeted by a Rococo-era facade—"eloquent as organ music" and impressively set off by a spectacular flight of 17th-century stairs, which rises from its own plaça. Inside, three smaller naves were compressed into one gigantic hall by the famed architect Guillermo Bofill in 1416. The change was typical of Catalan Gothic "hall" churches, and it was done to facilitate preaching to crowds. Note the famous silver canopy, or *baldaquí* (baldachin). The oldest part of the cathedral is the 11th-century Romanesque **Torre de Carlemany** (Charlemagne Tower).

The cathedral's 12th-century cloister has an obvious affinity with the cloisters in the Roussillon area of France. Inside the Treasury are a 10th-century copy of Beatus's manuscript *Commentary on the Apocalypse* (illuminated in the dramatically primitive Mozarabic style), the Bible of Emperor Charles V, and the celebrated *Tapís de la Creació* (Tapestry of the Creation), considered by most experts to be the finest tapestry surviving from the Romanesque era. It depicts the seven days of Creation as told in Genesis in the primitive but powerful fashion of early Romanesque art. Made of wool, with predominant colors of green, brown, and ocher, the tapestry once hung behind the main altar as a pictorial Bible lesson. The four seasons, stars, winds, months of the year and days of the week, plants, animals, and elements of nature circle around a central figure, likening paradise to the eternal cosmos presided over by Christ. In addition to its intrinsic beauty, the bottom band (which appears to have been added at a later date) contains two *iudeis,* or Jews, dressed in the round cloaks they were compelled to wear to set them apart from Christians. This scene is thought to be the earliest portrayal of a Jew (other than biblical figures) in Christian art. ✉ *Pl. de la Catedral s/n* ☎ *972/427189, 972/215814* 🌐 *www.catedraldegirona.org* 🎫 *€7 (free Sun.)* ⏲ *Apr.–Oct., daily 10–7:30; Nov.–Mar., daily 10–6:30.*

Museu d'Art. The Episcopal Palace near the cathedral contains the wide-ranging collections of Girona's main art museum. You'll see everything from superb Romanesque *majestats* (carved wood figures of Christ) to reliquaries from Sant Pere de Rodes, illuminated 12th-century manuscripts, and works of the 20th-century Olot school of landscape painting. ✉ *Pujada de la Catedral 12* ☎ *972/203834* 🌐 *www.museuart.com* 🎫 *€2* ⏲ *May–Sept., Tues.–Sat. 10–7, Sun. 10–2; Oct.–Apr., Tues.–Sat. 10–6, Sun. 10–2.*

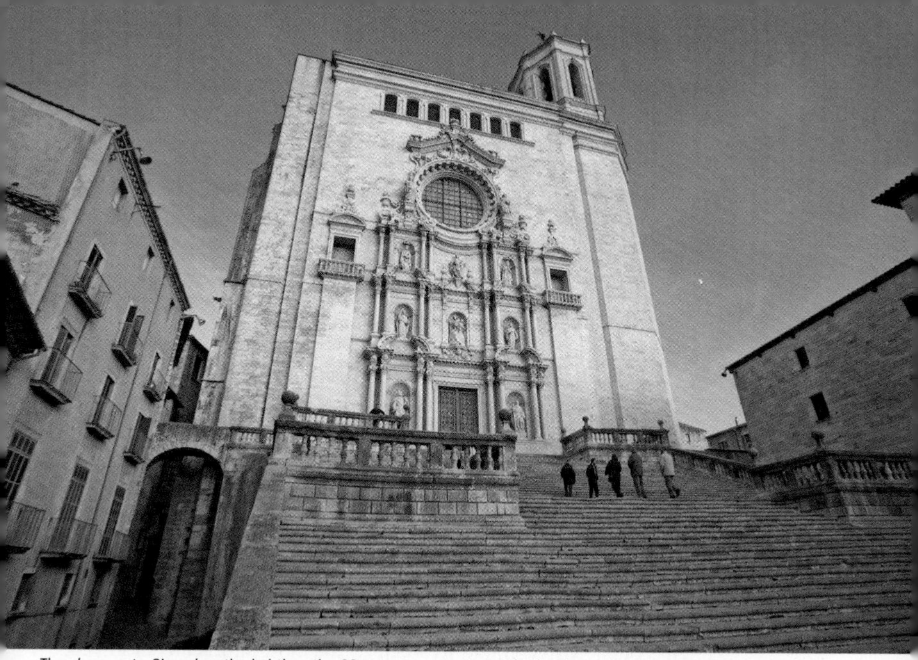

There's more to Girona's cathedral than the 90 steps to get to it; inside there's much to see, including the Treasury.

FAMILY **Museu del Cinema.** An interactive museum, this spot has artifacts and movie-related paraphernalia starting from Chinese shadows, the first rudimentary moving pictures, to Lyon's Lumière brothers. The Cine Nic toy filmmaking machines, originally developed in 1931 by the Nicolau brothers of Barcelona and now being relaunched commercially, allow even novices to put together their own movies. ✉ *Carrer de la Sèquia 1* ☎ *972/412777* 🌐 *www.museudelcinema.cat* 🎫 *€5)free 1st Sun. of month)* 🕓 *May, June, and Sept., Tues.–Sat. 10–8, Sun. 11–3; July and Aug., Tues.–Sun. 10–8; Oct.–Apr., Tues.–Fri. 10–6, Sat. 10–8, Sun. 11–3.*

8

WORTH NOTING

Banys Arabs (*Arab Baths*). A misnomer, the Banys Arabs were actually built by Morisco craftsmen (workers of Moorish descent) in the late 12th century, long after Girona's Islamic occupation (714–797) had ended. Following the old Roman model that had disappeared in the West, the custom of bathing publicly may have been brought back from the Holy Land with the Crusaders. These baths are sectioned off into three rooms in descending order: a *frigidarium,* or cold bath, a square room with a central octagonal pool and a skylight with cupola held up by two stories of eight fine columns; a *tepidarium,* or warm bath; and a *caldarium,* or steam room, beneath which is a chamber where a fire was kept burning. Here the inhabitants of the old Girona came to relax, exchange gossip, or do business. ✉ *Carrer Ferran el Catòlic s/n* ☎ *972/190797* 🌐 *www.banysarabs.cat* 🎫 *€2* 🕓 *Apr.–Sept., Mon.–Sat. 10–7, Sun. 10–2; Oct.–Mar., daily 10–2.*

Centre Bonastruc ça Porta. Housed in a former synagogue and dedicated to the preservation of Girona's Jewish heritage, this center organizes conferences, exhibitions, and seminars. The **Museu de Història dels Jueus** (Museum of Jewish History) contains 21 stone tablets, one of the finest collections in the world of medieval Jewish funerary slabs. These came from the old Jewish cemetery of Montjuïc, revealed when the railroad between Barcelona and France was laid out in the 19th century. Its exact location, about 1½ km (1 mile) north of Girona on the road to La Bisbal and known as La Tribana, is being excavated. The center also holds the **Institut d'Estudis Nahmànides,** with an extensive library of Judaica. ✉ *Carrer de la Força 8* ☎ *972/216761* 🌐 *www.girona.cat/call/eng/museu.php* 🎫 *€4* ⏲ *Sept.–June, Tues.–Sat. 10–6, Sun. and Mon. 10–2; July and Aug., Mon.–Sat. 10–8, Sun. 10–2.*

El Call. Girona is especially noted for its 13th-century Jewish Quarter, El Call, which can be found branching off Carrer de la Força, south of the Plaça Catedral. The word *call* (pronounced "kyle" in Catalan) may come from an old Catalan word meaning "narrow way" or "passage," derived from the Latin word *callum* or *callis*. Others suggest that it comes from the Hebrew word *qahal*, meaning "assembly" or "meeting of the community." Owing allegiance to the Spanish king (who exacted tribute for this distinction) and not to the city government, this once-prosperous Jewish community—one of the most flourishing in Europe during the Middle Ages—was, at its height, a center of learning. An important school of the Kabala was centered here. The most famous teacher of the Kabala from Girona was Rabbi Mossé ben Nahman (also known as Nahmànides), who wrote an important religious work based on meditation and the reinterpretation of the Bible and the Talmud.

The earliest presence of Jews in Girona is uncertain, but the first historical mention dates from 982, when a group of 25 Jewish families moved to Girona from nearby Juïgues. Today the layout of El Call bears no resemblance to what this area looked like in the 15th century, when Jews last lived here. Space was at a premium inside the city walls in Girona, and houses were destroyed and built higgledy-piggledy one atop the other.

QUICK BITES

La Vienesa. Fortify yourself for sightseeing with some superb tea and plump pastries at La Vienesa. One of the town's best-loved gathering points for conversation, this cozy spot is good place to regroup and reorient. ✉ ***Carrer La Pujada del Pont de Pedra 1*** ☎ ***972/486046.***

Museu d'Història de la Ciutat. On Carrer de la Força, this fascinating museum is filled with artifacts from Girona's long and embattled past. From pre-Roman objects to paintings and drawings from the notorious siege at the hands of Napoleonic troops, to the early municipal lighting system and the medieval printing press, there is plenty to see here. You will definitely come away with a clearer idea of Girona's past. ✉ *Carrer de la Força 27* ☎ *972/222229* 🌐 *www.girona.cat/museuciutat* 🎫 *€4 (free 1st Sun. of month)* ⏲ *Tues.–Sat. 10:30–5:30 (till 6:30 May–Sept.), Sun. 10:30–1:30.*

Passeig Arqueològic. The landscaped gardens of this stepped archaeological walk are below the restored walls of the Old Quarter (which you can walk, in parts) and have good views from belvederes and watchtowers. From there, climb through the Jardins de la Francesa to the highest ramparts for a view of the cathedral's 11th-century Charlemagne Tower.

Placeta del Institut Vell. In this small square on Carrer de la Força you can study a tar-blackened 3-inch-long, half-inch-deep groove carved shoulder-high into the stone of the right-hand doorpost as you enter the square. It indicates the location of a *mezuzah*, a small case or tube of metal or wood containing a piece of parchment with verses from the Torah (declaring the essence of Jewish belief in one God). Anyone passing through the doorway touched the mezuzah as a sign of devotion. Evidence of the labyrinthine layout of a few street ruts in the Old Quarter may still be seen inside the antiques store Antiguitats la Canonja Vella at Carrer de la Força 33.

Sant Feliu. The vast bulk of this structure is landmarked by one of Girona's most distinctive belfries, topped by eight pinnacles. One of Girona's most beloved churches, it was repeatedly rebuilt and altered over four centuries and stands today as an amalgam of Romanesque columns, Gothic nave, and Baroque facade. It was founded over the tomb of St. Felix of Africa, a martyr under the Roman emperor Diocletian. ✉ *Pujada de Sant Feliu 29* ☎ *972/201407* 🎫 *Included with €7 Cathedral admission ticket* ⏲ *Mon.–Sat. 10–5:30, Sun. 1–5:30.*

Torre de Gironella. A five-minute walk uphill behind the cathedral leads to a park and this four-story tower (no entry permitted) dating from the year 1190; the tower marks the highest point in the Jewish Quarter. Girona's Jewish community took refuge here in early August 1391, emerging 17 weeks later to find their houses in ruins. Even though Spain's official expulsion decree did not go into effect until 1492, this attack effectively ended the Girona Jewish community. Destroyed in 1404, reconstructed in 1411, and destroyed anew by retreating Napoleonic troops in 1814, the Torre de Gironella was the site of the celebration of the first Hanukkah ceremony in Girona in 607 years, held on December 20, 1998, with Jerusalem's chief Sephardic rabbi Rishon Letzion presiding. ✉ *Ctra. Sant Gregori 91.*

8

WHERE TO EAT

$$ TAPAS — ✕ **Bubbles Gastro Bar.** Excellent Catalan cuisine with Mediterranean-fusion touches is served here in an elegant setting just across the river from the Old City. Try the innovative tapas, or choose from two dinner tasting menus for €25 or €45. $ *Average main: €15* ✉ *Passeig José Canalejas 6* ☎ *972/226002* 🌐 *www.gastrobubbles.com* ⏲ *Closed Sun. and Mon.*

$$$$ CONTEMPORARY Fodor's Choice ★ — ✕ **Celler de Can Roca.** Annointed in 2013 by an international panel of food critics and chefs as the best restaurant in the world, Celler de Can Roca is a life-changing experience for anybody persistent enough to get a reservation. The Roca brothers, Joan, Josep, and Jordi, showcase their masterful creations in two tasting menus, at €155 and €190; consider your visit blessed if yours includes signature dishes like lobster

With its picturesque rivers, Girona is often called the Spanish Venice.

parmentier with black trumpet mushrooms, or Iberian suckling pig with pepper sauce and garlic and quince terrine, or Dublin Bay prawns with curry smoke (the Rocas pioneered the technique of roasting in the aromas of spices during the cooking process). For dessert, try any of maitre confectioner Jordi's spectacular innovations. Don't be embarrassed to ask Josep, the sommelier, for guidance through the encyclopedic wine list. *Average main: €38 Can Sunyer 48 972/222157 Reservations essential Closed Sun., Mon., and Aug.*

WHERE TO STAY

$$$$ RENTAL FAMILY Fodor's Choice ★ **Alemanys 5.** Award-winning architect Anna Noguera and partner Juan-Manuel Ribera transformed a 16th-century house steps from the cathedral into two extraordinary apartments: one for up to five people, the other for six. **Pros:** perfect for families or small groups; ideal location. **Cons:** difficult to reach by car; minimum stay required. *Rooms from: €250 Carrer Alemanys 5 649/885136 www.alemanys5.com 2 apartments No meals.*

$ HOTEL Fodor's Choice ★ **Hotel Històric y Apartaments Històric Girona.** Perfectly placed for exploring the Jewish Quarter, this boutique hotel occupies a 9th-century house, with remnants of a 3rd-century Roman wall and a Roman aqueduct on the ground floor and in one of the apartments. **Pros:** good location; historical features; top amenities and comforts. **Cons:** rooms and apartments are a little cramped; difficult to get a car in; no pets. *Rooms from: €114 Carrer Bellmirall 4A 972/223583 www.hotelhistoric.com 6 rooms, 7 apartments, 2 suites No meals.*

NIGHTLIFE AND THE ARTS

Girona is a university town, so the night scene is especially lively during the school year.

Platea. This nightspot, popular with students and visitors alike, has both disco and live bands in concert, depending on the day of the week. ✉ *Carrer Jeroni Real de Fontclara 4* ☎ *972/227288, 972/411902* ⏲ *Wed.–Sat. 10 pm–5:30 am.*

SHOPPING

Boutique Carlos Falcó. Men will find fine plumage here, from suits to accessories. ✉ *Carrer Josep Maluquer Salvador 16* ☎ *972/207156.*

Despiral. Young people stock up on threads at Despiral. ✉ *Carrer Santa Clara 43* ☎ *972/221448.*

Dolors Turró. Painter and sculptor Dolors Turró knows her angels: making them—in all shapes, sizes and styles—is what she does best. Drop in to her quirky atelier in the old city. ✉ *Carrer de les Ballesteries 19* ☎ *972/410193.*

Gluki. This chocolatier and confectioner has been in business since 1880. ✉ *Carrer Santa Clara 44* ☎ *972/201989.*

Llibreria 22. Girona's best bookstore has travel guidebooks and a selection of English fiction. ✉ *Carrer Hortes 22* ☎ *972/212395* 🌐 *www.llibreria22.net.*

Peacock. For shoes, go to one of Peacock's four Girona locations—the others are at Carrer Migdia 18, Plaça de Vi 4, and Carrer Pare Claret 29. ✉ *Carrer Nou 15* ☎ *972/226848* 🌐 *www.peacock.cat.*

FIGUERES

37 km (23 miles) north of Girona on the A7.

Figueres is the capital of the *comarca* (county) of the Alt Empordà, the bustling county seat of this predominantly agricultural region. Local people come from the surrounding area to shop at its many stores and stock up on farm equipment and supplies. Thursday is market day, and farmers gather at the top of La Rambla to do business and gossip, taking refreshments at cafés and discreetly pulling out and pocketing large rolls of bills, the result of their morning transactions. What brings the tourists to Figueres in droves, however, has little to do with agriculture—unless, of course, you use a broader definition of fertilizer: the jaw-dropping Dalí Museum, one of the most visited museums in Spain.

Artist Salvador Dalí is Figueres's most famous son. With a painterly technique that rivaled that of Jan van Eyck, a flair for publicity so aggressive it would have put P. T. Barnum in the shade, and a penchant for shocking (he loved telling people Barcelona's historic Barri Gòtic should be knocked down), Dalí enters art history as one of the foremost proponents of Surrealism, the movement launched in the 1920s by André Breton. His most lasting image may be the melting watches in his iconic 1931 painting *The Persistence of Memory.* The artist, who was born in Figueres and died there in 1989, decided to create a museum-monument to himself during the last two decades of his life.

CLOSE UP

Catalonia's National Dance

The *sardana*, Catalonia's national dance, is often perceived as a solemn and measured affair performed by older folks in front of the Barcelona Cathedral at midday on weekends. Look for an athletic young *colla* (troupe), though, and you'll see the grace and fluidity the sardana can create. The mathematical precision of the dance, consisting of 76 steps in sets of four, each dancer needing to know exactly where he or she is at all times, demands intense concentration. Said to be a representation of the passing of time, a choreography of the orbits and revolutions of the moon and stars, the circular sardana is recorded in Greek chronicles dating back 2,000 years. Performed in circles of all sizes and by dancers of all ages, the sardana is accompanied by an ensemble called the *cobla*: five wind instruments, five brass, and a director who plays a three-holed flute called the *flabiol* and a small drum, the *tabal*, which he wears attached to his flute arm (normally the right).

Dalí often frequented the Cafeteria Astòria at the top of La Rambla (still the center of social life in Figueres), signing autographs for tourists or just being Dalí: he once walked down the street with a French omelet in his breast pocket instead of a handkerchief.

GETTING HERE AND AROUND

Figueres is one of the stops on the regular train service from Barcelona to the French border. Local buses are also frequent, especially from nearby Cadaqués, with more than eight services daily. The town is sufficiently small to explore on foot.

ESSENTIALS

Visitor Information Figueres ✉ *Pl. del Sol s/n* ☎ *972/503155* 🌐 *en.visitfigueres.cat.*

EXPLORING

Castell de Sant Ferran. Just a minute's drive northwest of Figueres is this imposing 18th-century fortified castle, one of the largest in Europe. Only when you start exploring can you appreciate how immense it is. The parade grounds extend for acres, and the arcaded stables can hold more than 500 horses; the perimeter is roughly 4 km (2½ miles around. This castle was the site of the last official meeting of the Republican parliament (on February 1, 1939) before it surrendered to Franco's forces. Ironically, it was here that Lieutenant Colonel Antonio Tejero was imprisoned after his failed 1981 coup d'état in Madrid. ■ **TIP→ Call a day ahead and arrange for the "Catedral de l'Aiguas" 2-hour guided tour in English (€15), including a trip through the castle's subterranean water system by zodiac pontoon boat.** ✉ *Pujada del Castell s/n* ☎ *972/506094, 972/514585* 🌐 *www.lesfortalesescatalanes.info* 🎟 *€3* ⏲ *Apr.–June and mid-Sept.–Oct., daily 10–6; July–mid-Sept., daily 10–8; Nov.–Mar., daily 10–3. Last admission 1 hr before closing.*

The Dalí Museum in Figueres is itself a work of art. Note the eggs on the exterior: they're a common image in his work.

FAMILY **Museu del Joguet de Catalunya.** Hundreds of antique dolls and toys are on display here—including collections owned by, among others, Salvador Dalí, Federico García Lorca, and Joan Miró. It also hosts Catalonia's only *caganer* exhibit, from mid-December to mid-January in odd-numbered years. These playful little figures answering nature's call have long had a special spot in the Catalan *pessebre* (Nativity scene). Farmers are the most traditional figures, squatting discreetly behind the animals, but these days you'll find Barça soccer players and politicians, too. Check with the museum for exact dates. ✉ *Hotel Paris, Carrer de Sant Pere 1* ☎ *972/504585* 🌐 *www.mjc.cat* 🎫 *€6* ⏲ *June–Sept., Mon.–Sat. 10–7, Sun. 11–6; Oct.–May, Tues.–Sat. 10–6, Sun. 11–2.*

Fodor's Choice ★ **Teatre-Museu Dalí.** "Museum" was not a big enough word for Dalí, so he christened his monument a "Theater." And, in fact, the building was once the Old Town theater, reduced to a ruin in the Spanish Civil War. Now topped with a glass geodesic dome and studded with Dalí's iconic egg shapes, the multilevel museum pays homage to his fertile imagination and artistic creativity. It includes gardens, ramps, and a spectacular dropcloth Dalí painted for Les Ballets de Monte Carlo. Don't look for his greatest paintings here, although there are some memorable images, including *Gala at the Mediterranean,* which takes the body of Gala (Dalí's wife) and morphs it into the image of Abraham Lincoln once you look through coin-operated viewfinders. The sideshow theme continues with other coin-operated pieces, including *Taxi Plujós* (Rainy Taxi), in which water gushes over the snail-covered occupants sitting in a Cadillac once owned by Al Capone, or *Sala de Mae West,* a trompe-l'oeil vision in which a pink sofa, two fireplaces, and two paintings morph into the face of the onetime Hollywood sex symbol. Fittingly, another "exhibit" on view is Dalí's own crypt. When his friends considered what flag to lay over his coffin, they decided to cover it with an embroidered heirloom tablecloth instead. Dalí would have liked this unconventional touch, if not the actual site: he wanted to be buried at his castle of Púbol next to his wife, but the then-mayor of Figueres took matters into his own hands. All in all, the museum is a piece of Dalí dynamite. ✉ *Pl. Gala-Salvador Dalí 5* ☎ *972/677500* 🌐 *www.salvador-dali.org* 🎫 *€12* ⏲ *July–Sept., daily 9–7:15 (with night visits late July–late Aug., 10–12:15); Mar.–June and Oct., Tues.–Sun. 9:30–5:15; Nov.–Feb., Tues.–Sun. 10:30–5:15.*

OFF THE BEATEN PATH

Casa-Museu Gala Dalí. The third point of the Dalí triangle is the medieval castle of Púbol, where the artist's wife, Gala, is buried in the crypt. During the 1970s this was Gala's residence, though Dalí also lived here in the early 1980s. It contains paintings and drawings, Gala's haute-couture dresses, elephant sculptures in the garden, furniture, and other objects chosen by the couple. Púbol, roughly between Girona and Figueres, is near the C255, and is not easy to find. If you are traveling by train, get off at the Flaçà station on RENFE's Barcelona–Portbou line; walk or take a taxi 4 km (2½ miles) to Púbol. By bus, the Sarfa bus company has a stop in Flaçà and on the C255 road, some 2 km (1¼ miles) from Púbol. ✉ *Pl. Gala-Dalí s/n, Púbol* ☎ *972/488655* 🌐 *www.salvador-dali.org* 🎫 *€8* ⏲ *Mid-Mar.–mid-June and mid-Sept.–Oct., Tues.–Sun. 10–6; mid-June–mid-Sept., daily 10–8; Nov.–Dec., Tues.–Sun. 10–5. Last admission 45 mins before closing.*

WHERE TO STAY

$ HOTEL

Hotel Duràn. Dalí had his own private dining room in this former stagecoach relay station, and you can take a meal amid pictures of the great Surrealist. **Pros:** good central location; family-friendly. **Cons:** rooms lack character; parking inconvenient; no pets. [$] *Rooms from: €80* ✉ *Carrer Lasauca 5* ☎ *972/501250* 🌐 *www.hotelduran.com* *65 rooms* *No meals.*

$ HOTEL Fodor's Choice ★

Hotel Empordà. Just a mile north of town, this hotel houses the elegant restaurant run by Jaume Subirós that's been hailed as the birthplace of modern Catalan cuisine and has become a beacon for gourmands. **Pros:** historic culinary destination; convenient to the Teatre-Museu Dalí. **Cons:** on an unprepossessing roadside lot beside the busy N11 highway. [$] *Rooms from: €80* ✉ *Av. Salvador Dalí i Domènech 170, 1.5 km (1 mile) north of town* ☎ *972/500562* 🌐 *www.hotelemporda.com* *39 rooms, 3 suites* *No meals.*

BESALÚ

34 km (21 miles) north of Girona, 25 km (15 miles) west of Figueres.

Besalú, the capital of a feudal county until power was transferred to Barcelona at the beginning of the 12th century, remains one of the best-preserved medieval towns in Catalonia. Among its main sights are the 12th-century Romanesque fortified bridge over the Fluvià river; two churches, Sant Vicenç (set on an attractive, café-lined plaza) and Sant Pere; and the ruins of the convent of Santa Maria on the hill above town.

GETTING HERE AND AROUND

With a population of just over 2,400, the village is easily small enough to stroll through, with all the restaurants and sights within easy distances of each other. There is bus service to Besalú from Figueres and the surrounding Costa Brava resorts.

ESSENTIALS

Visitor Information Besalú ✉ *Carrer del Pont Vell 1* ☎ *972/591240* 🌐 *www.besalu.cat.*

Guided tours. Guided tours of Besalú, offered by the visitor information center (daily at 1 pm in English, setting out from Carrer Major), cover the churches of Sant Pere and Sant Vincenç, archaeological sites, the Jewish Quarter, and the bridge. A nighttime Medieval Tour (July and August, Wednesday at 10 pm), is led by a knight on horseback and a retinue of various characters in costume. Phone reservations are recommended. ■ **TIP→ At the Church of Sant Pere, which has a 13th-century ambulatory, you may hear Gregorian chant.** ☎ *972/591240* *Day tours €2.20 (30 mins) and €4.50 (1 hr), night tours €15.*

EXPLORING

Església de Sant Vicenç. Founded in 977, this pre-Romanesque gem contains the relics of St. Vincent as well as the tomb of its benefactor, Pere de Rovira. La Capella de la Veracreu (Chapel of the True Cross) displays a reproduction of an alleged fragment of the True Cross brought from Rome by Bernat Tallafer in 977 and stolen in 1899. ✉ *Carrer de Sant Vicenç s/n.*

Pont Fortificat. The town's most emblematic feature is this Romanesque 11th-century fortified bridge with crenellated battlements spanning the Fluvià River.

8

WHERE TO EAT

$$$ CATALAN Fodor's Choice ★ **Els Fogons de Can Llaudes.** A faithfully restored 10th-century Romanesque chapel holds proprietor Jaume Soler's outstanding restaurant, one of Catalonia's best. A typical main dish is *confitat de bou i raïm glacejat amb el seu suc* (beef confit au jus with glacé grapes). There is no à la carte menu; call at least one day in advance to reserve the €60 *menú de degustació* (tasting menu). *$ Average main: €25* ✉ *Prat de Sant Pere 6* ☎ *972/590858, 629/782388* *Reservations essential* *Closed Tues. and last 2 wks of Nov.*

OLOT

21 km (13 miles) west of Besalú, 55 km (34 miles) northwest of Girona.

Capital of the comarca (administrative region) of Garrotxa, Olot is famous for its 19th-century school of landscape painters and has several excellent Art Nouveau buildings, including the Casa Solà-Morales, which has a facade by Lluís Domènech i Montaner, architect of Barcelona's Palau de la Música. The Sant Esteve church at the southeastern end of Passeig d'en Blay is famous for its El Greco painting *Christ Carrying the Cross* (1605).

Besalú contains astonishingly well-preserved medieval buildings.

WHERE TO EAT AND STAY

$$$$ CATALAN ✕ **Ca l'Enric.** Chefs Jordi and Isabel Juncà have become legends in the town of La Vall de Bianya just north of Olot, where symposia on culinary matters such as woodcock preparation have inspired prizewinning books. Cuisine firmly rooted in local products, starring game of all sorts, is taken to another level here. What's on offer varies with the season; order the tasting menu (€90), and sample a full range of the Juncàs's virtuosity. *Average main: €30* *N260, Km 91, La Vall de Bianya* *972/290015* *www.calenric.net* *Reservations essential* *Closed Mon., Jan.1–17, and 1st 2 wks July. No dinner Sun.–Wed.*

$$$$ CATALAN ✕ **Les Cols.** Off the road east to Figueres, Fina Puigdevall has made this ancient *masia* (Catalan farmhouse) a design triumph. The sprawling 18th-century rustic structure is filled with glassed-in halls, intimate gardens, and wrought-iron and steel details. The cuisine is seasonal and based on locally grown products, from wild mushrooms to the extraordinarily flavorful legumes and vegetables produced by the rich, volcanic soil of La Garrotxa. There are five rooms for overnight stays. *Average main: €85* *Mas les Cols, Ctra. de la Canya s/n* *972/269209* *www.lescols.com* *Reservations essential* *Closed 1st 3 wks in Jan.*

RIPOLL

34 km (21 miles) west of Olot, 91 km (56 miles) north of Girona.

From Olot, it's an easy drive farther west on Route N260 to Ripoll—the wellspring, in a sense, of Catalonia's earliest history. The town's principal attraction is the Benedictine **Monastery of Santa Maria,** established in the late 9th century by Wilfred II—then Count of

Barcelona—who wrested the independence of the province from the control of the Frankish Empire. Founder of the first dynastic line of Catalan kings, he rejoiced in the historical nickname Guifré el Pelós: Wilfred the Hairy.

GETTING HERE AND AROUND

RENFE has 16 commuter trains daily from Sants Station in Barcelona—the trip takes about 2 hours. By car, it's quicker—you can drive to Ripoll from Barcelona on the C17/C33 highways in about 90 minutes, traffic permitting.

THE COSTA BRAVA

The Costa Brava (Wild Coast) is a nearly unbroken series of sheer rock cliffs dropping down to clear blue-green waters, punctuated with innumerable coves and tiny beaches on narrow inlets, called *calas*. It basically begins at Blanes and continues north along 135 km (84 miles) of coastline to the French border at Port Bou. Although the area does have spots of real-estate excess, the rocky terrain of many pockets (Tossa, Cap de Begur, and Cadaqués) has discouraged overbuilding. On a good day here, the luminous blue of the sea contrasts with red-brown headlands and cliffs, and the distant lights of fishing boats reflect on wine-color waters at dusk. Small stands of umbrella pine veil the footpaths to many of the secluded coves and little patches of white sand—often, the only access is by boat.

GETTING HERE AND AROUND

From Barcelona, the fastest way to the Costa Brava by car is to start up the inland AP7 *autopista* tollway toward Girona, then take *Sortida* (Exit) 10 for Blanes, Lloret de Mar, Tossa de Mar, Sant Feliu de Guíxols, S'Agaró, Platja d'Aro, Palamós, Calella de Palafrugell, and Palafrugell. From Palafrugell, you can head inland for La Bisbal and from there on to Girona, in the heart of Northern Catalonia. To head to the middle section of the Costa Brava, get off at Sortida 6, the first exit after Girona; this will point you directly to the Iberian ruins of Ullastret. To reach the northern part of the Costa Brava, get off the AP7 before Figueres at Sortida 4 for L'Estartit, L'Escala, Empúries, Castelló d'Empúries, Aïguamolls de l'Empordà, Roses, Cadaqués, Sant Pere de Rodes, and Portbou. Sortida 4 will also take you directly to Figueres, Peralada, and the Alberes mountains. The old national route, N11, is slow, heavily traveled, and more dangerous, especially in summer.

BLANES

The beaches closest to Barcelona are at Blanes (60 km [37 miles] northeast of Barcelona; 45 km [28 miles] south of Girona). The Costa Brava begins here with five different beaches, running from Punta Santa Anna on the far side of the port—a tiny cove with a pebbly beach at the bottom of a chasm encircled by towering cliffs, fragrant pines, and deep blue-green waters—to the 2½-km-long (1½-miles-long) S'Abanell beach, which draws the crowds. Small boats can take you from the harbor to Cala de Sant Francesc or the double beach at Santa Cristina between May and September.

DID YOU KNOW?

The artist Marc Chagall loved to vacation in Tossa de Mar and felt inspired by its vivid-blue ocean seascape.

The town's castle of Sant Joan, on a mountain overlooking the town, goes back to the 11th century. The watchtower on the coast was built in the 16th century to protect against Barbary pirates. Most travelers skip the working port of Blanes.

TOSSA DE MAR

The next stop north from Blanes on the coast road—by way of the mass-market resort of Lloret de Mar—is Tossa de Mar (80 km [50 miles] northeast of Barcelona, 41 km [25 miles] south of Girona), christened "Blue Paradise" by painter Marc Chagall, who summered here for four decades. Tossa's walled medieval town and pristine beaches are among Catalonia's best.

Set around a blue buckle of a bay, Tossa de Mar is a symphony in two parts: the Vila Vella, or Old Town—a knotted warren of steep, narrow, cobblestone streets with many restored buildings (some dating back to the 14th century)—and the Vila Nova, or New Town. The former is encased in medieval walls and towers, but the New Town is open to the sea and is itself a lovely district threaded by 18th-century lanes. Girdling the Old Town, on the Cap de Tossa promontory that juts out into the sea, the 12th-century walls and towers at water's edge are a local pride and joy, the only example of a fortified medieval town on the entire Catalan coast.

Ava Gardner filmed the 1951 British drama *Pandora and the Flying Dutchman* here (a statue dedicated to her stands on a terrace on the medieval walls). Things may have changed since those days, but this beautiful village retains much of the unspoiled magic of its past. The primary beach at Tossa de Mar is the Platja Gran (Big Beach) in front of the town beneath the walls, and just next to it is Mar Menuda (Little Sea), where the small, colorfully painted fishing boats—maybe the same ones that caught your dinner—pull up onto the beach.

The main bus station (the local tourist office is here) is on Plaça de les Nacions Sense Estat. Take Avinguda Ferran and Avinguda Costa Brava to head down the slope to the waterfront and the Old Town, which you enter via the Torre de les Hores, and head to the Vila Vella's heart—the Gothic church of Sant Vicenç—for a journey back in time to the Middle Ages.

WHERE TO EAT AND STAY

$$$ CATALAN ✕ **La Cuina de Can Simon.** Elegantly rustic, this restaurant right beside Tossa del Mar's medieval walls serves a combination of classical Catalan cuisine with up-to-date innovative touches. The menu changes with the season; two tasting menus (€68 and €98) provide more than enough to sample. The service is top-shelf, from the welcoming tapa with a glass of cava to the little pastries accompanying coffee. *Average main: €20* ✉ *Carrer del Portal 24* ☎ *972/341269* ⏲ *Closed Mon. and Tues., Nov. 7–26, last 2 wks of Jan., and Oct.–May. No dinner Sun.*

$ HOTEL **Hotel Capri.** The hotel is on the beach, in hailing distance of the old quarter in the medieval fortress, and proprietor Maria-Eugènia Serrat, a native Tossan, lavishes warm personal attention on every guest. **Pros:** family-friendly; perfect location; good value. **Cons:** rooms a little small;

8

minimal amenities; no private parking. *Rooms from: €93 ✉ Passeig del Mar 17 ☎ 972/340358 ⊕ www.hotelcapritossa.com 22 rooms ⊙ Closed Nov.–Mar. Breakfast.*

$$ HOTEL Fodor's Choice ★ **Hotel Diana.** Built in 1906 by architect Antoni Falguera, this Art Nouveau gem sits on the square in the heart of the old town, steps from the beach. **Pros:** attentive service; ideal location. **Cons:** minimal amenities; room rates unpredictable. *Rooms from: €165 ✉ Pl. de Espanya 6 ☎ 972/341886 ⊕ www.hotelesdante.com 20 rooms, 1 suite ⊙ Closed Nov.–Mar. Breakfast.*

SANT FELIU DE GUIXOLS

The little fishing port of Sant Feliu de Guixols, 23 km (15 miles) north of Tossa de Mar, is set in a small bay; handsome Moderniste mansions line the seafront promenade, recalling a time when the cork industry made this one of the wealthier towns on the coast. In front of them, a long crescent beach of fine white sand leads around to the fishing harbor at its north end. Behind the promenade, a well-preserved old quarter of narrow streets and squares leads to a 10th-century gateway with horseshoe arches (all that remains of a pre-Romanesque monastery); nearby, a church still stands that combines Romanesque, Gothic, and baroque styles. To get here, take the C65 highway from Tossa del Mar—though adventurous souls might prefer the harrowing hairpin curves of the G1682 coastal corniche.

WHERE TO EAT AND STAY

$ CATALAN **Can Segura.** Half a block in from the beach at Sant Feliu de Guixols, this restaurant serves home-cooked seafood and upland specialties; the *pimientos de piquillos rellenos de brandada* (sweet red peppers stuffed with codfish mousse) are first-rate, as are the rice dishes and the *escudella*. The dining room is always full, with customers waiting their turn in the street, but the staff is good at finding spots at the jovially long communal tables. Lunch menus at €11, €14, and €16 are a bargain. There are very basic rooms (doubles at €80, without breakfast) available for overnight sojourns. *Average main: €11 ✉ Carrer de Sant Pere 11, Sant Feliu de Guixols ☎ 972/321009 ⊙ Closed Nov.–June (except New Year's Eve weekend) No meals.*

$$$ CATALAN Fodor's Choice ★ **El Dorado.** Lluis Cruañes, who once owned superb Catalan restaurants in Barcelona and New York, returns to his roots in Sant Feliu. With his daughter Suita running the dining room and Iván Álvarez as chef, this smartly designed restaurant with contemporary lines, a block back from the beach, serves tasty dishes from *llom de tonyina a la plancha amb tomàquets agridolços, cebas i chíps d'escarchofa* (grilled tuna with pickled tomato, baby onions, and artichoke chips) to *llobarro rostít amb emulsió de cítrics i espàrrecs trigueros* (roast sea bass with a citric emulsion and wild asparagus), all cooked to perfection. Try the *patates braves* (new potatoes in *allioli* [garlic mayonnaise] and hot sauce). *Average main: €20 ✉ Rambla Vidal 19, Sant Feliu de Guixols ☎ 972/821414 ⊙ Closed Tues. No lunch Oct.–Easter.*

$$$ CATALAN **Villa Mas.** This Moderniste villa on the coast road from Sant Feliu to S'Agaró, with a lovely turn-of-the-20th-century zinc bar, serves up typical Catalan and seasonal Mediterranean dishes like *arròs a la cassola* (deep-dish rice) with shrimp brought fresh off the boats in Palamos, just up the coast. The terrace is a popular and shady spot just across the road from the beach. *Average main: €25 Passeig de Sant Pol 95 972/822526 Closed Mon. and mid-Dec.–mid-Jan. No dinner Tues.–Thurs. and Sun. Oct.–Mar.*

$ HOTEL **Hostal del Sol.** Once the summer home of a wealthy family, this Moderniste hotel has a grand stone stairway and medieval-style tower, as well as a garden and a lawn where you can take your ease by the pool. **Pros:** family-friendly; good value. **Cons:** bathrooms a bit claustrophobic; far from the beach; on a busy road. *Rooms from: €98 Ctra. a Palamós 194, Sant Feliu de Guixols 972/320193 www.hostaldelsol.cat/en 41 rooms Breakfast.*

S'AGARÓ

An elegant gated community on a rocky point at the north end of the cove, S'Agaró is 3 km (2 miles) north of Sant Feliu. The 30-minute walk along the **sea wall** from Hostal de La Gavina to Sa Conca Beach is a delight. Likewise, the one-hour hike from Sant Pol Beach over to Sant Feliu de Guixols for lunch and back offers a superb view of the Costa Brava at its best.

WHERE TO EAT AND STAY

$$$$ HOTEL Fodor's Choice ★ **L'Hostal de la Gavina.** Orson Welles, who used to spend weeks at a time here, called this the finest resort hotel in Spain. **Pros:** in a gated community; impeccable service and amenities; sea views. **Cons:** hard on the budget *and* habit-forming. *Rooms from: €410 Pl. de la Rosaleda s/n, S'Agaró 972/321100 www.lagavina.com 51 rooms, 23 suites Closed Nov.–Easter Breakfast.*

CALELLA DE PALAFRUGELL AND AROUND

Up the coast from S'Agaró, the C31 brings you to Palafrugell and Begur; to the east are some of the prettiest, least developed inlets of the Costa Brava. One road leads to **Llafranc,** a small port with waterfront hotels and restaurants, and forks right to the fishing village of **Calella de Palafrugell,** known for its July habaneras festival. (The *habanera* is a form of Cuban dance music brought to Europe by Catalan sailors in the late 19th century; it still enjoys a nostalgic cachet here.) Just south is the panoramic promontory of **Cap Roig,** with views of the barren Formigues Isles.

North along the coast lie **Tamariu, Aiguablava, Fornell, Platja Fonda,** and (around the point at Cap de Begur) **Sa Tuna** and **Aiguafreda.** There's not much to do in any of these hideaways (only Llafranc has a long enough stretch of seafront to accommodate a sandy beach), but you can luxuriate in the wonderful views and the soothing quiet.

WHERE TO EAT AND STAY

$$$ CATALAN Fodor's Choice ★ **Pa i Raïm.** "Bread and Grapes" in Catalan, this excellent restaurant in Josep Pla's ancestral family home in Palafrugell has one rustic dining room as well as another in a glassed-in winter garden. In summer the leafy terrace is the place to be. The menu ranges from traditional country cuisine to more streamlined contemporary fare such as strawberry gazpacho. The *canelón crujiente de verduritas y setas* (crisped cannelloni with young vegetables and wild mushrooms) and the prawn tempura with soy sauce emulsion are two standouts. *Average main: €18 Torres i Jonama 56, Palafrugell 972/304572 www.pairaim.com Closed Mon. and mid-Dec.–early Jan. No dinner Sun.; no lunch Mon. and Tues. July and Aug.*

$$$$ B&B/INN FAMILY **El Far Hotel-Restaurant.** Rooms in this 17th-century hermitage attached to a 15th-century watchtower have original vaulted ceilings, hardwood floors, and interiors accented with floral prints. **Pros:** friendly service; graceful architecture; spectacular views. **Cons:** longish drive from the beach; a bit pricy for the amenities. *Rooms from: €255 Muntanya de San Sebastia, Carrer Uruguai s/n, Llafranc–Palafrugell 972/301639 www.elfar.net 8 rooms, 1 suite Closed Jan. Breakfast.*

BEGUR AND AROUND

From Begur, you can go east through the calas or take the inland route past the rose-color stone houses and ramparts of the restored medieval town of **Pals.** Nearby **Peratallada** is another medieval fortified town with a castle, tower, palace, and well-preserved walls. North of Pals there are signs for **Ullastret,** an Iberian village dating from the 5th century BC.

Empúries. The Greco-Roman ruins here are Catalonia's most important archaeological site. This port is one of the most monumental ancient engineering feats on the Iberian Peninsula. As the Greeks' original point of arrival in Spain, Empúries was also where the Olympic Flame entered Spain for Barcelona's 1992 Olympic Games.

WHERE TO EAT AND STAY

$$$ CATALAN **Restaurant Ibèric.** This excellent pocket of authentic Costa Brava tastes and aromas serves everything from snails to woodcock in season. Wild mushrooms scrambled with eggs or stewed with hare are specialties, as are complex and earthy red wines made by enologist Jordi Oliver of the Oliver Conti vineyard in the Upper Empordà's village of Capmany. The terrace is ideal for leisurely dining. *Average main: €19 Carrer Valls 11, Ullastret 972/757108 Closed Mon., and Tues.–Wed. Nov.–Mar. No dinner Sun. Nov.–Mar.*

$$$$ HOTEL **El Convent Hotel and Restaurant.** Built in 1730, this elegant former convent is a 10-minute walk to the beach at the Cala Sa Riera—the quietest and prettiest inlet north of Begur. **Pros:** outstanding architecture; quiet and private. **Cons:** minimum stay required in summer. *Rooms from: €235 Ctra. de la Platja del Racó 2, Begur 972/623091 www.conventbegur.com 24 rooms, 1 suite Breakfast.*

$$$$ HOTEL FAMILY Fodor's Choice ★ **Hotel Aigua Blava.** What began as a small hostal in the 1920s is now a sprawling luxury hotel, run by the fourth generation of the same family. **Pros:** impeccable service; gardens and pleasant patios at every turn; private playground. **Cons:** lots of stairs to negotiate; no beach in the inlet. *Rooms from: €209 Platja de Fornells s/n, Begur 972/624562 www.aiguablava.com 66 rooms, 19 suites Breakfast.*

$$$ HOTEL **Parador de Aiguablava.** The vista from this modern white parador, 9 km (6 miles) north of Calella de Palafrugell, is the classic postcard Costa Brava: the rounded Cala d'Aiguablava wraps around the shimmering blue Mediterranean. **Pros:** magnificent views; good-size rooms. **Cons:** building itself lacks character; minimum stays required in summer; service can be perfunctory. *Rooms from: €188 Playa d'Aiguablava s/n, Begur 972/622162 www.parador.es 68 rooms, 10 suites Closed Jan. 6–Feb. 20 No meals.*

CADAQUÈS AND AROUND

Spain's easternmost town, Cadaqués, still has the whitewashed charm that transformed this fishing village into an international artists' haunt in the early 20th century. The Marítim bar is the central hangout both day and night; after dark, you might also enjoy the Jardí, across the square. Salvador Dalí's house, now a museum, is at Port Lligat, a 15-minute walk north of town.

EXPLORING

Cap de Creus. North of Cadaqués, Spain's easternmost point is a fundamental pilgrimage, if only for the symbolic geographical rush. The hike out to the lighthouse—through rosemary, thyme, and the salt air of the Mediterranean—is unforgettable. The Pyrenees officially end (or rise) here. New Year's Day finds mobs of revelers awaiting the first emergence of the "new" sun from the Mediterranean. Gaze down at heart-pounding views of the craggy coast and crashing waves with a warm mug of coffee in hand or fine fare on the table at **Bar Restaurant Cap de Creus**, which sits on a rocky crag above the Cap de Creus.

8

Casa Museu Salvador Dalí. This was Dalí's summerhouse and a site long associated with the artist's notorious frolics with everyone from poets Federico García Lorca and Paul Eluard to filmmaker Luis Buñuel. Filled with bits of the Surrealist's daily life, it's an important point in the "Dalí triangle," completed by the castle at Púbol and the Museu Dalí in Figueres. You can get here by a 3-km (2-mile) walk north along the beach from Cadaqués. Only small groups of visitors are admitted at any given time; reservations are required. *Port Lligat s/n 972/251015 www.salvador-dali.org €11 Mid-June–mid-Sept., daily 9:30–9; early Feb.–mid-June and mid-Sept.–early Jan., Tues.–Sun. 10:30–6.*

Castillo Púbol. Dalí's former home is now the resting place of Gala, his perennial model and mate. It's a chance to wander through another Dalí-esque landscape: lush gardens, fountains decorated with masks of Richard Wagner (the couple's favorite composer), and distinctive elephants with giraffe's legs and claw feet. Two lions and a giraffe stand guard near Gala's tomb. *Pl. Gala Dalí s/n, on Rte. 255,*

The popular harbor of Cadaqués

about 15 km (9 miles) east of A7 toward La Bisbal, Púbol-la Pera ☎ *972/488655* 🎫 *€8* ⏲ *Mid-June–mid-Sept., daily 10–8; mid-Mar.–mid-June and mid-Sept.–early Nov., Tues.–Sun. 10–6; early Nov.–Dec., Tues.–Sun. 10–5.*

Fodor's Choice ★ **Sant Pere de Rodes.** The monastery of Sant Pere de Rodes, 7 km (4½ miles) by car (plus a 20-minute walk) above the pretty fishing village El Port de la Selva, is one of the most spectacular sites on the Costa Brava. Built in the 10th and 11th centuries by Benedictine monks—and sacked and plundered repeatedly since—this Romanesque monolith, recently restored, commands a breathtaking panorama of the Pyrenees, the Empordà plain, the sweeping curve of the Bay of Roses, and Cap de Creus. (Topping off the grand trek across the Pyrenees, Cap de Creus is a spectacular six-hour walk from here on the well-marked GR11 trail.) One-hour guided visits to the monastery in English are available (€2.95). **■TIP→ In July and August, the monastery is the setting for the annual Festival Sant Pere (🌐 www.festivalsantpere.com ☎ 972/194233, 610/310073), drawing top-tier classical musicians from all over the world.** The website publishes the calendar of events (in Spanish); phone for reservations—and to book a postconcert dinner in the monastery's refectory-style restaurant. ✉ *Camí del Monestir s/n, El Porte de la Selva* ☎ *972/387559* 🌐 *www.mhcat.cat* 🎫 *€4.50* ⏲ *June–Sept., Tues.–Sun. 10–8; Oct.–May, Tues.–Sun. 10–5:30.*

WHERE TO EAT AND STAY

$$$$ SEAFOOD Fodor's Choice ★ **Casa Anita.** Simple, fresh, and generous dishes are the draw at this informal little eatery—an institution in Cadaqués for nearly half a century. It sits on the street that leads to Port Lligat and Dalí's house. Tables are shared, and there is no menu; the staff recites the offerings of the day, which might include wonderful local prawns and sardines a la plancha, mussels, and sea bass. There's also a fine selection of inexpensive regional wines. The walls are plastered with pictures of the celebrities who have made the pilgrimage here, including Dalí himself. Call for reservations, or come early and wait for a table. *Average main: €25 Carrer Miquel Rosset 16 972/258471 Reservations essential Closed mid-Oct.–Nov. and Mon. Sept.–May. No lunch Mon. in summer.*

$ HOTEL **Hotel Playa Sol.** Open for more than 50 years, this hotel sits in the cove of Es Pianc, just a five-minute walk from the village center. **Pros:** attentive, friendly service; family-friendly; great views. **Cons:** redecorated rooms in relentless white could use a splash of color; best rooms, with balcony and sea views, are hard to book. *Rooms from: €98 Riba Es Pianc 3 972/258100 www.playasol.com 48 rooms Closed mid-Nov.–mid-Feb. Breakfast.*

SOUTHERN CATALONIA AND AROUND VALENCIA

South of the Costa Brava, the time machine takes you back some 20 centuries. Tarragona, the principal town of southern Catalonia, was in Roman times one of the finest and most important outposts of the empire. Its wine was already famous and its population was the first *gens togata* (literally, the toga-clad people) in Spain, which conferred on them equality with the citizens of Rome. Roman remains, chief among them the Circus Maximus, bear witness to Tarragona's grandeur, and to this the Middle Ages added wonderful city walls and citadels.

Farther south lies Valencia, Spain's third-largest city and the capital of its region and province, equidistant from Barcelona and Madrid. If you have time for a day trip (or you decide to stay in the beach town of El Saler), make your way to the Albufera, a scenic coastal wetland teeming with native wildlife, especially migratory birds.

TARRAGONA

98 km (61 miles) southwest of Barcelona, 251 km (155 miles) northeast of Valencia.

With its vast Roman remains, walls, and fortifications and its medieval Christian monuments, Tarragona has been designated a World Heritage Site. The city today is a vibrant center of culture and arts, a busy fishing and shipping port, and a natural jumping-off point for the towns and pristine beaches of the Costa Daurada, 216 km (134 miles) of coastline north of the Costa del Azahar.

Though modern Tarragona is very much an industrial and commercial city, it has preserved its heritage superbly. Stroll along the town's

CLOSE UP

En Route: Museu Pau Casals

Museu Pau Casals. The family house of renowned cellist Pau Casals (1876–1973) is on the beach at Sant Salvador, just east of the town of El Vendrell. Casals, who left Spain in self-imposed exile after Franco seized power in 1939, left a museum of his possessions here, including several of his cellos, original music manuscripts, paintings and sculptures. Other exhibits describe the Casals campaign for world peace (Pau, in Catalan, is both the name Paul and the word for peace), his speech and performance at the inauguration of the United Nations in 1958 (at the age of 82), and his haunting interpretation of *El Cant dels Ocells* (*The Song of the Birds*), his homage to his native Catalonia. Across the street, the Auditori Pau Casals holds frequent concerts and, in July and August, a classical music festival. ✉ *Av. Palfuriana 67* ☎ *977/684276* 🌐 *www.paucasals.org* 🎟 *€6* 🕐 *Mid-June–mid-Sept., Tues.–Sat. 10–2 and 5–9, Sun. 10–2; mid-Sept.–mid-June, Tues.–Fri. 10–2 and 4–6, Sat. 10–2 and 4–7, Sun. 10–2.*

cliffside perimeter and you'll see why the Romans set up shop here: Tarragona is strategically positioned at the center of a broad, open bay, with an unobstructed view of the sea. As capital of the Roman province of Hispania Tarraconensis (from 218 BC), Tarraco, as it was then called, formed the empire's principal stronghold in Spain. St. Paul preached here in AD 58, and Tarragona became the seat of the Christian church in Spain until it was superseded by Toledo in the 11th century.

Entering the city from Barcelona, you'll pass the **Triumphal Arch of Berà,** dating from the 3rd century BC, 19 km (12 miles) north of Tarragona; and from the Lleida (Lérida) autopista, you can see the 1st-century **Roman aqueduct** that helped carry fresh water 32 km (19 miles) from the Gaià River. Tarragona is divided clearly into old and new by Rambla Vella; the Old Town and most of the Roman remains are to the north, while modern Tarragona spreads out to the south. You could start your visit at acacia-lined Rambla Nova, at the end of which is a balcony overlooking the sea, the **Balcó del Mediterràni.** Then walk uphill along Passeig de les Palmeres; below it is the ancient amphitheater, the curve of which is echoed in the modern, semicircular Imperial Tarraco hotel on the promenade.

GETTING HERE AND AROUND

Tarragona is well connected by train: there are half-hourly express trains from Barcelona (1 hour and 20 minutes: €7.50) and regular train service from other major cities, including Madrid.

The bus trip from Barcelona to Tarragona is easy; 7 to 10 buses leave Barcelona's Estación Vilanova-Norte every day. Connections between Tarragona and Valencia are frequent. There are also bus connections with the main Andalusian cities, plus Alicante, Madrid, and Valencia.

The €18 Tarragona Card, valid for two days, gives free entry to all the city's museums and historical sites, free rides on municipal buses, and discounts at more than 100 shops, restaurants, and bars. It's sold at the main tourist office and at most hotels.

Tarragona's cathedral is a mix of Romanesque and Gothic styles.

Tours of the cathedral and archaeological sites are conducted by the tourist office, located just below the cathedral.

ESSENTIALS

Visitor Information Tarragona ✉ *Carrer Major 39* ☎ *977/250795* 🌐 *www.tarragonaturisme.cat/en.*

EXPLORING

Amphitheater. Tarragona—the Emperor Augustus's favorite winter resort—had arguably the finest amphitheater in Roman Iberia. The remains of the amphitheater, built in the 2nd century AD for gladiatorial and other contests, have a spectacular view of the sea. You're free to wander through the access tunnels and along the tiers of seats. In the center of the theater are the remains of two superimposed churches, the earlier of which was a Visigothic basilica built to mark the bloody martyrdom of St. Fructuós and his deacons in AD 259. **■ TIP→ €11.05 buys a combination ticket card valid for all Tarragona archeological museums and sites.** ✉ *Parc de l'Amphiteatre Roma s/n* ☎ *977/242579, 977/242220* 🎫 *€3.30* ⏲ *Tues.–Sat. 10–7 (June–Sept. until 9), Sun. 10–3.*

Casa Castellarnau. Now an art and historical museum, this Gothic *palauet* (town house) built by Tarragona nobility in the 18th century includes stunning furnishings from the 18th and 19th centuries. The last member of the Castellarnau family vacated the house in 1954. ✉ *Carrer dels Cavallers 14* ☎ *977/242220* 🎫 *€3.30, €11.05 combination ticket with Circus Maximus and Praetorium* ⏲ *Tues.–Sun. 10–3.*

Catedral. Built between the 12th and 14th centuries on the site of a Roman temple and a mosque, this cathedral shows the transition from Romanesque to Gothic style. The initial rounded placidity of the Romanesque apse gave way to the spiky restlessness of the Gothic; the result is somewhat confusing. If no mass is in progress, enter the cathedral through the cloister, which houses the cathedral's collection of artistic and religious treasures. The main attraction here is the 15th-century Gothic alabaster altarpiece of St. Tecla by Pere Joan, a richly detailed depiction of the life of Tarragona's patron saint. Converted by St. Paul and subsequently persecuted by local pagans, St. Tecla was repeatedly saved from demise through divine intervention. ✉ *Pl. de la Seu s/n* ☎ *977/226935, 977/238685* 🎫 *€5* 🕒 *Weekdays 10–8, Sat. 10–7 (Apr.–Oct. until 7:30), Sun. for mass only.*

Circus Maximus. Students have excavated the vaults of the 1st-century AD Roman arena, near the amphitheater. The plans just inside the gate show that the vaults now visible formed only a small corner of a vast space (350 yards long), where 23,000 spectators gathered to watch chariot races. As medieval Tarragona grew, the city gradually engulfed the circus. ✉ *Pl. del Rei, Rambla Vella s/n* ☎ *977/251515* 🎫 *€3.30, €11.05 combination ticket with Casa Castellarnau and Praetorium* 🕒 *Apr.–Sept., Mon.–Sat. 10–9, Sun. 9–3; Oct.–Mar., Tues.–Sat. 10–7, Sun. 10–3.*

El Serrallo. The always entertaining fishing quarter and harbor are below the city near the bus station and the mouth of the Francolí River. Attending the afternoon fish auction is a golden opportunity to see how choice seafood starts its journey toward your table in Barcelona or Tarragona. Restaurants in the port, like Manolo (✉ *Carrer Gravina 61* ☎ *977/223484*), are excellent choices for no-frills fresh fish in a rollicking environment.

Museu Nacional Arqueològic de Tarragona. A 1960s neoclassical building contains this museum housing the most significant collection of Roman artifacts in Catalonia. Among the items are Roman statuary and domestic fittings such as keys, bells, and belt buckles. The beautiful mosaics include a head of Medusa, famous for its piercing stare. Don't miss the video on Tarragona's history. ✉ *Pl. del Rei 5* ☎ *977/236209* 🎫 *€2.40 combined entry ticket with the Necrópolis i Museu Paleocristìa* 🕒 *June–Sept., Tues.–Sat. 9:30–8:30, Sun. 10–2; Oct.–May, Tues.–Sat. 9:30–6, Sun. 10–2.*

Passeig Arqueològic. A 1.5-km (1-mile) circular path skirting the surviving section of the 3rd-century-BC Ibero-Roman ramparts, this walkway was built on even earlier walls of giant rocks. On the other side of the path is a glacis, a fortification added by English military engineers in 1707 during the War of the Spanish Succession. Look for the rusted bronze of Romulus and Remus. ✉ *Access from Via de l'Imperi Romà.*

Praetorium. This towering building was Augustus's town house, and is reputed to be the birthplace of Pontius Pilate. Its Gothic appearance is the result of extensive alterations in the Middle Ages, when it housed the kings of Catalonia and Aragón during their visits to Tarragona. The Praetorium is now the city's **Museu d'Història** (History Museum), with plans showing the evolution of the city. The museum's highlight

CLOSE UP

Reus: Birthplace of Modernisme

No city matches Barcelona for the sheer density of its Modernisme, but it all began in **Reus** (13 km [8 miles] northwest of Tarragona), where Antoni Gaudí was born and where his contemporary, Lluís Domènech i Montaner—lesser known but in some ways the more important architect—lived and worked for much of his early career. The oldest part of the city—defined by a ring of streets called *ravals*, where the medieval walls once stood—has narrow streets and promenades with many of Reus's smartest shops, boutiques, and coffeehouses. Inside the ring, and along the nearby Carrer de Sant Joan, are some 20 of the stately homes by Domènech, Pere Caselles, and Joan Rubió that make Reus a must for fans of the Moderniste movement.

Gaudí Centre. In this small museum showcasing the life and work of the city's most illustrious son, there are copies of the models Gaudí made for his major works and a replica of his studio. His original notebook—with English translations—is filled with his thoughts on structure and ornamentation, complaints about clients, and calculations of cost-and-return on his projects. A pleasant café on the third floor overlooks the main square of the old city and the bell tower of the Church of Sant Pere. The Centre also houses the **Tourist Office**; pick up information here about visits to two of Domènech's most important buildings: the Casa Navàs (by appointment) and the Institut Pere Mata (€5). ✉ *Pl. del Mercadal 3, Reus* ☎ *977/010670* 🌐 *www.gaudicentre.cat/en* 🎟 *€7* 🕒 *Early Jan.–mid-June and mid-Sept.–Dec., Mon.–Sat. 10–2 and 4–7, Sun. 11–2; mid-June–mid-Sept., Mon.–Sat. 10–8, Sun. 11–2.*

Getting Here An express bus service operates some 30 daily buses between Tarragona (main bus station) and Reus (Avenida Jaume I); the trip takes about 30 minutes each way. There are five daily buses between Barcelona and Reus (only two on Saturday one on Sunday), and regular train service connects Reus with Tarragona and other Catalonian and Andalusian destinations.

8

is the **Hippolytus Sarcophagus,** which bears a bas-relief depicting the legend of Hippolytus and Fraeda. You can access the remains of the Circus Maximus from the Praetorium. ✉ *Pl. del Rei* ☎ *977/221736, 977/242220* 🎟 *€3.30, €11.05 combination ticket with Casa Castellarnau and Circus Maximus* 🕒 *May.–Sept., Tues.–Sat. 10–9, Sun. 10–3; Oct.–Apr., Tues.–Sat. 10–7, Sun. 10–3.*

WHERE TO EAT AND STAY

$$$ CATALAN ✕ **Les Coques.** If you have time for only one meal in the city, take it at this elegant little restaurant in the heart of historic Tarragona. The menu is bursting with both mountain and Mediterranean fare. Start off with the *canelons d'aubergínia amb ànec* (eggplant and duck cannelloni); seafood fans should try the *tronc de lluç al forn amb patates* (oven-baked hake with potatoes). The prix fixe lunch at €18 is a bargain. [$] *Average main: €24* ✉ *Carrer Sant Llorenç 15* ☎ *977/228300* 🕒 *Closed Sun.*

$ CATALAN Fodor's Choice ★ **Les Voltes.** Built into the vaults of the Roman Circus Maximus, this out-of-the-way spot serves a hearty cuisine. You'll find Tarragona specialties, mainly fish dishes, as well as international recipes, with *calçots* (spring onions, grilled over a charcoal fire) in winter. (For the *calçotadas*, you need to reserve a day—preferably two—in advance.) *Average main: €11 Carrer Trinquet Vell 12 977/230651 www.restaurantlesvoltes.cat No dinner Sun.; no lunch Mon. Oct.–Mar.*

$ HOTEL **Imperial Tarraco.** Large and white, this half-moon-shape hotel has a superb position overlooking the Mediterranean. **Pros:** facing the Mediterrranean and overlooking the fishing port and the Roman amphitheater. **Cons:** on a very busy intersection with heavy traffic. *Rooms from: €85 Passeig Palmeres s/n 977/233040 www.hotelhusaimperialtarraco.com 151 rooms, 19 suites No meals.*

$ HOTEL **Plaça de la Font.** The central location and the cute rooms at this budget choice just off the Rambla Vella in the Plaça de la Font make for a comfortable base in downtown Tarragona. **Pros:** easy on the budget; comfortable, charming rooms. **Cons:** rooms are on the small side; rooms with balconies can be noisy on weekends. *Rooms from: €55 Pl. de la Font 26 977/240822 www.hotelpdelafont.com 20 rooms No meals.*

NIGHTLIFE AND THE ARTS

Nightlife in Tarragona takes two forms: older and quieter in the upper city, younger and more raucous down below. There are some lovely rustic bars in the Casc Antic, the upper section of Old Tarragona. Port Esportiu, a pleasure-boat harbor separate from the working port, has another row of dining and dancing establishments; young people flock here on weekends and summer nights.

Café L'Antiquari. For a dose of culture with your cocktail, this laid-back bar hosts readings, art exhibits, and occasional screenings of classic or contemporary movies. *Carrer Santa Anna 3 977/241843.*

Teatre Metropol. This is Tarragona's center for music, dance, theater, and cultural events ranging from *castellers* (human-castle formations, usually performed in August and September), to folk dances. *Rambla Nova 46 977/244795.*

SHOPPING

Carrer Major. You have to haggle for bargains, but Carrer Major has some exciting antiques stores. They're worth a thorough rummage, as the gems tend to be hidden. *Carrer Major.*

VALENCIA

351 km (210 miles) southwest of Barcelona, 357 km (214 miles) southeast of Madrid.

Valencia is a proud city. During the Civil War, it was the last seat of the Republican Loyalist government (1935–36), holding out against Franco's National forces until the country fell to 40 years of dictatorship. Today it represents the essence of contemporary Spain—daring design and architecture along with experimental cuisine—but remains

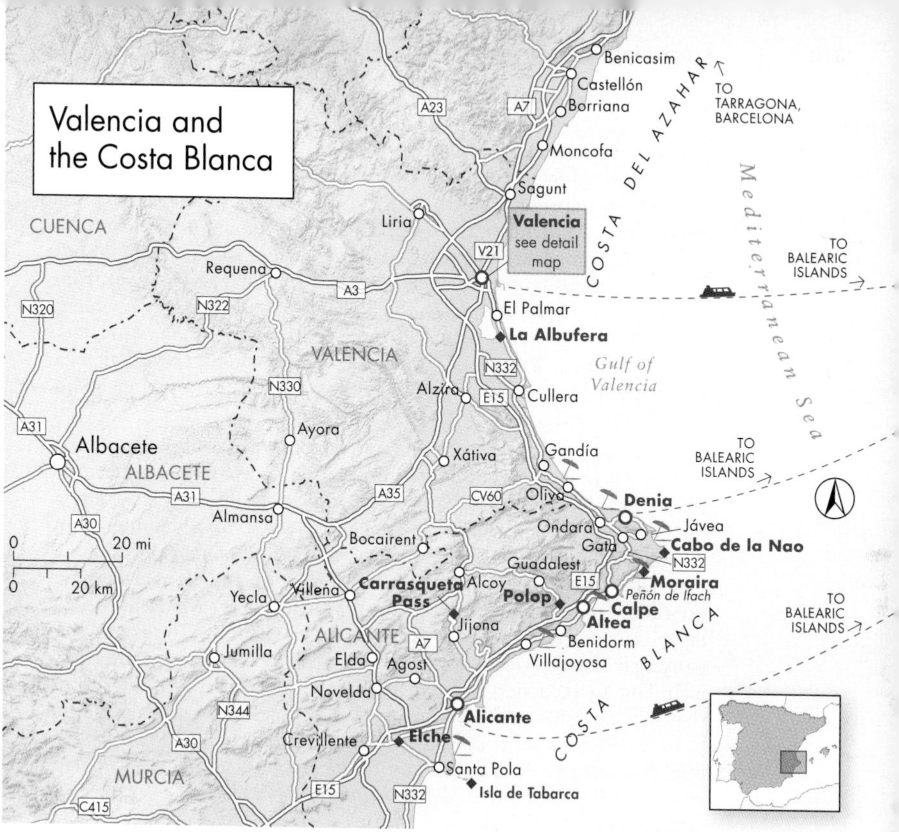

deeply conservative and proud of its traditions. Though it faces the Mediterranean, Valencia's history and geography have been defined most significantly by the River Turia and the fertile floodplain (*huerta*) that surrounds it.

The city has been fiercely contested ever since it was founded by the Greeks. El Cid captured Valencia from the Moors in 1094 and won his strangest victory here in 1099: he died in the battle, but his corpse was strapped into his saddle and so frightened the besieging Moors that it caused their complete defeat. In 1102 his widow, Jimena, was forced to return the city to Moorish rule; Jaume I finally drove them out in 1238. Modern Valencia was best known for its frequent disastrous floods until the River Turia was diverted to the south in the late 1950s. Since then the city has been on a steady course of urban beautification. The lovely bridges that once spanned the Turia look equally graceful spanning a wandering municipal park, and the spectacularly futuristic Ciutat de les Arts i les Ciències (City of Arts and Sciences), most of it designed by Valencia-born architect Santiago Calatrava, has at last created an exciting architectural link between this river town and the Mediterranean. If you're in Valencia, an excursion to Albufera Nature Park is a worthwhile day trip.

GETTING HERE AND AROUND

By car, Valencia is about 3½ hours from Madrid via the A3 motorway, and about the same from Barcelona on the AP7 toll road. Valencia is well connected by bus and train, with regular service to and from cities throughout the country, including nine daily AVE high-speed express trains from Madrid, making the trip in an hour and 40 minutes, and six Euromed express trains daily from Barcelona, taking about three-and-a-half hours. Valencia's bus station is across the river from the old town; take Bus 8 from the Plaza del Ayuntamiento. Frequent buses make the four-hour trip from Madrid and the five-hour trip from Barcelona. Dozens of airlines, large and small, serve Valencia airport, connecting the city with dozens of cities throughout Spain and the rest of Europe.

Once you're here, the city has an efficient network of buses, trams, and metro. For timetables and more information, stop by the local tourist office. The double-decker Valencia Bus Turístic runs daily 9:50 am–9 pm (10:30 to 6:50 in winter) and departs every 30 to 40 minutes from the Plaza de la Reina. It travels through the city, stopping at most of the main sights: a one-day ticket (€17) lets you get on and off at eight main boarding points, including the Institut Valencià d'Art Modern, Museo de Bellas Artes, and the Ciutat de les Arts i les Ciències. The same company also offers a two-hour guided trip (€16) to Albufera Nature Park, including an excursion by boat through the wetlands, departing from the Plaza de la Reina. In summer (and sometimes during the rest of the year) Valencia's tourist office organizes tours of Albufera. You see the port area before continuing south to the lagoon itself, where you can visit a traditional *barraca* (thatch farmhouse).

ESSENTIALS

Bus Station Valencia ✉ *Av. Menendez Pidal 3* ☎ *963/466266.*
Valencia–Estación del Norte ✉ *Xativa 24* ☎ *902/240505, 902/240202.*

Visitor Information Valencia ✉ *Pl. de la Reina 19* ☎ *963/153931* 🌐 *www.visitvalencia.com* ✉ *Pl. del Ayuntamiento s/n* ☎ *963/524908* 🌐 *www.turisvalencia.es.*

Tours Valencia Bus Turístic ✉ *Pl. de la Reina 8* ☎ *963/414400, 699/982514* 🌐 *www.valenciabusturistico.com.*

EXPLORING

Casa Museo José Benlliure. The modern Valencian painter and sculptor José Benlliure is known for his intimate portraits and massive historical and religious paintings, many of which hang in Valencia's Museo de Bellas Artes (Museum of Fine Arts). Here in his elegant house and studio are 50 of his works, including paintings, ceramics, sculptures, and drawings. On display are also works by his son, Pepino, who painted in the small, flower-filled garden in the back of the house, and iconographic sculptures by Benlliure's brother, the well-known sculptor Mariano Benlliure. ✉ *Calle Blanquerías 23* ☎ *963/911662* 🎫 *€2 (free Sun.)* ⏲ *Mid-Mar.–mid-Oct., Tues.–Sat. 10–2 and 3–7, Sun. 10–3; mid-Oct.–mid-Mar., Tues.–Sat. 10–2 and 3–6, Sun. 10–3.*

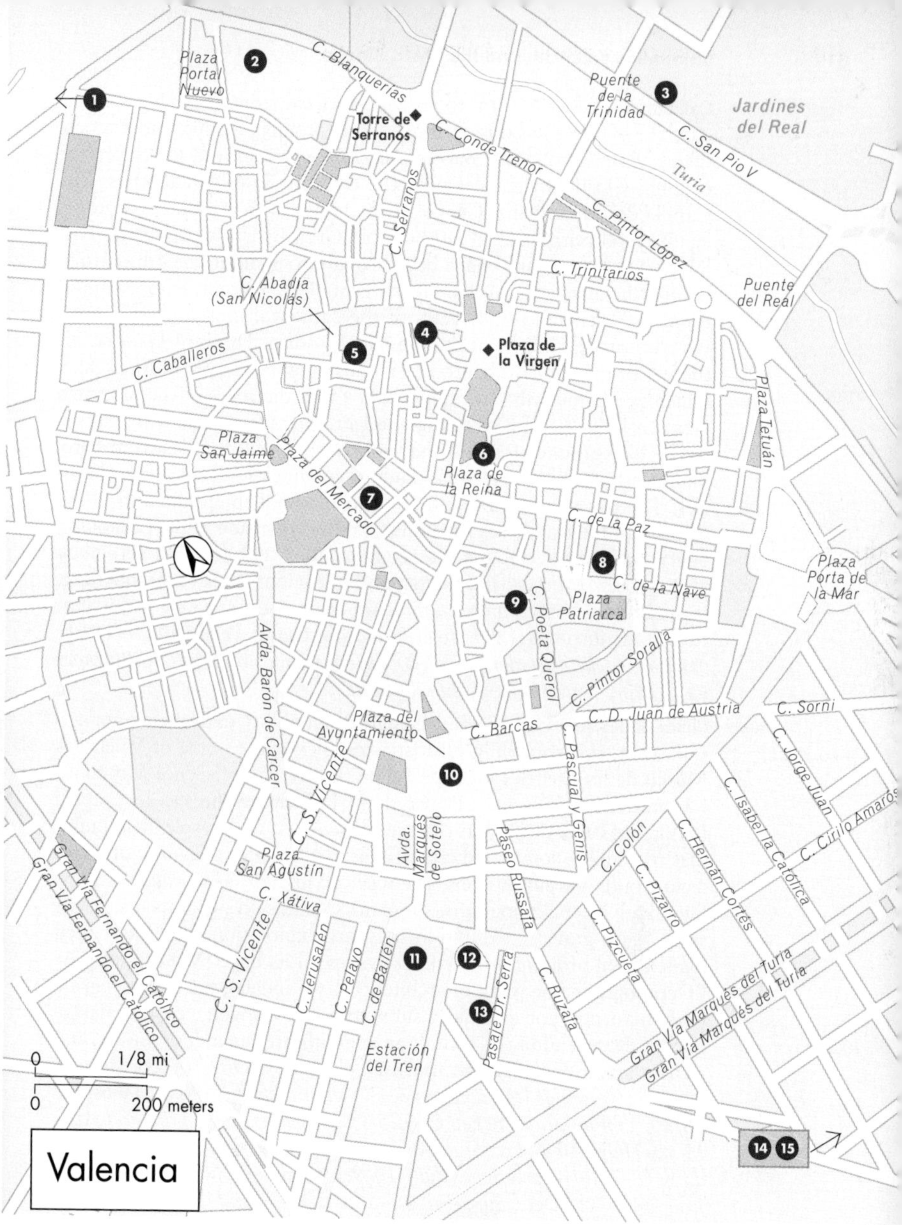

- Casa Museo José Benlliure ... **2**
- Cathedral ... **6**
- Ciutat de les Arts i les Ciències ... **15**
- Estación del Tren ... **11**
- Institut Valencià d'Art Modern (IVAM) ... **1**
- Lonja de la Seda ... **7**
- Museo de Bellas Artes ... **3**
- Museo Taurino ... **13**
- Palacio del Marqués de Dos Aguas (Ceramics Museum) ... **9**
- Palau de la Generalitat ... **4**
- Palau de la Música ... **14**
- Plaza del Ayuntamiento ... **10**
- Plaza de Toros ... **12**
- Real Colegio del Patriarca ... **8**
- San Nicolás ... **5**

Fodor's Choice ★ **Cathedral.** Valencia's 13th- to 15th-century cathedral is the heart of the city. The building has three portals—Romanesque, Gothic, and Rococo. Inside, Renaissance and Baroque marble was removed to restore the original Gothic style, as is now the trend in Spanish churches. The Capilla del Santo Cáliz (Chapel of the Holy Chalice) displays a purple agate vessel purported to be the Holy Grail (Christ's cup at the Last Supper) and thought to have been brought to Spain in the 4th century. Behind the altar you can see the left arm of **St. Vincent,** who was martyred in Valencia in 304. Stars of the cathedral **museum** are Goya's two famous paintings of St. Francis de Borja, Duke of Gandia. To the left of the cathedral entrance is the octagonal tower **El Miguelete,** which you can climb (207 steps) to the top: the roofs of the old town create a kaleidoscope of orange and brown terra-cotta, with the sea in the background. It's said that you can see 300 belfries from here, many with bright-blue cupolas made of ceramic tiles from nearby Manises. The tower was built in 1381 and the final spire added in 1736. **■ TIP→ The Portal de los Apostoles, on the west side of the Cathedral, every Thursday at noon is the scene of the 1,000-year-old ceremony of the Water Tribunal. The judges of this ancient court assemble here, in traditional costume, to hand down their decisions on local irrigation rights disputes.** ✉ *Pl. de la Reina s/n, Ciutat Vella* ☎ *963/918127* 🌐 *www.catedraldevalencia.es* 🎫 *Cathedral and museum €4.50, tower €2* ⏲ *Mon.–Sat. 10–6:30, Sun. 2–6:30.*

FAMILY Fodor's Choice ★ **Ciutat de les Arts i les Ciències.** Designed mainly by native son Santiago Calatrava, this sprawling futuristic complex is the home of Valencia's **Museu de les Ciències Príncipe Felipe** (Prince Philip Science Museum), **L'Hemisfèric** (Hemispheric Planetarium), **L'Oceanogràfic** (Oceanographic Park), and **Palau de les Arts** (Palace of the Arts). With resplendent buildings resembling combs and crustaceans, the Ciutat is a favorite of architecture buffs and curious kids. The Science Museum has soaring platforms filled with lasers, holograms, simulators, hands-on experiments, and a swell "zero gravity" exhibition on space exploration. The eye-shaped planetarium projects 3-D virtual voyages on its huge IMAX screen. At l'Oceanogràfic (the work of architect Felix Candela), the largest marine park in Europe, you can take a submarine ride through a coastal marine habitat. Recent additions include an amphitheater, an indoor theater, and a chamber-music hall. ✉ *Av. Autovía del Saler 7* ☎ *902/100031* 🌐 *www.cac.es* 🎫 *Museu de les Ciències €8, L'Oceanogràfic €27.90, L'Hemisfèric €8.80, combination ticket €36.25* ⏲ *Museum: early Jan.–mid-Apr., Mon.–Thurs. 10–6, Fri.–Sun. 10–7; mid-Apr.–June and early Sept.–Dec., daily 10–7; July–early Sept., daily 10–9. L'Oceanogràfic: early Jan.–mid-June and Oct.–Dec., Sun.–Fri. 10–6, Sat. 10–7; mid- to late June and mid- to late Sept., Sun.–Fri. 10–7, Sat. 10–8; early to mid-July and mid- to late Sept., daily 10–8; mid-July–Aug., daily 10–midnight. L'Hemisfèric: Sun.–Thurs. 10–8, Fri.–Sat. 10–9, with shows hourly from 11.*

Estación del Norte. Designed by Demetrio Ribes Mano in 1917, the train station—declared a National Historical-Artistic monement in 1983—is a splendid Moderniste structure decorated with motifs of Valencia oranges. The tops of the two towers seem to sprout like palm trees. ✉ *Calle Xátiva 24* ☎ *902/240202.*

Valencia's L'Oceanografi (City of Arts and Sciences) has amazing exhibits, as well as an underwater restaurant.

Institut Valèncià d'Art Modern (IVAM). Dedicated to modern and contemporary art, this blocky, uninspired building on the edge of the old city—where the riverbed makes a loop—houses a permanent collection of 20th-century avant-garde painting, European Informalism (including the Spanish artists Antonio Saura, Antoni Tàpies, and Eduardo Chillida), pop art, and photography. ✉ *Carrer de Guillem de Castro 118, Ciutat Vella* ☎ *963/863000* 🌐 *www.ivam.es* 🎟 *€2 (free Sun.)* ⏲ *July and Aug., Tues.–Sun. 10–8.*

Lonja de la Seda (*Silk Exchange*). On the Plaza del Mercado, this 15th-century building is a product of Valencia's golden age, when the city's prosperity as one of the capitals of the Corona de Aragón made it a leading European commercial and artistic center. The Lonja was constructed as an expression of this splendor. Widely regarded as one of Spain's finest civil Gothic buildings, its facade is decorated with ghoulish gargoyles, complemented inside by high vaulting and slender helicoidal (twisted) columns. Opposite the Lonja stands the **Iglesia de los Santos Juanes** (Church of the St. Johns), gutted during the 1936–39 Spanish Civil War, and, next door, the Moderniste **Mercado Central** (Central Market), with its wrought-iron girders and stained-glass windows. The bustling food market (at 8,160 square meters, one of the largest in Europe) is open Monday through Saturday 8 to 2; locals and visitors alike queue up at the 1,247 colorful stalls to shop for fruit, vegetables, meat, fish, and confections. ✉ *Pl. del Mercado s/n, Ciutat Vella* ☎ *963/525478, 926/085143* 🌐 *www.lonjadevalencia.com* 🎟 *€2* ⏲ *Tues.–Sat. 10–2 and 4:30–8:30, Sun. 10–3.*

Fodor's Choice ★ **Museo de Bellas Artes** (*Museum of Fine Arts*). Valencia was a thriving center of artistic activity in the 15th century—one reason that the city's Museum of Fine Arts, with its lovely palm-shaded cloister, is among the best in Spain. To get here, cross the old riverbed by the Puente de la Trinidad (Trinity Bridge) to the north bank; the museum is at the edge of the **Jardines del Real** (Royal Gardens; open daily 8–dusk), with its fountains, rose gardens, tree-lined avenues, and small zoo. The permanent collection of the museum includes many of the finest paintings by Jacomart and Juan Reixach, members of the group known as the Valencian Primitives, as well as work by Hieronymus Bosch—or El Bosco, as they call him here. The ground floor has a number of the brooding, 17th-century Tenebrist masterpieces by Francisco Ribalta and his pupil José Ribera, a Diego Velázquez self-portrait, and a room devoted to Goya. Upstairs, look for Joaquín Sorolla (Gallery 66), the Valencian painter of everyday Spanish life in the 19th century. ✉ *Calle San Pío V 9, Trinitat* ☎ *963/870300* 🌐 *www.museobellasartesvalencia.gva.es* 🎫 *Free* ⏲ *Tues.–Sun. 10–7, Mon. 11–5.*

Palacio del Marqués de Dos Aguas (*Ceramics Museum*). This building near Plaza Patriarca has gone through many changes over the years and now has elements of several architectural styles, including a fascinating baroque alabaster facade. Embellished with carvings of fruits and vegetables, the facade was designed in 1740 by Ignacio Vergara. It centers on the two voluptuous male figures representing the Dos Aguas (Two Waters), a reference to Valencia's two main rivers and the origin of the noble title of the Marqués de Dos Aguas. Since 1954, the palace has housed the **Museo Nacional de Cerámica,** with a magnificent collection of local and artisanal ceramics. Look for the Valencian kitchen on the second floor. ✉ *Calle Poeta Querol 2* ☎ *963/516392* 🌐 *www.mceramica.mcu.es* 🎫 *Palace and museum €3, free Sat. 4–8 and Sun.* ⏲ *Tues.–Sat. 10–2 and 4–8, Sun. 10–2. Night visits July–Aug., Sat. 10–midnight.*

Palau de la Generalitat. On the left side of the Plaza de la Virgen, fronted by orange trees and box hedges, is this elegant facade. The Gothic building was once the home of the Cortes Valencianas (Valencian Parliament), until it was suppressed by Felipe V for supporting the losing side during the 1700–14 War of the Spanish Succession. The two *salones* (reception rooms) in the older of the two towers have superb woodwork on the ceilings. Don't miss the Salon de los Reyes, a long corridor lined with portraits of Valencia's kings through the ages. Call in advance for permission to enter. ✉ *Calle Caballeros 2* ☎ *963/863461* ⏲ *Weekdays 9–2.*

Palau de la Música (*Music Palace*). On one of the nicest stretches of the Turia riverbed is this huge glass vault, Valencia's main concert venue. Supported by 10 arcaded pillars, the dome gives the illusion of a greenhouse, both from the street and from within its sun-filled, tree-landscaped interior. Home of the Orquesta de Valencia, the main hall also hosts touring performers from around the world, including chamber and youth orchestras, opera, and an excellent concert series featuring early, baroque, and classical music. For concert schedules, pick up a Turia guide or one of the local newspapers at any newsstand. To see the building without concert tickets, pop into the **art gallery,** which hosts free changing exhibits. ✉ *Paseo de la Alameda 30* ☎ *963/375020* 🌐 *www.palauvalencia.com* ⏲ *Gallery daily 10–1:30 and 5–9:30.*

Plaza del Ayuntamiento. With the massive baroque facades of the *Ayuntamiento* (City Hall) and the *Correos* (central Post Office) facing each other across the park, this plaza is the hub of city life. City Hall itself houses the municipal tourist office and a museum of paleontology. **TIP→ Pop in just for a moment to marvel at the Post Office, with its magnificent stained-glass cupola and ring of classical columns. They don't build 'em like that any more.** ✉ *Pl. del Ayuntamiento 1* ☎ *963/525478* ⏲ *Ayuntamiento weekdays 8:30–2:30.*

Plaza de Toros. Adjacent to the train station, this bullring is one of the oldest in Spain. The best bullfighters are featured during Las Fallas in March, particularly on March 18 and 19. ✉ *Calle Xátiva 28, Ciutat Vella* ☎ *963/519315*

Museo Taurino (*Bullfighting Museum*). This museum has bullfighting memorabilia, including bull heads and matador swords. ✉ *Pasaje Dr. Serra 10, Ciutat Vella* ☎ *963/883738* 🎟 *€2* ⏲ *Tues.–Sat. 10–6, Sun. and Mon. 10–2.*

Real Colegio del Corpus Christi (*Iglesia del Patriarca*). This seminary, with its church, cloister, and library, is the crown jewel of Valencia's Renaissance architecture and one of the city's finest sites. Founded by San Juan de Ribera in the 16th century, it has a lovely Renaissance patio and an ornate church, and its museum holds works by Juan de Juanes, Francisco Ribalta, and El Greco. ✉ *Calle de la Nave 3* ☎ *963/514176* 🎟 *€1.20* ⏲ *Daily 11–1:30.*

8

San Nicolás. A small plaza contains Valencia's oldest church, once the parish of the Borgia Pope Calixtus III. The first portal you come to, with a tacked-on, Rococo bas-relief of the Virgin Mary with cherubs, hints at what's inside: every inch of the originally Gothic church is covered with exuberant ornamentation. ✉ *Calle Caballeros 35* ☎ *963/913317* 🎟 *Free* ⏲ *Mon. 7:30 am–8 pm, Tues.–Sat. 9:30–11 and 6:30–8 pm, Sun. 10–1.*

WHERE TO EAT

$$$ SEAFOOD

✕ **El Timonel.** Decorated—nay, festooned—with nautical motifs, this restaurant two blocks east of the bullring serves outstanding shellfish. The cooking is simple but makes use of the freshest ingredients; try the grilled *lenguado* (sole) or *lubina* (sea bass). Also top-notch are the eight different kinds of rice dishes, including paella with lobster and arroz a banda, with peeled shrimp, prawns, mussels, and clams. For a sweet finale, try the house special *naranjas a la reina,* oranges spiced with rum and topped with *salsa de fresa* (strawberry sauce). Lunch attracts businesspeople, and dinner brings in a crowd of locals and visitors. $ *Average main: €18* ✉ *Carrer Félix Pizcueta 13, L'Eixample* ☎ *963/526300* 🌐 *www.eltimonel.com.*

$$ SPANISH

✕ **La Pepica.** Locals regard this bustling informal restaurant, on the promenade at the El Cabanyal beach, as the best in town for seafood paella. Founded in 1898, the walls of the establishment are covered with signed pictures of appreciative visitors, from Ernest Hemingway to

King Juan Carlos and the royal family. Try the *arroz marinero* (seafood paella) topped with shrimp and mussels or hearty platters of *calamares* (squid) and *langostinos* (prawns). Save room for the delectable tarts made with fruit in season. $ *Average main: €15* ✉ *Paseo Neptuno 6* ☎ *963/710366* 🌐 *www.lapepica.com* ⏲ *Closed last 2 wks Nov. No dinner Sun, and Mon.–Thurs. Sept.–May.*

$$ SPANISH ✕ **La Riuà.** A favorite with Valencia's well connected and well-to-do since 1982, this family-run restaurant a few steps from the Plaza de la Reina specializes in seafood dishes like *anguilas* (eels) prepared with *all i pebre* (garlic and pepper), *pulpitos guisados* (stewed baby octopus), and traditional paellas. Lunch begins at 2 and not a moment before. The walls are covered with decorative ceramics and the gastronomic awards the restaurant has won over the years. $ *Average main: €13* ✉ *Carrer del Mar 27, bajo* ☎ *963/914571* 🌐 *www.lariua.com* ✍ *Reservations essential* ⏲ *Closed Sun., Easter wk, and last 2 wks Aug. No dinner Mon.*

$$$$ MEDITERRANEAN ✕ **La Sucursal.** This thoroughly modern but comfortable restaurant in the Institut Valencià d'Art Modern is likely to put a serious dent in your budget, but it's unlikely you'll sample venison carpaccio anywhere else or partake of an *arroz caldoso de bogavante* (soupy rice with lobster) any better. All dinner menus are prix fixe, costing €45, €55, or €65. A great choice for lunch is the informal downstairs eatery, on the terrace of the museum, where the €12 prix-fixe lunch gets you a three-course feast. $ *Average main: €45* ✉ *Carrer Guillem de Castro 118, El Carmen* ☎ *963/746665* 🌐 *www.restaurantelasucursal.com* ✍ *Reservations essential.*

WHERE TO STAY

$ B&B/INN Fodor's Choice ★ **Antigua Morellana.** Run by four convivial sisters, this 18th-century town house provides the ultimate no-frills accommodations in the heart of the old city. **Pros:** friendly service; excellent location; complementary tea in the lounge. **Cons:** no parking; soundproofing leaves much to be desired. $ *Rooms from: €50* ✉ *C. En Bou 2, Ciutat Vella* ☎ *963/915773* 🌐 *www.hostalam.com* *18 rooms* *No meals.*

$ HOTEL **Hotel Husa Reina Victoria.** Valencia's grande dame is an excellent choice for traditional atmosphere and good location, just steps from the Plaza del Ayuntamiento. **Pros:** ideal location; walking distance to train station and major sights. **Cons:** soundproofing not up to par; not especially family-oriented. $ *Rooms from: €81* ✉ *Carrer Barcas 4* ☎ *963/520487* 🌐 *www.husareinavictoria.com* *96 rooms* *No meals.*

NIGHTLIFE AND THE ARTS

Valencianos have perfected the art of doing without sleep. The city's nocturnal way of life survives even in summer, when locals disappear on vacation and vie with the hordes of visitors for space on the beach. Nightlife in the old town centers on Barrio del Carmen, a lively web of streets that unfolds north of Plaza del Mercado. Popular bars and pubs dot Calle Caballeros, leading off Plaza de la Virgen; the Plaza del Tossal also has some popular cafés, as does Calle Alta, off Plaza San Jaime.

DID YOU KNOW?

Valencia's Las Fallas festival in March is a fabulous 19-day celebration. *Fallas* means "bonfires," and a highlight of the party is when the larger-than-life papier mâché effigies of various celebrities and political figures are torched to end the festival.

Some of the funkier, newer places are to be found in and around Plaza del Carmen. Across the river in the new town, look for appealing hangouts along Avenida Blasco Ibáñez and on Plaza de Cánovas del Castillo. Out by the sea, Paseo Neptuno and Calle de Eugenia Viñes are lined with loud clubs and bars most active during the summer. The monthly English-language nightlife and culture magazine *2/7 Valencia* is free at tourist offices and various bars and clubs around the city; leisure guides in Spanish include *Hello Valencia* and *La Guía Go.*

Café de la Seu. For quiet after-dinner drinks, try this jazzy, lighthearted bar, with contemporary art and animal-print chairs, open daily from 6. ✉ *Carrer Santo Cáliz 7, Ciutat Vella* ☎ *963/915715* 🌐 *www.cafedelaseu.com.*

Feria de Julio. Valencia's monthlong festival, in July, celebrates theater, film, dance, and music. 🌐 *www.feriadejulio.com.*

Fodor's Choice ★ **Las Fallas.** If you want nonstop nightlife at its frenzied best, come during the climactic days of this festival, March 15–19, when revelers throng the streets and last call at many of the bars and clubs isn't until the wee hours, if at all. 🌐 *www.fallas.com.*

Radio City. The airy, perennially popular, bar–club–performance space Radio City offers eclectic nightly shows featuring music from flamenco to Afro-jazz fusion. ✉ *Carrer Santa Teresa 19, Ciutat Vella* ☎ *963/914151.*

SHOPPING

A few steps from the Cathedral, off the upper end of Calle San Vicente Mártir, the newly restored **Plaza Redonda** (literally "Round Square") is lined with stalls selling all sorts of souvenirs and traditional crafts. Browse here for **ceramics,** and especially for embroidered table linens and children's clothing designed in the intricate Valencian style.

ALBUFERA NATURE PARK

11 km (7 miles) south of Valencia.

GETTING HERE AND AROUND

From Valencia, buses depart from the corner of Sueca and Gran Vía de Germanías every hour (every half hour in summer) daily 7 am to 9 pm.

EXPLORING

Albufera Nature Park. This beautiful freshwater lagoon was named by Moorish poets—*albufera* means "the sun's mirror." Dappled with rice paddies, the park is a nesting site for more than 250 bird species, including herons, terns, egrets, ducks, and gulls. Admission is free, and there are miles of lovely walking and cycling trails. Bird-watching companies offer boat rides all along the Albufera. For maps, guides, and tour arrangements, start your visit at the Park's information center, the Centre d'Interpretació Raco del'Olla in El Palmar. ✉ *Ctra. de El Palmar s/n, El Palmar* ☎ *961/627345* 🌐 *www.albufera.com* ⏲ *Tues.–Sun. 9–2.*

El Palmar. This is the major village in the area, with restaurants specializing in various types of paella. The most traditional kind is made with rabbit or game birds, though seafood is also popular in this region because it's so fresh.

WHERE TO EAT

$$ SPANISH **La Matandeta.** With its white garden walls and rustic interior, this restaurant is a culinary island in the rice paddies. Valencian families come here on Sunday, when many of the city's restaurants are closed. Host-owners Maria Dolores Baixauli and Rafael Gálvez preside over evening meals on the terrace, even as the next generation (Rubén Ruiz Vilanova in the kitchen and Helena Gálvez Baixauli as maître d') begin to contribute new energy. Fish fresh off the boats is grilled over an open fire, and the traditional main dish is the *paella de pato, pollo, y conejo* (rice with duck, chicken, and rabbit). Choose from 50 types of olive oil on the sideboard for your bread or salad. *Average main: €16 Ctra. Alfafar–El Saler (CV1045), Km 4 962/112184 www.lamatandeta.es Closed Mon.*

THE COSTA BLANCA

The stretch of coastline known as the Costa Blanca (White Coast) begins at Dénia, south of Valencia, and stretches down roughly to Torrevieja, below Alicante. It's best known for its magical vacation combo of sand, sea, and sun, and there are some excellent albeit crowded beaches here, as well as more secluded coves and stretches of sand. Alicante itself—with two long beaches, a charming Old Quarter, and mild and sunny weather most of the year—is a favorite destination for visitors from northern Europe.

DÉNIA

Dénia is the port of departure on the Coast Blanca for the ferries to Ibiza, Formentera, and Mallorca—but if you're on your way to or from the islands, you would do well to stay at least a night in the lovely little town in the shadow of a dramatic clifftop fortress. At the very least, spend a few hours wandering in the Baix la Mar, the old fishermen's quarter with its brightly painted houses, and exploring the historic town center.

ESSENTIALS

Visitor Information Dénia *Calle Jorge Juan 7 966/422367 www.denia.net.*

EXPLORING

Castillo de Dénia. Dénia's most interesting architectural attraction is the castle overlooking the town, and the **Palau del Governador** (Governor's Palace) inside. On the site of an 11th-century Moorish fortress, the Renaissance-era palace was built in the 17th century and was later demolished. A major restoration project is underway. The fortress has an interesting archaeological museum as well as the remains of a Renaissance bastion and a Moorish portal with a lovely horseshoe arch. *Calle San Francisco s/n 966/420656 €3 Apr. and May, daily 10–1:30 and 3:30–7; June, daily 10–1:30 and 4–7:30; July and Aug., daily 10–1:30 and 5–8:30; Sept., daily 10–1:30 and 4–8; Oct., daily 10–1 and 3–6:30; Nov.–Mar., daily 10–1 and 3–6.*

FAMILY **Cueva de las Calaveras** (*Cave of the Skulls*). Inland from Dénia, this 400-yard-long cave was named for the 12 Moorish skulls found here when it was discovered in 1768. The cave of stalactites and stalagmites has a dome rising to more than 60 feet and leads to an underground lake. ✉ *Ctra. Benidoleig–Pedreguera, Km 1.5, Benidoleig* ☎ *966/404235* 🌐 *www.cuevadelascalaveras.com* 🎫 *€3.50* ⏲ *June–Oct., daily 9–8; Nov.–May, daily 9–6.*

WHERE TO EAT

$ SEAFOOD ✕ **El Port.** In the old fishermen's quarter just across from the port, this classic dining spot features all kinds of fish fresh off the boats. There are also shellfish dishes and a full range of rice specialties, from *arros negre* (black rice) to a classic *paella marinera* (seafood and rice). The tapas here are ample and excellent. El Port is a favorite with locals, resident expats, and tour groups alike; in summer high season it gets hectic, which can sometimes put a strain on service and consistency. [$] *Average main: €10* ✉ *Esplanada Bellavista 12* ☎ *965/784973* ⏲ *Closed Thurs.*

$$ SEAFOOD ✕ **El Raset.** Across the harbor, this Valencian favorite has been serving traditional cuisine with a modern twist for about 25 years. From a terrace with views of the water you can choose from an array of excellent seafood dishes. House specialties include *arroz en caldero* (rice with monkfish, lobster, or prawns) and *gambas rojas* (local red prawns). A la carte dining can be expensive, but set menus are easier on your wallet. The same owners run a very comfortable and modern hotel three houses down on the same street (⇨ *see Where to Stay*). [$] *Average main: €16* ✉ *C. Bellavista 7* ☎ *965/785040* 🌐 *www.grupoelraset.com.*

$$$ SPANISH Fodor's Choice ★ ✕ **La Seu.** Under co-owners Fede and Diana Cervera and chef Xicu Ramón, this distinguished restaurant in the center of town continues to reinvent and deconstruct traditional Valencian cuisine. The setting is an architectural tour de force: a 16th-century town house transformed into a sunlit modern space with an open kitchen and a three-story-high wall sculpted to resemble a billowing white curtain. The tasting menus, available for lunch or dinner, include a selection of creative tapas—mini-courses, really, that might include a soup and/or a salad—and one rice dish or other main course, giving you a good idea of the chef's repertoire at an unbeatable price. [$] *Average main: €20* ✉ *Calle Loreto 59* ☎ *966/424478* 🌐 *www.laseu.es* ⏲ *Closed Mon. No dinner Sun.*

WHERE TO STAY

For expanded reviews, facilities, and current deals, visit Fodors.com.

$ B&B/INN 🏨 **Art Boutique Hotel Chamarel.** Ask the staff and they'll tell you that *chamarel* means a "mixture of colors," and this hotel, built as a grand family home in 1840, is certainly a genial blend of styles, cultures, periods, and personalities. **Pros:** friendly staff; individual attention; pet-friendly. **Cons:** no pool; not on the beach. [$] *Rooms from: €85* ✉ *Calle Cavallers 13* ☎ *966/435007* 🌐 *www.hotelchamarel.com* 🛏 *10 rooms, 5 suites* 🍽 *Breakfast.*

$ HOTEL Fodor's Choice ★ 🏨 **Hostal Loreto.** Travelers on tight budgets will appreciate this impeccable lodging, on a central pedestrian street in the historic quarter just steps from the Town Hall. **Pros:** great location; good value; broad comfy roof terrace. **Cons:** no elevator; no amenities. [$] *Rooms from:*

Dénia's massive fort overlooks the harbor and provides a dramatic element to the skyline, with the Montgü mountains in the background.

€70 ✉ Calle Loreto 12, Dénia ☎ 966/435419 🌐 www.hostalloreto.com ⇆ 43 rooms 🍴 No meals.

$$$ HOTEL **La Posada del Mar.** A few steps across from the harbor, this hotel in the 13th-century customs house has an inviting rooftop terrace and rooms with views. **Pros:** serene environment; close to center of town. **Cons:** pricey parking; no pool. *$ Rooms from: €180 ✉ Pl. de les Drassanes 2, Dénia ☎ 966/432966 🌐 www.laposadadelmar.com ⇆ 20 rooms, 11 suites 🍴 Breakfast.*

EN ROUTE The Playa del Arenal, a tiny bay cut into the larger one, is worth a visit in summer. You can reach it via the coastal road, CV736, between Dénia and Jávea.

CALPE (CALP)

35 km (22 miles) south of Dénia.

Calpe has an ancient history, as it was chosen by the Phoenicians, Greeks, Romans, and Moors as a strategic point from which to plant their Iberian settlements. The real-estate developers were the latest to descend upon it: much of Calpe today is overbuilt with high-rise resorts and urbanizaciónes (housing estates). But the Old Town is a delightful maze of narrow streets and small squares, archways and cul-de-sacs, houses painted in Mediterranean blue, red, ochre, and sandstone: wherever there's a broad expanse of building wall, you'll likely discover a mural. Calpe is, in short, a delightful place to wander.

ESSENTIALS

Calpe *✉ Pl. del Mosquit s/n ☎ 965/838532 🌐 www.calpe.es.*

EXPLORING

Fish Market. The fishing industry is still very important in Calpe, and every evening the fishing boats return to port with their catch. The subsequent auction at the Fish Market can be watched from the walkway of La Lonja de Calpe. ✉ *Port* ⏲ *Weekdays 4:30–8 pm.*

Mundo Marino. Choose here from a wide range of sailing trips, including cruises up and down the coast. Some of the vessels have glass bottoms, the better to observe the abundant marine life. ✉ *Esplanade Maritime s/n* ☎ *966/423066* 🌐 *www.mundomarino.es.*

Peñón d'Ifach. The landscape of Calpe is dominated by this huge rock more than 1,100 yards long, 1,090 feet high, and joined to the mainland by a narrow isthmus. The area has more than 300 species of plants and 80 species of land and marine birds. A visit to the top is not for the fainthearted; wear shoes with traction for the hike, which includes a trip through a tunnel to the summit. The views reach to Ibiza on a clear day. Check with the local visitor information center (✉ *Centro de Interpretación, C. Isla de Formentera s/n* ☎ *679/195912*) about guided tours for groups.

ALTEA

11 km (7 miles) southwest of Calpe.

Overbuilt along the beachfront, like much of the Costa Blanca during its orgiastic days of development, Altea is still well preserved on the heights above a truly lovely little old quarter, with narrow cobblestone streets and stairways, and gleaming white houses. At the center is the striking church of Nuestra Señora del Consuelo, with its blue ceramic-tile dome, and the Plaza de la Iglesia in front.

ESSENTIALS

Altea ✉ *Pl. José Maria Planella 7* ☎ *965/844114* 🌐 *www.altea.es.*

WHERE TO EAT AND STAY

$$$ CATALAN ✕ **La Costera.** This popular restaurant focuses on fine French and Catalan fare, with such specialties as house-made foie gras, roasted *lubina* (sea bass), and *fondue bourguignonne*. There's also a variety of game in season, including venison and partridge. Book a table on the small and leafy terrace for a particularly romantic dinner. [$] *Average main: €18* ✉ *Costera del Mestre la Música 8* ☎ *965/840230* 🌐 *www.lacosteradealtea.com* ⏲ *Closed Mon.*

$$ EUROPEAN ✕ **Oustau de Altea.** In one of the prettiest corners of Altea's old town, this eatery was formerly a cloister and a school. Today the dining room and terrace combine contemporary design gracefully juxtaposed with a rustic setting. Named for the Provençal word for inn or hostelry, Oustau serves polished international cuisine with a French flair. Dishes are named for classic films, such as *Love Story* (beef and strawberry coulis), and film stars, like the "Sophia Loren" tomato and mozarella salad. Contemporary artists display work here, so the art changes regularly. [$] *Average main: €12* ✉ *Calle Mayor 5, Casco Antiguo* ☎ *965/842078* 🌐 *www.oustau.com* ✍ *Reservations essential* ⏲ *Closed Feb. and Mon. No lunch Oct.–June.*

9

BILBAO AND THE BASQUE COUNTRY

with Navarra and La Rioja

WELCOME TO BILBAO AND THE BASQUE COUNTRY

TOP REASONS TO GO

★ **Explore the Basque coast:** From colorful fishing villages to tawny beaches, the Basque Coast always delights the eye.

★ **Eat tapas in San Sebastián:** Nothing matches San Sebastián's old quarter, with the booming laughter of tavern-hoppers who graze at counters heaped with colorful morsels.

★ **Appreciate Bilbao's art and architecture:** The gleaming titanium Guggenheim and the Museo de Bellas Artes (Fine Arts Museum) shimmer where steel mills and shipyards once stood, while verdant pastures loom above and beyond.

★ **Run with the bulls in Pamplona:** Running with a pack of wild animals (and people) will certainly get the adrenaline pumping, but you might prefer to be a spectator.

★ **Drink in La Rioja wine country:** Spain's premier wine-growing region is filled with wine-tasting opportunities and fine cuisine.

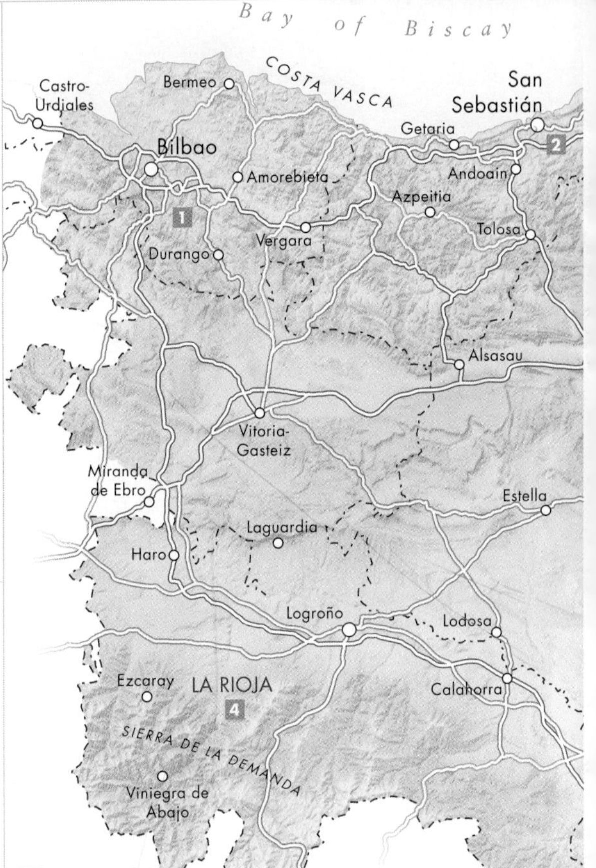

1 Bilbao and the Basque Country. The contrast between Bilbao and the rest of the Basque Country makes each half of the equation better: a city famous for steel and shipbuilding turned into a shimmering art and architecture hub, surrounded by sylvan hillsides, tiny fishing ports, and beautiful beaches.

2 San Sebastián to Hondarribia. San Sebastián lures travelers with its sophistication and a wide beach. Nearby Hondarribia is a fishing port on the Bidasoa river estuary border with France.

3 Navarra and Pamplona. This region offers much beyond Pamplona's running-with-the-bulls blowout party. The green Pyrenean hills to the north contrast with the lunar Bárdenas Reales to the southeast, and the wine country south of Pamplona leads to lovely Camino de Santiago way stations like Estella. Medieval Vitoria is the capital of Alava and the whole Basque Country, and is relatively undiscovered by tourists.

GETTING ORIENTED

Bordering the coastline of the Bay of Biscay, the Basque Country and, farther inland, Navarra and La Rioja are a Spain apart—a land of moist green foothills, lush vineyards, and rolling meadowlands. A fertile slot between the Picos de Europa and the Pyrenees mountain ranges that stretch from the Mediterranean Cap de Creus all the way to Finisterre (World's End) on the Atlantic in northwestern Galicia, this northern Arcadia is an often rainy but frequently comforting reprieve from the bright, hot Spanish *meseta* (high plain or tableland) to the south.

4 La Rioja. Spain's wine country is dedicated to tastes of all kinds. The Sierra de la Demanda mountain range offers culinary destinations such as Ezcaray's Echaurren or Viniegra de Abajo's Venta de Goyo, while the towns of Logroño, Haro, and Laguardia are well endowed with superb architecture and gastronomy.

By Suzanne Wales

Northern Spain is a misty land of green hills, low russet rooflines, and colorful fishing villages; it's also home to the formerly industrial city of Bilbao, reborn as a center of art and architecture. The semiautonomous Basque Country—with its steady drizzle (onomatopoetically called the *siri-miri*), verdant landscape, and rugged coastline—is a distinct national and cultural entity.

Navarra is considered Basque in the Pyrenees and Navarran in its southern reaches, along the Ebro River. La Rioja, tucked between the Sierra de la Demanda (a mountain range that separates La Rioja from the central Castilian steppe) and the Ebro River, is Spain's premier wine country.

Called the País Vasco in Castilian Spanish and Euskadi in the linguistically mysterious, non-Indo-European Basque language Euskera, the Basque region is more a country within a country, or a nation within a state (the semantics are much debated). The Basques are known to love competition—it has been said that they will bet on anything that has numbers on it and moves (horses, dogs, runners). Such traditional rural sports as chopping mammoth tree trunks and lifting boulders reflect the Basques' attachment to the land as well as an enthusiasm for feats of endurance. Even poetry and gastronomy become contests in Euskadi, as *bertsolaris* (amateur poets) improvise duels of sharp-witted verse, and gastronomic societies compete in cooking contests to see who can make the best *sopa de ajo* (garlic soup) or *marmitako* (tuna stew).

The much-reported-on Basque separatist movement is made up of a small but radical sector of the political spectrum. The terrorist organization known as ETA, or Euskadi Ta Askatasuna (Basque Homeland and Liberty), has killed nearly 900 people in almost four decades of violence. Conflict has waxed and waned over the years, though it has never affected travelers. When ETA declared a permanent cease-fire in April 2006, hope flared for an end to Basque terrorism until a late-December bomb at Madrid's Barajas airport brought progress to a halt. In 2009 Basque *lehendakari* (president) Juan José Ibarretxe and the PNV (Basque Nationalist Party) lost, albeit narrowly, the Basque presidency in favor of Patxi López of the PSOE (Spanish Socialist Party) in coalition with the PP (the right-wing Partido Popular), reflecting voter weariness with the nationalist cause. In October 2011, ETA declared a permanent renunciation of violence, received by the Spanish government with some skepticism, and two years later the Strasbourg's European Court of Human Rights ordered the release of many long-term ETA prisoners, much to the dissatisfaction of the Spanish government and victim's rights associations. But overall there is hope that Spain's greatest post-Franco tragedy is nearing an end.

PLANNING

WHEN TO GO

Mid-April through June, September, and October are the best times to enjoy the temperate climate and both the coastal and upland landscapes of this wet and grassy corner of Spain—though any time of year except August, when Europeans are on vacation, is nearly as good.

Pamplona in July is bedlam, though for hard-core party animals it's heaven.

The Basque Country is rainy in winter, but the wet Atlantic weather is always invigorating and, as if anyone needed it in this culinary paradise, appetite-enhancing. Much of the classically powerful Basque cuisine evolved with the northern maritime climate in mind.

The September film festival in San Sebastián coincides with the spectacular whaleboat regattas, while the beaches are still ideal and largely uncrowded.

When you're looking for a place to stay, note that the largely industrial and well-to-do north is an expensive part of Spain, which is reflected in room rates. San Sebastián is particularly pricey, and Pamplona rates triple during San Fermín in July. Reserve ahead for nearly everywhere in summer, especially Bilbao, where the Guggenheim is filling hotels.

FESTIVALS

Glitterati descend on San Sebastián for its international **film festival** in the second half of September (exact dates vary, check 🌐 *www.sansebastianfestival.com*). The same goes for the late-July **jazz festival** (🌐 *www.heinekenjazzaldia.com*), which draws many of the world's top performers. Saint's day is celebrated here January 19–20 with **La Tamborrada,** when 100-odd platoons of chefs and Napoleonic soldiers parade hilariously through the streets.

Pamplona's feast of **San Fermín** (July 6–14), made famous by Ernest Hemingway in *The Sun Also Rises,* remains best known for its running of the bulls. Bilbao's **Semana Grande** (Grand Week), in mid-August, is notorious for the largest bulls of the season and a fine series of street concerts.

Near San Sebastián, on August 7 every four years (the next will be in 2017), the fishing village of **Getaria** celebrates Juan Sebastián Elcano's completion of Ferdinand Magellan's voyage around the world. The fiesta includes a solemn procession up from the port of the weather-beaten, starving survivors and a week of feasts, dances, and street parties.

DID YOU KNOW?

The French sculptress Louise Bourgeois's (1911–2010) giant spider *Maman*, more than 30 feet tall, stands outside the back entrance to the Guggenheim.

Vitoria's weeklong **Fiesta de la Virgen Blanca** (Festival of the White Virgin) celebrates the city's patron saint with bullfights and more, August 4–9.

BEACHES

Between Bilbao and San Sebastián, the smaller beaches at Zumaia, Getaria, and Zarautz are usually quiet. San Sebastián's best beach, La Concha, which curves around the bay along with the city itself, is scenic and clean but packed in summer; Ondarreta, at the western end of La Concha, is often less crowded. Surfers gather at Zurriola on the northern side of the Urumea River.

GETTING HERE AND AROUND

AIR TRAVEL

Bilbao's airport serves much of this area, and there are smaller airports at Hondarribia (serving San Sebastián), Logroño, and Pamplona, which are generally only used by domestic carriers in high season.

Airports **Aeropuerto de Bilbao** 🌐 *www.aeropuertodebilbao.net.*

CAR TRAVEL

Even the remotest points are an easy one-day drive from Madrid, and northern Spain is superbly covered by freeways.

The drive from Madrid to Bilbao is 397 km (247 miles)—about five hours; follow the A1 past Burgos to Miranda del Ebro, where you pick up the AP68. Car rentals are available in the major cities: Bilbao, Pamplona, San Sebastián, and Vitoria. Cars can also be rented at Hondarribia (Fuenterrabía) and the San Sebastián (Donostia) airport.

TAXI TRAVEL

Taxis normally can be hailed on the street, though from more remote spots, such as Pedro Subijana's Akelaŕerestaurant on Igueldo above San Sebastián, you'll need to call a taxi.

TRAIN TRAVEL

Direct RENFE trains from Madrid run to Bilbao (at 8 am and 4:05 pm), San Sebastián (at 8 am and 4:05 pm), Pamplona (7:30 am, 9:40 am, 3:05 pm, 3:30 pm, and 7:30 pm), Vitoria (8 am, 8:48 am, 12:22 pm, and 4:05 pm), and Logroño (7:30 am, 12:30 pm, 3:30 pm, and 7:30 pm). A car is the most convenient way to get around here, but if this isn't an option, many cities are connected by RENFE trains, and the regional company FEVE runs a delightful narrow-gauge train that winds through stunning landscapes. From San Sebastián, lines west to Bilbao (the Ueskotren) and east to Hendaye depart from Estación de Amara; most long-distance trains use RENFE's Estación del Norte. ⇨ *See the Travel Smart chapter for more information about train travel.*

PLANNING YOUR TIME

A road trip through the Basque Country, Navarra, and La Rioja would require at least a week, but a glimpse, however brief, of Bilbao and its Guggenheim, can be done in two days. San Sebastián and its beach, La Concha, the Baztán Valley, Pamplona, Laguardia, and La Rioja's wine capital at Haro are the top must-see stops.

If you have more time, visit Mundaka and the coast of Vizcaya west of Bilbao; Getaria, Pasajes de San Juan, and Hondarribia near San Sebastián; and Logroño in La Rioja.

La Rioja's Sierra de la Demanda also has some of the finest landscapes in Spain, not to mention culinary pilgrimages to Echaurren in Ezcaray or Venta de Goyo in Viniegra de Abajo.

RESTAURANTS

Though top restaurants are expensive in Bilbao, some of what is undoubtedly Europe's finest cuisine is served here in settings that range from the traditional hewn beams and stone walls to sleekly contemporary international restaurants all the way up to the Guggenheim itself, where superstar chef Martín Berasategui runs a dining room as superb as its habitat.

Prices in dining reviews are the average cost of a main course at dinner or, if dinner is not served, at lunch.

HOTELS

Ever since the Guggenheim reinvented Bilbao as a design darling, the city's hotel fleet has expanded and reflected (in the case of the Gran Hotel Domine, literally) the glitter and panache of Gehry's museum. Boutique hotels, high-design hotels, and high-rise mammoths have made the older hotels look small and quaint by comparison. Despite new developments, the López de Haro remains one of the city's best lodging options, and many longtime Bilbao visitors prefer the storied halls of the Hotel Carlton to the glass and steel labyrinths overlooking Abandoibarra and the Nervión estuary.

Prices in lodging reviews are the lowest cost of a standard double room in high season.

BILBAO AND THE BASQUE COAST TO GETARIA (GUETARIA)

Starring Frank Gehry's titanium brainchild—the Museo Guggenheim Bilbao—Bilbao has established itself as one of Spain's 21st-century magnets. The area around the coast of Vizcaya and east into neighboring Guipúzcoa province to Getaria and San Sebastián is a succession of colorful ports, ocher beaches, and green hills.

BILBAO

34 km (21 miles) southeast of Castro-Urdiales, 116 km (72 miles) east of Santander, 397 km (247 miles) north of Madrid.

Time in Bilbao (Bilbo, in Euskera) may be recorded as BG or AG (Before Guggenheim or After Guggenheim). Never has a single monument of art and architecture so radically changed a city. Frank Gehry's stunning museum, Norman Foster's sleek subway system, the Santiago Calatrava glass footbridge and airport, the leafy César Pelli Abandoibarra park and commercial complex next to the Guggenheim, and the Philippe Starck Alhóndiga Bilbao cultural center have contributed to an unprecedented cultural revolution in what was once the industry capital of the Basque Country.

Greater Bilbao encompasses almost 1 million inhabitants, nearly half the total population of the Basque Country. Founded in 1300 by Vizcayan noble Diego López de Haro, Bilbao became an industrial center in the mid-19th century, largely because of the abundance of minerals in the surrounding hills. An affluent industrial class grew up here, as did the working-class suburbs that line the Margen Izquierda (Left Bank) of the Nervión estuary.

Bilbao's new attractions get more press, but the city's old treasures still quietly line the banks of the rust-color Nervión River. The **Casco Viejo** (Old Quarter)—also known as Siete Calles (Seven Streets)—is a charming jumble of shops, bars, and restaurants on the river's Right Bank, near the Puente del Arenal bridge. This elegant proto-Bilbao nucleus was carefully restored after devastating floods in 1983. Throughout the Old Quarter are ancient mansions emblazoned with family coats of arms, wooden doors, and fine ironwork balconies. The most interesting square is the 64-arch Plaza Nueva, where an outdoor market is pitched every Sunday morning.

Walking the banks of the Nervión is a satisfying jaunt. After all, this was how—while out on a morning jog—Guggenheim director Thomas Krens first discovered the perfect spot for his project, nearly opposite the right bank's Deusto University. From the Palacio de Euskalduna upstream to the colossal Mercado de la Ribera, parks and green zones line the river. César Pelli's Abandoibarra project fills in the half mile between the Guggenheim and the Euskalduna bridge with a series of parks, the Deusto University library, the Meliá Bilbao Hotel, and a major shopping center.

On the left bank, the wide, late-19th-century boulevards of the **Ensanche** neighborhood, such as Gran Vía (the main shopping artery) and Alameda de Mazarredo, are the city's more formal face. Bilbao's cultural institutions include, along with the Guggenheim, a major museum of fine arts (the Museo de Bellas Artes) and an opera society (ABAO: Asociación Bilbaína de Amigos de la Ópera) with 7,000 members from Spain and southern France. In addition, epicureans have long ranked Bilbao's culinary offerings among the best in Spain. Don't miss a chance to ride the trolley line, the Euskotram, for a trip along the river from Atxuri Station to Basurto's San Mamés soccer stadium, reverently dubbed "la Catedral del Fútbol" (the Cathedral of Football).

GETTING HERE AND AROUND

Bilbao's Euskotram, running up and down the Ría de Bilbao (aka River Nervión) past the Guggenheim to the Mercado de la Ribera, is an attraction in its own right: silent, swift, and panoramic as it glides up and down its grassy runway. The EuskoTren leaving from Atxuri Station north of the Mercado de la Ribera runs along a spectacular route through Gernika and the Urdaibai Nature Preserve to Mundaka, probably the best way short of a boat to see this lovely wetlands preserve.

The Creditrans ticket is good for tram, metro, and bus travel and is available in values of €5, €10, and €15, though the €5 ticket should suffice for the few subway hops you might need to get around town. Creditrans can be purchased at newspaper stands, bus stops, metro stations, and from some drivers. Pass your ticket through the machine as you get on and off metros, tramways, or buses and it is charged according to the length of your trip. Transfers cost extra. A single in-town (Zone 1) ride costs about €1.60 and can be purchased from a driver; with a Creditrans transaction the cost is reduced to about €1.10. Day passes are also available for €3.80.

Bilbobus provides bus service from 6:15 am to 10:55 pm. Plaza Circular and Plaza Moyúa are the principal hubs for all lines. Once the metro and normal bus routes stop service, take a night bus, known as a *Gautxori* (Night bird). Six lines run every 30 minutes between Plaza Circular and Plaza Moyúa and the city limits from 11:30 pm to 2 am Friday and until 7 am on Saturday.

Metro Bilbao is linear, running down the Nervión estuary from Basauri, above, or east of, the Casco Viejo, all the way to the mouth of the Nervión at Getxo, before continuing to the beach town of Plentzia. There is no main hub, but the Moyúa station is the most central stop and lies in the middle of Bilbao's Ensanche, or modern (post-1860) part. The second subway line runs down the left bank of the Nervión to Santurtzi. The fare is €1.50 within Zone 1.

TOURS

Bilbao's tourist office, Bilbao Turismo, conducts weekend guided tours in English and Spanish. The Casco Viejo tour starts at 10 am at the tourist office on the ground floor of the main office on the Plaza Circular. The Ensanche and Abandoibarra tour begins at noon at the tourist office to the left of the Guggenheim entrance. The tours last 90 minutes and cost €4.50.

Bilbao Paso a Paso arranges custom-designed visits and tours of Bilbao throughout the week.

Stop Bilbao leads visits and tours of Bilbao and the province of Vizcaya.

ESSENTIALS

Bus and Subway Informaton Bilbobus ☎ *944/790981* 🌐 *www.bilbobus.com.* **Metro Bilbao.** Customer services offices are in or near four stations: Areeta, San Inazio, Casco Viejo, and Ansio. Hours are weekdays 8:30–7:30, with the San Inazio location also open Saturday 8:30–3. ✉ *C. Navarra 2, Casco Viejo* ☎ *944/254025* 🌐 *www.metrobilbao.net.*

Bus Station Termibus Bilbao ✉ *Gurtubay 1, San Mamés* ☎ *944/395077* 🌐 *www.termibus.es.*

Tour Information Bilbao Paso a Paso ✉ *Egaña 17, 5th fl., Casco Viejo* ☎ *944/153892* 🌐 *www.bilbaopasoapaso.com.* **Bilbao Turísmo** ✉ *Alameda de Mazarredo 66 (next to Guggenheim Museum), Ensanche* ☎ *944/795760* 🌐 *www.bilbao.net* 🕑 *Mon.–Sat. 10–7, Sun. 10–3 (till 7 July and Aug.).* **Stop Bilbao** ✉ *Portuondo Auzoa 4, Mundaka* ☎ *944/424689* 🌐 *www.stop.es.*

Train Station Bilbao Turismo ✉ *Edificio Terminus, Pl. Circular 2, El Ensanche* ☎ *94/479–5760* 🌐 *www.bilbaoturismo.net* 🕑 *Daily 9–9.* **EuskoTren** ✉ *C. Atxuri 8, Casco Viejo* ☎ *902/543210* 🌐 *www.euskotren.es.*

The Guggenheim may be the most famous art museum in Bilbao these days, but the Museum of Fine Arts is also a very worthwhile destination.

9

TOP ATTRACTIONS

AlhóndigaBilbao. In the early 20th century this was a municipal wine-storage facility used by Bilbao's Rioja wine barons. Now, this city-block-size, Philippe Starck–designed civic center is filled with shops, cafés, restaurants, movie theaters, swimming pools, fitness centers, and nightlife opportunities at the very heart of the city. Conceived as a hub for entertainment, culture, wellness, and civic coexistence, it added another star to Bilbao's cosmos of architectural and cultural offerings when it opened in 2010. The complex regularly hosts film festivals and art exhibitions, and it's a cozy place to take refuge on a rainy afternoon. Locals lovingly call it "the meatball," because its name is one letter off from the Spanish word for meatballs, *albóndigas*. ✉ *Pl. Arriquibar 4, El Ensanche* ☎ *94/401–4014* 🌐 *www.alhondigabilbao.com* Ⓜ *Moyúa.*

OFF THE BEATEN PATH

Funicular de Artxanda. The panorama from the hillsides of Artxanda is the most comprehensive view of Bilbao, and the various typical *asadors* (roasters) here serve delicious beef or fish cooked over coals. ✉ *Pl. de Funicular s/n, Matiko* ☎ *94/445–4966* 💳 *€0.92* ⏲ *Weekdays 7:15 am–10 pm, weekends 8:15 am–10 pm (till 11 June–Sept.)* Ⓜ *Casco Viejo.*

Fodor's Choice ★

Museo de Bellas Artes (*Museum of Fine Arts*). Considered one of the top five museums in a country that has a staggering number of museums and great paintings, the Museo de Bellas Artes is like a mini-Prado, with representatives from every Spanish school and movement from the 12th through the 20th centuries. The museum's fine collection of Flemish, French, Italian, and Spanish paintings includes works by El Greco, Francisco de Goya y Lucientes, Diego Velázquez, Zurbarán,

José Ribera, Paul Gauguin, and Antoni Tàpies. One large and excellent section traces developments in 20th-century Spanish and Basque art alongside works by better-known European contemporaries, such as Fernand Léger and Francis Bacon. Look especially for Zuloaga's famous portrait of La Condesa Mathieu de Moailles and Joaquín Sorolla's portrait of Basque philosopher Miguel de Unamuno. A statue of Zuloaga outside greets visitors to this sparkling collection at the edge of Doña Casilda Park and on the left bank end of the Deusto bridge, five minutes from the Guggenheim. Three hours might be barely enough to appreciate this international and pan-chronological painting course. The museum's excellent Arbolagaña restaurant offers a stellar lunch to break up the visit. ✉ *Parque de Doña Casilda de Iturrizar, Museo Pl. 2D, El Ensanche* ☎ *94/439–6060* 🌐 *www.museobilbao.com* 🎟 *€6 (free Wed.); Bono Artean combined ticket with Guggenheim €13.50 (valid 1 yr)* ⏲ *Tues.–Sun. 10–8* Ⓜ *Moyúa.*

Fodor's Choice ★ **Museo Guggenheim Bilbao.** Described by the late Spanish novelist Manuel Vázquez Montalbán as a "meteorite," the Guggenheim, with its eruption of light in the ruins of Bilbao's shipyards and steelworks, has dramatically reanimated this onetime industrial city. How Bilbao and the Guggenheim met is in itself a saga: Guggenheim director Thomas Krens was looking for a venue for a major European museum, having found nothing acceptable in Paris, Madrid, or elsewhere, and glumly accepted an invitation to Bilbao. Krens was out for a morning jog when he found it—the empty riverside lot once occupied by the Altos Hornos de Vizcaya steel mills. The site, at the heart of Bilbao's steel and shipping port, was the perfect place for a metaphor for Bilbao's macro-reconversion from steel to titanium, from heavy industry to art, as well as a nexus between the early-14th-century Casco Viejo and the new 19th-century Ensanche and between the wealthy right bank and working-class left bank of the Nervión River.

Frank Gehry's gleaming brainchild, opened in 1997 and hailed as "the greatest building of our time" by architect Philip Johnson and "a miracle" by Herbert Muschamp of the *New York Times,* has sparked an economic renaissance in the Basque Country after more than a half century of troubles. In its first year, the Guggenheim attracted 1.4 million visitors.

At once suggestive of a silver-scaled fish and a mechanical heart, Gehry's sculpture in titanium, limestone, and glass is the perfect habitat for the contemporary and postmodern artworks it contains. The smoothly rounded jumble of surfaces and cylindrical shapes recalls Bilbao's shipbuilding and steel-manufacturing past, whereas the transparent and reflective materials create a shimmering, futuristic luminosity. With the final section of the La Salve bridge over the Nervión folded into the structure, the Guggenheim is both a doorway to Bilbao and an urban forum: the atrium looks up into the center of town and across the river to the Old Quarter and the tranquil green hillsides of Artxanda where livestock graze. Gehry's intent to build something as moving as a Gothic cathedral in which "you can feel your soul rise up," and to make it as playful and perfect as a fish—per the composer Franz Schubert's ichthyological homage in his famous "Trout Quintet"—is patent: "I wanted it to be more than just a dumb building; I wanted it to have a plastic sense of movement!"

Covered with 30,000 sheets of titanium, the Guggenheim became Bilbao's main attraction overnight. The enormous atrium, more than 150 feet high, connects to the 19 galleries by a system of suspended metal walkways and glass elevators. Vertical windows reveal the undulating titanium flukes and contours of this beached whale. The free Audio Guía explains everything you always wanted to know about contemporary art and the Guggenheim. Frank Gehry talks of his love of fish and how his creative process works, while the pieces in the collection are presented one by one.

The collection, described by Krens as "a daring history of the art of the 20th century," consists of more than 250 works, most from the New York Guggenheim and the rest acquired by the Basque government. The second and third floors reprise the original Guggenheim collection of abstract expressionist, cubist, surrealist, and geometrical works. Artists whose names are synonymous with the art of the 20th century (Wassily Kandinsky, Pablo Picasso, Max Ernst, Georges Braque, Joan Miró, Jackson Pollock, Alexander Calder, Kazimir Malevich) and European artists of the 1950s and 1960s (Eduardo Chillida, Tàpies, Jose Maria Iglesias, Francesco Clemente, and Anselm Kiefer) are joined by contemporary figures (Bruce Nauman, Juan Muñoz, Julian Schnabel, Txomin Badiola, Miquel Barceló, Jean-Michel Basquiat). The ground floor is dedicated to large-format and installation work, some of which—like Richard Serra's *Serpent*—was created specifically for the space. Claes Oldenburg's *Knife Ship,* Robert Morris's walk-in *Labyrinth,* and pieces by Joseph Beuys, Christian Boltanski, Richard Long, Jenny Holzer, and others round out the heavyweight division in one of the largest galleries in the world.

On holidays and weekends lines may develop, though no one seems too impatient. The longest lines tend to occur late morning through early afternoon, although you can buy tickets in advance online. The museum has no parking of its own, but underground lots throughout the area provide alternatives; check the website for information. ✉ *Abandoibarra Etorbidea 2, El Ensanche* ☎ *944/359080* 🌐 *www.guggenheim-bilbao.es* 🎫 *€11 (includes audio guide); Bono Artean combined ticket with Museo de Bellas Artes €13.50* ⏲ *July and Aug., daily 10–8; Sept.–June, Tues.–Sun. 10–8. Ticket office closes at 7:30* Ⓜ *Moyúa.*

FAMILY **Museo Marítimo Ría de Bilbao** (*Maritime Museum of Bilbao*). This carefully researched nautical museum on the left bank of the Ría de Bilbao reconstructs the history of the Bilbao waterfront and shipbuilding industry beginning from medieval times. Temporary exhibits range from visits by extraordinary seacraft such as tall ships or traditional fishing vessels to thematic displays on 17th- and 18th-century clipper ships or the sinking of the *Titanic.* ✉ *Muelle Ramón de la Sota 1, San Mamés* ☎ *94/608–5500* 🌐 *www.museomaritimobilbao.org* 🎫 *€6 (free Tues. Sept.–June)* ⏲ *May 16–Sept. 14, Tues.–Sun. 10–8; Sept. 15–May 15, Tues.–Fri. 10–6, weekends 10–8* Ⓜ *San Mamés.*

Fodor's Choice ★ **Museo Vasco (Euskal Museoa Bilbao)** (*Basque Museum of Bilbao*). One of the not-to-miss visits in Bilbao, this museum occupies an austerely elegant 16th-century convent. The collection centers on Basque ethnography, Bilbao history, and comprehensive displays from the lives of Basque shepherds, fishermen, and farmers—everything you ever wanted to know about this little-known culture. Highlights include *El Mikeldi* in the cloister, a pre-Christian, Iron Age, stone, animal representation that may be 4,000 years old; the Mar de los Vascos (Sea of the Basques) exhibit featuring whaling, fishing, and maritime activities; the second-floor prehistoric exhibit featuring a wooden harpoon recovered in the Santimamiñe caves at Kortezubi that dates from the 10th century BC. ✉ *Pl. Unamuno 4, Casco Viejo* ☎ *94/415–5423* 🌐 *www.euskal-museoa.org* 🎫 *€3 (free Thurs.)* ⏲ *Tues.–Sat. 11–5, Sun. 11–2* Ⓜ *Casco Viejo.*

Palacio de Euskalduna. In homage to the *astilleros Euskalduna* (Basque Country shipbuilders) who operated shipyards here beside the Euskalduna bridge into the late 20th century, this music venue and convention hall resembles a rusting ship, a stark counterpoint to Frank Gehry's shimmering titanium fantasy just up the Nervión. Designed by architects Federico Soriano and Dolores Palacios, Euskalduna opened in 1999 and is Bilbao's main opera venue and home of the Bilbao Symphony Orchestra. Free guided tours are offered on Saturday at noon on a first-come, first-served basis. Weekday tours (€4 per person) can also be booked ahead. ✉ *Av. Abandoibarra 4, El Ensanche* ☎ *94/403–5000* 🌐 *www.euskalduna.net* Ⓜ *San Mamés.*

Parque de Doña Casilda de Iturrizar. Bilbao's main park is a lush collection of exotic trees, ducks and geese, fountains, falling water, and great expanses of lawns usually dotted with lovers. It's a sanctuary from the hard-edged Ensanche, Bilbao's modern, post-1876 expansion. ✉ *El Ensanche* Ⓜ *San Mamés.*

Plaza Miguel de Unamuno. Named for Bilbao's all-time greatest intellectual, this bright and open space at the upper edge of the Casco Viejo honors Miguel de Unamuno (1864–1936)—a philosopher, novelist, and professor. De Unamuno wrote some of Spain's most seminal works, including *Del sentimiento trágico de la vida en los hombres y los pueblos* (*The Tragic Sense of Life in Men and Nations*); his *Niebla* (*Mist*) has been generally accepted as the first existentialist novel, published in 1914 when Jean-Paul Sartre was but nine years old. Remembrances to Unamuno in the Casco Viejo include the philosopher's bust here, his birthplace at No. 7 Calle de la Cruz, and the nearby Filatelia Unamuno, a rare stamp emporium that is a favorite of collectors. ✉ *Casco Viejo* Ⓜ *Casco Viejo.*

Plaza Nueva. This 64-arch neoclassical plaza seems to be typical of every Spanish city from San Sebastián to Salamanca to Seville. With its Sunday-morning flea market, its December 21 natural-produce Santo Tomás market, and its permanent tapas and restaurant offerings, Plaza Nueva is an easy place in which to spend a lot of time. It was finished in 1851 as part of an ambitious housing project designed to ease the pressure on limited mid-19th-century Bilbao space. Note the size of the houses' balconies: it was the measure—the bigger, the better—of the social clout of their inhabitants. The tiny windows near the top of the facades were

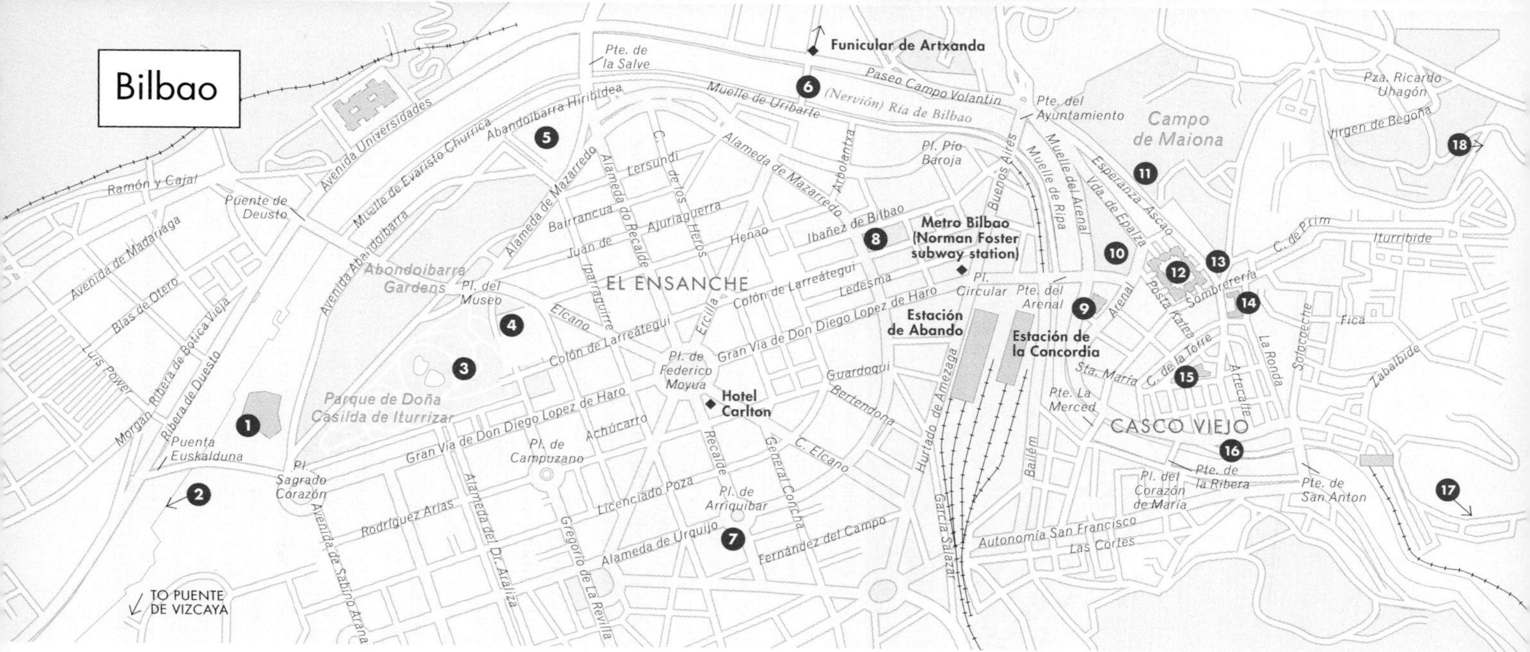

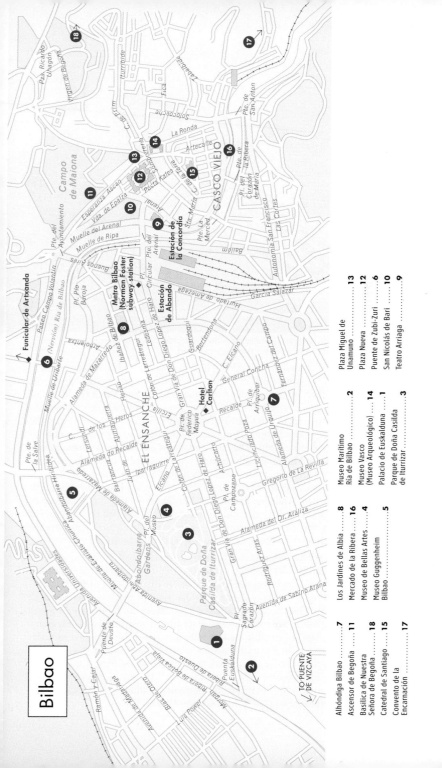

- Alhóndiga Bilbao **7**
- Ascensor de Begoña **11**
- Basilica de Nuestra Señora de Begoña **18**
- Catedral de Santiago **15**
- Convento de la Encarnación **17**
- Los Jardines de Albia **8**
- Mercado de la Ribera **16**
- Museo de Bellas Artes **4**
- Museo Guggenheim Bilbao **5**
- Museo Marítimo Ría de Bilbao **2**
- Museo Vasco (Museo Arqueológico) **14**
- Palacio de Euskalduna **1**
- Parque de Doña Casilda de Iturrizar **3**
- Plaza Miguel de Unamuno **13**
- Plaza Nueva **12**
- Puente de Zubi-Zuri **6**
- San Nicolás de Bari **10**
- Teatro Arriaga **9**

The exterior of the Bilbao Guggenheim is immediately recognized by many, but the interior is known for its large spaces, all the better for appreciating the stunning works of art.

servants' quarters. The building behind the powerful coat of arms at the head of the square was originally the Diputación, or provincial government office, but is now the **Academia de la Lengua Vasca** (Academy of the Basque Language). The coat of arms shows the tree of Guernica (the Basque spelling is Gernika), symbolic of Basque autonomy, with the two wolves representing Don Diego López de Haro (López derives from *lupus*, meaning wolf). The bars and shops around the arcades include two **Victor Montes** establishments, one for tapas at Plaza Nueva 8 and the other for more serious sit-down dining at Plaza Nueva 2. The **Café Bar Bilbao,** at Plaza Nueva 6, also known as Casa Pedro, has photos of early Bilbao, while the **Argoitia,** at No. 15 across the square, has a nice angle on the midday sun and a coat of arms inside with the *zatzpiakbat* ("seven-one" in Basque), referring to the cultural unity of the three French and four Spanish Basque provinces. ⊠ *Casco Viejo* Ⓜ *Casco Viejo.*

Puente de Zubi-Zuri. Santiago Calatrava's signature span (the name means "white bridge" in Euskera) connects Campo Volantín on the right bank with the Ensanche on the left. Just a few minutes east of the Guggenheim, the playful seagull-shape bridge swoops brightly over the dark Nervión. The Plexiglas walkway suggests walking on water, though wear-and-tear has reduced the surface from transparent to merely translucent. The airport just west of Bilbao at Loiu, also designed by Calatrava, resembles a massive, white Concorde plane and has been dubbed La Paloma (The Dove), despite more closely resembling a snow goose poised for takeoff. Calatrava's third Vizcaya creation, the bridge at Ondarroa, completes this troika of gleaming white structures exploring the theme of flight. ⊠ *El Ensanche* Ⓜ *Moyúa.*

San Nicolás de Bari. Honoring the patron saint of mariners, San Nicolás de Bari, the city's early waterfront church was built over an earlier eponymous hermitage and opened in 1756. With a powerful facade over the Arenal, originally a sandy beach, San Nicolás was much abused by French and Carlist troops throughout the 19th century. Sculptures by Juan Pascual de Mena adorn the inside of the church. Look for the oval plaque to the left of the door marking the high-water mark of the flood of 1983. ✉ *Pl. de San Nicolás 1, Casco Viejo* ☎ *94/416–3424* 🎫 *Free* ⏲ *Mon.–Sat. 10:30–1 and 5:30–8, Sun. 11:30–2* Ⓜ *Casco Viejo.*

Teatro Arriaga. About a century ago, this 1,500-seat theater was as exciting a source of Bilbao pride as the Guggenheim is today. Built between 1886 and 1890, when Bilbao's population was a mere 35,000, the Teatro Arriaga represented a gigantic per-capita cultural investment. Always a symbol of Bilbao's industrial might and cultural vibrancy, the original "Nuevo Teatro" (New Theater) de Bilbao was a lavish Belle Epoque, neo-baroque spectacular modeled after the Paris Opéra by architect Joaquín Rucoba (1844–1909). The theater was renamed in 1902 for the Bilbao musician thought of as "the Spanish Mozart," Juan Crisóstomo de Arriaga (1806–26).

After a 1914 fire, the new version of the theater opened in 1919. Following years of splendor, the Teatro Arriaga (along with Bilbao's economy) gradually lost vigor; it closed down in 1978 for restoration work that was finally concluded in 1986. Now largely eclipsed by the splendid and more spacious Palacio de Euskalduna, the Arriaga stages opera, theater, concerts, and dance events from September through June. Walk around the building to see the stained glass on its rear facade and the exuberant caryatids holding up the arches facing the river. ✉ *Pl. Arriaga 1, Casco Viejo* ☎ *944/792036* 🌐 *www.teatroarriaga.com* ⏲ *Ticket office Aug.–June, Sat.–Tues. 11:30–2 and 5–7, Wed.–Fri. 11:30–2 and 5–8:30; July, Mon.–Sat. 11:30–2* Ⓜ *Casco Viejo.*

9

WORTH NOTING

Basílica de Nuestra Señora de Begoña. Bilbao's most cherished religious sanctuary, dedicated to the patron saint of Vizcaya, can be reached by the 313 stairs from Plaza de Unamuno or by the gigantic elevator (the Ascensor de Begoña) looming over Calle Esperanza 6 behind the San Nicolás church. The church's Gothic nave was begun in 1519 on the site of an early hermitage, where the Virgin Mary was alleged to have appeared long before. Finished in 1620, the basilica was completed with the economic support of the shipbuilders and merchants of Bilbao, many of whose businesses are commemorated on the inner walls of the church. The high ground the basilica occupies was strategically important during the Carlist Wars of 1836 and 1873, and as a result La Begoña suffered significant damage that was not restored until the beginning of the 20th century. Comparable in importance (if not in geographical impact) to Barcelona's Virgen de Montserrat, the Basílica de la Begoña is where the Athletic Bilbao soccer team makes its pilgrimage, some of the players often barefoot, in gratitude for triumphs. ✉ *C. Virgen de Begoña 38, Begoña* ☎ *94/412–7091* 🌐 *www.basilicadebegona.com* 🎫 *Free* ⏲ *Mon.–Sat. 10:30–1:30 and 5:30–8:30, Sun. for mass only* Ⓜ *Casco Viejo.*

The streets of Bilbao's old town offer many welcoming shops, cafés, and restaurants.

Los Jardines de Albia. One of the two or three places all *bilbainos* will insist you see is this welcoming green space in the concrete-and-asphalt surfaces of this part of town. Overlooking the square is the lovely Basque Gothic **Iglesia de San Vicente Mártir,** its Renaissance facade facing its own Plaza San Vicente. The amply robed sculpture of the Virgin on the main facade, as the story goes, had to be sculpted a second time after the original version was deemed too scantily clad. The Jardines de Albia are centered on the bronze effigy of writer Antonio de Trueba by the famous Spanish sculptor Mariano Benlliure (1866–1947), creator of monuments to the greatest national figures of the epoch. ✉ *Calle Colón de Larreátegui s/n, El Ensanche* Ⓜ *Abando.*

Fodor's Choice ★ **Mercado de la Ribera.** This triple-decker ocean liner with its prow headed down the estuary toward the open sea is one of the best markets of its kind in Europe, as well as one of the biggest, with more than 400 retail stands covering 37,950 square feet. Like the architects of the Guggenheim and the Palacio de Euskalduna nearly 75 years later, the architect here was playful with this well-anchored, ocean-going grocery store in the river. From the stained-glass entryway over Calle de la Ribera to the tiny catwalks over the river or the diminutive restaurant on the second floor, the market is an inviting place. Look for the farmers' market on the top floor. ✉ *C. de la Ribera 20, Casco Viejo* ☎ *94/602–3791* 🌐 *www.mercadodelaribera.net* ⏲ *Mon.–Thurs. 8–2 and 4:30–7, Fri. 8–2 and 4:30–7.30, Sat. 8:30–2:30* Ⓜ *Casco Viejo.*

Hotel Carlton. Bilbao's grande-dame favorite *(⇨ see also Where to Stay)* has hosted top-tier celebrities over the last century, from Orson Welles and Ernest Hemingway to Ava Gardner, casting giant Gretchen

Rennell, and music czar John Court, not to mention Francis Ford Coppola. Opened in 1926, Architect Manuel María de Smith based this project on the London hotel of the same name, although the stained glass in the oval reception area is a reduced version of the one in Nice's Hotel Negresco. During the Spanish Civil War, this building was the seat of the Republican Basque government; later it housed a number of Nationalist generals. The hotel's bar, the Grill, has a clubby English feel to it, with murals painted by client Martinez Ortiz in 1947. The murals, representing an equestrian scene and some 10 bourgeois figures, are remarkable for the detailed painting of every hand and finger. ✉ *Pl. Federico Moyúa 2, El Ensanche* ☎ *94/416–2200* 🌐 *www.hotelcarlton.es* Ⓜ *Moyúa.*

NEED A BREAK?

Café La Granja. Founded in 1926, this café, near the Puente del Arenal, is a Bilbao classic, offering excellent coffee, cold beer, *tortilla de patata* (potato omelet), a good lunch menu—and free Wi-Fi. Hours are long (weekdays 7:30 am–12:30 am, Saturday 10:30 am–1:30 am), but it's closed Sunday. ✉ *Pl. Circular 3, Casco Viejo* ☎ *94/423–0813* 🌐 *www.grupoiruña.net* Ⓜ *Abando.*

OFF THE BEATEN PATH

Puente de Vizcaya. Commonly called the **Puente Colgante** (Hanging Bridge), this has been one of Bilbao's most extraordinary sights ever since it was built in 1893. The bridge, a transporter hung from cables, ferries cars and passengers across the Nervión, uniting two distinct worlds: exclusive, bourgeois Las Arenas and Portugalete, a much older, working-class town. (Dolores Ibarruri, the famous Republican orator of the Spanish civil war, known as "*La Pasionaria*" for her ardor, was born here.) Portugalete is a 15-minute walk from Santurce, where the quayside Hogar del Pescador serves simple fish specialties. *Besugo* (sea bream) is the traditional choice, but the grilled sardines are hard to surpass. To reach the bridge, take the subway to Areeta, or drive across the Puente de Deusto, turn left on Avenida Lehendakari Aguirre, and follow signs for Las Arenas; it's a 10- or 15-minute drive from downtown. ✉ *Barria 3, Las Arenas* ☎ *94/480–1012* 🌐 *www.puente-colgante.com* 🎫 *Pedestrians €0.35, car €1.35 (5 am–10 pm; price increases after 10 pm); tour with audio guide €9; observation deck €7* Ⓜ *Areeta.*

9

WHERE TO EAT

$$$$ SPANISH

✕ **Aizian.** Euskera for "in the wind," the hotel restaurant for the Meliá Bilbao, under the direction of chef José Miguel Olazabalaga, has become one of the city's most respected dining establishments. Typical bilbaino culinary classicism doesn't keep Olazabalaga from creating surprising reductions and contemporary interpretations of traditional dishes such as *rape con espuma de patata y trufa e infusión de champiñones* (monkfish with potato and truffle cream and infusion of wild mushrooms) and *falda de buey Wagyu en láminas, con ajos en texturas y zanahoria* (Wagyu beef with "textured" garlic and carrots) in escabeche. The clean-lined contemporary dining room and the streamlined, polished cuisine are a perfect match. 💲 *Average main: €40* ✉ *C. Lehendakari Leizaola 29, El Ensanche* ☎ *94/428–0039* 🌐 *www.restaurante-aizian.com* 🕒 *Closed Sun.* Ⓜ *San Mamés.*

$$$$ CONTEMPORARY Fodor's Choice ★ ✕ **Arbolagaña.** On the top floor of the Museo de Bellas Artes, this elegant space has bay windows overlooking the lush Parque de Doña Casilda. A devotee of the 'slow food' movement, chef Aitor Basabe's modern cuisine offers innovative versions of Basque classics such as codfish on toast, venison with wild mushrooms, or rice with truffles and shallots. The €45 *menú de degustación* (tasting menu) is a superb affordable luxury, while the abbreviated *menú de trabajo* (work menu) provides a perfect light lunch. $ *Average main: €30* ✉ *Museo de Bellas Artes, Alameda Conde Arteche s/n, El Ensanche* ☎ *94/442–4657* 🌐 *www.arbolagana.com* ✍ *Reservations essential* ⏲ *Closed Mon. No dinner Tues., Wed., and Sun.* Ⓜ *Moyúa.*

$$$$ BASQUE ✕ **Arriaga.** The cider-house experience is a must in the Basque Country, and Arriaga is a local institution, on the ground floor of an ancient tower where locals sing to the Virgin of Begoña on religious festival days. Cider *al txotx* (shot straight from the barrel), sausage stewed in apple cider, codfish omelets, *txuletón de buey* (beefsteaks), and Idiazabal cheese with quince jelly are the classic fare. Reserving a table is a good idea, especially on weekends. $ *Average main: €30* ✉ *C. Santa Maria 13, Casco Viejo* ☎ *94/416–5670* 🌐 *www.asadorarriaga.com* ⏲ *No dinner Sun.* Ⓜ *Casco Viejo.*

$ BASQUE ✕ **Berton.** Dinner is served until midnight in this sleek, contemporary but casual bistro in the Casco Viejo. Fresh wood tables with a green-tint polyethylene finish and exposed ventilation pipes give the dining room an industrial design look, while the classic cuisine ranges from Iberian ham to smoked salmon, foie gras, cod, beef, and lamb. $ *Average main: €15* ✉ *C. Jardines 8, Casco Viejo* ☎ *94/416–7035* Ⓜ *Casco Viejo.*

$$$$ SPANISH ✕ **Bistro Guggenheim Bilbao.** Complementing the Guggenheim's visual feast with more sensorial elements, this spot overseen by Martín Berasategui is on everyone's short list of Bilbao restaurants. Try the *lomo de bacalao asado en aceite de ajo con txangurro a la donostiarra i pil pil* (cod flanks in garlic oil with crab San Sebastián–style and emulsified juices), a postmodern culinary pun on Bilbao's traditional codfish addiction. A lobster salad with lettuce-heart shavings and tomatoes at a table overlooking the Nervión, the University of Deusto, and the heights of Artxanda qualifies as a perfect 21st-century Bilbao moment. If you don't feel like splurging on the full menu, there's also a cafeteria and bar that serve tapas versions of some of the most popular dishes, with the same views and at a quarter of the price. $ *Average main: €32* ✉ *Av. Abandoibarra 2, El Ensanche* ☎ *94/423–9333* 🌐 *www.restauranteguggenheim.com* ✍ *Reservations essential* ⏲ *Closed Mon. No dinner Tues., Wed., and Sun.* Ⓜ *Moyúa.*

$$ CAFÉ Fodor's Choice ★ ✕ **Café Iruña.** This is an essential Bilbao haunt on the Ensanche's most popular garden and square, Los Jardines de Albia. Famous for its interior design and boisterous ambience, the neo-Mudejar dining room overlooking the square is the place to be. (If they try to stuff you in the back dining room, resist or come back another time). The bar has two distinct sections: the elegant side near the dining room, and the older, more bare-bones Spanish side on the Calle Berástegui, with its plain marble counters and *pinchos morunos de carne de cordero* (lamb

brochettes) as the house specialty. $ *Average main: €17* ✉ *C. Berástegui 4, El Ensanche* ☎ *94/424–9059* 🌐 *www.grupoiruña.net* Ⓜ *Moyúa.*

$$ BASQUE Fodor's Choice ★ **Casa Rufo.** More than 100 years old, this place is a Bilbao institution that's actually a series of nooks and crannies tucked into a fine food, wine, olive-oil, cheese, and ham emporium. It has become famous for its *txuleta de buey* (beef or ox chops). Let the affable owners bring on what you crave. The house wine is an excellent *crianza* (two years in oak, one in bottle) from La Rioja, but the 1,000-strong wine list offers a good selection from Ribera del Duero, Somontano, and Priorat as well. $ *Average main: €18* ✉ *C. Hurtado de Amézaga 5, El Ensanche* ☎ *94/443–2172* 🌐 *www.casarufo.com* *Reservations essential* *Closed Sun.* Ⓜ *Abando.*

$$$ BASQUE Fodor's Choice ★ **El Perro Chico.** The global glitterati who adopted post-Guggenheim Bilbao favor this spot across the Puente de la Ribera footbridge below the market. Frank Gehry discovered the color "Bilbao blue"—the azure of the skies over Bilbao—on the walls here and used it for the Guggenheim's office building. Despite celebrity sightings, the restaurant retains its quaint style, with tiled floors and walls and authentic menu. Noteworthy are the *alcachofas a la plancha* (grilled artichokes) and the *bacalao con berenjena* (cod with eggplant). $ *Average main: €30* ✉ *C. Aretxaga 2, El Ensanche* ☎ *94/415–0519* *Reservations essential* *Closed Sun. and Mon.* Ⓜ *Casco Viejo.*

$$$$ BASQUE **Etxanobe.** This luminous top corner of the Euskalduna palace overlooks the Nervión River, the hills of Artxanda, and Bilbao. Fernando Canales creates homegrown, contemporary cuisine using traditional ingredients. Standouts are the five codfish recipes, the duckling with Pedro Ximenez sherry, poached eggs with lamb kidneys and foie gras, and the braised scallops with shallot vinaigrette. $ *Average main: €70* ✉ *Palacio de Euskalduna, Av. de Abandoibarra 4, El Ensanche* ☎ *94/442–1071* 🌐 *www.etxanobe.com* *Closed Sun.* Ⓜ *San Mamés.*

$$$$ BASQUE Fodor's Choice ★ **Guetaria.** With a wood paneled dining room decorated with antiques, this family operation is a local favorite for fresh fish and meats cooked over coals. Named for the fishing village west of San Sebastián known as *la cocina de Guipúzcoa* (the kitchen of Guipúzcoa province), Bilbao's Guetaria does its namesake justice. The kitchen, open to the clientele, cooks lubina, besugo, dorada, *txuletas de buey* (beef chops), and *chuletas de cordero* (lamb chops) to perfection in a classic *asador* (barbecue) setting. $ *Average main: €50* ✉ *Colón de Larreátegui 12, El Ensanche* ☎ *94/424–3923, 94/423–2527* 🌐 *www.guetaria.com* *Reservations essential* *Closed Easter wk* Ⓜ *Moyúa.*

$$$$ BASQUE Fodor's Choice ★ **Guria.** The late Genaro Pildain, founder of the restaurant, learned cooking from his mother in the tiny village of Arakaldo and always focused more on potato soup than truffles or caviar. Don Genaro's influence is still felt here in the restaurant's streamlined traditional Basque cooking that dazzles with its simplicity. Every ingredient and preparation is perfect, from *alubias "con sus sacramentos"* (fava beans, chorizo, and blood sausage) to *crema de puerros y patatas* (cream of potato and leek soup) to lobster salad with, in season, *perretxikos de Orduña* (wild mushrooms). $ *Average main: €50* ✉ *Gran Vía 66, El Ensanche* ☎ *944/415780* 🌐 *www.restauranteguria.com* *Reservations essential* *No dinner Sun.* Ⓜ *Indautxu.*

$$$ BASQUE Fodor's Choice ★ **Kiskia.** A modern take on the traditional cider house, this rambling tavern near the San Mamés soccer stadium serves the classic *sidrería* menu of chorizo sausage cooked in cider, codfish omelet, txuleta de buey, Idiazabal with quince jelly and nuts, and as much cider as you can drink. Actors, sculptors, writers, soccer stars, and Spain's who's who frequent this boisterous marvel. *Average main: €25 ✉ C. Pérez Galdós 51, San Mamés ☎ 94/442–0032 🌐 www.sidreria-kiskia-bilbao.com ⏲ No dinner Sun.–Tues. Ⓜ San Mamés.*

$ TAPAS **La Deliciosa.** For carefully prepared food at friendly prices, this simply designed, intimate space is one of the best values in the Casco Viejo. The *crema de puerros* (cream of leeks) is as good as any in town, and the *dorada al horno* (roast gilthead bream) is fresh from the nearby La Ribera market. *Average main: €12 ✉ C. Jardines 1, Casco Viejo ☎ 94/415–0944 Ⓜ Casco Viejo.*

$ BASQUE **La Taberna de los Mundos.** Sandwich-maker Ander Calvo is famous throughout Spain, and his masterpiece is a sandwich on ciabatta of melted goat cheese with garlic, wild mushrooms, organic tomatoes, and sweet red piquillo peppers on a bed of acorn-fed wild Iberian ham. Calvo's two restaurants in Bilbao and one in Vitoria include creative interpretations of the sandwich along with photography, art exhibits, travel lectures, and a global interest reflected in his obsession with early maps and navigational techniques. The tapas bar is open longer hours than the dining room. *Average main: €12 ✉ C. Lutxana 1, El Ensanche ☎ 94/416–8181, 94/441–3523 🌐 www.delosmundos.com Ⓜ Moyúa.*

$$$$ CONTEMPORARY **Public Lounge.** For designer cuisine in a designer setting, this Guggenheim-inspired lounge creates sleek, postmodern fare in an exciting environment. The VIP table serves diners on Versace crockery and Baccarat crystal, and the cooking is no less exquisite. The menu changes frequently but expect up-to-the-minute tricks such as meat or fish cooked at low temperatures (45°C), salads with contrasting textures and temperatures, and some of the best risottos in Bilbao. *Average main: €35 ✉ C. Henao 54, El Ensanche ☎ 94/405–2824 🌐 www.public-bilbao.com ⏲ Closed Sun. No dinner Mon.–Thurs. Ⓜ Moyúa.*

$$$$ BASQUE **Txakolí de Artxanda.** The funicular from the end of Calle Múgica y Butrón up to the mountain of Artxanda deposits you next to this excellent spot for a roast of one kind or another after a hike around the heights. Whether ordering lamb, beef, or the traditional Basque besugo, you would have a hard time going wrong at this picturesque spot with unbeatable panoramas over Bilbao. For weekend lunches, especially in springtime, it's best to call ahead or make a reservation—this is a popular spot for weddings. *Average main: €30 ✉ Ctra. Artxanda-Santo Domingo 19, El Arenal ☎ 94/445–5015 🌐 www.eltxakoli.net Ⓜ Abando.*

$$ TAPAS **Victor Montes.** On the ground floor, there's a deli and tapas bar where the well-stocked counter might offer anything from wild mushrooms to *txistorra* (spicy sausages), Idiazabal, or, for the adventurous, *huevas de merluza* (hake roe)—all taken with splashes of Rioja, *txakolí* (a young, white wine made from tart green grapes), or cider. There's a sprawling terrace and a dining room upstairs, but the bar is most popular. *Average main: €20 ✉ Pl. Nueva 8, Casco Viejo ☎ 94/415–7067*

www.victormontesbilbao.com *Reservations essential* *Closed Aug. 1–15. No dinner Sun.* *Casco Viejo.*

$ TAPAS **Xukela.** Amid bright lighting and a vivid palette of green and crimson morsels of ham and bell peppers lining his bar, chef Santiago Ruíz Bombin creates some of the tastiest and most interesting and varied pintxos in all of tapas-dom. Among the specialties are grilled mushrooms, stuffed with smoked cod and topped with apple cream, or other varieties topped with cured duck or salmon and liver. *Average main: €12* *C. El Perro 2, Casco Viejo* *94/415–9772* *www.xukela.com* *Casco Viejo.*

$$$$ SPANISH **Yandiola.** Within the Philippe Starck–designed Alhóndiga Bilbao complex in the Ensanche, Yandiola serves chic designer cuisine. The atmosphere is cool and casual, especially on the terrace, and the market cooking is creative but soundly based on quality products. The *croquetas caseras de hongos* (homemade wild mushroom croquettes) are not to be missed, while the *fideuà cremosa de coliflor y langostas al ajillo* (vermicelli noodle paella with cauliflour and garlicky prawns) is a delicious nod to Spain's east coast culinary canon. *Average main: €59* *Edificio Alhóndiga Bilbao, Pl. Arriquibar 4, Ensanche* *94/413–3636* *www.yandiola.com* *Reservations essential* *Closed Mon. No dinner Sun.* *Moyúa.*

$$$$ SPANISH **Zortziko.** An ultramodern kitchen housed in an ultrahistoric building, this fine dining restaurant is run by chef Daniel García, one of the Basque Country's culinary stars—with a Michelin star to prove it. García also offers a cooking exhibition for groups of 10 or more at a special table where diners can watch him in action. Reserve your table online. *Average main: €60* *C. Alameda Mazarredo 17, El Ensanche* *94/423–9743* *www.zortziko.es* *Reservations essential* *Closed Sun. and Mon.* *Moyúa.*

WHERE TO STAY

$ B&B/INN FAMILY **Artetxe.** With rooms overlooking Bilbao from the heights of Artxanda, this Basque farmhouse with wood trimmings and eager young owners offers excellent value and tranquility. **Pros:** a peaceful, grassy place from which to enjoy Bilbao and the Basque countryside; great service; plenty of space for children to play **Cons:** far from the center, the museums, and the action. *Rooms from: €65* *C. de Berriz 112, off Ctra. Enékuri–Artxanda, Km 7, Artxanda* *94/474–7780* *www.hotelartetxe.com* *12 rooms* *Breakfast.*

$$$$ HOTEL Fodor's Choice ★ **Castillo de Arteaga.** Built in the mid-19th century for Empress Eugenia de Montijo, wife of Napoleon III, this Neo-gothic limestone castle with rooms in the watchtowers and defensive walls is one of the most extraordinary lodging options in or around Bilbao. **Pros:** excellent wine and local food product tastings; views over the wetlands. **Cons:** somewhat isolated from village life and a half-hour drive to Bilbao. *Rooms from: €190* *Calle Gaztelubide 7, 40 km (24 miles) northwest of Bilbao, Gautegiz de Arteaga* *94/627–0440* *www.castillodearteaga.com* *7 rooms, 6 suites* *Closed late Dec.–early Jan.* *Multiple meal plans.*

$ HOTEL **Ercilla.** The taurine crowd fills this modern, hotel during Bilbao's Semana Grande in early August, partly because it's near the bullring and partly because it has taken over from the Carlton as the place to see and be seen. **Pros:** a Bilbao nerve center for journalists, politicians, and businesspeople. **Cons:** this might not be the place to stay if you're looking for a quiet getaway. *Rooms from: €89 C. Ercilla 37, Endantxu 94/470–5700 www.ercillahoteles.com 325 rooms Multiple meal plans Moyúa.*

$$$ HOTEL Fodor's Choice ★ **Gran Hotel Domine Bilbao.** As much modern design celebration as hotel, this Silken chain establishment directly across the street from the Guggenheim showcases the conceptual wit of Javier Mariscal, creator of Barcelona's 1992 Olympic mascot Cobi, and the structural know-how of Bilbao architect Iñaki Aurrekoetxea. **Pros:** at the very epicenter and, indeed, part of Bilbao's art and architecture excitement; the place to cross paths with Catherine Zeta-Jones or Antonio Banderas. **Cons:** hard on the wallet and a little full of its own glamour. *Rooms from: €150 Alameda de Mazarredo 61, El Ensanche 94/425–3300, 94/425–3301 www.granhoteldominebilbao.com 139 rooms, 6 suites Multiple meal plans Moyúa.*

$$$$ HOTEL Fodor's Choice ★ **Hotel Carlton.** This illustrious hotel exudes old-world grace and charm along with a sense of history—which it has aplenty *(⇨ see also Exploring)*. **Pros:** historic, old-world surroundings that remind you that Bilbao has an illustrious past. **Cons:** surrounded by plenty of concrete and urban frenzy. *Rooms from: €320 Pl. Federico Moyúa 2, El Ensanche 94/416–2200 www.hotelcarlton.es 136 rooms, 6 suites Breakfast Moyúa.*

$ HOTEL **Hotel Sirimiri.** A small, attentively run hotel near the Atxuri station, this modest spot has modern rooms with views over some of Bilbao's oldest architecture. **Pros:** handy to the Mercado de la Ribera, Casco Viejo, and the Atxuri train station; excellent buffet-style breakfast. **Cons:** tight quarters; lacking character of surrounding buildings. *Rooms from: €60 Pl. de la Encarnación 3, Casco Viejo 94/433–0759 www.hotelsirimiri.es 28 rooms Breakfast Casco Viejo.*

$ B&B/INN Fodor's Choice ★ **Iturrienea Ostatua.** Extraordinarily beautiful, with charm to spare, this hotel is in a traditional Basque town house one flight above the street in Bilbao's Old Quarter. **Pros:** budget-friendly; all nonsmoking; exquisite rustic style; free Wi-Fi. **Cons:** nocturnal noise on the front side, especially on summer weekend nights—try for an interior room or bring earplugs. *Rooms from: €70 Santa María 14, Casco Viejo 94/416–1500 www.iturrieneaostatua.com 19 rooms No meals Casco Viejo.*

$$ HOTEL **López de Haro.** This luxury hotel five minutes from the Guggenheim is under the same ownership as the Ercilla and, like its sister hotel, it's becoming quite a scene now that the city is a bona fide contemporary art destination. **Pros:** state-of-the-art comfort, service, and cuisine; traditional and aristocratic setting. **Cons:** a less than relaxing, slightly hushed and stuffy scene; not for the shorts and tank top set. *Rooms from: €100 Obispo Orueta 2–4, El Ensanche 94/423–5500 www.hotellopezdeharo.com 49 rooms, 4 suites Breakfast Moyúa.*

$$ HOTEL **Meliá Bilbao Hotel.** Designed by architect Ricardo Legorreta and inspired by the work of Basque sculptor Eduardo Chillida (1920–2002), this high-rise hotel was built over what was once the nerve center of Bilbao's shipbuilding industry, and it feels appropriately like a futuristic ocean liner. **Pros:** great views over the whole shebang if you can get a room facing the Guggenheim. **Cons:** a high-rise colossus that might be more at home in Miami or Malibu. *Rooms from: €105 C. Lehendakari Leizaola 29, El Ensanche 94/428–0000 www.melia.com 199 rooms, 12 suites No meals San Mamés.*

$$ HOTEL **Miró Hotel.** Perfectly placed between the Guggenheim and Bilbao's excellent Museo de Bellas Artes, this boutique hotel refurbished by Barcelona fashion designer Toni Miró competes with the reflecting facade of Javier Mariscal's Domine Bilbao just up the street. **Pros:** a design refuge that places you in the eye of Bilbao's art and architecture fiesta. **Cons:** not unpretentious; a hint of preciosity pervades these halls. *Rooms from: €110 Alameda de Mazarredo 77, El Ensanche 94/661–1880 www.mirohotelbilbao.com 50 rooms No meals Moyúa.*

$ HOTEL **Petit Palace Arana.** Across from the Teatro Arriaga in the Casco Viejo, this design hotel has a blended style of contemporary and antique. **Pros:** in the heart of traditional Bilbao. **Cons:** can be noisy at night on the street side of the building. *Rooms from: €83 Bidebarrieta 2, Casco Viejo 94/415–6411 www.hthoteles.com 64 rooms Multiple meal plans Casco Viejo.*

$ HOTEL **Pensión Méndez I & II.** This may be the best value in town, with small but impeccable and well-appointed rooms, some of which (nos. **Pros:** excellent value; location in the middle of the Casco Viejo. **Cons:** no a/c; rooms with best views are noisy at night. *Rooms from: €50 Santa María 13, 1st and 4th fl., Casco Viejo 94/416–0364 www.pensionmendez.com 24 rooms No meals Casco Viejo.*

$$ HOTEL FAMILY **Urgoiti Hotel Palacio.** This extraordinary hotel, occupying a reconstructed 17th-century country palace out toward the airport, is a great retreat for active travelers or families, with a nine-hole pitch and putt in the hotel gardens and other activities nearby. **Pros:** handy train service into Bilbao; nearly walking distance from the airport; elegant and peaceful environment; golf and water sports nearby. **Cons:** Bilbao and the Guggenheim a short excursion away; a particular flight path into the airport can be teeth-rattling. *Rooms from: €115 Arritugane Kalea s/n, 13 km (8 miles) west of Bilbao, 2 km (1.2 miles) from the airport, Mungia 94/674–6868 www.palaciourgoiti.com 42 rooms, 1 suite Breakfast.*

BULLFIGHTS

Bilbao's *Semana Grande* (Grand Week), in mid-August, is famous for scheduling Spain's largest bullfights of the season, an example of the Basque Country's tendency to favor contests of strength and character over art. (Note that in Barcelona, bullfights are no longer allowed under local legislation.)

Plaza de Toros Vista Alegre. Prices and times of the bullfights held here vary by event; check the website for listings. *Martín Agüero 1, San Mamés 94/444–8698 www.plazatorosbilbao.com San Mamés.*

9

SHOPPING

The main stores for clothing are found around Plaza Moyúa in the Ensanche, along streets such as Calle Iparraguirre and Calle Rodríguez Arias. The Casco Viejo has dozens of smaller shops, many of them handsomely restored early houses with gorgeous wooden beams and ancient stones, specializing in an endless variety of products from crafts to antiques. Wool items, foodstuffs, and wood carvings from around the Basque Country can be found throughout Bilbao. *Txapelas* (berets or Basque *boinas*) are famous worldwide and make fine gifts.

The city is home to international fashion names from Coco Chanel to Calvin Klein. The ubiquitous department store El Corte Inglés is an easy one-stop shop, if a bit routine.

MUNDAKA

37 km (22 miles) northeast of Bilbao.

Tiny Mundaka, famous with surfers all over the world for its left-breaking roller at the mouth of the Ría de Gernika, has much to offer nonsurfers as well. The town's elegant summer homes and stately houses bearing family coats of arms compete for pride of place with the hermitage on the Santa Catalina peninsula and the parish church's Renaissance doorway.

ESSENTIALS

Visitor Information Mundaka ✉ *Josepa Deuna kalea s/n* ☎ *94/617–7201* 🌐 *www.mundakaturismo.com.*

WHERE TO EAT AND STAY

$$$ BASQUE **Baserri Maitea.** In the village of Forua, about 11 km (7 miles) south of Mundaka and 1 km (½ mile) northwest of Guernica, this restaurant is in a stunning 18th-century *caserío* (Basque farmhouse). Strings of red peppers and garlic hang from wooden beams in the cathedral-like interior, and the kitchen is famous for its hearty fish and meat dishes prepared over a wood-fired grill. $ *Average main: €25* ✉ *BI635 to Bermeo, Km 2* ☎ *94/625–3408* 🌐 *www.baserrimaitea.com* ⏲ *No dinner Sun. July and Aug.; no dinner Sun.–Thurs. Sept.–June.*

$$$ SEAFOOD Fodor's Choice ★ **Casino de Mundaka.** Built in 1818 as a fish auction house for the local fishermen's guild, this building in the center of town, with wonderful views of Mundaka's beach, is now a fine restaurant and a well-known and respected eating club. The public is welcome, and it's a favorite place for lunches and sunset dinners in summer, when you can sit in the glassed-in, upper-floor porch. Don't be confused by the name—there's no gambling here ("casino" means something like a gentleman's club in Castilian). $ *Average main: €25* ✉ *Kepa Deunaren 1* ☎ *94/687–6005.*

$$$$ BASQUE **Portuondo.** Spectacular terraces outside a traditional *caserío* (Basque farmhouse) overlooking the Laida beach, the aromas of beef and fish cooking over coals, a comfortable country dining room upstairs, and an easy 15-minute walk outside Mundaka all make this a good stop for lunch or dinner (in summer—it's a good idea to book ahead). Offerings are balanced between meat and seafood, and the wine list

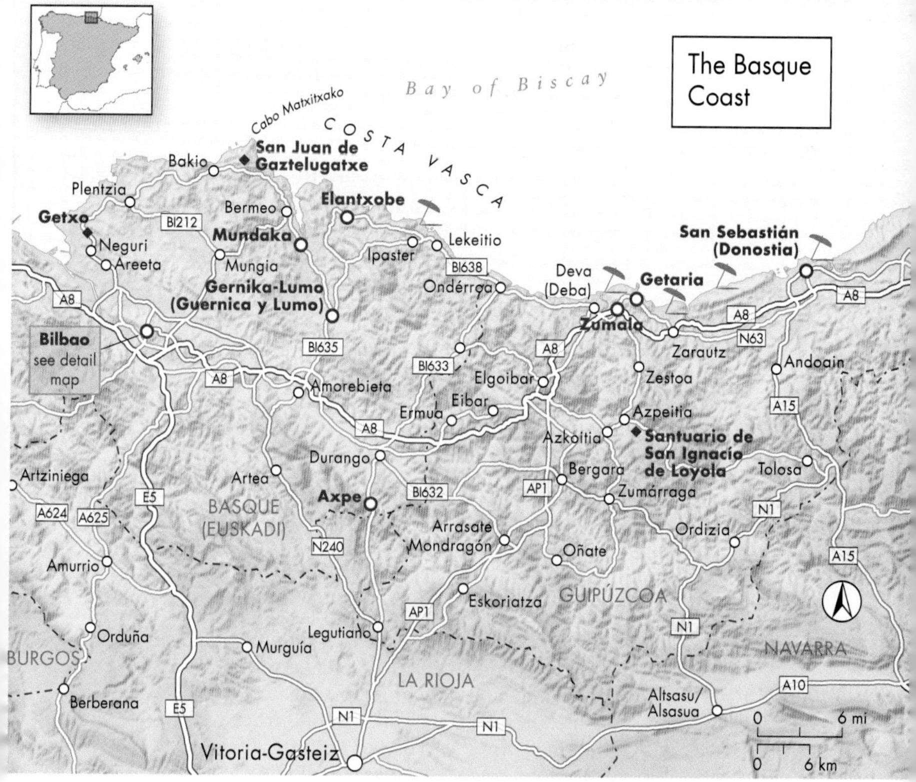

covers an interesting selection of wines from all over Spain. The tapas area downstairs crackles with life on weekends and during the summer. *Average main: €50* *Portuondo Auzoa 1, Ctra. Gernika–Bermeo (BI2235), Km 47* *94/687–6050* *www.restauranteportuondo.com* *Closed Mon.*

$$ **HOTEL** **Atalaya.** Tastefully converted from a private house, this 1911 landmark has become a big favorite for quick rail-getaway overnights from Bilbao—the 37-km (22-mile) train ride out is spectacular. **Pros:** intimate retreat from Bilbao's sprawl and bustle; friendly family service; weekend specials. **Cons:** tight quarters in some rooms. *Rooms from: €110* *Itxaropen Kalea 1* *94/687–6899* *www.atalayahotel.es* *13 rooms* *Multiple meal plans.*

$ **HOTEL** **Boliña.** Just a few steps from the Plaza de los Fueros in downtown Guernica, the Boliña is a pleasant and modern base camp for exploring the Vizcayan coast. **Pros:** comfortable and efficient; central location; good value. **Cons:** small rooms; restaurant seats 100 and is a local favorite for wedding receptions and gatherings. *Rooms from: €35* *Barrenkale 3* *94/625–0300* *www.hotelbolina.es* *16 rooms* *Multiple meal plans.*

$ **HOTEL** **Kurutziaga Jauregia.** Basque for Palacio de la Cruz, this elegant 18th-century town house is a perfect alternative to the Atalaya for an overnight getaway from Bilbao. **Pros:** cozy retreat in downtown Mundaka.

Cons: small rooms; tight streets; parking can be difficult. $ *Rooms from: €70 ✉ Kurtzio Kalea 1 ☎ 94/687–6925 🌐 www.kurutziagajauregia.com ⇨ 23 rooms 🍴 Multiple meal plans.*

OFF THE BEATEN PATH

Bosque de Oma. On the road to Kortezubi, 5 km (3 miles) from Guernica, stop off at the Urdaibai Natural Reserve for a stroll through the Bosque de Oma, also known simply as Bosque Pintado (Painted Forest) because of the rows of trees vividly painted by Basque artist Agustín Ibarrola. It's a striking and successful marriage of art and nature. The nearby **Cuevas de Santimamiñe** have important prehistoric cave paintings that can be accessed virtually at a visitor center. ✉ *Barrio Basondo, Kortezubi* ☎ *94/465–1657.*

ELANTXOBE

50 km (30 miles) northeast of Bilbao, 24 km (15 miles) east of Mundaka.

The tiny fishing village of Elantxobe (Elanchove in Spanish) is surrounded by huge, steep cliffs, with a small breakwater that protects its fleet from the storms of the Bay of Biscay. The view of the port from the upper village is breathtaking, and the lower fork in the road leads to it.

WHERE TO STAY

$ B&B/INN FAMILY

Casa Rural Arboliz. On a bluff overlooking the Bay of Biscay just outside of Elantxobe, this rustic, family-run inn is removed from the harborside bustle, offering a breath of country life on the Basque coast. **Pros:** bucolic setting. **Cons:** could be too isolated and quiet for some; breakfast not included in room rate. $ *Rooms from: €65 ✉ Arboliz 12, about 2 km (1 mile) along the road to Lekeitio, Elantxobe ☎ 94/627–6283 🌐 www.arboliz.com ⇨ 4 rooms, 2 suites 🍴 No meals.*

$ B&B/INN

Itsasmin Ostatua. At the foot of Monte Ogoño in the upper part of the charming and colorful fishing and seafaring village, this amicable place rents simple, cheery rooms and serves home-cooked Basque cuisine in its diminutive dining room. **Pros:** part of the hustle and bustle of village life; simple and comfortable. **Cons:** tight quarters in some rooms; rooms facing the square can be noisy on weekends. $ *Rooms from: €55 ✉ Nagusia 32, Elantxobe ☎ 94/627–6174 🌐 www.itsasmin.com ⇨ 12 rooms ⏲ Closed early Jan.–early Feb. 🍴 No meals.*

AXPE

47 km (28 miles) east of Bilbao, 42 km (26 miles) south of Elantxobe.

The village of Axpe, in the valley of Atxondo, nestles under the limestone heights of 4,777-foot Amboto—one of the highest peaks in the Basque Country outside the Pyrenees. Home of the legendary Basque mother of nature—Mari Urrika or Mari Anbotokodama (María, Our Lady of Amboto)—Amboto, with its spectral gray rock face, is a sharp contrast to the soft green meadows running up to the very foot of the mountain. According to Basque scholar and ethnologist José María de Barandiarán in his *Mitología Vasca* (*Basque Mythology*), Mari was "a beautiful woman, well constructed in all ways except for one foot, which was like that of a goat."

GETTING HERE

To reach Axpe from Bilbao, drive east on the A8/E70 freeway toward San Sebastián. Get off at the Durango exit 40 km (24 miles) from Bilbao and take the BI632 toward Elorrio. At Apatamonasterio turn right onto the BI3313 and continue to Axpe.

WHERE TO EAT AND STAY

$$$$ SEAFOOD Fodor's Choice ★ **Etxebarri.** Victor Arguinzoniz and his development of innovative techniques for cooking over coals have been hot news around the Iberian Peninsula for a decade now, with woods and coals tailored to different ingredients and new equipment such as a pan to char-grill angulas or caviar. Everything from clams and fish to meats and even the rice with langoustines is healthy, flavorful, and exciting as prepared and served in this blocky stone house in the center of a tiny mountain town. *Average main: €40 Pl. San Juan 1 94/658–3042 www.asadoretxebarri.com Reservations essential Closed Mon. and Aug. No dinner Tues.–Fri.*

$ HOTEL Fodor's Choice ★ **Mendigoikoa.** This handsome group of hillside farmhouses is among the province of Vizcaya's most exquisite hideaways. **Pros:** gorgeous setting; smart and attentive service. **Cons:** need a car to get here. *Rooms from: €80 Barrio San Juan 33 94/682–0833 www.mendigoikoa.com 11 rooms Closed Nov.–Easter Breakfast.*

GETARIA AND ZUMAIA

80 km (50 miles) east of Bilbao, 22 km (14 miles) west of San Sebastián.

Zumaia and Getaria are connected along the coast road and by several good footpaths.

ESSENTIALS

Visitor Information Getaria *Parque Aldamar 2 94/314-0957 www.getaria.net.* **Zumaia** *Pl. de Kantauri 13 94/314-3396 zumaia.net.*

EXPLORING

Cristóbal Balenciaga Museoa. Although his fashion house lives on in Paris, the haute-couture maestro Cristóbel Balenciaga (1895–1972) was born in Getaria. This museum dedicated to his life is a must see, not only for followers of fashion, but for anyone who believes in the transformative power of design. The collection gathers together 1,200 pieces that represent his life's work. *Aldamar Parkea 6 94/300–8840 www.cristobalbalenciagamuseoa.com €10 Nov.–Feb., Tues.–Fri. 10–3, weekends 10–5; Mar.–May and Oct., Tues.–Fri. and Sun. 10–5, Sat. 10–7; June and Sept., Tues.–Sun. 10–7; July and Aug., daily 10–7.*

Getaria (*Guetaria*). Getaria is known as *la cocina de Guipúzcoa* (the kitchen of Guipúzcoa province) for its many restaurants and taverns. It was also the birthplace of Juan Sebastián Elcano (1487–1526), the first circumnavigator of the globe and Spain's most emblematic naval hero. Elcano took over and completed Magellan's voyage after Magellan was killed in the Philippines in 1521. The town's galleonlike church has sloping wooden floors resembling a ship's deck. Zarautz, the next town over, has a wide beach and many taverns and cafés.

Zumaia. Zumaia is a snug little port and summer resort with the estuary of the Urola River flowing—back and forth, according to the tide—through town.

Museo Zuloaga. On the N634 at the eastern edge of town, this museum has an extraordinary collection of paintings by Goya, El Greco, Zurbarán, and others, in addition to works by the Basque impressionist Ignacio Zuloaga. The collection is housed in an ancient stone convent surrounded by gardens. With limited hours, the office phone often goes unanswered, so it's best to email with any requests. ✉ *Casa Santiago-Etxea 4* ☎ *67/707–8445* 🌐 *www.espaciozuloaga.com* *€5* ⏲ *Mid-Apr.–mid-Sept., Fri.–Sun. 4–8*

WHERE TO EAT AND STAY

$$ BASQUE

✕ **Bedua.** Zumaia natives like to access this rustic hideaway by boat when the tide is right, though you can also walk or drive. A specialist in *tortilla de patatas con pimientos verdes de la huerta* (potato omelet with homegrown green peppers), Bedua is also known for *tortilla de bacalao* (cod), *txuleta de buey* (beef chop), and fish of all kinds, especially the classic besugo cooked *a la donostiarra* (roasted and covered with a sauce of garlic and vinegar) and fresh baby eels, in season. $ *Average main: €15* ✉ *Cestona, Barrio Bedua, up Urola, 3 km (2 miles) from Zumaia* ☎ *94/386–0551* 🌐 *www.bedua.es.*

$$ SEAFOOD

✕ **Kaia Kaipe.** Suspended over Getaria's colorful and busy fishing port and with panoramas looking up the coast past Zarautz and San Sebastián all the way to Biarritz, this spectacular place puts together exquisite fish soups and serves fresh fish right off the boats—you can watch it being unloaded below. The town is the home of Txomin Etxaniz, the premier txakolí, and this is the ideal place to drink it. $ *Average main: €15* ✉ *General Arnao 4* ☎ *94/314–0500* 🌐 *www.kaia-kaipe.com* ⏲ *Closed Mon. Oct.–June.*

$$ B&B/INN FAMILY

Landarte. For a taste of life in a Basque caserío, spend a night or two in this lovely, restored, 16th-century, country manor house 1 km (½ mile) from Zumaia and an hour's walk from Getaria. **Pros:** Warm family-friendly atmosphere; traditional cuisine on request. **Cons:** Some top-floor rooms under the low roof eaves could be tricky for taller guests; breakfast costs €6 extra per person. $ *Rooms from: €88* ✉ *C. Artadi Anzoa 1, Zumaia* ☎ *94/386–5358* 🌐 *www.landarte.net* *6 rooms* ⏲ *Closed mid-Dec.–Feb.* *No meals.*

$$ HOTEL Fodor's Choice ★

Saiaz Getaria. For panoramic views over the Bay of Biscay, this 15th-century house on Getaria's uppermost street is a perfect choice. **Pros:** opportunity to stay in a noble house in a unique fishing village; free Wi-Fi; discounts at nearby spa and gym. **Cons:** rooms on the sea side are small and undistinguished except for the views. $ *Rooms from: €109* ✉ *Roke Deuna 25* ☎ *94/314–0143* 🌐 *www.saiazgetaria.com* *17 rooms* ⏲ *Closed Dec. 20–Jan. 6* *No meals.*

OFF THE BEATEN PATH

Pello Urdapilleta. For a look at an authentic Basque caserío where the Urdapilleta family farms pigs, sheep, cattle, goats, chickens, and ducks, take a detour up to the village of Bidegoian, on the Azpeitia–Tolosa road. Pello Urdapilleta (which means "pile of pigs" in Euskera) sells artisanal cheeses and sausages, depending on what's available on the day. ✉ *Elola Azpikoa Baserria, Bidegoian* ☎ *605/701204* 🌐 *www.urdapilleta.eu.*

SAN SEBASTIÁN TO HONDARRIBIA

Graceful, chic San Sebastián invites you to slow down: stroll the beach or wander the streets. East of the city is Pasajes, from which the Marquis de Lafayette set off to help the rebelling forces in the American Revolution and where Victor Hugo spent a winter writing. Just shy of the French border is Hondarribia, a brightly painted, flower-festooned port town.

SAN SEBASTIÁN

100 km (62 miles) northeast of Bilbao.

Fodor's Choice ★ San Sebastián (Donostia in Euskera) is a sophisticated city arched around one of the finest urban beaches in the world, **La Concha** (The Shell), so named for its resemblance to the shape of a scallop shell, with Ondarreta and Zurriola beaches at the southwestern and northeastern ends. The promontories of Monte Urgull and Monte Igueldo serve as bookends for La Concha, while Zurriola has Monte Ulía rising over its far end. The best way to see San Sebastián is to walk around: promenades and pathways lead up the hills that surround the city. The first records of San Sebastián date from the 11th century. A backwater for centuries, the city had the good fortune in 1845 to attract Queen Isabella II, who was seeking relief from a skin ailment in the icy Atlantic waters. Isabella was followed by much of the aristocracy of the time, and San Sebastián became a favored summer retreat for Madrid's well-to-do.

San Sebastián is divided by the **Urumea River,** which is crossed by three bridges inspired by late-19th-century French architecture. At the mouth of the Urumea, the incoming surf smashes the rocks with such force that white foam erupts, and the noise is wild and Wagnerian. The city is laid out with wide streets on a grid pattern, thanks mainly to the 12 different times it has been all but destroyed by fire. The last conflagration came after the French were expelled in 1813; English and Portuguese forces occupied the city, abused the population, and torched the place. Today, San Sebastián is a seaside resort on par with Nice and Monte Carlo. It becomes one of Spain's most expensive cities in the summer, when French vacationers descend in droves. It is also, like Bilbao, a center of Basque nationalism.

San Sebastián's neighborhoods include La Parte Vieja, tucked under Monte Urgull north of the mouth of the Urumea River; Gros (so named for a corpulent Napoleonic general), across the Urumea to the north; Centro, the main city nucleus around the cathedral; Amara, farther east toward the Anoeta sports complex; La Concha, at stage center around the beach; and El Antiguo, at the western end of La Concha. Igueldo is the high promontory over the city at the southwestern side of the bay. Alto de Miracruz is the high ground to the northeast toward France; Errenteria is inland east of Pasajes; Oiartzun is a village farther north; Astigarraga is in apple-cider country to the east of Anoeta.

GETTING HERE AND AROUND

San Sebastián is a very walkable city, though local buses (€1.60) are also convenient. Buses for Pasajes (Pasaia), Errenteria, Astigarraga, and Oiartzun originate in Calle Okendo, one block west of the Urumea River behind the Hotel Maria Cristina. Bus A-1 goes to Astigarraga; A-2 is the bus to Pasajes.

The EuskoTren, the city train, is popularly known as "El Topo" (The Mole) for the amount of time it spends underground. It originates at the Amara Viejo station in Paseo Easo and tunnels its way to Hendaye, France, every 30 minutes (€2.35; 45 mins). EuskoTren also serves Bilbao (€5.60; 2 hrs, 40 mins) hourly and Zarautz (€2.35; 40 mins) every half hour.

For the funicular up to Monte Igueldo (☎ *943/213525* ⊕ *www.monteigueldo.es* 🎫 *€1.70*) the station is just behind Ondarreta beach at the western end of La Concha.

ESSENTIALS

Bus Information Bus station (Estación de autobuses) ✉ *C. de Fernando Sasiaín 7* ☎ *94/346–9074* ⊕ *www.dbus.es.*

Car Rental Europcar ✉ *Aeropuerto de San Sebastián (Hondarribia [Fuenterrabía]), C. Gabarrari, 22* ☎ *94/366–8530* ⊕ *www.europcar.com.*

Train Information EuskoTren ☎ *90/254–3210* ⊕ *www.euskotren.es.*
San Sebastián train station ✉ *Estación de Amara, Pl. Easo 9* ☎ *90/254–3210* ⊕ *www.euskotren.es* ✉ *Estación del Norte (RENFE), Paseo de Francia 22* ☎ *90/224–3402* ⊕ *www.renfe.es.*

Visitor Information San Sebastián–Donostia ✉ *Erregina Erregentearen 3, Blvd. 8* ☎ *94/348–1166* ⊕ *www.sansebastianturismo.com.*

EXPLORING

Every corner of Spain champions its culinary identity, but San Sebastián's refined fare is in a league of its own. Many of the city's restaurants and tapas spots are in the **Parte Vieja** (Old Quarter), on the east end of the bay beyond the elegant **Casa Consistorial** (City Hall) and formal **Alderdi Eder** gardens. The building that now houses city hall began as a casino in 1887; after gambling was outlawed early in the 20th century, the town council moved here from the Plaza de la Constitución, the Old Quarter's main square.

FAMILY **Aquarium Donostia–San Sebastián.** For a stroll through and under some 6,000 fish—ranging from tiger sharks to sea turtles, with one participative pool where kids are encouraged to touch and try to pick up fish—this is a great resource on one of San Sebastián's many rainy days. The illustrated history of Basque whaling and boatbuilding is also fascinating. ✉ *Pl. Carlos Blasco de Imaz 1* ☎ *94/344–0099* ⊕ *www.aquariumss.com* 🎫 *€13* ⏲ *July and Aug., daily 10–9; Easter–June and Sept., weekdays 10–8, weekends 10–9; Oct.–Easter, weekdays 10–7, weekends 10–8.*

Catedral Buen Pastor (*Cathedral of the Good Shepherd*). Looking directly south from the front of Santa María, you can see the facade and of this 19th-century cathedral across town. With the tallest church

spire in the province, the Cathedral of the Good Shepherd was constructed in the neo-Gothic style. It's worth a glimpse inside at beautiful stained-glass windows. ✉ *Urdaneta Kalea 4, Pl. del Buen Pastor* ☎ *94/346–4516* 🎫 *Free* ⏲ *Weekdays 8:30–noon and 5–8, weekends for Mass only.*

Isla de Santa Clara. The tiny Isla de Santa Clara, right in the entrance to the bay, protects the city from Bay of Biscay storms, making La Concha one of the calmest beaches on Spain's entire northern coast. High promontories, Monte Urgull on the right and Monte Igueldo on the left, dominate the entrance to the bay. From June through September, ferries run from the mainland every 30 minutes, and are packed on summer weekends. There's a small bar at the ferry dock, and lifeguard service at a beach that reveals itself only at low tide. Bring sandals, as the coastline is rocky.

Kursaal. Designed by renowned Spanish architect Rafael Moneo and located at the mouth of the Urumea River, the Kursaal is San Sebastián's postmodern concert hall, film society, and convention center. The gleaming cubes of glass that make up this bright complex were conceived as a perpetuation of the site's natural geography, an attempt to underline the harmony between the natural and the artificial and to create a visual stepping-stone between the heights of Monte Urgull and Monte Ulía. It has two auditoriums, a gargantuan banquet hall, meeting rooms, exhibition space, a set of terraces overlooking the estuary and the Ni Neu restaurant *(⇨ see Where to Eat)*. For guided tours of the building, make arrangements in advance. ✉ *Av. de Zurriola 1, Gros* ☎ *94/300–3000* 🌐 *www.kursaal.org.*

Monte Igueldo. On the western side of the bay, this promontory is a must-visit. You can walk or drive up or take the funicular (€3.10 round-trip), with departures every 15 minutes. ☎ *94/321–3525 for funicular* 🌐 *www.monteigueldo.es* ⏲ *Funicular: Apr.–June, weekdays 11–8, weekends 10–9; July and Sept., daily 11–8; Oct.–Mar., Mon., Tues., Thurs., and Fri. 11–6, weekends 11–7; Aug., daily 10–10.*

Museo de San Telmo. In a 16th-century monastery behind the Parte Vieja, to the right (northeast) of the church of Santa María, the former chapel, now a lecture hall, was painted by José María Sert (1876–1945). The museum displays Basque ethnographic items, such as prehistoric steles once used as grave markers, and paintings by Zuloaga, Ribera, and El Greco. ✉ *Pl. de Ignacio Zuloaga 1, Parte Vieja* ☎ *94/348–1581* 🌐 *www.museosantelmo.com* 🎫 *€5* ⏲ *Tues.–Sun. and holiday Mon. 10–8.*

Santa María. Just in from the harbor, in the shadow of Monte Urgull, is this baroque church, with a stunning carved facade of an arrow-riddled St. Sebastian flanked by two towers. The interior is strikingly restful; note the ship above the saint, high on the altar. ✉ *C. 31 de Agosto 46 at C. Mayor* ☎ *94/342–3124* 🎫 *Free* ⏲ *Daily 10:15–1:15 and 4:45–7:45.*

WHERE TO EAT

$$$$ CONTEMPORARY

✕ **Akelare.** On the far side of Monte Igueldo (and the far side of culinary tradition, as well) presides chef Pedro Subijana, one of the most respected and creative chefs in the Basque Country. Prepare for tastes of all kinds, from Pop Rocks in blood sausage to mustard ice cream on tangerine peels. At the same time, Subijana's classical, dishes are monuments to traditional cookery: try the venison with apple and smoked chestnuts. Subijana also offers cooking classes; reserve online. [$] *Average main: €155* ✉ *Paseo del Padre Orkolaga 56, Igueldo* ☎ *94/331–1209* 🌐 *www.akelarre.net* ✍ *Reservations essential* ⏲ *Closed Mon. (and Tues Jan.–June), Feb., and Oct. 1–15. No dinner Sun.*

$$$$ BASQUE Fodor's Choice ★

✕ **Arzak.** Renowned chef Juan Mari Arzak's little house at the crest of Alto de Miracruz on the eastern outskirts of San Sebastián is internationally famous, so reserve well in advance. Here, traditional Basque products and preparations are enhanced to bring out the best in the natural ingredients. The ongoing culinary dialogue between Juan Mari and his daughter Elena, who share the kitchen, is one of the most endearing attractions here. The sauces are perfect, and every dish looks beautiful, but the prices (even of appetizers) are astronomical. [$] *Average main: €189* ✉ *Av. Alcalde Jose Elosegui 273, Alto de Miracruz* ☎ *94/327–8465, 94/328–5593* 🌐 *www.arzak.es* ✍ *Reservations essential* ⏲ *Closed Sun. and Mon., June 15–July 2, and 3 wks in early Nov.*

$$ BASQUE

✕ **Astelena.** In what was once a banana warehouse, chef Ander González has transformed narrow stone rooms into one of the finest spots for modern Basque dining at a very good price. The €24 daily menu and the €36 weekend tasting menu list changing seasonal specials like *taco de bacalao sobre verduritas asadas* (salt-cod taco with grilled vegetables) and *magret de pato* (duck breast) or *alcachofas rellenas de rabo* (artichokes stuffed with bull's tail). The restaurant is conveniently located in the old quarter, near the Victoría Eugenia theater and Kursaal. [$] *Average main: €15* ✉ *Euskal Herria 3, Parte Vieja* ☎ *94/342–5867* 🌐 *www.restauranteastelena.com* ⏲ *Closed Mon. No dinner Sun.–Wed.*

$ TAPAS

✕ **Bar Ganbara.** This busy favorite near Plaza de la Constitución is now run by the third generation of the same family. Specialty morsels range from shrimp and asparagus to Ibérico acorn-fed ham on croissants to anchovies, sea urchins, and wild mushrooms in season. [$] *Average main: €10* ✉ *C. San Jerónimo 21, Parte Vieja* ☎ *94/342–2575* 🌐 *www.ganbarajatetxea.com* ⏲ *Closed Mon. No dinner Sun.*

$ TAPAS

✕ **Bar Gorriti.** Next to open-air La Brecha Market, this traditional little pintxos bar is a classic, filled with good cheer and delicious tapas. [$] *Average main: €10* ✉ *C. San Juan 3, Parte Vieja* ☎ *94/342–8353* ⏲ *Closed Sun.*

San Sebastián's famed, curving La Concha beach

$ TAPAS **Bar San Marcial.** Nearly a secret, downstairs in the center of town, this is a very Basque spot with big wooden tables and a monumental bar filled with *cazuelitas* (small earthenware dishes) and tapas of all kinds. *Average main: €10 C. San Marcial 50, Centro 94/343–1720 Closed Tues.*

$$ TAPAS **Bergara Bar.** Winner of many a miniature cuisine award, this rustic tavern on the corner of Arteche and Bermingham offers a stylish take on traditional tapas and pintxos, and also serves meal-size roasts. *Average main: €20 General Arteche 8, Gros 94/327–5026 www.pinchosbergara.es.*

$ TAPAS **Bernardo Etxea.** This hangout for locals during the week and everyone else on weekends serves excellent morsels: fried peppers, octopus, salmon with salsa, and especially fine pimientos with anchovies. There's a dining room for sit-down meals in the back, but the bar is most popular with the tapas crowd. *Average main: €12 C. Puerto 7, Parte Vieja 94/342–2055 www.bernardoetxea.com Closed Thurs. No dinner Wed.*

$$ TAPAS **Casa Vallés.** Beloved by locals, the bar combines great value with excellent food. Freshly prepared tapas creations go up on the bar at midday and again in the early evening, but it's open throughout the day for meals or snacks. There's a wood-paneled formal dining room out back, and tables on the sidewalk terrace out front. *Average main: €15 C. Reyes Católicos 10, Amara 94/345–2210 www.barvalles.com Closed Wed. No dinner Tues.*

$$ TAPAS **Casa Vergara.** This cozy bar, in front of the Santa María del Coro church, is always filled with reverent tapas devotees—and the counter is always piled high with delicious morsels. *Average main: €15 C. Mayor/Nagusia 21, Parte Vieja 94/343–1073 www.casavergara.com Closed Wed.*

$ TAPAS **Goiz Argi.** The specialty of this tiny bar—and the reason locals flock here on weekends—is the crisp yet juicy prawn brochette. *Average main: €8 Fermín Calbetón 4, Parte Vieja 94/342–5204.*

$$$ TAPAS **La Cepa.** This boisterous tavern has been around virtually forever (it opened in 1948). The ceiling of the wood-beamed bar is lined with dangling jamónes, the walls covered with old photos of San Sebastian and the room probably packed with locals. Everything from the Ibérico ham to the little olive, pepper, and anchovy combos called "penalties" will whet your appetite. *Average main: €25 C. 31 de Agosto 7, Parte Vieja 94/342–6394 www.barlacepa.com Closed Tues. and 2nd half of Nov.*

$$$$ CONTEMPORARY Fodor's Choice ★ **Martín Berasategui.** One of the top restaurants in San Sebastián, sure bets here include the *lubina asada con jugo de habas, vainas, cebolletas y tallarines de chipirón* (roast sea bass with juice of fava beans, green beans, baby onions, and cuttlefish shavings), and the *salmón salvaje con pepino líquido y cebolleta a lost fruitos rojos y rábanos* (wild salmon with liquid cucumber and spring onion, red fruits and radish), but go with whatever Martín suggests. *Average main: €55 C. Loidi 4, Lasarte, 8 km (5 miles) south of town 94/336–6471, 94/336–1599 www.martinberasategui.com Reservations essential Closed Mon., Tues., and mid-Dec.–mid-Jan. No dinner Sun.*

$$$$ SPANISH Fodor's Choice ★ **Mugaritz.** This farmhouse in the hills above Errenteria, 8 km (5 miles) northeast of San Sebastián, is surrounded by spices and herbs tended by chef Andoni Aduriz and his crew. In a contemporary rustic setting with a bright and open feeling, Aduriz works to preserve and enhance natural flavors using avant-garde techniques such as *sous-vide* (cooking vacuum-packed foods slowly in low-temperature water) with pristine products from field, forest, and sea. The tasting menu is the only option here. *Average main: €170 Aldura Aldea 20, Otzazulueta Baserria, Errenteria 94/352–2455, 94/351–8343 www.mugaritz.com Reservations essential Closed Mon. and mid-Dec.–mid-Apr. No lunch Tues.; no dinner Sun.*

$$$ CONTEMPORARY **Ni Neu.** Chef Mikel Gallo's Ni Neu ("Me, Myself" in Euskera) occupies a bright corner of Rafael Moneo's dazzling Kursaal complex at the mouth of the Urumea River. The new formula here has been christened *bistronómico,* a term coined by French chef Sebastián Demorand to describe a less formal, family-bistro environment with more affordable and creative cuisine. Eggs fried at a low temperature with potatoes and codfish broth and pork ribs cooked for 40 hours and accompanied by creamy chicory and vanilla rice are two examples of comfort food with creative touches. The tapas-bar section of the restaurant is an excellent value. *Average main: €25 Avenida Zurriola 1, Gros 94/300–3162 www.restaurantenineu.com Closed Mon. No dinner Tues., Wed., and Sun.*

$$$ BASQUE **Sidrería Petritegui.** For hearty dining and a certain amount of splashing around in hard cider, make this short excursion southeast of San Sebastián to the town of Astigarraga. Gigantic wooden barrels line the walls, and *sidra al txotx* (cider drawn straight from the barrel) is classically accompanied by cider-house specialties such as tortilla de bacalao, txuleta de buey, the smoky local sheep's-milk cheese from the town of Idiazabal, and, for dessert, walnuts and *membrillo* (quince jelly). You can also buy cider in bulk, and take a tour of the factory.

$ *Average main: €30* ✉ *Ctra. San Sebastián–Hernani, Km 7, Astigarraga* ☎ *94/345–7188, 94/347–2208* 🌐 *www.petritegi.com* ▭ *No credit cards* ⏲ *Closed mid-Dec.–mid-Jan. No lunch Mon. and Tues.–Thurs. late Sept.–late June.*

$ TAPAS
Zeruko. It may look like just another tapas bar, but the pintxos served here are among the most advanced and beautiful concoctions in town. Don't miss the bacalao *al pil pil* that cooks itself on your plate. $ *Average main: €10* ✉ *Pescadería 10, Parte Vieja* ☎ *94/342–3451* 🌐 *www.barzeruko.com* ⏲ *Closed Mon. No dinner Sun.*

$$$$ BASQUE Fodor's Choice ★
Zuberoa. Working in a 15th-century Basque farmhouse 9.5 km (6 miles) northeast of San Sebastián outside the village of Oiartzun, Hilario Arbelaitz has long been one of San Sebastián's most celebrated chefs due to his original yet simple management of prime raw materials such as tiny spring cuttlefish, baby octopi, or woodcock. The *lenguado con verduritas y chipirones* (sole with baby vegetables and cuttlefish) is a tour de force. The atmosphere is unpretentious: just a few friends sitting down to dine simply—but very, very well. $ *Average main: €40* ✉ *Araneder Bidea, Barrio Iturriotz, Oiartzun* ☎ *94/349–1228* 🌐 *www.zuberoa.com* ⏲ *Closed Wed., and Sun. June–Oct. No dinner Sun., and Tues. Nov.–May.*

WHERE TO STAY

$ B&B/INN FAMILY
Aristondo. A 15-minute drive above San Sebastián on Monte Igueldo, this comfortable and rustic farmhouse hideaway is a scenic and economical place to stay. **Pros:** good value; great views; bucolic peace and quiet. **Cons:** far from the action; requires a lot of walking, riding the funicular, or driving up and down Monte Igueldo. $ *Rooms from: €58* ✉ *Camino de Pilotegui 70, Igueldo* ☎ *94/321–5558, 615/780682* 🌐 *www.aristondo.com* *16 rooms* *No meals.*

$$$ HOTEL Fodor's Choice ★
Hotel de Londres y de Inglaterra. On the main beachfront promenade overlooking La Concha, this stately hotel has a regal, old-world feel and Belle Époque aesthetic that starts in the elegant marble lobby, with its shimmering chandeliers, and continues throughout the hotel. **Pros:** sunsets from rooms on the Concha side are stunning; great location over the beach. **Cons:** street side can be noisy on weekends. $ *Rooms from: €129* ✉ *Zubieta 2, La Concha* ☎ *94/344–0770* 🌐 *www.hlondres.com* *139 rooms, 9 suites* *No meals.*

$$$$ HOTEL
Hotel María Cristina. The graceful beauty of the Belle Époque is embodied here, in San Sebastián's most luxurious hotel, which sits on the elegant west bank of the Urumea River. **Pros:** polished service; supreme elegance; *the* place to stay. **Cons:** staffers occasionally can be stiff. $ *Rooms from: €250* ✉ *Paseo República Argentina 4, Centro* ☎ *94/343–7600* 🌐 *www.hotel-mariacristina.com* *108 rooms, 28 suites* *Some meals.*

$$$ HOTEL
Hotel Parma. Overlooking the Kursaal concert hall and the Zurriola beach at the mouth of the Urumea River, this small but bright new hotel is also at the edge of the Parte Vieja, San Sebastián's prime grazing area for tapas and vinos. **Pros:** prime location; views; the crashing of the waves; free Wi-Fi. **Cons:** rooms are a bit cramped and cluttered; room style is efficient but drab. $ *Rooms from: €157* ✉ *Paseo de Salamanca 10, Parte Vieja* ☎ *94/342–8893* 🌐 *www.hotelparma.com* *27 rooms* *No meals.*

NIGHTLIFE

Bataplan. San Sebastián's top disco is near the western end of La Concha. Guest DJs and events determine the vibe, although you can count on high-energy dance music and enthusiastic drinking. ✉ *Paseo de la Concha s/n, Centro* ☎ *94/347–3601* 🌐 *www.bataplandisco.com* ⏲ *Thurs.–Sat. midnight–7 am.*

Bebop. This publike bar, on the edge of the Urumea River, has regular live Latin and jazz music. Hours vary; check the website for listings. ✉ *Paseo de Salamanca 3, Parte Vieja* ☎ *94/342–9869* 🌐 *www.barbebop.com.*

Kursaal. Home of the Orquesta Sinfónica (Symphony Orchestra) de Euskadi, this venue is also a favorite for ballet, opera, theater, and jazz. ✉ *Av. de la Zurriola, Gros* ☎ *94/300–3000* 🌐 *www.kursaal.com.*

La Rotonda. Across the street from Bataplan and below Miraconcha, this is a top nightspot. ✉ *Paseo de la Concha 6, Centro* ☎ *94/342–9095, 639/146268* 🌐 *www.rotondadisco.com.*

Teatro Victoria Eugenia. In a stunning 19th century building, this elegant venue offers varied programs of theater, dance and more. ✉ *Paseo de la República Argentina, 2, Centro* ☎ *94/348–1155, 94/348–1160* 🌐 *www.victoriaeugenia.com.*

SHOPPING

San Sebastián is a busy designer-shopping town. Wander Calle San Martín and the surrounding pedestrian-only streets to see what's in the windows.

Elkar. Previously known as Bilintx, this shop is one of the city's best bookstores—it's now part of the Basque bookstore chain Elkar. There's a decent selection of English-language books, as well as CDs, games, and stationary. ✉ *Fermin Calbeton Kalea 21, Parte Vieja* ☎ *902/115210* 🌐 *www.elkar.com.*

Maitiena. Stop by this stylish shop for a fabulous selection of chocolates, hot chocolate, teas, and other fixes for sweet-tooths. ✉ *Peña Florida 6, Centro* ☎ *94/342–4721* 🌐 *www.maitiana.com.*

Ponsol. The best place to buy Basque berets—the Leclerq family has been hatting (and clothing) the local male population for four generations, since 1838. It's closed between 1 and 4 pm, and all day Sunday. ✉ C. *Narrica 4 at C. Sarriegui 3, Parte Vieja* ☎ *94/342–0876* 🌐 *www.casaponsol.com.*

PASAJES DE SAN JUAN

7 km (4 miles) east of San Sebastián.

Generally marked as Pasai Donibane, in Euskera, there are actually three towns around the commercial port of Rentería: **Pasajes Ancho,** an industrial port; Pasajes de San Pedro, a large fishing harbor; and historic **Pasajes de San Juan,** a colorful cluster of 16th- and 17th-century buildings along the shipping channel between the industrial port of Rentería and the sea. Best and most colorfully reached by driving into Pasai de San Pedro, on the San Sebastián side of the strait, and catching a launch across the mouth of the harbor (about €1, depending on the time of day), this is too sweet a side trip to pass up.

In 1777, at the age of 20, General Lafayette set out from Pasajes de San Juan to aid the American Revolution. Victor Hugo spent the summer of 1843 here writing his *Voyage aux Pyrénées*. The **Victor Hugo House** is the home of the tourist office and has an exhibit of traditional village dress. **Ondartxo,** a center of maritime culture, is directed by Xavier Agote, who taught boatbuilding in Rockland, Maine. Pasajes de San Juan can be reached via Pasajes de San Pedro from San Sebastián by cab or bus. Or, if you prefer to go on foot, follow the red-and-white-blazed GR trail that begins at the east end of the Zurriola beach—you're in for a spectacular three-hour hike along the rocky coast. By car, take N1 toward France and, after passing Juan Mari Arzak's landmark restaurant, Arzak, at Alto de Miracruz, look for a marked left turn into Pasaia or Pasajes de San Pedro.

WHAT TO SEE

FAMILY **Barco Museo Mater** (*Mater Ship Museum*). A former Basque fishing boat now offers tours of the port, visits to a rowing club, and to the Victor Hugo house in Pasai Donibane, as well as a treasure hunt for young and old alike. You can join a one-hour trip or rent the ship out for the whole day (for groups of 10 or more). Book ahead, online or by phone. ✉ *Muelle Pesquero, Pasai San Pedro* ☎ *619/814225* 🌐 *www.itsasgela.org* 🎫 *One-hour trip €5* ⏲ *Tues.–Thurs. at 5 and 6, weekends at noon and 1.*

WHERE TO EAT

$$$$ SEAFOOD Fodor's Choice ★ ✕ **Casa Cámara.** Four generations ago, Pablo Cámara turned this 19th century fishing wharf on the Rentería narrows into a first-class seafood restaurant with classic fare. The dining room has lovely views over the shipping lane, and a central "live" tank that rises and falls with the tide and from which lobsters and crayfish can be hauled up for your inspection. A steaming *sopa de pescado* (fish soup) on a wet Atlantic day is a memorable event. Try *cangrejo del mar* (spider crab with vegetable sauce) or the superb *merluza con salsa verde* (hake in green sauce). 💲 *Average main: €37* ✉ *C. San Juan 79, Pasai Donibane* ☎ *94/352–3699* 🌐 *www.casacamara.com* ✍ *Reservations essential* ⏲ *Closed Mon., and Wed. Nov.–Easter wk. No dinner Sun.*

9

HONDARRIBIA

18 km (11 miles) east of Pasajes.

Hondarribia (Fuenterrabía in Spanish) is the last fishing port before the French border. Lined with fishermen's homes and small fishing boats, the harbor is a beautiful but touristy spot. If you have a taste for history, follow signs up the hill to the medieval bastion and onetime castle of Carlos V, now a parador.

ESSENTIALS

Visitor Information Hondarribia ✉ *Pl. de Armas 9* ☎ *94/364–3677* 🌐 *www.bidasoaturismo.com.*

WHERE TO EAT AND STAY

$$$$ BASQUE **Alameda.** The three Txapartegi brothers—Mikel, Kepa and Gorka—are the star chefs behind this restaurant, which opened in 1997 after the brothers' apprenticeship with, among others, Lasarte's master chef Martín Berasategui. The elegantly restored house in upper Hondarribia is a delight, as are the seasonally rotated combinations of carefully chosen ingredients, from fish to duck to vegetables. Both surf and turf selections are well served here, from Ibérico ham to fresh tuna just in from the Atlantic. *Average main: €50 Minasoroeta 1 94/364–2789 www.restaurantealameda.net No dinner Sun., and Mon. and Tues. late Dec.–early Feb.*

$ B&B/INN FAMILY **Casa Artzu.** Better hosts than this warm, friendly clan are hard to find, and their family house and barn—here in one form or another for some 800 years—offers modernized accommodations overlooking the Bidasoa estuary and the Atlantic. **Pros:** good value; friendly family. **Cons:** free parking; breakfast costs €3 extra. *Rooms from: €47 Barrio Montaña 94/364–0530 www.euskalnet.net/casartzu 6 rooms No meals.*

$$$$ HOTEL FAMILY Fodor's Choice ★ **Parador de Hondarribia.** You can live like a medieval lord in this 10th-century bastion, home in the 16th century of Spain's founding emperor, Carlos V—hence it's alternative name: Parador El Emperador. **Pros:** great sea views; impeccably comfortable. **Cons:** no restaurant. *Rooms from: €220 Pl. de Armas 14 94/364–5500 www.parador.es 36 rooms No meals.*

NAVARRA AND PAMPLONA

Bordering the French Pyrenees and populated largely by Basques, Navarra grows progressively less Basque toward its southern and eastern edges. Pamplona, the ancient Navarran capital, draws crowds with its annual feast of San Fermín, but medieval Vitoria, the Basque capital city in the province of Alava, is largely undiscovered by tourists. Olite, south of Pamplona, has a storybook castle, and the towns of Puente la Reina and Estella are visually indelible stops on the Camino de Santiago.

PAMPLONA

79 km (47 miles) southeast of San Sebastián.

Pamplona (Iruña in Euskera) is known worldwide for its running of the bulls, made famous by Ernest Hemingway in his 1926 novel *The Sun Also Rises.* The occasion is the festival of San Fermín, July 6–14, when Pamplona's population triples (along with hotel rates), so reserve rooms months in advance. Every morning at 8 sharp a rocket is shot off, and the bulls kept overnight in the corrals at the edge of town are run through a series of closed-off streets leading to the bullring, a 924-yard dash. Running before them are Spaniards and foreigners feeling festive enough to risk goring. The degree of peril in the running (or *encierro,* meaning "enclosing") is difficult to gauge. Serious injuries occur nearly every day during the festival; deaths are rare but always

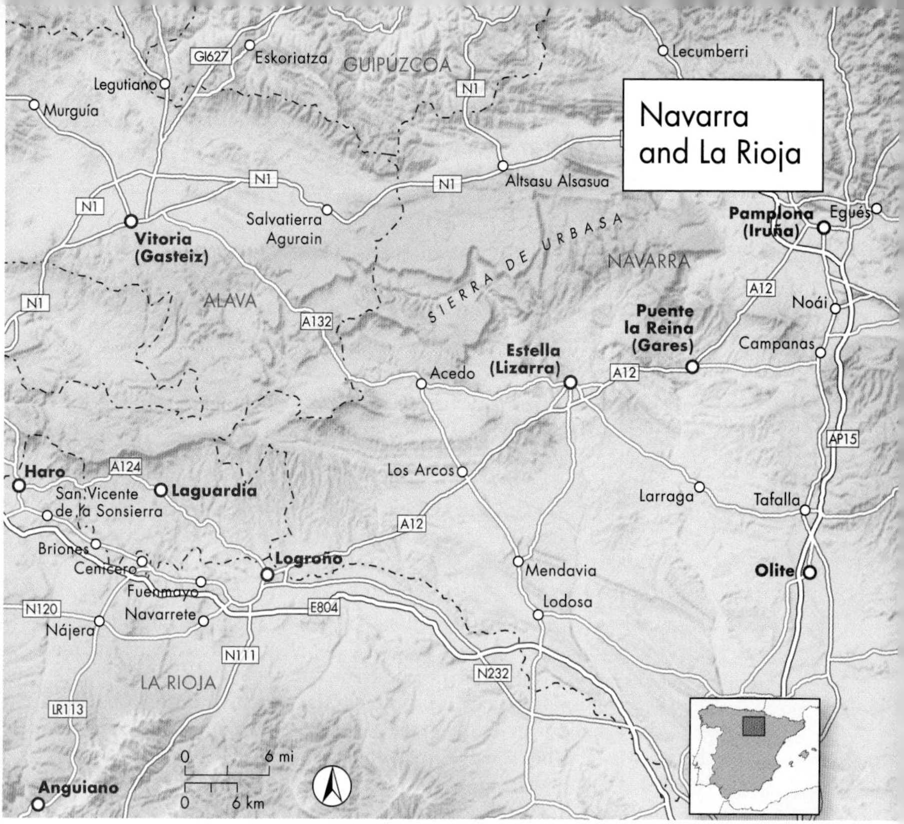

a possibility. What's certain is the sense of danger, the mob hysteria, and the exhilaration. Access to the running is free, but tickets to the bullfights (*corridas*) can be difficult to get.

Founded by the Roman emperor Pompey as Pompaelo, or Pampeiopolis, Pamplona was successively taken by the Franks, the Goths, and the Moors. In 750, the Pamplonians put themselves under the protection of Charlemagne and managed to expel the Arabs temporarily. But the foreign commander took advantage of this trust to destroy the city walls; when he was driven out once more by the Moors, the Navarrese took their revenge, ambushing and slaughtering the retreating Frankish army as it fled over the Pyrenees through the mountain pass of Roncesvalles in 778. This is the episode depicted in the 11th-century *Song of Roland*, although the anonymous French cast the aggressors as Moors. For centuries after that, Pamplona remained three argumentative towns until they were forcibly incorporated into one city by Carlos III (the Noble, 1387–1425) of Navarra.

ESSENTIALS

Bus Station Pamplona ✉ *C. Yanguas y Miranda 2* ☎ *90/202–3651*
🌐 *www.estaciondeautobusesdepamplona.com.*

Car Rentals Europcar ✉ *Blanca de Navarra Hotel, Av. Pio XII 43* ☎ *94/817-2523* 🌐 *www.europcar.com* ✉ *Aeropuerto de Pamplona (Noain), Carretera Bellaterra s/n* ☎ *94/831-2798* 🌐 *www.europcar.com.*

Train Information Pamplona ✉ *Estación de Pamplona, Pl. de la Estación s/n* ☎ *90/232-0320, 90/243-2343* 🌐 *www.adif.es.*

Visitor Information Pamplona. In addition to Pamplona's main tourist office, there's a tourist information kiosk in Plaza Consistorial from Easter through September, open 10–8 daily. ✉ *Av. Roncesvalles 4* ☎ *84/842-0420* 🌐 *www.turismodepamplona.es.*

EXPLORING

Archivo Real y General de Navarra. This Rafael Moneo-designed structure of glass and stone, ingeniously contained within a Romanesque palace, is Pamplona's architectural treasure. Containing papers and parchments going back to the 9th century, the archive holds more than 25,000 linear yards of documents and has room for more than 18,500 yards more. The library and reading rooms are lined with cherrywood and topped with a gilded ceiling. ✉ *C. Dos de Mayo s/n* ☎ *84/842-4667, 84/842-4623* 🌐 *www.cfnavarra.es/agn* 🎫 *Free* ⏲ *Weekdays 8:30–2:30.*

Ayuntamiento (*Town hall*). Pamplona's most remarkable civic building is the ornate town hall on the Plaza Consistorial, with its rich ocher facade setting off brightly gilded balconies. The interior is a lavish wood-and-marble display of wealth, reinforcing Navarra's historic status as a wealthy kingdom in its own right. The present building was erected between 1753 and 1759. You can appreciate it from the outside and even step inside the lobby, but the building is not otherwise open to visitors. ✉ *Pl. Consistorial s/n.*

QUICK BITES

Café Iruña. Pamplona's gentry has been flocking to this ornate, French-style café since 1888, but Ernest Hemingway made it part of world literary lore in *The Sun Also Rises* in 1926. You can still have a drink with a bronze version of the author at his favorite perch at the far end of the bar, or enjoy views of the plaza from an outdoor table on the terrace. It's closed on Saturday afternoon. ✉ ***Pl. del Castillo 44*** ☎ ***94/822-2064*** 🌐 ***www.cafeiruna.com.***

Cathedral. Near the portion of the ancient walls rebuilt in the 17th century, this is one of the most important religious buildings in northern Spain, thanks to the fragile grace and gabled Gothic arches of its cloister. Inside are the tombs of Carlos III and his wife, marked by an alabaster sculpture. The **Museo Catedralicio Diocesano** (Diocesan Museum) houses religious art from the Middle Ages and the Renaissance. Call in advance for guided tours in English. ✉ *C. Dormitaleria 3–5* ☎ *94/821-2594* 🌐 *www.catedraldepamplona.com* 🎫 *€5* ⏲ *Cathedral Mon.–Sat. 9–10:30 and 7–8:30, Sun. 10–2; museum Mon.–Sat. 10:30–5.*

Edificio Baluarte. The Palacio de Congresos y Auditorio de Navarra, built in 2003 by local architectural star Patxi Mangado, is a sleek assemblage of black Zimbabwean granite. It contains a concert hall of exquisite acoustical perfection, utilizing beechwood from upper Navarra's famed

Irati *haya* (beech) forest. Performances and concerts, from opera to ballet, are held in this modern venue, built on the remains of one of the five bastions of Pamplona's 16th-century Ciudadela. ✉ *Plaza del Baluarte* ☎ *94/806–6066* 🌐 *www.baluarte.com.*

Plaza del Castillo. One of Pamplona's greatest charms is the warren of small streets near the Plaza del Castillo (especially Calle San Nicolás), which are filled with restaurants, taverns, and bars. Pamplonicas are hardy, rough-and-tumble sorts, well known for their eagerness and capacity to eat and drink.

OFF THE BEATEN PATH

Fundación–Museo Jorge Oteiza. Just 8 km (5 miles) east of Pamplona on the road toward France, this museum dedicated to the father of modern Basque art is a must-visit. Jorge Oteiza (1908–2003), in his seminal treatise, *Quosque Tandem,* called for Basque artists to find an aesthetic of their own instead of attempting to become part of the Spanish canon. Oteiza created a school of artists of which the sculptor Eduardo Chillida (1924–2002) was the most famous. The building itself is a large cube of earth-colored concrete designed by Oteiza's longtime friend, Pamplona architect Francisco Javier Sáenz de Oiza. The sculptor's living quarters, his studio, and the workshop used for teaching divide the museum into three sections. ✉ *C. de la Cuesta 7, Alzuza, 8 km from Pamplona on N150* ☎ *94/833–2074* 🌐 *www.museooteiza.org* 🎫 *€4 (free Fri.)* ⏲ *July and Aug., Tues.–Sat. 11–7, Sun. 11–3; Sept.–June, guided tours by reservation only, Tues. and Sat. at 11 and 1.*

WHERE TO EAT AND STAY

$$$ SPANISH

✕ **Europa Restaurante.** Generally considered Pamplona's best restaurant, the Europa, in the hotel of the same name, offers a decidedly epicurean take on traditional Navarran cooking, with a Michelin star to show for it. The small and light first-floor dining room offers the perfect backdrop to dishes like slow-cooked lamb and pork, or the best bacalao al pil pil you may try on your trip. À la carte dining is reasonably priced, and there are excellent tasting menus available for €41, €48, and €60. 💲 *Average main: €20* ✉ *C. Espoz y Mina 11* ☎ *94/822–1800* 🌐 *www.hreuropa.com* ⏲ *Closed Sun.*

$ TAPAS

✕ **Gaucho.** A legendary address for *tapeo* (tapas grazing) and *txikiteo* (wine tippling), this small tavern serves some of the best tapas in Pamplona. Just off Plaza del Castillo, in the eye of the hurricane during San Fermín, there is a surprising sense of peace and quiet here, even as the fiesta spins out of control outside. Tapas range from the classical *chistorra* (spicy sausage) to contemporary creations such as the deconstructed *vieira* (scallop), an apt metaphor for Pamplona's blend of old and new. 💲 *Average main: €7* ✉ *C. Espoz y Mina 7* ☎ *94/822–5073* 🌐 *www.cafebargaucho.com.*

$ HOTEL Fodor's Choice ★

🏨 **Hotel Europa.** More famous for its world-class Michelin-starred restaurant on the ground floor, this modest hotel is one of Pamplona's best-kept secrets, just a block and half from the bullring and within shouting distance of party-central Plaza del Castillo. **Pros:** central location; good value; special restaurant offers for hotel guests. **Cons:** noisy during the fiesta unless you score an interior room; rooms on the small side. As with all Pamplona properties, prices can double during the San Fermín festival. 💲 *Rooms from: €88* ✉ *C. Espoz y Mina 11* ☎ *94/822–1800* 🌐 *www.hoteleuropapamplona.com* 🛏 *25 rooms* 🍽 *Breakfast.*

$$$ HOTEL Fodor's Choice ★ **Gran Hotel La Perla.** The oldest hotel in Pamplona, after several years of refurbishing, has reinvented itself as a luxury lodging option. **Pros:** read your worn copy of *The Sun Also Rises* in the place where the book was first conceived; impeccable comfort. **Cons:** round-the-clock mayhem during San Fermín. *Rooms from: €155* ✉ *Pl. del Castillo 1* ☎ *94/822–3000* 🌐 *www.granhotellaperla.com* *44 rooms* *Breakfast.*

$$$ HOTEL **Palacio Guendulain.** This 18th-century palace in the center of town has been restored to the original architecture and aristocratic style, including the wooden ceilings and the grand staircase. **Pros:** opportunity to stay in a historical monument; central location; outstanding service. **Cons:** provides little refuge from the mayhem during San Fermín; noise from the street is a problem on weekends; extra charge for parking. *Rooms from: €143* ✉ *Zapatería 53* ☎ *94/822–5522* 🌐 *www.palacioguendulain.com* *23 rooms, 2 suites* *Multiple meal plans.*

NIGHTLIFE

The city has a thumping student life year-round, especially along the length of Calle San Nicolas. Calle Estafeta is another hot spot.

Marengo. Dress up or you might flunk the bouncer's inspection at this barnlike rager, filled until dawn with young singles and couples. Cover charge depends on visiting DJs and events. ✉ *Av. Bayona 2* ☎ *94/826–5542* 🌐 *www.discotecamarengo.com* *Thurs.–Sat. 1:30 am–6 am.*

SHOPPING

Botas are the wineskins from which Basques typically drink at bullfights or during fiestas. The art lies in drinking a stream of wine from a bota held at arm's length without spilling a drop, if you want to maintain your mojo (not to mention your clean shirt).

Casa Torrens. Navarran favorites such as piquillo peppers and chistorra sausages are sold here. It's closed on Saturday afternoon and Sunday. ✉ *C. San Miguel 12* ☎ *94/822–4286* 🌐 *www.torrensalimentacion.com.*

Manterola. Here you can buy some toffee called "La Cafetera," a café con leche sweet known all over Spain. The shop also sells Navarran wine and other delicacies. ✉ *C. Tudela 5* ☎ *94/822–3174* 🌐 *www.casamanterola.es.*

OFF THE BEATEN PATH

Olite. An unforgettable glimpse into the Spain of the Middle Ages is the reward for journeying to this town. The 11th-century church of San Pedro is revered for its finely worked Romanesque cloisters and portal, but it's the town's castle—restored by Carlos III in the French style and brimming with ramparts, crenellated battlements, and watchtowers—that captures the imagination most. You can walk the ramparts, and should you get tired or hungry, part of the castle has been converted into a parador, making a fine place to catch a bite or a few Z's. ✉ *41 km (25 miles) south of Pamplona, Olite* ☎ *94/874–0000.*

DID YOU KNOW?

The distance from the corral where the bulls are kept to the bullring where they'll fight in the afternoon is 902 yards; the bulls cover this distance in about three minutes.

VITORIA-GASTEIZ

70 km (44 miles) northwest of Estella, 100 km (62 miles) west of Pamplona, 93 km (56 miles) north of Logroño, 101 km (62 miles) southwest of San Sebastián, 64 km (40 miles) southeast of Bilbao.

Vitoria-Gasteiz was chosen as the European Green Capital in 2012 because of its abundance of green space, including its six parks, all within the city center.

The capital of the Basque Country, and its second-largest city after Bilbao, Vitoria-Gasteiz is nevertheless in many ways Euskadi's least Basque city. Neither a maritime city nor a mountain enclave, Vitoria occupies the steppelike *meseta de Alava* (Alava plain) and functions as a modern industrial center with a surprisingly medieval Casco Medieval (Medieval Quarter), which serves as a striking example of the successful integration of early and contemporary architecture. Founded by Sancho el Sabio (the Wise) in 1181, the city was built largely of granite, so Vitoria's oldest streets and squares seem especially weathered and ancient.

GETTING AROUND

Vitoria is a big city, but the area you'll spend your time in is small, only about 1 km (½ mile) square, and easily walked.

ESSENTIALS

Bus Station Vitoria ✉ *Pl. España 1* ☎ *94/516–1598* 🌐 *www.vitoria-gasteiz.org* ⏲ *Oct.–June, Mon.–Sat. 10–9, Sun. 11–2; July–Sept., daily 10–8.*

Visitor Information Vitoria-Gasteiz ✉ *Pl. España 1* ☎ *94/516–1598* 🌐 *www.vitoria-gasteiz.org.*

EXPLORING

Artium. Officially titled Centro-Museo Vasco de Arte Contemporáneo, this former bus station was opened in 2002 by King Juan Carlos, who called it "the third leg of the Basque art triangle, along with the Bilbao Guggenheim and San Sebastián's [now closed] Chillida Leku." The museum's permanent collection—including 20th- and 21st-century paintings and sculptures by Jorge Oteiza, Chillida, Agustín Ibarrola, and Nestor Basterretxea, among many others—makes it one of Spain's finest treasuries of contemporary art. ✉ *C. Francia 24* ☎ *94/520–9020* 🌐 *www.artium.org* 🎫 *€6 (suggested donation Wed. and weekends following exhibit openings)* ⏲ *Tues.–Fri. 11–2 and 5–8, weekends 11–9.*

Bibat. The 1525 Palacio de Bendaña and the adjoining bronze-plated building are home to one of Vitoria's main attractions, the Bibat, which combines the Museo Fournier de Naipes (Playing-Card Museum) with the Museo de la Arqueología. The project, by Navarran architect Patxi Mangado, is a daring combination of old and new architecture, though it was dubbed "the chest" because of its dark facade. The palacio houses the playing-card collection of Don Heraclio Fournier, who, in 1868, founded a playing-card factory and eventually found himself with 15,000 sets. As you survey rooms of hand-painted cards, the distinction between artwork and game piece is scrambled. The oldest sets date from the 12th century, and the story parallels the history of printing. The Archeology Museum, in the newest building, has Roman art and

The Plaza de la Virgen Blanca is surrounded by impressive buildings.

artifacts and the famous stele of the horseback rider, an early Basque tombstone. ✉ *C. Cuchillería 54* ☎ *94/520–3707* 🎫 *€3 (free 1st Sat. of every month)* ⏲ *Tues.–Fri. 10–2 and 4–6:30, Sat. 10–2, Sun. 11–2.*

Catedral de Santa María. Dating back to the 14th century, the cathedral is currently being restored but is still open for visitors—in fact, that's part of the fun. Tour guides hand out hardhats, and show you around the site. A prominent and active supporter of the project is British novelist Ken Follett, whose novel *World Without End* is about the construction of the cathedral. A statue of the author has been placed on one side of the cathedral. ✉ *C. Cuchillería 95* ☎ *94/512–2160, 94/525–5135* 🌐 *www.catedralvitoria.com* 🎫 *€8.50, €10.50 including tower* ⏲ *Daily 10–2 and 4–7.*

Museo de Bellas Artes (*Museum of Fine Arts*). Paintings by Ribera, Picasso, and the Basque painter Zuloaga are among the collection here. ✉ *Paseo Fray Francisco de Vitoria 8* ☎ *94/518–1918* 🎫 *€3* ⏲ *Tues.–Fri. 10–2 and 4–6:30, Sat. 10–2 and 5–8, Sun. 10–2.*

Museo Provincial de Armería (*Provincial Arms Museum*). Just south of the park, this museum has prehistoric hatchets, 20th-century pistols, and a reproduction of the 1813 battle between the Duke of Wellington's troops and the French. ✉ *Paseo Fray Francisco de Vitoria 3* ☎ *94/518–1925* 🎫 *€3* ⏲ *Tues.–Fri. 10–2 and 4–6:30, Sat. 10–2, Sun. 11–2.*

Palacio de los Alava Esquivel. One of Vitoria's most splendid buildings, this palace was erected in 1488 and reformed in 1535 and 1865. It's reached from the Plaza de la Virgen Blanca along Calle de Herrería. ✉ *C. de la Soledad s/n.*

Palacio Villasuso. Don't miss this austere palace, built in 1538 across from the church of San Miguel. ✉ *Pl. del Machete 1* ☎ *94/516–1260* ⏲ *Weekdays 8:30 am–9 pm (8:30–1:30 in summer).*

Plaza de la Virgen Blanca. In the southwest corner of old Vitoria, this plaza is ringed by noble houses with covered arches and white-trim glass galleries. The monument in the center commemorates the Duke of Wellington's victory over Napoléon's army here in 1813.

Plaza del Machete. Overlooking Plaza de España, this plaza is named for the sword used by medieval nobility to swear allegiance to the local *fueros* (special Basque rights and privileges).

San Miguel Arcángel. A jasper niche in the lateral facade of this Gothic church contains the Virgen Blanca (White Virgin), Vitoria's patron saint. ✉ *Pl. Virgen Blanca s/n* ☎ *94/516–1598.*

Torre de Doña Otxanda. This 15th-century tower houses Vitoria's **Museo de Ciencias Naturales**, which contains botanical, zoological, and geological collections along with amber from the nearby archaeological site at Peñacerrada-Urizaharra. ✉ *C. Siervas de Jesús 24* ☎ *94/518–1924* 🌐 *€3* ⏲ *Tues.–Fri. 10–2 and 4–6:30, Sat. 10–2, Sun. 11–2.*

WHERE TO EAT AND STAY

$$$ SPANISH Fodor's Choice ★

✕ **El Portalón.** With dark, creaky wood floors and staircases, bare brick walls, and ancient beams, pillars, and coats of arms, this rough and rustic 15th-century inn turns out classical Castilian and Basque specialties that reflect Vitoria's geography and social history. Try the *cochinillo lechal asado* (grilled suckling pig) or any of the *rape* (anglerfish) preparations. The wine cellar is a gold mine. Call 48 hours ahead to reserve any of the special tasting menus, a good value ranging between €35 and €61. Once a month the restaurant organizes a theater night (€65), where performers surround your table. [$] *Average main: €22* ✉ *C. Correría 147* ☎ *94/514–2755* 🌐 *www.restauranteelportalon.com* ⏲ *No dinner Sun.*

$$$$ CONTEMPORARY

✕ **Zaldiarán.** Vitoria's most recent culinary star serves contemporary interpretations of classics and daring combinations of prime ingredients from black truffles to to lobster in a sleek environment. The tasting menu (€55) changes seven times a year. [$] *Average main: €55* ✉ *Av. Gasteiz 21* ☎ *94/513–4822* 🌐 *www.restaurantezaldiaran.com* ⏲ *Mon., Thurs.–Sat. 1–3:30 and 9–11:30, Wed. and Sun. 1–3:30.*

$$ HOTEL

NH Canciller Ayala. This modern hotel is handy for in-town comfort, two minutes from the old quarter next to the lush Parque de la Florida. **Pros:** clean comfort; reliable chain brand. **Cons:** lacking any historical character. [$] *Rooms from: €110* ✉ *C. Ramón y Cajal 5* ☎ *94/513–0000, 90/257–0368* 🌐 *www.nh-hotels.com* *184 rooms, 1 suite* *No meals.*

$$$ HOTEL

Parador de Argómaniz. This 17th-century palace has panoramic views of the Alava plains and retains a sense of romance with long halls peppered with antiques. **Pros:** contemporary rooms and comforts; gorgeous details and surroundings. **Cons:** isolated, about a 15-minute drive from Vitoria. [$] *Rooms from: €120* ✉ *N1, Km 363, east of Vitoria off N104 toward Pamplona, Argómaniz* ☎ *94/529–3200* 🌐 *www.parador.es* *53 rooms* *No meals.*

LAGUARDIA

66 km (40 miles) south of Vitoria, 17 km (10 miles) northwest of Logroño.

Founded in 908 to stand guard—as its name suggests—over Navarra's southwestern flank, Laguardia is on a promontory overlooking the Ebro River and the vineyards of the Rioja Alavesa wine country north of the Ebro in the Basque province of Alava. Flanked by the Sierra de Cantabria, the town rises shiplike, its prow headed north, over the sea of surrounding vineyards.

ESSENTIALS

Visitor Information Laguardia ✉ *C. Mayor 52* ☎ *94/560–0845* 🌐 *www.laguardia-alava.com.*

EXPLORING

Starting from the 15th-century Puerta de Carnicerías, or Puerta Nueva, the central portal off the parking area on the east side of town, the first landmark is the 16th-century **ayuntamiento** (town hall), with its imperial shield of Carlos V. Farther into the square is the current town hall, built in the 19th century. A right turn down Calle Santa Engracia takes you past impressive facades—the floor inside the portal at No. 25 is a lovely stone mosaic, and a walk behind the triple-emblazoned 17th-century facade of No. 19 reveals a stagecoach, floor mosaics, wood beams, and an inner porch. The Puerta de Santa Engracia, with an image of the saint in an overhead niche, opens out to the right, and on the left, at the entrance to Calle Víctor Tapia, No. 17 bears a coat of arms with the Latin phrase "Laus Tibi" ("Praise Be to Thee").

Fodor's Choice ★ **Herederos de Marqués de Riscal.** The village of Elciego, 6 km (4 miles) southeast of Laguardia, is the site of the historic Marqués de Riscal winery. Tours of the vineyards as well as the cellars are conducted in many languages, including English. Reservations are required. The estate also includes the stunning Frank Gehry-designed **Hotel Marqués de Riscal** (⇨ *see Where to Eat and Stay*), crafted out of waves of metal reminiscent of his Guggenheim Bilbao. ✉ *C. Torrea 1, Elciego* ☎ *94/560–6000* 🌐 *www.marquesderiscal.com* 🎟 *€10.25 includes tour and tasting of two wines* ⏲ *Tours daily, but hrs vary; book ahead.*

Santa María de los Reyes. Laguardia's architectural crown jewel is Spain's only Gothic polychrome portal, on this church. Protected by a posterior Renaissance facade, the door centers on a lifelike effigy of La Virgen de los Reyes (Virgin of the Kings), sculpted in the 14th century and painted in the 17th by Ribera. To see it, ask at the tourist office. ✉ *C. Mayor s/n.*

WHERE TO EAT AND STAY

$$$$ BASQUE ✕ **Marixa.** Aficionados travel great distances to dine in this restaurant, known for its excellent roasts, views, and value, in the Marixa hotel. The heavy, wooden interior is ancient, and the cuisine is Vasco-Riojano, combining the best of both worlds. House specialties are Navarran vegetable dishes and meat roasted over coals. There are also 10 guest rooms, which offer good-value half- or full-board terms, with meals taken in the restaurant. $ *Average main: €30* ✉ *C. Sancho Abarca 8* ☎ *94/560–0165* 🌐 *www.hotelmarixa.com.*

9

$$$$ HOTEL Fodor's Choice ★ **Hotel Marqués de Riscal.** Frank Gehry's post-Guggenheim Iberian eruption of genius looks as if a colony from outer space had taken up residence (or crashed) in the middle of La Rioja's oldest vineyards (⇨ *see Exploring*). **Pros:** dazzling architecture; 5-star environment; superb dining. **Cons:** expensive. *Rooms from: €300 ✉ C. Torrea 1, 6 km (4 miles) southwest of Laguardia, Elciego ☎ 94/518–0880 🌐 www.hotel-marquesderiscal.com 43 rooms Breakfast.*

$$ HOTEL Fodor's Choice ★ **Posada Mayor de Migueloa.** This 17th-century palace is a beauty, with stone entryway floors and guest rooms that have original, rough-hewn ceiling beams. **Pros:** beautiful rooms; off-season specials. **Cons:** in a pedestrianized area a long way from your car; rooms on the front side exposed to boisterous racket on weekends. *Rooms from: €92 ✉ C. Mayor de Migueloa 20 ☎ 647/212947 🌐 www.mayordemigueloa.com 8 rooms Closed Jan. 8–Feb. 8 Breakfast.*

LA RIOJA

A natural compendium of highlands, plains, and vineyards drained by the Ebro River, La Rioja (named for the River Oja) has historically produced Spain's finest wines. Most inhabitants live along the Ebro, in the cities of Logroño and Haro, though the mountains and upper river valleys hold many treasures. A mix of Atlantic and Mediterranean climates and cultures with Basque overtones and the meseta's arid influence, La Rioja is composed of the Rioja Alta (Upper Rioja), the moist and mountainous western end, and the Rioja Baja (Lower Rioja), the lower, dryer eastern extremity, more Mediterranean in climate. Logroño, the capital, lies between the two.

LOGROÑO

85 km (53 miles) southwest of Pamplona.

A busy industrial city of 153,000, Logroño has a lovely old quarter bordered by the Ebro and medieval walls, with **Breton de los Herreros** and **Muro Francisco de la Mata** the most characteristic streets.

Near Logroño, the Roman bridge and the *mirador* (lookout) at **Viguera** are the main sights in the lower Iregua Valley. According to legend, Santiago (St. James) helped the Christians defeat the Moors at the **Castillo de Clavijo,** another panoramic spot. The **Leza (Cañon) del Río Leza** is La Rioja's most dramatic canyon.

Logroño's dominant landmarks are the finest sacred structures in Rioja.

ESSENTIALS

Bus Station Logroño ✉ *Av. España 1 ☎ 94/123–5983.*

Train Station Logroño ✉ *Estación de Logroño, Av. de Colón 83 ☎ 90/243–2343, 90/232–0320 🌐 www.adif.es.*

Visitor Information Logroño ✉ *Portales 50 ☎ 94/129–1260 🌐 www.logroturismo.org.*

EXPLORING

Catedral de Santa María de La Redonda. Noted for its twin baroque towers, the present-day cathedral was rebuilt in the 16th century in a Gothic style, on top of the ruins of a 12th-century Roman church. ✉ *C. Portales 14* ☎ *94/125–7611* 🌐 *www.laredonda.org* ⏲ *Daily 8:30–1 and 6–9.*

Puente de Piedra (*Stone Bridge*). Many of Logroño's monuments, such as this elegant bridge, were built as part of the Camino de Santiago pilgrimage route.

San Bartolomé. The oldest still-standing church in Logroño, most of San Bartolomé was built between the 13th and 14th-centuries in a French Gothic style. Highlights include the 11th-century Mudejar tower and an elaborate 14th-century Gothic doorway. Some carvings on the stone facade depict scenes from the Bible. This is also a landmark on the Camino de Santiago pilgrimage path. ✉ *Pl. San Bartolomé 2.*

Santa María del Palacio. This 11th-century church is known as La Aguja (the Needle) for its pyramid-shape, 45-yard Romanesque-Gothic tower. ✉ *C. del Marqués de San Nicolás 30.*

Santiago el Real (*Royal St. James's Church*). Reconstructed in the 16th century, this church is noted for its equestrian statue of the saint (also known as Santiago Matamoros, or St. James the Moorslayer), which presides over the main door. ✉ *C. Barriocepo 6* ☎ *94/120–9501.*

WHERE TO EAT AND STAY

For tapas, **Calle and Travesía del Laurel** or *el sendero de los elefantes* (the path of the elephants)—an allusion to *trompas* (trunks), Spanish for a snootful—offers bars with signature specialties: Bar Soriano for "*champis*" (*champiñones,* or mushrooms), Blanco y Negro for "*matrimonio*" (a green pepper–and–anchovy sandwich), and La Travesía for potato omelet. If you're ordering wine, a crianza brings out the crystal, a young cosecha comes in small glasses, and reserva (selected grapes aged three years in oak and bottle) elicits snifters for proper swirling, smelling, and tasting.

$$ SPANISH ✕ **Asador Emilio.** The Castilian rustic interior here includes a coffered wood ceiling that merits a long look. Roast lamb cooked over wood coals is the specialty, but *alubias* (kidney beans) and *migas de pastor* (literally, "shepherd's bread crumbs," cooked with garlic and sausage) are hard to resist. The wine list, not surprisingly, is stocked with most of La Rioja's top finds, from Roda I to Barón de Chirel Reserva. [$] *Average main: €20* ✉ *C. República Argentina 8* ☎ *94/125–8844* 🌐 *www.asadoremilio.com* ⏲ *Closed Aug. No dinner Sun.*

$$$ SPANISH ✕ **El Cachetero.** Local fare based on roast lamb, goat, and vegetables is the rule at this local favorite in the middle of Logroño's main food and wine preserve. Coming in from Calle del Laurel is something like stepping through the looking glass: from street pandemonium to the peaceful hush of this culinary sanctuary. Though the dining room is classical and elegant, with antique furnishings and a serious look, the cuisine is homespun, based on seasonally changing raw materials. *Patatas a la riojana* (potatoes stewed with chorizo) is a classic dish here. [$] *Average main: €25* ✉ *C. Laurel 3* ☎ *94/122–8463* 🌐 *www.cachetero.com* ⏲ *Closed Tues. and 1st 2 wks in Aug. No dinner Sun.*

The fertile soil and fields of the Ebro River Valley make some of Spain's most colorful landscapes.

$$ SPANISH Fodor's Choice ★ **Tondeluna.** Francis Paniego's "gastro-bar," with David Gonzalez as chef de cuisine, strives to bring haute cuisine to everyone, and everyone into the kitchen. There are only six tables, and all have views into the kitchen. Gonzalez makes an excellent croqueta de jamón from Echaurren or La Zapatilla, a grilled open ham canapé. *Average main: €15* *C. Muro de la Mata 9* *94/123–6425* *www.tondeluna.com.*

$ HOTEL **Marqués de Vallejo.** Close to the food- and wine-tasting frenzy of nearby Calle del Laurel, this small but trendy hotel within view of the cathedral is nearly dead center amid the most important historic sites and best architecture that Logroño has to offer. **Pros:** central location; traditional Logroño architecture with very modern, renovated interior. **Cons:** streetside rooms can be noisy in summer when windows are open. *Rooms from: €80* *Marqués de Vallejo 8* *94/124–8333* *www.hotelmarquesdevallejo.com* *50 rooms* *No meals.*

LA RIOJA ALTA

The Upper Rioja, the most prosperous part of La Rioja's wine country, extends from the Ebro River to the Sierra de la Demanda. La Rioja Alta has the most fertile soil, the best vineyards and agriculture, the most impressive castles and monasteries, a ski resort at Ezcaray, and the historic economic advantage of being on the Camino de Santiago.

Ezcaray. Enter the Sierra de la Demanda by heading south from Santo Domingo de la Calzada on LR111. Your first stop is the town of Ezcaray, with its aristocratic houses emblazoned with family crests, of which the **Palacio del Conde de Torremúzquiz** (Palace of the Count of Torremúzquiz) is the most distinguished. Excursions from here are the Valdezcaray ski station; the source of the River Oja at Llano de la Casa; La Rioja's highest point, the 7,494-foot Pico de San Lorenzo; and the Romanesque church of Tres Fuentes, at Valgañón. The hamlet is famous for its wild-mushroom-gathering residents—and the resulting tapas too. ✉ *Ezcaray.*

Nájera. This town, 15 km (9 miles) west of Navarrete, was site of the court of the kings of Navarra and capital of Navarra and La Rioja until 1076, when La Rioja became part of Castile and the residence of the Castilian royal family. The monastery of **Santa María la Real** (☎ *941/363650* 🌐 *www.santamarialareal.net* 🎫 *€3* ⏲ *Tues.–Sat. 10–1 and 4–5:30 [till 7 in summer], Sun. and holidays 10–1 and 4–7*), the "pantheon of kings," is distinguished by its 16th-century *Claustro de los Caballeros* (Cavaliers' Cloister), a flamboyant Gothic structure with 24 lacy, Plateresque Renaissance arches overlooking a patio. The sculpted 12th-century tomb of Doña Blanca de Navarra is the monastery's best-known sarcophagus, while the 67 Gothic choir stalls dating from 1495 are among Spain's best. ☎ *94/136–1083.*

Navarrete. From Logroño, drive 14 km (8 miles) west on the A12 to Navarrete to see its noble houses and 16th-century Santa María de la Asunción church. ✉ *La Rioja.*

Fodor's Choice ★ **San Millán de la Cogolla.** This town, southeast of Santo Domingo de la Calzada, has two monasteries on the UNESCO World Heritage sites list. Take LR205 southeast through Berceo to the **Monasterio de Yuso** (☎ *941/373049* 🌐 *www.monasteriodeyuso.org* 🎫 *€6* ⏲ *Easter–Sept., Tues.–Sun. 10–1:30 and 4–6:30 [also Mon. in Aug.]; Oct.–Easter, Tues.–Sat. 10–1 and 3:30–5:30, Sun. 10–1*), where a 10th-century manuscript on St. Augustine's *Glosas Emilianenses* contains handwritten notes in what is considered the earliest example of the Spanish language, the vernacular Latin dialect known as Roman Paladino. The nearby Visigothic **Monasterio de Suso** (☎ *941/373082* 🌐 *www.monasteriodesanmillan.com/suso* 🎫 *€3* ⏲ *Tues.–Sun. 9:55–1:25 and 3:55–5:25; obtain required reservation at Yuso ticket office*) is where Gonzalo de Berceo, recognized as the first Castilian poet, wrote his 13th-century verse in the Castilian tongue, now the language of more than 300 million people around the world. ✉ *San Millán de la Cogolla.*

Santo Domingo de la Calzada. This town has always been a key stop on the Camino. Santo Domingo was an 11th-century saint who built roads and bridges for pilgrims and founded the hospital that is now the town's parador. The **cathedral** (✉ *Pl. del Santo 4* ☎ *941/340033*) is a Romanesque-Gothic pile containing the saint's tomb, choir murals, and an altarpiece carved by Damià Forment in 1541. The live hen and rooster in a stone chicken coop commemorate a legendary local miracle in which a pair of roasted fowl came back to life to protest the innocence of a pilgrim hanged for theft. Stroll through the town's beautifully preserved medieval quarter. ✉ *20 km (12 miles) west of Nájera on the N120.*

WHERE TO STAY

$$$ HOTEL Fodor's Choice ★ **Echaurren.** This rambling roadhouse, 7 km (4 miles) below Valdezcaray, La Rioja's best ski resort, is famous for its restaurants, El Portal, showcasing fine traditional cuisine engineered by Marisa Sánchez, and her son Francis Paniego's Bistrot Comilón. **Pros:** traditional building

(though modernized inside); comfortable beds; family service. **Cons:** the bells from the church across the way. *Rooms from: €140 Padre José García 19, Ezcaray 94/135–4047 www.echaurren.com 25 rooms Some meals.*

$$ HOTEL **Hospedería del Monasterio de San Millán.** Declared a World Heritage Site by UNESCO, this magnificent inn occupies a wing of the historic Monasterio de Yuso, famous as the birthplace of the Spanish language. **Pros:** historic site; graceful building. **Cons:** somewhat isolated; monastic interiors. *Rooms from: €120 Monasterio de Yuso, San Millán de la Cogolla 94/137–3277 www.sanmillan.com 22 rooms, 3 suites Breakfast.*

HARO

49 km (29 miles) west of Logroño.

Haro is the wine capital of La Rioja. Its Casco Viejo (Old Quarter) and best taverns are concentrated along the loop known as La Herradura (the Horseshoe), with the Santo Tomás church at the apex of its curve and Calle San Martín and Calle Santo Tomás leading down to the upper left-hand (northeast) corner of Plaza de la Paz. Up the left side of the horseshoe, Bar La Esquina is the first of many tapas bars. Bar Los Caños, behind a stone archway at San Martín 5, is built into the vaults and arches of the former church of San Martín and serves excellent local crianzas and reservas and a memorable pintxo of quail egg, anchovy, hot pepper, and olive.

ESSENTIALS

Visitor Information Haro *Pl. de la Paz 94/130–3580 www.haroturismo.org.*

EXPLORING

Bodegas (*wineries*). Haro's century-old bodegas have been headquartered in the *barrio de la estación* (train-station district) ever since the railroad opened in 1863. Guided tours and tastings, some in English, can be arranged at the facilities themselves or through the tourist office.

Santo Tomás. The architectural highlight of Haro is the church of Santo Tomás, a single-naved Renaissance and late Gothic church completed in 1564, with an intricately sculpted Plateresque portal on the south side and a Baroque organ facade towering over the choir loft. *C. Santo Tomás 5.*

WHERE TO EAT AND STAY

$$ SPANISH **Terete.** A local favorite, this rustic spot has been roasting lamb in wood ovens since 1877 and serves a hearty *menestra de verduras* (vegetables stewed with ham) that is revered as a regional institution. With wooden tables distributed around dark stone, the medieval stagecoach-inn environment matches the traditional roasts. The wine cellar is a virtual museum stocked with some of the Rioja's best reservas and crianzas. *Average main: €20 C. Lucrecia Arana 17 94/131–0023 www.terete.es Closed Mon., 1st 2 wks in July, and last 2 wks in Nov. No dinner Sun.*

$ HOTEL **Los Agustinos.** Across the street from the tourist office, Haro's best hotel is built into a 14th-century monastery with a cloister (now a beautiful covered patio) that's considered one of the best in La Rioja.

Pros: gorgeous public rooms; convivial hotel bar; close to town center but in a quiet corner; free Wi-Fi. **Cons:** unexciting room interiors; staff not very helpful. *Rooms from: €87* *San Agustín 2* *94/131–1308* *www.hotellosagustinos.com* *60 rooms, 2 suites* *Some meals.*

THE HIGHLANDS

The rivers forming the seven main valleys of the Ebro basin originate in the Sierra de la Demanda, Sierra de Cameros, and Sierra de Alcarama. **Ezcaray** is La Rioja's skiing capital in the **valley of the Rio Oja,** just below Valdezcaray in the Sierra de la Demanda. The upper **Najerilla Valley** is La Rioja's mountain sanctuary, an excellent hunting and fishing preserve. The Najerilla River, a rich chalk stream, is one of Spain's best trout rivers. Look for the Puente de Hiedra (Ivy Bridge), its heavy curtain of ivy falling to the surface of the Najerilla. The **Monasterio de Valvanera,** off C113 near Anguiano, is the sanctuary of La Rioja's patron saint, the Virgen de Valvanera, a 12th-century Romanesque wood carving of the Virgin and Child. **Anguiano** is renowned for its Danza de los Zancos (Dance of the Stilts), held July 22, when dancers on wooden stilts plummet down through the steep streets of the town into the arms of the crowd at the bottom. At the valley's highest point are the Mansilla reservoir and the Romanesque Ermita de San Cristóbal (Hermitage of St. Christopher).

The upper **Iregua Valley,** off N111, has the prehistoric Gruta de la Paz caves at Ortigosa. The artisans of **Villoslada del Cameros** make the region's famous patchwork quilts, called *almazuelas.* Climb to **Pico Cebollera** for a superb view of the valley. Work back toward the Ebro along the River Leza, through Laguna de Cameros and San Román de Cameros (known for its basket weavers), to complete a tour of the Sierra del Cameros. The upper **Cidacos Valley** leads to the **Parque Jurásico** (Jurassic Park) at Enciso, famous for its dinosaur tracks. The main village in the upper **Alhama Valley** is **Cervera del Rio Alhama,** a center for handmade *alpargatas* (espadrilles).

9

WHERE TO EAT AND STAY

$$ SPANISH — **La Herradura.** High over the ancient bridge of Anguiano, this is an excellent place to try the local specialty, *caparrones colorados de Anguiano con sus sacramentos* (small, red kidney beans stewed with sausage and fatback) made with the much-prized hometown bean. Family-run La Herradura ("horseshoe") is a local favorite, usually filled with trout fishermen taking a break from the river. *Average main: €15* *Ctra. de Lerma, Km 14, Anguiano* *94/137–7151.*

$ B&B/INN Fodor's Choice ★ — **Venta de Goyo.** A favorite with anglers and hunters in season, this cheery spot across from the mouth of the Urbión River has wood-trim bedrooms with red-check bedspreads and an excellent restaurant specializing in venison, wild boar, and game of all kinds. **Pros:** excellent game and mountain cooking; charming rustic bar; unforgettable homemade jams. **Cons:** next to road; hot in summer. *Rooms from: €42* *Puente Rio Neila 2, Ctra. LR113, Km 24.6, Viniegra de Abajo* *941/378007* *www.ventadegoyo.es* *22 rooms* *Some meals.*

TRAVEL SMART BARCELONA

GETTING HERE AND AROUND

Finding your way around in Barcelona can be simple, with some planning. All of Barcelona's Ciutat Vella (Old City), including the Barri Gòtic (Gothic Quarter), can be explored on foot. Your transport needs will be mainly to get to Sarrià, Gràcia, Park Güell, Gaudí's Sagrada Família, and the Auditori near Plaça de les Glòries. The metro system will normally get you wherever you need to go. The commuter trains on the Catalan regional government's FGC system are also handy. The municipal metro lines are useful, air-conditioned, and safe. Buses are practical for certain runs, and taxis are rarely much more than around €15 for a complete crosstown ride.

Modern Barcelona, above Plaça de Catalunya, is built on a grid system. The Old City, however, from Plaça de Catalunya to the port, is a labyrinth of narrow streets, so you'll need a good street map and good shoes to explore it. You'll probably want to avoid driving in the city. (⇨ *For information about driving, see Car Travel.)* Maps of the bus and metro routes are available free from the Tourist Information office in Plaça de Catalunya.

ADDRESSES

Abbreviations used in the book for street names are Av. for *avinguda* (in Catalan; *avenida* in Spanish) and Ctra. for *carreter* (*carretera* in Spanish). The letters *s/n* following an address mean *sin número* (without a street number). *Carrer* (*calle* in Spanish) is often dropped entirely or not abbreviated at all. *Camí* (*camino* in Spanish) is abbreviated to C. *Passeig* (*paseo* in Spanish) is sometimes abbreviated as P., but is usually written out in full. Plaça/plaza is usually not abbreviated (in this book it is abbreviated as Pl.).

Addresses in Barcelona may include the street name, building number, floor level, and apartment number. For example, Carrer Balmes 155, 3°, 1ª indicates that the apartment is on the *tercero* (third) floor, *primera* (first) door. In older buildings, the first floor is often called the *entresuelo*; one floor above it is *principal* (sometimes called the *planta baja*), and above this, the first floor (*primera*). The top floor of a building is the *ático*; occasionally there is a floor above that, called the *sobreàtico*. In more modern buildings there is often no *entresuelo* or *principal.*

AIR TRAVEL

Transatlantic flying time to Barcelona is about seven hours from New York, depending on the wind. Other U.S. cities with direct flights to Barcelona are Atlanta, Chicago, Miami, Newark, and Philadelphia. A nonstop flight from Chicago to Madrid is about eight hours. There are several transit combinations from Los Angeles; one is by way of New York (five and a half hours), and then to Madrid (seven hours). Flying from other cities in North America also usually involves a connection.

Nonstop flights from London to Barcelona are two and a quarter hours. Flights from the United Kingdom to a number of destinations in Spain are frequent and offered at competitive fares, particularly on low-cost carriers such as Ryanair or easyJet. **TIP→ Beware of low-cost flights to "Barcelona" that, in fact, land in Girona, a 45-minute taxi ride north of Barcelona; often the taxi costs more than the flight.** Flights to and from the major cities in Europe and Spain also fly into and out of Bilbao's Loiu airport. There are no direct flights to Barcelona or anywhere in Spain from Australia or New Zealand.

Flying from Sydney, you can connectfirst in Johannesburg (14 hours) for Madrid (10 hours) and change again there for Barcelona.

For air travel within the regions covered in this book there are numerous regular flights, but rates tend to be high, so consider alternative ways of getting around. Bilbao, Pamplona, and San Sebastián all have small airports, and flights do run from Barcelona to each of them. For travel between those cities, given the short distances involved, most people elect to go by train or car.

Iberia operates a shuttle, the *puente aereo*, between Barcelona and Madrid from 6:45 am to 9:45 pm; planes depart from Terminal 1 hourly, and more frequently in the morning and afternoon commuter hours. Flying time is about an hour and a half. You don't need to reserve ahead; you can buy your tickets at the counter when you get to the airport.

Arriving two hours in advance is more than enough for Spanish security. Arriving fewer than 40 minutes in advance is no longer possible for either domestic or international flights.

Airlines and Airports AirlineandAirportLinks.com. This site has links to many of the world's airlines and airports. 🌐 *www.airlineandairportlinks.com.*

Airline Security Issues Transportation Security Administration *(TSA).* The TSA has answers for almost every security question. 🌐 *www.tsa.gov.*

AIRPORTS

Most flights arriving in Spain from the United States and Canada pass through Madrid's Barajas (MAD), but the major gateway to Catalonia and other regions in this book is Spain's second-largest airport, Barcelona's spectacular glass, steel, and marble El Prat del Llobregat (BCN). The T1 terminal, which opened in 2009, is a sleek ultramodern facility that uses solar panels for sustainable energy and offers a spa, a fitness center, restaurants and cafés, and more VIP lounges. This airport is served by numerous international carriers, but Catalonia also has two other airports that handle passenger traffic, including charter flights. One is just south of Girona, 90 km (56 miles) north of Barcelona and convenient to the resort towns of the Costa Brava. Bus and train connections from Girona to Barcelona work well and cheaply, provided you have the time. The other Catalonia airport is at Reus, 110 km (68 miles) south of Barcelona and a gateway to Tarragona and the beaches of the Costa Daurada. Flights to and from the major cities in Europe and Spain also fly into and out of Bilbao's Loiu (BIL) airport. For information about airports in Spain, consult 🌐 *www.aena.es.*

Airport Information Aeroport de Girona–Costa Brava *(GRO).* ✉ *Girona* ☎ *913/211000, 972/186600.* **Aeropuerto de Reus** *(REU).* ✉ *Autovia Tarragona–Reus, Reus* ☎ *902/404704, 913/211000.* **Aeropuerto Internacional de Bilbao** *(BIL).* ✉ *Ctra. Aeropuerto, Loiu* ☎ *902/404704, 913/211000.* **Barajas Aeropuerto de Madrid** *(MAD).* ✉ *Av. de la Hispanidad s/n, Madrid* ☎ *902/404704, 913/211000.* **El Prat de Llobregat** *(BCN).* ✉ *Barcelona* ☎ *91/3211000, 902/404704.*

GROUND TRANSPORTATION

Check first to see if your hotel in Barcelona provides airport-shuttle service. Few do: visitors normally get into town by train, bus, taxi, or rental car.

The Aerobus leaves the airport for Plaça de Catalunya every 10 minutes between 6 am and 1 am. From Plaça de Catalunya the bus leaves for the airport every 10 or 20 minutes between 5:30 am and 12:30 am. The fare is €5.90 one-way and €10.20 round-trip. Aerobuses for terminals 1 and 2 pick up and drop off passengers at the same stops en route, so if you're outward bound make sure that you board the right one. The A1 Aerobus for Terminal 1 is two-tone light and dark blue; the A2 Aerobus for Terminal 2 is dark blue and yellow.

Cab fare from the airport into town is €30–€35, depending on traffic, the part of town you're heading to, and the amount of baggage you have (there's a €1 surcharge for each suitcase that goes in the trunk). If you're driving your own car, follow signs to the Centre Ciutat, from which you can enter the city along Gran Vía. For the port area, follow signs for the Ronda Litoral. The journey to the center of town can take 25–45 minutes, depending on traffic.

If you have to get to the airport by car or taxi during rush hour, allow yourself plenty of extra time, as the ring roads are likely to be jammed.

The train's only drawback is that it's a 10- to 15-minute walk from your gate through Terminal 2 over the bridge. From Terminal 1 a shuttle bus drops you at the train. Trains leave the airport every 30 minutes between 5:42 am and 11:38 pm, stopping at Estació de Sants, for transfer to the Arc de Triomf, then at Passeig de Gràcia and finally at El Clot-Aragó. Trains going to the airport begin at 5:22 am from the Clot station, stopping at Passeig de Gràcia at 5:27 am, and Sants at 5:32 am. The trip takes about half an hour, and the fare is €3.80. But the best bargain is the T10 subway card; it gives you free connections within Barcelona plus nine more rides, all for €9.80. Add an extra hour if you take the train to or from the airport.

TRANSFERS BETWEEN AIRPORTS

To get to Girona Airport from Barcelona Airport by train you have to first catch the RENFE train that leaves from the airport and then change at Barcelona Sants station. From Barcelona Sants you need to catch the train for Figueres and get off at Girona, two stops before. From there you will then have to take a bus or a taxi to the airport. Allow yourself 30 minutes from the RENFE Girona station to the airport.

Sagales runs the Barcelona Bus shuttle buses between Girona airport and Estació del Nord in Barcelona (€15 one-way, €25 round-trip; valid 30 days), the trip takes about 1 hour and 15 minutes. The schedules, set up to coincide with RyanAir arrivals and departures at Girona, are a bit twisty; consult the Sagales website or call ☎ *902/130014* for bus information.

Contact Sagales ☎ *902/130014*
🌐 *www.sagales.com.*

FLIGHTS

If you are traveling from North America, consider flying a British or other European carrier, especially if you are traveling to Barcelona or Bilbao. Though you may have to change planes in London, Paris, Amsterdam, Zurich, or even Rome, savings can be significant.

The least expensive airfares to Barcelona are priced for round-trip travel and must usually be purchased in advance. Airlines generally allow you to change your return date for a fee; most low-fare tickets, however, are nonrefundable.

If you buy a round-trip transatlantic ticket on the Spanish carrier Iberia, you might want to buy an Iberiabono España pass, good for major discounts on domestic flights during your trip. The pass must be purchased outside Spain at the time you purchase your international ticket. All internal Spain flights must be booked in advance. On certain days of the week, Iberia also offers minifares (*minitarifas*), which can save you 40% on domestic flights. Tickets must be purchased at least two days in advance, and you must stay over at your destination on a Saturday night.

American, United/Continental, Delta, and Iberia fly to Madrid and Barcelona; US Airways and Air Europa fly to Madrid. Within Spain, Iberia is the main domestic airline; two independent airlines, Air Europa and Vueling, fly a number of domestic routes at somewhat lower prices.

BOAT TRAVEL

There are regular ferry services between the United Kingdom and northern Spain. Brittany Ferries sails from Portsmouth to Santander, and P&O European Ferries sails from Plymouth to Bilbao. Spain's major ferry line, Trasmediterránea, links mainland Spain (including Barcelona) with the Balearics and the Canary Islands. Trasmediterránea's fast catamaran service takes half the time of the standard ferry, but catamarans are often canceled because they can navigate only in very calm waters.

You can pick up schedules and buy tickets at the ferry ticket office in the port.

From the U.K. Brittany Ferries ☎ *0871/2440744 in U.K., 902/108147 in Spain* 🌐 *www.brittany-ferries.com*. **P&O European Ferries** ☎ *08716/642121 in U.K.* 🌐 *www.poferries.com*.

In Spain Trasmediterránea ☎ *902/454645* 🌐 *www.trasmediterranea.es*.

CRUISE TRAVEL

Barcelona is one of Europe's busiest cruise ports. Vessels dock at the Port Vell facility, which has seven terminals catering to cruise-ship traffic. All terminals are equipped with duty-free shops, telephones, bar/restaurants, information desks, and currency-exchange booths. The ships docking closest to the terminal entrance are a 10-minute walk from the southern end of Las Ramblas (the Rambla), but those docked at the farthest end require passengers to catch a shuttle bus (the Autobús Azul, a distinctive blue bus) to the port entrance. The shuttle, which runs every 20 minutes, links all terminals with the public square at the bottom of the Rambla. If you walk up Las Ramblas, after about 10 minutes you'll reach Drassanes metro station for onward public transport around the city. The shuttle runs about every 30 minutes A single metro or bus ticket is €2; a day ticket (T-Dia) is €7.

If you intend to explore Barcelona, don't rent a car. Public transportation and taxis are by far the most sensible options. City buses run daily from 5:30 am to 11:30 pm. The FGC (Ferrocarril de la Generalitat) train is a comfortable commuter train that gets you to within walking distance of nearly everything in Barcelona; transfers to the regular city metro are free. The Barcelona Tourist Bus is another excellent way to tour the city. Three routes (Red, Blue, and Green) cover just about every place you might want to visit, and you can hop on and off whenever you want. Buses run from 9 am to 7 pm, and a one-day ticket costs €24; you can buy advance tickets online at 🌐 *www.barcelonabusturistic.cat*.

If you plan to explore the Spanish coast or countryside, a vehicle would be beneficial, but even an economy car (manual transmission) is expensive at approximately €50 per day. Allow for plenty of time to get back to your ship, as Barcelona traffic is always heavy.

GETTING TO THE AIRPORT

Barcelona's main airport is El Prat de Llobregat, 14 km (9 miles) south of Barcelona. If you choose not to purchase airport transfers from your cruise line, the simplest way to get from the airport to the cruise port is to take a taxi from the airport to the port (about €30). There are public transport options, but transfers between bus, metro, or rail stations do involve up to 10 minutes of walking, and this may be impractical with many pieces of luggage. If you only have light baggage, this will certainly be a less expensive option.

The RENFE airport train is inexpensive and efficient, but also runs only every 30 minutes. From the airport, the RENFE station is a 10- to 15-minute walk (with moving walkway) from the port gates. Trains run between 5:30 am and 12:45 am, stopping at the Estació de Sants. The one-way fare is €2.

Barcelona Guide Bureau (☎ *93/2682422* 🌐 *www.barcelonaguidebureau.com*) provides private transfers between El Prat and the cruise port. A round trip costs around €45 per person.

BUS TRAVEL

Barcelona's main bus station for intra-Spain routes is Estació del Nord, a few blocks east of the Arc de Triomf. Buses also depart from the Estació de Sants for long-distance and international routes, as well as from the depots of Barcelona's various private bus companies. Spain's major national long-haul company is Alsa-Enatcar. Grup Sarbus serves Catalonia and, with its subsidiary Sarfa, the Costa Brava. Bus timetables are complicated and confusing; trying to get information by phone will probably get you put on interminable hold. Better to plan your bus trip online or through a local travel agent, who can quickly book you the best way to your destination.

Within Spain, private companies provide comfortable and efficient bus services between major cities. Fares are lower than the corresponding train fares, and service is more extensive: if you want to get somewhere not served by rail, you can be sure a bus will go there. ⇨ *See the planner sections in Chapters 8 and 9 for companies serving the rest of Catalonia and the Basque Country.*

Most larger bus companies have buses with comfortable seats and adequate legroom; on longer journeys (two to three hours or more) a movie is shown on board, and earphones are provided. Except for smaller, regional buses that travel short hops, buses have bathrooms on board. Smoking is prohibited. Most long-haul buses stop at least once every two to three hours for a snack and bathroom break. Although buses are subject to road and traffic conditions, highways in Catalonia and the Basque Country, particularly along major routes, are well maintained. That may not be the case in more rural areas, where you could be in for a bumpy ride.

You can get to Spain by bus from London, Paris, Rome, Frankfurt, Prague, and other major European cities. It is a long journey, but the buses are modern and inexpensive. Eurolines, the main carrier, connects many European cities with Barcelona.

Alsa-Enatcar, Spain's largest national bus company, has two luxury classes in addition to its regular coach services. The top of the line is Supra Clase, with roomy leather seats, free Wi-Fi internet connection, and onboard meals; in this class you also have the option of *asientos individuales*, single-file seats along one side of the bus. The next class is the Eurobus, with comfy seats and plenty of legroom, but no asientos individuales or onboard meals. The Supra Clase and Eurobus cost up to one-third and one-fourth more, respectively, than the regular coaches.

Some smaller, regional bus lines (Sarfa, for example, which connects Barcelona to destinations on the Costa Brava) offer multitrip bus passes, which are worthwhile if you plan on making multiple trips between two destinations. Generally, these tickets offer a savings of 20% per journey; you can buy them only in the bus station (not on the bus).

The general rule for children is that if they occupy a seat, they pay.

In Barcelona you can pick up schedule and fare information at the Tourist Information offices in Plaça de Catalunya, Plaça Sant Jaume, or at the Sants train station. A better and faster solution is to check online at 🌐 *www.barcelonanord.com*.

At bus-station ticket counters, major credit cards (except for American Express) are universally accepted. You must pay in cash for tickets purchased on the bus. Traveler's checks are almost never accepted.

During peak travel times (Easter, August, and Christmas), it's always a good idea to make a reservation at least three to four days in advance.

City buses run daily 5:30 am–11:30 pm. Route maps are displayed at bus stops. Note that those with a red band always stop at a central square—Catalunya, Universitat, or Urquinaona—and blue indicates a night bus. Barcelona's 17 night buses generally run until about 5 am.

Bus Information

Alsa-Enatcar ☎ *902/422242* 🌐 *www.alsa.es.* **Grup Sarbus** ✉ *Estació d'Autobusos Barcelona-Nord, Carrer d'Alí Bei 80, Eixample* ☎ *902/302025* 🌐 *www.sarfa.com.* **Julià Travel** ✉ *Ronda Universitat 5, Eixample* ☎ *93/317-6454* 🌐 *www.juliatravel.com.*

Bus Terminals Estació del Nord ✉ *Carrer d'Ali Bei 80, Eixample* ☎ *902/260606* 🌐 *www.barcelonanord.com.* **Estació de Sants** ✉ *Pl. dels Països Catalans s/n, Eixample* ☎ *902/240202, 902/240505 International.*

From the U.K. Eurolines/National Express ☎ *08717/818178 in the U.K.* 🌐 *www.nationalexpress.com.*

International Bus Companies
Eurolines ✉ *Av. Roma 13–15, Eixample* ☎ *93/367–4400* 🌐 *www.eurolines.es* ✉ *Estació del Nord, Carrer d'Ali Bei 80, Eixample* ☎ *93/265–0788* 🌐 *www.eurolines.es* ✉ *Barcelona Sants, Carrer de Viriat s/n, Eixample* ☎ *93/367–4400* 🌐 *www.eurolines.es.* **Linebus** ✉ *Estació del Nord, Carrer d' Alí Bei 80, Eixample* ☎ *93/265–0700, 902/335533* 🌐 *www.linebus.es.*

CABLE CAR AND FUNICULAR TRAVEL

The Montjuïc Funicular is a cog railway that runs from the junction of Avinguda Paral.lel and Nou de la Rambla (Ⓜ *Paral.lel*) to the Miramar station on Montjuïc. It operates 10 am–6 pm in winter and 10 am–9 pm in summer; the fare is €2, or one ride on a T10 card. A *telefèric* (cable car) then takes you up to Montjuïc Castle. The telefèric runs daily, 10 am–6 pm in winter (November through March), 10 am–9 pm in summer (June through September), and 10 am–7 pm the rest of the year. One-way fare is €7.30; round-trip fare is €10.30.

A Transbordador Aeri del Port (Harbor Cable Car) runs between Miramar and Montjuïc across the harbor to Torre de Jaume I, on Barcelona's *moll* (quay), and on to Torre de Sant Sebastià, at the end of Passeig Joan de Borbó in Barceloneta. You can board at either stage. One-way fare is €11; round-trip fare is €16.50. The car runs every 15 minutes, November through February, daily noon–5:30 pm, and March through October 10:30 am–8 pm.

To reach the summit of Tibidabo, take the metro to Avinguda de Tibidabo, then the Tramvía Blau (€3 one-way, €4.70 round-trip) to Peu del Funicular, and finally the Tibidabo Funicular (€7.70 round-trip; €4.10 with purchase of admission to the Tibidabo Amusement Park) from there to the top. The Tramvia runs daily March through December, and weekends only in February. Generally when running it's every 15–30 minutes, beginning at 10 am and finishing at dusk (around 6 pm in winter and 8 pm in summer).

CAR TRAVEL

Major routes throughout Spain bear heavy traffic, especially in peak holiday periods, so be extremely cautious. Spain's roads are shared by a mixture of local drivers, Moroccan immigrants traveling between northern Europe and northern Africa, and non-Spanish travelers on vacation, some of whom are more accustomed to driving on the left-hand side of the road. Watch out, too, for heavy truck traffic on national routes. Expect the near-impossibility of on-street parking in the major cities. Parking garages are common and affordable, and provide added safety to your vehicle and possessions.

The country's main cities are well connected by a network of four-lane *autovías* (freeways). The letter N stands for a national route (*carretera nacional*), either four- or two-lane. An *autopista* (AP) is a toll road. At the tollbooth plazas (the term in Castilian is *peaje*; in Catalan, *peatge*), there are three systems to choose from—*automàtic,* with machines for credit cards or coins; *manual,* with an attendant; or *telepago,* an automatic chip-driven system mostly used by Spanish drivers.

GETTING AROUND AND OUT OF BARCELONA

Arriving in Barcelona by car from the north along the AP7 autopista or from the west along the AP2, follow signs for the Ronda Litoral (the coastal ring road—but beware: it's most prominently marked "Aeroport," which can be misleading) to lower and central Barcelona along the waterfront, or the Ronda de Dalt (the upper ring road) along the edge of upper Barcelona to Horta, the Bonanova, Sarrià, and Pedralbes. For the center of town, take the Ronda Litoral and look for Exit 21 ("Paral.lel–Les Ramblas") or 22 ("Barceloneta–Via Laietana–Hospital de Mar"). If you are arriving from the Pyrenees on the C1411/E9 through the Tunel del Cadí, the Tunels de Vallvidrera will put you on the upper end of Via Augusta with off-ramps to Sarrià, Pedralbes, and La Bonanova. The Eixample and Ciutat Vella are 10–15 minutes farther if traffic is fluid. Watch out for the new variable speed limits on the approaches to Barcelona. While 80 kph (48 mph) is the maximum speed on the rondas, flashing signs over the motorway sometimes cut the speed limit down to 40 kph (24 mph) during peak hours.

Barcelona's main crosstown traffic arteries are Diagonal (running diagonally through the city) and the midtown avenues, Carrer d'Aragó, and Gran Via de les Corts Catalanes, both cutting northeast–southwest through the heart of the city. Passeig de Gràcia, which becomes Gran de Gràcia above Diagonal, runs all the way from Plaça de Catalunya up to Plaça Lesseps, but the main up-and-down streets, for motorists, are Balmes, Muntaner, Aribau, and Comtes d'Urgell. The general urban speed limit is 50 kph (30 mph).

Getting around Barcelona by car is generally more trouble than it's worth. It's better to walk or travel via subway, taxi, or bus.

Leaving Barcelona is not difficult. Follow signs for the rondas, do some advance mapping, and you're off. Follow signs for Girona and França for the Costa Brava, Girona, Figueres, and France. Follow Via Augusta and signs for Tunels de Vallvidrera or E9 and Manresa for the Tunel del Cadí and the Pyrenean Cerdanya valley. Follow Diagonal west and then the freeway AP7 signs for Lleida, Zaragoza, Tarragona, and Valencia to leave the city headed west. Look for airport, Castelldefells, and Sitges signs to head southwest down the coast for these beach points on the Costa Daurada. This C32 freeway to Sitges joins the AP7 to Tarragona and Valencia.

For travel outside Barcelona, the freeways to Girona, Figueres, Sitges, Tarragona, and Lleida are surprisingly fast. The distance to Girona, 97 km (58 miles), is a 45-minute shot. The French border is an hour away. Perpignan, at 188 km (113 miles) away, is an hour and 20 minutes.

GASOLINE

Gas stations are plentiful and often open 24 hours, especially around Barcelona's rondas. Most stations are self-service, though prices are the same as those at full-service stations. At the tank, punch in the amount of gas you want (in euros, not in liters), unhook the nozzle, pump the gas, and then pay. At night, however, you must pay before you fill up. Some stations allow for credit cards at the pump. Most pumps offer unleaded gas and diesel fuel, so be careful to pick the right one for your car. Unleaded gas (*gasolina sin plomo*) is available in two grades, 95 and 98 octanes. Prices per liter (🌐 *www.elpreciodelagasolina.com)* vary little between stations: €1.40 for sin plomo (95 octane) and €1.52 for unleaded (98 octane). Diesel fuel, known as *gas-oleo*, is about €1.37 a liter and, what's more, gets you farther per liter, so renting a car with a diesel engine will save you major fuel money.

PARKING

Barcelona's underground parking lots (posted "Parking" and symbolized by a white P on a blue background) are generally safe and convenient. Garage prices vary; expect close to €4 an hour and €25–€40 per 24-hour day. Airport parking runs from €3.50 for up to two hours to €18.75 per day for up to four days and €15 per day thereafter. The long-term parking located between Terminal 1 (T1) and Terminal 2 (T2) costs €13.55 per day up to 5 days and €12 per day after that.

Barcelona's street-parking system runs 9 am–2 pm and 4 pm–8 pm (with on-call attendants) weekdays and all day Saturday. Park in the specially marked blue spaces (about €2.60 per hour in the most expensive zones), and look for a nearby ticket vending machine. Tickets are valid for one, two, or three hours, but renewable in half-hour increments. The ticket must be displayed on the front dashboard. On the streets, do not park where the pavement edge is yellow or where there is a private entry (*gual* or *vado*). Parking signs marked "1–15" or "15–30" signify you can park on those dates of the month on the side of the street where indicated. Whenever you feel you have found an open space, be alert for triangular yellow stickers on the pavement that indicate a tow-away zone—the spot might not be so lucky after all. If your car is towed in Barcelona, you will find one of these yellow triangles, with the phone number and address of the municipal car deposit where your vehicle now resides, on the pavement where you left your car. A taxi will know where to take you to get it back.

Costs are presently €147.50, plus the fine for the parking infraction (fines range €45–€95), reduced by half if you pay the same day, and car storage by the hour (€1.99 per hour or €19.86 per day). To avoid risking this annoying and expensive catastrophe, park in a parking lot or garage. If your car is towed in Bilbao, contact the *ayuntamiento*, or town hall.

Towing Contact Information

Barcelona ☎ *901/513151.* **Bilbao Ayuntamiento (Town Hall)** ☎ *94/420–4200.*

RENTAL CARS

Currently, one of the best ways to rent a car, whether you arrange it from home or during your travels, is through the company's website—the rates are the best and the arrangements the easiest.

Generally you'll get a better deal if you book a car before you leave home. Avis, Hertz, Budget, and the European agency Europcar all have counters at the airports in Barcelona and Bilbao and in other cities. National companies work through the Spanish agency Atesa. Smaller, local companies offer lower rates. Cars with automatic transmission are less common, so specify your need for one in advance. A SatNav system programmable in English is likely to be well worth the cost of the option. Rates for pickup at Barcelona airport can start as low as €13 a day and €30 a week for an economy car with air-conditioning, manual transmission and unlimited mileage, booked online, but commonly run at least twice that amount. This does not include the tax on car rentals, which is 21%.

Your own driver's license is valid in Spain, but you may want to get an International Driver's Permit (IDP) for extra assurance. Permits are available from the American or Canadian Automobile Association, or, in the United Kingdom, from the Automobile Association or Royal Automobile Club. Check the AAA website for more info as well as for IDPs ($15) themselves.

If you are stopped you will be asked to present your license and passport (or photocopy). In Spain anyone over 18 with a valid license can drive; however, some rental companies will not rent a car to drivers under 21.

The cost for a child's car seat is €3.50 a day; the cost per day for an additional driver is approximately €4.50 per day.

Automobile Associations

American Automobile Association (*AAA*). Member services are provided through state and regional affiliates. ☎ *800/222–3395* 🌐 *www.aaa.com.* **National Automobile Club.** Individual membership is open to California residents only. ☎ *650/294–7000* 🌐 *www.thenac.com.*

Local Agencies in Barcelona **Atesa** ✉ *Aeropuerto El Prat, El Prat del Llobregat* ☎ *93/521–9095* 🌐 *www.atesa.es* ✉ *Muntaner 45, Eixample* ☎ *93/323–0701* 🌐 *www.atesa.es.* **Vanguard** ✉ *Viladomat 297, Eixample* ☎ *93/439–3880* 🌐 *www.vanguardrent.com.*

Major Agencies Avis *Estació de Sants, Eixample 902/110293 Còrsega 293–295, Eixample 902/110275 www.avis.es.* **Europcar** *Viladomat 214, Eixample 93/ 439–8403 www.europcar.es Estació de Sants, Eixample 93/491–4822 www. europcar.es.* **Hertz** *Estació de Sants, Eixample 902/998707 www.hertz.com Centro Comercial L'Illa, Av. Diagonal 549, Eixample 93/410–0134 www.hertz.com.*

ROAD CONDITIONS

You can reach all major cities and destinations by high-speed autopistas, two- and three-lane freeways where 110 kph (63 mph) is the legal speed limit. Tolls are steep, sometimes as high as €20 for two-to-three hour sections, but these freeways are spectacular touring tracks with terrific views of the countryside (billboards are prohibited), *and* they make the Iberian Peninsula into a relatively small piece of geography. Once you are off these major roads, all bets are off. Trucks can hold up long lines of traffic, and averaging 60 kph (36 mph) can be challenging. Still, the scenery, by and large, remains superb.

Signage on autopistas can be erratic and the lettering too small to decipher early enough to make decisions. Add to this the different languages (Spanish, Catalan, Euskera) appearing on road signs within a few hours of each other, and a certain amount of confusion is guaranteed. Only slower speeds can alleviate this problem by giving motorists more time to react.

Traffic jams (*atascos*) can be a problem in and around Barcelona, where the travel on the rondas slows to a standstill at peak hours. If possible, avoid the rush hours, which can last from 7 am until 9:30 am and 7 pm to 9 pm.

Long weekends, called *puentes* (literally, bridges), particularly on Friday, routinely provoke delays leaving Barcelona. Avoiding the rondas in favor of the Tunels de Vallvidrera (straight out Via Augusta) can save time if you're headed north. Most of Barcelona vacation during August, so if you're hitting the road at the beginning or end of this month you'll likely encounter lots of traffic, particularly on the roads heading up or down the coast.

ROADSIDE EMERGENCIES

The rental agencies Hertz and Avis have 24-hour breakdown service. If you belong to an auto club (AAA or CAA), you can get emergency assistance from their Catalan counterpart, the Reial Automovil Club de Catalunya (RACC), or the Spanish branch Real Automovil Club de España (RACE). There are emergency telephones on all autopistas, every 2 km (1 mile), with service stations generally found every 40 km (25 miles).

Traveling with a European cell phone is essential for safety and convenience, keeping in mind that coverage in the mountains is erratic.

If your rental car breaks down, be especially wary of anyone who stops to help you on the road: highway robbery has been known to be all too literal here on occasion, as bands of thieves puncture tires and steal belongings (nearly always on toll roads and freeways, sometimes at knife- or gunpoint) while pretending to offer assistance.

Emergency Services Real Automovil Club de Catalunya (*RACC*). *Diagonal 687, Diagonal 93/495–5152, 902/106106 for emergency aid www.racc.es.* **Real Automovil Club de España** (*RACE*). *Muntaner 107, Eixample 93/451–1551, 902/111–2222 for emergency aid www.race.es.*

RULES OF THE ROAD

In Spain, motorists drive on the right. Horns are banned in cities, but that doesn't seem to keep irate drivers from blasting away.

Children under 10 may not ride in the front seat, and seat belts are compulsory. Speed limits are 50 kph (31 mph) in cities; 100 kph (62 mph) on N roads; 110 kph (68 mph) on the autopistas and autovías; and, unless otherwise signposted, 70 kph (44 mph) on secondary roads. Barcelona's rondas now limit motorists to 80 kph (48 mph) and sometimes, at peak hours, cut the speed limit down to 40 kph (24 mph).

Right turns on red are not permitted. In the cities people are more often stopped for petty rule-breaking such as crossing a solid line or doing a U-turn than for speeding. However, Spanish highway police are especially vigilant regarding speeding and illegal passing, generally interpreted as crossing the solid line; fines start at €100 and, in the case of foreign drivers, police are empowered to demand payment on the spot.

On freeway ramps, expect to come to a full stop at the red stop (not yield) triangle at the end of the on-ramp and wait for a break in the traffic. Expect no merging to the left lane, especially from trucks, which, by law, must remain in the right lane.

Drunk-driving tests are becoming more prevalent. It is illegal to drive with an alcohol level that exceeds 0.5% BAC (blood-alcohol count) or 0.25 on a breath test; this is about three medium-size glasses of wine or three beers for a man of average height and weight, but it's best to be extra cautious. Fines vary from one region of Spain to another.

METRO TRAVEL

In Barcelona the underground metro, or subway, is the fastest, cheapest, and easiest way to get around. Metro lines run Monday through Thursday and Sunday 5 am to midnight, Friday to 2 am Saturday and holiday evenings all night. The FGC trains run 5 am to just after midnight on weekdays and to 1:52 on weekends and the eves of holidays. Sunday trains run on weekday schedules.

When switching from a metro line to the FGC (or vice versa), merely insert the card through the slot and the turnstile will open without charging you for a second ride provided less than an hour and 15 minutes has elapsed since you punched in initially. Maps showing bus and metro routes are available free from the Tourist Information office in Plaça de Catalunya.

TICKET/PASS	PRICE
Single Fare	€2
10-Ride Pass	€9.80

Subway Info **Transports Metropolitans de Barcelona** (*TMB*). ☎ *93/298-7000* 🌐 *www.tmb.net.*

TAXI TRAVEL

In Barcelona taxis are black and yellow and show a green rooftop light on the front right corner when available for hire. The meter currently starts at €2.05 and rises in increments of €0.98 every kilometer. These rates apply 6 am to 10 pm weekdays. At hours outside of these, the rates rise 20%. There are official supplements of €1 per bag for luggage.

Trips to or from a train station, or the quay where the cruise ships put in, entail a supplemental charge of €2.10; airport runs add a supplemental charge of €4.20, as do trips to or from a football match. There are cabstands (*parades*, in Catalan) all over town, and you can also hail cabs on the street, though if you are too close to an official stand they may not stop. You can call for a cab by phone 24 hours a day. Drivers do not expect a tip, but rounding up the fare is standard.

Taxi Companies **Barna Taxi** ☎ *93/322-2222* 🌐 *www.barnataxi.com.* **Cooperativa Radio-Taxi Metropolitana Barcelona** ☎ *93/225000.* **Radio Taxi** ☎ *93/225-0000.* **Taxi Class Rent** ☎ *93/307-0707.* **Teocar Mercedes** ☎ *93/308-3434.*

TRAIN TRAVEL

International overnight trains to Barcelona arrive from many European cities, including Paris, Grenoble, Geneva, Zurich, and Milan; the route from Paris takes 11½ hours. Almost all long-distance trains arrive at and depart from Estació de Sants, though many make a stop at Passeig de Gràcia that comes in handy for hotels in the Eixample or in the

Ciutat Vella. Estació de França, near the port, handles only a few regional trains within Catalonia. Train service connects Barcelona with most other major cities in Spain; in addition a high-speed Euromed route connects Barcelona to Tarragona and Valencia.

A new twice-daily high-speed train, linking Barcelona and Paris in just six and a half hours, went into service in December 2013. Only the 200-km (124-mile) section of track between Perpignan and Nîmes is still unable to handle the TGV speed; when that section is brought up to standard (which could take another ten years), travel time will be cut to just five and a half hours—making the downtown-to-downtown journey by train palpably competitive, time-wise, with a flight.

Spain's intercity services (along with some of Barcelona's local train routes) are the province of the government-run railroad system—RENFE (Red Nacional de Ferrocarriles Españoles). The high-speed AVE train now connects Barcelona and Madrid (via Lleida and Zaragoza) in less than three hours. (Spain has more high-speed track in service than any other country in Europe.) The fast TALGO and ALTARIA trains are efficient, though local trains remain slow and tedious. The Catalan government's FGC (Ferrocarril de la Generalitat de Catalunya) also provide train service, notably to Barcelona's commuter suburbs of Sant Cugat, Terrassa, and Sabadell.

Smoking is forbidden on all RENFE trains.

Information on the local/commuter lines (*rodalies* in Catalan, *cercanias* in Castilian) can be found at 🌐 *www.renfe.es/cercanias*. Rodalies go, for example, to Sitges from Barcelona, whereas you would take a regular RENFE train to, say, Tarragona. It's important to know whether you are traveling on RENFE or on rodalies (the latter distinguished by a stylized C), so you don't end up in the wrong line.

Both Catalonia and the Basque Country offer scenic railroad excursions. The day train from Barcelona to Madrid runs through bougainvillea-choked towns before leaping out across Spain's central meseta to Zaragoza and Madrid, arriving in less than three hours. The train from Barcelona's Plaça de Catalunya north to Sant Pol de Mar and Blanes runs along the edge of the beach.

First-class train service in Spain, with the exception of the *coche-cama* (Pullman) overnight service, barely differs from second class or *turista*. The TALGO or the AVE trains, however, are much faster than second-class carriers like the slow-poke Estrella overnight from Barcelona to Madrid. Legroom and general comforts are about the same (that is, mediocre). The AVE is the exception: between Barcelona and Madrid or between Madrid and Sevilla, these sleek bullets with their tinted windows are superlative moving observation platforms. Some 30 AVE trains a day connect Barcelona and Madrid, with departures from 5:50 am to 10:20 pm. Ticket prices in tourist class start at €125.90 and vary depending on peak hours. Trips take from 2 hours 30 minutes to 3 hours 10 minutes.

After buses, trains are the most economical way to travel. Within the RENFE pricing system, there are 20% discounts on long-distance tickets if you buy a round-trip ticket, and there are 20% discounts for students and senior citizens (though they usually have to carry cards issued by the local government, the Generalitat, so they are not intended for tourists).

If you're planning extensive train travel, look into rail passes. If Spain is your only destination, consider a Spain Flexipass. Prices begin at $165 for three days of second-class travel within a two-month period and $215 for first class. Other passes cover more days and longer periods. The 10-day pass costs $365 in second class, $460 in first class. (Beware when you order online; broker's quotations can vary considerably.)

Spain is one of 17 European countries in which you can use Eurail Global Passes, which buy you unlimited first-class rail travel in all participating countries for the duration of the pass. If you plan to rack up the miles and go between countries, get a standard pass; these are available for 15 days ($454), 21 days ($585), one month ($720), two months ($1,015), and three months ($1,252). If your needs are more limited, look into a Regional Pass, which costs less than a Eurail Pass and buys you a limited number of travel days in a limited number of countries (France, Italy, and Spain, for example), during a specified time period.

In addition to standard Eurail Passes, Rail Europe sells the Eurail Youthpass (for those under age 26), the Eurail Saverpass (which gives a discount for two or more people traveling together), a Eurail Flexipass (which allows a certain number of travel days within a set period), the Euraildrive Pass (four days of train travel and two days of Avis or Hertz car rental), and the Europass Drive (which combines three days travel by train and two by rental car). Whichever pass you choose, remember that you must buy your pass before you leave for Europe.

■ TIP→ **Many travelers assume that rail passes guarantee them seats—not so: you need to reserve seats in advance even if you're using a rail pass.** Seat reservations are required on some European trains, particularly high-speed trains, and are wise on any train that might be crowded. You'll also need a reservation if you want sleeping accommodations. All reservations require an extra fee.

For schedules and fares, call RENFE. The easiest way for non–Spanish speakers to get schedule information is to go the RENFE website (🌐 *www.renfe.es*).

Train services to Barcelona from the United Kingdom are not as frequent, fast, or affordable as flights, and you have to change trains (and stations) in Paris. From Paris it's worth paying extra for a TALGO express to avoid having to change trains again at the Spanish border. Journey time to Paris (from London via Eurostar through the Channel Tunnel) is around three hours; from Paris to Barcelona takes six and a half hours more. Allow at least two hours in Paris for changing trains.

Although overnight trains have comfortable sleeper cars for two or four in coche-cama, first-class fares that include a sleeping compartment are comparable to airfares.

The Estrella, the overnight train from Barcelona to Madrid, takes nine hours. A tourist-class seat costs €44.40. A bunk in a compartment with three other people, called *clase turista damas-caballeros* (tourist class), separates travelers by gender and costs another €57 for a total of €101.40. (But be warned: windows do not open and the heat can be suffocating.) The air shuttle (or a scheduled flight) between Madrid and Barcelona can, if all goes well, get you door to door in less than three hours. Prices vary enormously, depending on the carrier and the time of day: At best you can fly for less than half the cost of the overnight train; at worst you can pay more than twice as much. For shorter, regional train trips, you can often buy your tickets directly from machines in the main train stations. For a one-way ticket, ask for, in Catalan, *anada* (in Spanish it's *ida*); or for a round-trip ticket, *anada i tornada*. In Spanish, it's *ida y vuelta*.

Most travel agencies can sell you train tickets (though not for same-day travel), which saves standing in line at the station *taquilla* (ticket office).

Lines at Sants can be long. Look for the counters marked *salida inmediata* (next departure), where you can buy same-day tickets more quickly.

Visa and MasterCard are universally accepted at station ticket counters.

During peak travel times (Easter, August, and Christmas), it's important to make a reservation weeks or even months in advance; on routes between major cities (Barcelona to Bilbao or Madrid, for example), it's a good idea to reserve well in advance, especially for overnight trips.

You can make reservations over the phone by calling RENFE, online, or by waiting at the station ticket counter, preferably in Barcelona's Passeig de Gràcia, where lines are often shorter.

The easiest way to make reservations is to use the TIKNET service on the RENFE website. TIKNET involves registering and providing your credit-card information. When you make the reservation, you will be given a car and seat assignment and a *localizador* (translated as "localizer" on the English version of the site). Print out the reservations page or write down car number, seat number, and localizer. When traveling, go to your assigned seat on the train. When the conductor comes around, give him the localizer, and he will issue the ticket on the spot. You will need your passport and, in most cases, the credit card you used for the reservation. The AVE trains check you in at the gate to the platform, where you provide the localizer. You can review your pending reservations online at any time.

Caveats: The first time you use TIKNET, you must pick up the tickets at a RENFE station; you can go to a RENFE booth at the airport as you get off your plane. A 15% cancellation fee is charged if you cancel more than two hours after making the reservation. You cannot buy tickets online for certain regional lines or for commuter lines (*cercanias*). Station agents cannot alter TIKNET reservations: you must do this yourself online. If a train is booked, the TIKNET process doesn't reveal this until the final stage of the reservation attempt. Then it gives you a cryptic error message in a little box, though if you reserve a few days in advance it's unlikely you'll encounter this problem except at Easter or Christmas or in the first week of August.

There is no line per se at the train station for advance tickets (and often for information); you take a number and wait until it is called. Ticket clerks at stations rarely speak English, so if you need help or advice in planning a more complex train journey, you may be better off going to a travel agency that displays the blue-and-yellow RENFE sign. A small commission (American Express Viajes charges €3.75) should be expected.

General Information Estació de França ✉ *Av. Marquès de l'Argentera 1, Born-Ribera* ☎ *902/240202, 902/320320* 🌐 *www.renfe.es.* **Estació de Passeig de Gràcia** ✉ *Passeig de Gràcia/Carrer Aragó, Eixample* ☎ *902/240202.* **Estació de Sants** ✉ *Pl. dels Països Catalans s/n, Eixample* ☎ *902/240202, 902/432343.* **Ferrocarrils de la Generalitat de Catalunya (FGC)** ☎ *93/2051515* 🌐 *www.fgc.es.* **RENFE** ☎ *902/240202* 🌐 *www.renfe.es.*

Information and Passes Eurail 🌐 *www.eurail.com.* **Rail Europe** ✉ *44 S. Broadway, White Plains, New York* ☎ *800/622-8600* 🌐 *www.raileurope.com* ☎ *905/602-4195 in Canada, 800/361-7245* 🌐 *www.raileurope.ca.*

From the U.K. Eurostar ☎ *01233/617575 in the U.K., 0843/218-6186* 🌐 *www.eurostar.co.uk.* **National Rail Enquiries** ☎ *0845/748-4950 in the U.K.* 🌐 *www.nationalrail.co.uk.* **Voyages-sncf** ✉ *193 Piccadilly, London, England* ☎ *0844/848-5484 in the U.K.* 🌐 *uk.voyages-sncf.com/en.*

Channel Tunnel Car Transport Eurotunnel ☎ *08443/353535 in U.K., 902/307315 in Spain, 810/630304 in France* 🌐 *www.eurotunnel.com.*

Channel Tunnel Passenger Service Eurostar ☎ *08432/186186 in U.K., 1233/617575 from outside U.K.* 🌐 *www.eurostar.co.uk.* **Rail Europe** ☎ *800/622-8600 in U.S., 08448/484-064 in U.K.* 🌐 *www.raileurope.com.*

ESSENTIALS

COMMUNICATIONS

INTERNET

Internet access via Wi-Fi is available in virtually all Barcelona hotels. In addition, many cafés and bars are Internet hot spots and have signs indicating it in their windows. Easy Internet Café near the top of La Rambla is one of the city's most complete and convenient cybercafés, with 300 computers available from 8:30 am to 2:30 am daily. An important piece to pack is the adapter that translates flat-edged plugs or triple plugs to round dual ones. Most Internet cafés have no equipment to get your laptop online, but Wi-Fi access is common throughout Barcelona.

Cybercafé Resources **Crepsi.** Internet café. ✉ *Carrer Rosselló 227, Eixample* ☎ *93/415–3677.* **Friends on Line** ✉ *Carrer Còrsega 197, Eixample* ☎ *93/363–0754.*

PHONES

Calling out to anywhere from your hotel almost always incurs a hefty surcharge. Pre-paid cards can help you keep costs to a minimum, but only if you purchase them locally. And then there are mobile phones: if you have one that's Skype-compatible, your financial worries are over.

The country code for Spain is 34. To phone home from Spain, 00 gets you an international line; country codes are 1 for the United States and Canada, 61 for Australia, 64 for New Zealand, and 44 for the United Kingdom.

CALLING WITHIN SPAIN

Spain's telephone system is efficient, and direct dialing is the norm everywhere. Only cell phones conforming to the European GSM standard will work in Spain.

All Spanish area codes begin with a 9; for instance, Barcelona is 93 and Bilbao is 94. The 900 code indicates a toll-free number. Numbers starting with a 6 indicate a cellular phone; note that calls from landlines to cell phones (and vice versa) are significantly more expensive.

For general information in Spain, dial 1–18–18. The operator for international information and assistance is at 1–18–25 (some operators speak English). Barcelona information of all kinds, including telephone information, is available at 010, where many operators speak English.

Calls within Spain require dialing 8, 9, or 10 digits (beginning with a 2- or 3-digit regional code), even within the same area code.

Making a long-distance call within Spain simply requires dialing the 8, 9, or 10-digit number including the provincial area code and number.

Between phone booths (ask for a *cabina telefónica*) and public phones in bars and restaurants, telephone communication in Spain functions as well as anyplace in the world. Many phones have digital screens, so you can see your money ticking away. You need at least €0.20 in coin for a local call, €1 to call another province. Pick up the phone, wait for the dial tone, and only then insert coins before dialing. Rates are reduced on weekends and after 8 pm on weekdays.

CALLING OUTSIDE SPAIN

The best way to phone home is to use a public phone that accepts pre-paid cards (available from tobacconists and most newsagents) or make your call from a *locutorio* (phone center). The best thing about the locutorio is the quiet, private booth. If the call costs more than €5, you can often pay with Visa or MasterCard.

To make an international call yourself, dial 00, then the country code, then the area code and number. Ask at a tourist office for a list of locutorios and Internet centers that include phone service.

Before you go, find out your long-distance company's access code in Spain.

Access Codes **AT&T** ☎ *900/990011.* **MCI WorldPhone** ☎ *800/099357.* **Sprint International Access** ☎ *900/990013.*

CALLING CARDS

Pay phones work with a pre-paid card (*tarjeta telefónica*), of which there are several varieties that you can buy at any tobacco shop (*tabac*) or newsagent. The Euro Hours Card, sold at many tobacco shops for €6, is good for 350 minutes' worth of international calls.

MOBILE PHONES

If you have a multiband phone and your service provider uses the world-standard GSM network (as do T-Mobile, Cingular, and Verizon), you can probably use your phone pretty much anywhere abroad—roaming fees can be steep, however. And overseas you can get stuck with toll charges for incoming calls. It's almost always cheaper (but confirm with your carrier) to send a text message than to make a call, since text messages have a low set fee (often less than €0.05). To avoid roaming fees completely, select airplane mode or turn off data roaming until you are in a Wi-Fi hot spot, where you can check email or use the Web at much lower costs (often free). If you were to do either while roaming, your bill would show it: an email with a five-megapixel photo, for example, would require your phone to download about 2 megabytes of data at a cost of about $20 per MB from either Verizon or AT&T.

If you just want to make local calls, consider buying a new SIM card (note that your provider may have to unlock your phone for you to use a different card) and a pre-paid service plan in your destination.

Cell Phone Rentals Rent A Phone ✉ *Numancia 212, Barcelona* ☎ *93/280–2131.* **Telecon Iberica** ☎ *93/228–9110.*

Contacts Cellular Abroad. This company rents and sells GMS phones and sells SIM cards that work in many countries. ☎ *800/287–5072 in the U.S.* 🌐 *www.cellularabroad.com.* **Mobal.** This company rents mobiles and sells GSM phones (starting at $29) that will operate in 140 countries. Per-call rates vary throughout the world. ☎ *888/888–9162* 🌐 *www.mobalrental.com.* **Planet Fone.** This company rents cell phones, but unlike with most other providers, you have to pay for incoming calls. ☎ *888/988–4777* 🌐 *www.planetfone.com.*

ELECTRICITY

The electrical current in Spain is 220 volts, 50 cycles alternating current (AC); wall outlets take continental-type plugs, with two round prongs. An adapter from flat to round prongs is a must for computers and hair dryers.

EMERGENCIES

You can expect local residents to be helpful if you have an emergency. For assistance, dial the pan-European emergency phone number 112, which can connect you to an English-speaking operator. Otherwise, dial the emergency numbers below for national police, local police, fire department, or medical services. On the road, there are emergency phones at frequent regular intervals on autovías and autopistas. They are marked S.O.S.

If your documents are stolen, contact both the police and your consulate or embassy *(⇨ below)*. If you lose a credit card, phone the issuer immediately *(⇨ Money)*.

To find out which pharmacies are open late at night or 24 hours on a given day, look on the door of any pharmacy or in any local newspaper under "*Farmacias de Guardia*" or dial 010.

In Barcelona, Tourist Attention, a service provided by the local police, can help if you're the victim of a crime or need medical assistance. English interpreters are on hand.

MAIL

The postal system in Spain, called *Correos,* does work, but delivery times can vary widely. An airmail letter to the United States may take four days to reach its destination, or it may take two weeks. Mail to the United Kingdom may range from overnight delivery to four days. Delivery to other places worldwide is equally unpredictable. Sending letters by special delivery (*urgente*) will ensure speedier delivery.

Post offices are usually open 8:30–8:30 on weekdays, and 10–2 on Saturday. Barcelona's main post office, on Pl. Antonio López at the port end of Via Laietana, is open all day, 8:30 am–9:30 pm weekdays, and 8:30–2:30 on Saturday.

Airmail letters to Australia, New Zealand, the United States, and Canada cost €0.90 up to 20 grams. Letters to the United Kingdom and other EU countries cost €0.75 up to 20 grams. Postcard rates are identical. An urgente sticker costs €2.84. Letters within Spain are €0.37. You can buy stamps at post offices and at licensed tobacco shops.

To have mail held at the Barcelona post office, have it addressed to *Lista de Correos* (the equivalent of Poste Restante), Oficina Central de Correus i Telecomunicacions, Pl. Antonio López 1, 08002. Provincial postal addresses should include the name of the province in parentheses, for example, Figueres (Girona). For Barcelona, this is not necessary.

Main Branch Oficina Carrer Aragó ✉ *Aragó 282, Eixample* ☎ *93/216–0453* Ⓜ *Passeig de Gràcia.*

MONEY

Barcelona has long been Spain's most expensive city, but prices are still lower than they are an hour north across the French border. Coffee or beer in a bar generally costs €1.50 (standing) or €1.75 (seated). Small glass of wine in a bar: around €1.50. Soft drink: €2 to €3 a bottle. Ham-and-cheese sandwich: €5 to €8. Two-kilometer (1-mile) taxi ride: about €5, but the meter keeps ticking in traffic jams. Local bus or subway ride: €2. Movie ticket: €8.60. Foreign newspaper: €4.50 to €6.50.

Prices throughout this guide are given for adults. Substantially reduced fees are almost always available for children, students, and senior citizens.

TIP→ Banks never have every foreign currency on hand, and it may take as long as a week to order. If you're planning to exchange funds before leaving home, don't wait till the last minute.

CREDIT CARDS

It's a good idea to inform your credit-card company before you travel. Otherwise, the credit-card company might put a hold on your card if their computer flags a purchase it considers "unusual" activity. Record all your credit-card numbers—as well as the phone numbers to call if your cards are lost or stolen—and keep them in a safe place. Both MasterCard and Visa have general numbers you can call (collect if you're abroad) if your card is lost, but you're better off calling the issuing bank; the number is usually printed on your card.

If you plan to use your credit card for cash advances, you'll need to apply for a PIN at least two weeks before your trip.

Dynamic currency conversion programs are becoming increasingly widespread. Merchants who participate in them are supposed to ask whether you want to be charged in dollars or the local currency, but they don't always do so. And even if they do offer you a choice, they may well avoid mentioning the additional surcharges. With American Express cards, DCC simply isn't an option. But note that in Spain, many restaurants don't accept American Express.

Reporting Lost Cards American Express ☎ *800/528–4800 in U.S., 336/393–1111 collect from abroad* 🌐 *www.americanexpress.com.* **Diners Club** ☎ *800/234–6377 in U.S., 303/799–1504 collect from abroad* 🌐 *www.dinersclub.com.* **MasterCard** ☎ *800/627–8372 in U.S., 636/722–7111 collect from abroad* 🌐 *www.mastercard.com.* **Visa** ☎ *800/847–2911 in U.S., 301/967–1096 collect from abroad* 🌐 *www.visa.com.*

Toll-Free Numbers in Spain
American Express ☎ *900/814500.* **Diners Club** ☎ *900/801331 24-hr, 514/877–1577 for U.S. customer service* 🌐 *www.dinersclub.es.* **MasterCard** ☎ *900/971231, 900/974445.* **Visa** ☎ *900/991124, 301/967–1096.*

CURRENCY AND EXCHANGE

On January 1, 2002, the European monetary unit, the euro (€), went into circulation in Spain and the other countries that have adopted it (Austria, Belgium, Finland, France, Germany, Greece, Ireland, Italy, Luxembourg, the Netherlands, and Portugal). Euro notes come in denominations of 5, 10, 20, 50, 100, 200, and 500 euros; coins are worth 1 cent of a euro, 2 cents, 5 cents, 10 cents, 20 cents, 50 cents, 1 euro, and 2 euros. (€500 notes don't really circulate. Shops and restaurants won't accept them, and they tend to carry a whiff of the underground economy.) All coins have one side with the value of the euro on it; the other side has each country's own national symbol. Banknotes are the same for all European Union countries. At this writing exchange rates were U.S. $1.33, U.K. £0.83, Australian $1.42, Canadian $1.40, New Zealand $1.62, and 13.82 South African rands to the euro.

TIP→ Even if a currency-exchange booth has a sign promising no commission, there's going to be a fee. You're better off getting foreign currency at an ATM.

Currency Conversion

Google *www.google.com*. **Oanda.com** *www.oanda.com*. **XE.com** *www.xe.com*.

PASSPORTS

Visitors from the United States, Australia, Canada, New Zealand, and the United Kingdom need a valid passport to enter Spain. No visa is required for U.S. passport holders for a stay of up to three months; for stays exceeding three months, contact the Consulate of Spain nearest you. Australians require a visa for stays longer than one month; you should obtain it from the Spanish Embassy before you leave.

TAXES

Value-Added Tax (similar to sales tax) is called IVA (for *Impuesto sobre el valor añadido*) in Spain. It is levied on services, such as hotels and restaurants, and on consumer products. When in doubt about whether tax is included, ask, "*Está incluido el IVA* ("ee-vah")?"

The IVA rate for hotels and restaurants is 10%. Menus will generally say at the bottom whether tax is included (*IVA incluido*) or not (*más 7% IVA*). While food and basic necessities are taxed at the lowest rate, most consumer goods are taxed at 21%. In shops displaying the Tax-Free Shopping sticker, non–EU citizens can request a Tax-Free Cheque on purchases of at least €90.16. This Cheque must be stamped at the airport customs office. After this is done, present it to one of the Caixa or Banco de España offices in the airport. The bank issues a certified check or credits the amount to your credit card.

Global Refund is a Europe-wide service with 225,000 affiliated stores and more than 700 refund counters at major airports and border crossings. Its refund form, called a Tax-Free Cheque, is the most common across the European continent. The service issues refunds in the form of cash, check, or credit-card adjustment. The company's center in the departure lobby of Terminal 1 at Barcelona's El Prat airport is open daily 7 am to 11 pm. Note that Global Refund takes a handling fee for processing your refund.

V.A.T. Refunds Global Refund *800/566–9828* *www.globalrefund.com*.

TIPPING

A certain gallantry keeps Spanish service workers from seeming to care about your small change, but waiters and other service people expect to be tipped, and you can be sure that your contribution will be appreciated. On the other hand, if you experience bad or surly service, don't feel obligated to leave a tip.

Restaurant checks always include service. The bill may not tell you that the service is included, but it is. An extra tip of 5% to 10% of the bill is icing on the cake. Leave tips in cash, even if paying by credit card. If you eat tapas or sandwiches at a bar, just round up the bill to the nearest euro. Tip cocktail servers €0.50 a drink, depending on the bar. In a fancy establishment, leave no more than a 10% tip even though service is included—likewise if you had a great time.

Taxi drivers expect no tip and are happy if you round up in their favor. A tip of 5% of the total fare is considered generous. Long rides or extra help with luggage may merit a tip, but if you're short of change, you'll never hear a complaint. On the contrary, your driver may sometimes round down in *your* favor instead of ransacking his pockets for exact change.

Tip hotel porters €1 a bag, and the bearer of room service €1. A doorman who calls a taxi for you gets €1. If you stay in a hotel for more than two nights, tip the maid about €1 per night. A concierge should receive a tip for service, from €1 for basic help to €5 or more for special assistance such as getting reservations at a popular restaurant.

Tour guides should be tipped about €2, barbers €1, and women's hairdressers at least €2 for a wash and style. Restroom attendants are tipped €1 or whatever loose change is at hand.

TOURS

SPECIAL-INTEREST TOURS

ART TOURS

The Ruta del Modernisme (Moderniste Route), a self-guided tour, provides an excellent guidebook (available in English) that interprets 116 Moderniste sites from the Sagrada Família and the Palau de la Música Catalana to Art Nouveau building facades, lampposts, and paving stones. The €12 Guide, sold at the Plaça de Catalunya Tourist Office, Pavellons Güell, and Hospital de Sant Pau, comes with a book of vouchers good for discounts up to 50% on admission to most of the Moderniste buildings and sites in the Guide in Barcelona and 13 other towns and cities in Catalonia, as well as free guided tours in English at Pavellons Güell (daily 10:15 and 12:15) and the Hospital de Sant Pau (daily at 10, 11, noon and 1).

The Palau de la Música Catalana offers guided tours in English every hour on the hour from 10 to 3:30. Sagrada Família guided tours cost extra. Casa Milà offers one guided tour daily (6 pm weekdays, 11 am weekends). Architect Dominique Blinder of Urbancultours specializes in explorations of the Barcelona Jewish Quarter but can also provide tours of the Sagrada Família or virtually any architectural aspect of Barcelona.

Contacts Centre del Modernisme, Centre d'Informació de Turisme de Barcelona ✉ *Pl. de Catalunya 17 soterrani, Eixample* ☎ *93/285–3834* 🌐 *www.rutadelmodernisme.com.* **Centre del Modernisme, Hospital de la Santa Creu i Sant Pau** ✉ *C. Sant Antoni Maria Claret 167, Eixample* ☎ *93/268–2444* 🌐 *www.rutadelmodernisme.com* Ⓜ *Sant Pau/Dos de Maig.* **Centre del Modernisme, Pavellons Güell** ✉ *Av. de Pedralbes 7, Pedralbes* ☎ *93/317–7652, 93/256–2504* 🌐 *www.rutadelmodernisme.com* Ⓜ *Palau Real.* **Urbancultours** ✉ *info@urbancultours.com* 🌐 *www.urbancultours.com.*

CULINARY

Aula Gastronómica (Cooking Classroom) has different culinary tours, including tours of the Boqueria and Santa Catarina markets with breakfast, cooking classes, and tastings, for €12 per person and up. The locals you'll meet on the tours may struggle a bit in English, but between the guides and the help of fellow travelers, everyone manages. Jane Gregg, founder of Epicureanways, offers gourmet and wine tours of Barcelona and Catalonia. Teresa Parker of Spanish Journeys organizes cooking classes, seasonal specials, custom cultural or culinary tours, corporate cooking retreats, or off-the-beaten-path travel.

Contacts Aula Gastronómica ✉ *Sagristans 5, Barri Gòtic* ☎ *93/301–1944* 🌐 *www.aulagastronomica.com.* **Epicureanways** ✉ *1208 Wellford St., Charlottesville, Virginia* ☎ *434/738–2293 in the U.S., 93/802–2688 in Spain* 🌐 *www.epicureanways.com.* **Spanish Journeys** ✉ *805 Long Pond Rd., Wellfleet, Massachusetts* ☎ *508/349–9769* 🌐 *www.spanishjourneys.com.*

DAY TOURS AND GUIDES

BOAT TOURS

Golondrina harbor boats make short trips from the Portal de la Pau, near the Columbus monument. The fare is €7 for a 40-minute "Barcelona Port" tour of the harbor and €14.80 for the "Barcelona Sea" 90-minute ride out past the beaches and up the coast to the Fòrum at the eastern end of Diagonal. Departures are spring and summer (Easter week through September), daily 11:15 to 5:15 for the Port tour, 12:30 and 3:30 for the Sea tour; fall and winter, weekends and holidays only, 11 to 5. It's closed mid-December through early January.

Fees and Schedules Las Golondrinas and Trimar y Ómnibus ✉ *Plaza Portal de la Pau s/n, Rambla* ☎ *93/4423106* 🌐 *www.lasgolondrinas.com* Ⓜ *Drassanes.*

BUS TOURS

The Bus Turístic (9 or 9:30 am to 7 or 8 pm every 5–25 minutes, depending on the season), sponsored by the tourist office, runs on three circuits that pass all the important sights. The blue route covers upper Barcelona; the red route tours lower Barcelona; and the green route runs from the Port Olímpic along Barcelona's beaches to the Fòrum at the eastern end of Diagonal (April through September only). A one-day ticket, which you can buy online (with a 10% discount) for €23.40 (a two-day ticket is €30.60), or on the bus for €26 (€34 for two days), also covers the fare for the Tramvía Blau, funicular, and Montjuïc cable car across the port. You receive a booklet with discount vouchers for various attractions. The blue and red bus routes start at Plaça de Catalunya near Café Zurich. The green route starts at Port Olímpic next to the Hotel Arts. Passengers can jump off and catch a later bus at any stop along the way; some stops are "hubs" where you can switch to a bus on one of the other routes. Audio coverage is provided in 10 languages. A competing bus tour, Barcelona Tours, also leaves from Plaça de Catalunya near the corner of Ronda de la Universitat.

The product and prices are all but identical, though the Bus Turístic is the official Tourist Office tour, offering discount vouchers and superior service. In the event of long lines or delays on the Bus Turístic, Barcelona Tours is a good alternative.

Contacts Bus Turístic ✉ *Pl. de Catalunya 3, Barcelona* ☎ *93/285–3832* 🌐 *www.barcelonabusturistic.cat.* **Julià Tours** ✉ *Ronda Universitat 5, Eixample* ☎ *93/402–6951* 🌐 *www.juliatravel.com/en/tours-barcelona.html.* **Pullmantur** ✉ *Gran Vía 645, Eixample* ☎ *902/240070* 🌐 *www.pullmantur.es.*

PRIVATE GUIDES

Guides from the organizations listed below are generally competent, though the quality of language skills and general showmanship may vary. For customized tours, including access to some of Barcelona's leading chefs, architects, art historians, and artists, Heritage Tours will set it all up from New York.

Contacts Associació Professional d'Informadors Turístics. Book half-day or full-day tours with an English-speaking guide, for Moderniste Barcelona, Barri Gòtic, and/or the major museums. ☎ *93/319–8416* 🌐 *www.informadoresturisticos.com/index.html.* **Barcelona Guide Bureau.** Book here for five-hour coach tours (from €59) of the major sites in Barcelona, offered daily, and get fast-track entrance to museums and popular venues like the Sagrada Familia. ✉ *Via Laietana 54, Barcelona* ☎ *93/268–2422, 93/315–2261* 🌐 *www.barcelonaguidebureau.com.* **Heritage Tours.** Contact Heritage for upscale personalized tours, planned in advance. ✉ *121 W. 27th St., Ste. 1201, New York, New York* ☎ *800/378–4555, 212/206–8400 in U.S.* 🌐 *www.htprivatetravel.com.*

WALKING TOURS

Turisme de Barcelona offers weekend walking tours of the Barri Gòtic, the Waterfront, Picasso's Barcelona, Modernisme, a shopping circuit, and Gourmet Barcelona in English (at 10:30 am). Prices range from €15 to €21, with 10% discounts for purchases online. The Picasso tour, which includes the entry fee for the Picasso Museum, is a real bargain. Tours depart from the Plaça de Catalunya tourist office. For private tours, Julià Tours and Pullmantur *(⇨ Bus Tours)* both lead walks around Barcelona. Tours leave from their offices, but you may be able to arrange a pick-up at your hotel. Prices per person are €35 for half a day and €90 for a full day, including lunch.

For the best English-language walking tour of the medieval Jewish Quarter, Dominique Tomasov Blinder, of Urban Cultours *(⇨ Art Tours)* is an architect with 13 years experience in Jewish heritage. Her tour of Jewish Barcelona is a unique combination of history, current affairs, and personal experience; learn more at *www.urbancultours.com* or email her at *info@urbancultours.com*.

Contact Turisme de Barcelona *Pl. de Catalunya 17, soterrani, Eixample* *93/285-3834* *www.barcelonaturisme.com.*

SEGWAY TOURS

Barcelona Segway Tours, with an office near the Cathedral, puts you up on one of its futuristic two-wheelers for a 2-hour tour (€59) of the Barri Gòtic, La Rambla and the seafront; its longer 3-hour excursion (€79) includes the Ciutadella Park as well. Tours depart daily at 9 and 10 am, and 12:30, 4, 6:30 and 9 pm; the Early Bird tour, at 8 am, includes breakfast. Helmets are provided; children must be over 10 years of age; learn more at *www.barcelonasegwaytour.com*.

VISITOR INFORMATION

The Tourist Office of Spain (and its website) provides valuable practical information about visiting the country. Turisme de Barcelona has two main locations: Plaça de Catalunya, in the center of town, open daily 8:30 to 8:30; and Plaça Sant Jaume, in the Gothic Quarter, open weekdays 8:30 to 8, Saturday 9 to 7, and Sunday 9 to 2. Other tourist information stands are near the top of La Rambla just below Carrer Tallers, at the port end of La Rambla (just beyond the Columbus monument) and at the main entrance of the Sagrada Família. There are smaller facilities at the Sants train station, open daily 8 to 8; the Palau de la Virreina, open Monday through Saturday 9 to 9 and Sunday 10 to 2; and the Palau de Congressos, open daily 10 to 8 during trade fairs and conventions only. For general information in English, dial *010* between 8 am and 10 pm any day but Sunday.

El Prat Airport has an office with information on Catalonia and the rest of Spain, open Monday through Saturday 9:30 am to 8 pm and Sunday 9:30 am to 3 pm. The tourist office in Palau Robert, open Monday through Saturday 10 to 7, specializes in provincial Catalonia. From June to mid-September, information aides patrol the Barri Gòtic and La Rambla area 9 am to 9 pm. They travel in pairs and are recognizable by their red shirts, white trousers or skirts, and badges.

Barcelona Tourist Offices Plaça Sant Jaume *Ciutat 2, Barri Gòtic* *93/285-3834.* **Sants Estació** *Pl. dels Països Catalans s/n, Eixample* *93/285-3834.* **Servei d'Informació Cultural–Palau de la Virreina** *La Rambla 99, Rambla* *93/316-1000, 93/316-1111* *www.bcn.cat/cultura.*

Regional Tourist Offices
El Prat–Barcelona Airport *93/378-8175 for Terminal 1, 93/378-8149 for Terminal 2.* **Palau Robert** *Passeig de Gràcia 107, at Diagonal, Eixample* *93/238-8091* *www.gencat.net/probert.*

SPANISH VOCABULARY

WORDS AND PHRASES

When touring from Barcelona to Bilbao, you can be faced with a daunting number of languages, from Barcelona's Catalan to Bilbao's pre–Indo-European Basque, or Euskera. Of course, the most universal and widely known form of Spanish (Castilian), which you will find in the following vocabulary pages, will serve you throughout Spain, but a word or two of Catalan or Euskera will immediately make you into a local hero and elicit an entirely different (and much warmer) response.

Below are some English words and phrases translated into Catalan and Euskera. Following that are translations into Spanish.

Hello (*Hola!/Kaixó!*); Good morning (*Bon dia/Egun on*); Good afternoon (*Bona tarda/Arratsalde on*); Goodnight (*Bona nit/Gabon*); Thank you (*Gràcies/Eskerrik asko*); Please (*Si us plau/Mesedez*); Excuse me (*Perdó/Barkatu*); Yes (*Sí/Bai*); No (*No/Ez*); How much is this? (*Cuan val?/Zenbat da?*).

ENGLISH	SPANISH	PRONUNCIATION

BASICS

Yes/no	Sí/no	see/no
Please	Por favor	pohr fah-vohr
Thank you (very much)	(Muchas) gracias	(moo-chas) grah-see-as
You're welcome	De nada	deh nah-dah
Excuse me	Con permiso/perdón	con pehr-mee-so/ pehr-dohn
Pardon me/what did you say?	¿Perdón?/Mande?	pehr-dohn/mahn-deh
I'm sorry	Lo siento	lo see-en-to
Good morning!	¡Buenos días!	bway-nohs dee-ahs
Good afternoon!	¡Buenas tardes!	bway-nahs tar-dess
Good evening!	¡Buenas noches!	bway-nahs no-chess
Goodbye!	¡Adiós!/ ¡Hasta luego!	ah-dee-ohss/ ah-stah-lwe-go

NUMBERS

1	un, uno	oon, oo-no
2	dos	dohs
3	tres	tress
4	cuatro	kwah-tro

ENGLISH	SPANISH	PRONUNCIATION
5	cinco	sink-oh
6	seis	saice
7	siete	see-et-eh
8	ocho	o-cho
9	nueve	new-eh-veh
10	diez	dee-es
20	veinte	vain-teh
50	cincuenta	seen-kwen-tah
100	cien	see-en
200	doscientos	doh-see-en-tohss
500	quinientos	keen-yen-tohss

USEFUL PHRASES

Do you speak English?	¿Habla usted inglés?	ah-blah oos-ted in-glehs
I don't speak Spanish	No hablo español	no ah-bloh es-pahn-yol
I don't understand (you)	No entiendo	no en-tee-en-doh
I understand (you)	Entiendo	en-tee-en-doh
Yes, please/	Sí, por favor/	see pohr fah-vor/
No, thank you	No, gracias	no grah-see-ahs
When?	¿Cuándo?	kwahn-doh
What?	¿Qué?	keh
Where is . . . ?	¿Dónde está . . . ?	dohn-deh es-tah
. . . the subway station?	. . . la estación del metro?	la es-ta-see-on del meh-tro
. . . the hospital?	. . . el hospital?	el ohss-pee-tal
. . . the bathroom?	. . . el baño?	el bahn-yoh
Here/there	Aquí/allá	ah-key/ah-yah
Open/closed	Abierto/cerrado	ah-bee-er-toh/ ser-ah-doh
I'd like . . .	Quisiera . . .	kee-see-ehr-ah

ENGLISH	SPANISH	PRONUNCIATION
How much is this?	¿Cuánto cuesta?	kwahn-toh kwes-tah
I am ill	Estoy enfermo(a)	es-toy en-fehr- moh(mah)
Please call a doctor	Por favor llame un médico	pohr fah-vor ya- meh oon med-ee-koh
Help!	¡Ayuda!	ah-yoo-dah

DINING OUT

Bill/check	La cuenta	lah kwen-tah
Is the tip included?	¿Está incluida la propina?	es-tah in-cloo-ee-dahah pro-pee-nah
Menu	La carta, el menú	lah cart-ah, el meh-noo
Please give me . . .	Por favor déme . . .	pohr fah-vor deh-meh

INDEX

A

B

C

N

O

P

PHOTO CREDITS

Front Cover: Travel Pix Collection/AWL Images [Description: Rooftop chimneys, Casa Batlló]. Back cover (from left to right), © JACQUES Pierre / age fotostock; Steven Newton/Shutterstock; Public Domain. Spine: (c) Jacekkadaj I Dreamstime.com. 1, Bjorn Svensson/age fotostock. 2-3, Joan Miro Foundation, Barcelona. Catalonia, Spain. 5, Solodovnikova Elena/Shutterstock. Chapter 1: Experience Barcelona: 8-9, Carsten Leuzinger/age fotostock. 10, José LópezJauregi/Restaurante Arzak. 11 (leftrubiphoto/ Shutterstock. 11 (right), Oriol Gassó/age fotostock. 13, Vladimir Melnik/Shutterstock. 14, Philip Lange/ Shutterstock. 15 (left), A. WWW.viajar24h.com/Flickr. 15 (right) and 16, Philip Lange/ Shutterstock. 17 (left), gary718/Shutterstock. 17 (right), iladm/Shutterstock.18 (left), Steven NeWton/ Shutterstock. 18 (top center), Quim Roser/age fotostock. 18 (bottom center), Xcaballe/Wikipedia.org. 18 (right), David Davies/Flickr. 19 (top left), Javier Larrea/age fotostock.19 (bottom left), Andoni Canela/age fotostock. 19 (bottom center), Ken Welsh/age fotostock. 19 (right), Randi Utnes/Shutterstock. 20. Kevin Krejci/ Flickr. 21, Brian K./Shutterstock. 24, Oso Media/Alamy. 25, Pavel Kirichenko/iStock photo. 26 (top left), Public Domain. 26 (bottom left), Alfonso de Tomás/Shutterstock. 26 (top right), Zina Seletskaya/ Shutterstock. 26 (center right), Amy Nichole Harris/Shutterstock. 26 (bottom right), Luis M. Seco/ Shutterstock. 27 (left), IWona Grodzka/Shutterstock. 27 (top right), zvonkomaja/Shutterstock. 27 (center right), Public Domain. 27 (bottom right), Smackfu/Wikipedia.org. 28 (top left), synes/Flickr. 28 (bottom left), rubiphoto/Shutterstock. 28 (right), Solodovnikova Elena/Shutterstock. 29 (top), Quim Roser/age fotostock. 29 (bottom), Jan van der Hoeven/Shutterstock. 31 (left), robertpaulyoung/Flickr. 31 (right), Ronald Sumners/Shutterstock. Chapter 2: Exploring Barcelona: 33, Javier Larrea/age fotostock. 34, GARDEL Bertrand/age fotostock. 36, Bruno Perousse/age fotostock. 39, Wolfcomm/Flickr. 41, Matz Sjöberg/age fotostock. 45, JACQUES Pierre/age fotostock.48, böhringer friedrich/Wikipedia.org. 51, böhringer friedrich/Wikipedia.org. 54, Xavier Caballé/Wikipedia.org. 59, Rafael Campillo/age fotostock. 61, travelstock44/LOOK/age fotostock. 63, Lalupa/Wikipedia.org. 64,

Rafael Campillo/ age fotostock. 67, BORGESE Maurizio/age fotostock. 70, Yearofthedragon/Wikipedia.org. 73, Mikhail Zahranichny/Shutterstock. 74, Quim Roser/age fotostock.75, maveric2003/Flickr. 76 and 78, Ken Welsh/age fotostock. 82, Vinicius Tupinamba/Shutterstock. 85, Philip Lange/Shutterstock. 86, Petr Svarc/age fotostock. 88, Juergen Richter/age fotostock. 90, Juergen Richter/age fotostock. 93, Yuriy Chertok/Shutterstock. 94, Marco Cristofori/age fotostock. 99, Raquel Gisbert Gil/age fotostock. 100, José Fuste Raga/age fotostock. 101, Robert Harding Productions/age fotostock. 102 (left), Jose Fuste Raga/age fotostock. 102 (top right), Sylvain Grandadam/age fotostock. 102 (center right), Javier Larrea/age fotostock. 102 (bottom right), Siobhan O'Hare. 103 (top), ccchan 19/Flickr. 103 (bottom), Pep Daudé/Temple de la Sagrada Família. 104 (top), Jsome1/Flickr. 104 (bottom), Pepe Navarro/ Temple de la Sagrada Família. 105 (top), Hans Blosseyimagebro / age fotostock. 105 (bottom), (c) Achimhb | Dreamstime.com. 106 (top), Jose Antonio Sanchez/Shutterstock. 106 (2nd from top), Rafael Campillo/ age fotostock. 106 (3rd from top), MM Images/age fotostock. 106 (bottom) and 107 (top), Temple de la Sagrada Família. 107 (2nd from top), Harmonia Amanda/Wikipedia.org. 107 (3rd from top), Achim Prill/iStockphoto. 107 (bottom), ARCO/P Svarc/age fotostock. 108 (top), Wikipedia.org. 111, peresanz/ Shutterstock. 113, Jan van der Hoeven/Shutterstock. 116, Factoria Singular/age fotostock. 119, posztos (colorlab.hu)/Shutterstock. 121, Canaan/Wikipedia.org. 125, Solodovnikova Elena/Shutterstock. 127, Jordi Puig/age fotostock. 129, Philip Lange/Shutterstock. 130, Elan Fleisher/age fotostock. 132, Jordi Puig/age fotostock. Chapter 3: Where to Eat: 135, robertpaulyoung/Flickr. 136, atanas.dk/Shutterstock. 138, Elan Fleisher/age fotostock. 139 (top), jynus/Wikipedia.org. 139 (bottom), Javier Lastras/ Wikipedia.org. 153, OSOMEDIA/age fotostock. 159, Elan Fleisher/ age fotostock. 165, Ioseba Egibar/age fotostock. 166, Javier Larrea/age fotostock. 168 (top left), Daniel P. Acevedo/age fotostock. 168 (bottom left), Sam Bloomberg-Rissman/age fotostock. 168 (right), Javier Larrea/age fotostock. 169, J.D. Dallet/age fotostock. 170 (top), PHB.cz (Richard Semik)/Shutterstock. 170 (2nd from top), Javier Larrea/age fotostock, 170 (3rd from top), Jakub Pavlinec/Shutterstock, 170 (4th from top), J.D. Dallet/age fotostock. 170 (5th from top), Fresnel/Shutterstock. 170 (6th from top), J.D. Dallet/age fotostock. 170 (bottom), Marta Menéndez/Shutterstock. 171 (top left), Mauro Winery. 171 (top 2nd from left), Cephas Picture Library/Alamy. 171 (top 3rd from left), Alvaro Palacios Winery. 171 (top right), Mas Martinet Winery. 171 (bottom), Mike Randolph/age fotostock. Chapter 4: Where to Stay: 191, StarWood Hotels & Resorts. 192, Rafael Vargas. Chapter 5: Nightlife and the Arts: 211, alterna2/Flickr. 212, Josep Renalias/Wikipedia.org. 216, Rene Mattes/age fotostock. 217 (top), Juan David Ferrando Subero/ Shutterstock. 217 (bottom), Hemis /Alamy. 219, Quim Roser/age fotostock. 231, Elan Fleisher/age fotostock. Chapter 6: Sports and the Outdoors: 237, sportgraphic/Shutterstock. 238, Carlos Neto/Shutterstock. 240, Mikhail Zahranichny/ Shutterstock. 241 (top), Regien Paassen/ Shutterstock. 241 (bottom), Philip Lange/Shutterstock. Chapter 7: Shopping: 245, Peter Horree/Alamy. 246, Wili_hybrid/Flickr. 252, Xavier Subias/age fotostock. 258, Daderot/Wikipedia.org. Chapter 8: Catalonia Highlights: 271, Hermes/age fotostock. 272, Helio San Miguel. 273, VRoig/Flickr. 274, Patty Orly/Shutterstock. 275 (top), Mauricio Pellegrinetti/Flickr. 275 (bottom), Ana Abadla/age fotostock. 276, Helio San Miguel. 285, Oscar García Bayerri/age fotostock. 288, Carlos S. Pereyra/ age fotostock. 291, B&Y Photography Inc./age fotostock. 294, Oscar García Bayerri/age fotostock. 296, José Fuste Raga/age fotostock. 302, Helio San Miguel. 305, Alberto Paredes/age fotostock. 313, Nils-Johan Norenlind/age fotostock. 317, Igor Gonzalo Sanz/age fotostock. 321, Charles Bowman/age fotostock. 323, Hidalgo & Lopesino/age fotostock. 325, Alan Copson/Jon Arnold/age fotostock. Chapter 9: Excursion to Bilbao: 327, Jerónimo Alba/age fotostock. 328, Javier Larreda/age fotostock. 329, (top), Juan Carlos Muñoz/ age fotostock. 329 (bottom), Javier Larreda/age fotostock. 330, Javier Gil/ Shutterstock. 332, Adriaan Thomas Snaaijer/Shutterstock. 337, Gonzalo Azumendi/age fotostock. 342, Atlantide S.N.C./age fotostock. 344, John Miller/age fotostock. 361, Toño Labra/age fotostock. 371, Graham Lawrence/age fotostock. 373, Wojtek Buss/age fotostock. 378. Brigitte Merz/age fotostock.

ABOUT OUR WRITERS

Jared Lubarsky is a university teacher and freelance travel journalist who has been writing for Fodor's since 1997, first on Japan, where he lived for 30 years, and more recently—having relocated to Barcelona—on Spain. His credits include in-flight and general interest travel magazines, guidebooks, and newspapers. Jared updated our Experience, Exploring, Where to Stay, Sports and the Outdoors, Travel Smart, and Catalonia, Valencia, and Costa Blanca chapters.

Originally from Australia, **Suzanne Wales** arrived in Barcelona in 1992 and immediately became captivated with the city's rich architecture, sunny weather, and strong coffee. She regularly writes travel and arts features, generally with a focus on design and architecture, for top European and U.S. publications between leading tours on the city's most original shops and design destinations. Suzanne updated the Shopping, Nightlife and the Arts, and Bilbao and the Basque Country chapters.

Steve Tallantyre is a British journalist and copywriter. He moved from Italy to Barcelona in the late 1990s, just in time to witness Spain's rise as a global culinary superpower. Married to a Catalan native, with two "Catalangles" children, Steve writes about the region's recipes, restaurants, and food culture for a number of international publications. He also owns a popular blog about Barcelona cuisine (🌐 *www.foodbarcelona.com*) and works as a consultant for several travel companies. Steve updated our Where to Eat chapter.

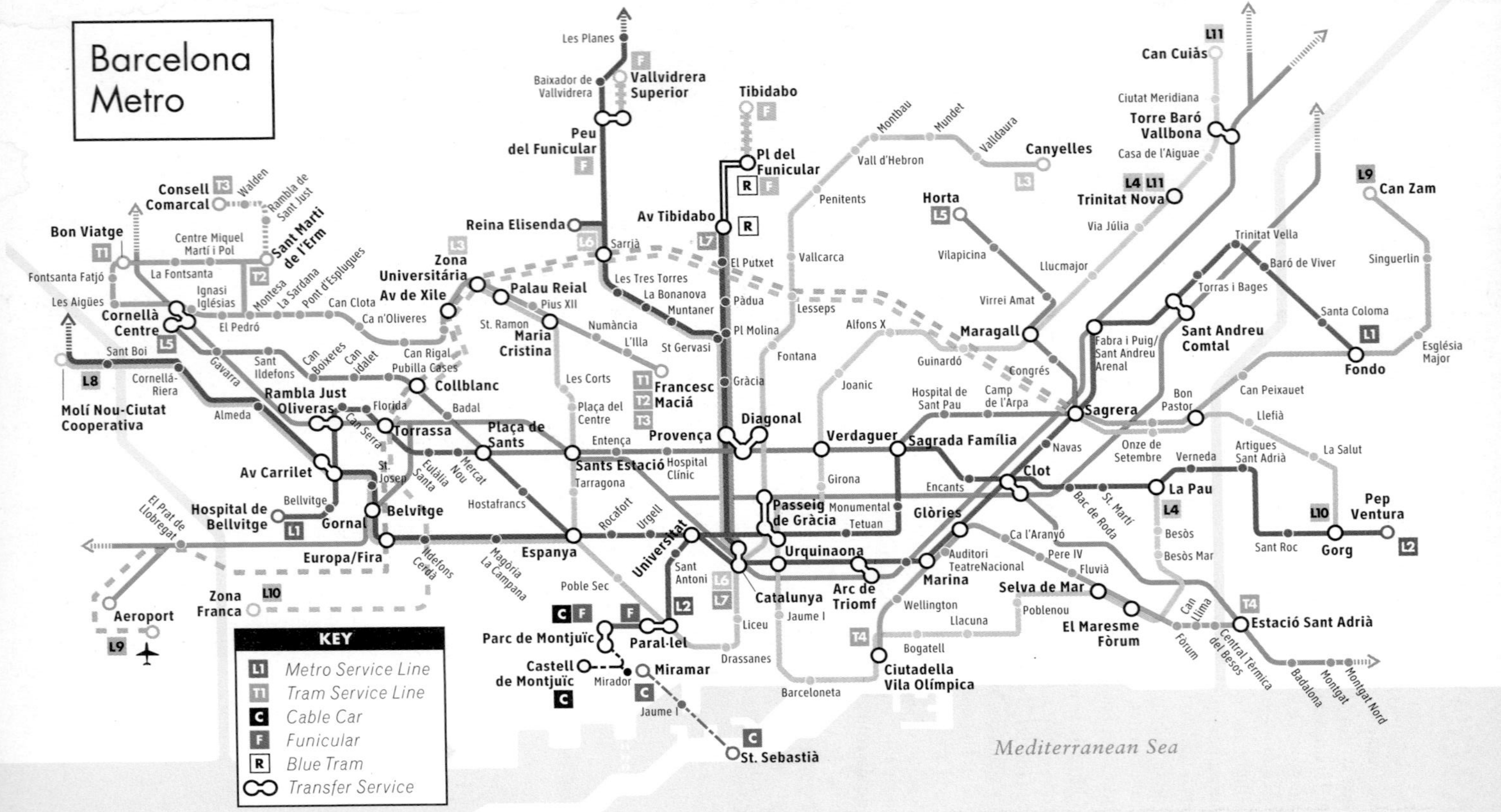
Barcelona Metro
KEY
L1 Metro Service Line
T1 Tram Service Line
C Cable Car
F Funicular
R Blue Tram
Transfer Service
Mediterranean Sea
Les Planes
Baixador de Vallvidrera
Vallvidrera Superior
Peu del Funicular
Tibidabo
Pl del Funicular
Av Tibidabo
Reina Elisenda
Sarrià
El Putxet
Pàdua
Pl Molina
Gràcia
Les Tres Torres
La Bonanova
Muntaner
St Gervasi
Consell Comarcal
Walden
Rambla de Sant Just
Sant Martí de l'Erm
Bon Viatge
Centre Miquel Martí i Pol
Fontsanta Fatjó
La Fontsanta
Ignasi Iglésias
Montesa
La Sardana
Pont d'Espluges
Les Aigües
Cornellà Centre
El Pedró
Can Clota
Ca n'Oliveres
Zona Universitària
Av de Xile
Palau Reial
Pius XII
St. Ramon
Maria Cristina
Numància
L'Illa
Francesc Macià
Les Corts
Plaça del Centre
Sant Boi
Cornellà-Riera
Molí Nou-Ciutat Cooperativa
Gavarra
Sant Ildefons
Can Boixeres
Can idalet
Can Rigal
Pubilla Cases
Collblanc
Badal
Almeda
Rambla Just Oliveras
Florida
Can Serra
Torrassa
Plaça de Sants
Entença
Sants Estació
Hospital Clínic
Tarragona
Provença
Diagonal
Av Carrilet
St. Josep
Eulàlia Santa
Mercat Nou
Hostafrancs
Hospital de Bellvitge
Bellvitge
Gornal
Belvitge
El Prat de Llobregat
Europa/Fira
Ildefons Cerdà
Magòria La Campana
Espanya
Rocafort
Urgell
Universitat
Sant Antoni
Poble Sec
Zona Franca
Aeroport
Parc de Montjuïc
Paral·lel
Castell de Montjuïc
Mirador
Miramar
Jaume I
St. Sebastià
Drassanes
Liceu
Catalunya
Jaume I
Barceloneta
Passeig de Gràcia
Urquinaona
Arc de Triomf
Monumental
Tetuan
Girona
Verdaguer
Sagrada Família
Hospital de Sant Pau
Camp de l'Arpa
Joanic
Fontana
Lesseps
Vallcarca
Penitents
Vall d'Hebron
Montbau
Mundet
Valldaura
Canyelles
Horta
Vilapicina
Virrei Amat
Maragall
Alfons X
Guinardó
Congrés
Llucmajor
Via Júlia
Trinitat Nova
Casa de l'Aiguae
Torre Baró Vallbona
Ciutat Meridiana
Can Cuiàs
Can Zam
Singuerlin
Església Major
Fondo
Santa Coloma
Baró de Viver
Trinitat Vella
Torras i Bages
Sant Andreu Comtal
Fabra i Puig/ Sant Andreu Arenal
Sagrera
Bon Pastor
Can Peixauet
Llefià
La Salut
Onze de Setembre
Navas
Encants
Clot
Glòries
Marina
Auditori TeatreNacional
Ca l'Aranyó
Pere IV
Fluvià
Selva de Mar
El Maresme Fòrum
Poblenou
Llacuna
Wellington
Bogatell
Ciutadella Vila Olímpica
Verneda
La Pau
Bac de Roda
St. Martí
Besòs
Besòs Mar
Artigues Sant Adrià
Sant Roc
Gorg
Pep Ventura
Can Llima
Fòrum
Central Tèrmica del Besos
Estació Sant Adrià
Badalona
Montgat
Montgat Nord